FASHIONING MASCULINITIES

THE ART OF MENSWEAR

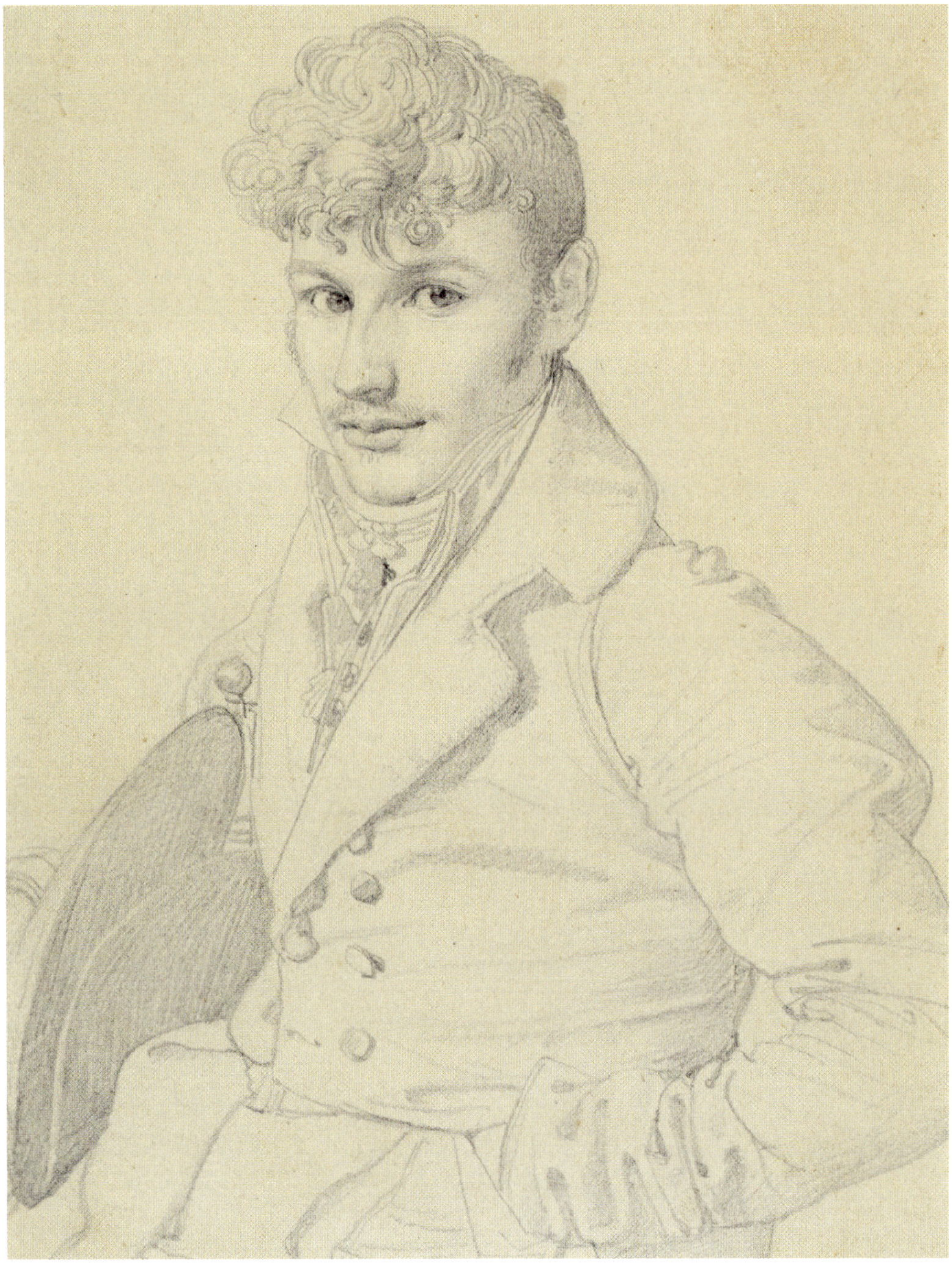

FASHIONING MASCULINITIES

THE ART OF MENSWEAR

EDITED BY
ROSALIND McKEVER & CLAIRE WILCOX
WITH MARTA FRANCESCHINI

V&A PUBLISHING

In partnership with

GUCCI

With support from

AMERICAN EXPRESS

First published by V&A Publishing to accompany the exhibition *Fashioning Masculinities: The Art of Menswear* on view from 19 March to 6 November 2022 at the Victoria and Albert Museum, South Kensington, London SW7 2RL

Distributed in North America by Abrams, an imprint of ABRAMS

The moral right of the authors has been asserted.

ISBN 9781838510114

10 9 8 7 6 5 4 3 2 1
2026 2025 2024 2023 2022

A catalogue record for this book is available from the British Library.

Design: Fraser Muggeridge studio
Copyeditor: Rebeka Cohen
Proofreader: Linda Schofield
Indexer: Nic Nicholas

New photography: Kieron Boyle, V&A Photo Studio

Printed in Italy

FSC www.fsc.org MIX Paper from responsible sources FSC® C013123

Front cover illustration: Omar Victor Diop (1980–), after Anne-Louis Girodet (1767–1824), *Jean-Baptiste Belley*. Pigment inkjet print on Harman by Hahnemühle paper, 120 × 80 cm. Senegal, 2014. Magnin-A, Paris. © Omar Victor Diop. Courtesy Magnin-A Gallery, Paris

Back cover illustration: Michelangelo's *David* in the Accademia di Belle Arte, Florence. Photograph, gelatin silver print mounted on card, 33 × 26.7 cm. Italy, late 19th to early 20th century. V&A: 1548-1953

p. 2: Possibly by or after Jean-Auguste-Dominique Ingres (1780–1867), *Portrait of a man*. Pencil on paper, 17.14 × 13.65 cm. France, *c*.1805–20. V&A: CAI.261

p. 5: Chris Steele-Perkins (1947–), *Ted with comb, Market Tavern, Bradford*. Photograph, gelatin silver print, 23.1 × 34.1 cm. England, 1977. V&A: PH.880-1980

p. 22: Ruffle-fronted shirt. Linen and cotton. Great Britain, 1800–10. V&A: T.16-2019

p. 25: Gérard Audran (1640–1703), 'Belvedere Antinous' (detail), *The Proportions of the Human Body* (London, 1718). V&A: National Art Library 194.C.33

p. 80: Waistcoat. Silk, wool, linen, silver-gilt thread. Great Britain, 1730–5. V&A: T.36-2019

p. 83: Pompeo Batoni (1708–1787), *John, Lord Mountstuart, later 4th Earl and 1st Marquess of Bute* (detail), Oil on canvas, 236.4 × 144.7 cm. Italy, 1767. The Bute Collection at Mount Stuart

p. 160: Coat. Wool and silk velvet. USA, 1845–53. V&A: T.176&A-1965. Waistcoat. Silk damask, cotton. England, 1850–3. Given by Miss C.M. Higgs. V&A: T.121-1949. Cravat. Satin. England, 1840–50. Given by Miss C. Wigginton. V&A: T.215-1966

p. 163: Janette Beckman (1959–), London Rude Boy twins Chuka and Dubem Okonkwo, published in *The Face* (London, May 1980)

V&A Publishing

Supporting the world's leading museum of art and design, the Victoria and Albert Museum, London

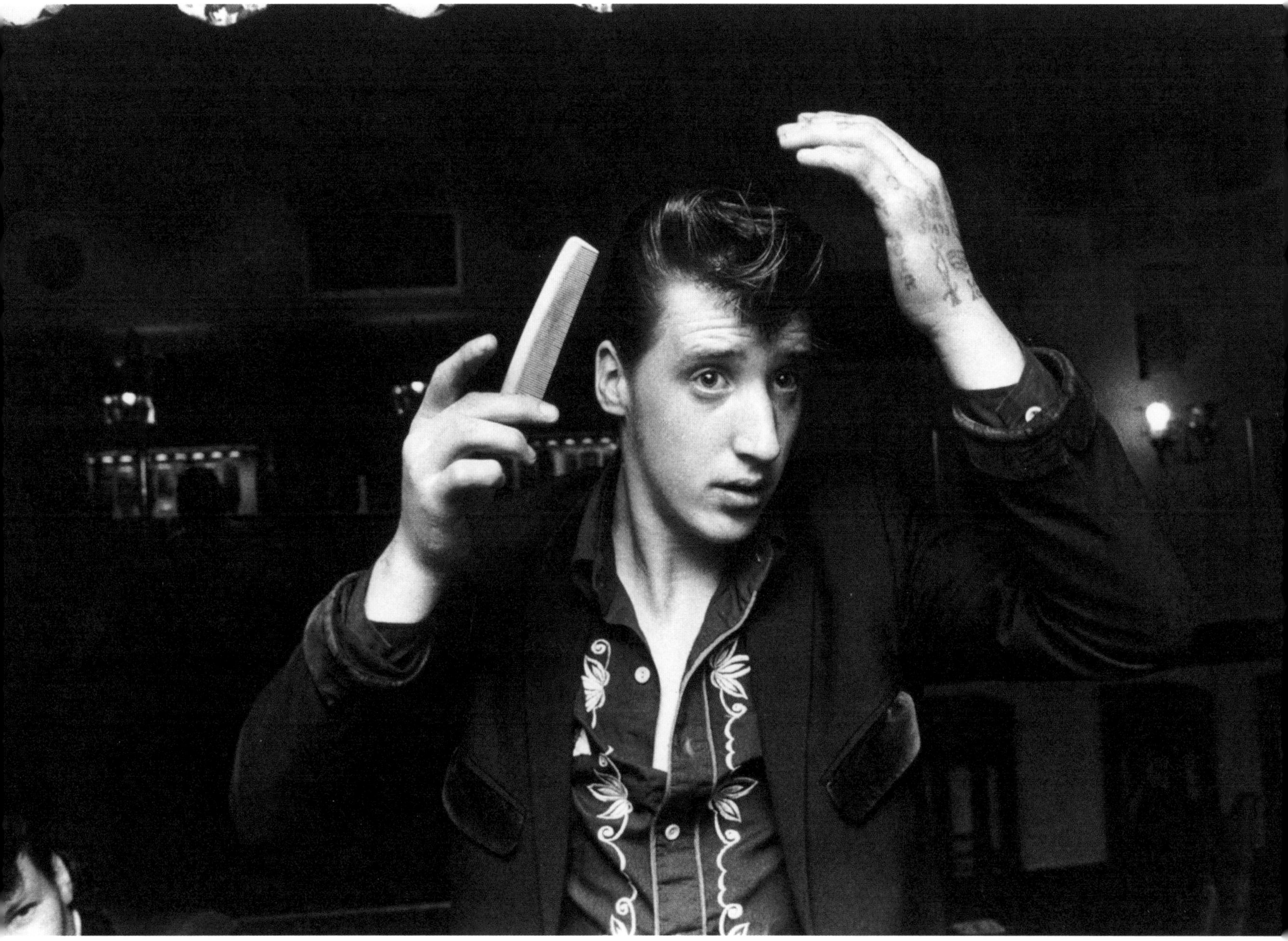

8
SPONSOR'S FOREWORD
Alessandro Michele

9
DIRECTOR'S FOREWORD
Tristram Hunt

10
DO CLOTHES MAKE THE MAN?
Rosalind McKever

UNDRESSED

26
MARBLE MARVELS AND CLASSICAL IDEALS
Sarah Goldsmith

44
A POLISHED IMPRESSION
Alun Withey

48
BEHIND CLOTHES: FASHIONING MEN AT THE MUSEUM
Satish Padiyar

60
A DEVELOPED PHYSIQUE
Zorian Clayton

68
UNDERPINNINGS: THE NEXT BEST THING TO NAKED
Shaun Cole

OVERDRESSED

84
YOUNG ENGLISHMEN BEHAVING BADLY (AND DRESSING OUTRAGEOUSLY)
Susan North

98
A WELL-TURNED LEG
Elisabeth Gernerd

104
BRAGGADOCIO: A BRIEF HISTORY OF SWAGGER
Elizabeth Currie

114
FINE AND DANDY
Claire Wilcox

130
SARTORIAL ENCOUNTERS: THE KIMONO AND MASCULINE STYLE
Anna Jackson

142
ORLANDO AS A BOYETTE
Rosalind McKever

154
A HIBISCUS PRINT
Cher Potter

REDRESSED

164
MONOCHROME MAN
Christopher Breward

186
A FULL MONTY
Miriam Phelan

192
A SUITABLE HAT
Oriole Cullen

196
THE HYBRID OF IT ALL:
THE MAKING OF BLACK BRITISH STYLE
Ekow Eshun

208
A TAILORED SARI
Avalon Fotheringham

214
A BROKEN SUIT
Marta Franceschini

222
THE JACKET
ERODED, BORROWED, EVOLVED
Alistair O'Neill

236
WHAT EVER HAPPENED TO
CONTEMPORARY MENSWEAR?
Charlie Porter

246
EPILOGUE
Gus Casely-Hayford

250
FASHIONING THE FUTURE

252
AFTERWORD
Virgil Abloh

254
NOTES

260
BIBLIOGRAPHY

267
PICTURE CREDITS

268
ACKNOWLEDGEMENTS

269
CONTRIBUTORS

270
INDEX

SPONSOR'S FOREWORD

ALESSANDRO MICHELE
CREATIVE DIRECTOR
GUCCI

An excerpt from the statement released to coincide with the Autumn/Winter 2020 menswear collection

In a patriarchal society, masculine gender identity is often moulded by violently toxic stereotypes. A dominant, winning, oppressive masculinity model is imposed on babies at birth. Attitudes, languages and actions end up progressively conforming to a macho virility ideal that removes vulnerability and dependence. Any possible reference to femininity is aggressively banned, as it is considered a threat against the complete affirmation of a masculine prototype that allows no divergencies. There is nothing natural in this drift. The model is socially and culturally built to reject anything that does not comply with it.

Therefore, it seems necessary to suggest a desertion, away from patriarchal plans and uniforms. Deconstructing the idea of masculinity as it has been historically established. Opening a cage. Throwing a chant. It is time to celebrate a man who is free to practice self-determination, without social constraints, without authoritarian sanctions, without suffocating stereotypes.

DIRECTOR'S FOREWORD

TRISTRAM HUNT
DIRECTOR
V&A

Fashioning Masculinities: The Art of Menswear is the first major exhibition at the V&A to celebrate the power, artistry and variety of male attire and appearance and deconstruct norms and forms of masculinity.

The V&A's unrivalled fashion collections reflect the constant refashioning of menswear. They have been enriched over the past century by donations from pioneering wearers and collectors, from the historical treasure troves of the painter Talbot Hughes to the wardrobe of twentieth-century art patron Edward James, and the generous recent donations of fashion aficionados Mark Reed and Charlie Porter.

This exhibition and catalogue threads together the fashion cultures of Europe and the Global South with painting, sculpture and photography on an unprecedented scale. In the crafting of this exhibition the V&A has benefitted greatly from the expertise of colleagues who have helped cast a critical, historical eye from contemporary viewpoints. This volume brings together thoughtful contributions, academic insights and personal perspectives on the powerful influence of menswear in shaping our understanding of gender and identity.

Contemporary designers are leading the way in rethinking masculinity in fashion. We are fortunate to have had the great privilege of working with Alessandro Michele, Creative Director at Gucci, whose vision eschews machismo to spotlight vulnerability, self-determination and diversity on the runway. It gives me particular pleasure to thank our sponsors Gucci, without whom this exhibition would not have been possible. I also wish to express my gratitude to the curators for their rigorous exploration of this timely topic and for realizing the expansive ambition of this project.

DO CLOTHES MAKE THE MAN?

ROSALIND McKEVER

Vestis virum facit.
Clothes make the man.
Erasmus, 1500

Masculine clothing's capacity to fashion its wearers has repeatedly drawn comment. Erasmus' maxim echoes through the English literary canon, from William Shakespeare's *Hamlet* to Thomas Carlyle's *Sartor Resartus* to Virginia Woolf's *Orlando*.[1] The phrase's ambiguity reflects menswear's expressive and restrictive powers, simultaneously inviting anyone to construct a masculine identity through dress while reducing people to their apparel and appearance. It is usually in the latter vein that it manifests itself in the written and unwritten dress codes which have defined and redefined masculine fashions for five centuries. A litany of advice has been penned by those trying to get men to take their attire seriously. As Lord Chesterfield put it in a now famed letter to his son in 1745:

> dress is a very foolish thing; and yet it is a very foolish thing for a man not to be well dressed, according to his rank and way of life; and it is so far from being a disparagement to any man's understanding, that it is rather a proof of it, to be as well dressed as those whom he lives with.[2]

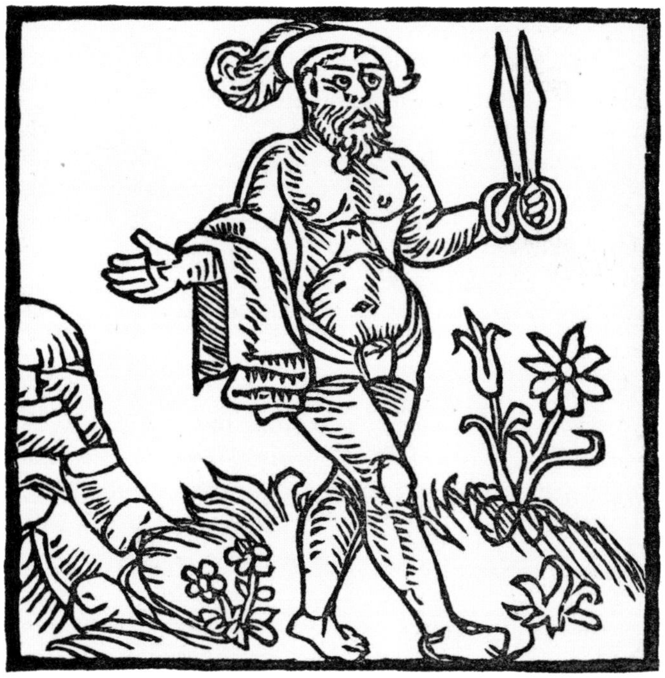

1. 'The Englishman who loves new fashions', from Andrew Boorde's *The Fyrst Boke of the Introduction of Knowledge* (1542). V&A: National Art Library Forster L8VO 2674

The trope of a naked man ready to cut his cloth to the latest fashions developed in sixteenth-century European books of costume. Here a bearded figure wears only a loincloth and a fine feathered hat, with a bolt of fabric and a pair of shears in hand. As in this illustration accompanying a poem by Andrew Boorde, this fickle follower of fashion was often English, ever adaptable to the taste of other countries.

For all the literature on what men should and should not wear, for all the portraits of 'great men' flaunting their sartorial mores, from swaggering silks modelled in oils to sedate tailoring captured through photography, the topic has received less attention from fashion historians and museums than its supposedly more glamorous sister. In recent years menswear has stepped out of the closet. An upsurge in studies and a flurry of exhibitions has coincided with wider societal reflection on masculinity and a period of unprecedented vitality in the men's fashion industry.[3]

This outpouring of creativity among designers is multifaceted, fuelled by the desire to deconstruct menswear's established forms, imbue it with emotion and poetry, diversify its references and reduce its environmental footprint. A shared goal – with precedent in the kaleidoscopic bursts of peacockery initiated by every post-war subculture – is to liberate wearers from a limiting model of masculinity. Pioneering fashion designers Giorgio Armani, Tom Ford and Raf Simons paved the way for a generation of creatives embracing a more fluid approach, including Jonathan Anderson, Alessandro Michele, Adebayo Oke-Lawal, Harris Reed and Grace Wales Bonner. Crucially, the performers bringing ever more attention to fashion industry's push beyond the binary – from Bimini Bon Boulash to Billy Porter, Sam Smith to Harry Styles – represent a broader spectrum of identities in the public eye.

Indeed, the enhanced visibility of the relationship between menswear and masculinity has not been confined to the world of high fashion. From images of Gareth Southgate dressed in his signature waistcoat comforting the England men's football team, to Netflix's reboot of makeover show *Queer Eye* shot in the American Midwest, the positive possibilities of fashion's transformative effects are in the spotlight.

This book, and the exhibition it accompanies, chooses this moment to offer some reflections on whether clothes make the man. Our authors, with expertise ranging from the early modern to the contemporary, do not attempt a linear menswear history. Instead, whether inspired by a single object or examining a larger theme, they trace resonant connections across and beyond European menswear histories. Bringing together fashion with artistic, photographic, literary, cinematic and cultural histories places an

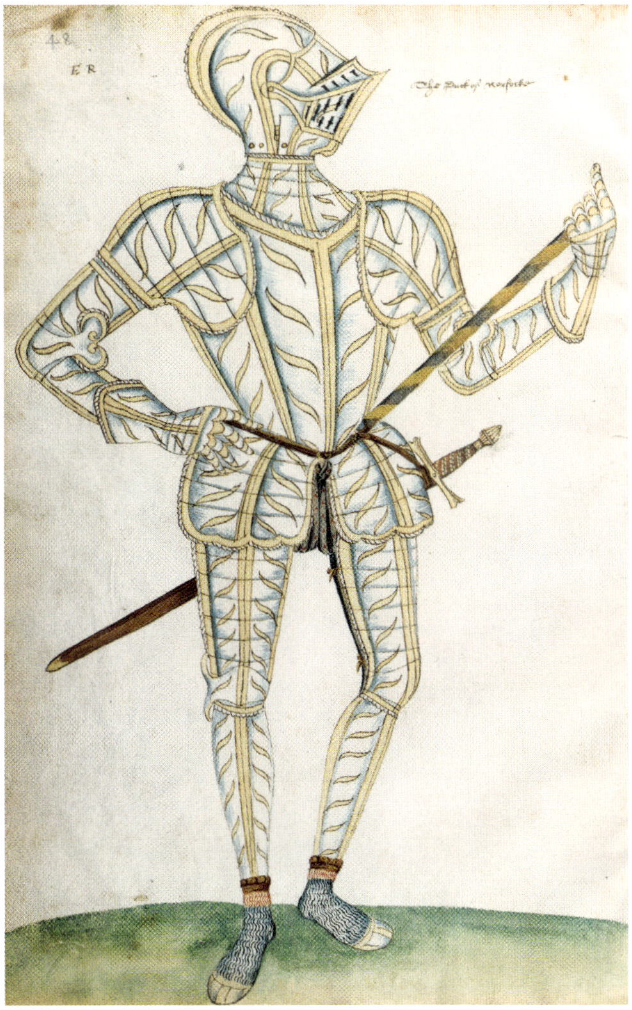

2. Jacob Halder (active 1556–1608), 'Armour for William Brooke, 10th Baron Cobham' in the Almain Armourers' Album. Pen, ink and watercolour on paper, 86.2 × 58.5 cm (double page). London 1557–87. V&A: D.597&A-1894

For Elizabethan courtiers like Baron Cobham, armour was a fashion statement, a way to show off when covered head to toe. The slashes of gold across this design mimic the trend for cutting garments to reveal layers beneath, itself likely inspired by the torn clothes of soldiers returning from war. The taste for armour decorations produced at the English Royal Armoury in Greenwich was captured in vivid detail by Master Armourer Jacob Halder.

emphasis on individuals, on the designers, tailors and artists – plus their clients, models and sitters – who have constructed and performed masculinity and unpicked it at the seams. This accumulation of voices seeks to provide a choral response as layered, contingent and diverse as the subject itself.

The essays are grouped into three sections reflecting the tripartite structure of the exhibition. These undress, overdress and then redress – or rather unmake, make and remake – the man. *Undressed* reveals the role of the body and underwear in fashioning masculinities. Chapters follow the shaping of classical models from the Grand Tour to Times Square, the boxing gym to the barber's shop, the artist's studio to the art museum. *Overdressed* explores the power dynamics of sartorial bravado, from the battlefield to the city streets. Authors address people flouting and remixing the dress codes that have sought to keep them in their place. *Redressed* pieces together the modern masculine uniform: the black suit. Essays spanning the high-street tailor to the fashion-week runway disassemble the suit garment by garment, as wearers and designers erode the monolithic model of gender it embodies.

Writing on masculinity through menswear when many within and beyond the fashion industry are calling for the end of gendered dressing altogether, and during a year when sartorial habits and awareness of unjust power structures have irrevocably shifted, has permeated this book with both elegiac reflection and revolutionary zeal. Janus-faced, we look to the past to inspire a future of creating clothes that make the people we wish to be.

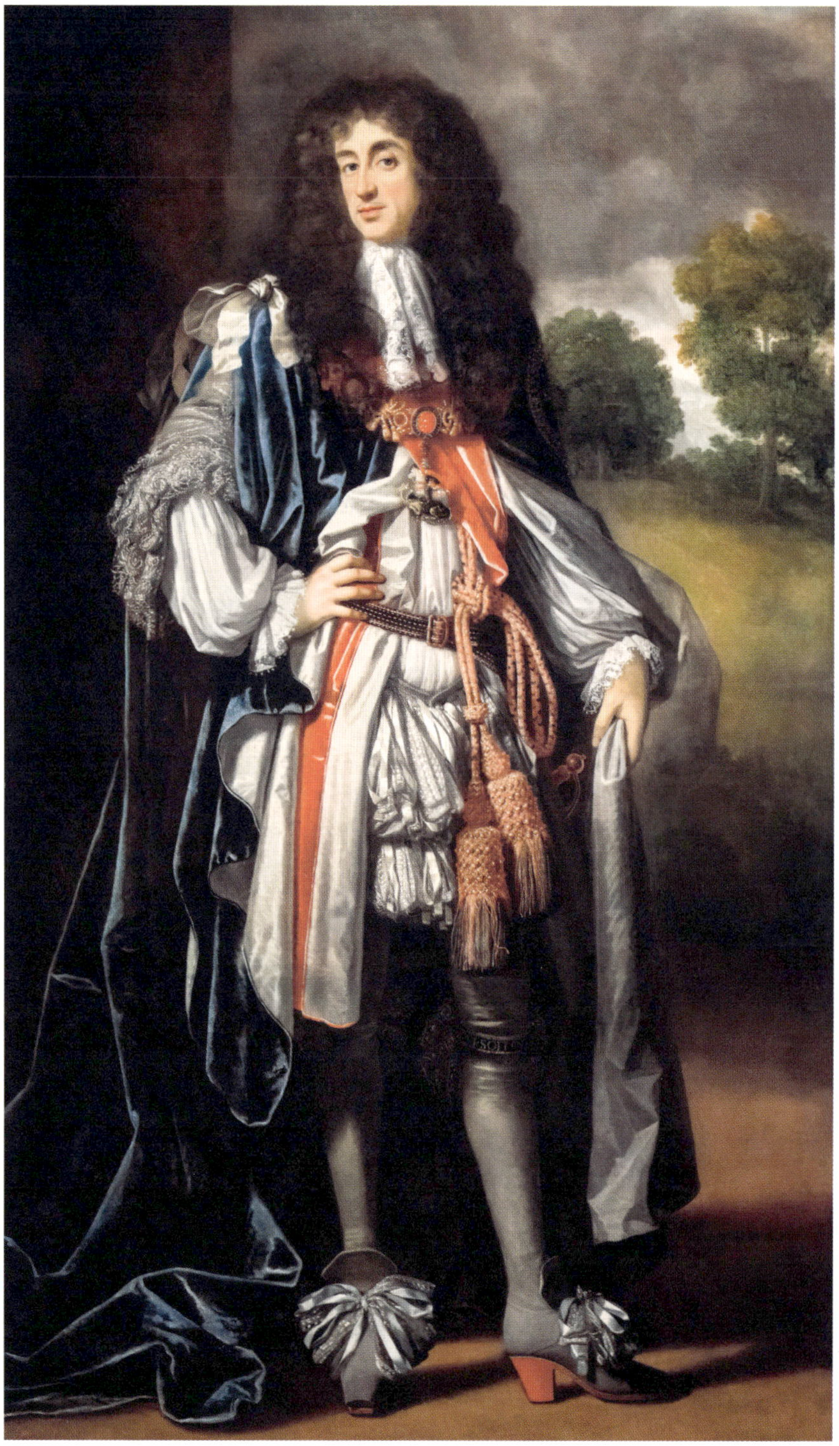

3. Simon Verelst (1644–1721), *Charles II.* Oil on canvas, h. 219 cm. England, *c.*1677–85. Royal Collection Trust: RCIN 409151

Charles II's clothing choices struck a balance between Restoration pageantry and post-Civil War restraint. For portraits he often adopted the sumptuous robes and insignia of the Order of the Garter, combining this historicizing garb with the red high heels favoured by his cousin Louis XIV. This masculine footwear fashion was inspired by the Persian riding boot. Charles' more understated innovation, the three-piece suit, was also associated with a Persian style of vest.

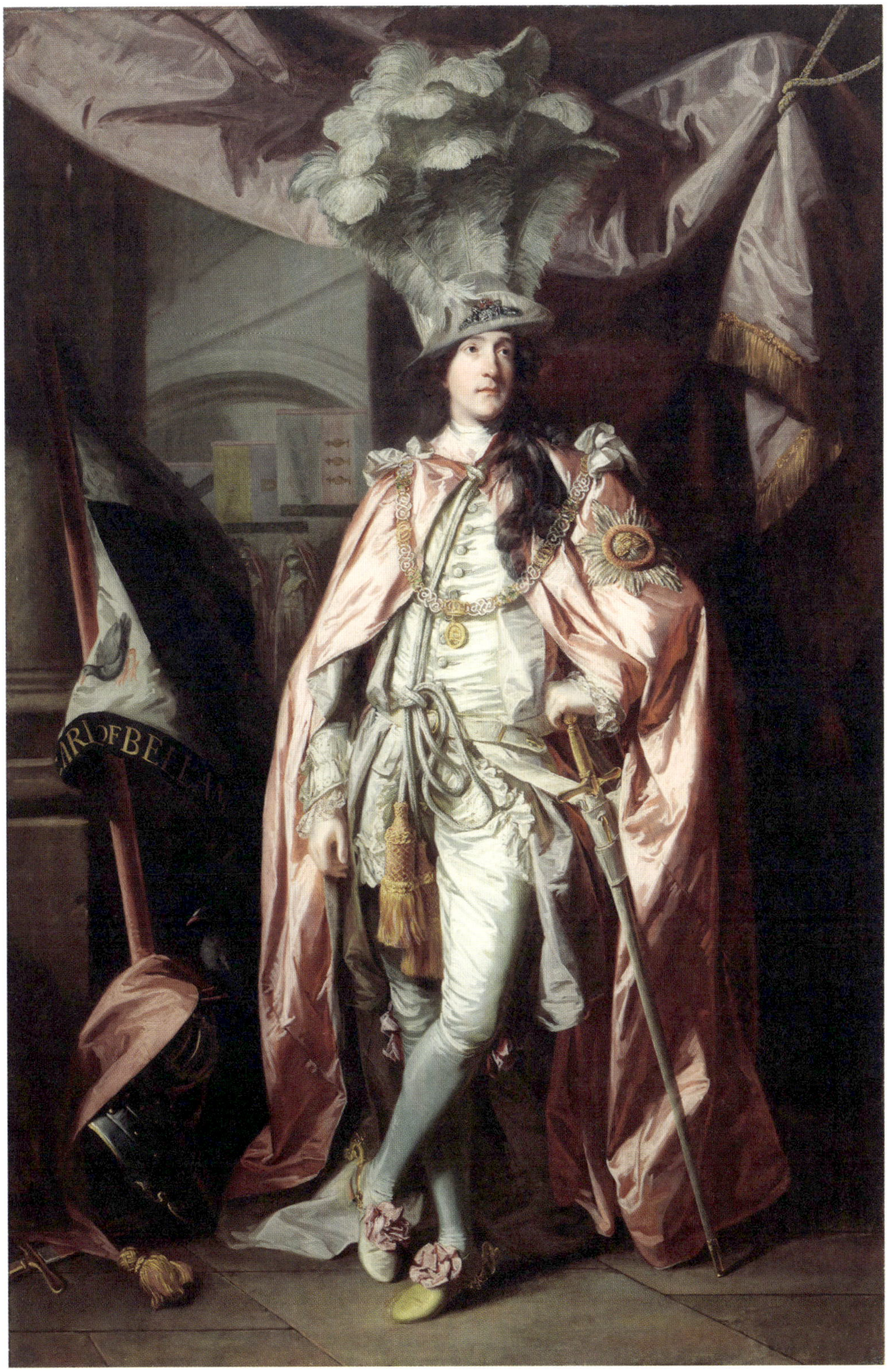

4. Sir Joshua Reynolds PRA (1723–1792), *Charles Coote, 1st Earl of Bellamont, in Robes of the Order of the Bath*. Oil on canvas, 245 × 162 cm. Great Britain, 1773–4. National Gallery of Ireland, Dublin: NGI.216

Charles Coote's reputation as a vain and pompous womanizer permeates this typically aggrandizing portrait by Sir Joshua Reynolds. Depicted in the ceremonial robes of the Order of the Bath, he exudes patriarchal power from plumed headdress to lolling passementerie to beribboned shoes. Yet the fading of the pigment used for the scarlet cape to pale pink has transformed this picture. Ironically, Reynolds rarely painted dress in detail because he considered it too transient.

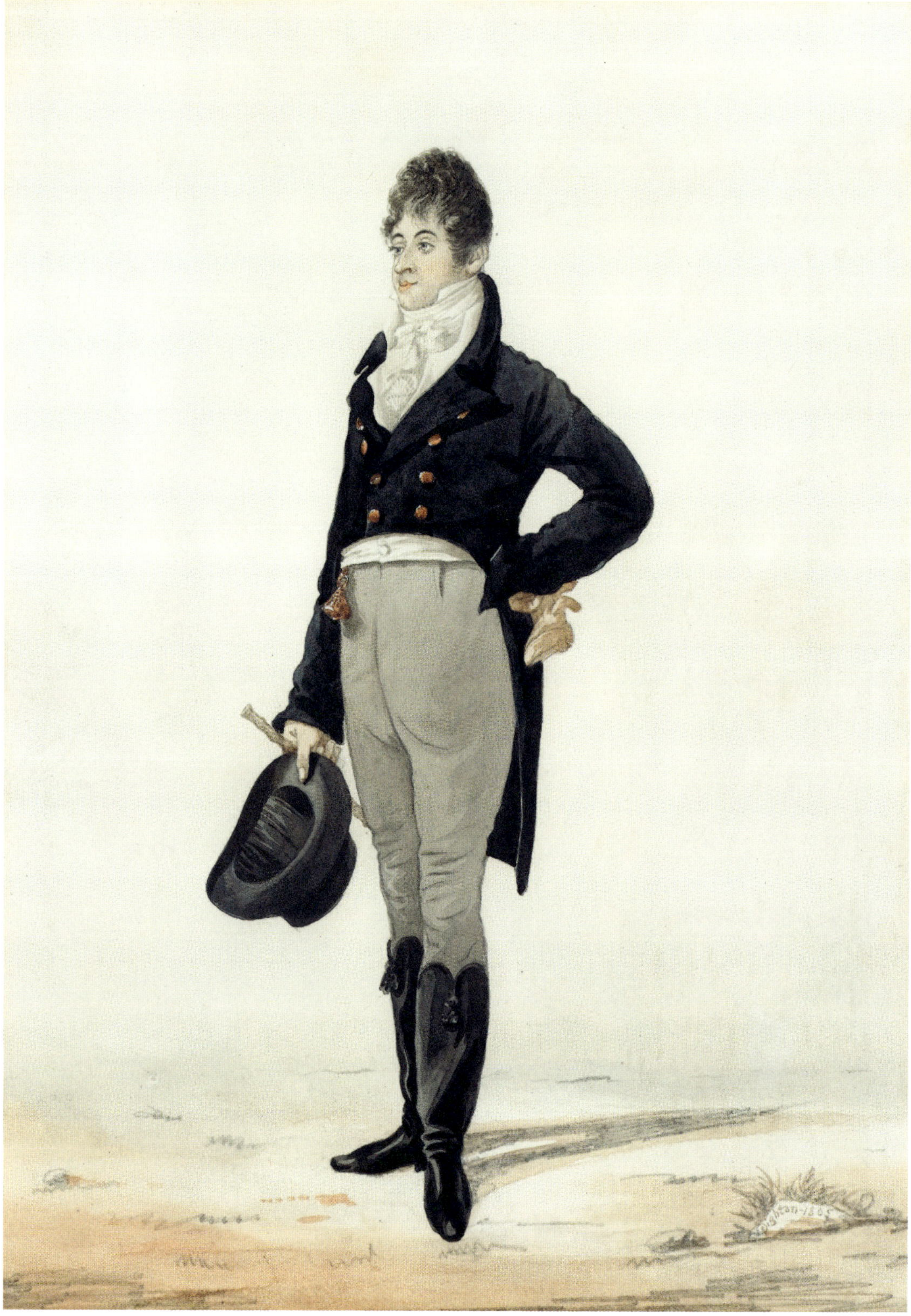

5. Robert Dighton (1752–1814), *Beau Brummell*.
Watercolour on paper, 32.5 × 23.5 cm. England, 1805.
Private collection

George Bryan 'Beau' Brummell was the premier dandy of early nineteenth-century London. He revolutionized menswear by advocating simplicity, quality and fit. For a man famed for his appearance, he left surprisingly few portraits. Dighton's watercolour captures not only the precision of his artfully tied cravat and his Hussar-inspired high-cut navy coat and skin tight breeches, but also the haughty attitude that shamed the rest of society into following his sartorial lead.

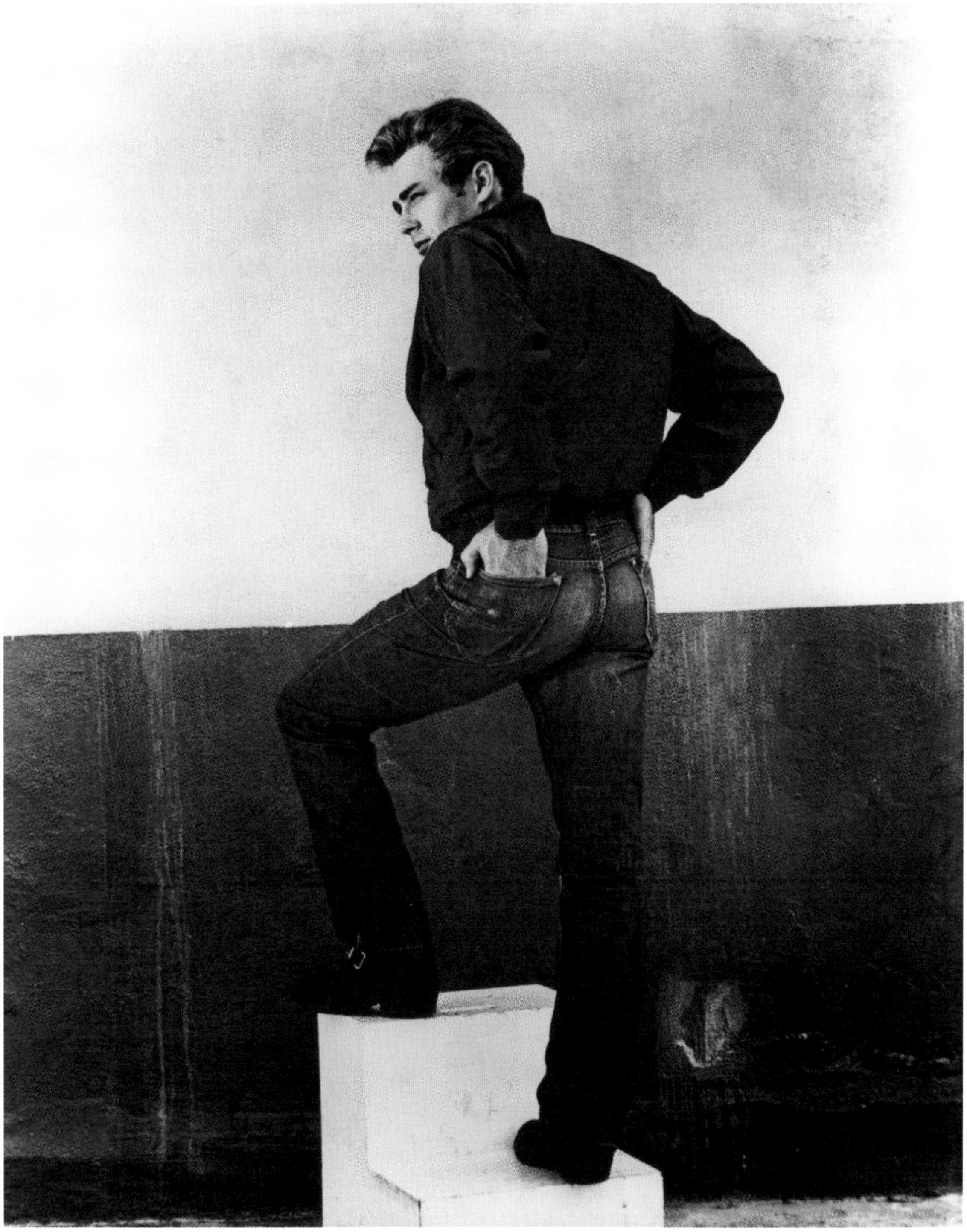

6. James Dean in a publicity portrait for *Rebel Without a Cause* (1955), dir. Nicholas Ray

Actor James Dean created the iconic look of youthful rebellion in 1950s Hollywood. He focused on functionality and fit. His crisp white T-shirts, blouson and biker jackets, minimalist knitwear and straight-cut denim jeans – not to mention his quiff – defined casual style for his generation. The ubiquity of his look today betrays its radicality in the 1950s. Dean transformed humble garments – jeans associated with labourers, and the T-shirt, previously an item of underwear – into enduring wardrobe staples.

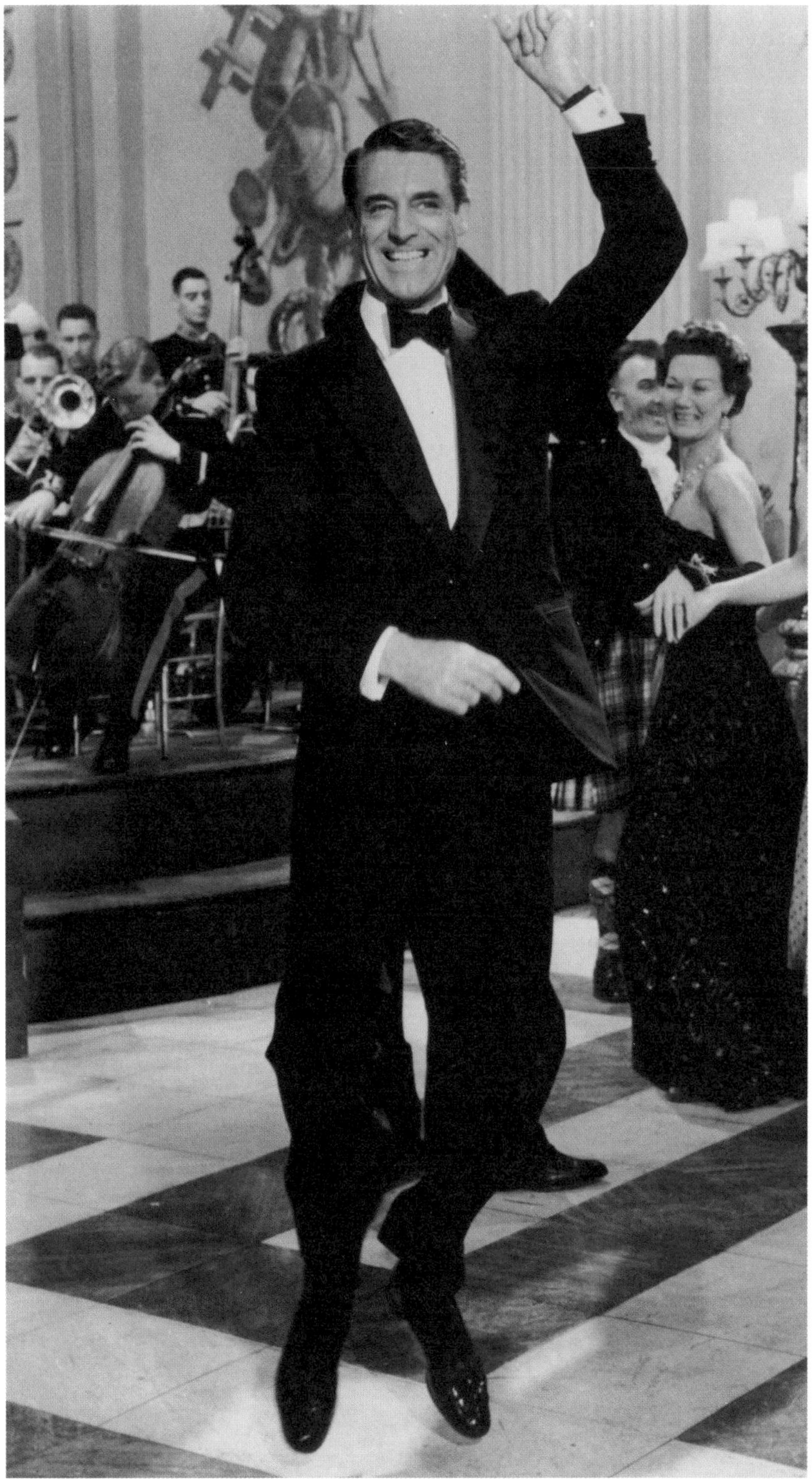

7. Cary Grant in *Indiscreet* (1958), dir. Stanley Donen

British actor Cary Grant popularized Savile Row style in America and beyond. He tailored his suits to his characters, considering his own proportions and their physicality to ensure an ever-elegant appearance. His tuxedo jacket in *Indiscreet* (1958) gives him the freedom of movement required to dance a jig. His grey flannel, single-breasted suit in Alfred Hitchcock's *North by Northwest* (1959) plays a central role in the case of mistaken identity. His everyman appearance has been much imitated.

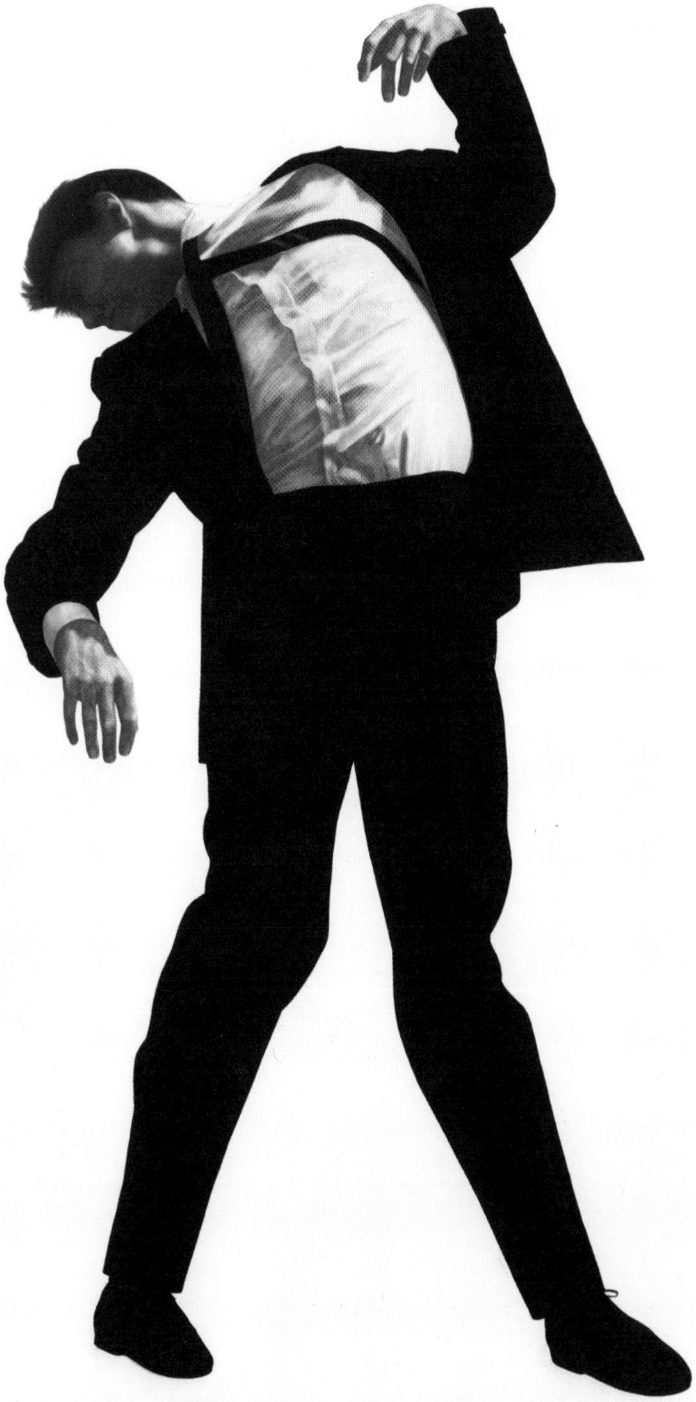

8. Robert Longo (1953–), *Men in the Cities*.
Graphite on paper, 244 × 152.5 cm.
United States, 1981. Thaddaeus Ropac

Robert Longo used his friends as models, photographing them on the rooftop of his New York studio. He pummelled them with balls and pulled them with ropes to create contorted poses. The resulting drawings twist the clean lines of their No wave, Film noir attire. Longo's imagery is associated with the conformity and anguish of city executives, from the opening sequence to TV show *Mad Men* (2007–15) to Mary Harron's film adaptation of Bret Easton Ellis's novel *American Psycho* (1991).

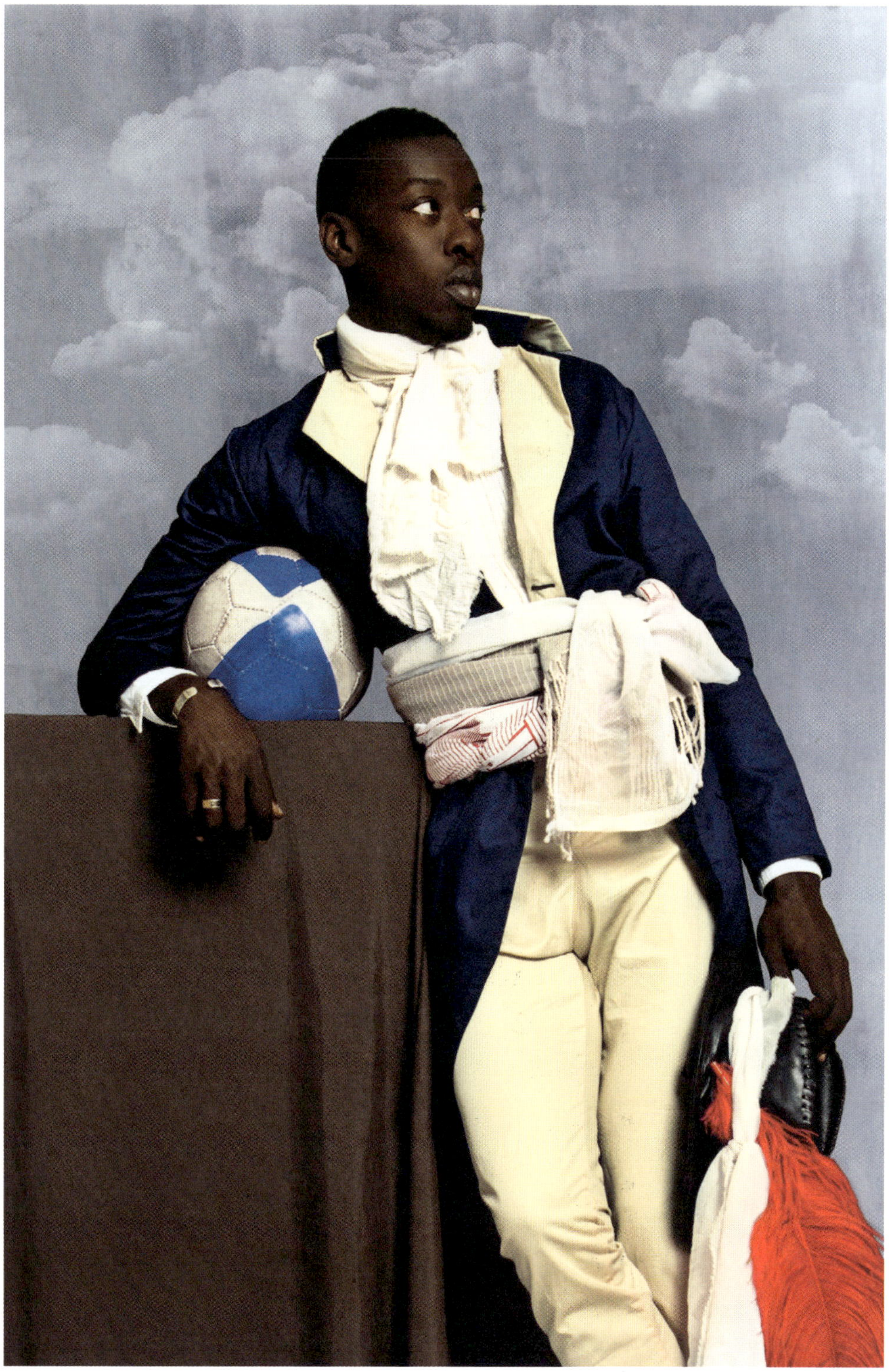

9. Omar Victor Diop (1980–),
after Anne-Louis Girodet (1767–1824), *Jean-Baptiste Belley*.
Pigment inkjet print on Harman by Hahnemühle paper, 120 × 80 cm.
Senegal, 2014. Magnin-A, Paris

In his 'Diaspora' series, photographer Omar Victor Diop restages European portraits of Black men with himself as the sitter, incorporating football-related props to signal the hero-worship and exclusion faced by Black footballers in Europe today. This is a reimagining of a 1797 portrait of Jean-Baptiste Belley, the first Black deputy in the French government, wearing his parliamentary uniform. Belley, born in Senegal, bought his freedom from enslavement and fought in the Haitian Revolution.

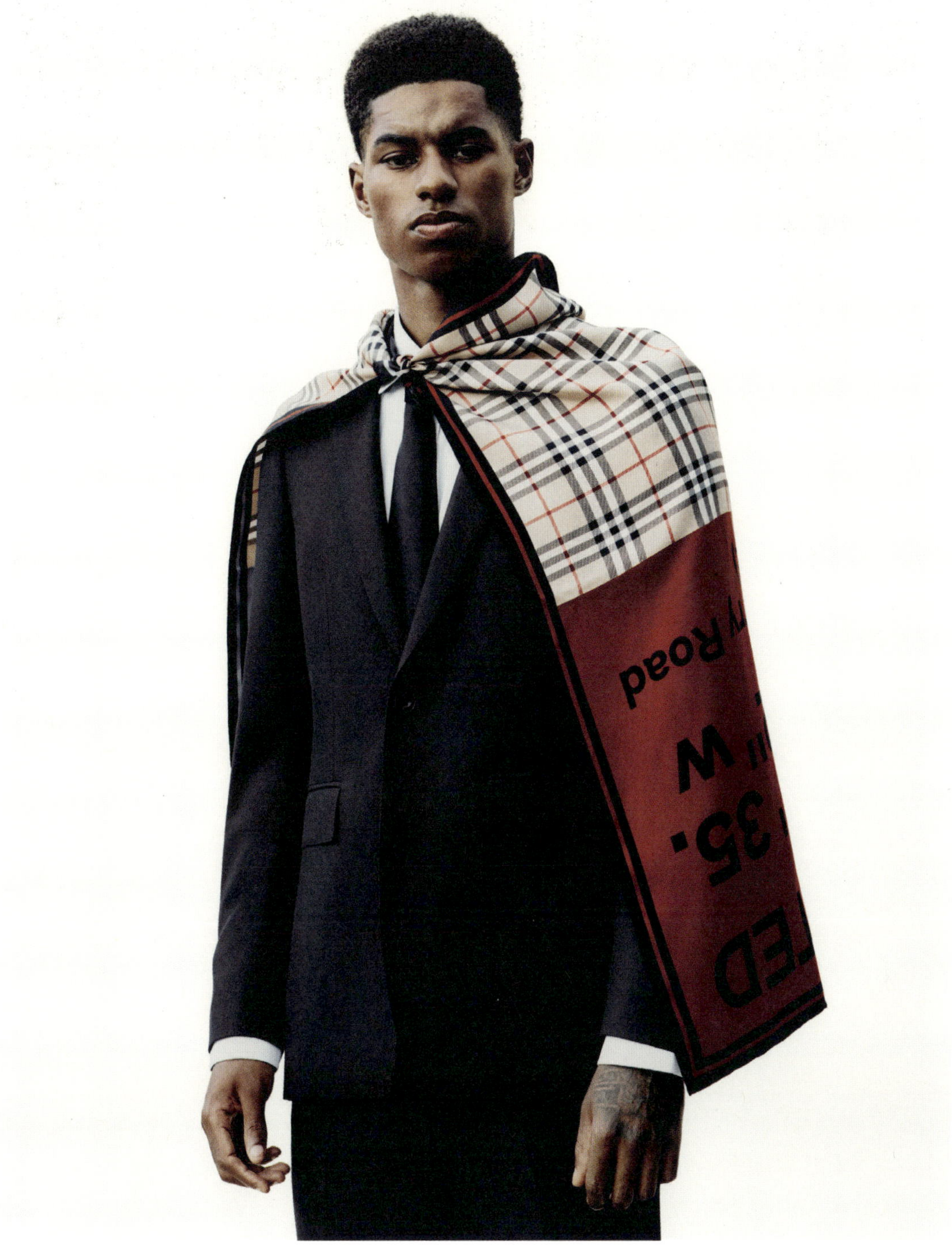

10. Marcus Rashford (1997–),
in Burberry festive campaign, 2020.
Photo by Rafael Pavarotti

Footballer Marcus Rashford uses his platform across the worlds of sport and fashion to campaign for social justice. He appeared on the cover of British *Vogue* in September 2020, and has modelled for Off-White × Nike and Burberry, the latter connected to an initiative to support youth charities. He has become a role model on and off the pitch for challenging racism and advocating for children in underserved communities.

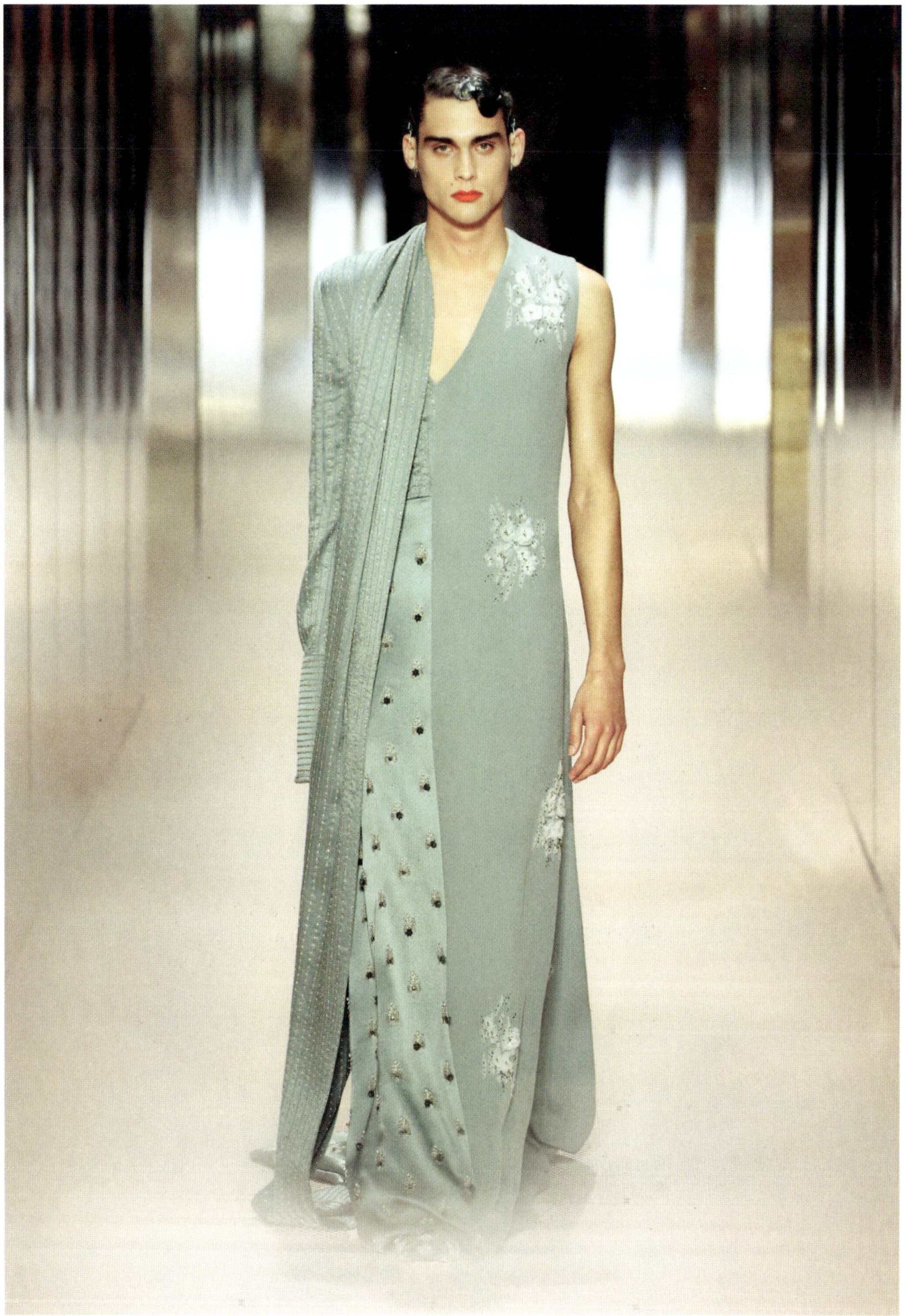

11. Kim Jones (1979–) for Fendi Couture. Dress. Spring/Summer 2021. Model: Ludwig Wilsdorff

The male catwalk model is transforming with the fashion industry's approach to gender. Ludwig Wilsdorff wore this Kim Jones dress in a Fendi womenswear collection inspired by Virginia Woolf's novel *Orlando* (1928). Jones, better known for menswear, used models of all genders for this androgynous runway presentation. Modelling remains one of the few industries in the world where women are paid more than men, yet male models can expect longer careers.

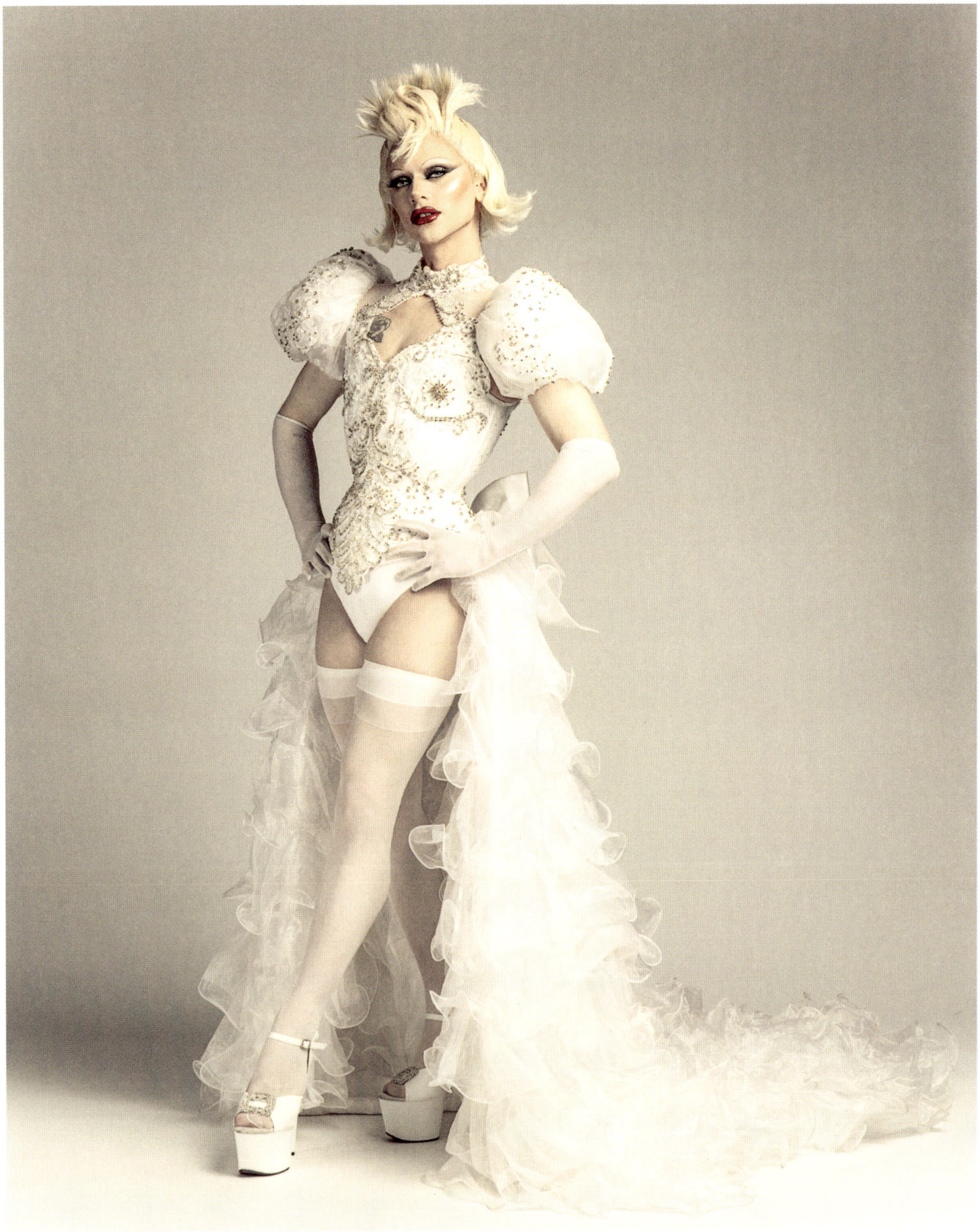

12. Bimini Bon Boulash (1993–)
wearing a wedding look by Ella Lynch for
the final episode of *RuPaul's Drag Race UK* season 2.
Photo by Jakub Koziel

Drag has growing mainstream visibility and fashion crossover. Drag queen Bimini Bon Boulash, who found fame on *RuPaul's Drag Race UK* season 2, now works as a professional model. On the show, her looks were fashion-forward and inspired by couture as much as punk. She wore a wedding dress for the finale to honour the traditional end of a fashion show. Performer Tommy speaks openly about their own non-binary gender identity.

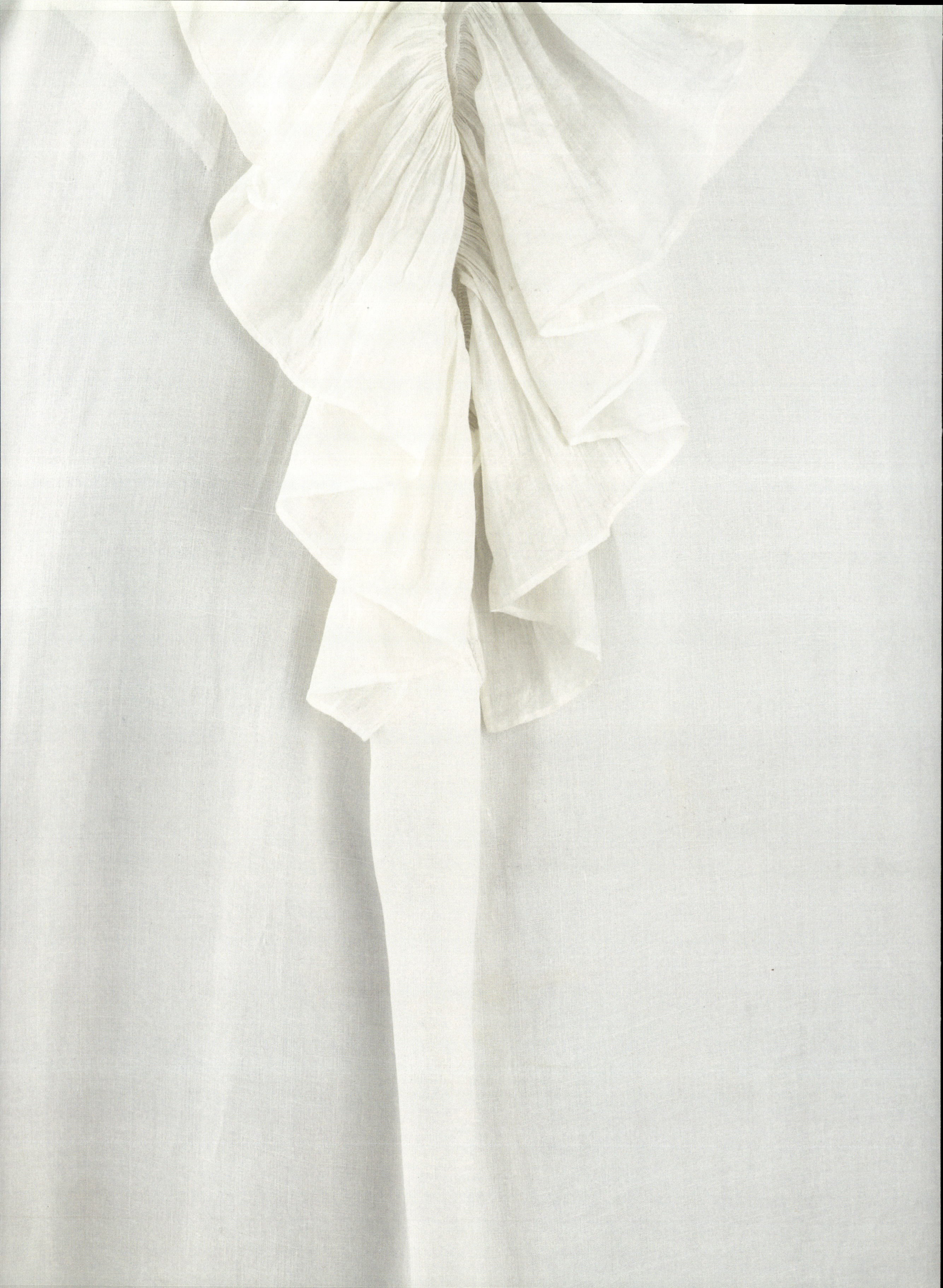

UNDRESSED

HIS BODY IS AN ANALOGUE OF THE WORLD

LEONARDO DA VINCI

*c.*1490

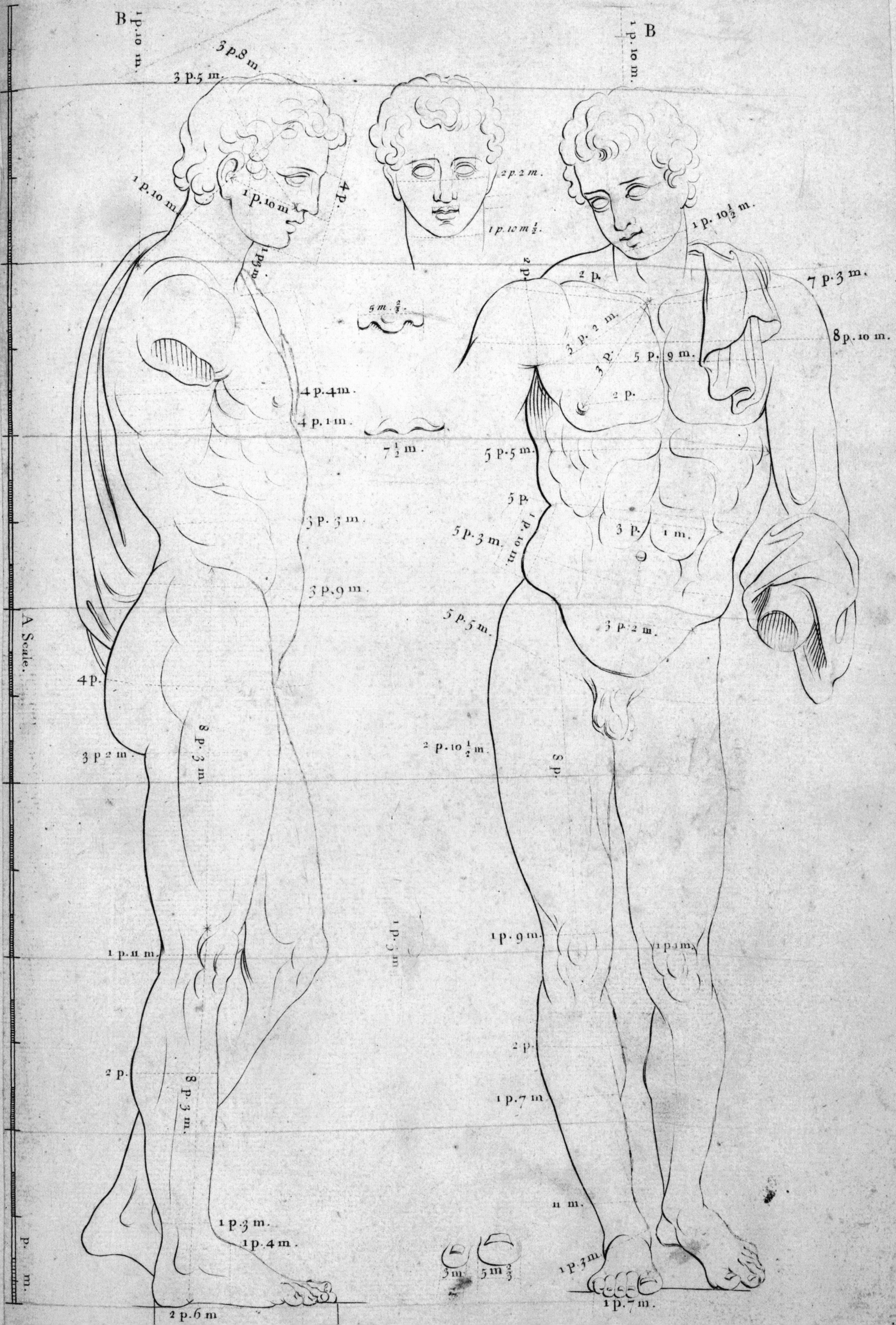

B
1 p. 10 m.
3 p. 8 m.
3 p. 5 m.
1 p. 10 m.
1 p. 10 m.
4 p.
2 p. 2 m.
1 p. 10 m ½.
1 p. 10 ½ m.
7 p. 3 m.
8 p. 10 m.
2 p.
3 p. 2 m.
3 p.
5 p. 9 m.
5 m. ⅔
4 p. 4 m.
4 p. 1 m.
7 ½ m.
5 p. 5 m.
5 p.
5 p. 3 m.
1 p. 10 m.
3 p. 1 m.
3 p. 3 m.
3 p. 9 m.
5 p. 5 m.
3 p. 2 m.
A Scale.
4 p.
8 p. 3 m.
3 p. 2 m.
2 p. 10 ½ m.
8 p.
1 p. 9 m.
1 p. 11 m.
1 p. 3 m.
2 p.
2 p.
8 p. 3 m.
1 p. 7 m.
11 m.
1 p. 3 m.
1 p. 4 m.
3 m.
5 m ⅔
1 p. 3 m.
1 p. 7 m.
2 p. 6 m.
p.
m.

MARBLE MARVELS AND CLASSICAL IDEALS

SARAH GOLDSMITH

Throughout the eighteenth century, the galleries and courtyards of Rome's Vatican, Villa Borghese and Palazzo Farnese, along with the Medici family's ducal collections in Florence, rang with the footsteps and appreciative voices of visitors from across Europe. They came to admire the 'beautiful Originals of the Ancients': marble sculptures that have been revered as the pinnacle of artist achievement and exemplars of aesthetic human beauty in the Global North since the Renaissance and that continue to exert a profound influence in contemporary culture.[1] In among goddesses, nymphs, animals and vases sat sculptures depicting the epitome of the male body: the divine splendour of the Roman god *Apollo Belvedere*, caught in the motion of drawing his bow; the soft naturalism of the beautiful youth *Belvedere Antinous*, then believed to portray Emperor Hadrian's lover; the fragmented beauty of the muscular *Belvedere Torso*; the dynamic form of the Hellenistic swordsman known as the *Borghese Gladiator*; and the enormous figure of the Roman hero and demi-god the *Farnese Hercules*, to name but a few.[2]

A common visitor to these galleries and courtyards was the young British gentleman on the Grand Tour (13). This was a rite of passage undertaken by privileged and wealthy young men in their late teens and early twenties. It often lasted three to four years, covering the cities, courts and environs of France, the Netherlands and Low Countries, the German principalities, Austria, Switzerland and Italy. Its purpose was to ensure that its participants returned formed in the skills, virtues and adult masculine identities of Britain's ruling classes. This was (hopefully) achieved via a wide variety of expensive, time-consuming itineraries that included learning to ride, fence and dance, purchasing the latest fashions, reviewing troops and military encampments, inspecting the latest in industry and innovation, and launching themselves into the swirl of European society. Italy was an undoubted high point. Here, a youthful elite, taught from childhood to admire republican Greece and Rome as the zenith of civilization, was able to view and embrace the classical remnants found in Florence, Rome and Naples as its own heritage and birthright.[3] While some tourists were too immature to appreciate the experience, many more wrote enthusiastic letters and diaries, describing days that overflowed with architecture and monuments, bas reliefs and medals, vases and mosaics, and, of course, sculpture.[4]

These tourists did not limit themselves to admiring the artefacts *in situ*. Facilitated by a flourishing international art market and by their family's coffers, and gripped by a fashion for the classical, generations of British nobility brought home replicas, casts and (more rarely) original pieces. Sculpture was in particularly fierce demand, so much so that the moulds of the most popular statues, like the only cast of the *Borghese Gladiator*, were quite worn out by the end of the century. Reports that Prince Borghese was reluctant to risk the original by allowing further moulds to be taken were therefore potential sources of dismay.[5] Back in Britain, the ambitious collecting and architectural projects of the nobility and gentry were aided by the British artists and architects who journeyed to Italy to receive their professional training and subsequently embedded the classical into their own designs. Together, they ensured that classical motifs and imagery were ever-present in eighteenth-century culture. On private and public display as replicas and casts, the most famous sculptures were also cited in publications, incorporated into satirical prints, and inspired contemporary works of art. From aesthetic discourse to political satire, architecture to anatomy, and literary novels to accounts of cricket matches, eighteenth-century culture was littered with casual references to specific examples of antique sculpture. Somewhat ironically, this familiarity extended to contemporary travel literature. Even at the start of the period, Maximilien Misson, author of the enduringly popular *A New Voyage to Italy* (1691, English translation 1695), decided that Rome's most famous sculptures were so well known that only a brief mention was needed.[6]

William Hogarth's print 'The Sculpture Yard' in his treatise *The Analysis of Beauty* (1753) exemplifies the ubiquity of classical marble sculptures in eighteenth-century Britain (14). At the yard's centre stands the *Medici Venus*, surrounded by replicas of the most famous antique statues of the male form. Her gaze falls on the *Apollo Belvedere* to her right. Just below her plinth, facing away from the viewer, sits the *Belvedere Torso*. The *Farnese Hercules* also faces away from the viewer, on a towering plinth to the left but with a separate bust of his head facing forwards on the far left. Next to his plinth stands the *Belvedere Antinous*. To his right, and behind the *Venus*, the *Laocoön* sits beneath tripod scaffolding. In declining to provide any introductory explanations in his accompanying discussions, Hogarth evidently expected his eighteenth-century audience to be intimately familiar with these sculptures and their significance.

'THE BEAUTIES OF MEN'

But why were these statues so esteemed? On the one hand, eighteenth-century viewers deeply admired the translucent white qualities of marble itself, an admiration that conflated marble's aesthetic properties with

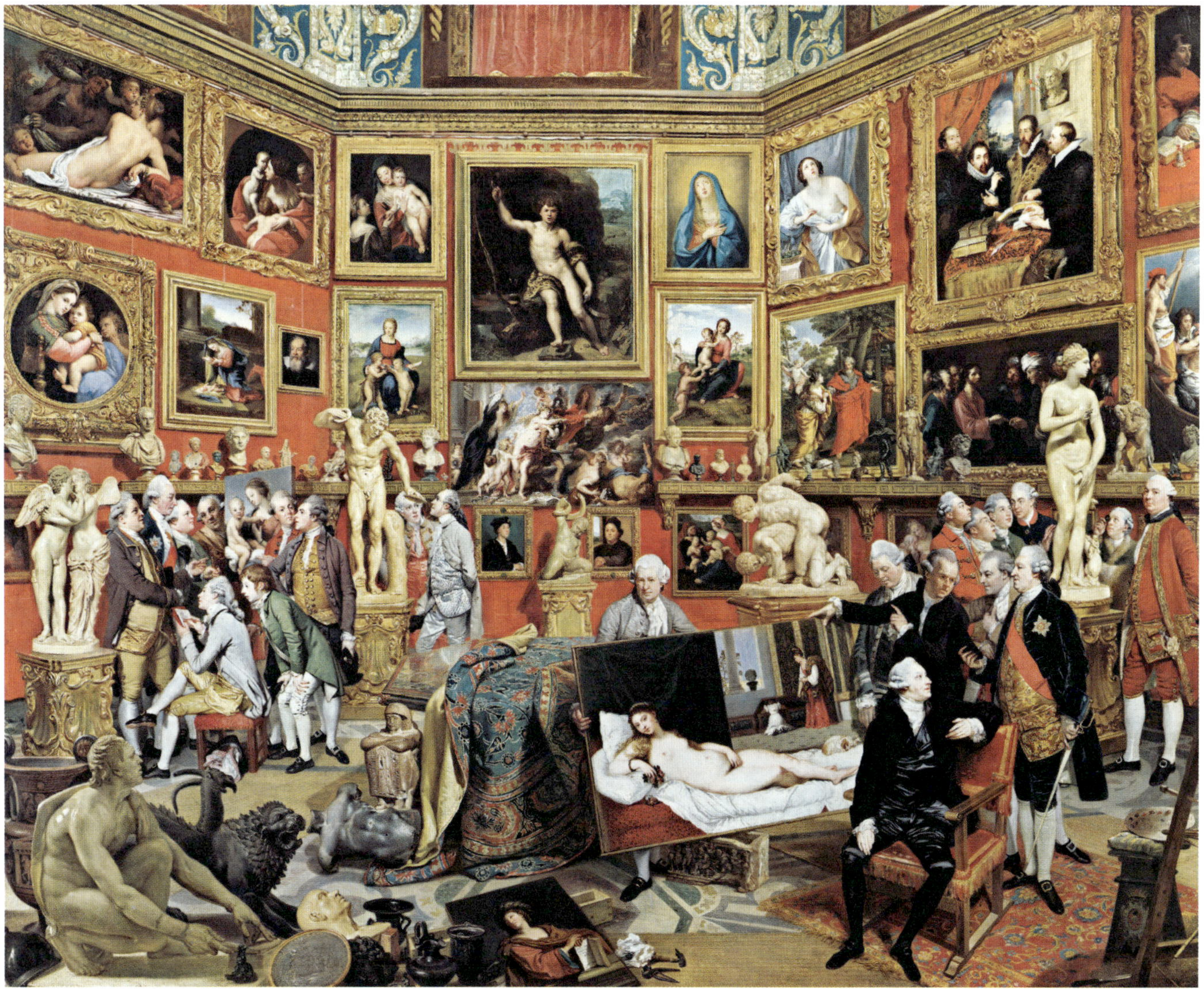

13. Johan Joseph Zoffany RA (1733–1810), *The Tribuna of the Uffizi*.
Oil on canvas, 123.5 × 155 cm. Florence, 1772–7.
Royal Collection Trust: RCIN 406983

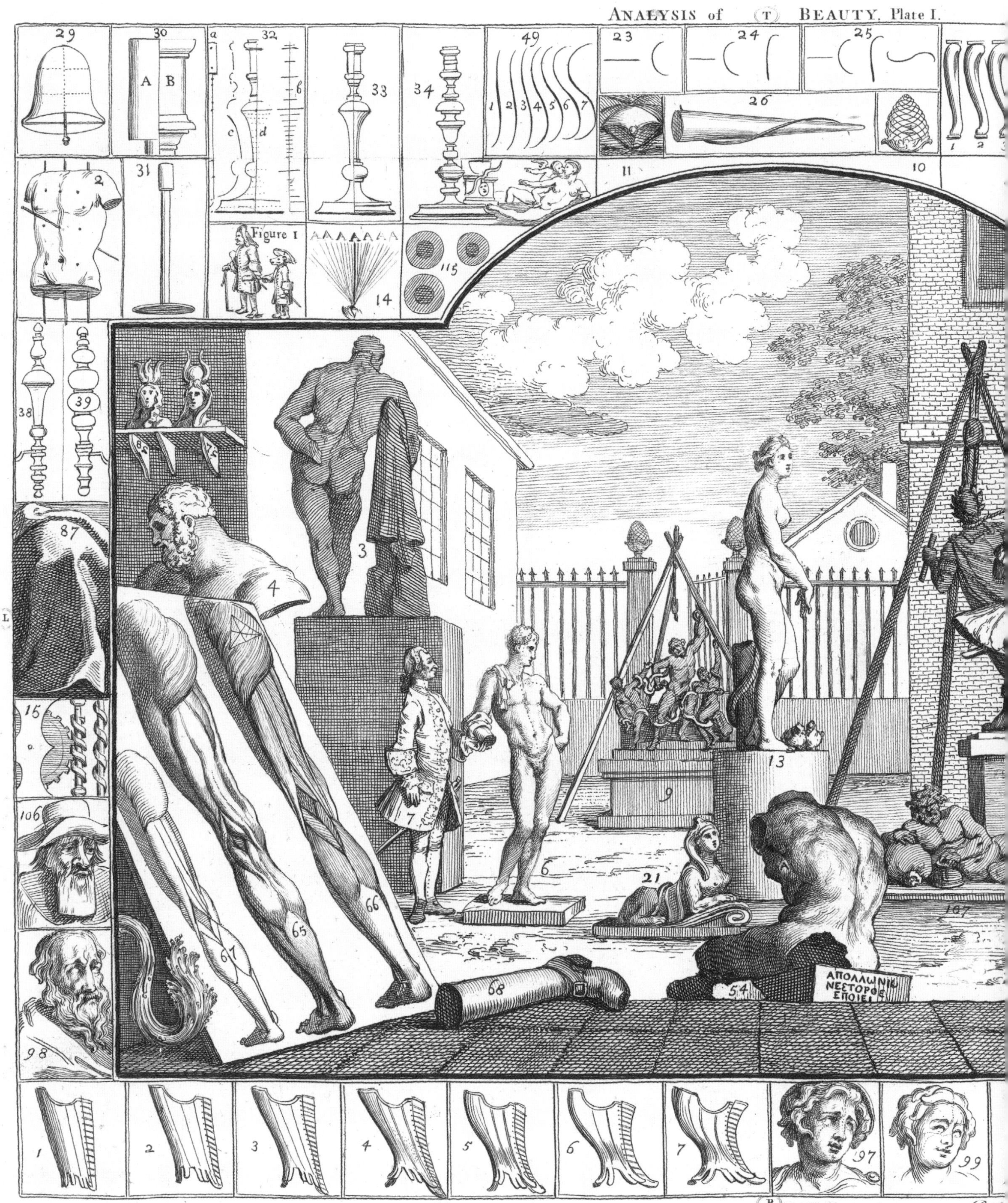

14. William Hogarth (1697–1764), 'The Sculpture Yard',
The Analysis of Beauty (London, 1753).
Forster Bequest. V&A: F.118:124

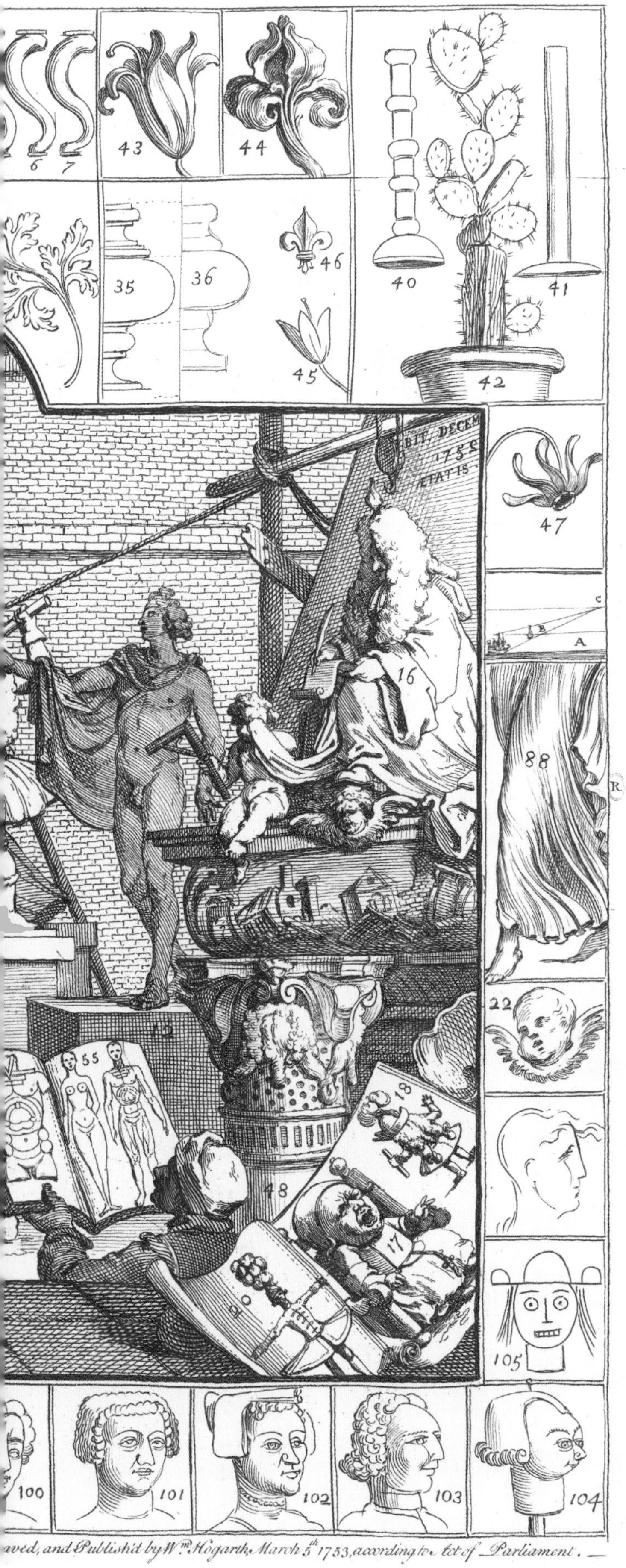

the supposedly superior beauties of white skin. By the nineteenth century, this admiration involved wilfully ignoring the growing evidence that these sculptures would have been painted in bright colours with a wide range of skin tones reflective of a Roman empire that at its height stretched from North Africa to Scotland. This deliberate whitewashing was underpinned by, and in turn enabled, a set of assumptions about western cultural, aesthetic and racial superiority that continue to this day.[7] On the other hand, the male canon of antique statues was consistently celebrated for its depiction of the ideal male body as strong, well-proportioned and athletic. Eighteenth-century commentators also noted that the canon contained a spectrum of physiques to admire. These ranged from heavy muscularity to sinewy litheness to athletic fitness with a degree of softness, while remaining within the parameters of this ideal.

In 1723 the French clergyman and writer François Raguenet, for example, drew comparisons between the *Apollo Belvedere* and *Belvedere Antinous*. They both represented men 'about the same Age' and were 'two of the most beautiful Bodies of a Man that ever was made'.[8] The *Antinous* was particularly celebrated for the natural, graceful and gentle sweep of the body, and for simply depicting 'a Man' with 'nothing in him but what is natural'.[9] In contrast, the *Apollo* was 'full of Lineaments sensibly divine' and 'sublimely superhuman'.[10] This was a statue of a divine male body that ravished its viewers, but the *Apollo's* physique was more than merely overwhelming.[11] It was also praised for combining 'the charming manliness of maturity with graceful youthfulness', with 'as much of softness in all of that is consistent with strength'.[12] This juxtaposition of a 'manly-soften'd Form' was admired well into the nineteenth century. In 1870 the German writer Leopold von Sacher-Masoch wrote in his *Venus in Furs*, for example, of that intoxicating combination of 'slender, steely musculature' and 'delicate features'.[13]

Sitting midway between the human and divine was the *Farnese Hercules*. In 1755 Joseph Spence, a scholar and Grand Tour tutor, drew attention to the extremity of muscularity and size: 'That breadth of his shoulder; this spaciousness of his chest; the vastness of his size, and the firmness of the muscles all over him.'[14] This was an example of a beautiful male body formed by a life of labour: 'a Man the most robust that ever was', 'Without being gigantick, or like a *Colossus*'.[15] Other sculptures were also celebrated for their beautiful muscularity. Johann Joachim Winckelmann, often considered the father of art history, exclaimed over the 'Abused and mutilated' *Belvedere Torso*'s 'powerful raised chest' and thigh muscles, claiming that 'Such a balanced fleshiness is to be found in no other figure'.[16] Commentators were divided over whether the *Torso* depicted the demi-divine body of Hercules, but there was no such debate over the *Borghese Gladiator* and the *Wrestlers* (which appears to the centre right of Johan Joseph Zoffany's painting). Like the *Antinous*, these were appreciated as representations of human bodies. As Misson enthused over the *Gladiator* in 1691, 'The Figure is an Imitation of the most exquisite Proportions of Nature: It represents a Man in the Vigour of his Age.'[17] Raguenet waxed lyrical over how:

> There is not one part of his [the *Gladiator's*] Body that does not shew that he has collected all its Force against his Adversary; all his Muscles from the Head to the Foot are stretched, swoln with Spirits, and employd to furnish him with that Vehemence he would make use of against his Enemy.[18]

Thus, while the *Antinous* was celebrated for its stillness, the *Gladiator's* reputation rested on its explosive sense of powerful motion, which captured man's ultimate athletic capacities.[19]

It has long been understood that eighteenth-century elite British men viewed these cold marble representations of gods, demi-gods, heroes and athletes through the lens of Whig political and cultural ideologies that positioned Georgian Britain as heir to the glories of the classical past. These statues were seen as the physical manifestations of the abstract concept of ideal beauty and the embodiment of the political, cultural and artistic perfection of Hellenic Greece and Republican Rome.[20] Political and aesthetic theorists argued that by admiring and displaying these artefacts, elite men could simultaneously demonstrate their taste in classical aesthetics, develop their virtue and spur themselves and others to honourable, disinterested acts of civic mindedness.[21]

While scholars have argued that this indicates a deeply disinterested gaze that prized the statues' 'Beauties and Excellence of Virtue' over their 'corporeal Beauty', there is plenty of evidence that suggests the two were admired together.[22] Certainly, when it came to classical sculptures of women's bodies, eighteenth-century dilettante and antiquarian practices had distinctly erotic undertones that clearly conflated beautiful marble and flesh.[23] This is implied in Zoffany's painting (13), in which Grand Tourists gaze admiringly up at the *Venus'* rear and reach out to touch her leg, and, more irreverently, in Thomas Patch's *A Gathering of the Dilettanti around the Medici Venus* (c.1760–1), which features a young dilettante clambering up onto the plinth to embrace her. Likewise, exemplars of aesthetic male beauty evoked romantic and/or erotic passion in their male and female viewers. In 1723 Raguenet desired the 'fair Sex' to view the *Apollo Belvedere* and state whether 'all the fine Images they ever form'd of the Beauties of Men are not very short of what this Statue presents them with.'[24] In 1754 Winckelmann's erotically charged descriptions mused that the *Apollo's* musculature was 'supple, and blown like molten glass in hardly visible undulations that are more apparent to the feeling than to the sight'.[25] As more women began to travel, they recorded their own reactions to the *Apollo*. In 1820 Charlotte Eaton outlined her raptures in *Rome, in the Nineteenth Century*, before recounting the tale of a French damsel who 'lost at once her heart and her reason', gazing, sighing and weeping at the statue until she died.[26]

Eighteenth-century society was unabashed in using these statues as a yardstick for real male bodies. Hogarth's 'Sculpture Yard', for example, makes an unfavourable visual comparison between the customer's body and that of the *Farnese Hercules* and *Belvedere Antinous*, in whose shadows he stands (14). Hogarth drove his point home by writing disapprovingly of 'the common notion that a person should be as straight as an arrow, and perfectly erect', mockingly imagining how a dancing master would 'cry shame' on 'the easy and gracefully-turned attitude of the Antinous ... and tell him he looked as crooked as a ram's horn.'[27] Arguing for the beauty of the natural form, Hogarth indicated that contemporary men could achieve this beauty, and do so by emulating the pose of classical sculpture. Their dancing masters may have cried shame on them, but the work of the highly popular Grand Tour portraitist Pompeo Batoni indicates that elite young men were doing exactly this. Based in Rome, Batoni produced around 225 tour portraits from the 1750s to the 1770s. These portraits were meant to capture young men at a significant coming of age moment, and Batoni excelled in presenting his sitters at ease with the grandeur of classical Rome. In many cases, their informal, dynamic poses were directly adapted from classical sculpture, such as the *Apollo Belvedere*.[28]

Batoni's quest to make a favourable comparison between his subjects and classical sculpture was aided by men's fashions. From the mid-century onwards, the three-piece suit became tighter, swaddling the body from neck to ankle to create a closely wrapped silhouette that was, like the portraits, intended to echo the classical male form.[29] In Batoni's 1759 Grand Tour portrait of Richard Milles, the long line of the sitter's body is on full display, outlined in his marble-white silk waistcoat, which clings tightly to the torso before flaring out at the hips, and by the well-fitting red breeches (15). Milles's choice of waistcoat was probably not intended to emulate marble perfection, but the convention of sheathing one's calves in fine knitted white silk stockings to create a sleek, translucently pale look most certainly was.[30]

By the Regency period, even more of the male body was on show as sculpted, close-fitting woollen broadcloth jackets, smooth doeskin pantaloons, shorter waistcoats and long coat tails all conspired to cling tightly and expose the thighs, groin and waist (16). As the fashion theorist Anne Hollander has argued, this style sought to fashion a body that was 'part English country gentleman, part innocent natural Adam, and part naked Apollo'.[31] The idealized bodily proportions of classical statues were even present in the nineteenth-century shift towards standard sizing and mass production. The German mathematician Dr Henry

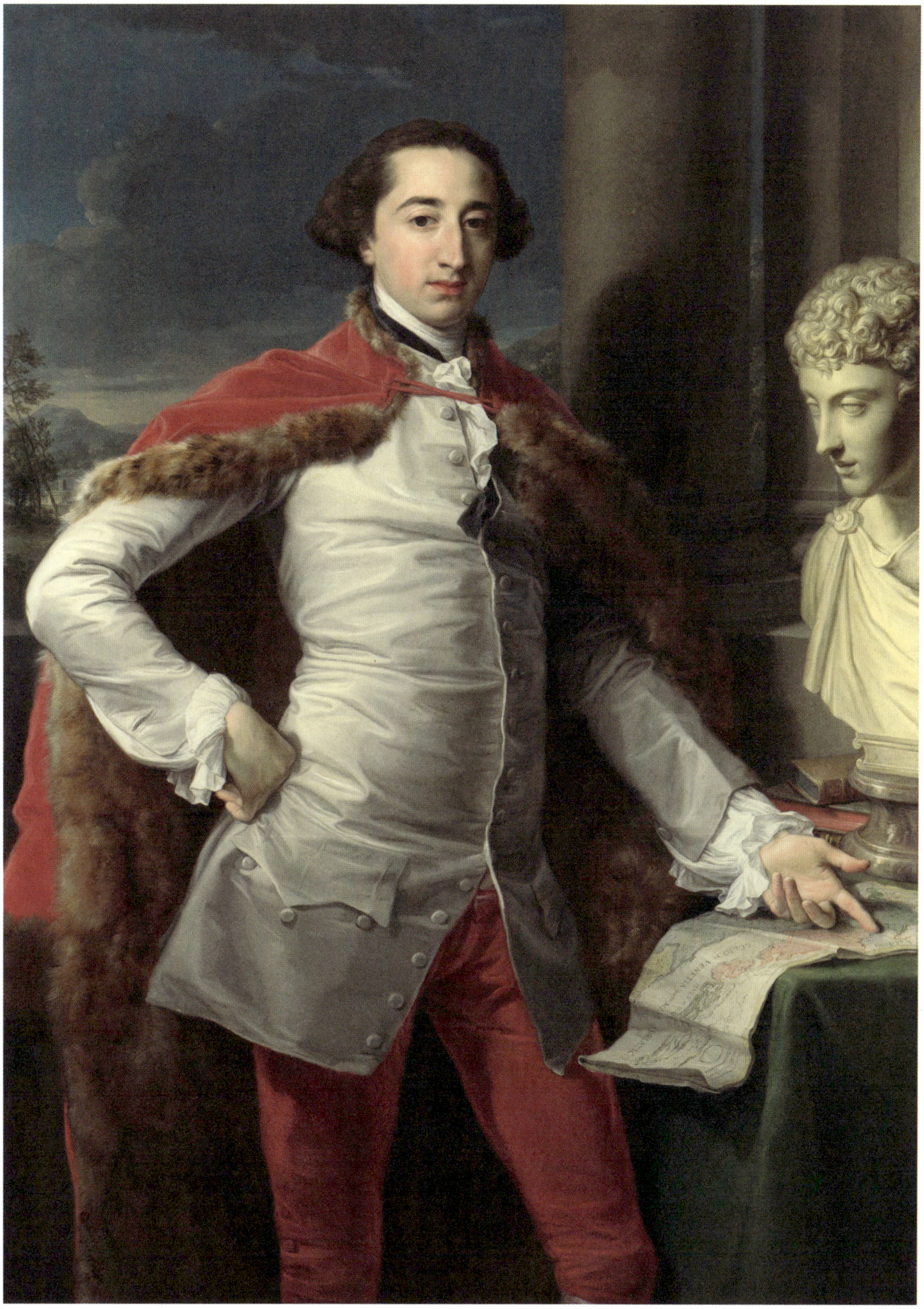

15. Pompeo Batoni (1708–1787), *Richard Milles*.
Oil on canvas, 134.6×96.3cm. Italy, *c.*1759.
National Gallery, London: NG6459

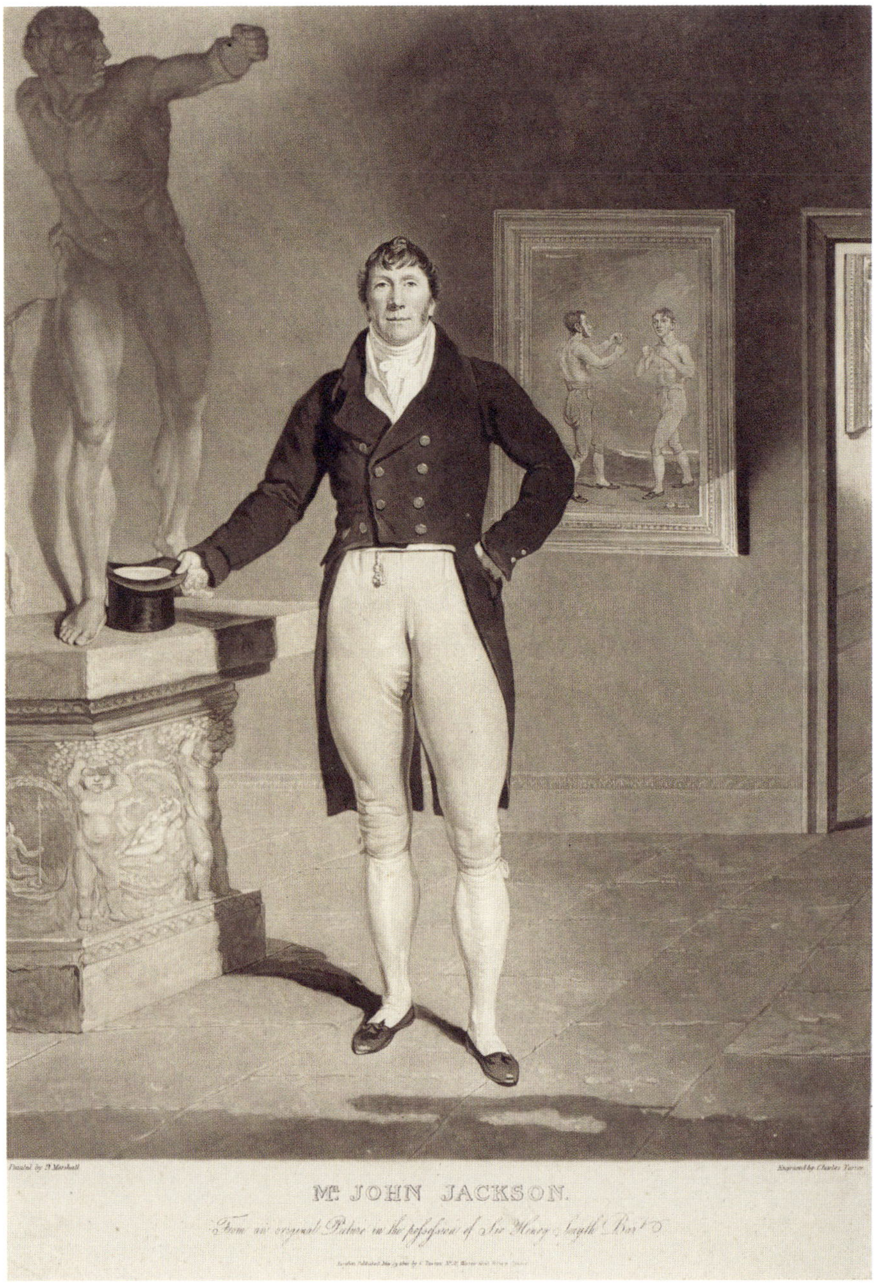

16. Charles Turner ARA (1774–1857), after Benjamin Marshall,
Mr John Jackson. London, 1810. Mezzotint, 68.8×49.5cm. V&A: 22031

Wampen, whose work was influential in the calculations required for this shift, described how the naked male form in its perfect 'classical' state and his early measurements of 'certain statues' were informative in creating his rules of proportion for the design of male clothing.[32]

As importantly, favourable comparisons were drawn between classical figures, sculpture and contemporary men as a way of praising physical male beauty and skill. Horace Walpole, for example, compared Henry Fiennes Pelham-Clinton, the 9th Earl of Lincoln, to a young Hercules: 'He was tall, well-made, and his complexion of a manly brown. He had eery feature and limb that promised strength and vigour.'[33] The expanding sport industry of the eighteenth century also looked to classical models. James Dance's comic *Cricket: A Heroic Poem* (1744), for example, described a game between Kent and 'All England' in which Richard Newland's bowling arm was comparable to '*Alcmena's* sinew'd Son' (Hercules), and Val Rumney's speed like '*Hermes* ... Whose winged Feet like nimble Lightning move!'[34] Boxers repeatedly used classical references in an effort to highlight their sport's ancient Olympic origins. For example, John Hamilton Mortimer's mid-eighteenth-century portrait of the champion boxer Jack Broughton shows him stripped to the waist and poised to fight, his muscular torso, arms and thighs framing the bas-relief of *The Wrestlers* behind him (17). Less than 50 years later, another boxing champion, John 'Gentleman' Jackson, also sought to make a direct comparison between his fight prowess and a classical precedent. In Benjamin Marshall's portrait, Jackson appears dressed in the

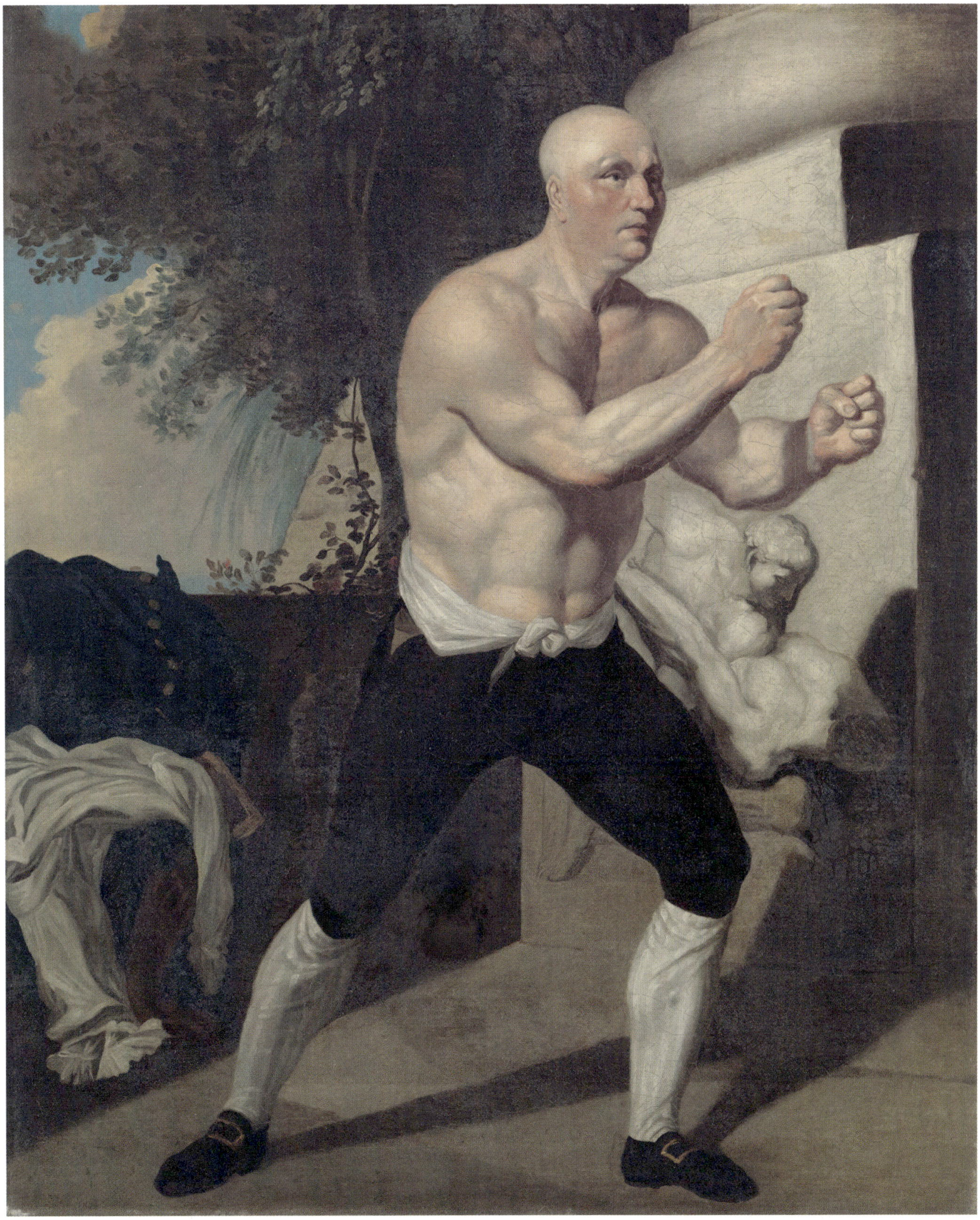

17. John Hamilton Mortimer ARA (1740–1779), *Jack Broughton, the Boxer*. Oil on canvas, 76.2×63.5cm. Great Britain, *c.*1767. Yale Center for British Art, Paul Mellon Collection, New Haven: B1981.25.462

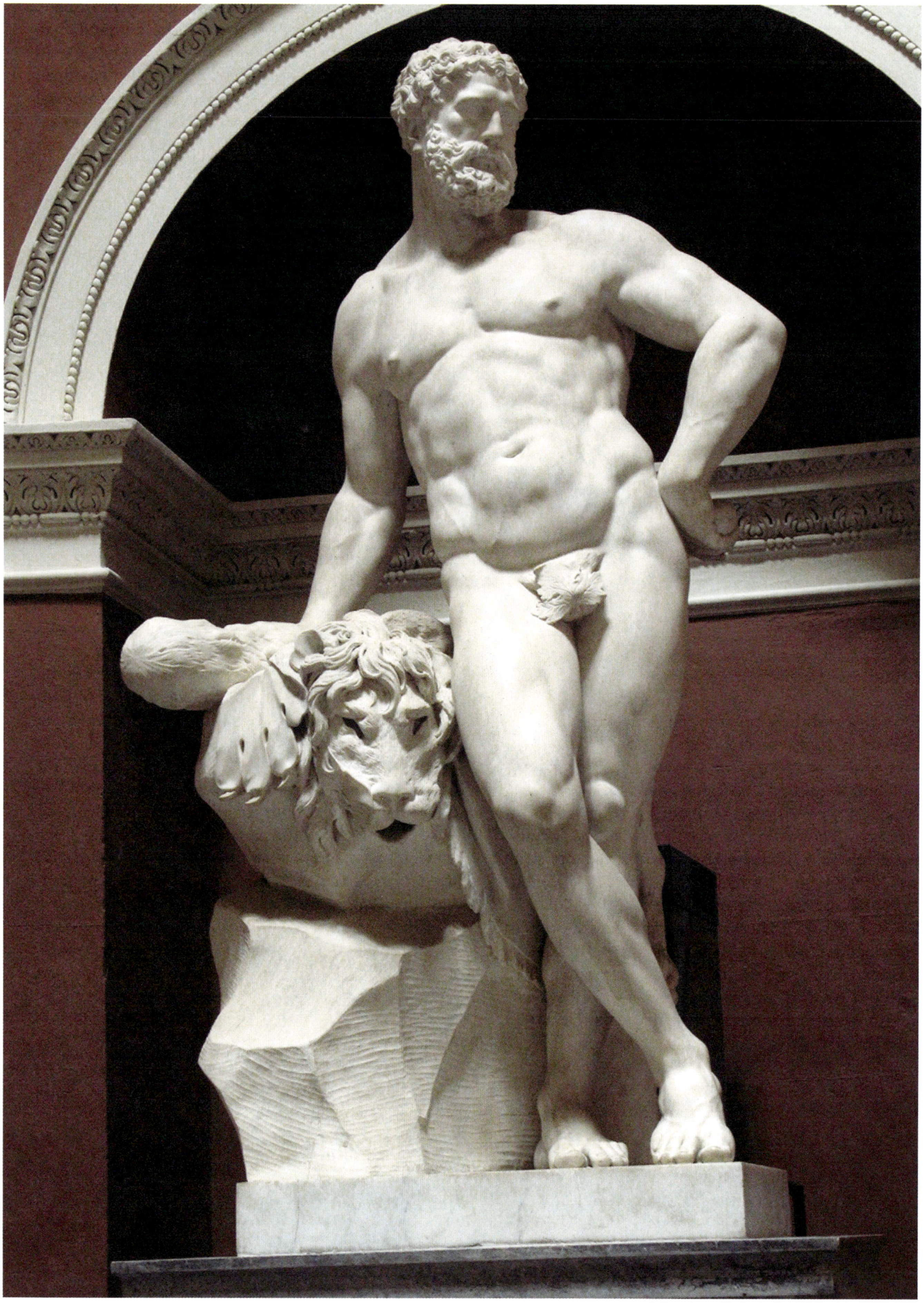

18. John Michael Rysbrack (1694–1770), *Hercules*. Marble, h.185.5cm.
London, 1756. Stourhead, Wiltshire. National Trust: 562911.1

latest Regency fashions with a framed print of his famous 1795 victory against Daniel Mendoza (16). The viewer's gaze, however, is directed to how Jackson's stance, one powerful leg slightly in front of the other, one arm reaching out with his hat, the other resting on his hip, carefully mirrors the *Borghese Gladiator*'s dynamic pose.

These comparisons were presumably made at the sitter's request, but artists themselves made eager use of the parallels between boxers' bodies and classical sculpture. One of the more curious comparisons was John Michael Rysbrack's sculpture of *Hercules* at Stourhead, created in 1756 as an experiment in Plato's abstract concept of the ideal (18).[35] Rysbrack used the *Farnese Hercules* for his rule of proportion but modelled the figure on 'one of the famous fighting boxers', George the Coachman. In addition, he selected 'the most beauty-full, or the most perfect parts' from six other named men, mingling and matching body parts to create an ideal whole. While very much an exploration of ideal beauty, this sculpture was nevertheless also a celebration of the living, breathing beauty of contemporary bodies that he deemed comparable to the *Farnese Hercules*. These seven men were sourced from Broughton's boxing amphitheatre, which was a mere ten minutes' walk from St Martin's Academy (the predecessor to the Royal Academy). They included Broughton himself who provided 'the belly & lower parts', and John Ellys, a portrait painter and senior figure at St Martin's, who provided a fantastic pair of legs.[36]

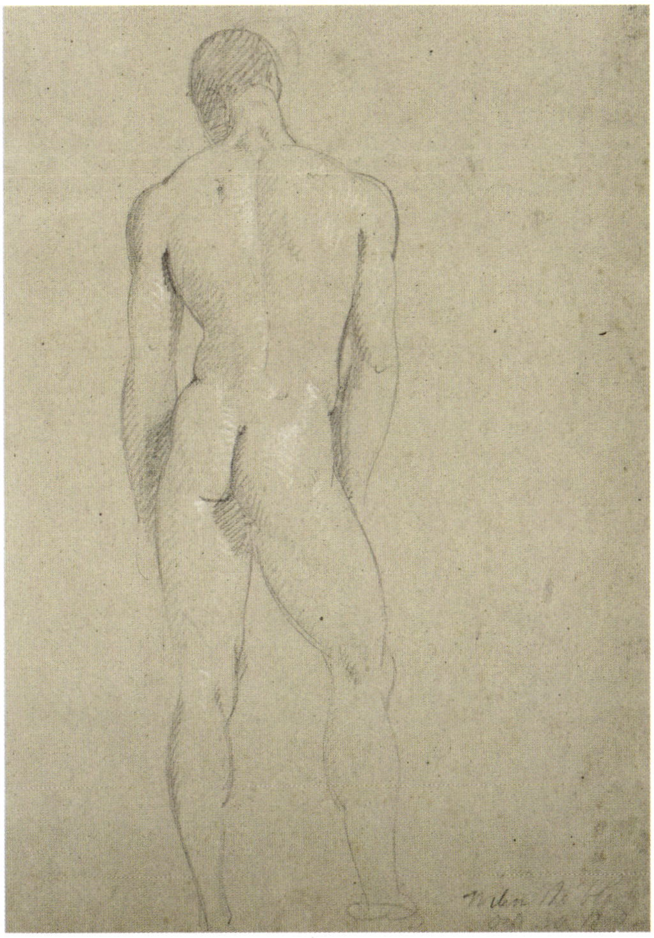

19. Benjamin Robert Haydon (1786–1846), *Nude male figure, study of the black sailor Wilson*. Black chalk, heightened with white, on brown paper, 53×38.3cm. London, 30 October 1810. The British Museum, London: 1881,0709.528

Yet another set of comparisons were made in the summer of 1808, when Jackson helped Anthony Carlisle, a surgeon and professor of anatomy at the Royal Academy, organize an appraisal of the recently acquired Parthenon marbles, highlighting their astonishing anatomical accuracy.[37] The arrival and, from 1817, permanent display of the marbles at the British Museum was part of the nineteenth-century Greek Revival. This was a significant shift in classical taste in which the ancient Greek (as opposed to the Roman) male body – as depicted in the marbles and other sculptures, such as Myron's *Discobolus* and Polykleitos' *Doryphoros*, *Diadumenos* and *Discophoros* – became widely celebrated for its naturalism, athleticism and beautiful proportions.[38] During the first meeting, artists, medical experts and gentlemen closely examined 'Gregson, the Pugilist, stripped naked', who was deemed 'the finest figure the persons present had seen'.[39] At the second meeting, held at Lord Elgin's house, Gregson posed nude among the marbles. This was repeated at the final meeting, which concluded with bouts of exhibition sparring between four leading boxers: John Gulley, Jem Belcher, Dutch Sam and Jackson himself. In 1810 Carlisle spotted yet another man with a classically beautiful body, a Black sailor from Boston called Wilson. The leading artists of the day were enamoured as Wilson posed in the nude (19). Thomas Lawrence thought that he combined 'the character & perfection of many of the Antique Statues', exclaiming that 'When His arm was suspended it appeared like that of Antinous, when contracted for exertion it was like the Farnese Hercules.'[40] As art historian Hugh Honour observes, Black men were increasingly employed as artist's models from the early nineteenth century onward, joining a group of men drawn from professions like boxing, the military and elsewhere, whose work-hardened labouring bodies were admired for their classical qualities.[41] Such admiration involved an often unacknowledged tension; identifying the body beautiful with labourers and Black men threatened a hierarchy that indicated that power and perfection should be the preserve of elite white men.

'FROM A WEAKLING TO A HERCULES'

In the nineteenth and twentieth centuries, the tendency towards comparison and emulation of the classical ideals continued to be guided by antique sculpture that was both Greek and Roman in origin. This was furthered by three key movements that encouraged a nutritious diet and exercise, not just for health but for beauty.

Firstly, there was the early nineteenth-century rise and spread of German gymnasium culture. This began under the late eighteenth-century educationalist

Johann Friedrich GutsMuths, who taught gymnastics at Schnepfenthal. In 1793 he published *Gymnastik für die Jugend* (translated into English in 1800) in which he argued that the 'beautiful and manly firmness' and 'symmetry of form' that exemplified ancient Greek bodies could be replicated by the 'constant employment of the mind, and corporeal exertions'.[42] This movement rapidly spread beyond German schools. In 1811 Friedrich Ludwig Jahn opened the first public gymnasium outside of Berlin, and by the 1820s two of his protégés, Peter (originally 'Phokion') Heinrich Clias and Carl Voelker, had brought the movement to London. Voelker's two gymnasiums, established in 1825 near the new Regent's Park and at Worship Street, Finsbury Square, quickly had over 700 subscribers.[43]

The second movement, often referred to as Muscular Christianity, was the preserve of the upper-middle classes. It developed in mid-century English public schools and spread rapidly to universities in Britain and America and the growing world of professional athletics. This 'cult of sporting manliness' promoted new forms of 'athleticism' as ways of instilling manly values, team spirit, physical prowess and religious piety, and made frequent references to bodily ideals encapsulated in classical sculpture.[44] This included casual usages in ephemera such as the Oxford–Cambridge Boat Race dinner programme, which featured an image of the *Discobolus*, but it also provided a quasi-scientific baseline of perfection in the growing relationship between athleticism, anthropometry and eugenics. For example, the physician Samuel Messenger Bradley used the proportions of the *Apollo Belvedere* when stipulating that a man's lower and upper body should be 618.03cm and 381.97cm respectively.[45]

From the 1890s onwards, Britain saw the rise of the physical culture movement. Focused on self-cultivation and affordable activities such as gymnastics and weightlifting, this third development appealed to a broader range of social backgrounds.[46] It was part of a wider international health and life reform movement, but it also originated out of the strong-men tradition of Victorian show halls. These men made a living by displaying their bodies and selling the ideal of physical perfection to a mass global market. Built around the rise of body consumerism and a flourishing physical culture press, this movement resulted in a fully fledged health and strength economy that developed in conjunction with the twentieth-century bodybuilding culture and which endures to this day.[47]

One influential founding figure was Friedrich Müller, better known as the German strongman, Eugen Sandow. Sandow attained global celebrity during the 1890s in which his physical attractiveness was crucial to his phenomenal success.[48] Alongside being described by the *New York World* (1893) as 'absolutely beautiful as a work of art', he was repeatedly compared to statues of *Achilles*, the *Discobolus*, the *Borghese Gladiator* and *Hercules*.[49] Sandow deliberately played up this comparison by chalking his body to appear more marble-like and borrowing poses from sculptures in order to become a 'living' classical figure (20).[50] In various interviews he described his epiphany while visiting Italy: 'my eyes were opened. The Greek and Roman statues I saw there inspired me with envy and admiration.'[51] Sandow went on to establish four gymnasiums, physique competitions and a lucrative business selling the ability to transform himself and others 'From a Weakling to a Hercules' via physique training apparatus, books and magazines. The French physical culturists Albert Surier and Edmond Desbonnet profited from similar promises in their 1904 illustration (21). Here, a thin man gazes longingly upon the *Farnese Hercules*, before entering a gymnasium. Subsequent panels document his physical transformation and increasing strength, before showing him standing once more before the statue as its physical equal. Sandow's generation of strongmen were succeeded by entrepreneurial physical culturalists and bodybuilders, including John M. Hernic, who retired in the 1920s to establish 'The Apollo Art Studios', a mail-order photographic gallery featuring the lead bodybuilders of the day.[52]

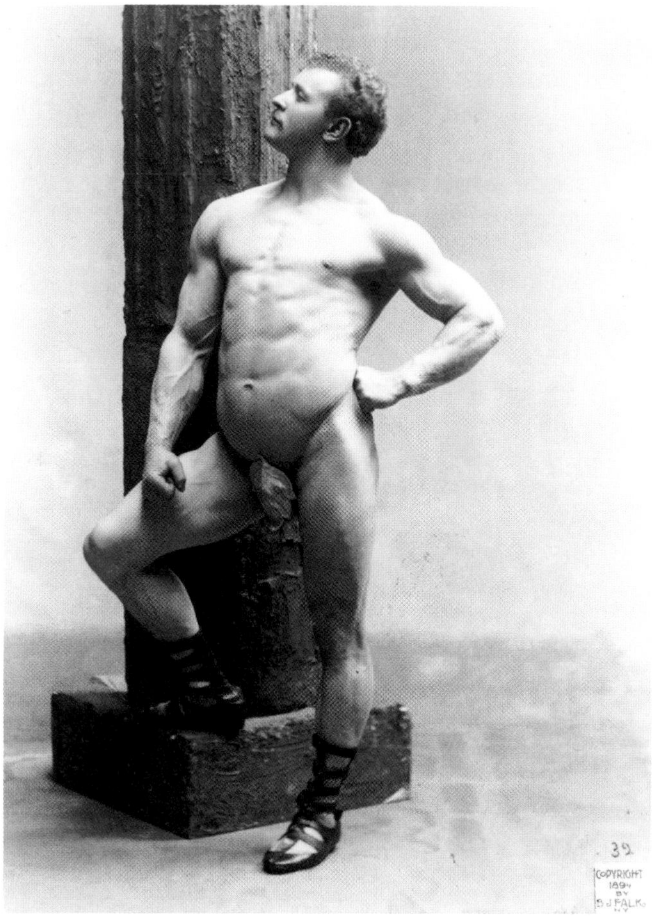

20. Benjamin J. Falk (1853–1925), Eugen Sandow. Photograph, albumen silver print. *c.*1894. Library of Congress, Washington DC

Herculean musculature and the sensuality and softness of the *Apollo* and *Antinous* continued to be celebrated in twentieth-century culture. However, twentieth-century modernity was particularly fixated on the cult of the thin, healthy and sportive aesthetic body. Following the horrors and mutilations of the First World

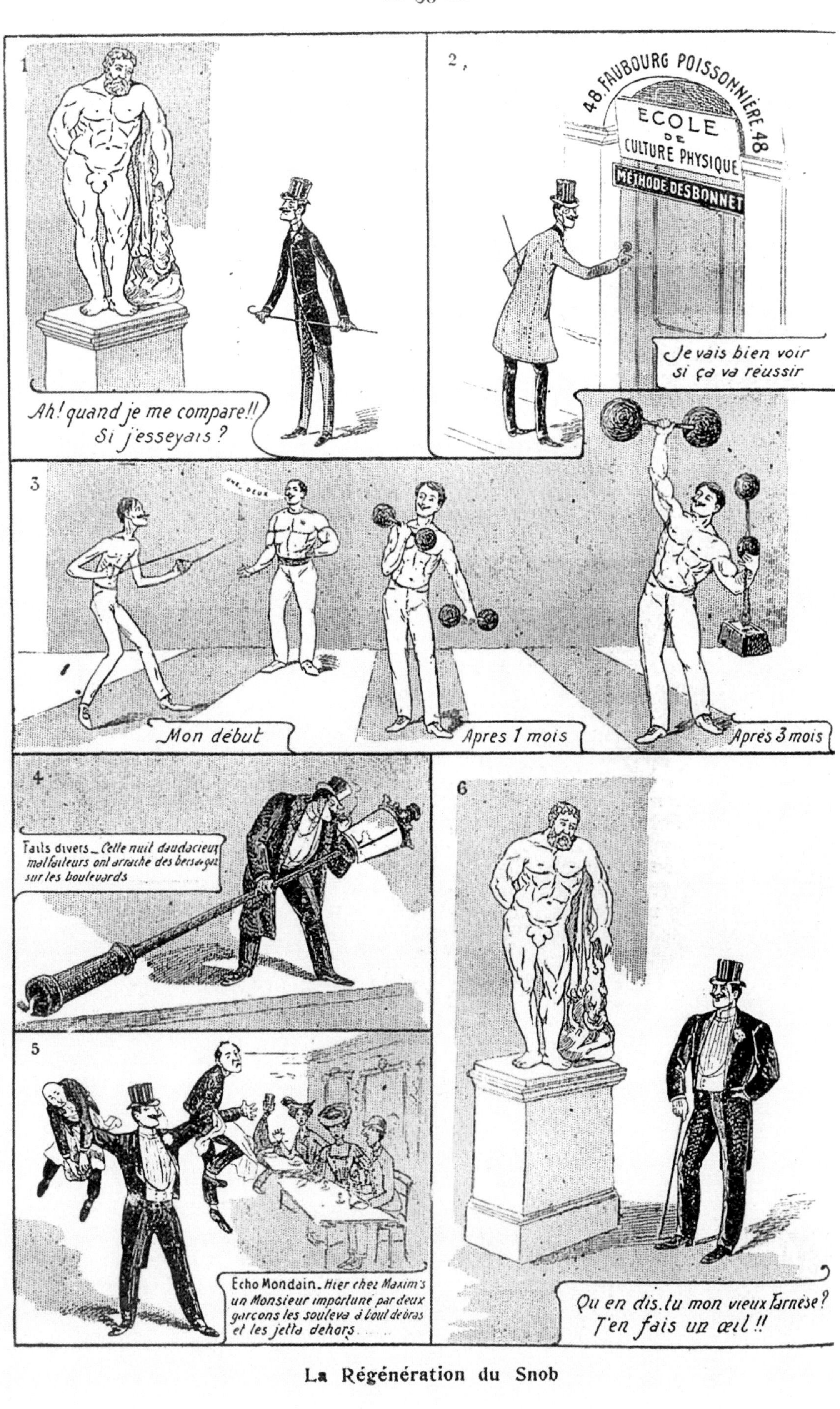

21. Albert Surier (1871–1944) and Edmond Desbonnet (1867–1953), ‘La Régénération du Snob’, *La Culture Physique* (Paris, March 1904). Wellcome Library, London

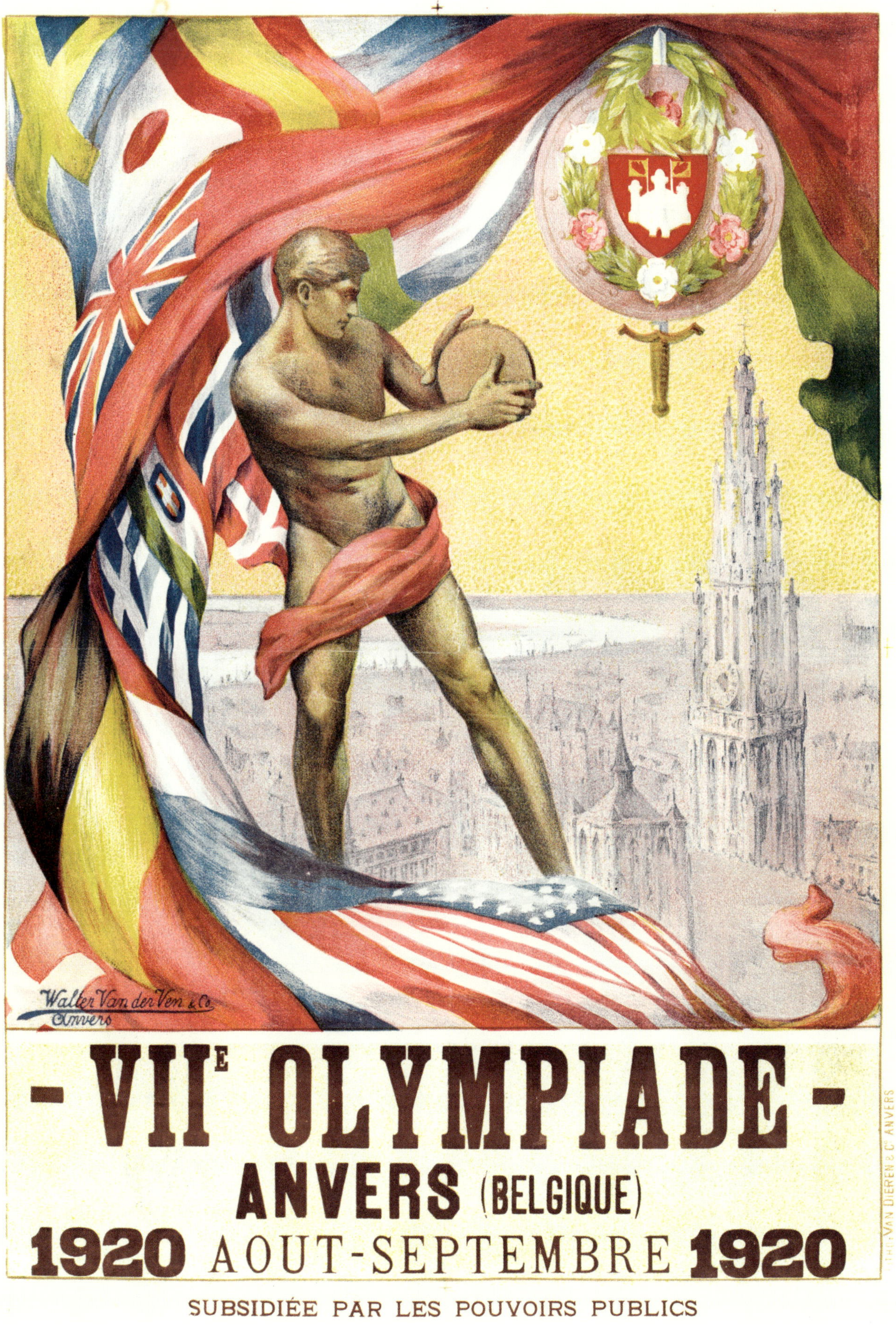

22. Walter van der Ven (1898–1958), Poster for the Games of the 7th Olympiad in Antwerp. Lithograph, 85.4 × 62 cm. Belgium, 1920. V&A: E.229-2006

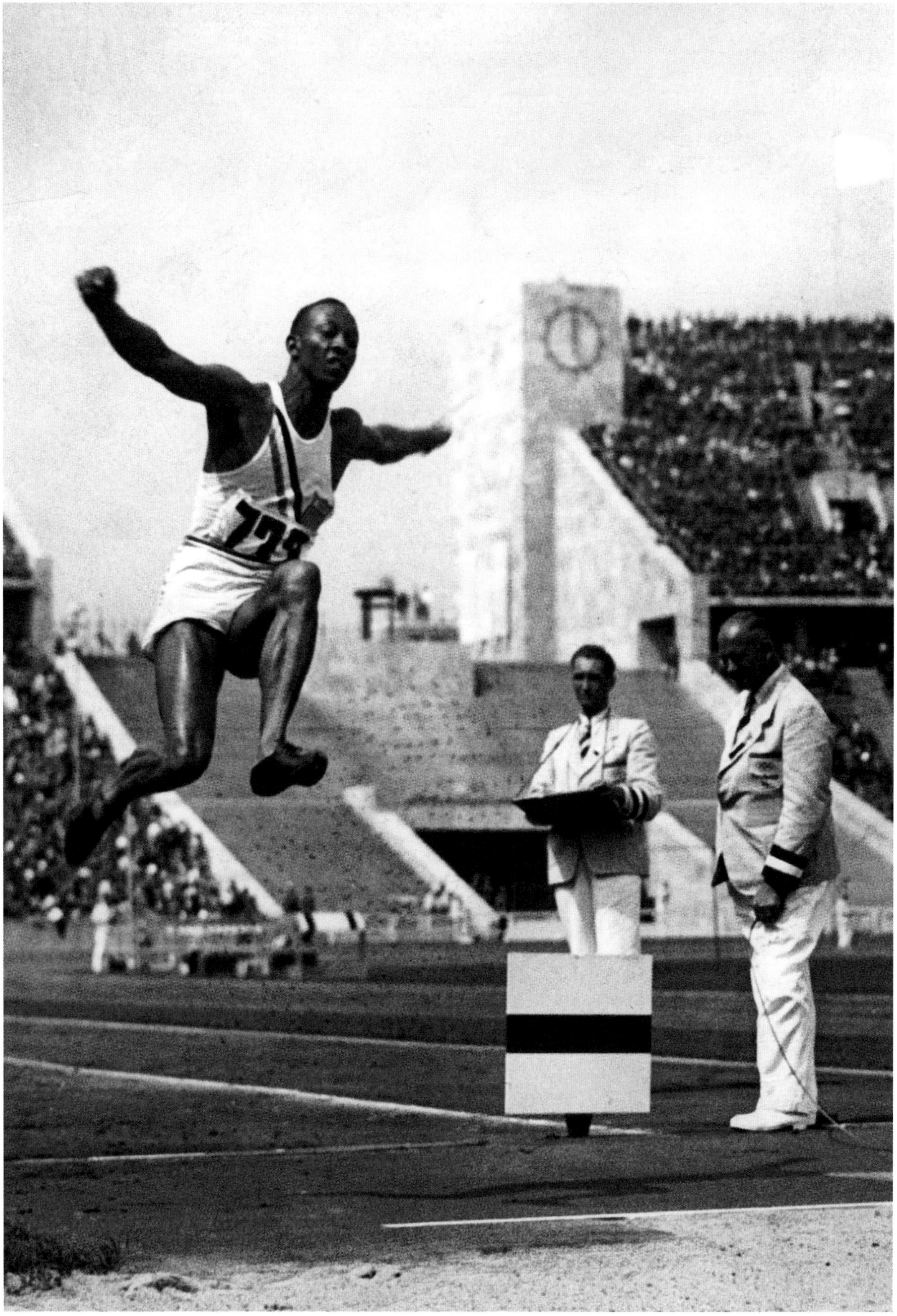

23. American athlete Jesse Owens during the Olympic Games in Berlin, 1936

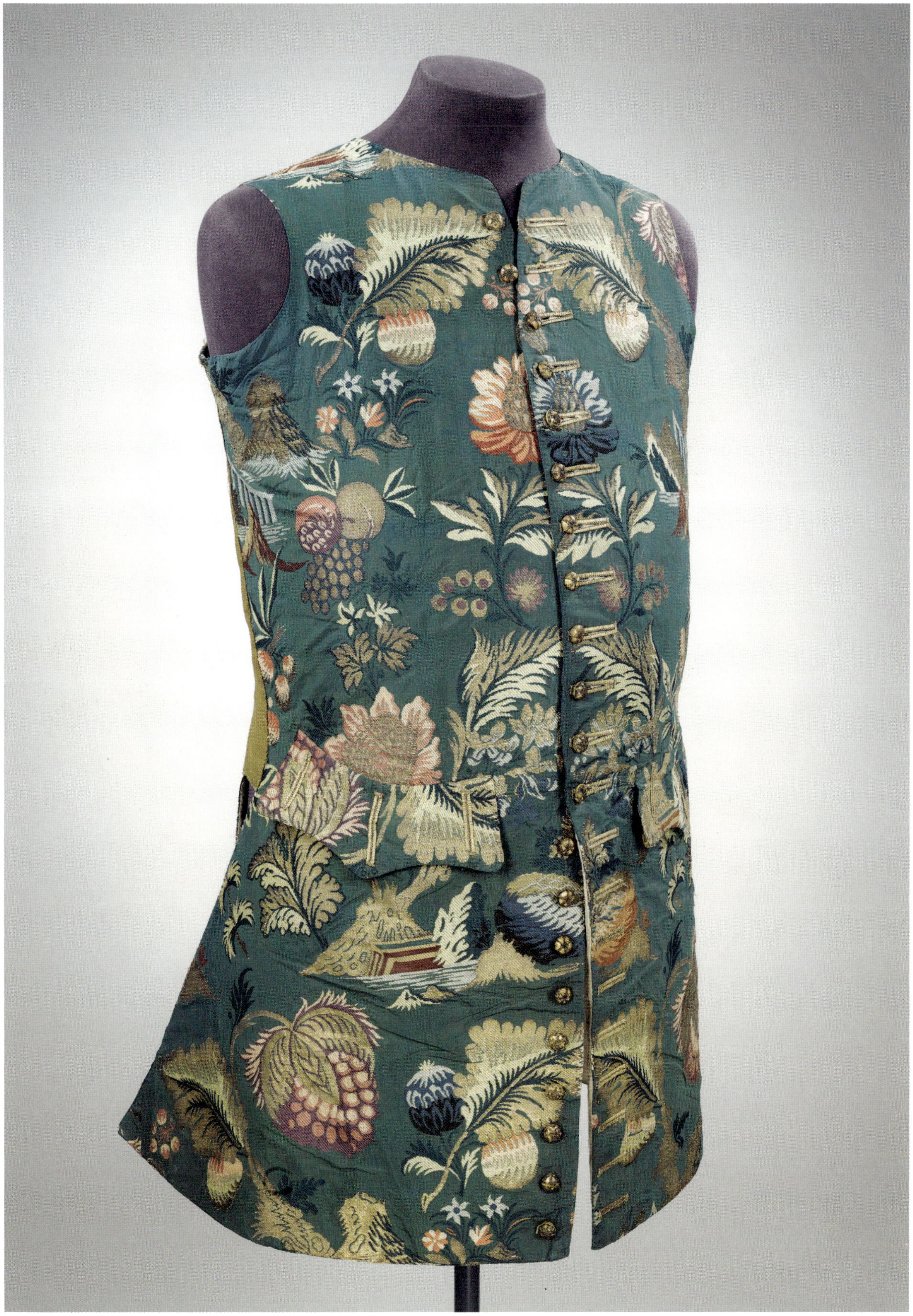

24. Waistcoat (front). Silk, wool, linen, silver-gilt thread.
Great Britain, 1730–5. V&A: T.36-2019

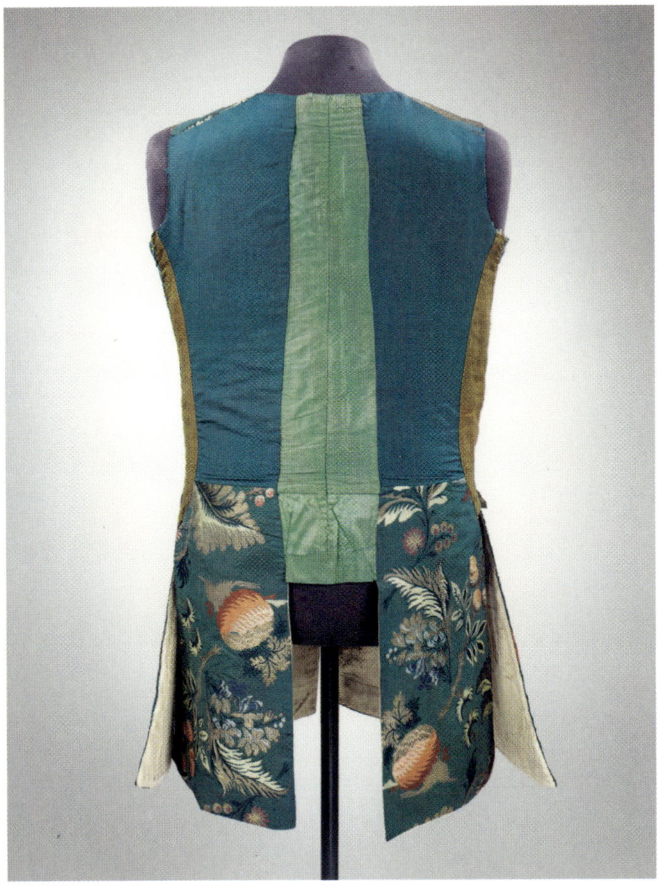

25. Waistcoat (back). Silk, wool, linen, silver-gilt thread. Great Britain, 1730–5. V&A: T.36-2019

War and inspired by new technologies, western society dreamt of disciplined, machine-like bodies characterized by a sleek, lithe musculature, fierce speed and agile dynamism as depicted in the *Borghese Gladiator* and the *Discobolus*.[53] Nowhere is this more apparent than in the modern Olympics, which were first held in Athens in 1896, with the *Discobolus* as its symbol (22). The troubling ties between this bodily ideal and the fascist movement are particularly evident in the 1936 Berlin Olympic games organized by Nazi Germany, and the resultant film, *Olympia* (1938), directed by Leni Riefenstahl. Among shots of smooth, rhythmic displays of masculine physical power, Nazi Germany's claim as the modern heir to the perfect classical Greek body was made clear as the *Discobolus* metamorphosed into the German discus thrower Erwin Huber.

Riefenstahl's *Olympia* makes an ideologically charged artistic statement on the male body, but it was also a documentary of the 1936 Olympic Games. Somewhat jarringly, this meant that a considerable proportion of the film was devoted to the athletic prowess and victories of the African American athlete Jesse Owens, who won four gold medals in the track and field and beat the German champion Luz Long in the long jump (23).[54] Owens's presence in Riefenstahl's *Olympia*, like the early nineteenth-century London artistic community's admiration for Wilson's body, is an example of the beauty and physical skills of the non-European male body being favourably compared with the classical epitome. Such comparisons, although at times grudgingly done, contravene western society's aesthetic, and at times explicitly racist, fixation on the translucent purities of classical sculpture's (fictitious) white marble as a key criterion of beauty.

The ideal male form repeatedly championed by western society over three centuries also gives precious little space for physiques that stray beyond certain physical proportions. Bodies that are too weighty/thin, too tall/small, too crooked or with missing limbs have been presented as the unacceptable opposites to the classical ideal, and subject to centuries of mockery, distrust and exclusion. Fashion, medicine and technology have often ruthlessly combined to forcibly reshape such forms into more acceptable silhouettes.[55] These quietly remain in place today. Take for example, the ongoing popularity of male fashion aids such as Spanx's Zoned Performance Shapewear (56 and 57). The control that this garment exerts over the male form is not dissimilar to the aids incorporated into an eighteenth-century waistcoat in the V&A collection (24 and 25). Alongside the extra panels of fabrics added to the back to allow for the girth of a larger man, the waistcoat also had cardboard inserted to control his silhouette.[56]

Policing the boundaries between ideal and unacceptable male bodies requires an impressively rigorous commitment to double standards. Just as archaeologists and classicists have known since at least the nineteenth century that the whiteness of marble skin would have been polychrome, artists and anatomists have known since the Renaissance that the canon of antique sculptures are *not* entirely anatomically or proportionally correct. Nevertheless, statues like the *Apollo Belvedere* continue to be widely revered as ideals to aspire to and emulate.

'HE LOOKS LIKE A GREEK GOD'

Even within a society that is slowly giving credence to representing and celebrating bodies that sit outside of restrictive classical standards, a harmful blindness to the realities behind attaining a 'perfect ideal' remain. This is a matter of growing concern, particularly as the lines between the attainable and the unattainable become increasingly blurred. Faced with the scrutiny of social media and a developing market in grooming and exercise, twenty-first-century men have an ever-growing fixation on the body beautiful. Gym membership is at a record high, magazines such as *Men's Health* sell in huge numbers, and hashtags like #shredded steadily trend on social media. Cosmetic muscularity – the current ideal male body – is highly muscular and extremely lean with a minimum amount of body fat. This physique is time consuming, costly and frequently impossible to achieve without a degree of chemical intervention. As such, studies from 2003 onwards have consistently found that increasing numbers of boys and men are anxious about their appearance. Steroid usage for aesthetic enhance-

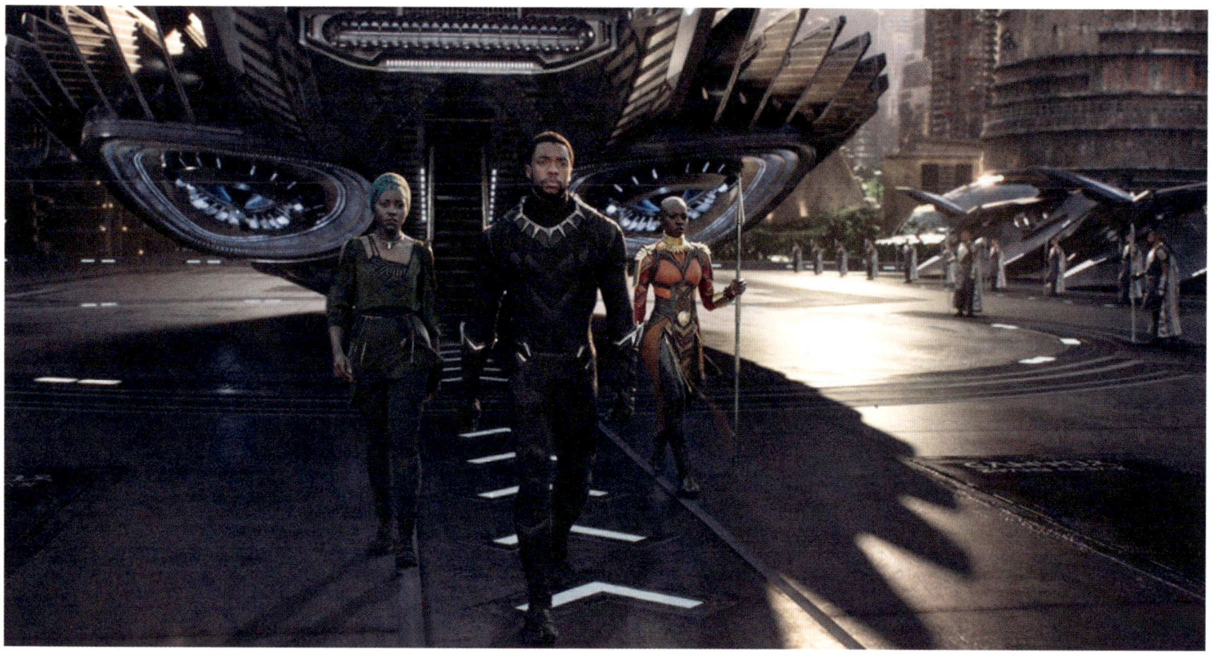

26. Lupita Nyong'o, Chadwick Boseman and Danai Gurira in *Black Panther* (2018), dir. Ryan Coogler

ment is skyrocketing, and more men are resorting to compulsive exercise, strict diets, laxatives or other means to achieve these ideals.[57]

A brief glance at *Men's Health* or the many regime websites online shows that sportsmen and actors are often seen to embody this modern ideal. In the last decade, those actors have almost inevitably been associated with the Marvel or DC superhero movie franchises: Chris Evans (Captain America) (27), Chris Hemsworth (Thor), Henry Cavill (Superman), Michael B. Jordan (Erik Killmonger), Chadwick Boseman (Black Panther) and David Bautista (Drax the Destroyer), to name just a few.[58] Part of the appeal of worlds like Marvel is that many of the characters are modern-day demi-gods: heroes who achieve divinity or have it thrust upon them. As the heir, and later king of Wakanda, T'Challa (aka Black Panther) (26), for example, comes by his powers via drinking the 'heart-shaped herb'; Steve Rogers (aka Captain America) gains his transformation via a 'super soldier serum'. This 'wimp to warrior' transformation is calculated to appeal to an all-too-human male audience, but the creation of the Marvel films has taken this another step further in conflating the protagonists' journey with the remarkable physical transformation of their actors. Indeed, Marvel's publicity strategy centres on 'before and after' pictures, exercise magazine cover shoots and open discussions of the actors' strict regimes.[59]

As comic-book heroes have become flesh and blood, the distinction between a hypermasculine fantasy and a natural, attainable ideal has become fundamentally confused, particularly as audiences have failed (or been unwilling) to comprehend the very heavy assistance given by flattering camerawork, stunt doubles, costume, make-up and CGI in making these bodies a reality.[60] Caught between their contractual studio obligations, the promotion of self-image and their moral duties, the actors themselves have frequently wavered between desiring a franker commentary on the unhealthy elements of this process and needing to maintain a certain mystique.

Even here, the legacy of classical sculpture is never far away. In the 2011 film *Captain America: The First Avenger*, as his new superhero body is unveiled, the cinematography places Evans/Captain America on a plinth. Lit from above, he is displayed to an admiring crowd of scientists and military personnel who even reach out to touch the gleaming musculature. Celebrity and fitness websites refer to Evan's 'chiselled, Adonis-like physique' that supposedly fits the Adonis Golden Ratio's pseudo-scientific waist/shoulder ratio of 1:618.[61] Fellow actors, like his Captain America co-star Anthony Mackie (Falcon/Captain America), described awestruck and envious reactions: 'he looks like a Greek god ... well shit, I gotta work out more'.[62] Irrespective of whether Evans is off or on camera, his body continues to be placed on a metaphorical plinth, as the *GQ* journalist Edith Zimmerman's tongue-in-cheek opening to her 2011 interview reveals: 'Chris Evans pecs. how do they FEEL? like smooth stone from the souvenir shop?'[63]

Zimmerman's opening, a text message from an enthusiastic friend, points towards the ongoing visual, tactile and erotic associations made between the marble texture of classical sculpture and the living bodies of admired contemporary men. If we cast our minds back to the wandering hands of Johan Joseph Zoffany and Thomas Patch's dilettantes, the breathless imaginings of Johann Winkelmann or the thrilled gaze of Charlotte Eaton, one cannot help but feel that they, at the very least, might well have understood the sentiment.

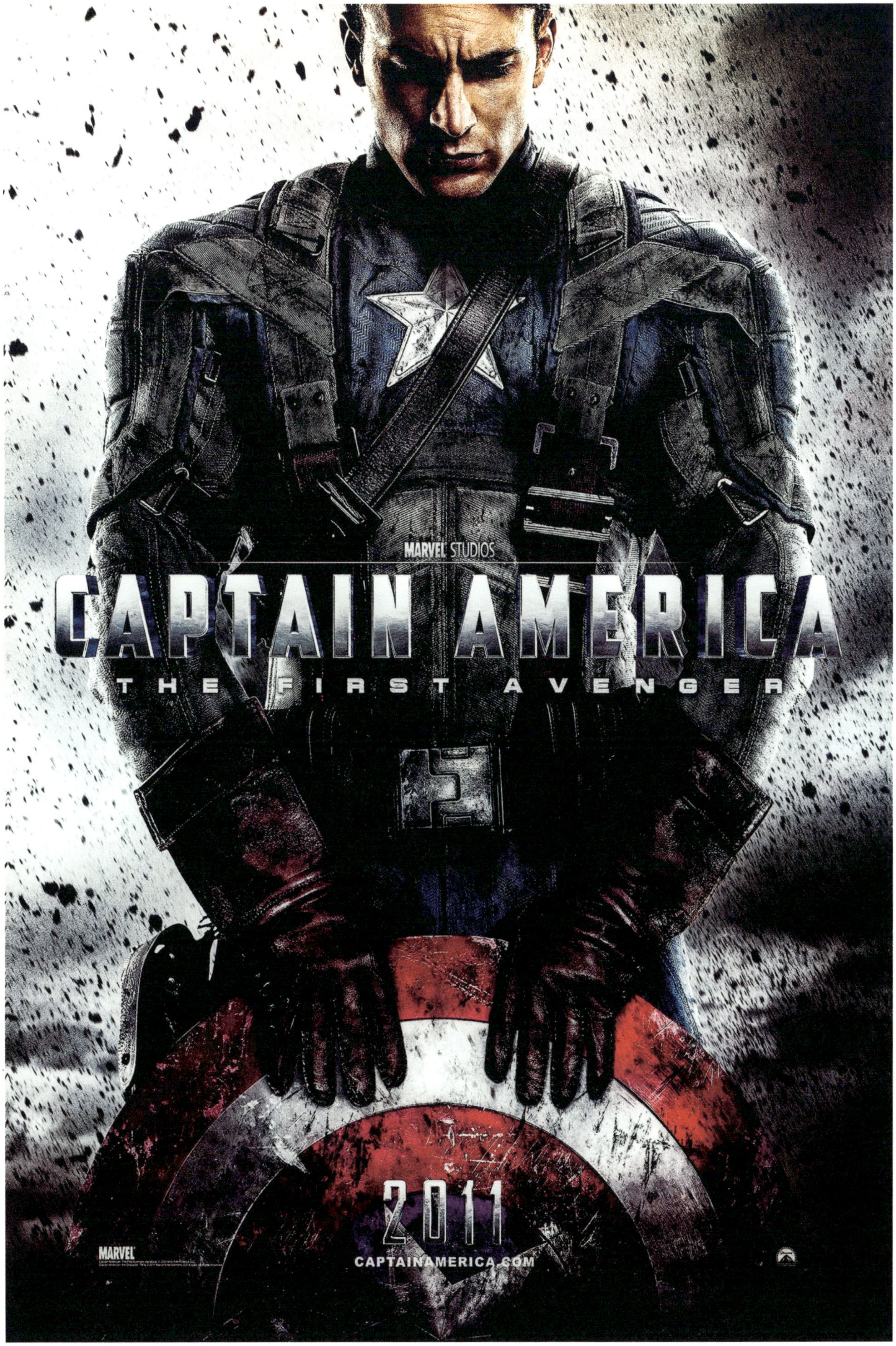

27. Chris Evans in *Captain America: The First Avenger* (2011), dir. Joe Johnston

A POLISHED IMPRESSION

ALUN WITHEY

The eighteenth century was a period of significant change in terms of masculinity and ideals of male appearance. This was predominantly an era of polite gentlemanliness, when characteristics such as neatness, elegance and refinement were prized. The body was central in the conveyance of politeness, as made clear by an essay in *The Universal Magazine* in 1775, which argued that it was a holistic concept which not only covered 'temper of mind and tenour of conduct', but also bodily appearance, posture and mien.[1] If an individual man's body did not meet these new, lofty ideals, it was his duty to shape and refine it to create a pleasing and harmonious whole. This period saw the proliferation and increasing acceptance of grooming practices and the paraphernalia involved with them.

Many aspects of daily life served to mark the Georgian body, from the dirt and smuts of the urban environment to the lack of regular washing. Other habits such as snuff-taking begrimed hands and faces in particular (see p. 117). Since neatness and elegance were central in conveying inner character and sensibility, attending to unsightly marks, blemishes and stains, pulling out errant hairs, picking food particles from the teeth or clipping mangled fingernails – anything that disturbed the overall harmony of appearance – was of signal importance.[2] The keyword was management. More often than not, bodies needed careful attention, and sometimes even force, in order to enable them to meet expectations of the polite body.

Before 1700, men had been actively discouraged from paying too much attention to their appearance, beyond keeping basically neat and tidy. Too much pluming and powdering was at best considered finicky but at worst potentially effeminate. Individual men had generally relied on the barber to undertake a range of bodily tasks from shaving and haircutting to scraping tongues and ears, picking teeth and lancing boils. But the eighteenth century increasingly saw the individual man (or, if he was wealthy enough, his servant) begin to take more responsibility for personal grooming.

As evident in the trade card of the London razor-maker Henry Patten from the 1750s, a whole range of products was available to assist in refining the body, and men were an important group of consumers (28). Set within its florid Rococo surrounds was his diverse range of products for the body, including open (cut-throat) razors, cases of multiple razors (which could be swapped each day to reduce the need for sharpening), various combs and cases, pince-nez spectacles, 'fleams' or lancets for bloodletting, and even surgeons' instruments. Patten was one of the increasing number of similar artisan makers and retailers in London, selling all manner of products for the body to discerning customers.

Of all the male grooming tasks, shaving was perhaps the most important. Since the late seventeenth century, facial hair had declined in popularity and, by the mid-eighteenth century, had come to signify a rough and rustic masculinity. As this occurred, shaving grew in significance and was a task increasingly undertaken by individual men rather than the barber. From the early 1750s, razor advertisements began to specifically target 'gentlemen who shave themselves'. New technologies in steelmaking made for sharper and more durable, but also aesthetically pleasing, razors. Steel goods were in fact highly fashionable and became an essential part of the aspiring gentleman's kit. Razor-makers played on the use of new technology in their advertisements, and appealed to gentlemanly interests in science, using metaphors of steely hardness and temper to echo desirable male characteristics. Steel razors were often sold alongside a range of other small instruments for refining the body. The six open razors in a luxurious grooming set are high-end instruments, with tortoiseshell handles inlaid with silver, illustrating how razors had transcended their prosaic function to become elegant and desirable (29).

But it was not only shaving instruments that grew in importance. At the same time, a new range of cosmetic shaving products – including soaps, powders, pastes, oils and creams – became available, some sweetly perfumed and stressing unctuousness and luxury as well as utility. Advertisements for exotically named products such as the 'Mellifluous shaving soap' offered an 'exquisite delicacy of complexion' and promised to be kind to tender faces. In doing so, makers of such products were offering an alternative, and somewhat contradictory, version of manliness – one that focused on sensuality and delicacy, rather than manly hardness and control.[3] This heralded an important shift in terms of the rise of a market for cosmetic products created solely for men, and a version of masculinity that could be linked to their consumption and use.

The eighteenth century also saw new interest in physiognomy: the reading of bodily characteristics for signs of character. The shape of a person's eyebrows was considered as a particularly important indicator: the ideal shape for eyebrows was arched; thick, bushy eyebrows were viewed as a potential sign of clownishness; while those pointing downwards suggested malice. Eyebrows that met in the middle were considered a deformity and one that, according to the French physician and author Nicolas Andry, gave the face an 'unlucky look'.[4] Given the visibility of eyebrows, and the need to create a favourable impression on first meeting, the use of tweezers to shape brows, but also remove unsightly hairs from the face, nose and ears, was con-

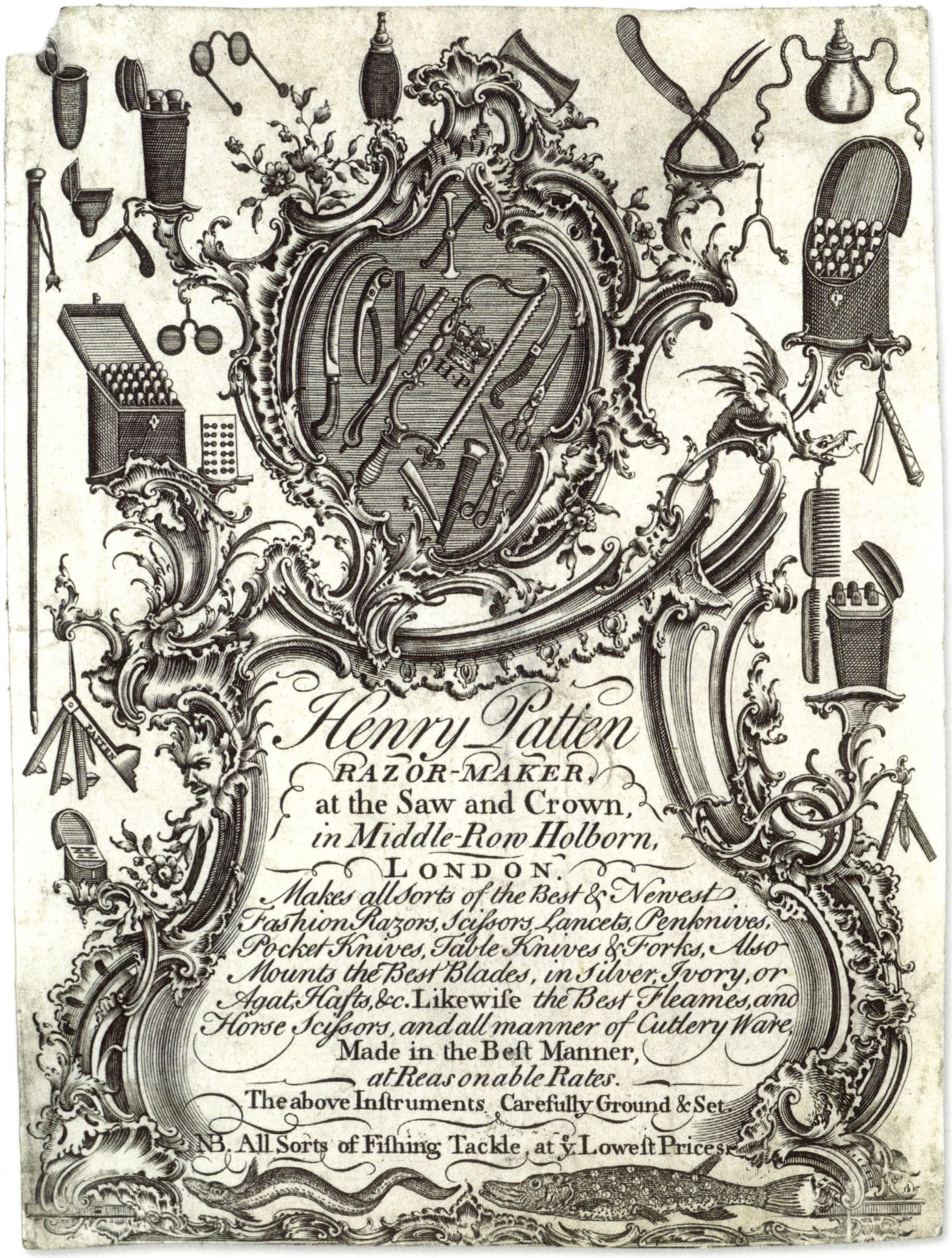

28. Edward Warner (active *c.*1750), Trade card for Henry Patten, razor-maker and cutler. Engraving, 19×14.5cm. London, *c.*1750. Bequeathed by Hugh Phillips. V&A: E.571-1976

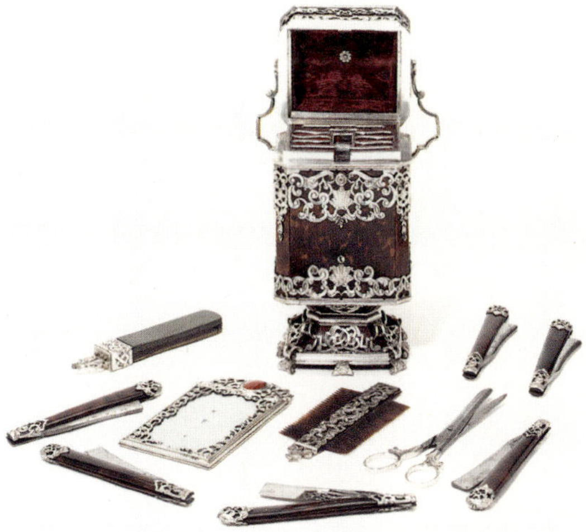

29. Shaving set. Silver, tortoiseshell, steel. Netherlands, 1700–30. V&A: 192:1-1881

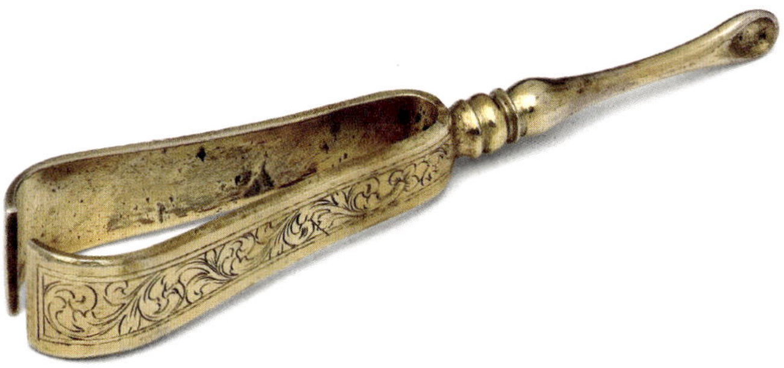

30. Tobias Baur (active *c.*1695), Tweezers, part of a toilet service. Engraved silver gilt. Augsburg, *c.*1695. The Rosalinde and Arthur Gilbert Collection on loan to the Victoria and Albert Museum, London. V&A: LOAN: GILBERT.566-2008

sidered an acceptable practice for men, as well as women. These elaborately decorated silver-gilt tweezers are part of a larger set of toilette instruments made by the German artisan Tobias Baur, one of Augsburg's leading makers of such sets during the seventeenth century (30).

As well as the face, hands were another important indicator of politeness, and well-kept fingernails in particular suggested attention to detail and pride in appearance. An important part of a gentleman's toilette routine was therefore to trim his fingernails. Before the eighteenth century, one of the most common means was to pare fingernails with a penknife. But the invention of nail nippers (clippers) made the task easier and more comfortable. Again, steel was a key material of choice for makers, and nippers could be worn on modish steel chains attached to a waistcoat, on which could also be found watches, seals and other trinkets. Trimming the nails was even something that could be done in public, ensuring that corporeal standards were always maintained.

Another key instrument in the construction of the polite body was the toothpick. The eighteenth century saw changes in attitudes towards the smile, which made it more socially acceptable to show the teeth. Given the rising consumption of sugar among middling and elite Georgians in particular, and the ministrations of practitioners of varying levels of skill, teeth were often in poor repair. Nevertheless, appearing in public with particles of food stuck between the teeth was considered a social faux pas. A range of toothpicks made from wood and steel, as well as silver and gold, were available to enable men to attend to this area of the face.[5] Their importance was highlighted by the elegant cases created to carry them around in, such as this example by Josiah Wedgwood featuring a neoclassical scene in cameo (31).

Rather than taking the time and trouble to purchase individual items, men were able to buy ready-made sets containing all the necessary instruments for their daily toilette. In 1778 the perfumer Richard Sangwine of the Strand, London, for example, sold a wide range of goods, including shaving and dressing equipment 'fit for gentlemen who travel or go on sea voyages' and 'a complete set of Teeth instruments to allow gentle- men to clean their own teeth'.[6] Also available were stylish dressing cases in which a gentleman's equipage could be kept. The example opposite, made of satinwood, contains separate compartments for razors, strops (sharpeners), shaving soap, as well as space for other useful items such as inkpots and cutlery (32). The quality and workmanship of such sets, and the expense of purchasing them, highlights the lengths to which wealthier men went in the pursuit of refining their bodies.

Personal grooming was an increasingly commodified practice in the eighteenth century. Georgian middling and elite men were prepared to devote greater time and expense in an effort to meet new masculine ideals, assisted by the growing range of specialist instruments and products sold by high-end makers. No longer simply a quotidian practice to be endured before the day began, attending to, and refining, the body was a matter of pride, as well as a marker of politeness.

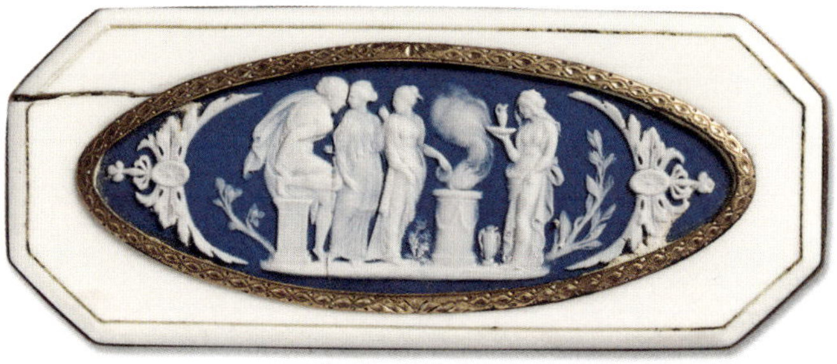

31. Josiah Wedgwood and Sons, Toothpick and cover. Ivory with jasperware plaque in chased gold and inlaid. Etruria (Stoke-on-Trent), *c.*1780–1800. Given by Lady Charlotte Schreiber. V&A: 414:1289/&A-1885

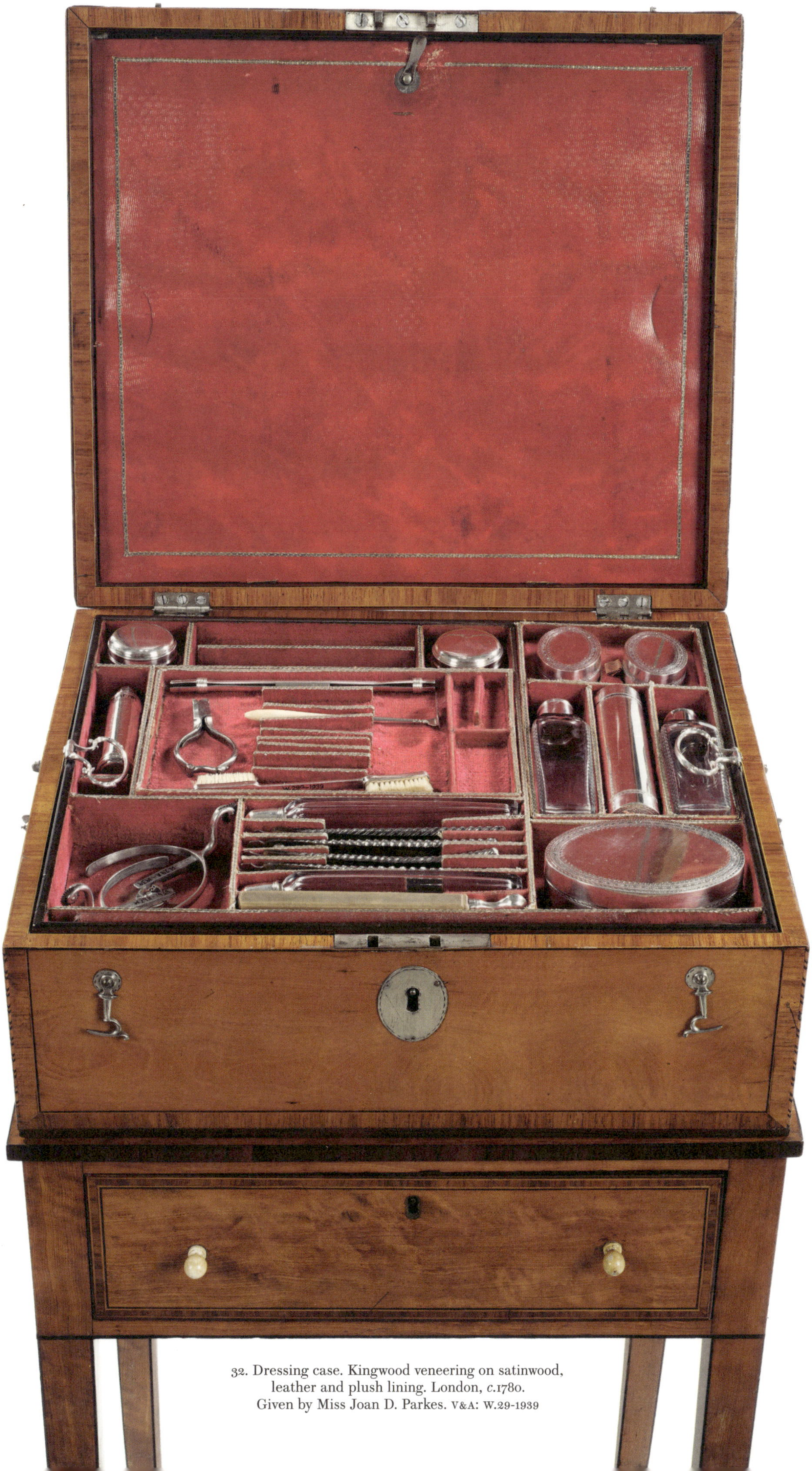

32. Dressing case. Kingwood veneering on satinwood, leather and plush lining. London, *c.*1780. Given by Miss Joan D. Parkes. V&A: W.29-1939

BEHIND CLOTHES: FASHIONING MEN AT THE MUSEUM

SATISH PADIYAR

Can a visit to a museum transform the way a man dresses? On 4 December 1852, Charles Dickens's journal *Household Words* featured a short story, penned by Henry Morley, entitled 'A House Full of Horrors'. 'I have been a very miserable man for the last five weeks', blurts Mr Crumpet, explaining his shift of mood since he had gone to the premises of the Department of Practical Art at Marlborough House in Pall Mall, to look over the new museum of ornamental art.[1] This was an interesting London venture that, opened just months earlier by the ambitious Henry Cole, was a combination of government art school, library and public museum (known as the Museum of Ornamental Art). In 1857 this conglomerate was renamed the South Kensington Museum; in 1899 it came to be known, in its final incarnation, as the Victoria and Albert Museum, with Cole as its founding Director.

The inaugural exhibition of the Museum of Ornamental Art in the spring of 1852 threw out a challenge. On entering the building, and before one arrived at the museum proper, Cole had curated a compact introductory section of objects demonstrating 'Examples of False Principles in Decoration'.[2] The point of this was to encourage in the British public a sense of good design, through comparative example, contrasting the worst taste in Victorian domestic objects – drinking glasses, scissors, candlesticks, carpets and patterned textiles for upholstery and clothing – with the best that could be produced by the advanced manufacturing industries of the day. The popular press of the day nicknamed the first part of the exhibition a 'Chamber of Horrors'. Perhaps it gained this notoriety because the visiting public, while exhorted to embrace good design in the main museum, actually saw itself in the very objects Cole had branded, passingly, as 'horrific'. 'I have acquired some Correct Principles of Taste', Crumpet admits, but 'my dressing gown and slippers torture me... I could have cried, sir. I was ashamed of the pattern of my own trousers, for I saw a piece of them hung up there as a horror.' Crumpet returns home from the visit, only to find himself aghast by the sight of his friend's 'literally demonical' attire, and distraught at the cloth of his own trousers: 'for I, too, had worn horizontal bars upon my trousers.' The museum's mission to transform the look of the entire population of Britain extended to the often tasteless specimens of Victorian garbed men inhabiting the streets around it. Part of the social mission of such educational nineteenth-century museums was to *refashion* men.

The problem with the 'horizontal bars' on the fashionable trousers of the 1850s – we see them on the figure on the left in a fashion plate of 1852 that admiringly records such a garment (33) – was that they contradicted the natural verticality of the male leg which they clothed.[3] One dogma of Cole's principles of good design – or, as he called it, 'good taste' – was that 'ornament should arise out of, and be subservient to Construction.'[4] In the case of men's clothes, the 'construction' was – and remains – the naked male body prior to any adornment. Men's fashion has forever been more or less ingrained with a minimum body-consciousness, even when it is least form-hugging, and even when it performs, on occasion, some audacious departure from the underlying construction. For centuries, the body under the clothes was in itself the object of an intense fashioning.

In the nineteenth century, specimens of exemplary male legs *au naturel* – and indeed any other crucial part of the male body – could be observed in all their constructed perfection in art schools. Flourishing across Britain, government art schools were one of the few places where a plethora of undressed male bodies could be scrutinized, unashamedly (hypersensitive to what lay underneath 'trousers', polite Victorians declined even to utter that word in public, resorting to the euphemism 'unmentionables').[5] The Renaissance invention of the life-drawing class had survived into the eighteenth and nineteenth centuries: a linchpin of this academic – which is to say, sanctioned and collective – art training was the focus on the naked male body. In the V&A collection there is a fascinating and previously unpublished photograph, *Life Drawing Class ... South Kensington Museum*, taken in 1897 (34).[6] It depicts the bustling activity of the art school which was at the heart of an institution whose original remit of extending design education to men and to women of all classes distinguished it. By contrast, the nearby Royal Academy was a professionalized, insistently male and relatively exclusive institution.[7]

The anonymous photographer has positioned us as if we were one of the students ranged on rows of benches, each with drawing book in hand, and we are plunged headlong into the arena of the fashioning of masculinities that was the world of the life-drawing class. The Italian word *disegno* describes the conceptual inseparability of 'drawing' and 'design'; *disegno* was both practice and idea. It was embraced by the fledgling V&A but not without argument. Cole had been derisive about training 'little girls ... to draw thigh bones'.[8] But ultimately, it was recognized that across Britain – unlike in France with its centralized Parisian École des Beaux-Arts – a disconnect between 'fine' artists (and their expertise in the ideal male nude), and decorative artists

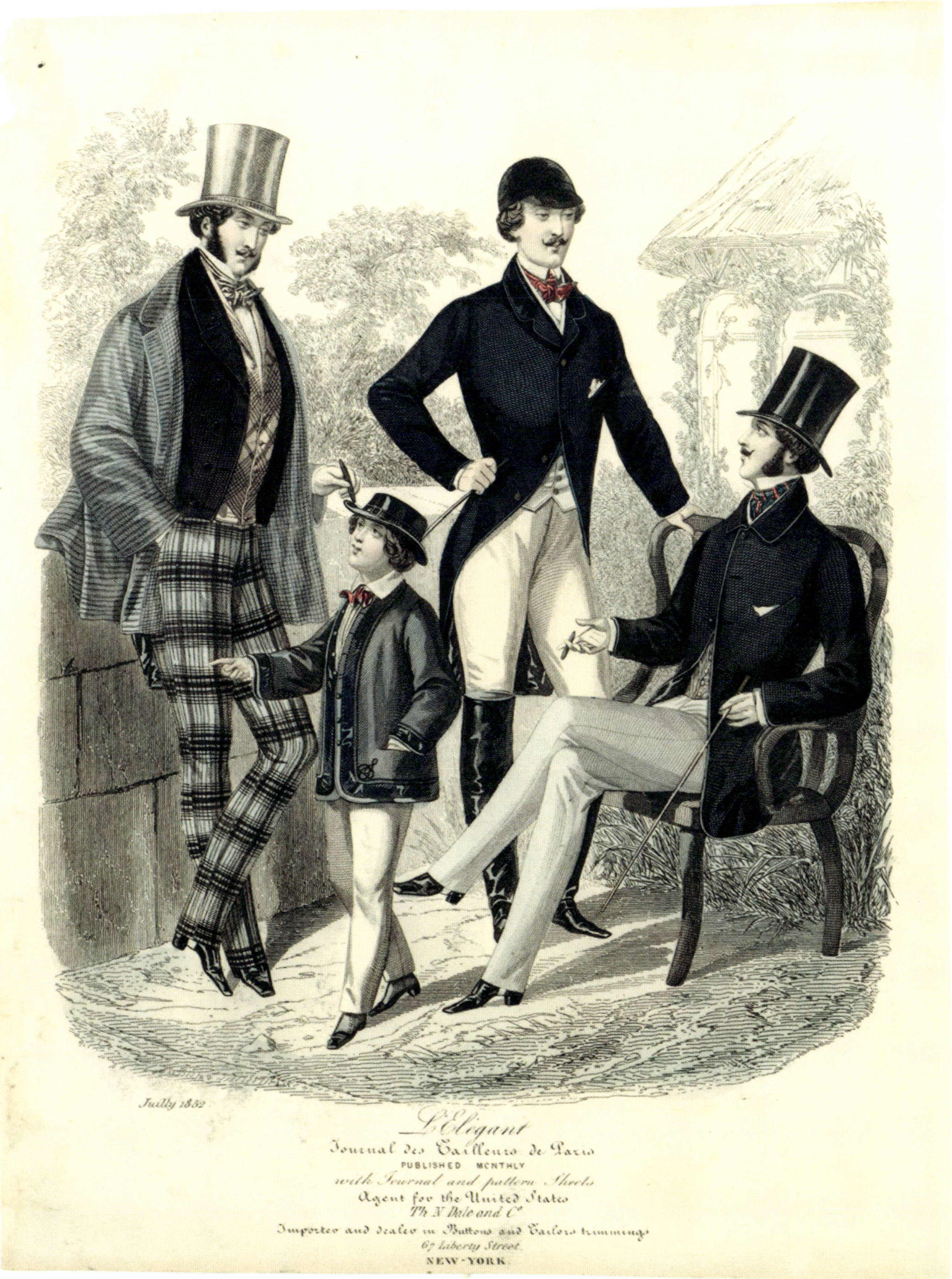

33. 'L'Elégant', *Journal des Tailleurs de Paris* (New York, July 1852).
Costume Institute, Metropolitan Museum of Art, New York
Digital Collections: B1750 9853

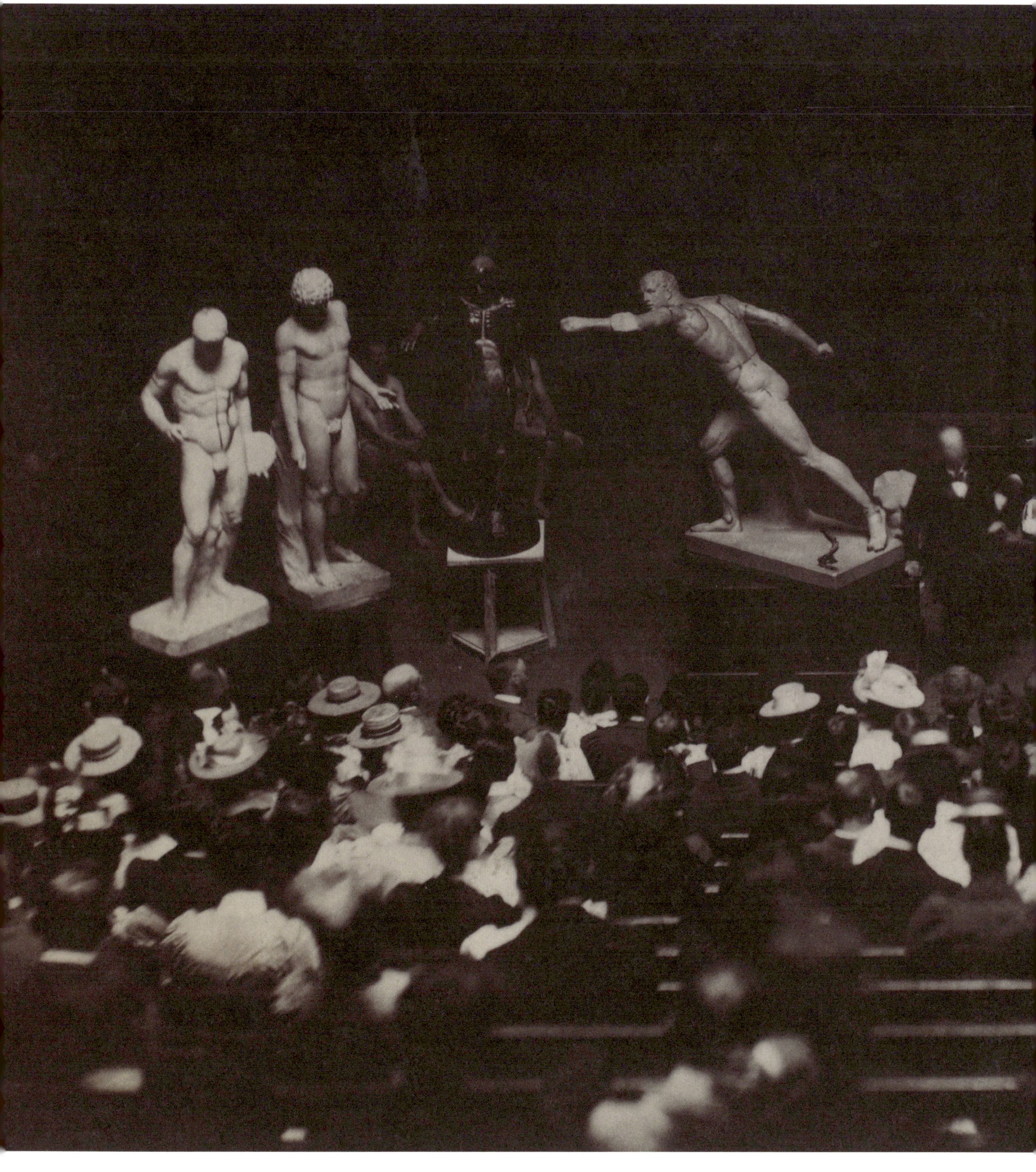

34. Life Drawing Class for the National Art Training School in the Lecture Theatre of the South Kensington Museum. Photograph. London, 6 December 1897. V&A: Guard Books 17937

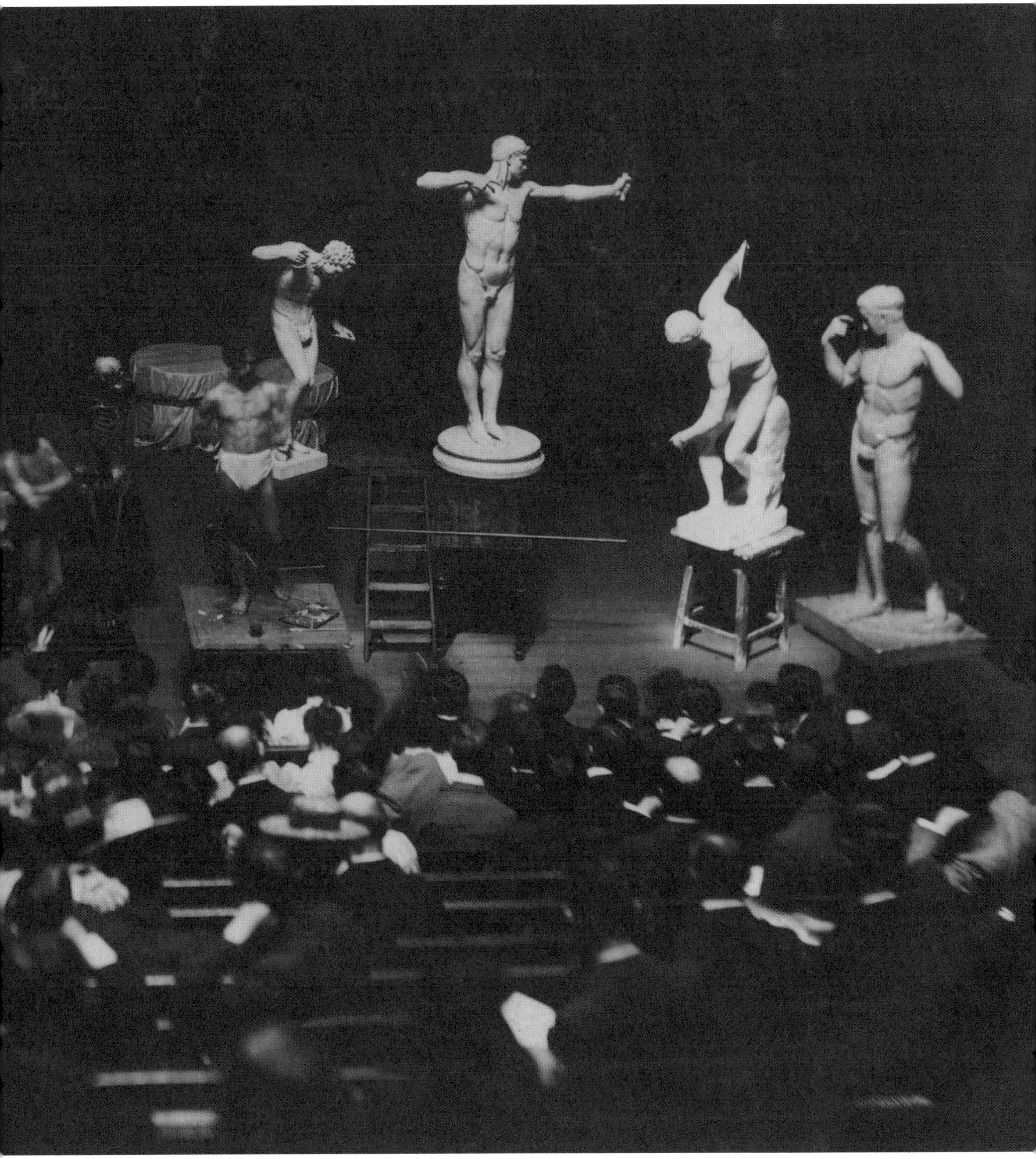

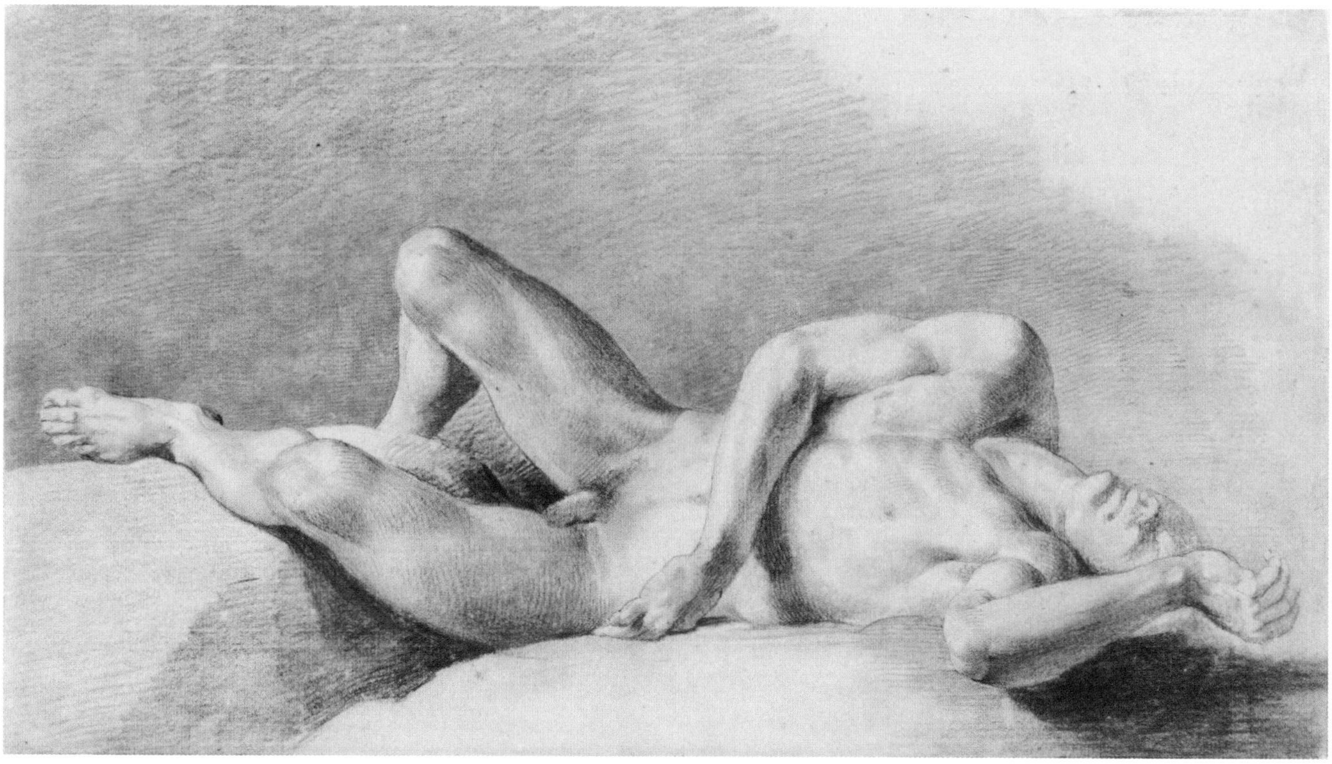

35. John Hamilton Mortimer (1740–1779), *Study of a reclining male nude.* Black chalk with white heightening on paper, 20.6×37cm. Great Britain, *c.*1758–9. V&A: D.99-1887

and designers for manufacture, had been harmful; too many British designers were deficient in the knowledge of the human figure and its anatomical details, which was precisely where skill in *disegno* had traditionally attained its heights. With the art school at the South Kensington Museum, a heretofore gentlemanly life class was imported into a reformist and demotic agenda to revolutionize the design of manufacture: what we see in the blurry photograph is this experiment in action.[9]

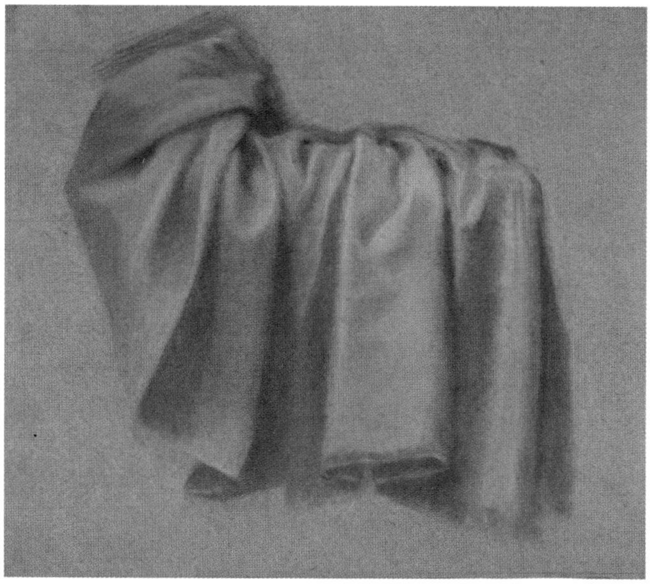

36. Pierre Paul Prud'hon (1758–1823), *Study of drapery.* Black and white chalk with stumping on paper, 25.5×26cm. France, *c.*1813. Purchase, Guy Wildenstein Gift, 2008. The Metropolitan Museum of Art, New York: 2008.44

Across the room, dressed students face naked male models. On stage, we see seven white plaster casts of sculptures of the male nude. They include, at its centre, the lunging *Borghese Gladiator*, and to its right the Victorian sculptor Sir William Hamo Thornycroft's starkly right-angled *Teucer*, with its insistent focus on the verticality of taut muscular legs and thighs (the original bronze was made in 1881). Three young scantily clad male models wait to pose, while the professor disquisitions at the foot of the *Gladiator*. What connects the majority of these figures on stage, plaster and flesh, classical and modern, taut and relaxed, is of course their radical lack of clothing. It is a theatre of male exposure. What assumptions lay behind this collective project to get *underneath* and *behind* clothing?

THE MAN BEHIND THE CLOTHES

'Before dressing a man we first draw him nude, then we enfold him in draperies', wrote Leon Battista Alberti in his *Della Pittura* (On Painting) in 1435.[10] The statement was pregnant, establishing a procedure that became the norm in post-Renaissance art academies across Europe. The myriad drawings of male nudes – or, as they came to be known, *académies* – that survive in their thousands today demonstrate this idea of drawing as pre-dressing (35), upon which 'construction' could later be overworked enfolded layers of 'draperies'. In fact, in European art academies, draughtsmen would graphically produce the male nude and the drapery as dis-

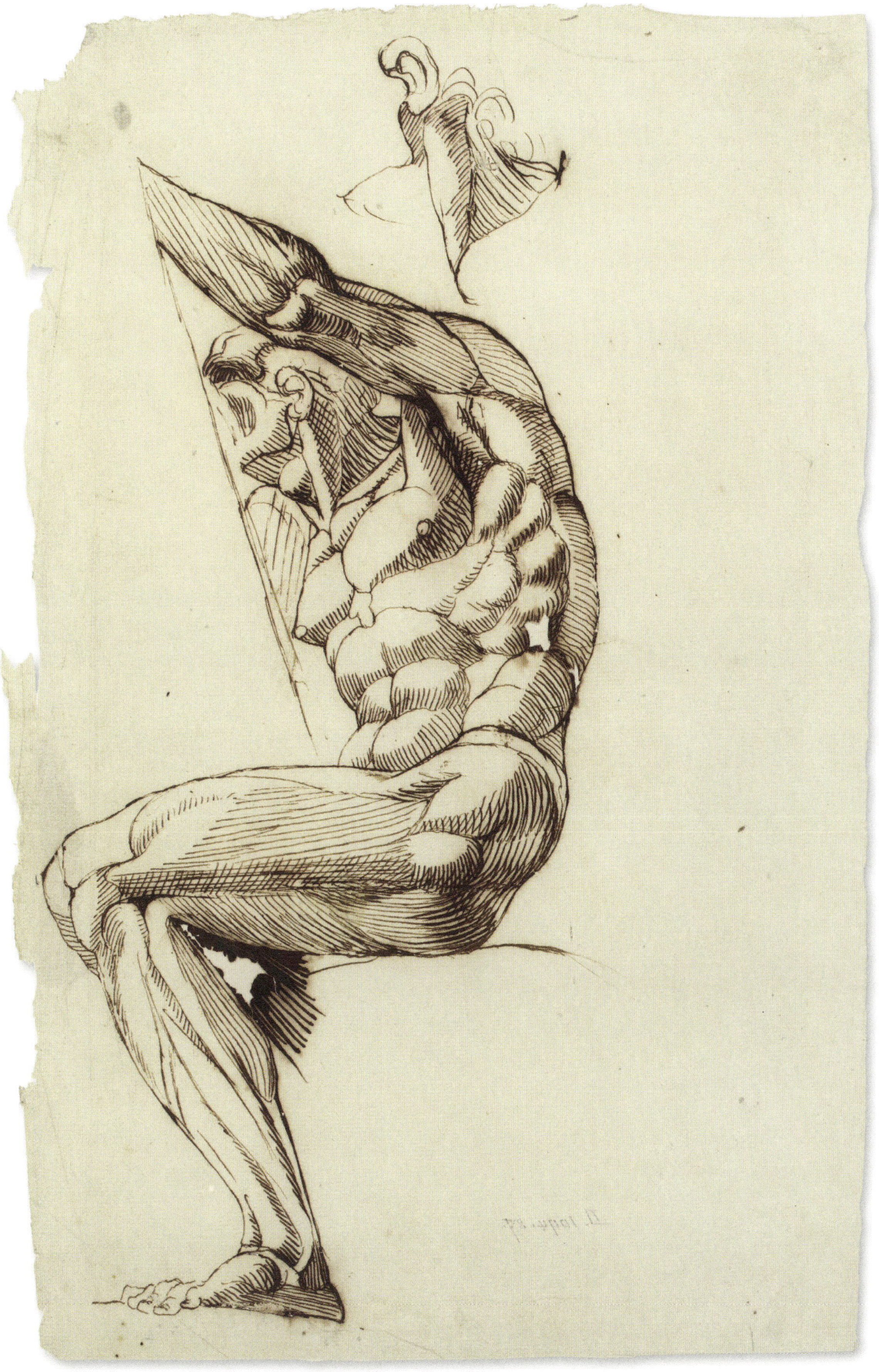

37. Henry Fuseli (1741–1825), *Seated male nude: anatomical study.* Pen and ink on tracing paper, 30×13cm. Great Britain, *c.*1770–8.
V&A: D.1094-1887

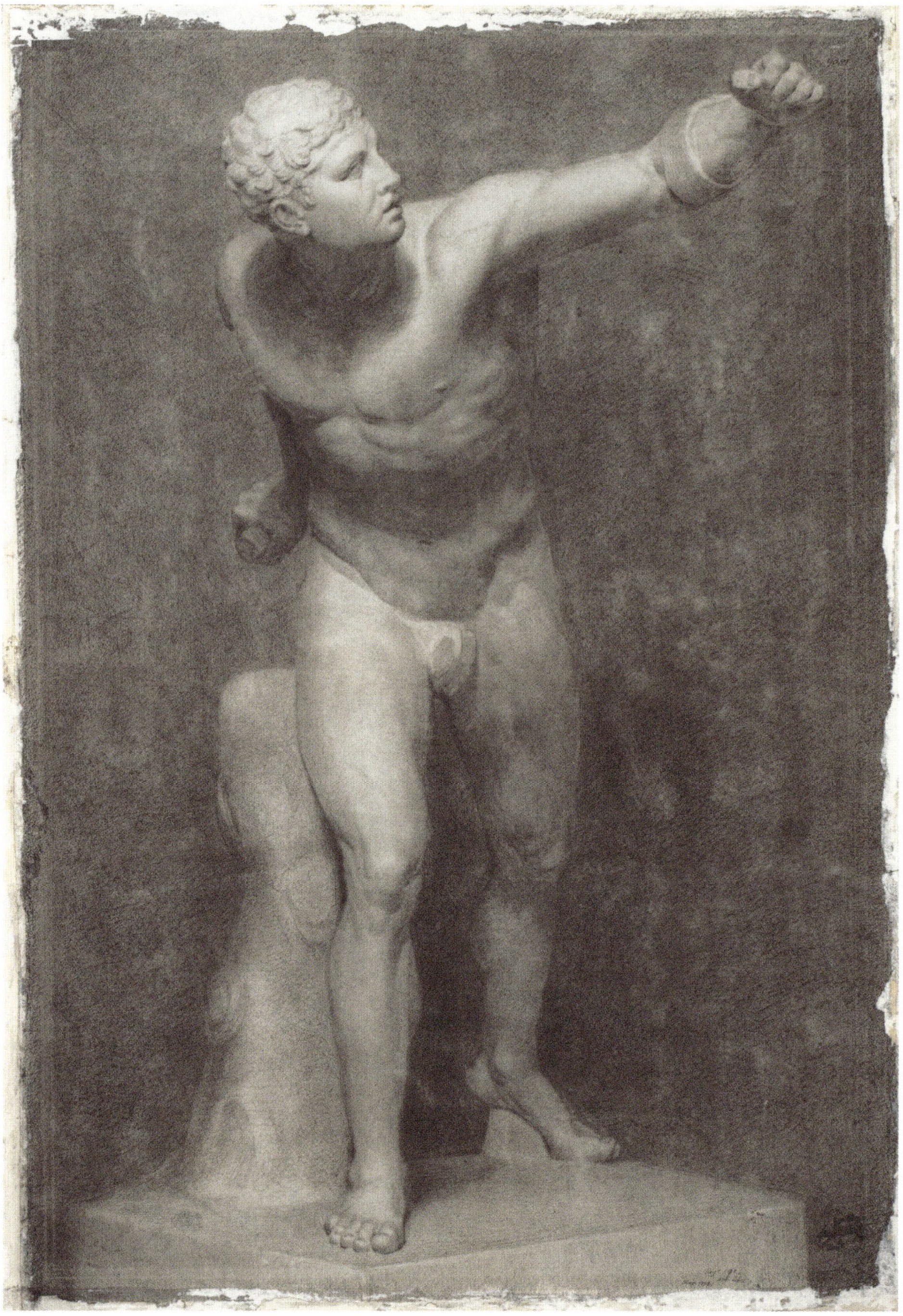

38. Maria Brooks (1837–1913), *Study of a plaster cast of the Borghese Gladiator.* Stamped with 'Department of Science and Art' stamp, and 'ESK' (Examined at South Kensington). Black chalk on paper, 73.8×53.2cm. London, 1872. V&A: D.150-1885

tinct entities (36). By the protocols of learning to draw, from the Renaissance to the nineteenth century, flesh and cloth were originally sundered.[11]

The cleavage not only privileged human skin over the garment – in art training, the study of drapery was accessory to the principal focus on the nude – but it was also a stage towards a deeper exposure of the male body. Just as the action of draping a body comes only after the pre-eminence of seeing the nude, 'so', Alberti continued, 'in painting the nude we place first his bones and muscles which we then cover with flesh so that it is not difficult to understand where each muscle is beneath.'[12] One of the roles of drawing was to chart this complex territory beneath the skin. In the Swiss-born artist Henry Fuseli's *Seated male nude*, of 1770–8, we can see how the skin has shed its opacity (37). Fuseli maintains the coherence of the tensed body through a firm delineation of the bodily contour: within it his pen describes the striations of tendons and larger muscles that constitute an interior landscape of the body. The building up of the male body in art was indubitably imagined as if from the inside out.

This type of forensic insight into what lay underneath skin and clothes guaranteed the art student a

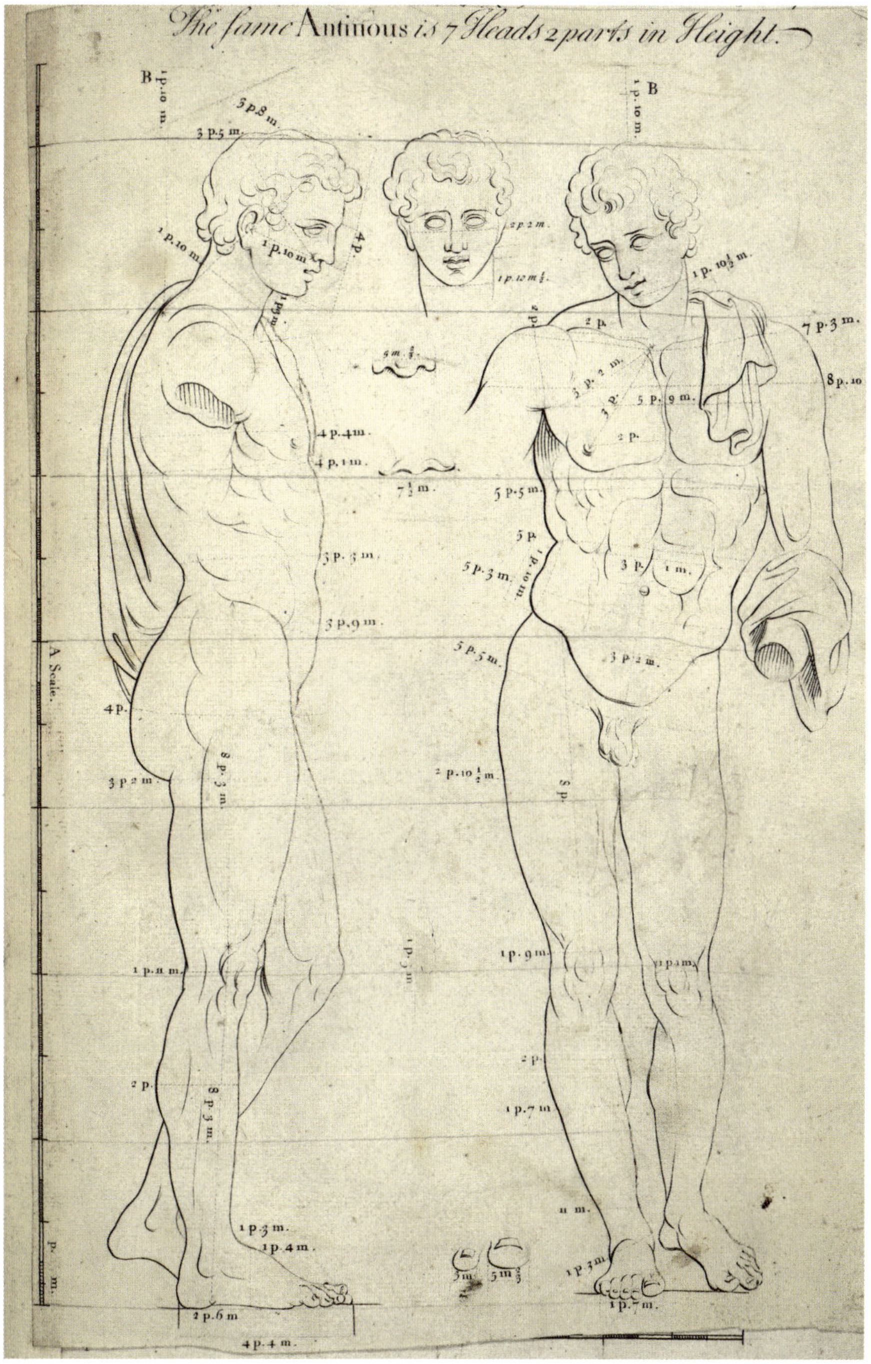

39. Gérard Audran (1640–1703), 'Belvedere Antinous',
The Proportions of the Human Body (London, 1718).
V&A: National Art Library 194.C.33

firm knowledge of the foundational structure of the human body. But in itself it could not bestow on the nude male form the quality, much desired, of perfect corporeal beauty. And nor could live models, who, however handsome, were invariably imperfect. For that, draughtsmen were guided to antique Greek and Roman statuary. Most artists from the seventeenth to the nineteenth centuries would have experienced such statuary through plaster cast reproductions: in the seven white casts we see in the photograph of the life-drawing class at South Kensington we glimpse the early museum's focus on building up its important collections in this area.[13] Not the least of the benefits of plaster casts was that they enabled female art students to scrutinize naked males at a time when a female gaze upon the live male model was largely proscribed (38).

A scientific exactitude was focused upon the exterior form of classical statues. Gérard Audran's engraving of the second-century Roman marble *Belvedere Antinous* (since identified as Hermes) (39–40) appeared in his influential volume *Les Proportions du Corps Humain, Mesurées sur les Plus Belles Figures de l'Antiquité* (1683) (*The Proportions of the Human Body, Measured from the Most Beautiful Statues of Antiquity*). Audran produced

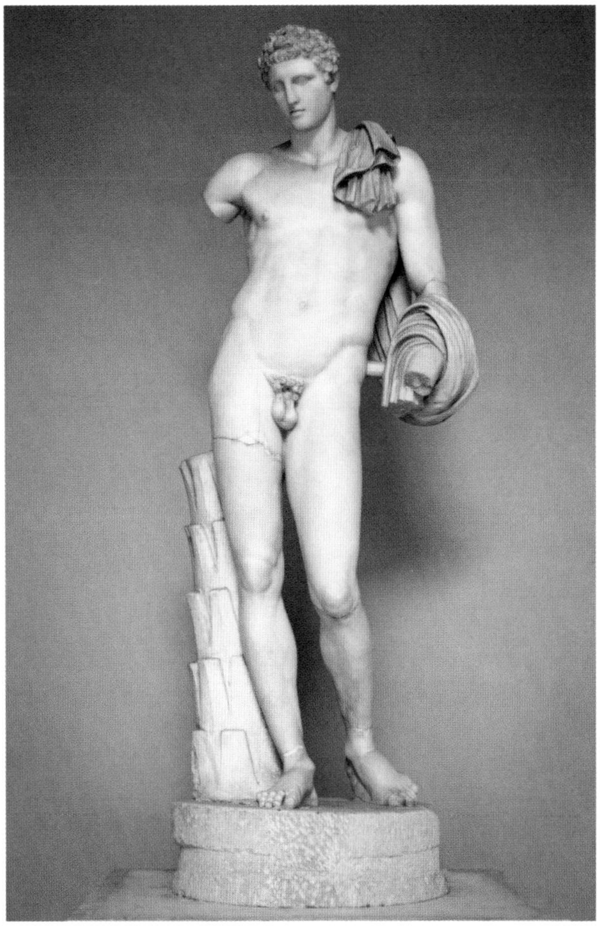

40. *Hermes* (formerly known as *Belvedere Antinous*). Marble, h.195cm. Roman, 2nd century. Museo Pio-Clementino, Vatican City: 907

this book as a tool for students of sculpture and drawing. In his introduction he offered a vestimentary metaphor to explain its rationale: as a constructed garment has a correct relationship to a particular body, so must there be an appropriate fit between the different members of the body.[14] The rationalism of the era led Audran in search of a general standard of male bodily perfection, and he selected canonical antique statues for probing analysis. His examples presented ideal types of masculinity. In addition to the graceful *Antinous* – until the nineteenth century this marble was considered the epitome of youthful male beauty – he drew the brawny *Farnese Hercules*, the majestic *Apollo Belvedere*, the tragic *Laocoön* and the athletic *Borghese Gladiator*.[15] In the spirit of a widespread culture of measurement in early modernity, each was submitted to rigorous examination. Audran brought the severity of the compass to the precision of the pencil. Together, they constituted a powerful investigative tool, rigidly mapping the body. Audran's project sought to evade the vagaries of the infinite variation of real male bodies, as well as the distorting fantasy of the artist. Ultimately, this cultural fascination with measuring antique statues – which can be traced back to earlier efforts by Leonardo da Vinci and Albrecht Dürer – was turned to judging the proportions of real men. In the nineteenth century tailors would construct their patterns for made-to-measure men's clothes on the model of the *Apollo Belvedere*; men pressed to conform to this calculated male beauty.[16] In this way, the 'correction of drawing', and a sculptural practice that modelled itself on ancient statuary, became implicated in a normalizing construction of masculinities.[17]

AGAINST CLOTHES

In his drawing of *Antinous*, Audran faithfully records the sculptor's minimal but striking use of cloth: the drapery that, in the antique marble, erotically hovers above the left pectoral, drops down the back and wraps round the stub of the forearm (40). This is the only part of Audran's drawing unmarked with purposeful measurements. Cloth is represented as subtly marginal: present, but there as an excess to his project.

Indeed, for all the richness of depicted cloth and clothes in the history of western art, it is possible to trace a long history of underrating – or suppressing – clothes display, in theory if not in practice. Lecturing to students at the Royal Academy in 1773, Sir Joshua Reynolds inhibited any incipient vestimentary exhibitionism in them: 'In the same manner as the historical

Painter never enters into the detail of colours,' Reynolds warned, 'so neither does he debase his conceptions with minute attention to the discriminations of Drapery.' And he continued, 'It is the inferior style that marks the variety of stuffs. With him [Reynolds means the mature historical painter], the clothing is neither woolen, nor linen, nor silk, satin, or velvet: it is drapery; it is nothing more.'[18] Drapery thus drained of the sensual pleasures of texture and tint, which is to say masculinized, as an excess of colour and pattern was since the seventeenth century associated with femininity.[19] Reynolds would repeat these strictures when later he spoke of the medium of sculpture. He contrasted its perceived gravity with what he saw as the transience of modern dress: 'Working in stone is a very serious business,' Reynolds cautions, 'and it seems to be scarce worthwhile to employ such durable materials in conveying to posterity a fashion of which the longest existence scarce exceeds a year.'

This male notion of attire as something to be subtly suppressed was buttressed by centuries-old beliefs in philosophy and theology. Today, we are likely to see a diaphanous shirt, or a T-shirt lifted to reveal honed muscle and smooth skin, as a matter of sex and sexiness. But removing a man's clothes in earlier times could be a profoundly symbolic and serious act. Stripping the male body for the ancient Greeks and Romans was not only an elite and erotic performance, but was also an ethical act associated with the manifestation of civic virtue.[20] If the most famous male nude of all, Christ, is usually represented, on the cross or in his mother's arms, as a pool of naked luminosity among gloriously draped figures, minimally clothed in translucent loincloth, it is so that the beholder may sense the truths he lived in an unobstructed way.[21] In his treatise *Émile* (1762), Enlightenment philosopher Jean-Jacques Rousseau decried the way boys, forced into constricting breeches at age four, were prematurely being turned into men and recommended a liberating attire that would develop free movement.[22] A philosophical antithesis between the stripped body and the constraining artificiality of fitted clothes is perfectly encapsulated in Berlin-based artist Daniel Chodowiecki's engraving *Natur und Afectation* (*Nature and Affectation*) (1779) (41). Chodowiecki graphically undresses a couple – it is the same couple on left and right – to persuade his enlightened public that the symbolic removal of clothes might bring about an internal moral reformation. A cultural fantasy of freedom *from* dress has for millennia been just as powerful as one of the freedom to dress up.

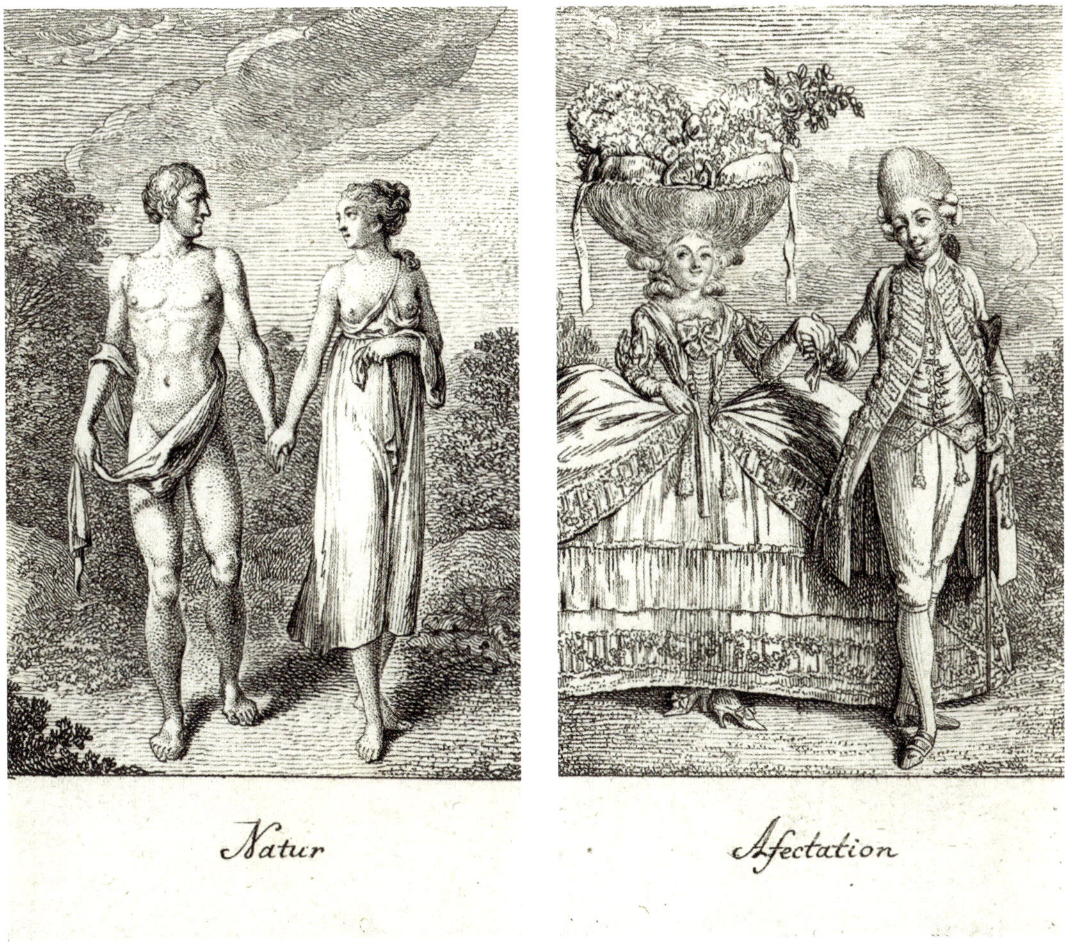

41. Daniel Chodowiecki (1726–1801), *Natur und Afectation*.
Etching, two of twelve published in *Göttinger Taschenkalender* (1779).
The British Museum, London: 1863,0613.643-654

DRAPERY AS A FANTASY

Nevertheless, the persistent cultural association between masculinity and radical nudity was more often than not subtly infringed upon by the presence of cloth, in the form – and compelling idea – of drapery. For post-Renaissance society, the drapery that was discovered on classical statues was perhaps the only form of vestment that could effectively suspend that modern moral choice between clothed and unclothed. For, uniquely, drapery offered a relationship between flesh and cloth that could maintain the nude male body in all its autonomy. In drapery, academic art theorists taught, the body was never overcome by the weight of material, never drowned in a quantity of folds. Drapery respected the natural joins of the parts of the male body, reverberated to its contours: one could glimpse the flow and the structure of the male nude *better* through the drapery.[23] Minimal cloth, transparent body. In reality, and in conditions of urban modernity, the ideal was of course impossible. At the end of the era of neoclassicism, the philosopher Georg Wilhelm Friedrich Hegel contrasted the restrictive cut of men's tailoring of his day, in which cloth is crudely 'dragged up and down the various parts of the body, and their movements', with an irrecoverable classical drapery, that 'environment in which man can move in freedom'.[24]

During the second half of the twentieth century the artist Robert Mapplethorpe was, like Hegel, captivated by classical statuary (and by masters and slaves). But he could comment only ironically on the disjunction between ideal drapery and a newly assertive contemporary masculinity.[25] In his 1976 *Arnold Schwarzenegger* (42), body and drapery are deliberately split apart, no longer in concert. The striation of muscles on the bodybuilder's skin is captivating, yet the ornamented drape's calm and simple folds on the left are a retort to the tense and hyperbolic performance of masculinity on the right. This deconstructs the neoclassical fantasy – longheld – of a seamless fit between naked masculinity and cloth. It is a fantasy that has haunted western modernity as well as the efforts of modern museums to pursue the refashioning of men.

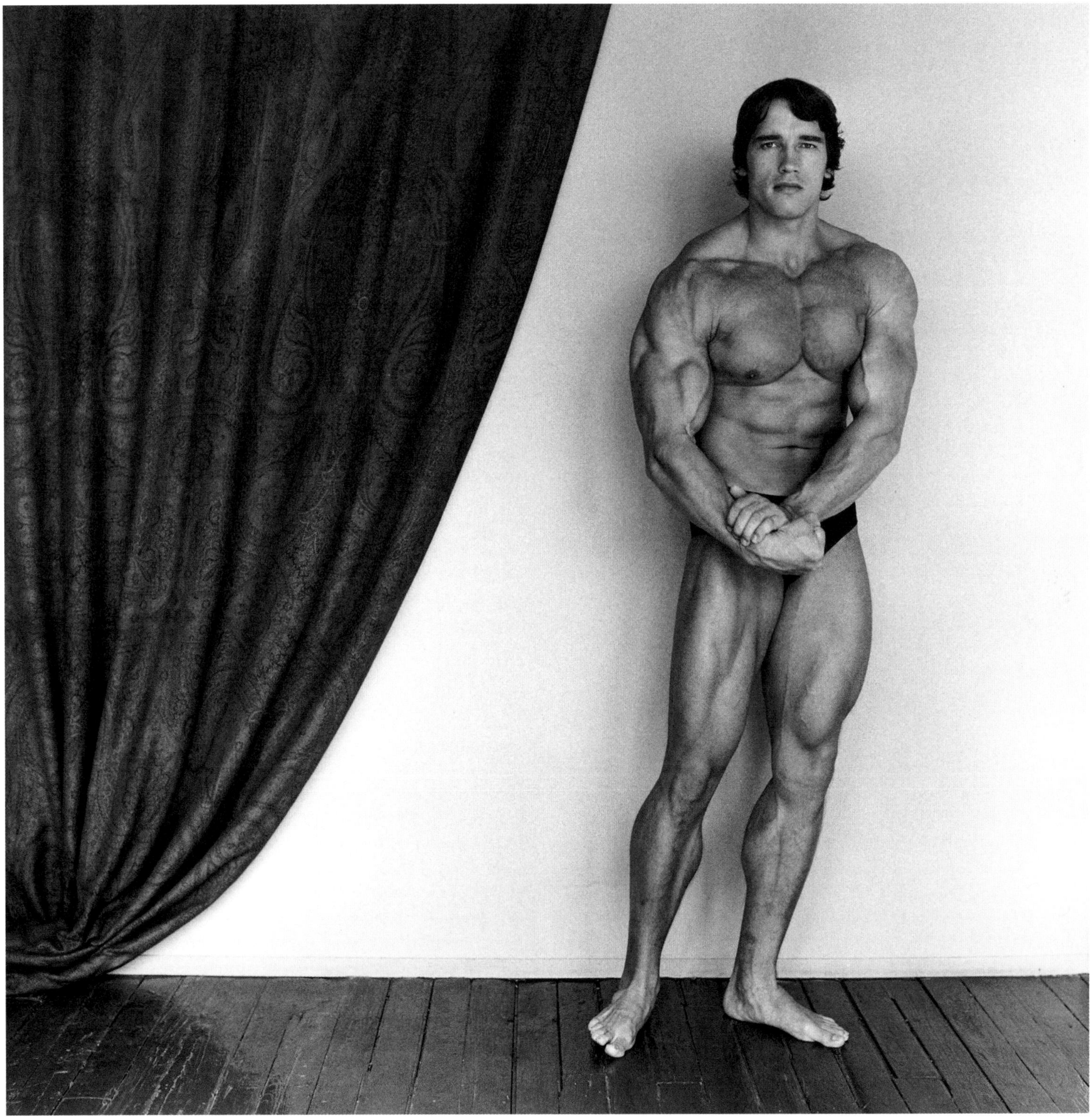

42. Robert Mapplethorpe (1946–1989), *Arnold Schwarzenegger*. Photograph, gelatin silver print on paper, 34.1×34.1cm. USA, 1976, printed 2005. Acquired jointly with the National Galleries of Scotland through The d'Offay Donation with assistance from the National Heritage Memorial Fund and the Art Fund 2008, Tate and National Galleries of Scotland: AR00213

A DEVELOPED PHYSIQUE

ZORIAN CLAYTON

Photography of the male nude has been connected to queer sensibilities since the invention of the medium in the 1830s. Turning the male gaze on the male body, many of the best-known practitioners have been gay or bisexual men. From Victorian Pictorialism through to contemporary performance art, homoerotic aesthetics have created a rich tapestry of queer threads passing through history. Photographers working across a century of societal change and artistic practices have developed affinities in the iconography of the male nude or queer body. Taking frequent inspiration from gods of the ancient world, and with intersections around the globe, it becomes somewhat transcendent of time and place. The pioneering creation and brave dissemination of such work has helped shape emerging queer identities and desires.

Living in a time when homosexuality and the creation of explicit photography could easily lead to incarceration or the death of a career, George Platt Lynes's studios in Paris and the USA became discreet hubs of homoerotic production. Platt Lynes worked in the heart of New York high society as a fashion photographer and principal documenter of the New York City Ballet during the first half of the twentieth century. However, he felt the more overt material was his masterwork and kept it carefully under wraps during his lifetime. Knowing that society was not ready to openly appreciate it, his archive of some 2,000 negatives and 600 prints of homoerotic works, featuring a broad variety of men (friends, lovers and paid models), was covertly donated to the custodians of the Kinsey Institute at Indiana University where its long-term safety could be guaranteed.[1] Even so, some images at the lighter end of his queer spectrum were released during his lifetime, such as this dream-like youth who appeared in a prominent 1937 publication, *Modern Masters of Photography* (43).[2]

The athletic figure emerging from the branches recalls both the young Spartan Hyacinthus, lover of the Greek god Apollo, who turned his dying body into a flower, and the Christian martyr Saint Sebastian, traditionally depicted tied to a tree as he is shot by arrows. Burgeoning with desire and queer coding, the image passes as acceptable by staying within the boundaries of art historical iconography.

Long is the list of gods who have fuelled the imaginations of artists eager to evoke the flexed posturing of naked Olympians and the classical world. Celebrated sculptor of the male physique Sir William Hamo Thornycroft stated, however, that the camera did not give 'the proper value of tone', praising sculpture as the medium with which to honour 'the exquisite gradations of light and shade which the nude presents to you'.[3] Lithe archers and well-built warriors were the subjects of the New Sculpture movement, but such imagery was also at the heart of kitsch physique magazines. Now read as a cornerstone in the formation of certain gay male aesthetics and communities, this niche form of print media played a key role in the shift towards broader definitions of gay cultural identities from the late 1940s until gay liberation in the late 1960s.

This pair evoke the classical bronze runners of the *Villa dei Papiri* at Herculaneum (44). Some physique magazines contained these sorts of outdoor shots, oily studio affairs with tridents, plinths and posing pouches, produced largely under the guise of art appreciation. When acquired by the V&A in 1955, they were catalogued as 'anatomical life studies'. Their true sexual purpose was hiding in plain sight behind a thin veil of sports and classical art. The old rules insisting that homosexuality equalled effeminacy in men were being dismantled as visions of classic masculinity (the lumberjack, the cowboy, the biker etc.) were recoded as queer, making way for the concept of the butch clone and the rise of the leather scene. These notions were cultivated even further by the fruitful fantasy drawings of artists like Tom of Finland and George Quaintance, whose careers were launched in the pages of such physique magazines.

The classified ads in these magazines allowed men to get in touch with others under the pretence of being interested in art photography.[4] One of the best-known American titles, which was published quarterly from 1951 to 1990, *Physique Pictorial*, claimed that it was primarily an art reference book.[5] *Grecian Guild Pictorial* went one step further with a pledge of allegiance: 'I seek a sound body in a sound mind that I may be a complete man; I am a Grecian.' Grecian has long been a byword for gay tastes and homoerotic customs. As the historian Robert Aldrich has explained, 'at times when homosexuality was condemned as sinful, dangerous, and unmanly, the Greek prototype provided an unparalleled and glorious image of man's desire for other men.'[6]

Fred Holland Day's photographs were highly praised by his contemporaries as 'exquisitely harmonious ... distinctly Greek'.[7] A wealthy dilettante and philanthropist, his subject matter and lifestyle can be compared with contemporaries of the 1890s, such as Wilhelm von Gloeden. Fixated on creating romanticized images of Sicilian teenagers embellished with the same garb of laurel wreaths, lyres and loincloths, it is widely thought that Gloeden's work was destined only for the secret collections of an aristocratic clientele. However, both envisaged and succeeded in having their homoerotic figure studies proudly displayed in galleries internationally.

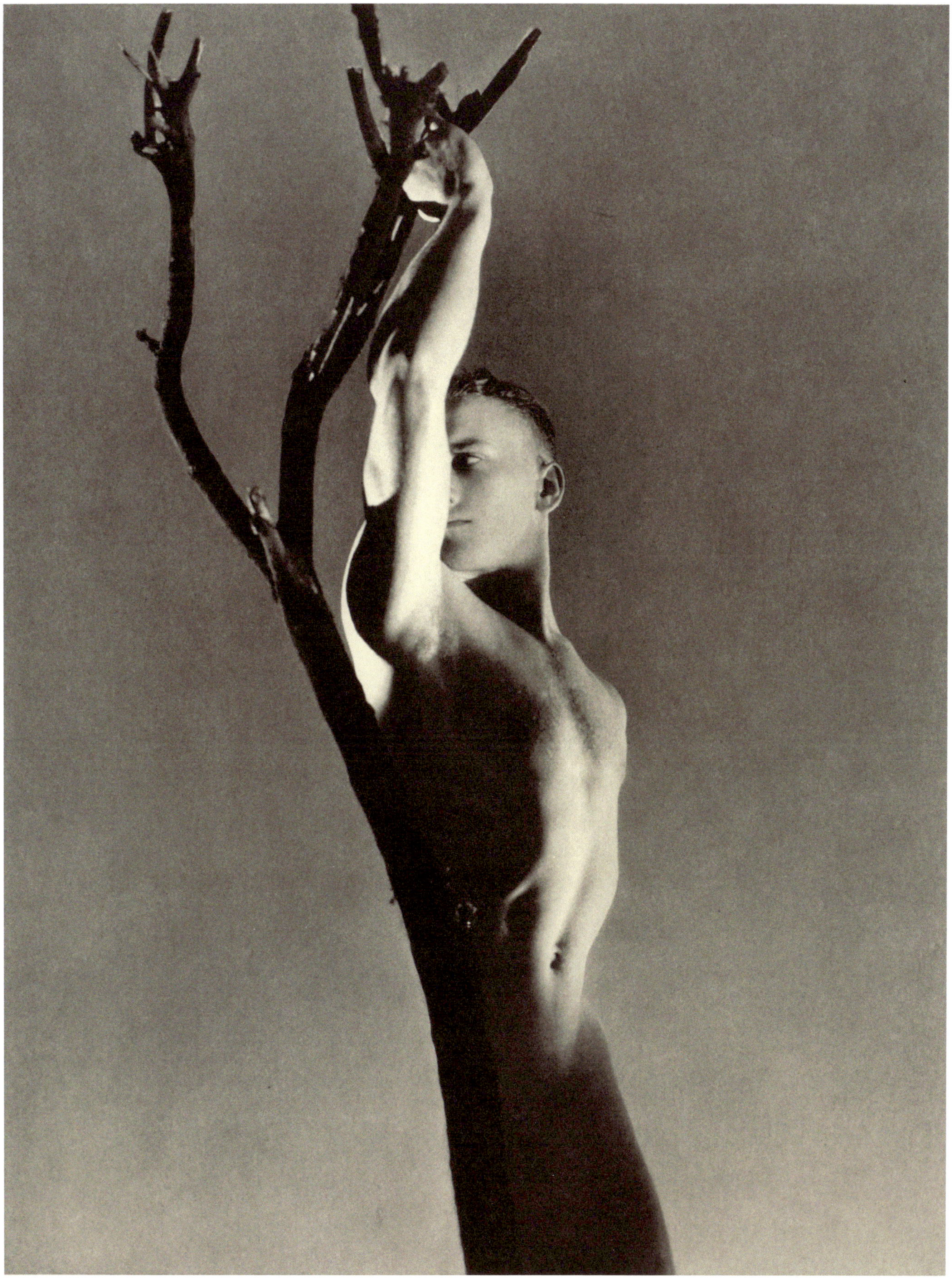

43. George Platt Lynes (1907–1955), *Nude Boy*.
Photograph, photogravure, 36×28cm. USA, 1937.
V&A: RPS.801:30-2020

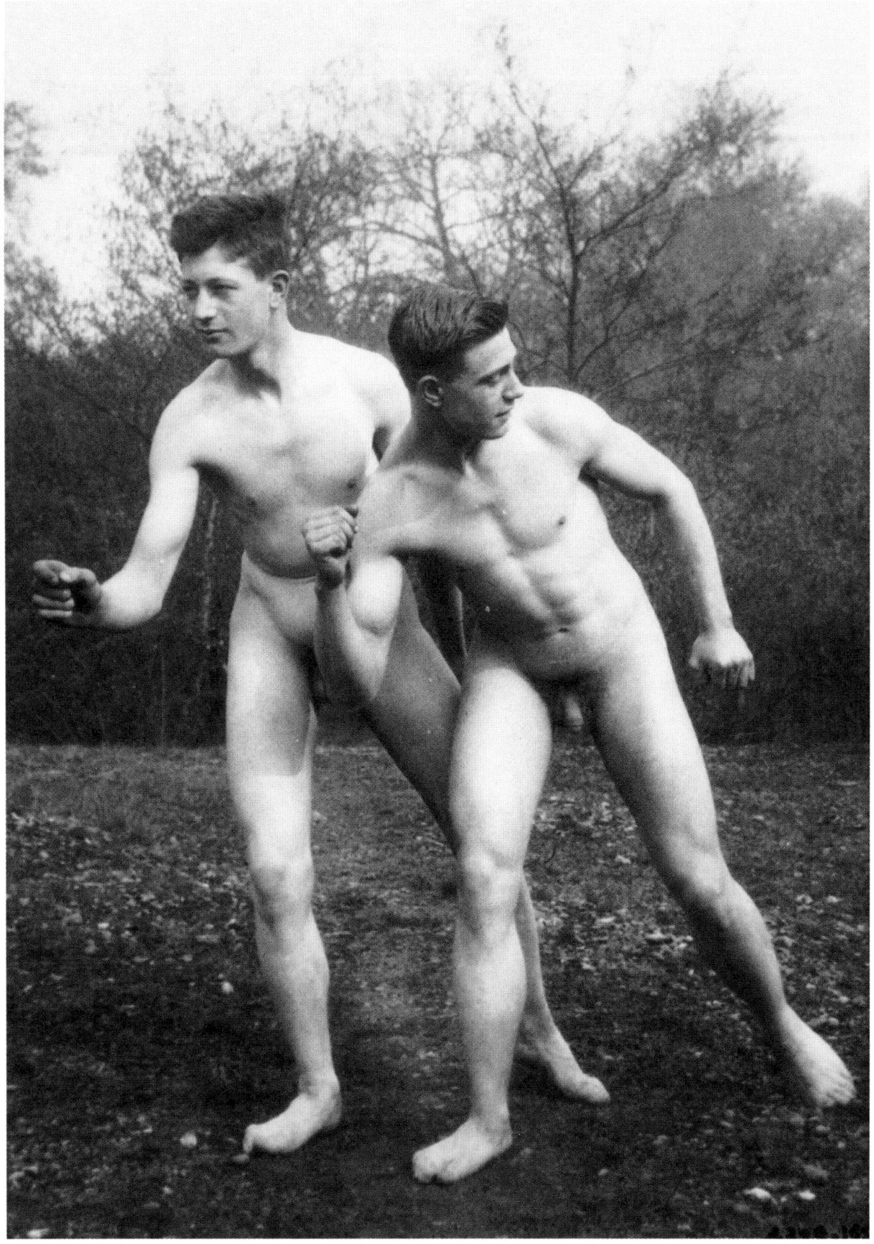

44. Two naked men poised for a race. Photograph, 15.6×12cm.
Great Britain, *c.*1950. V&A: 4328–1955

Aligned with the early aesthetic movement of Pictorialism, Day hired young working-class men to pose for him in pastoral settings. One such woodland series depicts fellow artist Nicholas Giancola languidly embodying the god Orpheus, who held the power to charm all living things (45). His toned body adorned only with the usual props, the photographer's fantasy is captured in Day's trademark platinum print, said to last for a thousand years. This divine Eros is thus frozen in time like a silent male siren; as Platt Lynes put it in his poem *Orpheus and Eros* of 1936: 'the camera guards the moment ... inters the god in winding light and shadow'.[8]

Heralded as an early proponent of photography as a fine art form, Day is also credited as one of the first to upend the 'ethnocentric fantasy that there was only one "race" of human beings who represented what was good and true and beautiful.'[9] His images of men of colour in the 1890s depict his sitters as kings and noblemen, celebrating contemporary tales of European colonial defeat in Ethiopia.

New parallels are being drawn between the work of Day and Rotimi Fani-Kayode, with their staging of photographs and attraction to homoeroticism and religious iconography. Indeed, Day was such 'a crucial touchstone in a queer counterhistory of photography',[10] and the links are so pronounced that perhaps 'Kayode was reactivating a lineage in which he was signalling himself as a part.'[11]

Fani-Kayode's 1983 arrival in Brixton, London, sparked the beginning of a tragically short but electrifying career, and the creation of a uniquely sensual and spiritual body of photographic work. The power of the medium is laid bare in his declaration: 'It is photogra-

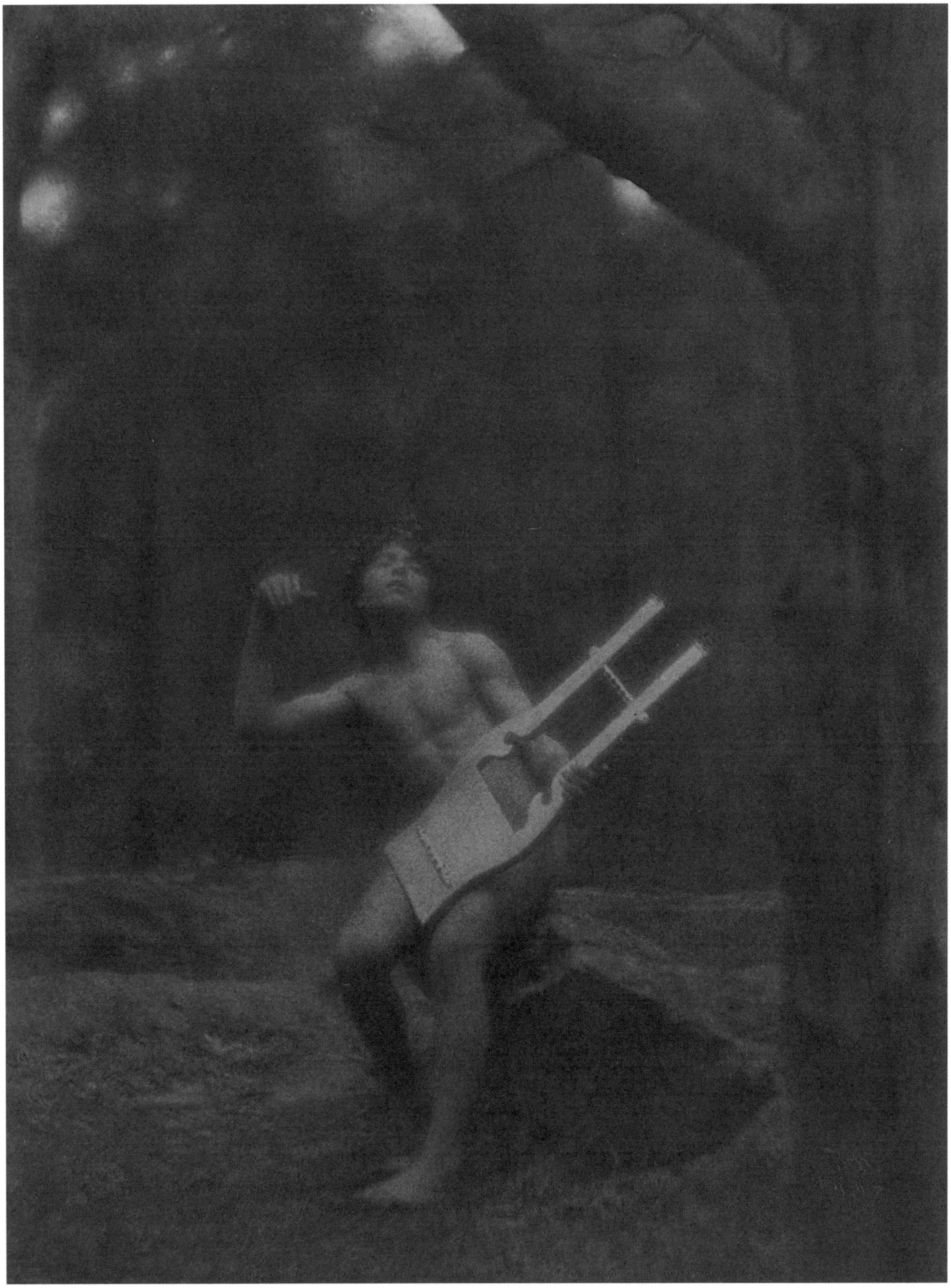

45. Fred Holland Day (1864–1933), *Orpheus.*
Photograph, platinum print, 24.2×18.7cm. USA, 1907.
Library of Congress, Washington DC: 96512538

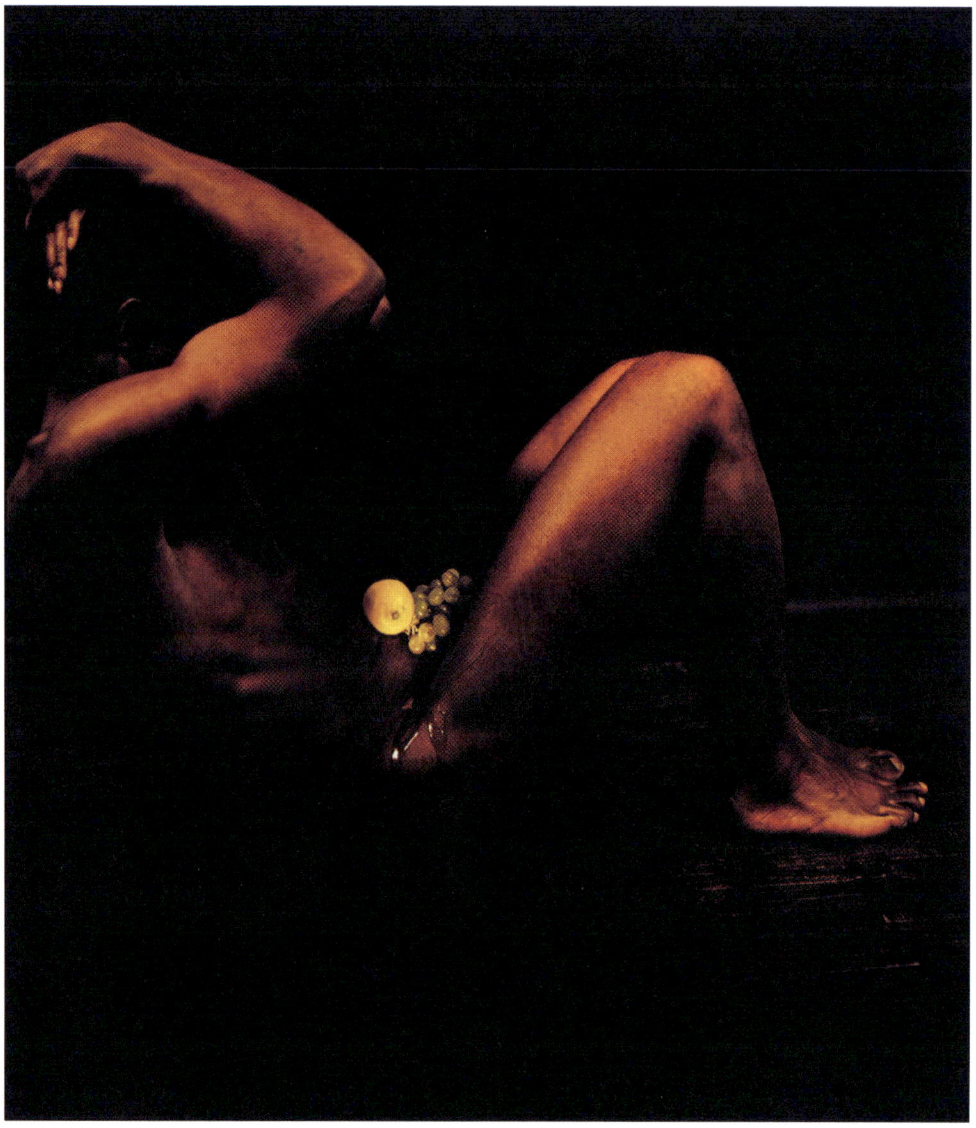

46. Rotimi Fani-Kayode (1955–1989), *Nothing to Lose XII.*
Photograph, Ilfochrome dye destruction print, 32.7×26cm.
London, 1989. V&A: E.1084-1996

phy, therefore – black, African, homosexual photography – which I must use not just as an instrument, but as a weapon if I am to resist attacks on my integrity and, indeed, my existence on my own terms.'[12] He felt a sense of liberation in his multi-layered outsider status, encapsulated in the title of his final series, 'Nothing to Lose (Bodies of Evidence)' (46). Bacchanalian yet bittersweet, this portrait was made in the year of his death during the AIDS epidemic. The AIDS crisis fuelled the urgency to visualize and support a community that had long been forced into the shadows, stealing the lives of many of the artists who had been at the forefront of this radical new wave.[13]

Among these was Robert Mapplethorpe who died in the same year (see p.58). It seems almost impossible for photographers focusing on the male nude to escape comparison with this gay, gothic heavyweight. Even with renewed criticism of the fraught fetishization in his visual diary of sexual exploits,[14] and endless examples of racist bigotry in interviews over the years, consumption of his work shows no sign of slowing. However, the aperture is widening beyond the usual fixations on sex and censorship to challenge the racist implications more directly. For example, the 2020 Guggenheim Museum exhibition, *Implicit Tensions: Mapplethorpe Now*, sought to reframe him in the context of a more diverse group of LGBTIQ artists: Rotimi Fani-Kayode, Lyle Ashton Harris, Glenn Ligon, Zanele Muholi, Catherine Opie and Paul Mpagi Sepuya.

Fani-Kayode admired some of Mapplethorpe's work, but saw no real connection between them beyond the fact that they both worked predominantly with Black male models. Arguably both used photography as a tool to tap into higher realms, putting erotic energy at the heart of their creative inspiration. Mapplethorpe described his discoveries of the perfect male form as 'a manifestation of the divine',[15] pulling us above the mere man once again towards a god-like plane. Fani-Kayode tapped into the rich iconography of the Yoruban Orisha (òrìṣà), sifting out narratives on gender fluidity and

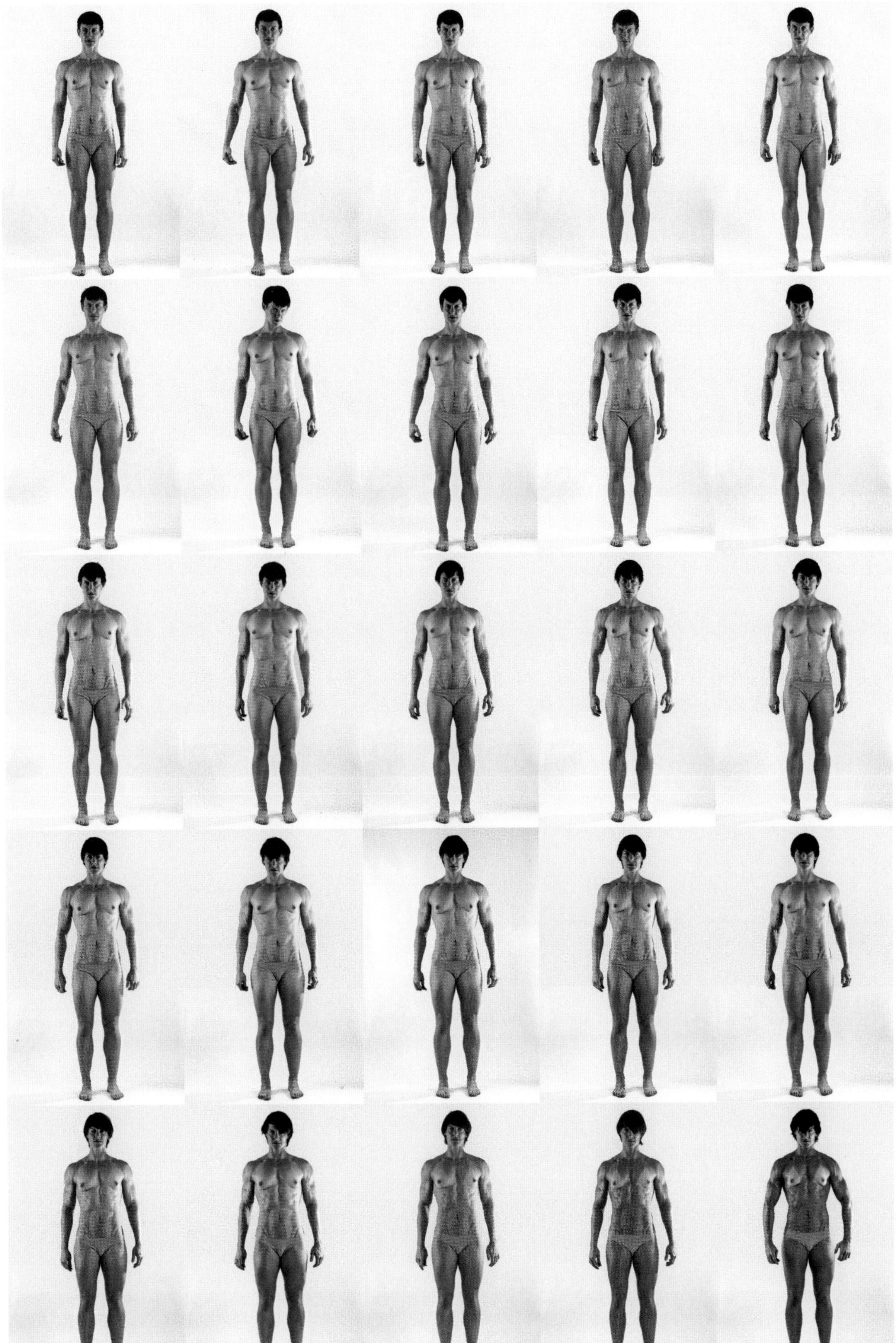

47. Cassils, *Cuts: A Traditional Sculpture: Time Lapse* (front). Photograph, archival pigment print, 152.4×101.6cm. USA, 2011. Courtesy of the artist

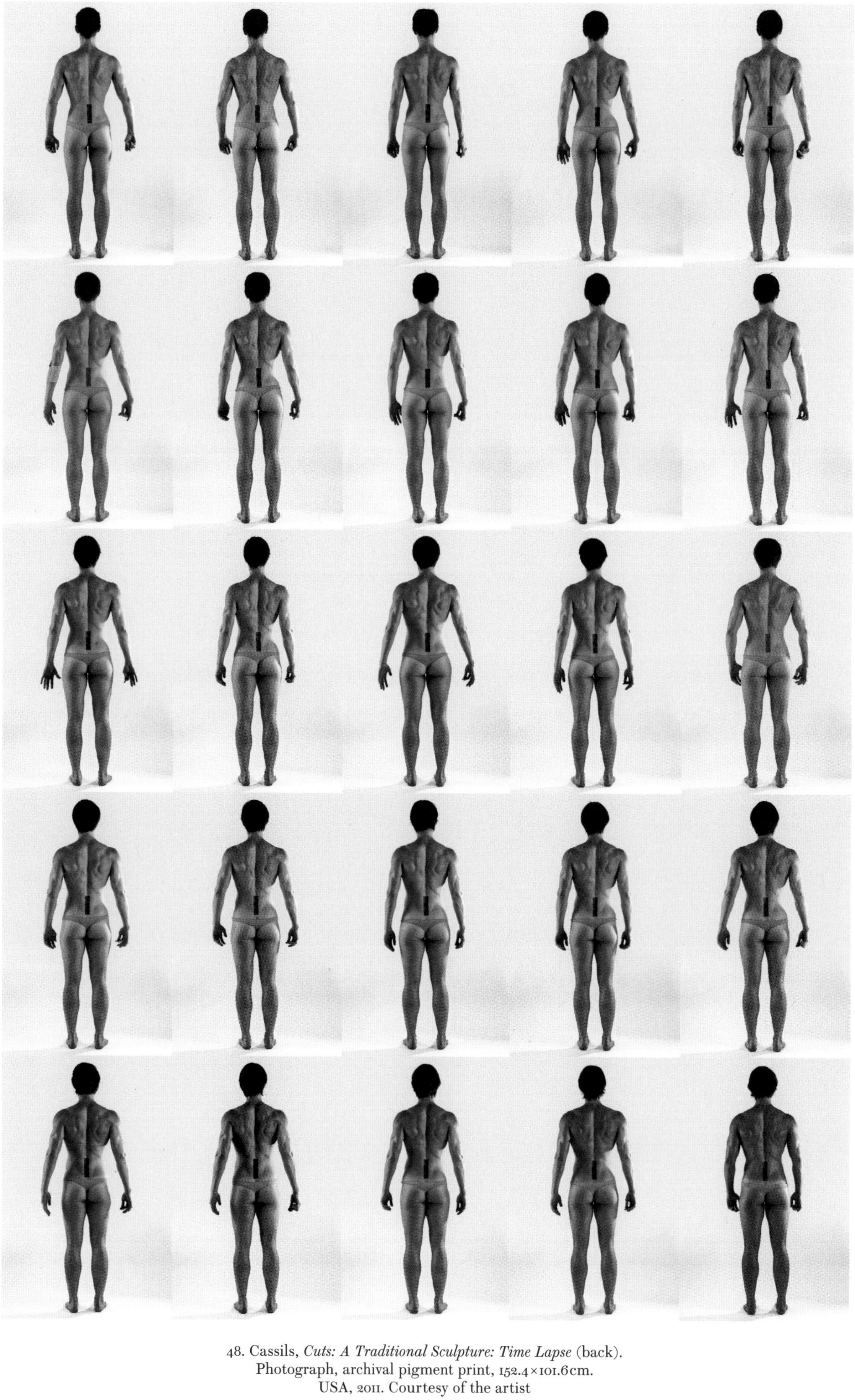

48. Cassils, *Cuts: A Traditional Sculpture: Time Lapse* (back).
Photograph, archival pigment print, 152.4 × 101.6 cm.
USA, 2011. Courtesy of the artist

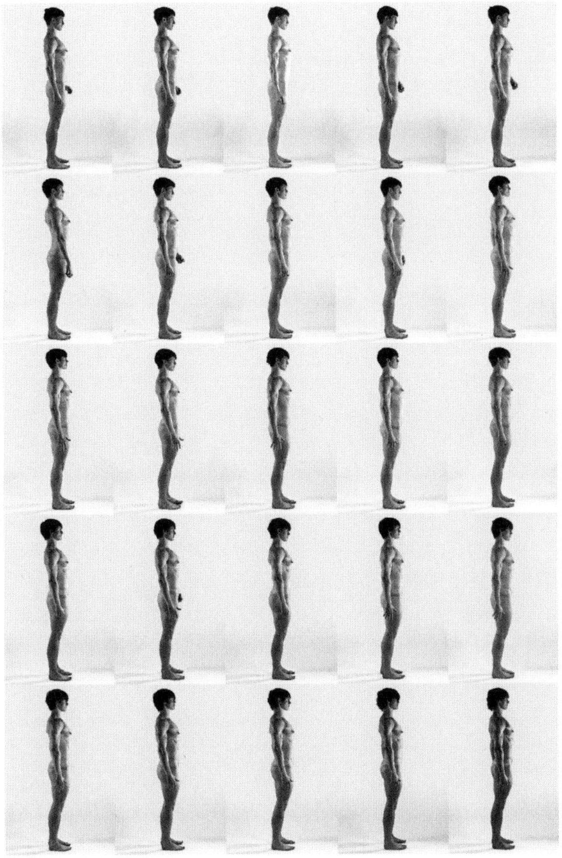

49. Cassils, *Cuts: A Traditional Sculpture: Time Lapse* (right). Photograph, archival pigment print, 152.4 × 101.6 cm. USA, 2011. Courtesy of the artist

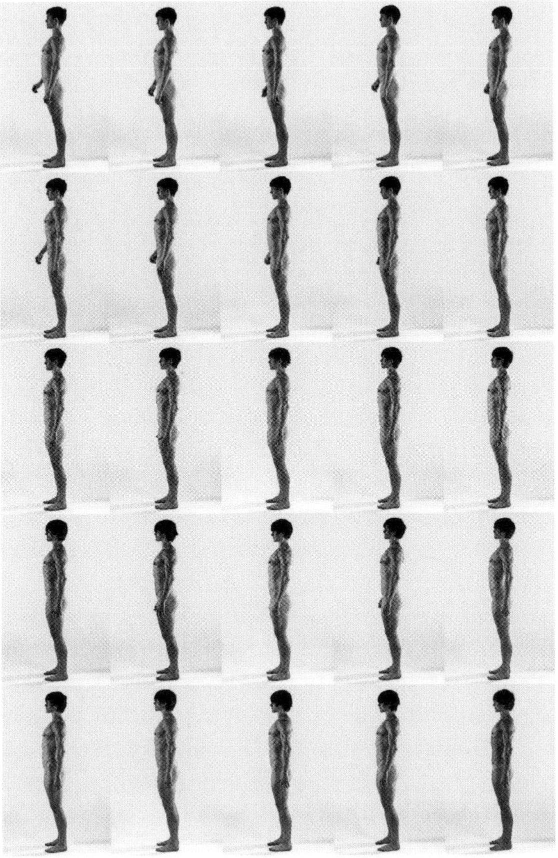

50. Cassils, *Cuts: A Traditional Sculpture: Time Lapse* (left). Photograph, archival pigment print, 152.4 × 101.6 cm. USA, 2011. Courtesy of the artist

sexual potency as tools to induce trance-like ecstasy and a connection to the spirit realm.[16]

The 1980s saw an explosion of queer visibility as artists began to publish and exhibit explicit work more widely. Despite insidious political attempts such as Section 28, designed to prohibit the 'promotion' of homosexuality, progress was nevertheless marching on.[17] As these photographers and their contemporaries started to carve out new space for queer narratives in galleries and museums, magazines such as *The Face* and *i-D* saw heterosexual men actively cultivated with more emotionally expressive yet narcissistic ways of being.[18] The rise of the so-called *new man* revealed fresh potential to flirt with androgyny and more flamboyant fashions. The consumption of images around male desirability was gradually gravitating away from a predominantly gay subculture and into a more mainstream marketplace.

Concurrently, a growing number of out trans, non-binary and intersex photographers came to the fore in the late twentieth-century. Del LaGrace Volcano, Amos Mac and Texas Isaiah are just a few who have taken up the mantle, wrenching back control of the narrative by documenting themselves and their communities with greater authenticity.

The artist Cassils has made their name as a pioneer in this critique of the binary, boldly centring their queer trans body in a performative practice, combating body normativity and the patriarchal hierarchy. Their piece entitled *Cuts: A Traditional Sculpture* (2011) (47–50) is a queer marriage of sculpture, photography and intense performance art. Inspired by a 1972 body transformation piece by Eleanor Antin, here too we find references to the Greeks. Antin described her photographic documentation of weight loss over a 45-day period as 'classical Greek sculpture (peeling small layers off an overall body image ... refined to the point of aesthetic satisfaction).' Cassils takes another path and in the process also bucks the perceived norm that transition equals surgery. To be cut can mean having hard defined muscles as well as to go under a surgeon's knife. Over a gruelling 23 weeks, they gained 23 pounds of muscle. The resulting multiple images, titled *Time Lapse*, are reminiscent of Eadweard Muybridge's analyses of human locomotion in the 1880s. Cassils uses their impressive form to create further large-scale portraits such as the provocatively titled *Lady Face Man Body*, citing Lynda Benglis's phallus-wielding nude self portrait *Centerfold* (1974), another artistic touchstone in debunking fears around gender diversity and equality.

Restrictive gender roles negatively affect every corner of society, reflected in the international constancy of gender-based violence and the wide-reaching damage of what is currently termed 'toxic masculinity'. Cassils deconstructs the traditional limitations and prejudices bound up with a rigid gender binary, becoming a vision of twenty-first-century masculinity on their own terms, and breathing new life into photography of the nude masculine form.

UNDERPINNINGS: THE NEXT BEST THING TO NAKED

SHAUN COLE

Underwear is the most intimate of garments, pressed close to the body, whether it is exposed publicly or kept privately hidden beneath an outer layer. A person wearing underwear is 'simultaneously dressed and undressed'.[1] Historically, those garments we now popularly understand as underwear were predominantly publicly unseen in keeping with the prevailing attitude of 'out of sight, out of mind'. Today, while still primarily private, men's underwear has become increasingly visible and public, particularly through advertising and in popular visual culture.

Men's underwear has performed multiple purposes: for protection, modesty and adornment; as an indicator of social status; and for support and for sexual or erotic purposes. Protection, of the body from the environment and abrasion of outer clothes, as well as those garments from the body. Modesty, in keeping the body covered in socially and morally acceptable forms. Adornment, through the decoration of visible parts of undergarments. Social status, as indicated through the number of garments owned and visibly displayed beneath outerwear. Men's underwear has supported the genitals as well as shaping the waist, torso and legs. It reflects and enhances sexuality and sensuousness, particularly when considered in the context of the role that concealment plays in the eroticism of clothing, calling attention to the body beneath the clothes.

'KEEP YOUR SHIRT ON!': FROM UNDER TO OUTER – SHIRTS AND T-SHIRTS

Until the early twentieth century, shirts were regarded as undergarments, serving the purposes of protection and modesty, and as indicators of wealth or social status. From the mid-sixteenth century, clean white linen had increasingly been seen as the marker of the courtier and changing the shirt daily became normal for men in court circles.[2] At the beginning of the nineteenth century, ruffle-fronted shirts had become the general fashion for both day and evening, and indicated that a man was not a manual worker (51). During the 1820s these frill-fronted shirts began to lose their popularity for daywear and were replaced by a front panel with vertical pleats or tucks. By the 1840s the daywear shirt front had become increasingly plain, and with the combination of a high-cut waistcoat and cravat, was practically hidden. The high buttoning of waistcoats and coats continued throughout the nineteenth century for formal day wear, leaving just the collar and cuffs showing. By the early twentieth century, with a change to less formal outerwear, the shirt had lost its status as underwear to become a key component of a man's outerwear wardrobe.

The 1840s saw the introduction of the woollen vest or 'under-vest', which was 'generally made of fine calico'.[3] Even though this 'undershirt' was worn next to the skin and under the shirt, it retained the name given to flannel under-waistcoats that had previously been worn for extra warmth. Knitted or flannel undershirts were worn by labouring men because, as well as keeping them warm in winter, they absorbed sweat and were easily washable. Such undershirts were also worn by sailors, and their transformation to the T-shirt has been attributed to naval adoption and adaption. In the years after the Second World War, most men still wore their T-shirts underneath their shirts. Enhanced by popular cinema-screen portrayals by Marlon Brando in *A Streetcar Named Desire* (1951) and *The Wild One* (1953), and James Dean in *Rebel Without a Cause* (1955), the T-shirt became part of the uniform of a rebellious teenager, and was transformed into outerwear. Fashion historian Valerie Steele described the T-shirt as, 'the most significant and pervasive example of underwear as outerwear', which 'flaunted rules about hidden clothing' and challenged 'taboos ... against male sexual display.'[4]

'SO COMFORTABLE, SO SMOOTH TO THE SKIN': HEALTH, HYGIENE AND COMFORT

A change in attitudes towards notions of personal cleanliness in the late eighteenth century ran alongside developments in cleaning techniques. George Bryan 'Beau' Brummell (5), credited with spearheading the move towards the pared-down dandy styles, advocated 'very fine linen, plenty of it, and country washing',[5] where 'cleanliness was the touchstone upon which [Brummell's] acquaintances were invariably tried.'[6] A shirt collar's cleanliness continued to be a marker of a gentleman throughout the nineteenth and into the early twentieth century, and novelists such as Arnold Bennett often used a description of a protagonist's collar to comment on character or social situation. For example, in *Riceyman Steps* (1923), Bennett describes the protagonist, second-hand bookseller Henry Earlforward, wearing 'a neat dark-grey suit, which must have been carefully folded at nights, a low, white, starched collar, and a "made" black tie that completely hid the shirt-front; the shirt-cuffs could not be seen... He gave an appearance of quiet, intelligent, refined and kindly prosperity'.[7]

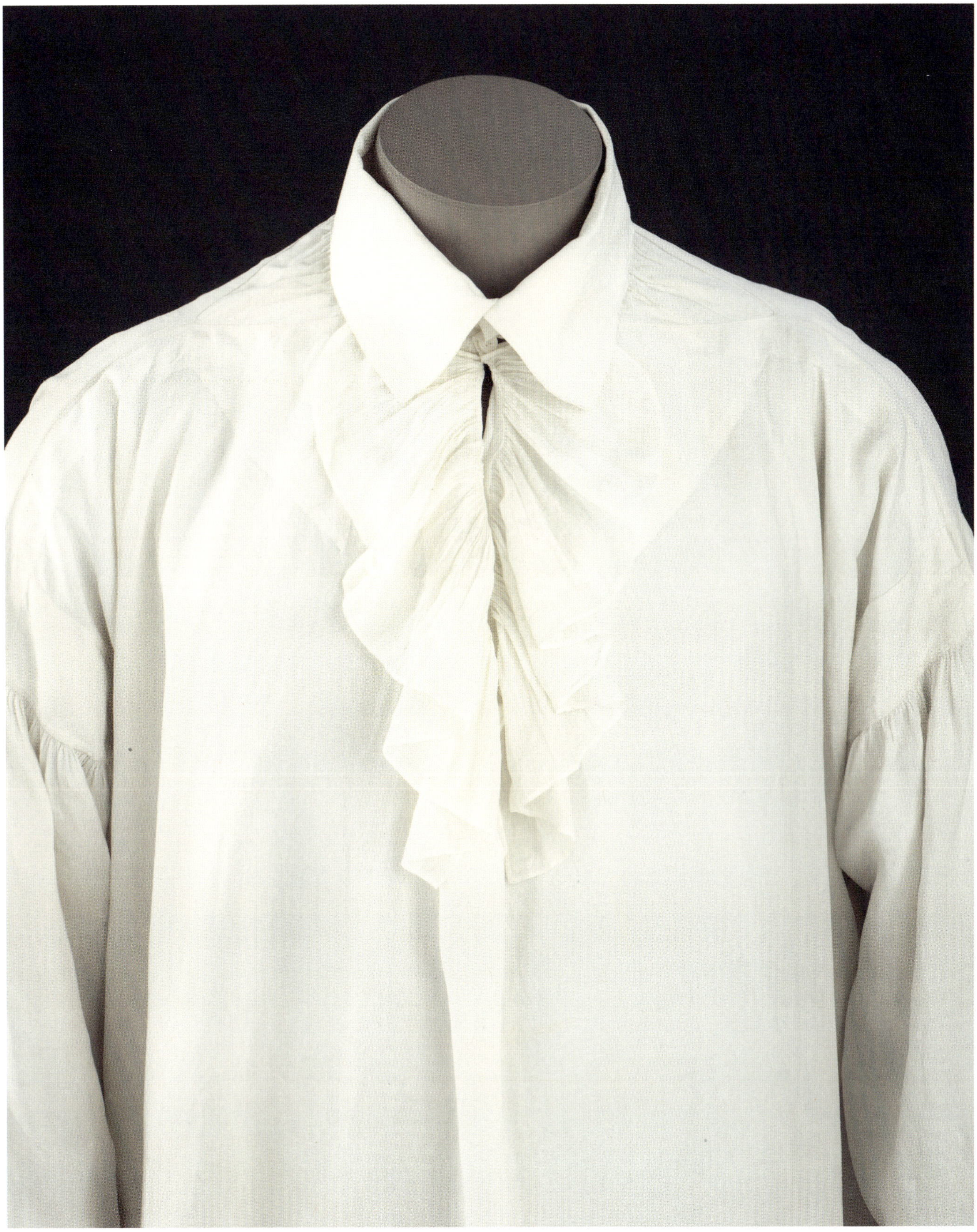

51. Ruffle-fronted shirt. Linen and cotton.
Great Britain, 1800–10. V&A: T.16-2019

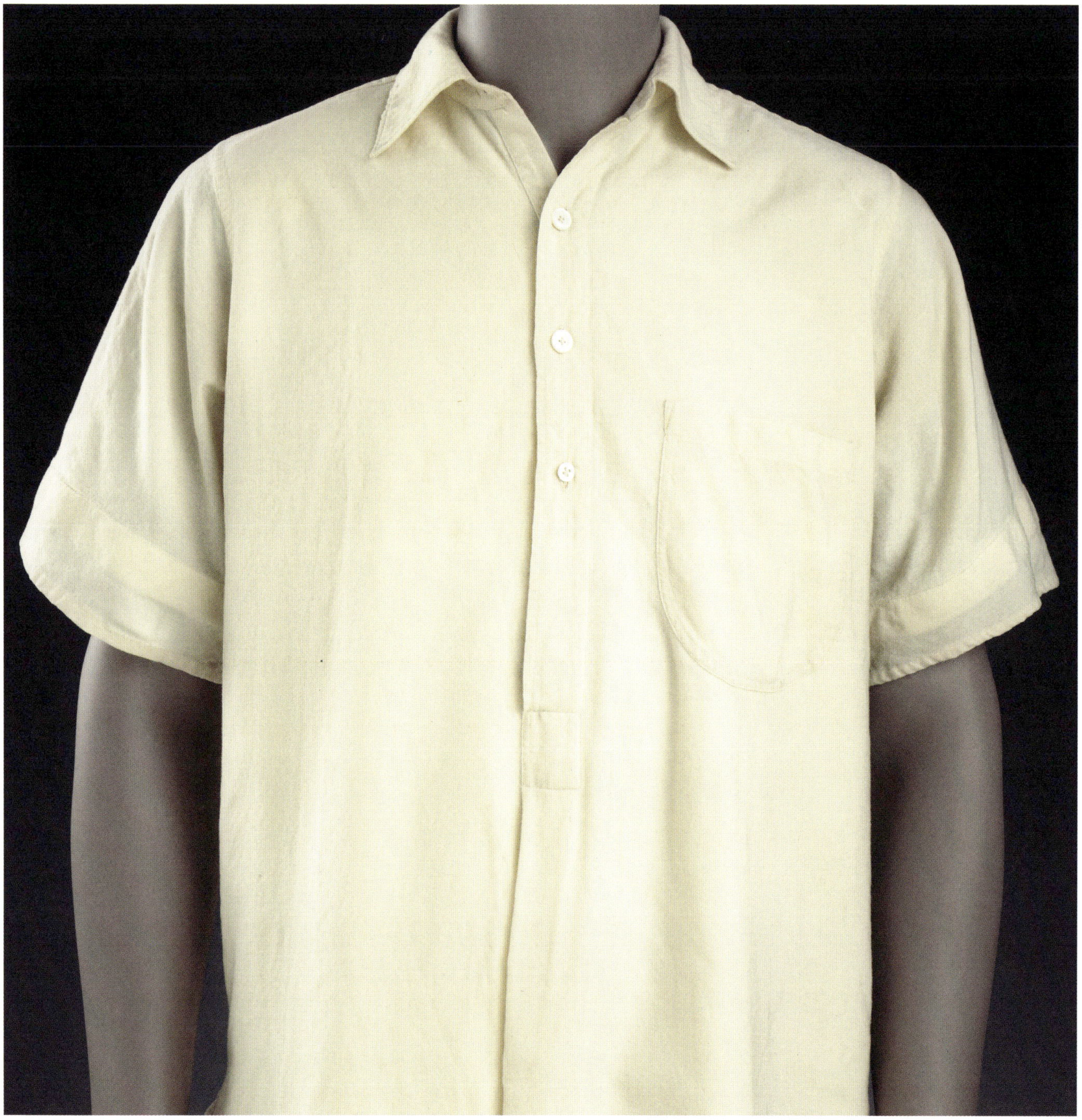

52. Dr Jaeger's Co. Ltd., Short sleeved shirt. Wool. Worn by the playwright and critic George Bernard Shaw. Great Britain, *c.*1884–1900. Given by the British Theatre Museum Association. V&A: S.1417-1984

The nineteenth century saw great developments in the approach to personal cleanliness, reflected in theories about 'hygienic dress'. German doctor and zoologist Hans Gustav Jaeger argued that it was crucial to wear wool next to the skin in order to encourage perspiration.[8] As Jaeger objected to dyes, his woollen garments were all undyed and available in creamy white, a variety of light browns and dark brown (52). Most of the customers for Jaeger's designs were enlightened, upper-class puritans, or else progressive intellectuals such as playwright George Bernard Shaw, who embraced Jaeger's principles and ordered his first Jaeger suit on 19 June 1885.[9]

By the early twentieth century, opinions about the health properties of fabrics were changing to reflect general ideas about health and fitness. Alongside this demand for comfort, leading companies saw the benefit of patenting their innovations and promoting their brands through advertising. In 1937 the British clothes manufacturer Sunspel developed and patented a lightweight, breathable, woven, open (mesh-like) fabric, known as Quality 14 (Q14), and other companies also produced garments in similar fabrics (53). In addition to knitted cellular cottons, new man-made fibres such as rayon (developed in 1905) offered a lighter-weight and more comfortable alternative to the traditional heavier fabrics and were promoted in quasi-scientific terms. These particularly appealed to younger men,

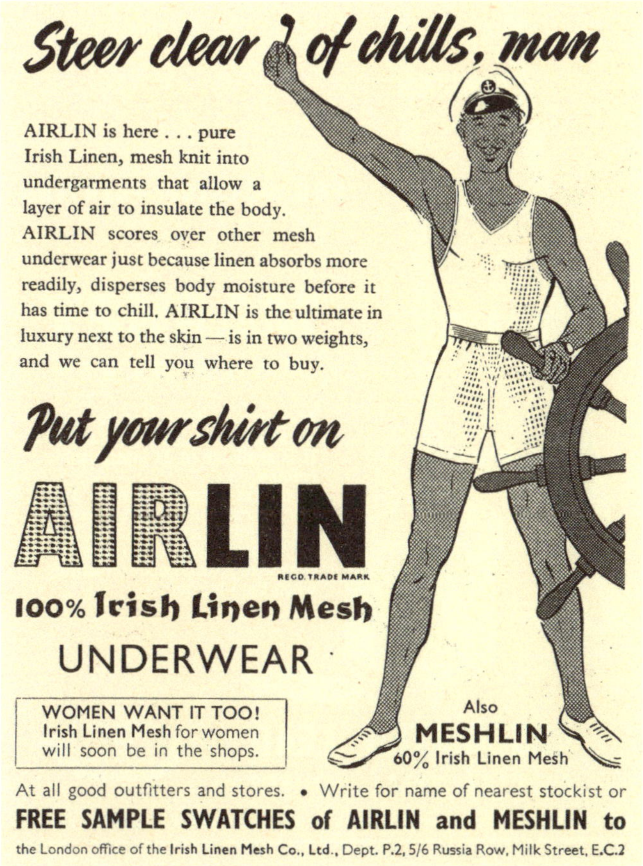

53. Advertisement for AIRLIN mesh underwear, 1953

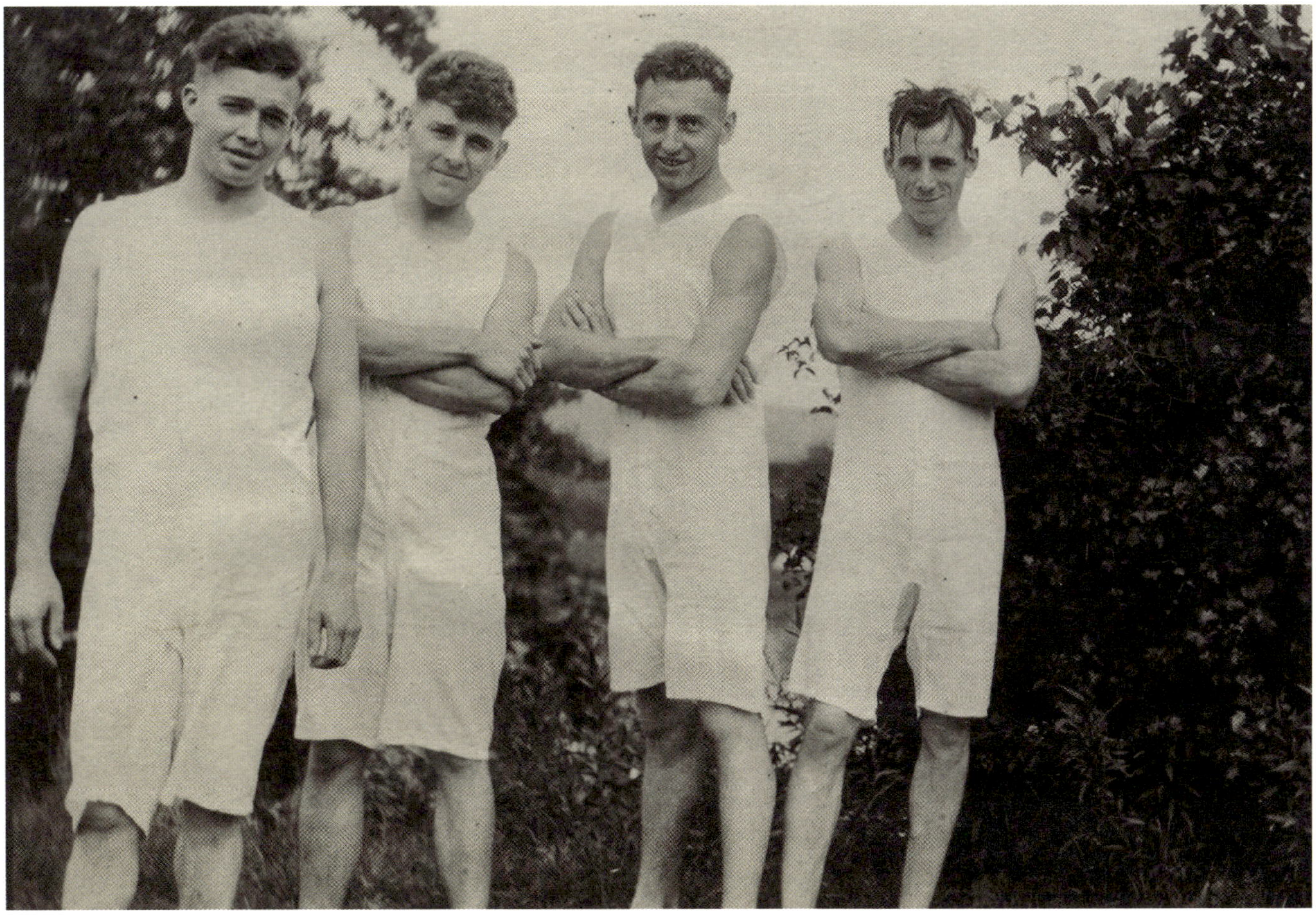

54. Four men wearing athletic union suits, USA, 1914

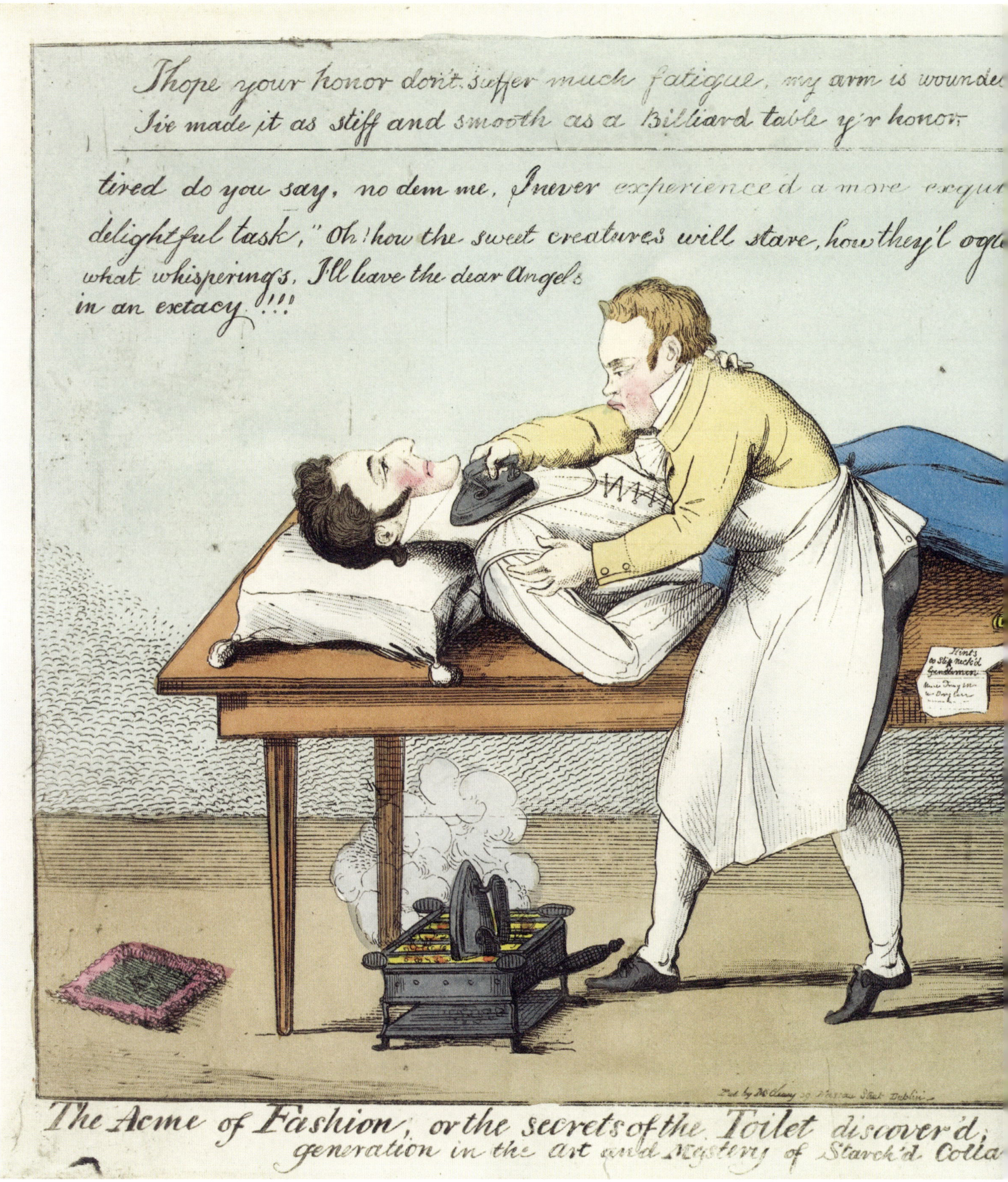

55. *The Acme of Fashion, or the secrets of the Toilet discover'd, intended as a lesson for the Stiff Neck'd generation in the art and mystery of Starch'd Collars by a nobleman.* Etching, coloured by hand, 25×34cm. Dublin, *c.*1820. Given by Mr Geoffrey A. Whittall. V&A: E.467-1955

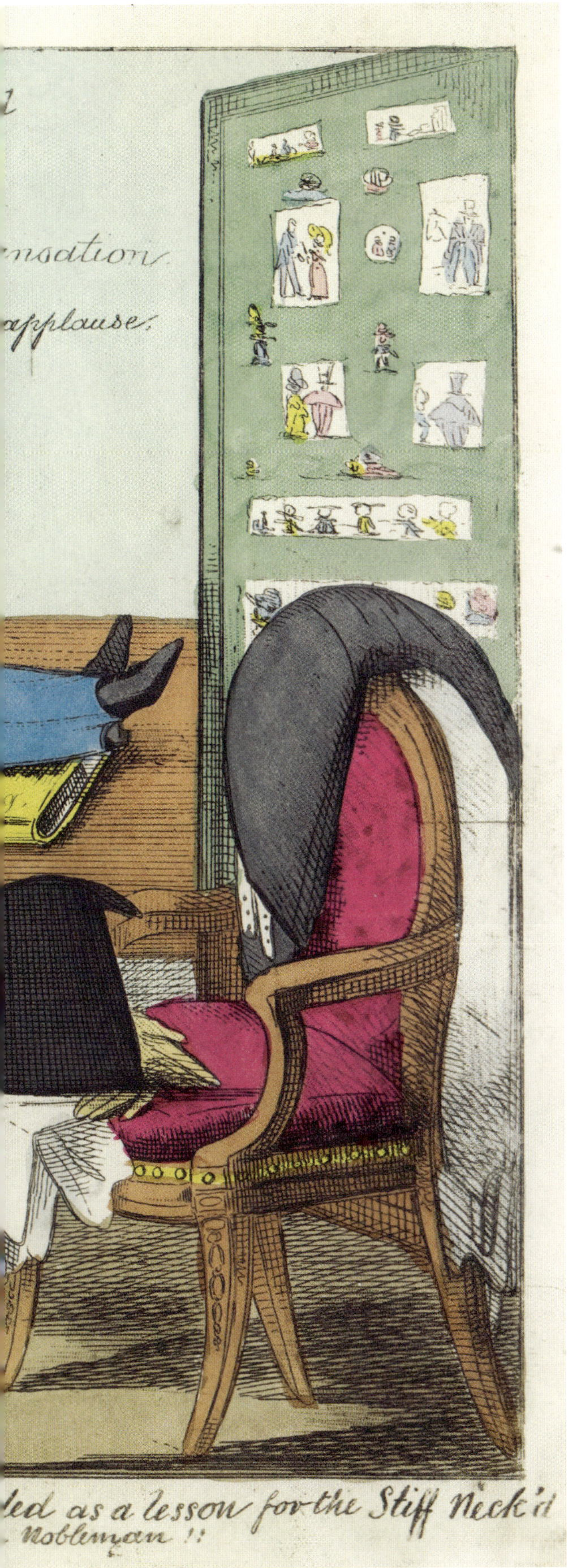

who were casting off outdated forms of outerwear. The increasing desire for comfort in men's underwear led to changes in the full-body, often cumbersome, one-piece woollen union suit. In 1914 the American underwear company B.V.D. introduced a sleeveless union suit with quarter-length legs, and by the 1920s this athletic union suit (so called because it resembled athletes' shorts and vests) was available in a variety of lighter-weight fabrics such as cotton, silk and poplin (54).

In achieving its protective function, the materiality of men's underwear was, and is, key. As a garment that sits directly upon the body, its physical contact with the skin was undeniable in its relevance. As what sociologist Elizabeth Shove has called a 'boundary object',[10] underwear creates a protective layer, both between the delicate corporeal surface and outer garments and from a cultural discomfort associated with nudity or nakedness. The choice of fabric, determined by scales of economy or fashionability, was key to the sense of comfort, an element emphasized in many underwear advertisements.

Mirroring the interest in athletic underwear of the 1920s and 1930s, the last decade of the twentieth century saw a revival of interest in underwear designed to embrace healthy lifestyles, personal fitness and exercise. The inclusion of Lycra and new polyamide microfibres with moisture-wicking qualities, as well as seamless knitting technologies, reduced the build-up of sweat and minimized chafing.[11] The continuing rise of sportswear had an impact on the design and presentation of underwear, and the language used to promote it emphasized the importance of the body as the site for which the garments were designed. This led to a preference for the use of the term 'bodywear'.

'DESIGN IS ONE THING, FIT IS THE OTHER ... IN SITUATIONS LIKE THIS YOU SHOULD BE ABLE TO RELY ON YOUR UNDERWEAR': SHAPING THE MALE BODY

Prior to the late nineteenth century, padding and corsetry were employed by men to create an ideal fashionable body shape beneath outer layers. Stays or corsets were occasionally worn by army officers, fops and dandies to promote a smart appearance, as well as to attain the correct and fashionable posture. A pinched-in waist and high collar were staples of the fashionable dandy image in the early nineteenth century, caricatured in the etching *The Acme of Fashion*, showing 'y'r honor' lying on a table having his collar and cravat ironed to make it 'as stiff and smooth as a Billiard table' (55). This rigidity is reflected in the visible laced corset the nobleman wears over his shirt. *The Workwoman's Guide* of 1840 noted that corsets were worn by men during athletic activities such as horseback riding and hunting and 'violent exercise', echoing the servant's concern in *The Acme of Fashion* that 'y'r honor don't suffer much fatigue'. Similar caricatures also demonstrate the

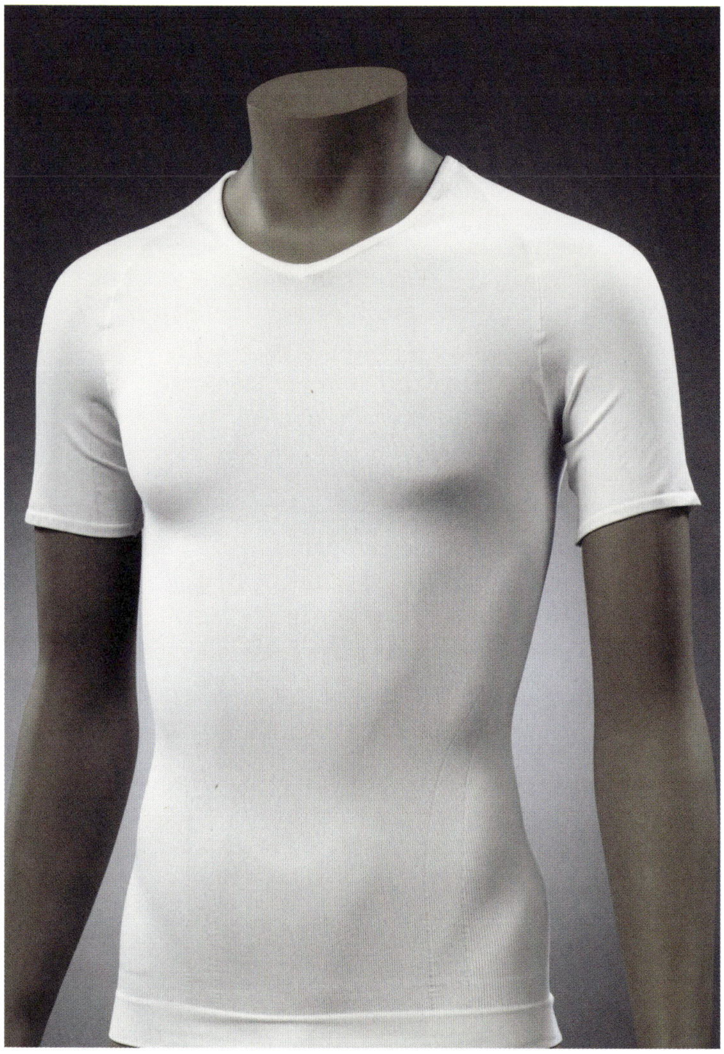

56. Sara Blakely (1971–) for Spanx, Zoned Performance V-Neck T-shirt. Nylon, elastane. USA, 2010. V&A: T.214:1-2016

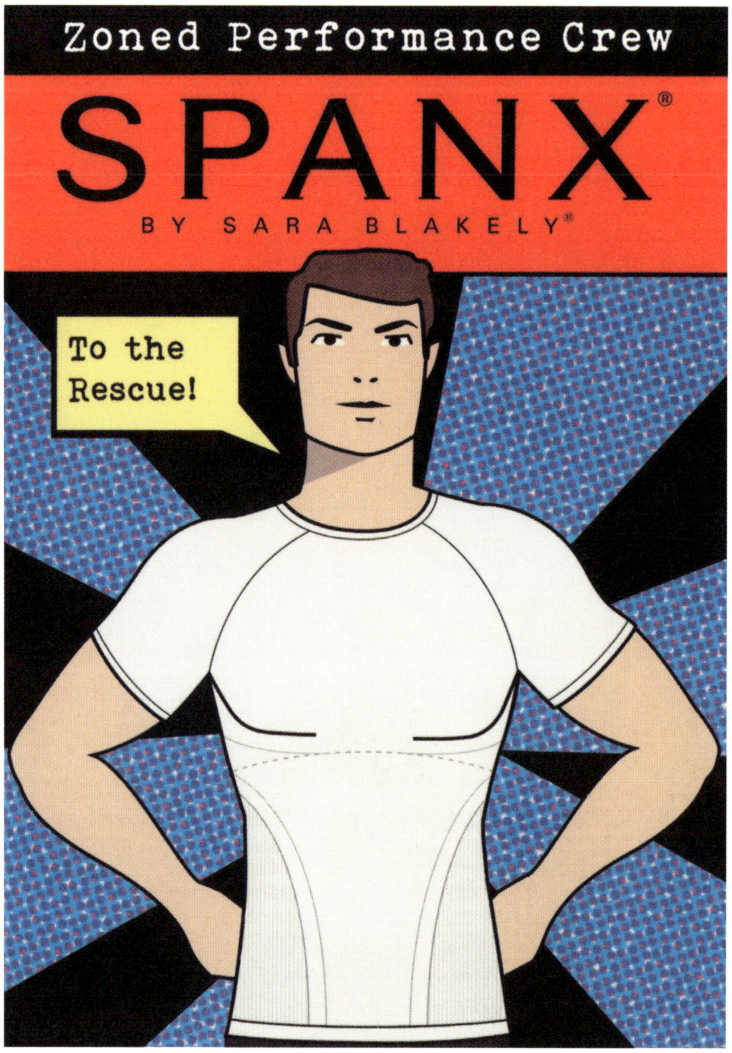

57. Packaging for Spanx Zoned Performance V-Neck T-shirt. Card, 14.1×9cm. USA, 2010. V&A: T.214:2-2016

lengths dandies and their fashionable precursors, the macaronis, would go to achieve a shapely leg, through the use of false calf pads, made from parchment or flannel, that could be strapped onto the leg under a man's stockings.

The early twenty-first century has seen a return to underwear that enhances or 'constructs' the idealized male physique. In 2008 Andrew Christian released underpants with 'Anti-Muffin Top elastic' designed to help reduce the appearance of love handles. Such 'compression' technology was also used in undershirts and vests to 'transform the torso and chest', making the wearer 'look sharper, stand taller and feel stronger', as claimed on the packaging for Spanx's 2010 shapewear T-shirt (56 and 57). Many compression garments (for both upper and lower body) were designed to support muscles and reduce injury during exercise, move moisture away from the body and provide anti-bacterial qualities, as well as body shaping.

New developments in the design of underpants enhanced the male body, particularly the crotch. In 2007 Australian brand aussieBum introduced the 'Wonderjock', developed in response to customers who 'expressed an interest in looking bigger, just like women using the Wonderbra'.[12] The Wonderjock used seams around the pouch and an additional pocket within the pouch front to 'push up' the genitals. Garments from Gregg Homme and C-IN2 included padding built into the pouch front, or integrated 'rings' that encircled the genitals pushing them upwards and forwards. This emphasis on the crotch and male virility in underwear was not new in the early 2000s. Comparisons can clearly be made to codpieces of the fifteenth and early sixteenth centuries that drew attention to the genital area and were often highly decorated. Codpieces were noteworthy not as sexual invitations to women but rather as symbols of social, temporal and territorial power. Writing in the 1960s about the new crotch-hugging trousers of that decade, and the skimpier underwear required for a good fit, journalist Rodney Bennett-England observed that 'once again, we have a codpiece, albeit a concealed one, to give a fellow self-assurance' and produce 'an overt bulge of masculinity'.[13] The recent trend for enhancement underwear demonstrates

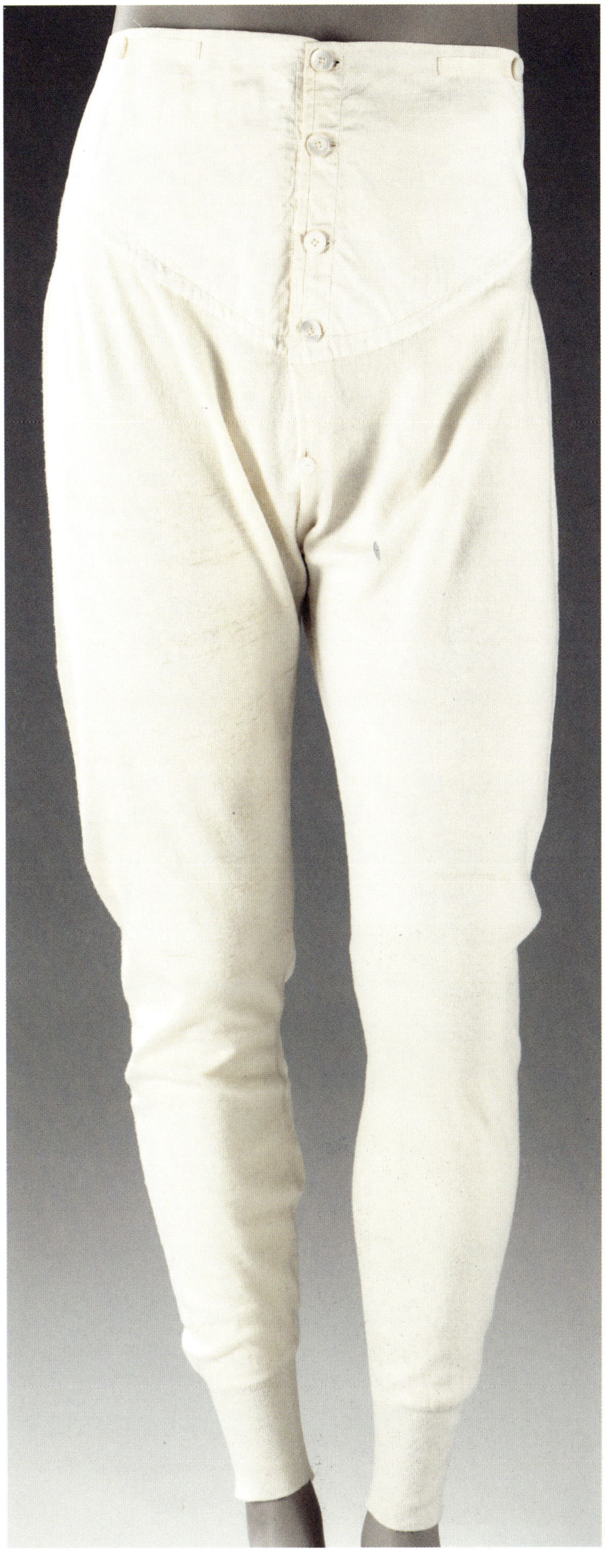

58. Long underpants (front). Machine-knitted wool. England, mid-nineteenth century. V&A: T.56-1959

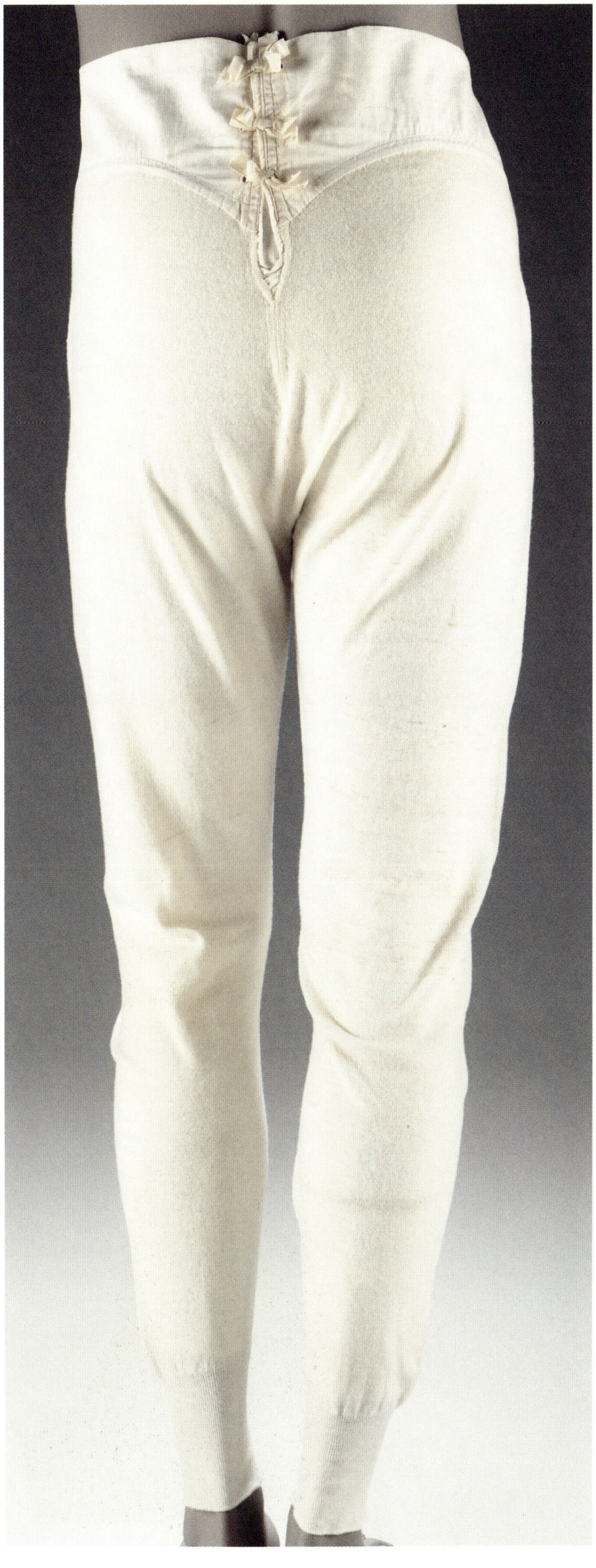

59. Long underpants (back). Machine-knitted wool. England, mid-nineteenth century. V&A: T.56-1959

the concern that men have about their crotches, and references the supposed power that is associated with a large penis as a signifier of a more masculine man.

'IT'S AN EROGENOUS ZONE THAT WE CAN BRAND LITERALLY': FROM PRIVATE TO PUBLIC – DESIGNING AND PROMOTING MEN'S UNDERPANTS

Until the 1930s men's underwear was generally concealing of the body beneath. Nineteenth-century underpants were of two lengths: short to be worn under breeches, and long for wearing under pantaloons and trousers. Variously made of knitted or woven linen, cotton, wool or silk, these followed shapes that had been developed in previous centuries to accommodate the fashionable styles of men's outer clothing. Of course, not all men wore such garments; those from lower classes often used their shirt tails pulled between their legs for protection and cleanliness. Changes in production and the increase in commercial manufacture resulted in innovations for front fastenings, back openings, ribbing for ankles and loops on the waistband for braces to pass through (58 and 59). Around the end of the nineteenth century, commercial manufacturers began to advertise their new, often patented, undergarments, highlighting their fit, comfort and construction. Sometimes these advertisements used the idealized male bodies of classical sculpture rather than real men's bodies, to avoid concerns about representation of the semi-clothed male body.

The American hosiery and underwear company Cooper's launched the Jockey Y-front in 1935, which marked a significant moment of change in men's underwear. Cooper's had previously introduced innovative additions to its garments, such as their union suit's Klosed Krotch back opening that was advertised by a painting entitled *Man on a Bag* by American illustrator J.C. Leyendecker. The Y-front was based on the style of French briefs, or 'slips', and swimwear that Cooper's vice president Arthur Kneibler had seen on a postcard. Unlike many previous styles, Y-fronts provided 'masculine support' through the lastex (a form of elastic) leg openings and waistband (with the name woven into it), and knitted cotton fabric. Such support had previously only been available in an athletic supporter or 'jock strap', hence the name Jockey. Patented in 1887 by C.F. Bennett's Bike Web Company to provide support to bicycle riders on the cobbled streets of Boston, the jock strap comprised a cup of fabric with a waistband and straps that ran across the buttocks (60). As well as providing comfort and support, Cooper's jockey short had a patented overlapping inverted Y-shaped seamed fly opening. This was revolutionary in that it drew attention to the male genitals through its innovatively shaped seams around the fly (61).

To promote its garments, Cooper's (who changed its name to Jockey Menswear Inc. in 1971) licensed its designs in the United Kingdom and Australia, and produced advertisements that combined illustrations and photographs with witty straplines and comparisons, such as a 1941 campaign that compared the Jockey 'Modern Man' to three classical Greek statues,

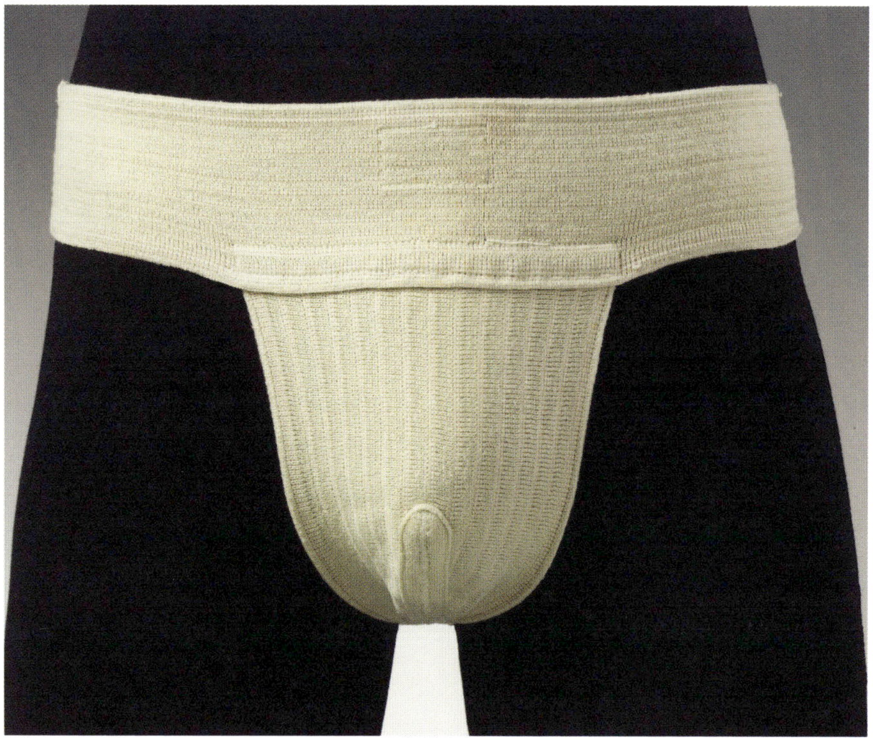

60. Duribilknit, Jockstrap. Wool and surgical elastic. New York, *c.*1947. Given by Mr and Mrs Anthony J. Drexel Biddle III. V&A: T.139-2015

Doryphoros, *Discobolus* and *The Praying Boy*. Curators Richard Martin and Harold Koda made a connection between the 1935 Jockey launch and that year being one in which increasing numbers of American beaches allowed men to go topless, as the 'erotics of the male were undergoing change'.[14] Although many other brands produced versions of briefs and patented various cuts and fly openings, Jockey remained a leading international producer until fashion designer Calvin Klein launched his own version of briefs in 1982.

The design of Klein's underpants was almost identical to Jockey's classic brief, but differed through the closer fit, lower rise and name woven into the waistband. Klein intended that it should be sexier and less practical than existing American men's styles, believing that 'underwear was pure sex'.[15] A series of three advertisements featuring Olympic pole-vaulter Tom Hintnaus photographed by Bruce Weber were produced. In one, which appeared on a 16-metre high billboard in New York's Times Square, a bare-chested Hintnaus leans against a white chimney with his hands resting upon his thighs and his eyes closed, with his white cloth-clad crotch as the main focus point (62). In a second image Hintnaus was photographed from a similar angle, caught in the act of removing an undershirt that covers his face, and stretching out his abdominal muscles. The third had Hintnaus in a singlet and briefs, on all fours in profile against the angles of a building. These latter two are less controversial than the first, better-known, image, following the traditions of underwear advertising with the 'model' wearing an undershirt, albeit in one he is removing it to reveal his tanned muscular torso. Klein, Weber and Hintnaus's collaboration proposed a picture of contemporary masculinity in which Hintnaus became the passive subject of the viewer's gaze as he stands, leans or crouches 'engrossed in reverie and sensation'.[16]

In 1992 Calvin Klein again produced a set of controversial underwear advertisements, this time with photographer Herb Ritts, advertising boxer briefs worn by rapper, later actor, 'Marky' Mark Wahlberg. Marky Mark was offered the contract to appear in Calvin Klein adverts following his inadvertent promotion of Calvin Klein underwear in stage shows and magazine photo shoots, where the waistband of his branded underpants showed above his low-slung jeans and below his perfectly formed six-pack. The Ritts adverts included images with model Kate Moss, and controversially, with Marky Mark grabbing his crotch through his white cotton boxer briefs. This hybrid between boxer shorts and briefs combined the leg length of boxer shorts with the fit and support of the brief to create a hybrid trunk. The style of low-slung jeans worn by Marky Mark was popular among American rap stars and as an inner-city African-American style. Believed to have originated amongst prisoners, where jeans hung below the waist because of the ban on belts (to prevent prisoners using them as a tool for suicide), the style was quickly adopted outside prisons and became an international trend among young urban men (63). Visibly branded waistbands had a marked impact upon designs for men's underpants and became a form of advertisement. Following Klein's success other underwear brands and designers followed his lead and added their name or

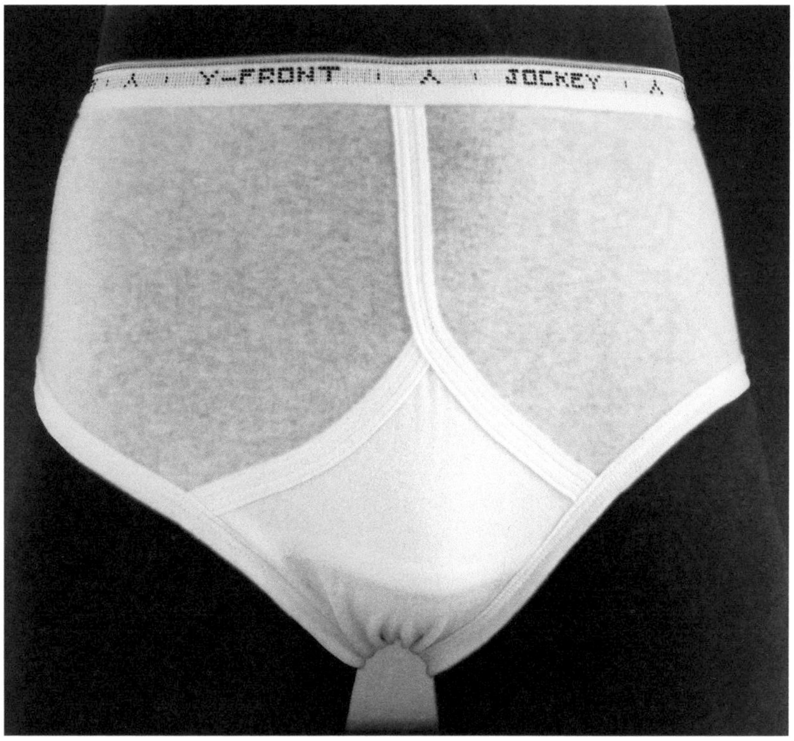

61. Jockey, Y-front underpants. Cotton. England, *c.*1986–7.
Given by the manufacturer. V&A: T.44-1987

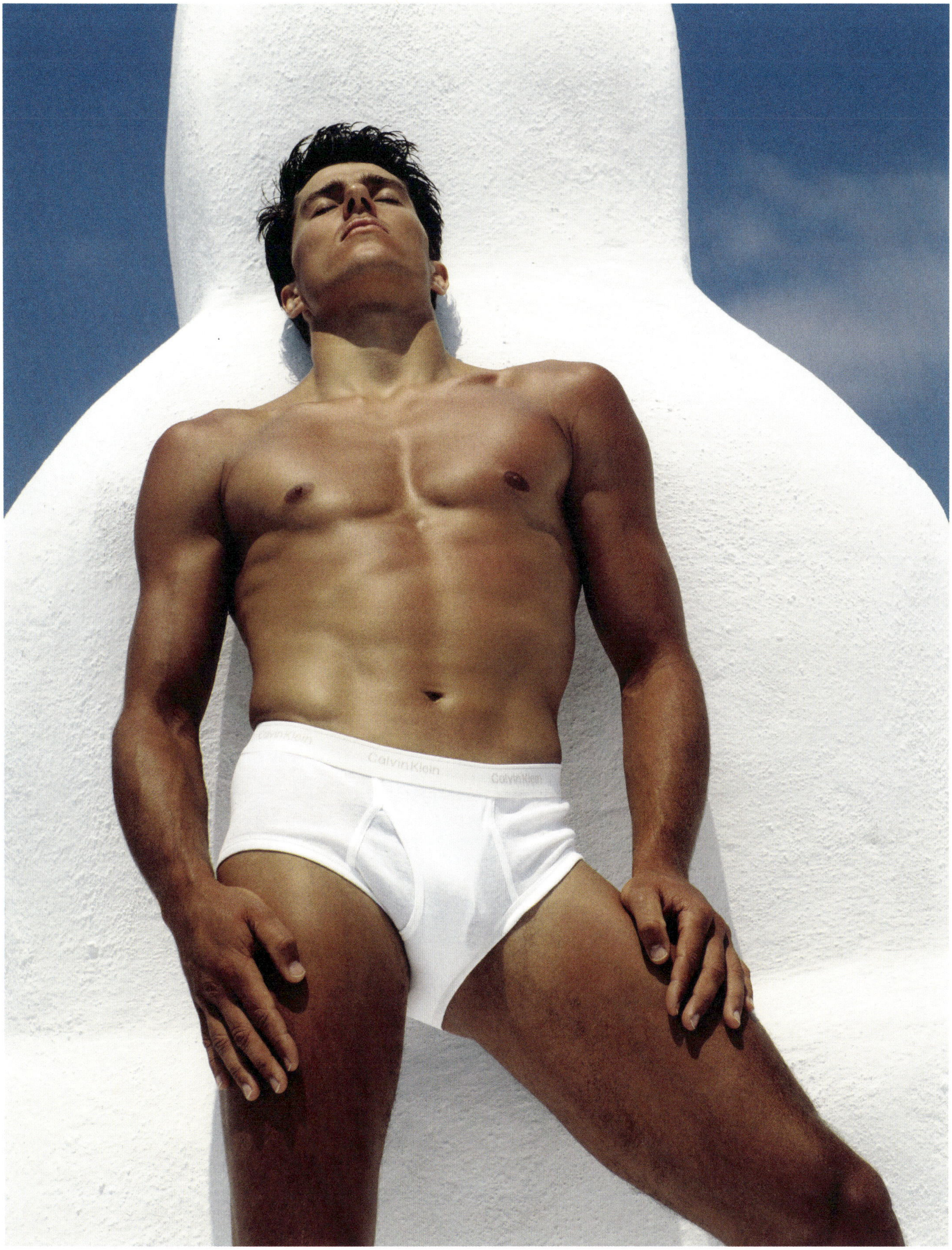

62. Bruce Weber (1946–),
Advertising campaign for Calvin Klein underwear, 1982.
Model: Tom Hintnaus

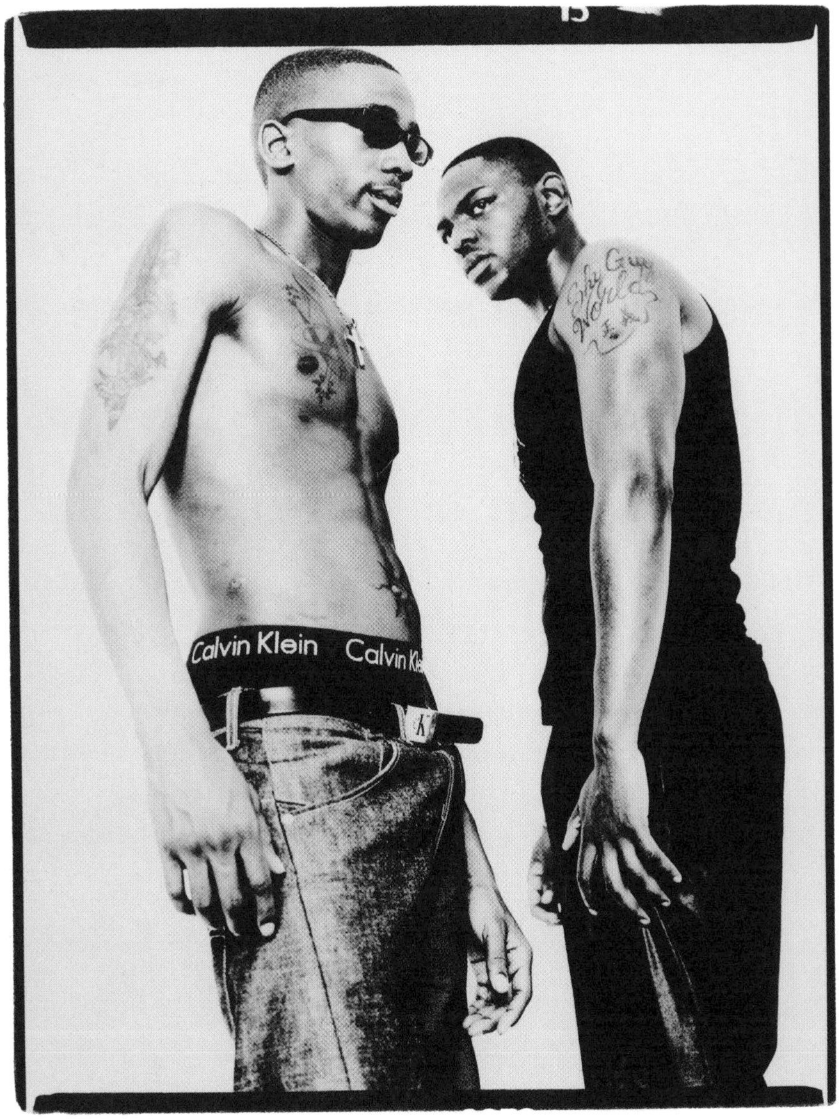

63. Jennie Baptiste (1971–), *Brixton Boyz*. Photograph, photo lithograph, 50.8×40.6cm. London, 2001. Supported by the National Lottery Heritage Fund. V&A: E.971-2010

logo to the outside of their garments. Italian fashion designer Franco Moschino was unimpressed with the banal commerciality of this trend and produced a line of underwear with the ironic waistband slogan 'To Be Shown in Public'.

'AN OVERT BULGE': UNDERWEAR AND ARCHETYPAL MASCULINITIES

Fashion writer Iain R. Webb noted that the 1980s 'were the time when men's underwear stopped being merely functional and became fashionable and sexy.'[17] This is attributable not only to the innovations in fabric and cut of men's underwear, but also to a cultural change in how men's bodies were portrayed and consumed through advertising and other popular culture representations. Contemporary underwear advertising has a direct relation to sexual attraction and the attractiveness of the male body. Garments are frequently portrayed as being designed to highlight the wearer's genitals, rather than focusing on innovation or fit and comfort. This led art critic Melody Davis to argue that the penis 'is even more present if it is concealed or disguised' and 'transforms to the phallus'. This, she continues, in turn becomes the man, who in turn 'represent[s] both the "power of the product" and that of the purchaser of that product'.[18] Despite historic associations of men's underwear as plain and functional, the innovation, design and stylistic changes that have occurred, as well as the profusion of advertising images that present particular forms of masculinity through semi-clothed models, demonstrate the relevance and enduring influence of male underpinnings.

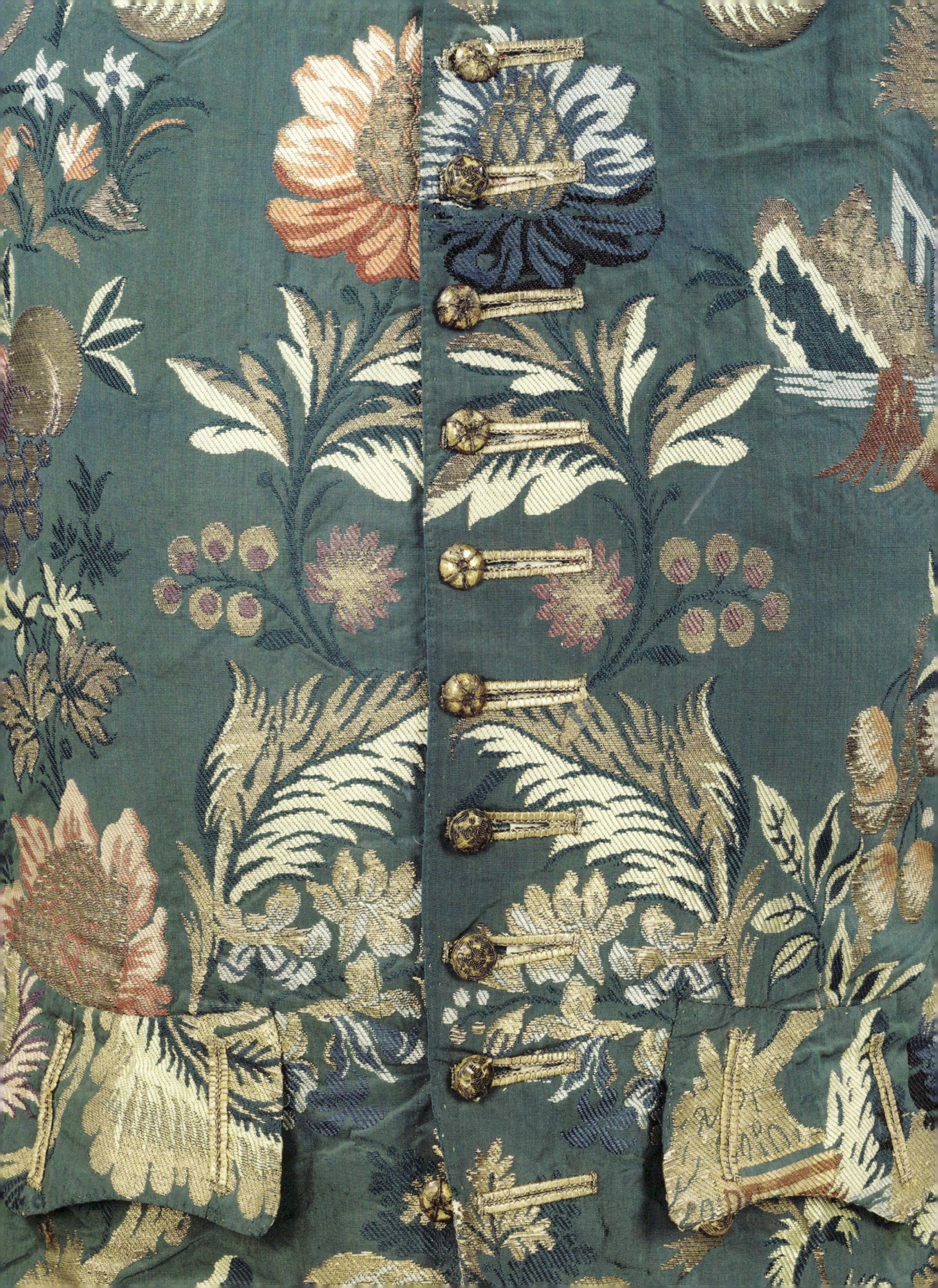

OVERDRESSED

TWO YARDS OF PINK CLOTH CAN MAKE A GENTLEMAN

NICCOLÒ MACHIAVELLI
1526

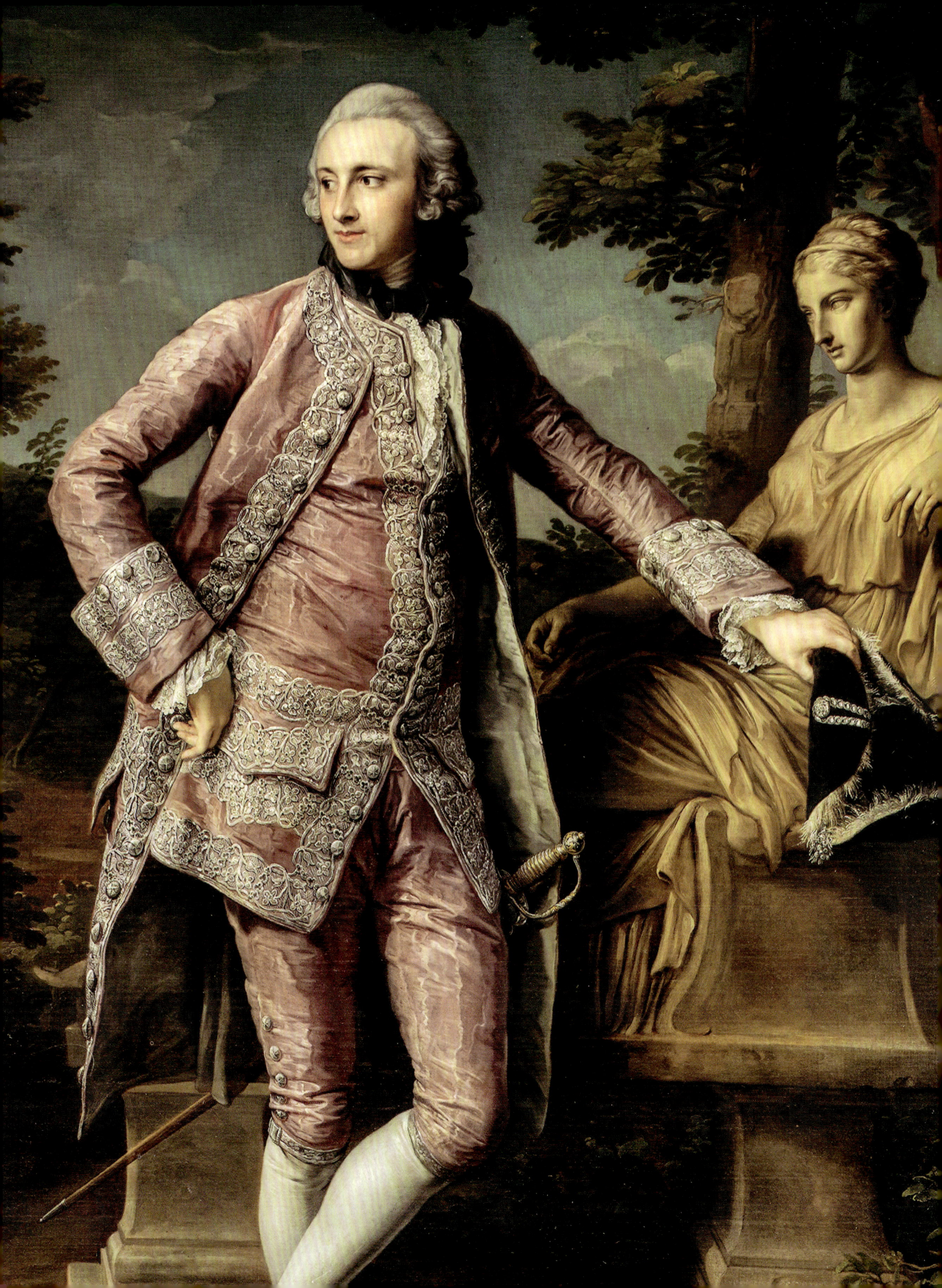

YOUNG ENGLISHMEN BEHAVING BADLY (AND DRESSING OUTRAGEOUSLY)

SUSAN NORTH

Dress is grown of great use in the conduct of life, as so much civility and respect is paid to appearance: it is a passport, which carries men into polite conversation, and a varnish, which makes what a man says conspicuous... The appearance of an easy fortune is necessary to get one.[1]

Fashion is a perennial flashpoint in the definitions of what it means to be a man, and this was particularly true of early modern England, compounded not only by issues of gender, but also by age and social status.[2] Although men governed early modern England at all levels of society, from family to nation, contemporary literature reveals a remarkable lack of confidence in their grasp of this authority. Descriptions of men's roles in society are riddled with anxiety and insecurity about those eligible for these responsibilities and the personal qualities required to carry them out. Civility, honesty, prudence, sobriety, thrift and, above all, self-control comprised appropriate manliness, for those unable to govern themselves could not be put in charge of others. Not all men were eligible for such leadership; a significant number such as apprentices, bachelors and servants were excluded from the role of patriarch for either part of or all their lives. While the disadvantage of youth would be outgrown eventually, one's place in society was not so easily overcome. Nevertheless, changing economic and political circumstances spurred upward social mobility in English society between 1500 and 1800 (and beyond).[3]

Dressing appropriately to his station was a visual indication that a man was prudent and sober, while slavishly indulging in frivolous fashions loudly signposted the opposite. Early modern moralists agonized over the dress and behaviour of youth, parental guides offered a stream of dos and don'ts on raising little boys, and should these fail, advice to young men reinforced what society expected of them. Sumptuary laws and guild regulations attempted to control the appearance of men according to their station. Those straying outside, or wilfully ignoring, these directions were satirized on stage in the roles of gulls, gallants, rakes, beaux and fops. All these media focused primarily on perceived undesirable extremes of manliness and faulty expressions of manhood. The dutiful, quiet, responsible, prudent and soberly dressed man – likely the vast majority of Englishmen – did not attract much attention (in print, at least).

Sixteenth-century sumptuary laws attempted to restrict luxurious fabrics and fashions to the aristocracy – only they could wear 'Imbroderie, or Taylers worke, hauing Golde, or Siluer, or Pearle therin' – and 'monstruous and outragious greatnesse of hosen' were forbidden.[4] Local authorities such as London's Common Council reiterated and attempted to enforce these laws with suitable punishments for transgression.[5] Noting the excessive 'stitching', 'cuttinge' (slashing), 'edginge' and 'garnishing', on ruffs, frills, girdles and garters in 1582, London insisted on an austere alternative for apprentices: a '"most plaine" pair of breeches, shirt, doublet, coat, cloak, and a woollen cap, all made from the poorest cloth and held together by "plaine stringes"'.[6] Inevitably such regulations could never keep up with new fashions. By 1611 the Council was insisting on hat brims 'no broader' than three inches, the fabric for ruffs and bands was not to exceed three yards, gloves costing more than a shilling and Spanish leather shoes were banned, all on pain of 18 hours in Little Ease prison.[7]

Other cities with large numbers of male apprentices were similarly troubled. The Merchant Adventurers Company of Newcastle-upon-Tyne, whose members included shopkeepers and warehousemen, complained: 'But whan as nowe, lewde libertye, in sted of the former virtuous life, haithe of late taken place in apprentizes ... what garded cotes, jagged hose, lyned with silke, and cutt shoes.'[8] Apprentices were to wear only coarse woollen cloth, with no slashing or pinking or decorative borders allowed.[9] By 1603 stylish ruffs were causing outrage and revised rules insisted on 'fallinge bands' only and these 'plaine, withoute laice, stitche, or anie kind of sowen worck' (65). Inappropriate footwear in the form of 'pumppes, pantofles' and 'corked shoes' was also proscribed.[10]

Contemporary moral advice echoed sumptuary regulation. In 1583 Philip Stubbes waxed apoplectic about 'great and monstrous ruffes, made either of Cambrick, holland, lawn or else of some other the finest cloth'.[11] Equally outrageous were the doublets 'being so hard-quilted, and stuffed, bombasted and sewed, as they can verie hardly stoupe downe' (66).[12] Bewildering varieties of cloaks – in the Spanish, French and Dutch fashions – proliferated in 'diverse and sundry colors' (67).[13] Stubbes condemned these and outlandish accessories – hats of every shape and height garnished with sprays of garishly dyed feathers – along with silk stockings knitted with gold and silver threads, and all manner of flimsy footwear.[14] He was very careful to exclude from his exhortation those entitled to such finery: 'I wold not be so understood, as though my speaches extended, to any, either noble, honorable, or worshipful'.[15] His primary complaint was that the 'confuse mingle mangle of apparell'

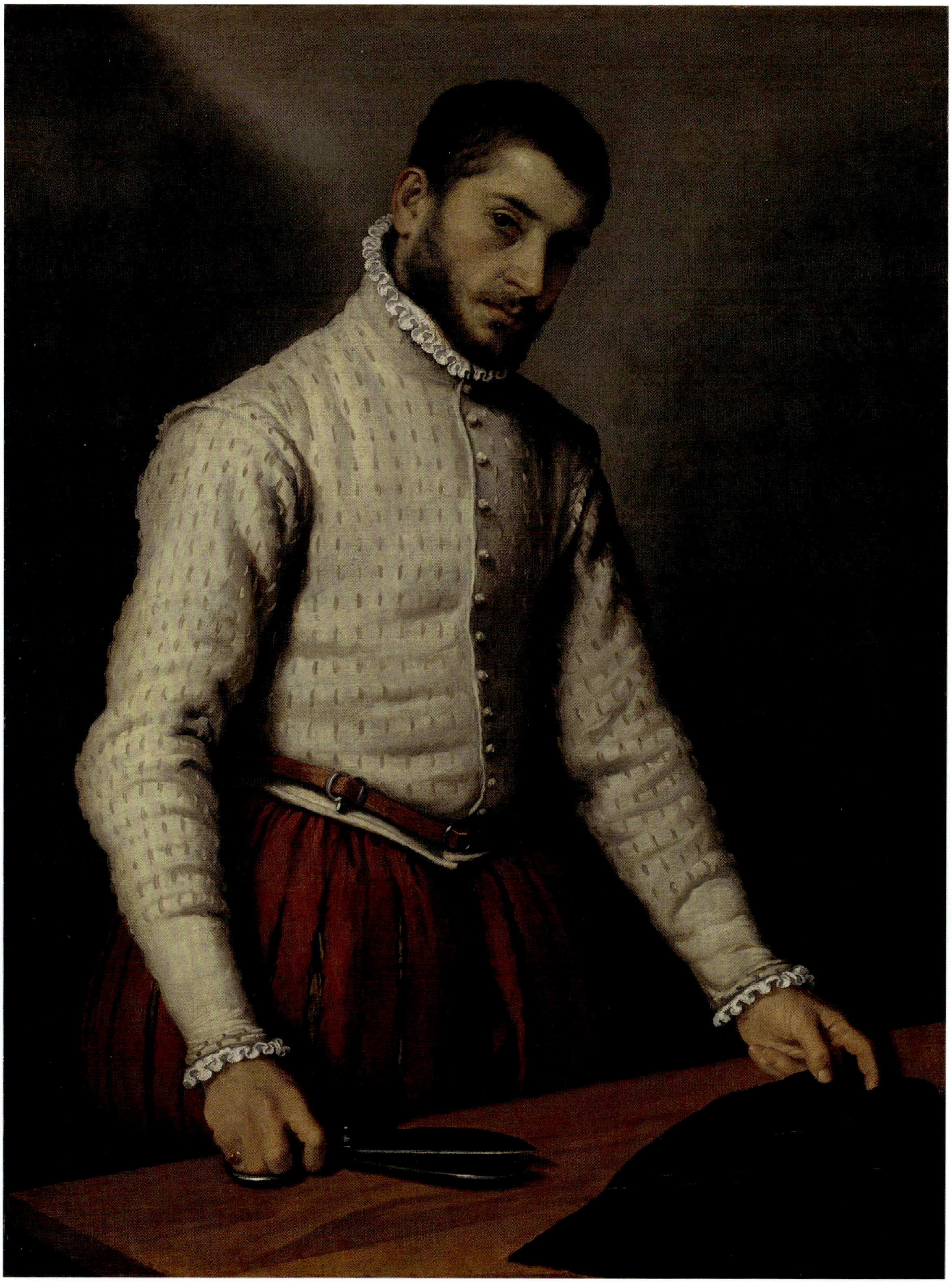

64. Giovanni Battista Moroni (1520/4–1579), *The Tailor ('Il Tagliapanni')*.
Oil on canvas, 99.5 × 77 cm. Italy, 1565–70.
The National Gallery, London: NG697

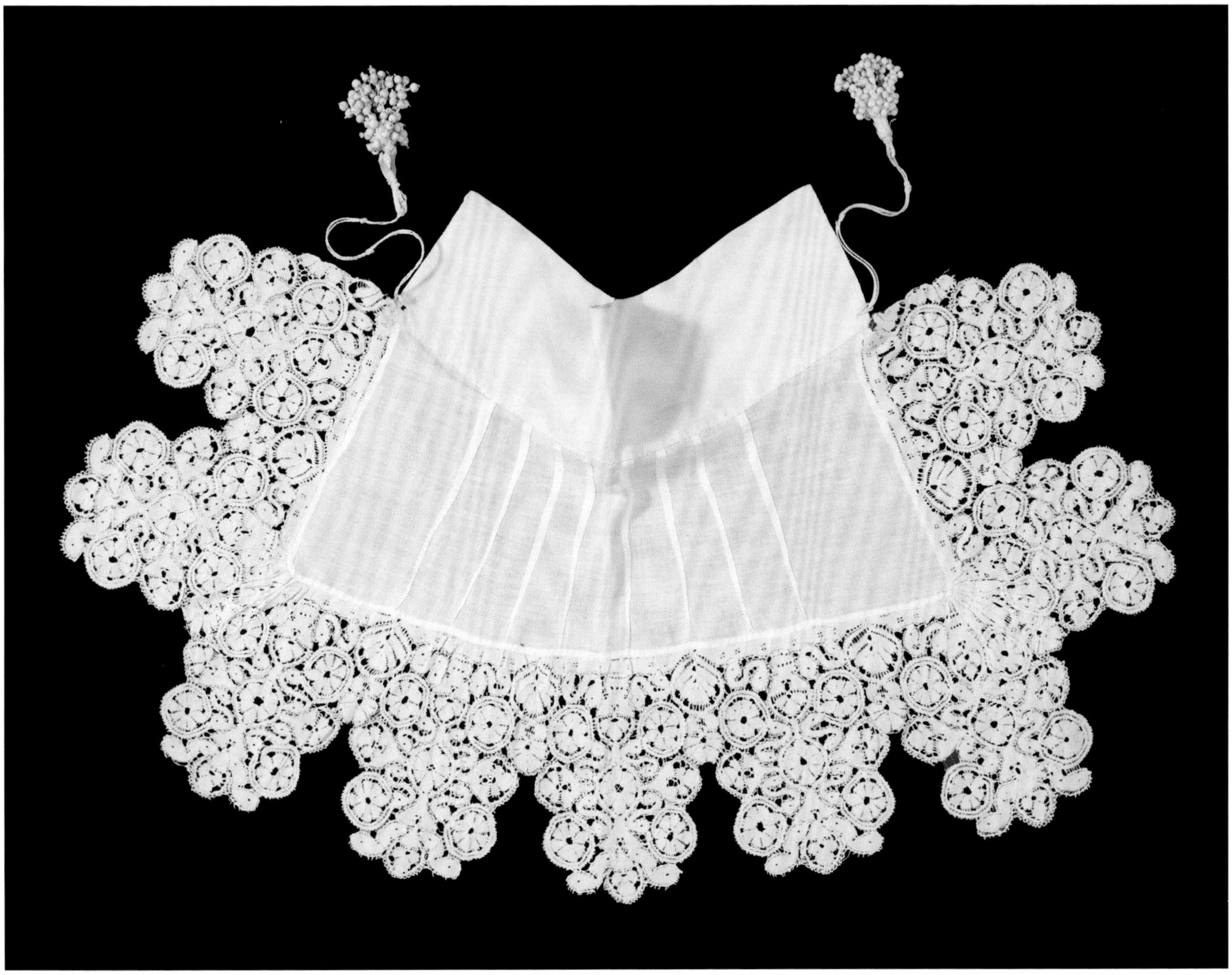

65. Falling band. Linen, edged with bobbin lace.
England, 1630–40. V&A: 1126-1903

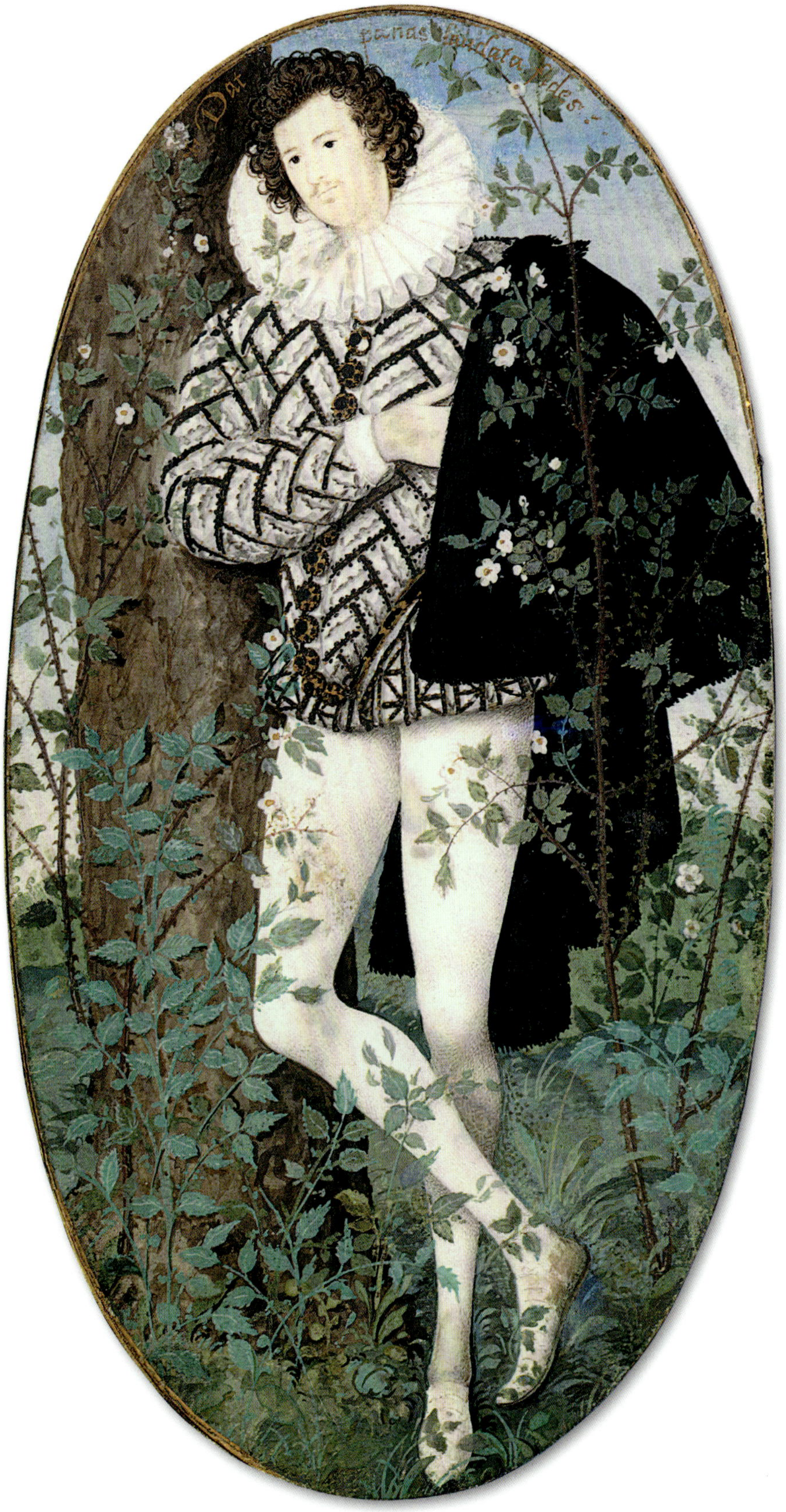

66. Nicholas Hilliard (1547–1619), *Young Man among Roses*.
Watercolour on vellum, 13.5 × 7.5 cm. England, *c.*1587.
Bequeathed by George Salting. V&A: P.163-1910

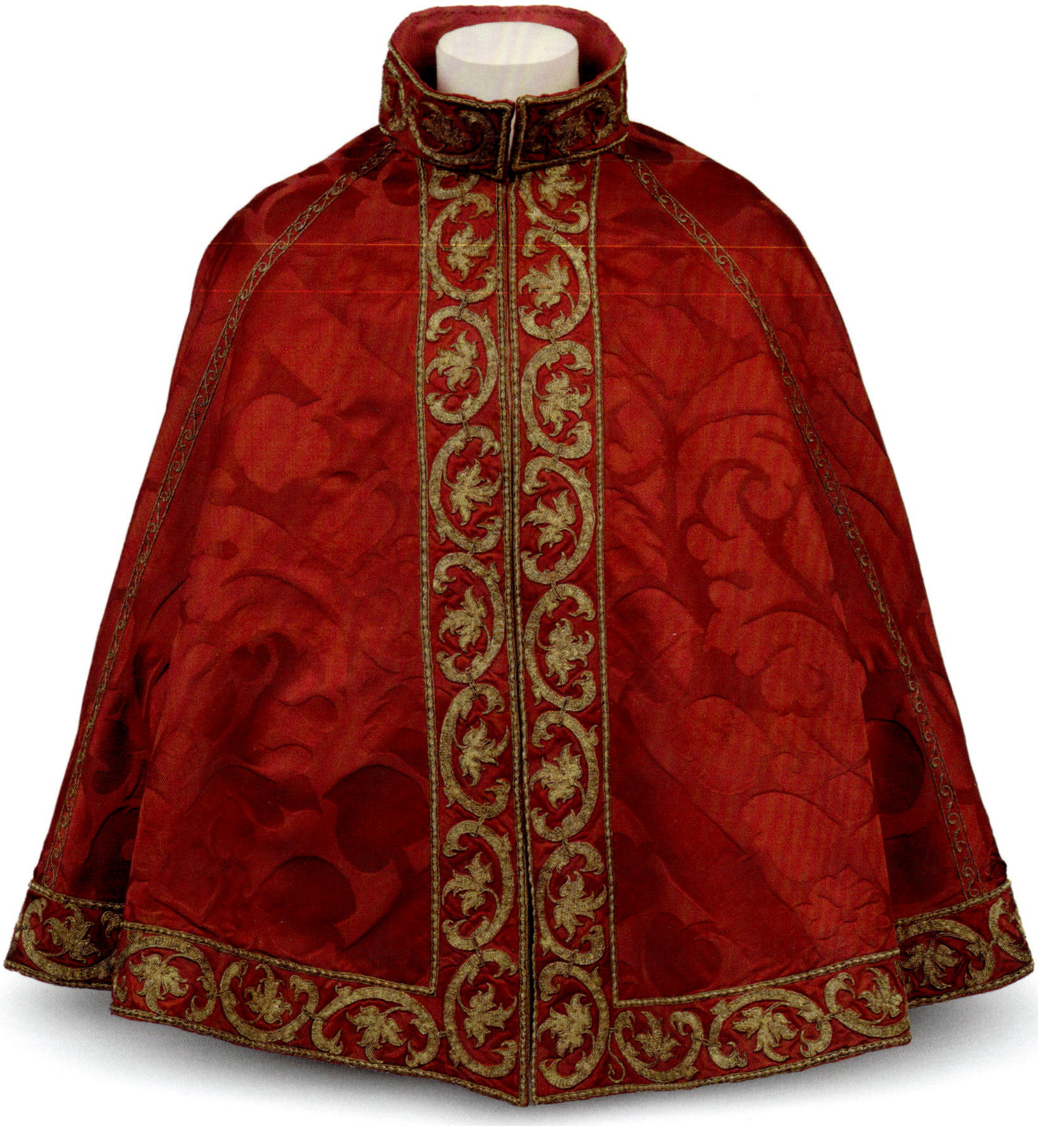

67. Cloak. Silk damask, applied silver-gilt embroidery.
Spain, 1575–1605. V&A: T.202-1965

made 'it is verie hard to knowe, who is noble, who is worshipfull, who is a gentleman' and, most importantly, 'who is not'.[16] The aristocratic young man among the roses in Nicholas Hilliard's miniature was allowed a voluminous ruff; humble apprentices were not (66).

PURPOSE OF DRESS

Throughout the early modern period, moralists agreed that the purpose of dress, beyond modesty and protection, was to signify gender, occupation and social status:

> A third end of Apparel is the distinguishing or differencing of persons, and that first in respect of Sex, secondly, in respect of qualities... God hath placed some in a higher condition than others and in proportion to their condition it befits their cloathes ... let every man cloath himself in such sober attire as befit his place and calling.[17]

Someone dressing above his station made 'himself a mocking stocke to the worlde, who shyneth a far of in his scarlets, and glistering gold lace, like a king of a Stage plaie', but without the 'sutable companie of followers, nor a living to maintain that bravery'.[18] However, the definition of a gentleman was not irrevocably linked to birth; as early as 1555 it was acknowledged that it included good character and appropriate behaviour. The 'gentle gentle' were well born and bred, but a commoner could aspire to being 'ungentle gentle'; his honourable behaviour and industriousness earned him a better place in society and made his sons gentlemen.[19] Such observations, along with the overall prosperity of sixteenth-century England, suggest that upward mobility was an option open to some men, perhaps not always through virtue, but certainly via fancy clothes.

Unspoken in any of these texts were the consequences of mistaking someone common for someone noble. In small towns, where everyone knew each other, the crime of dressing above one's station would be immediately obvious to all. However, a city as large as London was full of strangers, so 'People where they are not known, are generally honour'd according to their Cloaths and other Accoutrements'.[20] This was particularly important when passing strangers on the street, as etiquette demanded certain courtesies, such as removing, or at least tipping, one's hat to those of equal or higher social status, and granting them 'the wall', that is, the side of the street next to buildings and away from the mud and splatter at its centre.[21] What early modern authors never confessed in print was the horror that, when encountering a well-dressed stranger on the street, they might inadvertently give way to a lowly draper's apprentice.

Other aspects of young men's appearance were a target for middle-aged wrath, such as hair and weaponry. Newcastle-upon-Tyne apprentices were forbidden from sporting beards in 1555, and by 1603 disapproval focused on long hair, or on the even more scandalous lovelock: short hair with one long lock of hair trailing elegantly over the shoulder. Tyneside Merchant Adventurers barred 'haire longe' and 'locks on their eares like ruffians'.[22] In 1628 the Puritan author William Prynne devoted a whole book, *The Unlovelinesse of Love-lockes*, to this sinful and ominously effeminate hairstyle.

While long hair made young men look too much like women, with all the disasters this confusion of gender entailed, wearing rapiers and daggers inclined them to aggressive behaviour and duelling.[23] The alarm of the Newcastle-upon-Tyne merchants over 'daggers used by theim worn crosse overthwarte their backs' distinguished the ordinary knives worn and employed by all men for various professions and purposes, including eating, from the dangerously fashionable weapons for duelling: daggers and rapiers imported from Italy in the mid-sixteenth century.[24] Worn for civilian self-defence, rapiers and daggers were as elaborately decorated as doublets and hose (68). In damascened steel inlaid with silver and gold, set with jewels and sheathed in fabrics matching a gentleman's fashionable ensemble, rapiers were soon added to sumptuary laws, which attempted to restrict their length and decoration. This proliferation of aristocratic weaponry and the heightened sense of honour and insult that accompanied their use thoroughly alarmed the authorities:

> And now when the rapier and dagger dispatcheth a man quickly, neither he lives to heare his owne fame, nor no man living can let fall a good word of the quarrell, begun of such trifles, maintain'd with such terror, and ended with such madnes.[25]

Not only did the rapier confer the status of gentleman on those who wore them, but it did so to those wounded as well. In early modern England, violence as well as clothing were hierarchically structured: a horsewhip to punish a servant, the noose to execute a common thief, the executioner's sword for a rebellious courtier. The young Englishmen wearing rapiers and daggers not only sought to present themselves as gentlemen, but also to receive any defeat or injury in a manner appropriate to a gentleman.[26]

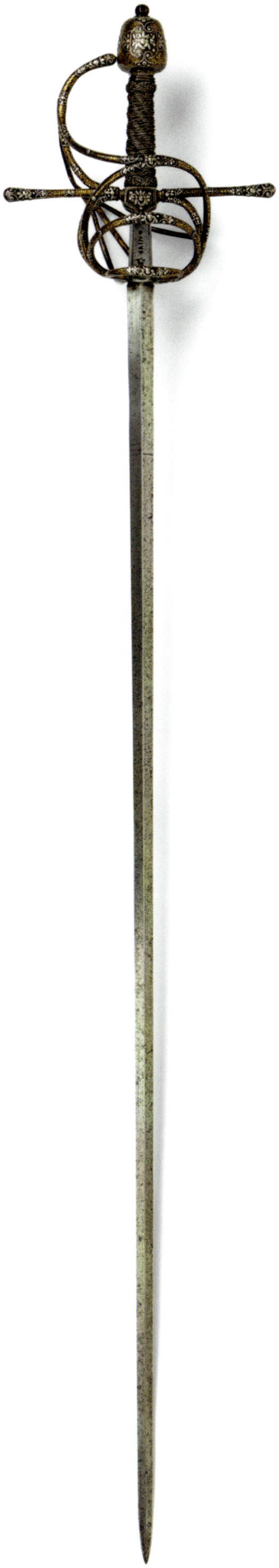

68. Swept-hilt rapier. Steel, damascened in gold and encrusted with chiselled silver. England, *c.*1600. F Mallett Bequest. V&A: M.51-1947

THE GALLANT

These performances of gentility were satirized on the Jacobean stage in the character of the gallant, as seen in Ben Jonson's city plays *Everyman out of his Humour* (1599) and *The Devil is an Ass* (1616), as well as Thomas Middleton's *Michaelmas Term* (1604) and *Your Five Gallants* (1607). Theatre costume during this period was predominately fashionable clothing donated by aristocratic patrons or purchased second-hand. For moralists, the stage was a festering hotbed of sartorial abuses, allowing the low-born to dress as gentlemen in their roles as such, glorifying gallants as characters and encouraging the audience of apprentices and serving-men to imitate them.[27]

> A Gallant is one that was born and shapt for his Cloathes ... and takes great delight in his walke to heare his Spurs gingle... He is a kind of walking Mercers Shop, and shewes you one Stuffe to day, and another to morrow, an ornament to the roomes he comes in, as the faire bed and Hangings be.[28]

The gallants' style was considerably cramped by the closure of the theatres in 1642, the Civil Wars in England and the subsequent establishment of the Commonwealth. Since the sixteenth century, the moral condemnation of fashionable dress had been driven by religious belief; the Puritans in particular, denounced it as evidence of the sins of pride and vanity. The restoration of Charles II in 1660, however, introduced an era of religious tolerance and secularism, as well as hedonism and material prosperity. The concerns of fathers and masters about the appearance and behaviour of young men remained much the same as those of their grandfathers, but the reasons for them changed. Admonishments to dress appropriately to one's station were now couched in terms of modesty and good sense. 'Clothe your self answerable to your condition, decently and cleanly, but never gawdily.'[29]

This change in tone reflects a wider shift in post-Restoration definitions of polite society and a gentleman's role within it. The emphasis was on propriety and decorum, an agreeable nature and generosity.[30] 'He is extremely natural and easy in all his Actions. They always fall into a sort of harmonious Order, by perfect Habit of Good-Breeding.'[31] The danger was taking such politeness to the extreme of effeminacy and ending up a beau or, more famously, a fop who spent his day 'in the idle pursuit of Modes and Fashions, in contriving his Cloaths... The first three Hours of every Day, are constantly dedicated to the setting his Wig and Cravat, rolling his Stockings, redning his Lips, and painting his nauseous Phiz. [physiognomy/face]'.[32]

THE FOP

Like the gallant, the fop was soon entrenched as a theatrical caricature.[33] In a cast of other stereotypes typical of Restoration comedy, he was immediately identified by name, such as Sir Fopling Flutter in George Etherege's *Man of Mode* (1676), Sir Novelty Fashion in Colley Cibber's *Love's Last Shift* (1696) and Lord Foppington in John Vanbrugh's *The Relapse* (1696). Like the earlier gallant, the fop was obsessed with fashionable dress, but he developed behavioural traits deemed effeminate: delicacy of taste, physical weakness and cowardice. In an exchange between Mr Callow, 'A Fop of the Town lately come from Travel', and his attorney, Pickquarrel, in *The roving husband reclaim'd* (1706), Callow is outraged that a rival has thrown a glass of wine in his face:

> Pickquarrel: Did he draw Blood of your Honour?
> Mr Callow: No, but Ten times worse, for he stain'd my Pink-colour'd Bourdash [sash], and spoil'd my Sword-knot, and Wastecoat, which was given me by a very fine Lady; and that which vexes me most of all is, spatter'd my New Pearl-colour'd Stockings.[34]

The fop flourished off stage as well (69). Fancily dressed even when out of the public eye; he could 'be barely content to flourish in a Lac'd Coat, and a Full-bottom Perriwig', but was 'equally Modish, and Tawdry in that Undress, taking a gay Cap and Slippers, with a Scarff and Party-Coloured Gown'.[35]

OTHER UNDESIRABLE MODELS OF MASCULINITY

The path to correct manliness was very narrow, with fops and beaux on the one side and equally undesirable extremes on the other. A lack of attention to one's appearance was the hallmark of the 'rustick', a long-running trope in contemporary conduct literature. Those 'deepely rooted in rusticitie' with 'clownish speech and other ungentlemanly jestures' were as abhorrent as the gallant or fop.[36] 'I would not have my Son practise Rusticity in his Apparel, or be careless therein to a Pitch of Nastiness (1699).'[37] Libertines and rakes were not to be emulated, nor were 'romantic criminals' such as highwaymen and pirates, accounts of whom became a popular literary genre. John Gay's *The Beggar's Opera* in 1728, with highwayman Captain Macheath as lead character, was a huge success.[38] Macheath proved an inspiration for many young highwaymen, including Paul Lewis, who went to the gallows in 'a white Cloth Coat, blue silk waistcoat trimmed with Silver, a silver laced hat, white Stockings and Silk Breeches' in 1763.[39] Daniel Defoe's account of the lives and exploits of 'famous pirates, highwaymen, murderers, street-robbers' included pirate Bartholomew Roberts who:

> ... made a gallant Figure ... being dressed in a rich Crimson Damask Waistcoat and Breeches, a red Feather in his Hat, a Gold Chain round his Neck, with a Diamond Cross belonging to it, a Sword in his Hand, and two Pair of Pistols hanging at the End of a Silk Sling, flung over his Shoulders, according to the Fashion of Pirates.[40]

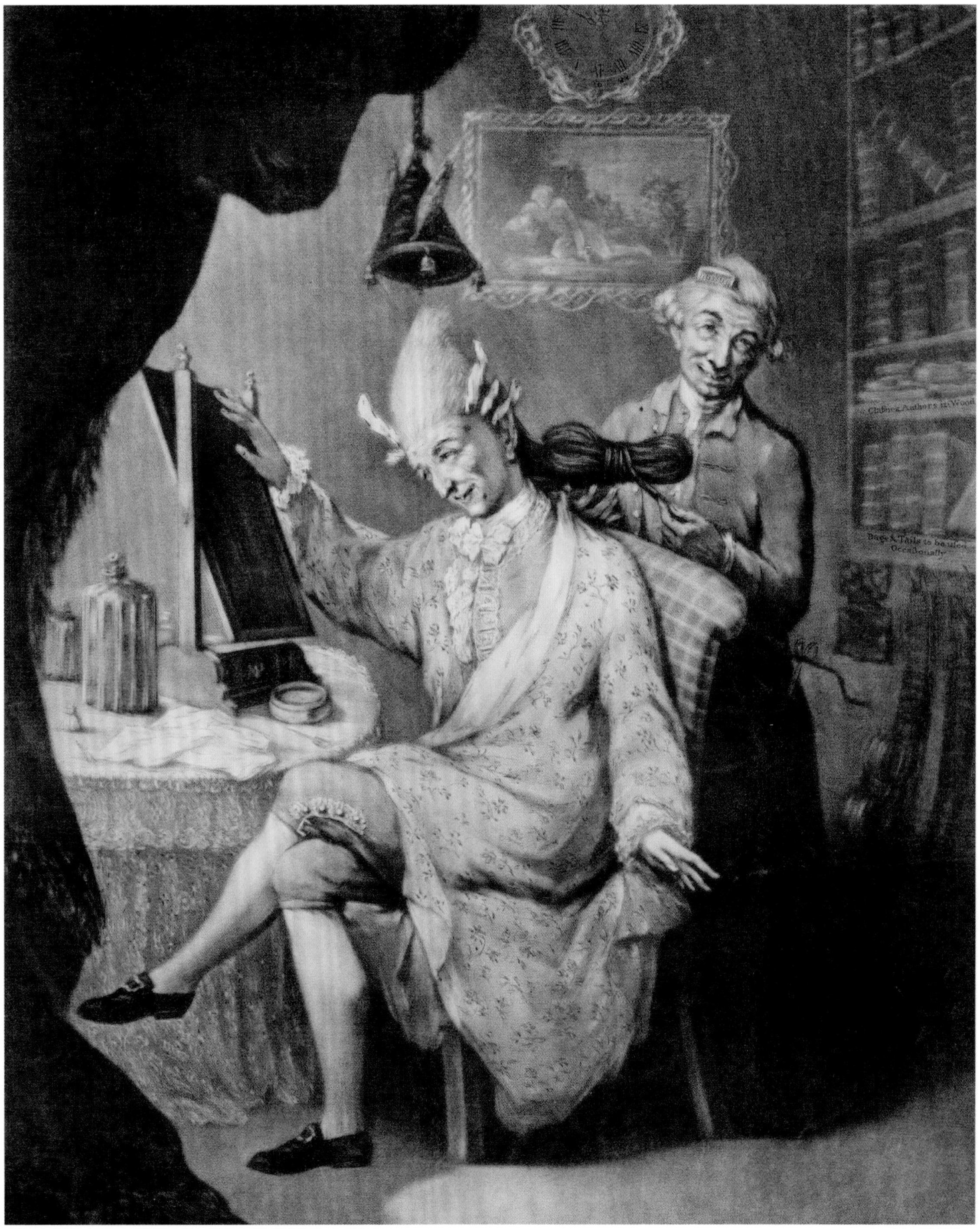

69. John Dixon (1740–*c.*1811), *The Old Beau in an Extasy*.
Mezzotint, 46.2×30 cm. London, 13 July 1773.
Given by Mrs E.B. Westwood. V&A: E.325-1959

Advice literature fretted over the imitative nature of young boys and their susceptibility to such dangerous role models. Warnings that nurses and tutors of little boys 'not suffre in the childes presence to be shewed any acte or tache [task?] dishonest – or any wanton or unclene worde to be spoken' appeared in 1531 and were repeated over the centuries.[41] One author worried that young boys 'early accustomed to manly Amusements, might justly be apprehended to be in great Danger of imbibing an early Taste for Extravagance, and plunging into manly Vices.'[42] He also cautioned parents they must not dress boys 'in the gayest Colours, and load them with the most unmeaning Ornament', a habit that 'though trifling in Appearance, has very serious Consequences'.[43]

However, *not* following fashion was equally objectionable, marking a young man as singular and yet another strand of instruction spelt out the dangers of such nonconformity:

> And if all men els, doe weare their heads powled
> [cut short]: it shalbe an ill sight for thee alone,
> to weare a longe bushe of haire. And where other
> men, make muche of their beardes and weare
> them longe: thou shalt not doe well to cut thine off,
> or shave it… For this singularitie, beyond all other
> ill customes, makes us generally spited of all men.[44]

Such counsel continued through the seventeenth and eighteenth centuries: 'the best rule we can observe for the fashion of our cloaths, is the Mode; to that it is we must submit all our own fancy and reason; observing still what is generally worn, and following their fashion without further dispute.'[45] 'A certain Mediocrity' was even recommended when it came to dress, but not *too* old-fashioned, lest one be mistaken for a 'stalking antick, or an Image broke loose from an old piece of Arras' (antique tapestry showing historical figures).[46]

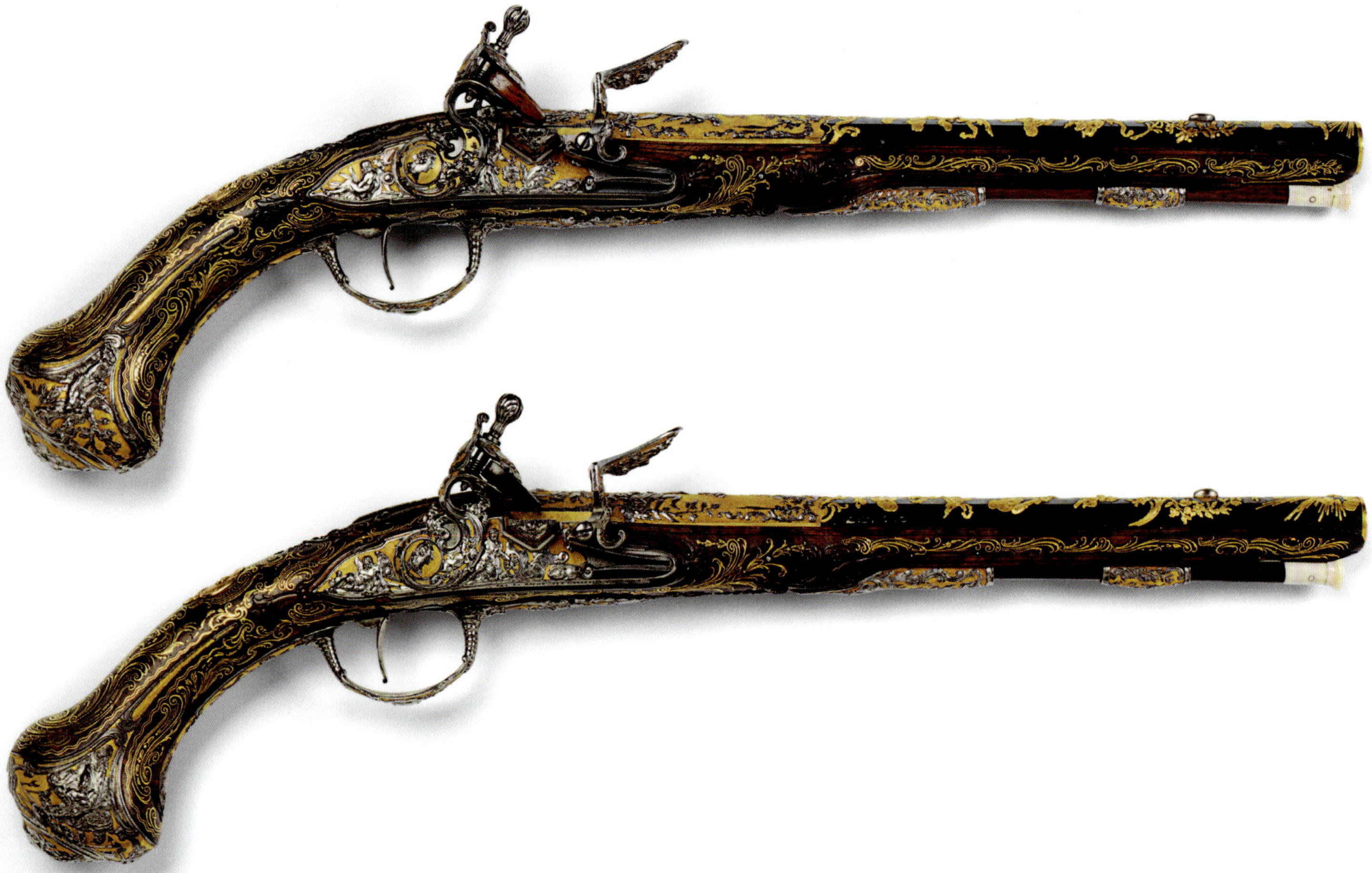

70. Jean Baptiste La Roche (active 1740–69), Pair of flintlock pistols.
Carved walnut, blued steel, chased gold and silver, silver inlay.
Paris, 1750–60. V&A: 2243&A-1855

FASHION AS A NECESSITY

Post-Restoration society was mercantile and upwardly mobile, so tradesmen were targeted for sartorial improprieties, including 'the Baker, the Barber, the Blacksmith, and every mean working Fellow, that can set up with little, has the Impudence, with the first Money he gets, to dress himself and Family like a Tradesman of great Substance.' Also guilty was 'every little Wretch, who plays upon a Pen in an Office, or on an Instrument at the Theatre, must have his large lac'd Hat, and open-sleeve Coat to expose the Gold or Silver Orrice on that of his Waistcoat.'[47] More thoughtful authors admitted that certain tradesmen such as coachmakers, hairdressers (see 75), jewellers, perfumers, tailors and wig-makers required a stylish appearance to ensure their customers' confidence in their taste, craft and products.[48] The sixteenth-century tailor in Moroni's portrait wears a fashionably slashed doublet, but the sumptuary laws noted above make clear that this was forbidden to ordinary apprentices (64). A mercer in particular:

> ...must be a very polite Man, and skilled in all
> the Punctilios of City-good-breeding; he ought,
> by no Means to be an aukward clumsey Fellow.
> He must dress neatly and affect a Court Air...
> Our mercer must have a great deal of the Frenchman
> in his Manners, as well as a large Parcel of French
> Goods in his Shop.[49]

FOREIGN INFLUENCES

Throughout the early modern period, English moralists blamed foreigners as the source of the frivolous fashions and behaviours that young men were following. 'The Frencheman deliteth in coloures so manye as be in the raine bow... The Spanyard excedeth with the most, and passeth the bondes of measure in costly array... The Dutchman and the lance-knight ... abound in many iagges, cuttes, & superfluous slopes.'[50] The later frivolities of the fop, especially clothing and dancing, were blamed entirely on the French, as detailed in Sir Fopling Flutter's account of those who made the ensemble he recently purchased in Paris:

> Emilia: He wears nothing but what are Originals
> of the Most Famous hands in Paris.
> Sir Fopling: You are in the right Madam.
> Lady Townley: The Suit.
> Sir Fopling: Barroy
> Emilia: The Garniture [matching set of sword,
> buttons, buckles, etc].
> Sir Fopling: Le Gras—
> Sir Medley: The Shooes!
> Sir Fopling: Piccar!
> Dorimant: The Perriwig!
> Sir Fopling: Chedreux.
> Lady Townley and Emilia: The Gloves!
> Sir Fopling: Orangerii![51]

On the other hand, the Grand Tour – visiting continental Europe to experience its art and culture and learn other languages – was considered essential to a young gentleman's education.[52] Opinion was divided as to whether this improved young Englishmen or turned them into fops. 'A young man may be polished indeed out of his rusticity; yet, if he have no better rule to go by, than the fashion of the place, where he lives, he may easily wear himself into the contrary defect, an effeminate and unmanly foppery.'[53] Nevertheless, the 'perfect Knowledge of the World' necessary to gentlemen, professionals and merchants could only be learned through visiting other countries, particularly Europe. While there, they took the opportunity to buy the luxury fabrics and laces for which France and Italy were renowned, goods that were heavily taxed in Britain as imports. In Paris, the architect Robert Adam purchased 'one of the genteelest and richest embroidered Vests that I ever saw' with wide silver-gilt embroidery 'upon rich, rich, vast rich thick silks of a Red colour'.[54] Edward Curtis, son of a Bristol sugar merchant, acquired equally glorious silks when he passed through Lyons en route to Rome where he was painted wearing them in 1750 (71 and 72).

WEARING IT WELL

Examining the social status of the authors and audience of this incessant and contradictory dialogue provides another perspective. Very few of the moralists and none of the playwrights were of noble birth, but men of the middling sorts, telling other men of roughly similar station what they should and should not do and wear. On occasion, these exchanges take on the form of an inside joke or rather competitive insult. The challenge with flamboyant fashions – then as now – is being able to carry them off convincingly. Upon seeing a young man dressed in the same beribboned style as the Duke of Bavaria (73), John Evelyn disparaged:

> It was a fine silken thing which I spied walking
> th' other day through Westminster-Hall, that had
> as much Ribbon on him as would have plundered
> six shops, and set up twenty Country Pedlers:
> All his Body was dres't like a May-Pole, or a Tom-a
> Bedlam's Cap. A Fregat newly rigg'd kept not half
> such a clatter in a storme, as this Puppets Streamers
> did when the Wind was in his Shroud's; the Motion
> was Wonderfull to behold, and the Colours were Red,
> Orange, and Blew, of well gum'd Sattin, which argu'd
> a happy fancy.

He finished this scathing assessment with the equally scornful observation 'that whether he were clad with this Garment, or (as a Porter) only carried it, was not to be resolv'd'.[55] Any sartorial extreme required confidence and panache in order to wear it well and inspire either envy or imitation (or both) in one's peers. Competitive exchanges about dress between young men appeared – anonymously, of course – occasionally in print. In 1675 *The Character of a Town-gallant* was described as 'made up of Complements,

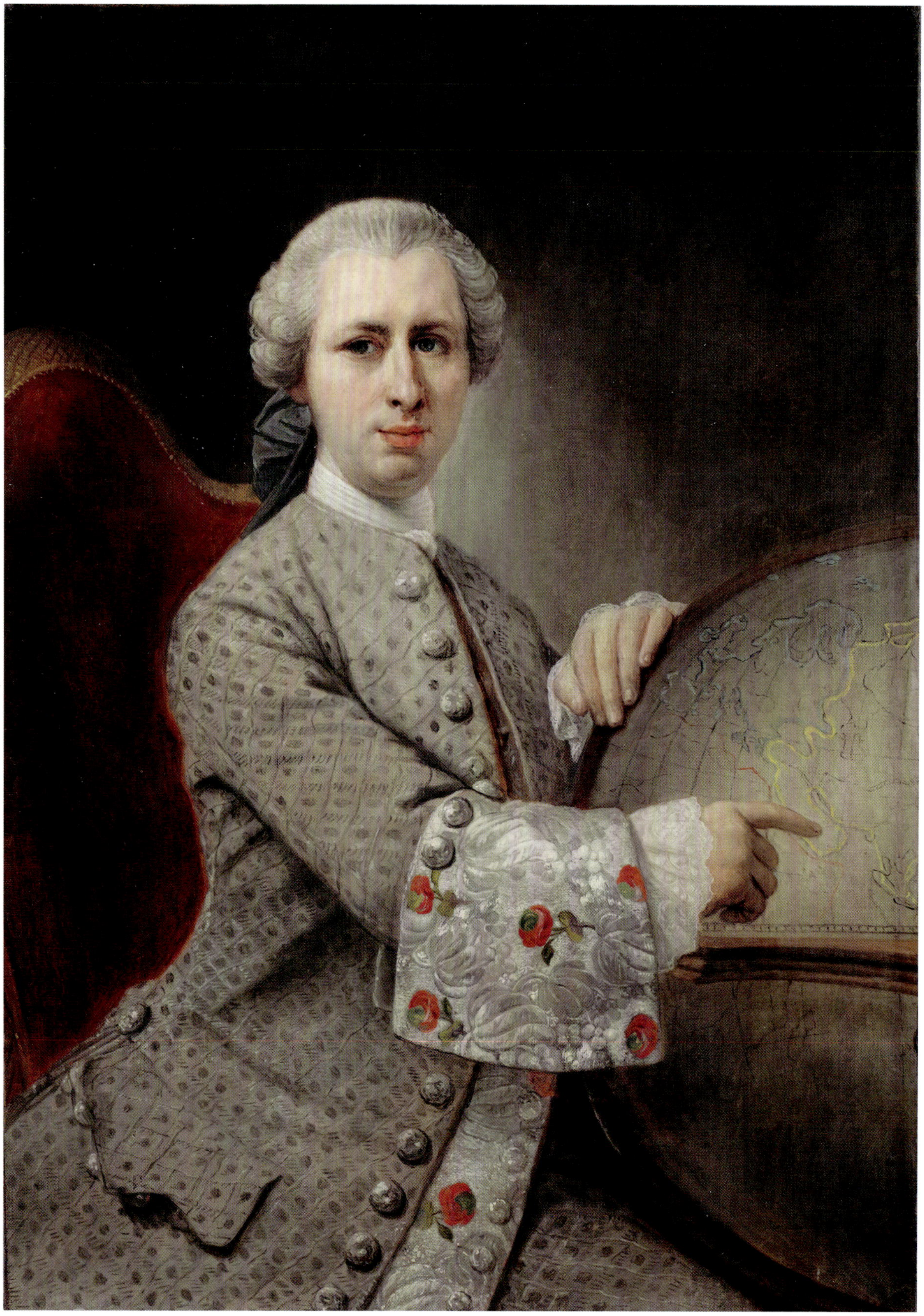

71. Marco Benefial (1684–1764), *Edward Curtis*.
Oil on canvas, 96 × 69.5 cm. England, 1750. V&A: E.381-2019

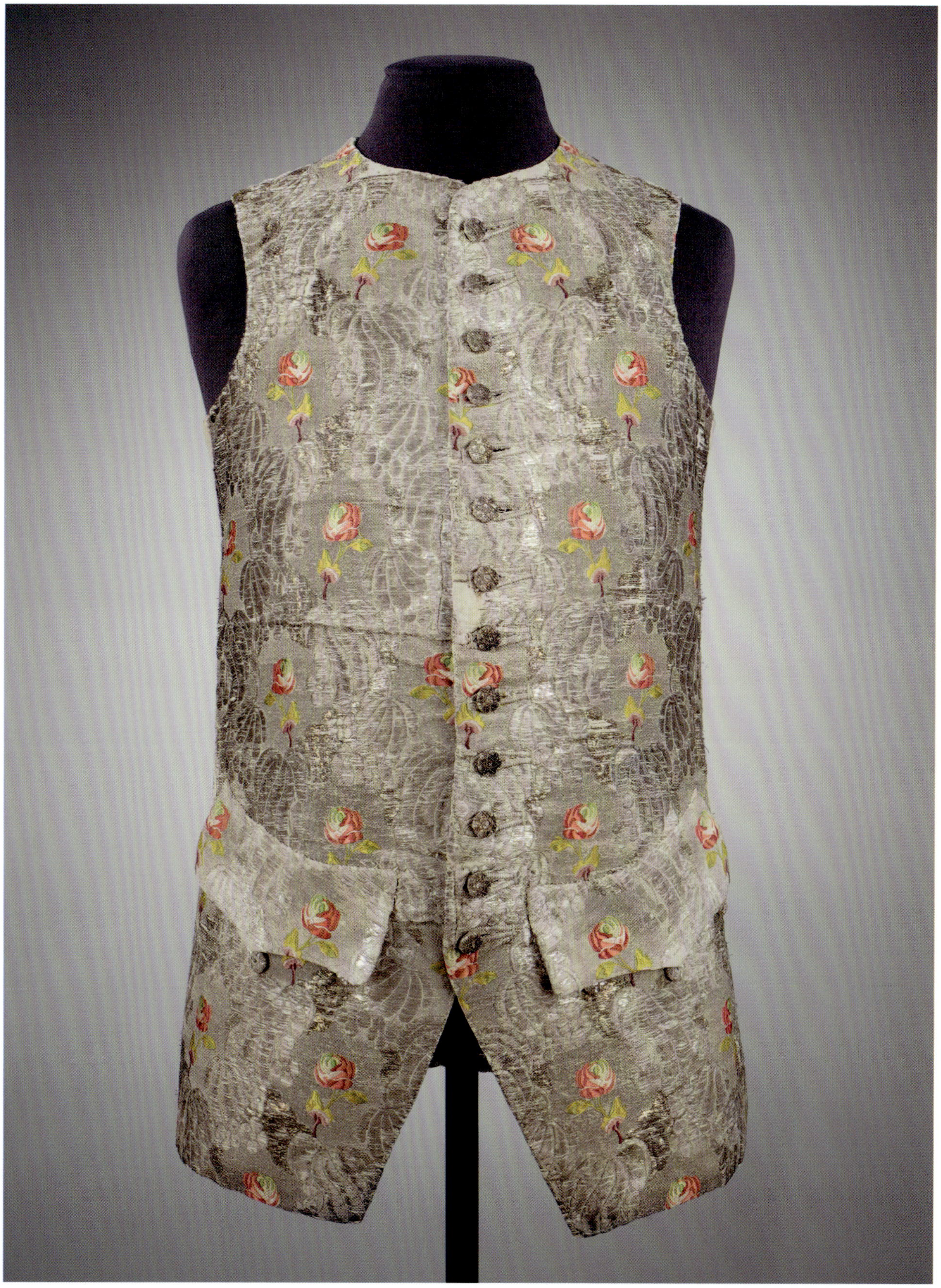

72. Waistcoat. Brocaded *Gros de Tours* taffeta.
Worn by Edward Curtis. France, 1745–50. V&A: T.22-2019

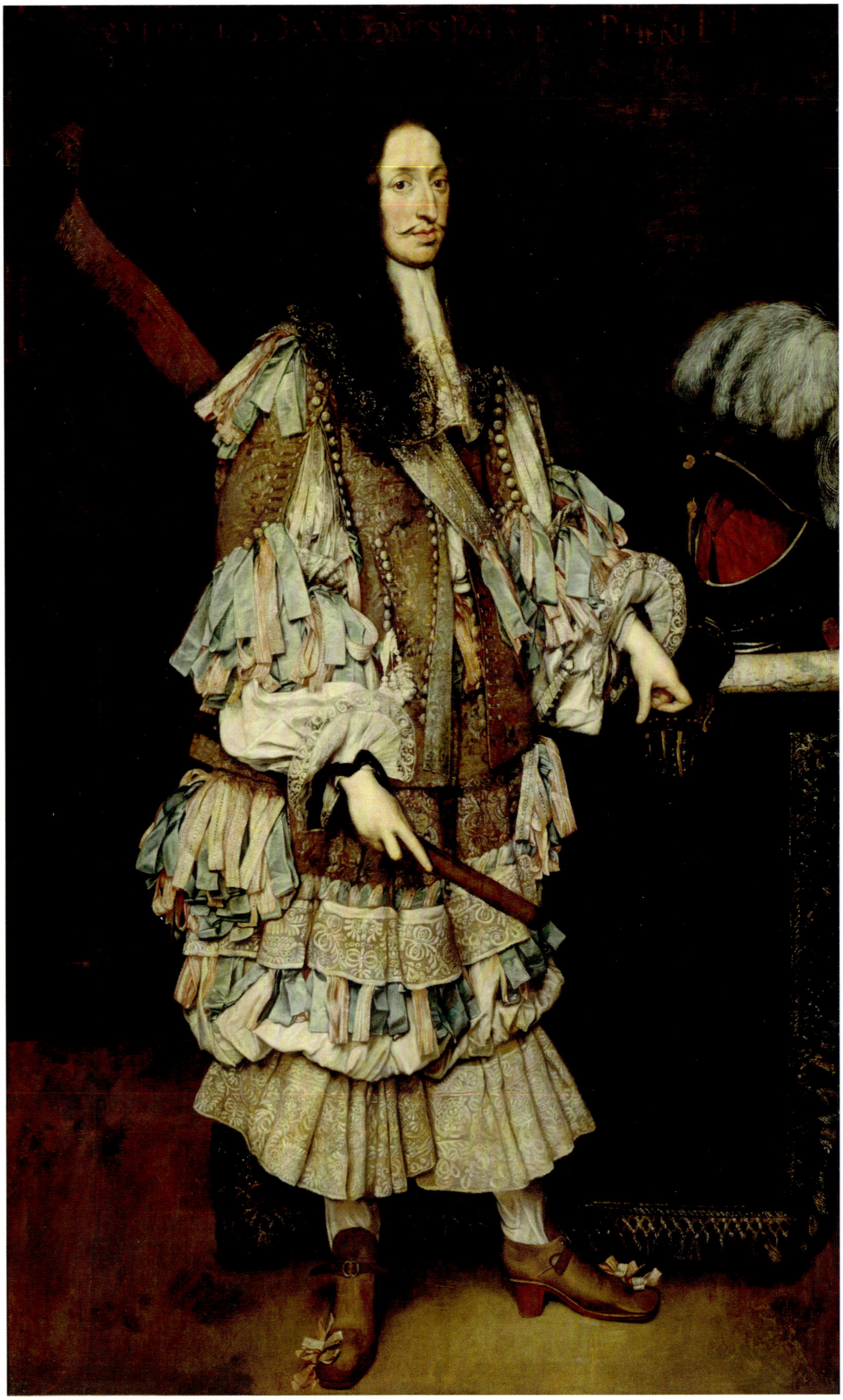

73. Copy of (?) Sebastiano Bombelli (1635–1719),
Duke Maximilian Philipp of Bavaria. Oil on canvas, 212 × 130 cm.
Europe, 1666. Gemäldegalerie, Dresden: 638

Cringes, Knots, Fancies, Perfumes, and a thousand French Apish Tricks, which render him only fit to be set on a Farmers Hovel to scare away Crows'.[56] Its anonymous author was outed as a cobbler in a responding anonymous pamphlet that satirically praised the gallant:

> To tye the Knot of ones Muff Ribbon, to the best advantage; to walk with such a pleasing Gate that your Swinging Arm may keep true time with your Feet, which must Dance to the Musick of the Points, Ratling on your Pantaloons...
>
> You know full well Gentlemen! tis no such easie business, to discern how much of the Hand-kerchief ought to hang out of the Right Pocket, and how to Poise it Mathematically, with the Tortoiseshell Comb on the Left.[57]

The fop of Restoration comedy was created and performed in the same spirit of competitive exaggeration and insult. Authors of these plays – Colley Cibber, David Garrick and Samuel Foote – both wrote and acted their own versions of fops as well as playing this role in the works of others.[58]

How men should dress appropriately to their station and roles as governors of family, town and nation vexed moralists for over two-and-a-half centuries. Slavishly following fashion revealed a shallow, frivolous character, while refusing to conform with contemporary style indicated a suspiciously 'singular' stubbornness. Lurking between these extremes were dangerous models of sartorial error in the guise of romantic criminals. The fleeting change of fashion meant that no sooner was one outlandish collar decried than another extravagant style of neckwear took its place and moralists had to start all over again. The passage of every generation saw a flash young man in his elegant coat, stylish hair and fashionable lace transformed into a careworn father, his hair thin and greying, his waistline expanding, his suit old-fashioned, fretting about his sons, apprentices and youth in general, their outlandish behaviour and obsession with dress, and what dangers these heralded for the future of the nation.

On the painted canvas, a man's posture was the construction of the painter; off the canvas, his body language was the product of a dancing master. Study with a dancing master was a necessity for not only learning the minuet, but also for shaping a young man's corporeal language. Hogarth visualized the central role of the dancing master in the formation of a man's character in Plate 2 of *A Rake's Progress* (77). Amid the gaggle of instructors of the gentlemanly arts, the dancing master is placed at the forefront of the ensemble. With a petite violin in hand and a preening smile across his face, he extends his right leg, effortlessly pointing the toe of his buckled shoe and inviting his distracted pupil to imitate. For those unable to afford personal tutelage, attitudes could be learned from illustrated etiquette books, like François Nivelon's *The Rudiments of Genteel Behavior* (1737). The gestures of dance were vital for learning how to carry oneself, a sentiment often repeated by Lord Chesterfield in his letters to his son:

> If you dance genteelly, I presume you walk, sit, and stand genteelly too; things which are much more easy, though much more necessary, than dancing well ... a man of fashion makes himself easy, and appears so, by leaning gracefully, instead of lolly supinely; and by varying those easy attitudes, instead of that stiff immobility of a bashful booby.[16]

Chesterfield emphasized that possessing a refined and confident carriage was vital for a man's position in society, underscoring the fundamental relationship between dance, dress and the expression of masculinity.

The connection between the body, dance and dress in shaping and challenging contemporary ideals of masculinity has echoed across the centuries, often highlighted by sartorial subversion. Like the macaroni's striped stockings, which threatened the masculine norm, we witness a similar subversion in the iconic footwear of one of music's most flamboyant and provocative performers. Prince Rogers Nelson, better known simply as Prince, utilized dress and body language to challenge gender norms in the late twentieth century, three centuries after his macaroni counterparts. His custom-made heeled ankle boots were his sartorial trademark, one of many examples of his ownership of traditionally feminine articles of dress, which he imbued with hyper-masculine sex appeal (78).[17] The black satin floral-patterned boots, accented with his gender-fluid 'love symbol #2', were one of 3,000 pairs owned by the artist.[18] Reinforced with metal braces that facilitated his fervent and physically demanding stage performance, his boots were a symbol of power, sexuality and subversion – his own unique brand of masculinity (79).

The silhouette of Prince's boots echoes the high-heeled shoes once worn by elite men in early-modern Europe. First introduced from Persia, high-heeled shoes were an embodiment of power, status and leisure, physically curtailing the wearer from extensive walking and physical labour while exaggerating the shapeliness of the calf.[19] As seen in the 1666 portrait of the Duke of Bavaria, seventeenth-century men's shoes were not only heeled, but also accented with rosettes of ribbon, known as shoe-roses (73). The red high-heel prominently displayed by the Duke's out-turned foot became the sartorial emblem of the Sun King, Louis XIV, who restricted their wear to the nobility of the French court.[20] Red high-heels were likewise worn by British royalty and the seventeenth-century court, although they were circumscribed to ceremonial court footwear over the course of the eighteenth century, visually surviving in state portraits of coronations and investitures of the Order of the Garter (3).[21] By the 1710s, red heels were arguably the footwear of fops and beaus. A frequent target of Joseph Addison and Richard Steele's didactic narratives of *The Tatler* and *The Spectator*, red heels were repeatedly ridiculed as one of the sartorial 'symptoms' of 'the Beau Species', falling out of fashion by the 1740s.[22]

Red heels reappeared when young men returned to continental Europe on the Grand Tour and adopted elements of European court dress. Leather and silk red-heeled shoes accent sitters' feet in numerous portraits by Batoni and made a marked entrance back into London society.[23] At a court drawing room on 4 June 1771, a newspaper noted that 'Mr. Charles James Fox had red heels to his shoes, though that fashion had been exploded above half a century'.[24] Like brazenly striped, green or even flesh-coloured stockings, red heels became a sartorial identifier of the macaronis.[25] Although the heels had lost their height compared with the century before, the thin-soled, slipper-like shoe of the macaroni could make an equally lofty impression.[26] In addition to the flash of a red heel, increasingly large shoe buckles made of diamonds, paste and precious stones, topped with silk rosettes, drew attention to the foot. One court observer of a birthday ball reflected:

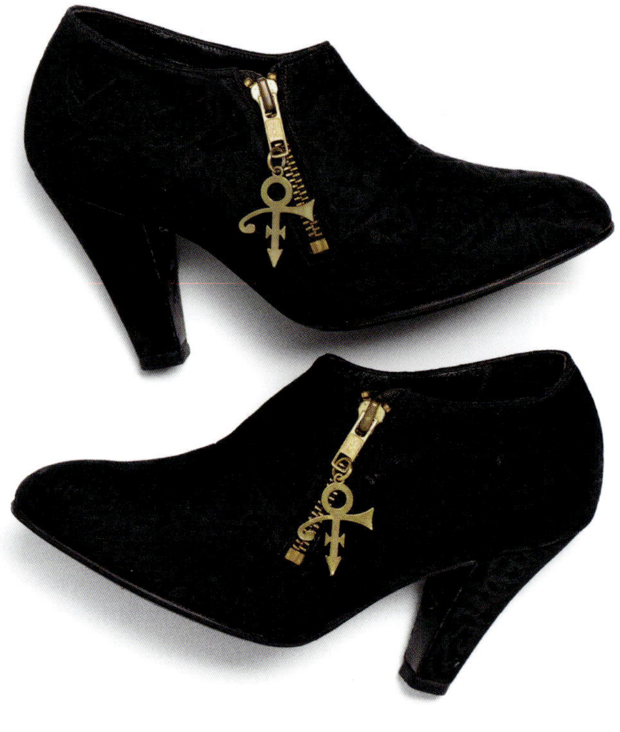

78. Satin floral-patterned heeled boots. Worn by Prince. USA, *c.*1994. V&A: S.1012:1,2-2017

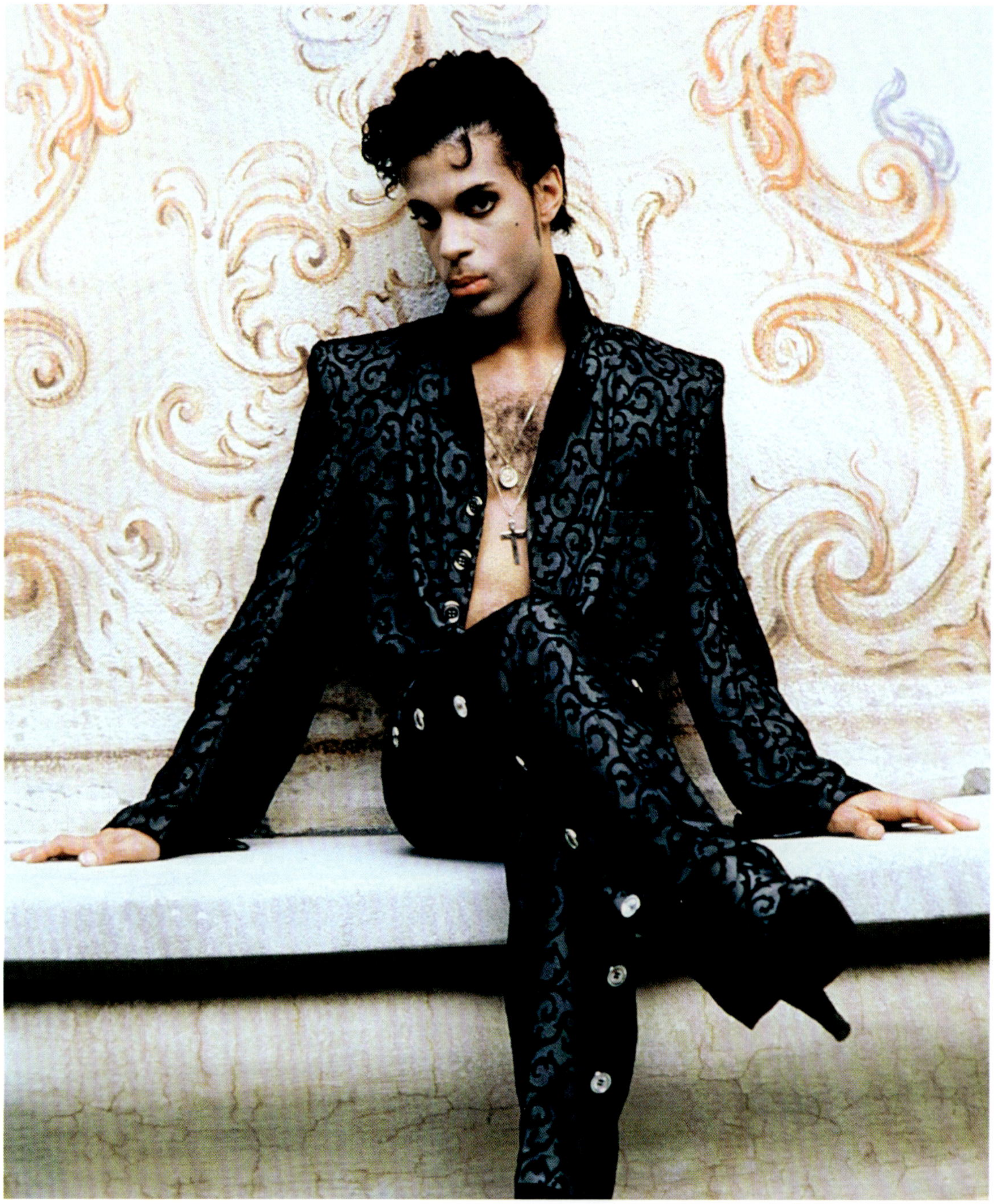

79. Prince in *Under the Cherry Moon* (1986), dir. Prince

> … 'tis a Pity that so many Gentlemen from the Hands of the Dancing-Master should not have learned to walk better. Several Gentlemen cut very conspicuous Figures in the Buckle Way, which almost eclipsed the Shoe: But, alas! what affected my Feelings most was, to see so many British Youths sinking into Effeminacy, as the Appearance of red Heels most strongly denotes.[27]

The lower leg and foot were loaded sites on the male body, embodying connotations of class and gender. As Peter McNeil and Giorgio Riello have argued, a man's shoe 'acted as a type of emphatic punctuation stop at the end of silk-stockinged legs which marked out his gender distinction from young boys and women, and his class distinction from working men wearing leather or cloth protective leggings, ragged shoes, and clogs.'[28] While the material elements of stockings and shoes signified status and varying modes and subversions of masculinity, corporeal presentation was equally important in their expression. Prince's boots would connote far less of the musician's subversive masculinity if they had not been animated by his electric dance moves, nor would an eighteenth-century man's footwear and stockings carry such weight had they not been presented in a well-turned fashion. As Lord Chesterfield imparted to his son: 'if your motions and carriage are not graceful, genteel, and natural, your fine clothes will only display your awkwardness the more.'[29] For Prince and the eighteenth-century man alike, masculinity began from the feet up.

BRAGGADOCIO: A BRIEF HISTORY OF SWAGGER

ELIZABETH CURRIE

Dressed in all your fancy clothes
Sneakers looking fresh to death,
I'm loving those Shell Toes
Walking that walk, talk that slick talk
I'm liking this American boy, American boy
'American Boy' by Estelle, featuring Kanye West (2008)[1]

'American Boy' is an upbeat, girl-meets-boy song with an original take on hip-hop brag. The above lyrics contain a typical checklist of male bravado: from the swagger to the designer clothes and pristine Adidas trainers. The American boy's ability to 'talk that slick talk' is as impressive as his sartorial status symbols. Here and throughout the song, language and fashion are shown to be complementary ways of communicating masculine strength and success. As a duet, 'American Boy' is unusual in offering two distinct perspectives on male boasting. While Kanye claims to be the 'hottest in the world right now', Estelle undercuts his hyperbole by telling him to 'cool down'. Generally referred to as braggadocio, similar themes have characterized hip-hop and rap music since the 1970s. A recent survey of rap lyrics from the 2010s suggests over 80 per cent of songs included them.[2] This chapter explores the close relationship between male fashion and bravado, and traces its origins back over four centuries. It shows how masculine identities have long been shaped by swagger and one-upmanship through words, song and clothing.

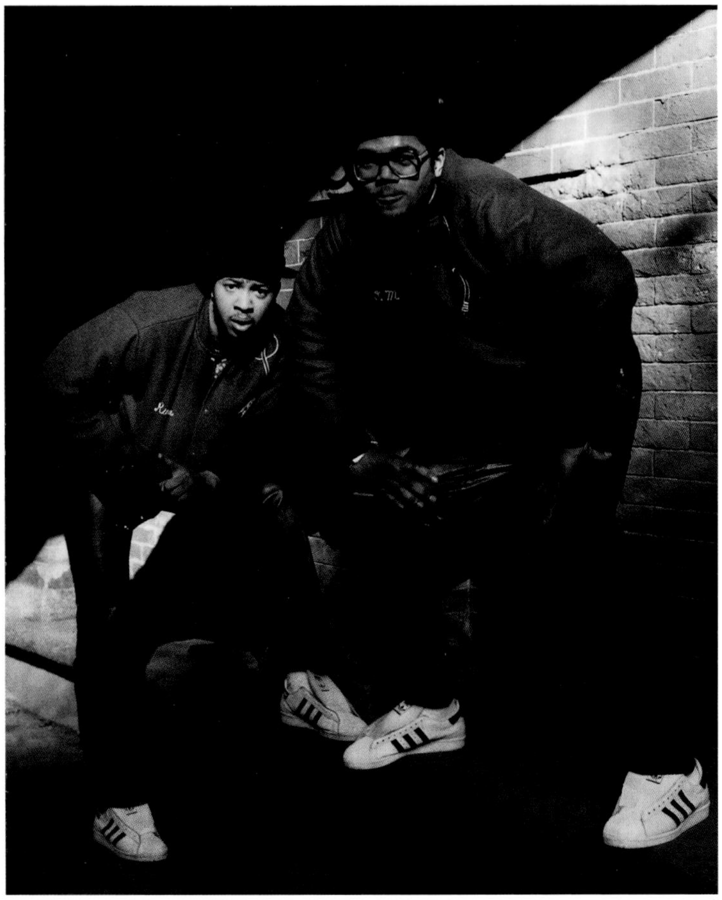

80. Run-DMC's Joseph 'Run' Simmons and Darryl 'DMC' McDaniels pose in Central Park, New York, 1984

FLAUNTING FASHION

Rivalry has propelled the evolution of hip-hop culture and rap music. Alongside more staged activities, including dance and vocal battles, musicians have developed their style and image to outdo their competitors. From the late 1980s, statement jewellery has been one of the most popular forms of materialist bragging. Early examples, such as Flavor Flav's clock pendants or the Beastie Boys' Mike D's VW chain, embraced a punk-like spirit of bricolage and played irreverently with the standard norms of ostentation. As the hip-hop industry proved increasingly lucrative for successful groups, these were replaced by eye-wateringly expensive pieces of jewellery, from multiple layers of heavy rope chains, gold and gem-encrusted pendants to teeth grills.[3] Following on the heels of the 1999 track 'Bling Bling' by B.G. featuring Cash Money Millionaires, the slang term entered mainstream and celebrity culture. Unique, custom-made pendants represent the pinnacle of bling, their impact enhanced by the fact that many still encapsulate a hint of irony, through slogans, oversized designs or puns on the materials used to make them, such as Method Man's diamond ice-pick pendant. In choosing diamonds, an undisputed marker of material wealth, male hip-hop and rap artists were overturning stereotypes that link gemstones with more conservative and often female consumers.[4] More crucially, bling created a new form of hypervisibility over which the wearer had full control. Author and activist bell hooks has discussed the pursuit of overt wealth linked with some strands of hip-hop culture, underlining the way it models and reinforces the aspirations of a white, capitalist patriarchy.[5] In her 2012 interview with Jay-Z, Zadie Smith offered another perspective on these materialistic trends, arguing that 'those taught that they deserve nothing rightly enjoy it when they succeed in terms the culture understands'.[6]

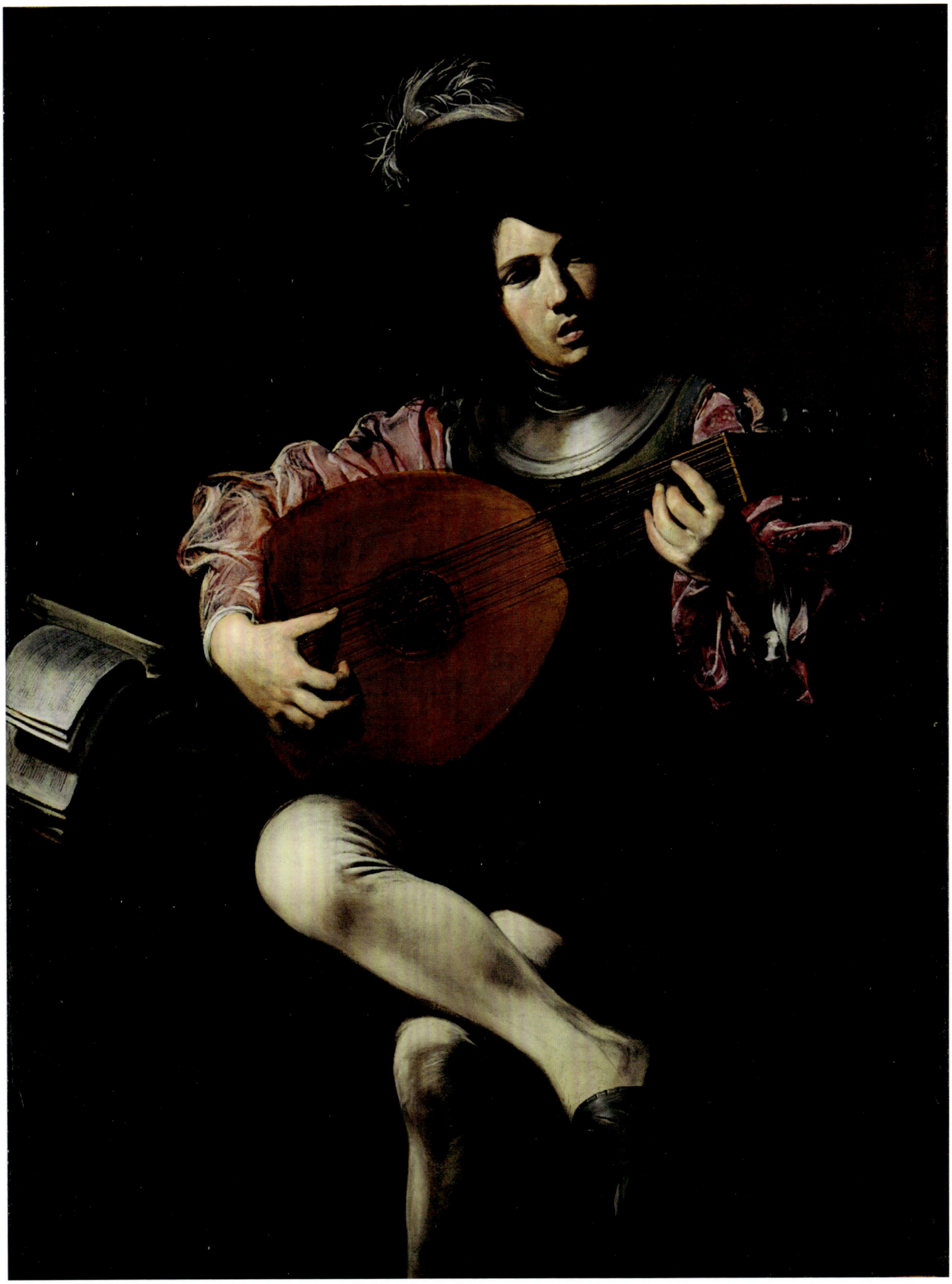

81. Valentin de Boulogne (1591–1632), *The Lute Player*.
Oil on canvas, 128.3 × 99.1 cm. Rome, *c.*1625–6.
Purchase, Walter and Leonore Annenberg Acquisitions Endowment Fund;
Director's Fund; Acquisitions Fund; James and Diane Burke and
Mr and Mrs Mark Fisch Gifts; Louis V. Bell, Harris Brisbane Dick,
Fletcher, and Rogers Funds and Joseph Pulitzer Bequest, 2008.
The Metropolitan Museum of Art, New York: 2008.459

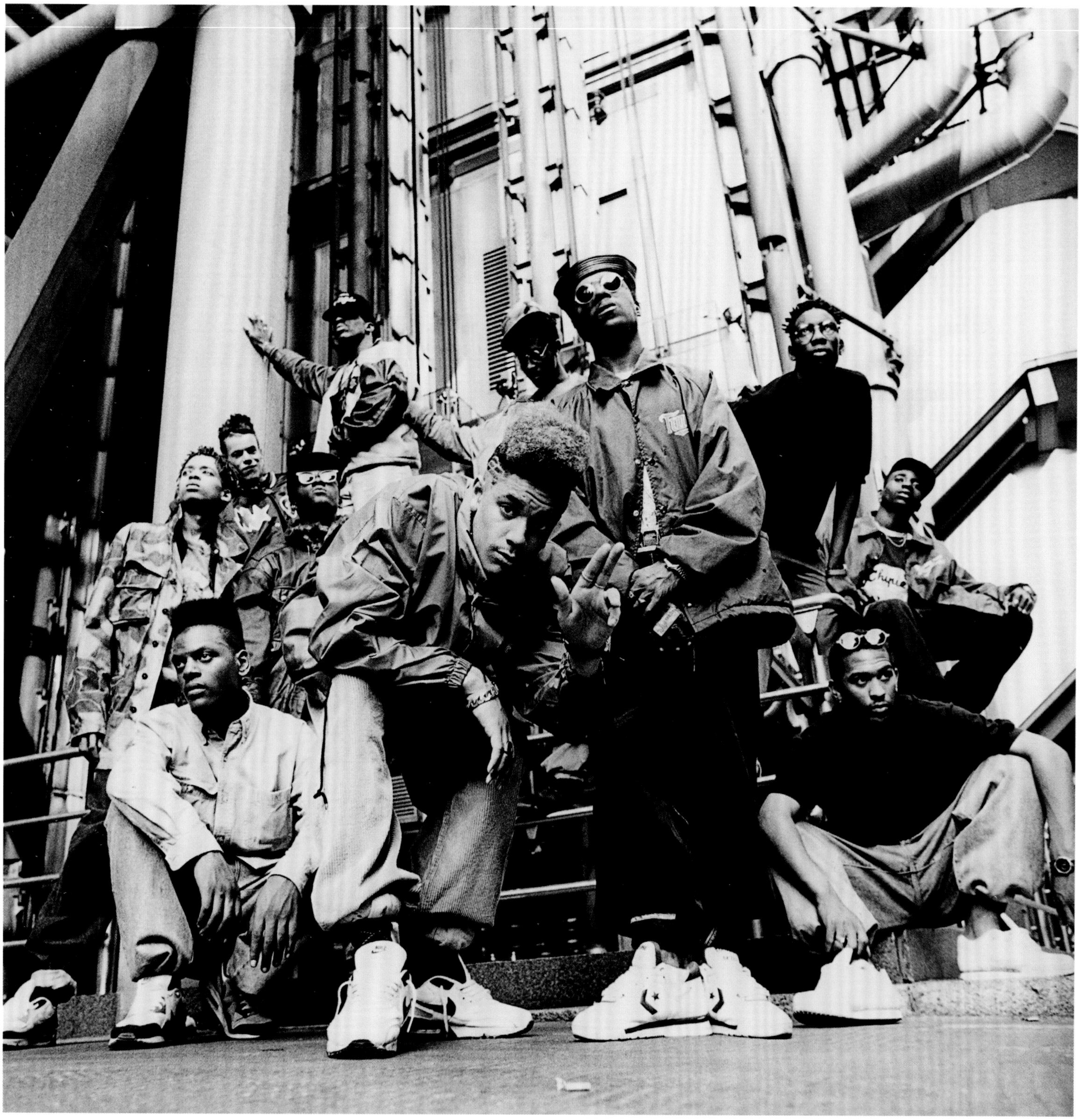

82. Normski (1966–), *Silver Bullet Posse – The Lloyds Building, London.*
Photograph, Fujifilm C-type print, 49×46cm. London, 1989, printed 2011.
Supported by the National Lottery Heritage Fund. V&A: E.113-2012

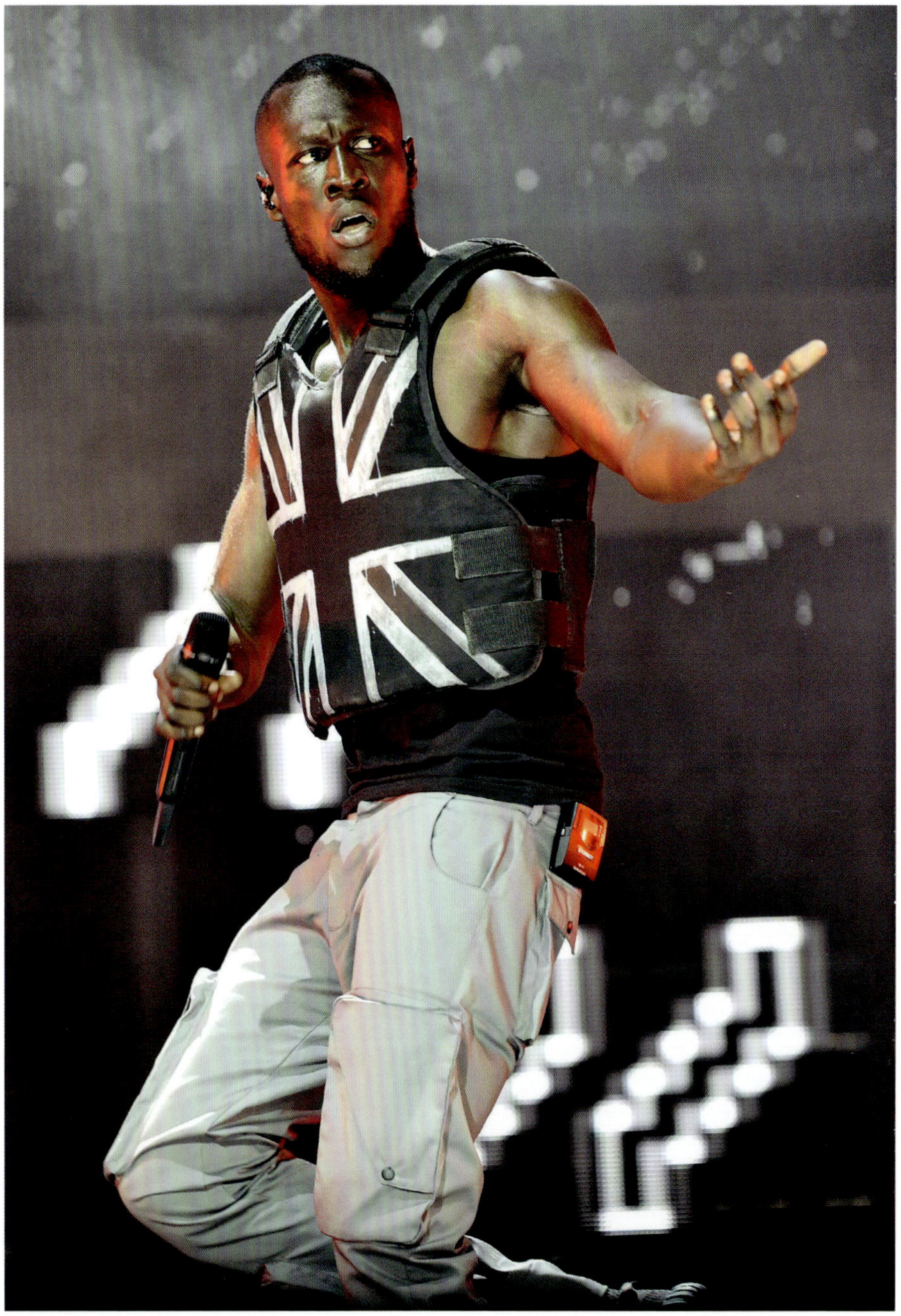

83. Stormzy performing on the Pyramid stage at Glastonbury Festival, 28 June 2019

The self-referential aspects of these music genres are well documented, expressed in the tendency to sample melodies and lyrics from previous hits.[7] The recurring materialist brag, whereby musicians' long-standing brand loyalties reinforce the desirability and recognizability of designer goods, is another manifestation of this. In 1986 Run-DMC recorded 'My Adidas', providing publicity that the sportswear label fostered with an endorsement deal and collaboration. Members of the group have been repeatedly photographed in different versions of the brand's classic Superstars (80). The reappearance of the shell toe trainer in 'American Boy' from 2008 highlights the longevity of its popularity. As hip-hop's influence on the garment industry escalated, artists and groups began to launch their own clothing lines, one of the first being Wu-Tang Clan's Wu-Wear in 1995. Fashion name-dropping became a staple feature of song lyrics, with the merits of these labels extolled alongside established mainstream designers. Braggadocious attitudes spilled over into marketing, as seen in the brand story of Jay-Z's Rocawear, founded in 1999: 'white hot from the start' it set out to be 'not just any player – the biggest player – in the fashion game'.[8]

IMPROVIZED STYLES AND ACTIVISM

Some of the most recognizable fashion statements popularized by rap and hip-hop artists have involved the reinvention and subversion of a garment's original appearance or function. Susan B. Kaiser et al. analyze similar strategies in their exploration of African American style to highlight the significance of improvization.[9] As Robin M. Chandler and Núrí Chandler Smith put it, this can be a case of: 'Take something and make it hip-hop.'[10] Kangol hats were turned back to front and multiple layers of T-shirts were worn under oversized bomber jackets, adding bulk and enhancing the impression of physical strength. Even blatant displays of wealth could be reinterpreted in ways that reflected the wearer's authentic street credentials. New York hip-hop artists modelled their own version of the logomania of the 1980s, in the form of 'knockups' from Harlem designer Daniel Day's Dapper Dan's Boutique.[11] Day outstripped the ostentation of luxury brands, including Gucci, Fendi and Louis Vuitton, by creating garments and accessories plastered with prints featuring their logos, such as Eric B. & Rakim's panelled jackets worn on the cover of their debut album *Paid in Full* (1987). These designs epitomized a spirit of self-reliance, successfully offering an alternative to the mainstream fashion brands' systems of supply and production.[12] Additionally, the function of garments was reinterpreted, rendering them useless for their original purposes as work or sportswear. These forms of reappropriation constituted an act of defiance, sometimes as a reaction to cultural stereotyping and inequalities in the labour market. Trainers, for example, were preferably spotless and unlaced, as seen in the prominent line-up of gleaming white Nike and Converse sneakers in Normski's 1989 photograph of UK rapper Silver Bullet and posse (82). Jeans were worn low slung and sagging, a look capitalized upon by underwear brands such as Calvin Klein for its advertising potential (63).

Several of these trends conjure up a very recognizable 'hard guy' image, intentionally bearing a trace of their roots within tough, sometimes combative, environments. Hip-hop artists have often mixed elements of military uniforms with street styles and the clothing of political activism, as in the case of the Black Panther-style berets and army fatigues worn by members of the group Public Enemy on stage in the late 1980s. The stab vests worn by 50 Cent and other exponents of the 1990s subgenre of gangsta rap were another overt response to violence. Although intended principally for protection, the vest became particularly symbolic for 50 Cent, serving to underline his death-defying reputation while embodying a spirit of bravado and intimidation. In 2019, for his headline set at Glastonbury, Stormzy wore a stab vest emblazoned with a Union Jack, its dark red tones and dripping paint reminiscent of dried blood (83). It transpired that the vest had been made by street artist and political commentator Banksy. In this setting, the garment signified far more than the individual wearer's swagger or aggression, becoming an emblem for escalating street violence and social exclusion. The cover for Stormzy's second album, *Heavy is the Head* (2019), showing the musician with head bent contemplating the vest, similarly reverses expectations. Intentionally evoking a Renaissance painting, a kind of modern-day *Pietà*, the album cover undercuts a strong, muscular version of manhood with a sense of loss and sacrifice.[13]

THE BIRTH OF BRAGGADOCIO

The braggadocio look is linked with certain types of music and individual, well-known artists. Yet many of its key elements have evolved from street styles that have a much wider significance and represent traits traditionally associated with masculinity. Nowadays, the word braggadocio rarely spills into everyday speech but it has a long history, being thought to derive from the name of Braggadocchio, a character in Edmund Spenser's poem *The Faerie Queene* (1590): a boastful, flaunting figure of fun who pretends to be brave but fails when he is put to the test.[14] Bravery, a fundamental male attribute or virtue in Spenser's time, was displayed through a combination of looks and deeds. It was necessary to visually demonstrate or perform bravery and the adjective 'brave' was used to describe finery and ostentation. In Spenser's poem, for example, we learn that armour is often 'brave', Gloriana, the Faerie Queen, is 'brave embellished with royall robes' and a horse's bridle is 'rung with golden bels and bosses brave'.[15] Spenser created Braggadocchio's name by adding the Italian suffix *occio* to the word braggart, and he possibly also drew inspiration from the *bravo*, sometimes described in English as a 'soldier of fortune', a figure who loomed large in Italian art and literature in the late sixteenth and early seventeenth centuries.

An Italian–English dictionary of 1611 translates *bravo* as 'a braver, swaggerer' and 'brave, gallant or fine', while the verb *bravare* means 'to boast, to brag, to vaunt, to swagger, to flaunt it'.[16] Writings from this period often use pejorative terms to describe *bravi*, linking them with violence and social unrest, yet their negative reputation also stemmed from their marginalized status and the fact that they were usually, to some extent, itinerant. *Bravi* were part of street life and so had disproportionately high visibility. Many fought as mercenary soldiers during the prolonged wars between France, Spain and Italy in the sixteenth century. During peacetime they were forced to rely on their wits to find other ways of making a living. A very small proportion of them were probably excluded on the grounds of ethnicity, as they are sometimes depicted as members of the Romani communities who travelled through western Europe from the fifteenth century onwards, and who bore the brunt of increasingly punitive legal measures.[17] Laws were also passed in some cities, for example in Milan in 1583, with the intention of driving out *bravi*.[18] Despite these tensions, landowners and members of the aristocracy frequently hired *bravi* for protection or other purposes.

The Italian painter Michelangelo Merisi da Caravaggio and his followers depicted *bravi* in taverns and other meeting places, often playing music or cards or in the act of pickpocketing. *The Lute Player* (*c.*1625–6), a painting by the French artist Valentin de Boulogne, who lived and worked in Rome, depicts their typical clothing (81). The young musician's air of confidence is mirrored in his dress. His adherent silk stockings, immaculately white despite the difficulties of laundering clothing during this period, are as much of a statement as a pair of box-fresh trainers. At a time when professional men and courtiers often favoured

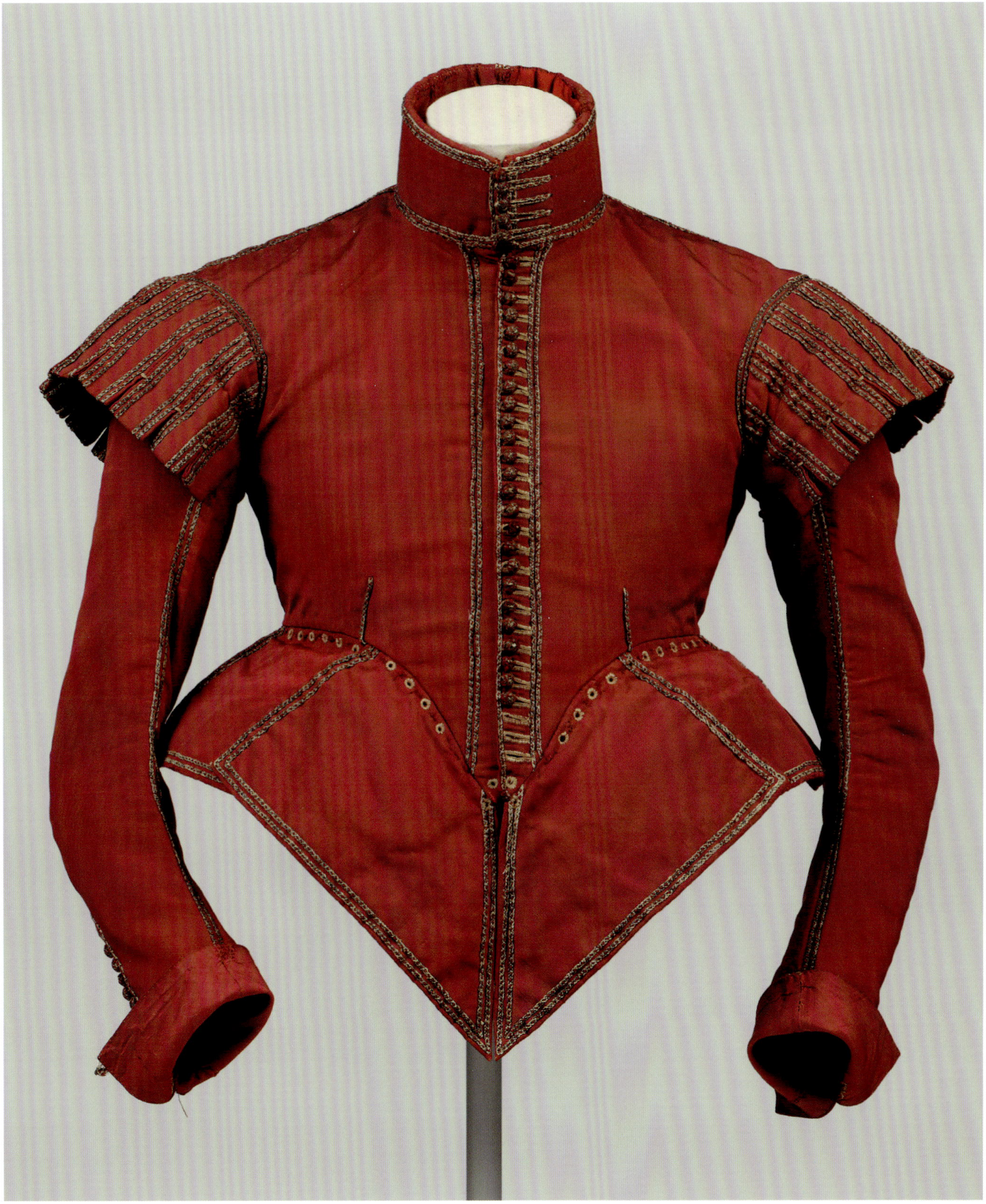

84. Doublet. Silk grosgrain. England, *c.*1620. V&A: 268-1891

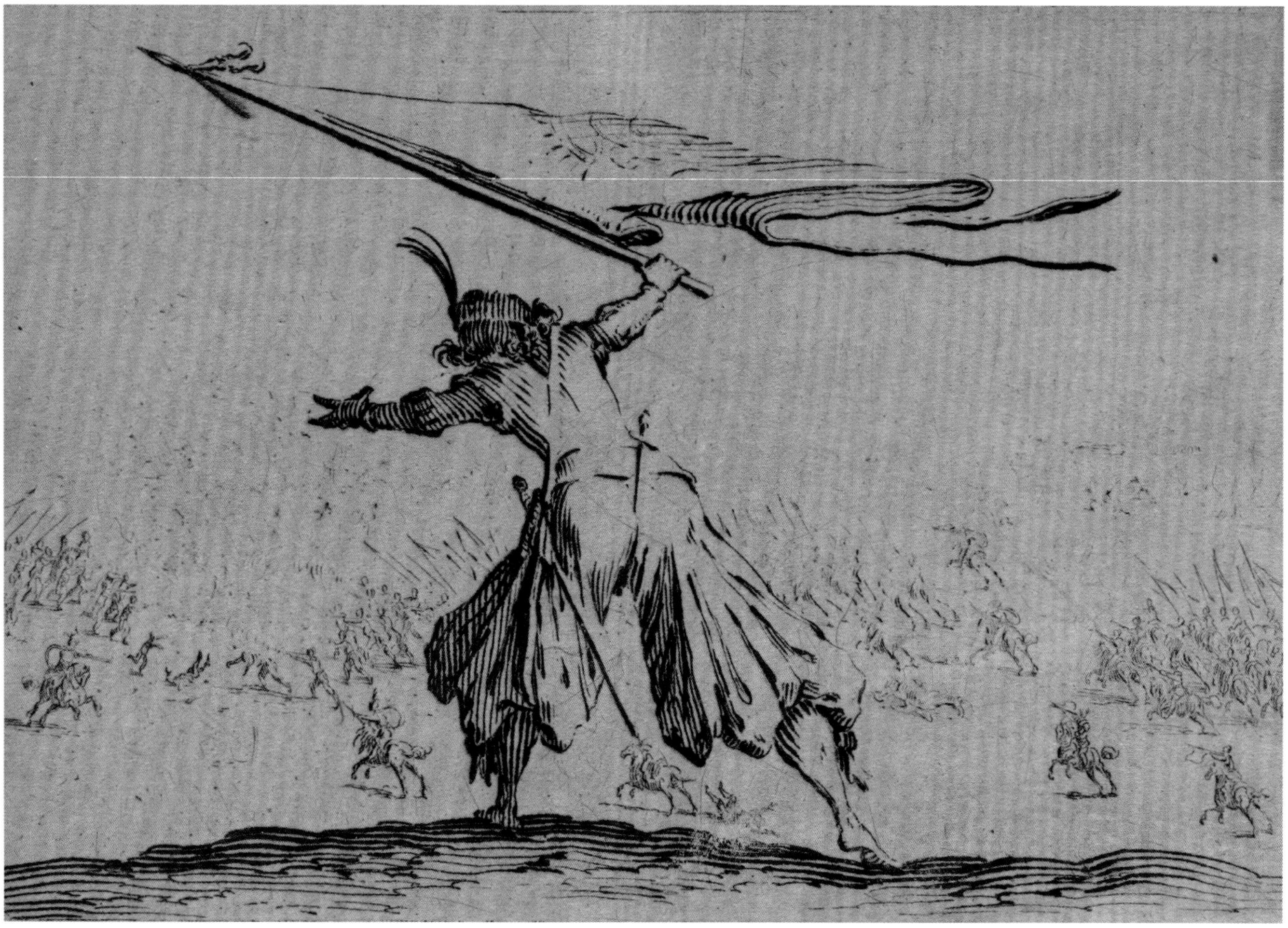

85. Jacques Callot (1592–1635), *A Flag Bearer from 'Capricci di varie figure di Iacopo Callot'*. Engraving, 5.5 × 8 cm. Nancy, 1617. Harry R. Beard Collection, given by Isobel Beard. V&A: S.1593-2012

dark, sombre colours, his sleeves are a flamboyant pink. Deep pink or red male garments, like this crimson silk doublet originally belonging to a wealthy Englishman, were linked with bravery and robustness in sixteenth-century theories on medicine and colour (84).[19] The Mantuan courtier Fulvio Pellegrino Morato explained that soldiers chose to wear red because it was thought to draw inner fire to the surface.[20] *Bravi* were often shown wearing bright silks, probably the vestiges of household or military liveries left over from periods of time when they wore the heraldic colours of the nobility they served. These expensive fabrics reflected their social limbo, as they were partly subservient yet unbound by some of the constraints that shaped other men's experiences.

COMBAT CLOTHING

Soldiers were widely known for their ostentatious appearance. Given the hypermasculine nature of their lives, they were exempt from the criticisms of contemporary moralists who thought that bright colours and decorative effects were effeminate. One figure particularly encapsulated this conjunction between finery and courage: the military standard-bearer whose eye-catching clothing and banner were intended to raise the morale of his fellow soldiers. French artist Jacques Callot, who produced many images of the hardships of war, gives an impression of the energy of the standard-bearer and his role as a beacon on the battlefield (85). It is more common, however, to find standard bearers posing in the style of a fashion plate, as in this engraving by the German artist Daniel Hopfer, where the second figure from the right is enveloped in his flag, flanked by other splendidly dressed soldiers (86). All wear doublets and breeches highly decorated with different forms of slashing and panes, or strips of fabrics, that allow the linings underneath to show through. This technique is thought to have been inspired by the ragged, torn clothing of soldiers in combat. Of course, the carefully placed cuts and pinking made by tailors to grace costly garments were a far cry from the tatters of those who actually took part in warfare. Other memorable sixteenth-century fashions also originated on the battlefield. The codpiece emerged in order to cover the gap between separate leg hose or armour worn by soldiers, deemed particularly useful for those on horseback.[21] While the examples in Hopfer's engraving of soldiers are relatively modest affairs, until its demise towards the end of the sixteenth century, the codpiece was designed in a bewildering variety of shapes and sizes that encapsulated the very essence of flaunting.[22]

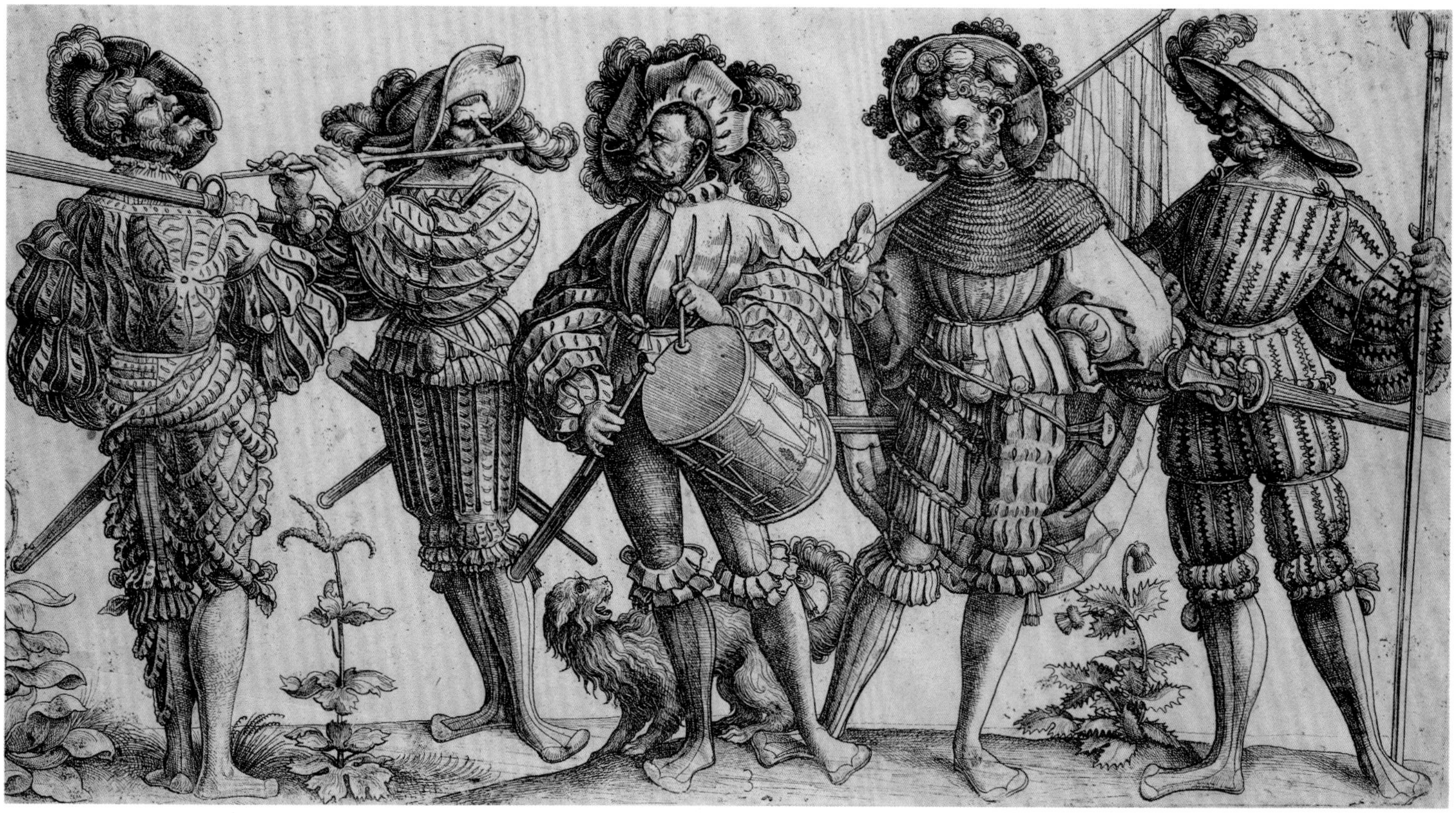

86. Daniel Hopfer (1471–1536), *Five German Soldiers*. Etching, 20.6×38.1cm.
Augsburg, early sixteenth century, printed *c.*1910. V&A: E.6292A-1910

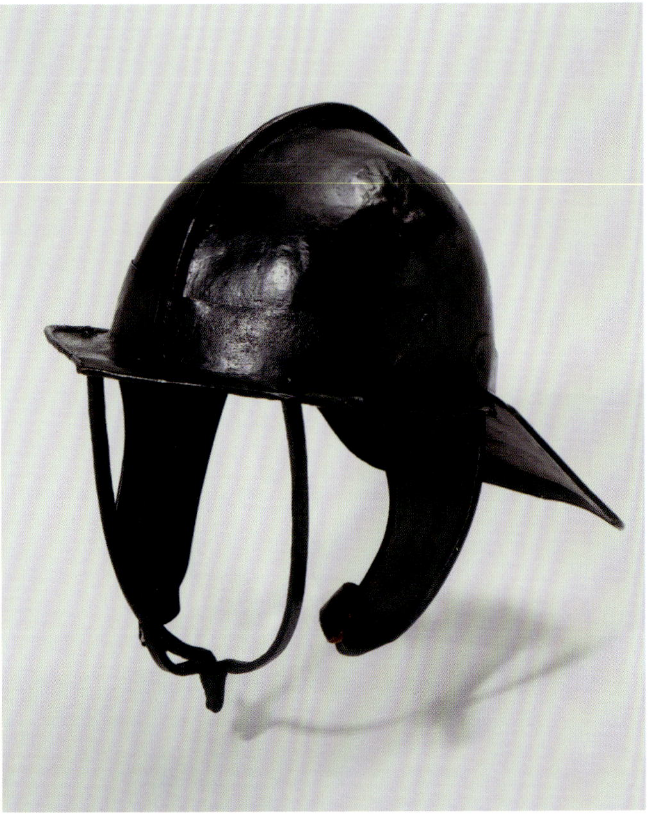

87. Lobster-tailed pot helmet. England, 1650–60.
Bequeathed by Major Victor Alexander Farquharson. V&A: M.597-1927

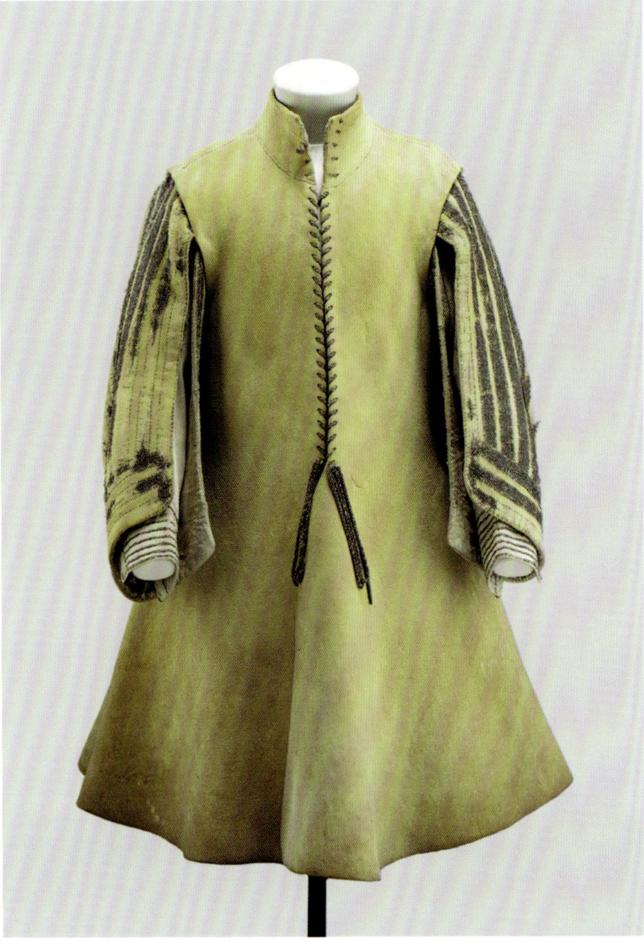

88. Buff coat. Leather, silk, baleen, silver gilt. England, 1640–50.
V&A: T.34-1948

The Lute Player projects some of this soldierly swagger. Like many other *bravi* and soldiers who were depicted with a drum or other instruments, he shows off his musical talents and his open mouth suggests that his likeness has been captured mid-song. Several elements of his clothing point to a combative life. His sleeves have black laces, or arming points, at the shoulders, which could be used to fasten on a breastplate, and he wears a gorget, a form of plate armour intended to protect the throat. These were some of the essential pieces of armour provided to the lower military ranks, including foot soldiers and civilian militia.[23] They tended to be primarily functional in design, like this lobster-tailed pot helmet, a type associated with the New Model Army regiments who fought in the English Civil War (87). Worn by an army of soldiers, their hard, skull-like, blackened metal exteriors would have created an intimidating sight. In civilian life, the use of single pieces of armour offered some protection in case a fight broke out. More significantly, they hinted that the wearer, no stranger to violence, was always ready for action.

The Lute Player's leather jerkin is connected to one of the most controversial male garments of the period. Prized for its hardwearing, resilient nature, leather was increasingly used to make garments for military combat or other situations that entailed physical risk. As types of warfare changed, full body armour was predominantly replaced by less unwieldy thick buff coats, which were named after the buffalo hide initially used to make them. These were expensive and covetable garments, often combining ornament with protection. The sleeves of this coat from around 1640 are decorated with silver-gilt braid, while the collar is reinforced with whalebone and the thickest areas of the leather have been reserved to make the coat's ample skirts to provide maximum coverage for the legs (88). However, unless they were worn underneath a breastplate their efficacy was limited, as demonstrated by the bullet hole through the chest of the buff coat worn by Gustavus Adolphus, King of Sweden, when he was killed at the battle of Lützen in 1632.[24]

Short leather jerkins or doublets were more practical alternatives to the buff coat, worn in everyday life and on city streets, and could be regarded as the stab vests of their day. In England in 1579 a law forbade the wearing of 'doublets of defence, thereby intending to quarrel and make frays on others unarmed'.[25] In Italy, thick leather jerkins padded with a variety of materials 'designed as protection rather than ordinary garments' were also prohibited in 1585.[26] This plated jack or armoured doublet, now without its sleeves, dates from around 1580 (89). Given that it is reinforced with overlapping metal plates encased between two layers of linen and wool padding, it would presumably have been illegal to wear it in everyday life. The military associations of such garments probably increased their appeal and leather jerkins can be seen in many sixteenth-century portraits of noblemen. However, in these images they are usually made from thin, supple leather and sometimes pierced with decorative patterns, so their original, defensive function was entirely lost.

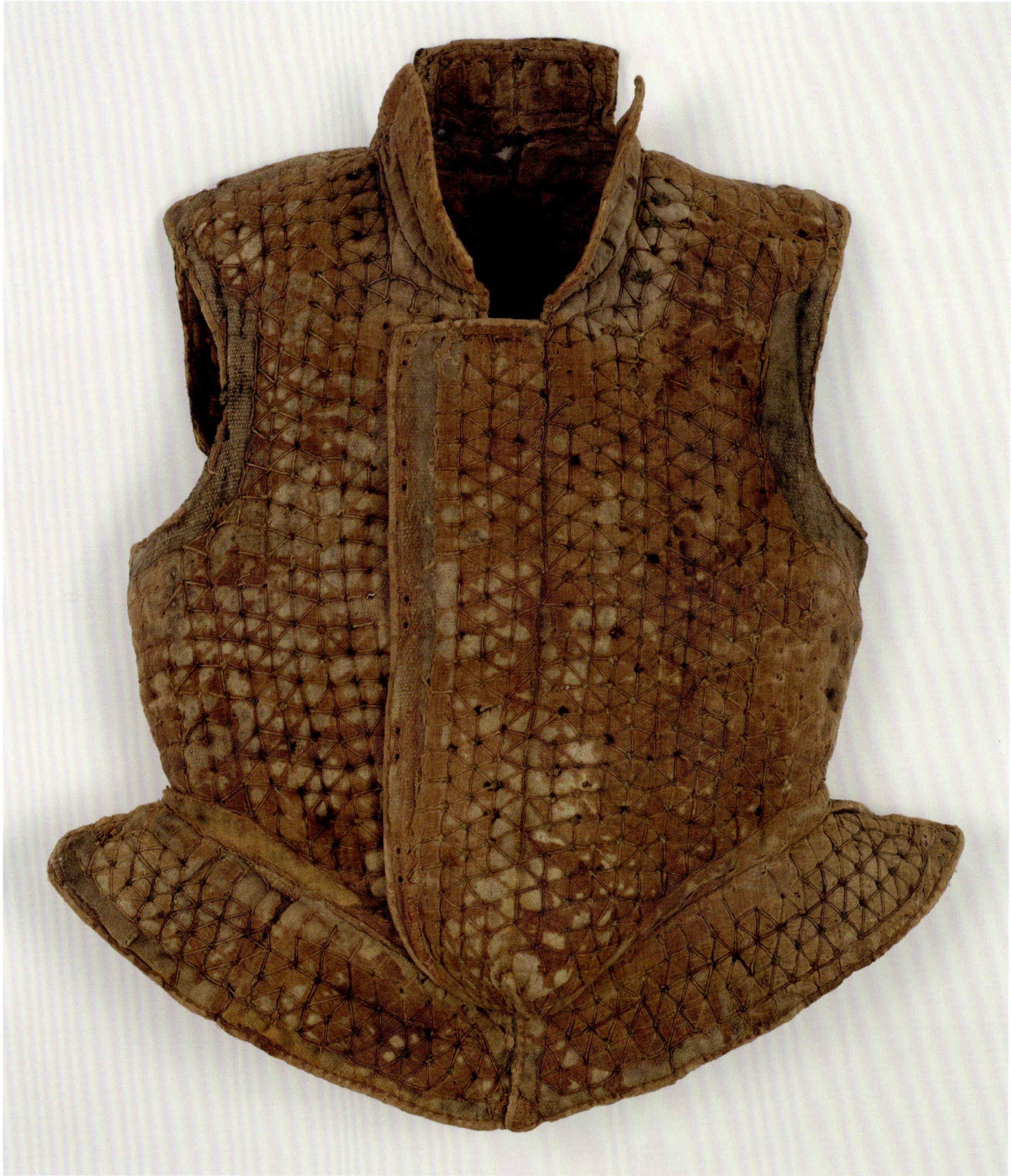

89. Plated jack. Linen, wool, metal, twine.
England, 1580–90. V&A: T.48-2017

Despite being separated by several centuries, these different manifestations of male swagger have much in common, embedded in the urban landscape and connected with the sounds and spaces of the streets. Both involve dress styles and identities that became highly desirable commodities. Sixteenth- and seventeenth-century elites imitated the fashions of *bravi* and foot soldiers and the appearance of the standard-bearer was a source of fascination for artists and patrons alike for many decades. In a similar vein, wealthy corporate brands have profited hugely from the politically and culturally subversive styles of hip-hop, while the tough-guy stereotype is often inflated in rap lyrics in order to sell records. However, in their initial forms, these types of bravado combined swagger with resilience, using self-aggrandizement to carve out status and be heard. Although a stereotypical form of masculine competition, braggadocio can also be regarded as a very visible form of risk-taking and resistance.

FINE AND DANDY

CLAIRE WILCOX

This brief collection of observations brings the enjoyment of fashion and its flourishes – whether subtle or flamboyant – into the realm of the personal. It examines the way individual wearers have taken possession of their treasured artefacts: pocketed their vanities, embroidered their initials, reclaimed their stolen watch, gifted or received a snuffbox, posed for the camera, presented themselves as a history man, or one who is botanically bold. Finally, fashion is shown as a collective pleasure as a twenty-first-century designer gives agency to her communities of menfolk, whether pictured in gilded frames or crowned in bouffant wigs.

PEPYS'S POCKETS

On 6 April 1661 Samuel Pepys ran into Thomas Townshend, Clerk of the King's Wardrobe, who 'told of his mistake the other day, to put both his legs through one of his knees of his breeches, and went so all day.'[1] Knee-length and often festooned with ribbons, petticoat breeches – so named for their resemblance to women's skirts – not only invited such sartorial mishaps but also questions about a man's masculinity. Pepys's friend and fellow diarist John Evelyn referred to them as 'a kind of Hermaphrodite and of neither Sex' in his essay *Tyrannus, or, The Mode,* in which he also decried the English addiction to extravagant French fashions.[2]

At a time when doublets were short and close fitting, breeches offered deep and capacious side pockets, invaluable for the paraphernalia of a fashionable man about town. Pepys's diaries are sprinkled with references to things he carried about him, from the quotidian, such as money, letters and keys – on one occasion getting locked out of his office when he left his keys in another pocket – to the bucolic: wandering in the garden of a friend, he fills his pockets with 'filberts' (hazelnuts). Other items were connected to his attendance at court, such as lace handkerchiefs and fancy gloves, or to his work as administrator for the navy; a folding rule for measuring ship's timber invented by Pepys was 'certainly the best and most commodious for carrying in one's pocket'.[3] An inveterate bibliophile, he pocketed John Webster's *The Duchess of Malfi* (1623) to read on his river commute and, bored by a long sermon, spied on the congregation with his new 'pocket glasse'.

On 28 October 1665 Pepys noted 'The King and Court, they say, have now finally resolved to spend nothing upon clothes, but what is the growth of England'.[4] A year later, Charles II introduced long, straight waistcoats, suppressing the buoyancy of such troubling garments as petticoat breeches. This eventually led to the adoption of the coat, waistcoat and knee breeches that dominated men's fashion for more than a century. Scattered about the suit, pockets still played their part, but were never as accommodating again.

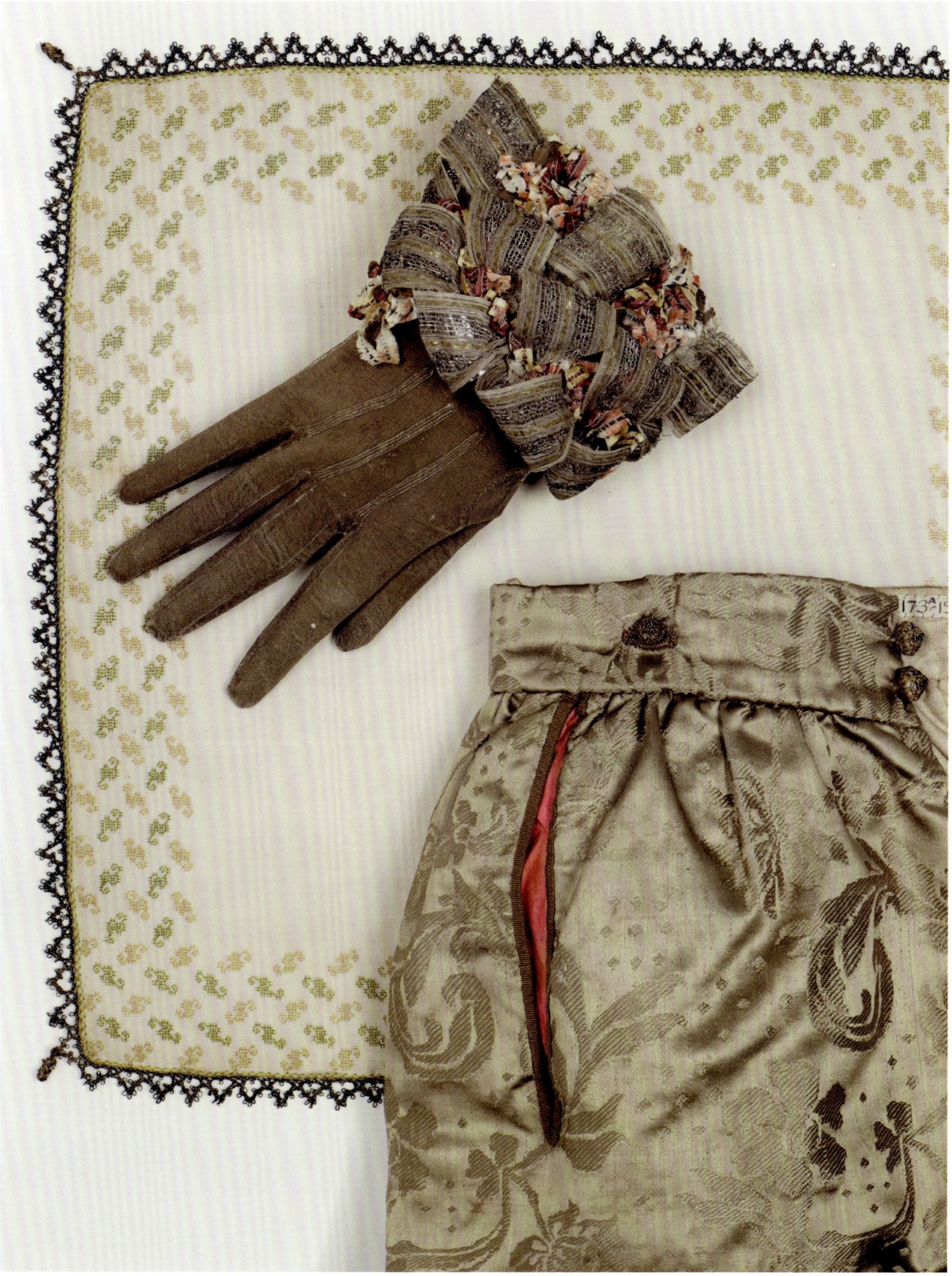

90. Petticoat breeches. Silk. England, 1680s. V&A: 173&A-1900.
Beribboned gloves. Leather, silk, silver. England, 1660–80. Acquired with the assistance of the National Heritage Memorial Fund, The Art Fund and contributors to the Margaret Laton Fund. V&A: T.229:1, 2-1994.
Handkerchief. Linen and metal. England, 1600–30. V&A: T.99-1954

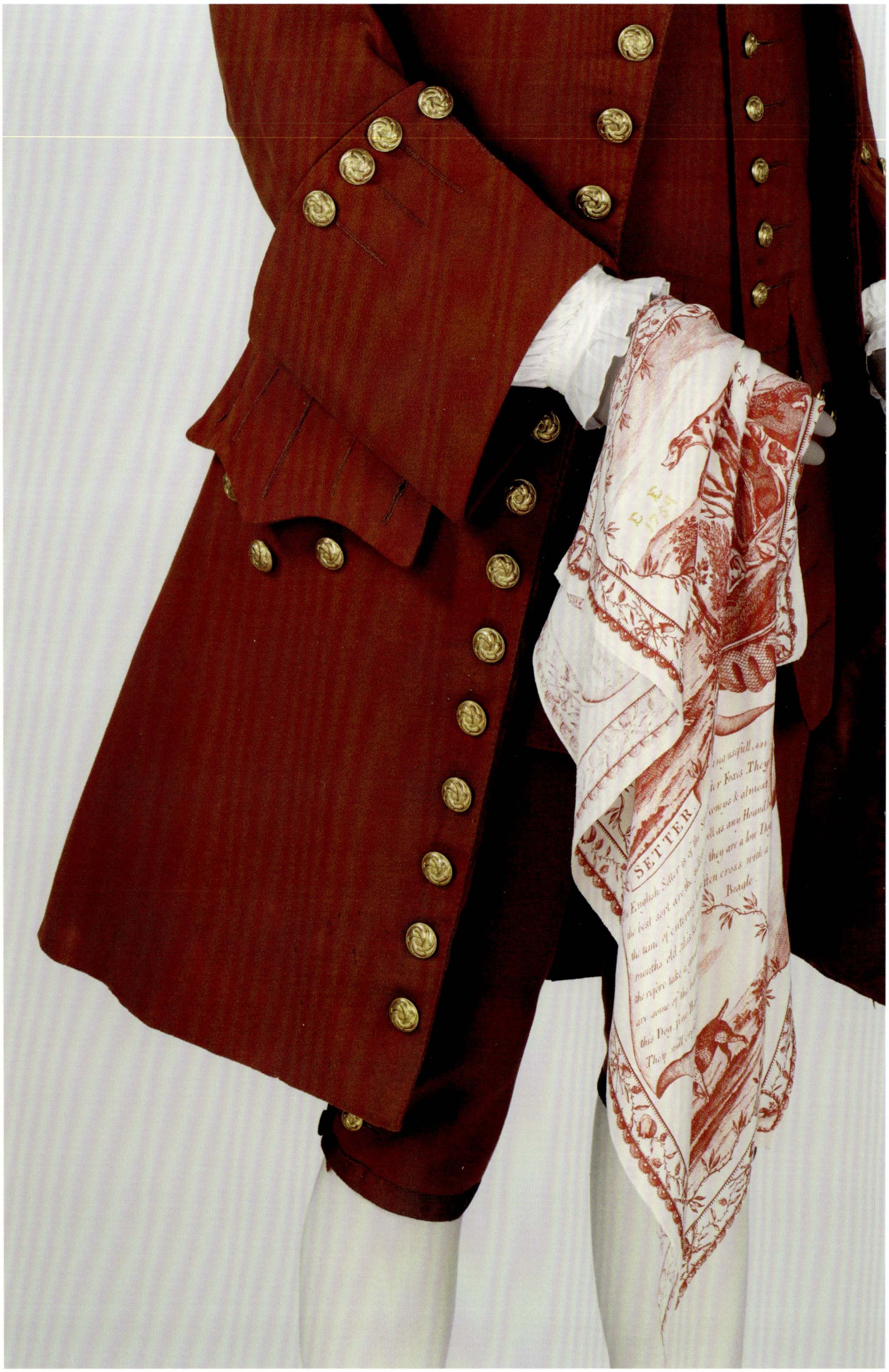

91. Suit. Wool and cast and gilt silver. Great Britain, 1750s. V&A: T.329 to D-1985. Hunting dog handkerchief. Printed cotton. England, 1760s. V&A: T.42-2021

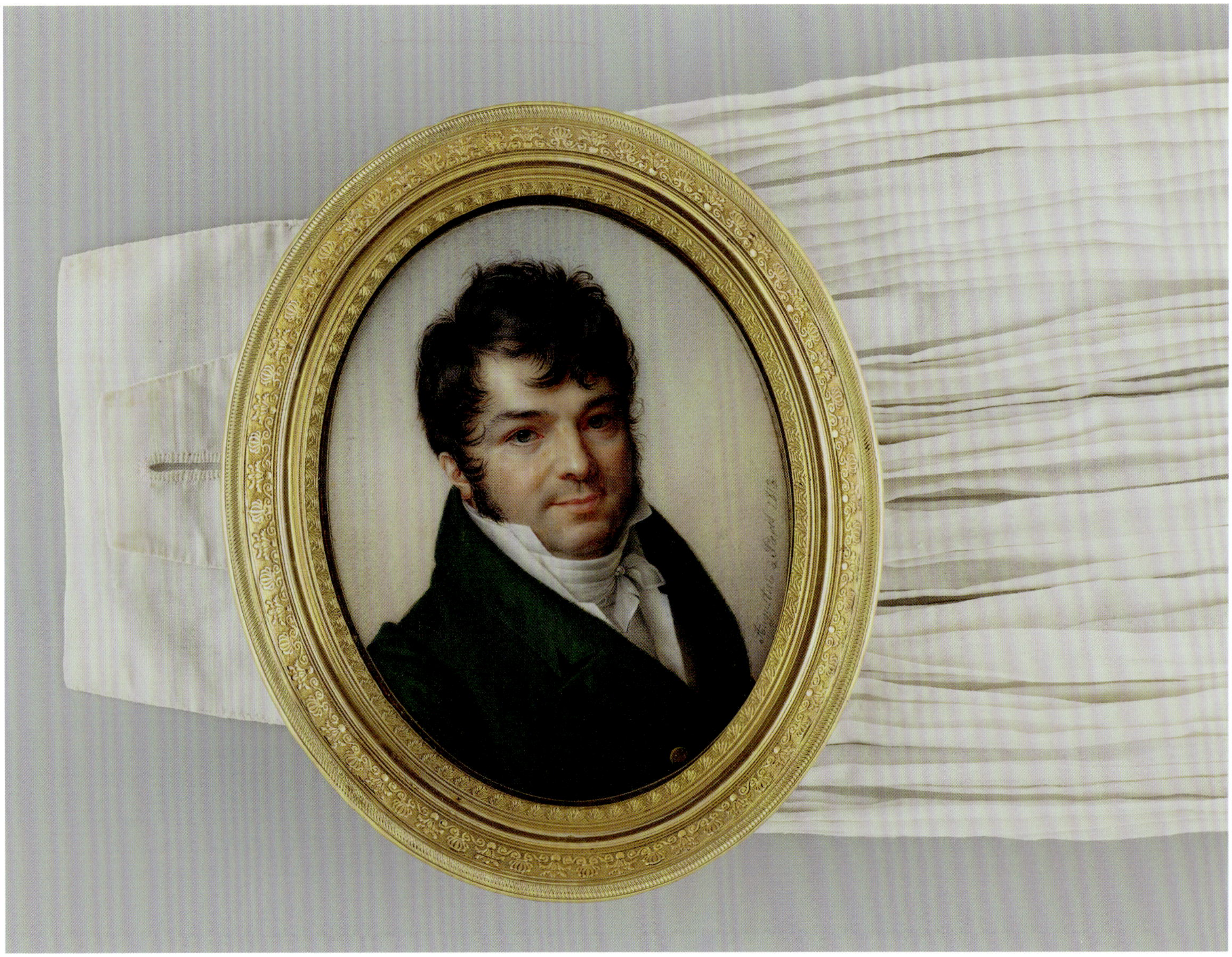

94. Lawn stock. Pleated linen. Britain, *c.*1800. Given by Jonathan Anderson. V&A: T.44-2021. Jean-Baptiste Augustin (1759–1832), Self portrait (?). Watercolour on paper, 9.3 × 7.4 cm. France, 1813. V&A: P.11-1958

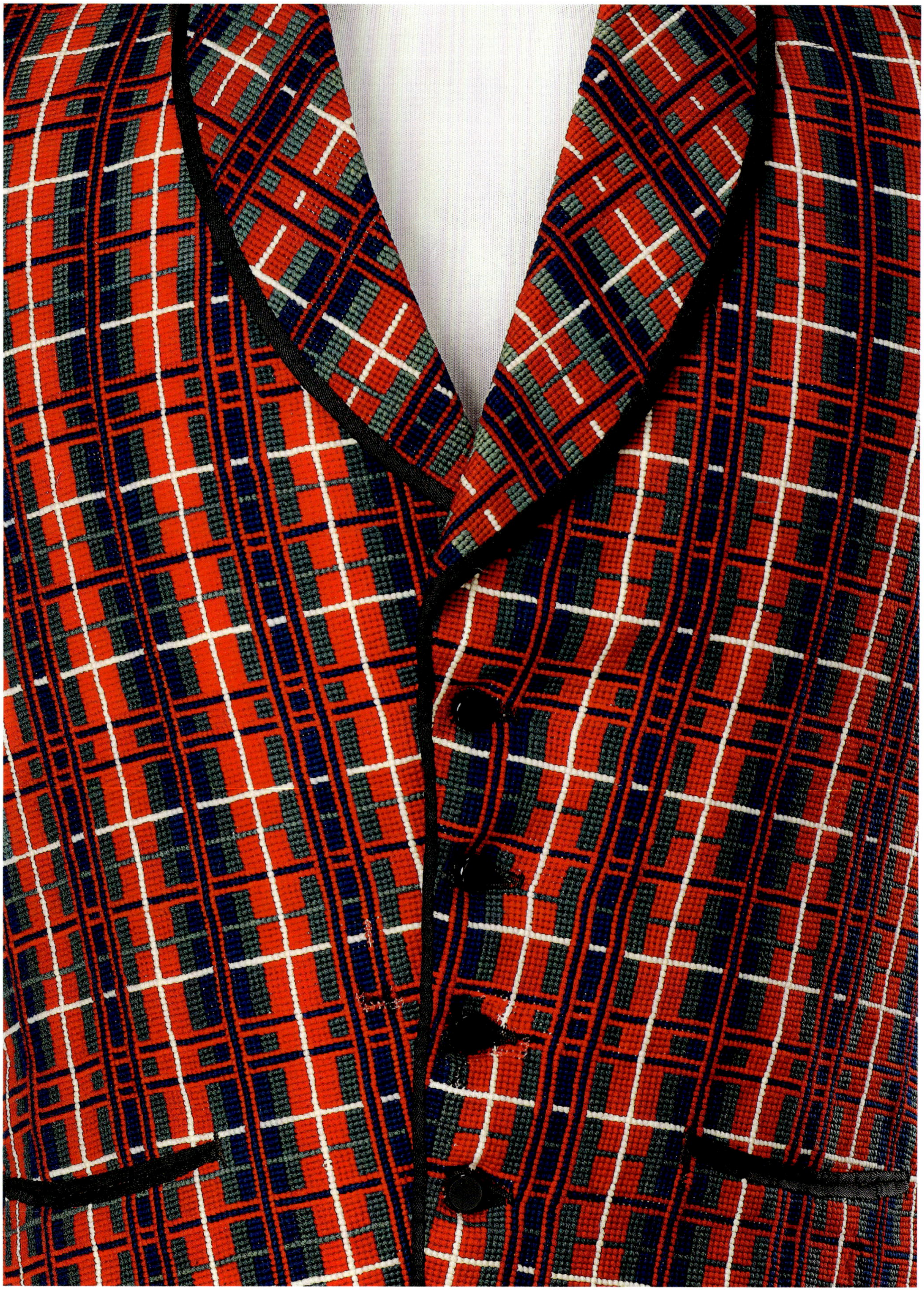

95. Waistcoat. Wool on canvas ground, cotton twill.
Great Britain, *c*.1850. The John Bright Collection

THE TASTE FOR TARTAN

Unfortunately, he takes no interest in anything but clothes, and again clothes.[19]

Prince Albert, 1858

Anxieties about over-fashionable men have been a recurring theme in the history of menswear. One of the most visible upholders of propriety in the nineteenth century was Albert, Prince Consort. In his guidance to those appointed to attend his eldest son, the Prince of Wales, he advised:

> The appearance, deportment and dress of a gentleman consist perhaps more in the absence of certain offences against good taste... He will borrow nothing from the fashions of the groom or the gamekeeper, and whilst avoiding the frivolity and foolish vanity of dandyism, will take care that his clothes are of the best quality, well-made, and suitable to his rank and position...[20]

Yet not every man concurred, particularly when they were of an artistic or literary bent. In 1835 politician and novelist Benjamin Disraeli was described as 'very showily attired in a dark bottle-green frockcoat, a waistcoat of the most extravagant pattern, the front of which was almost covered with glittering chains, and in fancy-pattern pantaloons'.[21] In 1842 Charles Dickens was also noted for his profusion of gold watch chains and satin waistcoats 'with very gay and variegated colours' that stood out among a sea of men in black. As one witness opined, 'His whole appearance is foppish, and partakes of the flash order.'[22]

Although Prince Albert eschewed the more outrageous garb of some of his contemporaries, following their purchase of Balmoral Castle in 1852 he and Queen Victoria did popularize in England one fabric that has permeated menswear styles ever since: tartan. While many were content to wear a waistcoat made of similar materials to their coat or trousers, or favoured delicate woven or embroidered patterns, others were braver. The design of this waistcoat is based on the Fraser of Lovat tartan and is worked in Berlin wool work, a popular form of all-over embroidery using a worsted woollen yarn on a canvas ground. The bright colours would have stood out against a dark cloth coat while the pattern is shaped on the cross for greater impact and to achieve a flattering line. The Prince Consort's achievements go far beyond fashion, but his particular passion for photography helped record it. In March 1861 Albert posed in a frockcoat and boldly striped waistcoat.[23] Thousands of copies of the photograph were sold following his untimely death, an event that perpetuated the sobriety of male fashion well into the twentieth century, inextricably linking it to mourning wear and suppressing the taste for flashy waistcoats.

FLOWERFUL MEN

It was a gorgeous day and I dressed elegantly
in a flowered shirt, open at the neck,
and faded denim jacket...[24]

Sir Roy Strong, 11 May 2004

The taste for floriferous menswear in the 1700s did not reflect an ambiguity about the wearer's masculinity but was instead an expression of status. In Lyons, the centre of France's silk-weaving industry, complex naturalistic motifs were informed by an increasing interest in floriculture and the publication of scientific works such as Carl Linnaeus's *Systema Naturae* (1735). Meanwhile in England, Anna Maria Garthwaite's meticulous designs for Spitalfields weavers reflected her botanical eye. Plant and seed collectors travelled the world, sending specimens to the Royal Botanic Gardens at Kew, which opened to the public in the 1840s, while new parks and arboreta played a fundamental role in urban life, encouraging social morality and a pride in appearance: as the Select Committee on Public Walks of 1833 explained 'a man walking out with his family among his neighbours of different ranks will naturally be desirous to be properly clothed'.[25] Intricate and orderly displays of bedding plants perhaps found reprisal in the craze for Berlin wool work as vast quantities of colourful waistcoats, braces and slippers were embroidered and enjoyed in the comfort of the home.

In spite of the efforts of William Morris, home embroidery declined and pattern and colour had to be found in print, aided by new synthetic dyes. In March 1895 the *Tailor & Cutter* referred to neckwear as being the 'saving touch from the monotony of sombreness ... bows, scarves and ties seem to get more and more varied, and, in the majority of styles, prettier and more artistic',[26] a trend that eventually saw fruition in the kipper ties and psychedelics of the 1960s. Shops such as I Was Lord Kitchener's Valet offered Oscar Wilde-type velvets and paisleys; Liberty & Co. produced dainty floral shirts with matching ties; and Aubrey Beardsley and Art Nouveau inspired prints gave women's and menswear a new homogeneity. Ossie Clarke designed chiffon shirts and dresses for men, while the tailor and dandy Mr Fish – who opened his shop on London's Clifford Street in 1966 – was the purveyor of a range of 'peacock' styles, including frockcoats and flares, heels and homburgs, and Byronic tunics worn by Mick Jagger. Another client was the plantsman, historian and dedicated follower of fashion Sir Roy Strong, whose friendship with that other great dandy of the twentieth century, Sir Cecil Beaton, was informed by their shared love of gardening. Their sartorial mores were naturally as well-tended as the blowsy roses and clipped parterres that distinguished their botanical style.

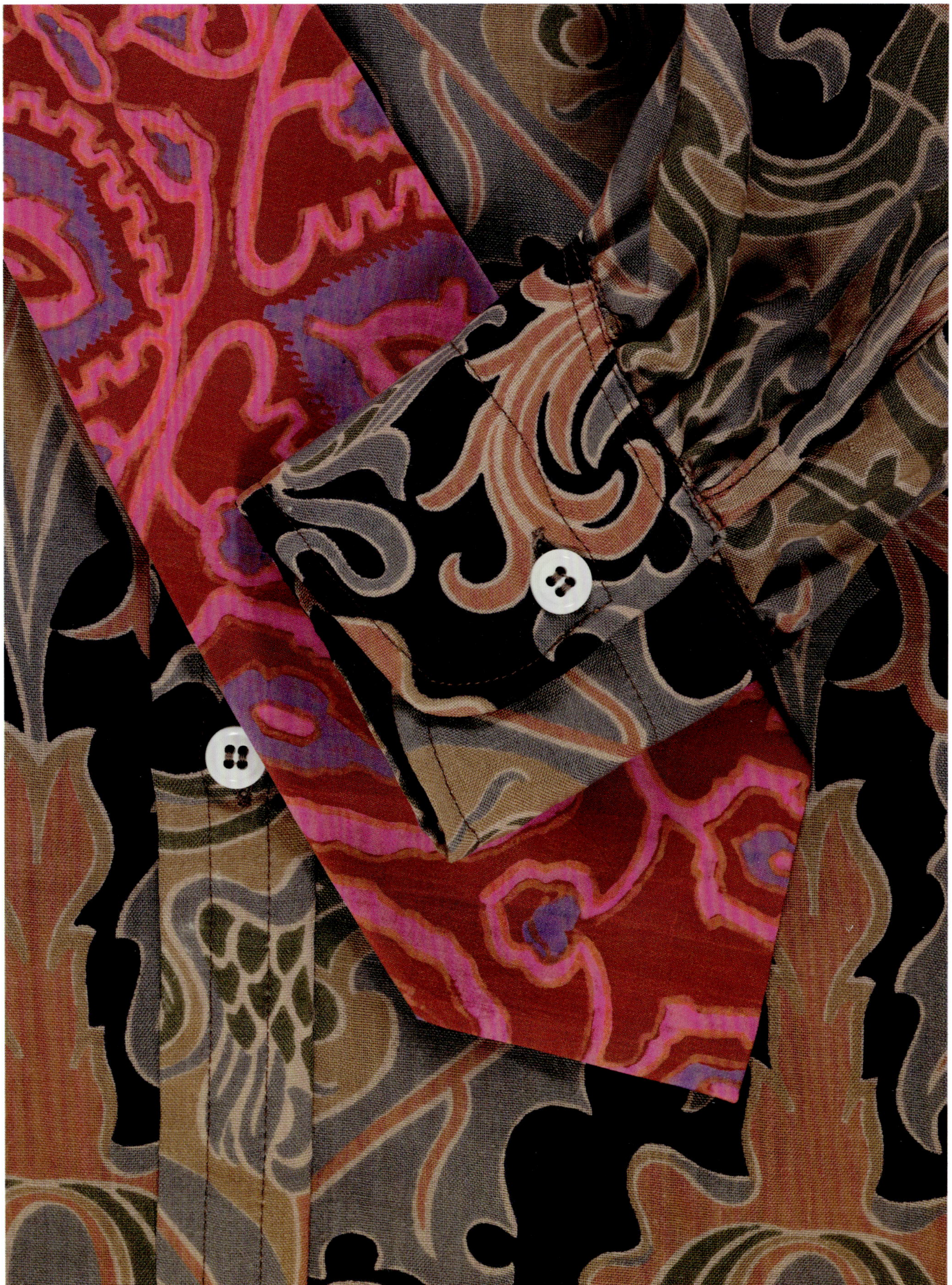

96. Take 6, shirt. Printed viyella. England, *c.*1970. Given by Sir Roy Strong. V&A T.107-1985. Austin Reed Ltd, tie. Printed silk. England, *c.*1966. Given by Sir Roy Strong. V&A T.200-1979

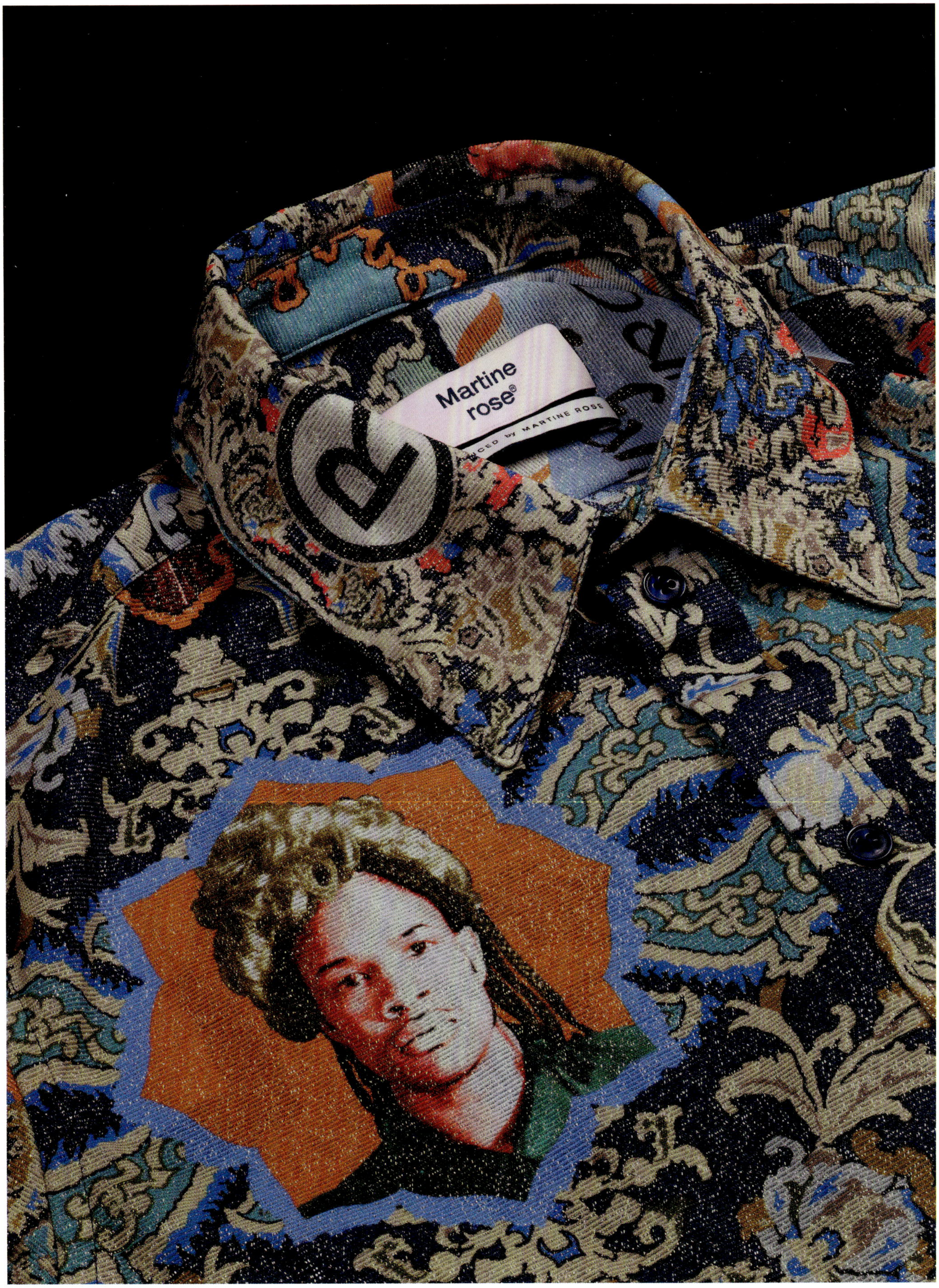

97. Martine Rose (1980–). Shirt. Printed lurex. Autumn/Winter 2020.
Given by the designer. V&A T.2443:1-2021

SHIRTSLEEVES

What I do is tell a story about masculinity.
All different versions – including
awkward and weird.[27]

Martine Rose

A dress shirt by London designer Martine Rose hijacks the codes of designer fashion with its ironic 'R' logo and reference to Versace's baroque silk print shirts of the 1990s. In its place, it draws attention to the cult of community, and to the music and clubbing subcultures that inform Rose's work, along with her Jamaican British heritage. The fabric features a gallery of portraits of bewigged male models framed in organic forms and rococo flourishes reflecting the artifice and hierarchies of the past. The print nods to lineage, for it was based on the street-cast men and women who walked in a previous collection, Spring/Summer 2020. Here, Rose staged her catwalk inspired by 1960s protest T-shirts, rave culture and football kits on a rooftop in the corporate heart of the city in a protest against the divisiveness of Brexit.

Like the T-shirt, the shirt was once an undergarment, not to be revealed in public. Since being outed, the former has often taken on the role of billboard, while the latter has tended to maintain the status quo for, like much of the male wardrobe, its structure contains residues of the past. The breast pocket, for example, appeared in the 1960s when waistcoats were abandoned, while the turn-down collar was to house the near-obsolete tie. Using the conventions of this wardrobe staple, Rose asks where her community stands and what its aspirations are; she invites her wearers – and models – to stand up and stand out.

But her designs are not just for the underground. Dropping in on the establishment, she created bubble-gum pink trainers for Nike, loosened up Balenciaga's menswear line and partnered with Italian casual brand Napapijri. Cool, clubby and questioning, Rose's designs reframe masculinity through an intergenerational lens, offering what *Vogue* described as 'cultural notes remade for a young generation to arm itself against disunity'.[28]

SARTORIAL ENCOUNTERS: THE KIMONO AND MASCULINE STYLE

ANNA JACKSON

In the 2019 BBC drama series, *The Trial of Christine Keeler*, society osteopath Stephen Ward, played by James Norton, is shown wearing a kimono while relaxing in his flat in Wimpole Mews (98). Women in kimono can sometimes be seen in film and television, but it is more unusual to find a man in the garment. This costume choice was made perhaps to suggest the louche character of the morally dubious, but ultimately tragic figure at the centre of the Profumo scandal. Its presence on the screen also revealed the fluidity, both literal and figurative, of an item of Japanese clothing that has, for many centuries, blurred cultural, gender and behavioural boundaries.

STYLE AND SUBVERSION

Full-length, straight-seamed garments constructed with minimal cutting from a single bolt of cloth, kimono are worn wrapped left side over right and secured around the waist with a sash called an obi. While in western dress, cut and construction emphasize or suppress the body shape, in Japanese clothing, the body is irrelevant. It is the flat surface of the kimono that is important, with colour, pattern and technique indicating wealth, status and taste. Kimono have a long history, but by the Edo period (1615–1869) the kimono was the principal item of dress for everyone in Japan, regardless of gender or social status.[1] Men, however, occupied the public arena of official life, where clothing conventions and sumptuary edicts regularly issued by the *shōgun* (military ruler) were more strictly enforced. The scope for personal expression was thus more limited with male garments being predominantly characterized by dark hues and subtle decoration. Despite this, men could still cut a dash, particularly through fashionable accessories such as tobacco pouches and *inrō* (small, tiered containers) that hung from the obi (99). Men could also subvert the rules more consciously by choosing a bold under-kimono (*juban*) or a colourful lining for their kimono jacket (*haori*), which would add flamboyant, but concealed, layers to otherwise restrained ensembles. Particular aesthetic concepts such as *date*, describing a style that was extravagant yet always elegant, and *kabuki*, meaning exciting and unconventional, were used to describe more daring expressions of masculine style.

Kabuki derives from the verb 'kabuku', meaning 'to slant' or 'to deviate'. In the early seventeenth century, the term *kabukimono* was used to describe outlandish rogues, gangs of young men from the fringes of samurai society and those left masterless by many years of civil war.[2] Infamous for their wild behaviour, *kabukimono* wore outrageous, gaudy, and occasionally women's, clothing. Kabuki is also the name given to the popular theatre that developed in this period, in which gender ambiguity and cross-dressing played an important part. Kabuki initially featured female performers, but in 1629 their participation was prohibited and young men, or *wakashū*, took on the role and, like the women before them, often sold their sexual services. *Wakashū* simply means adolescent male. They did not have the social responsibility of adult men, but they were sexually active and would often have relationships with older men, as well as with women of their own age and older.[3] Their kimono was similar to young women's and *wakashū* were often only distinguishable by their swords and the fact that the crown of their head was shaved.[4] The *wakashū* in this woodblock print is wearing fairly subdued clothing, although the red of his undergarment is seductively revealed at hem and sleeve ends (99). He carries chrysanthemums and looks coquettishly over his fan, which bears the lines of an eighth-century Chinese poem.[5]

Wakashū were banned from the stage in the 1660s but continued to serve as entertainers and sex workers. Despite the exclusion of female and young male actors, the kabuki theatre continued to operate as a subversive and seductive space.[6] Along with the licensed brothel districts, the theatres were at the heart of the floating world (*ukiyo*) of entertainment and eroticism that developed in the urban centres of Edo-period Japan. The leading actors were the great celebrities of their day, and the colours, patterns and styles they wore were eagerly emulated. The adult male actors who specialized in female roles were known as *onnagata* and were seen to embody ideal femininity. Many chose to live their lives as women off-stage as well as on.[7]

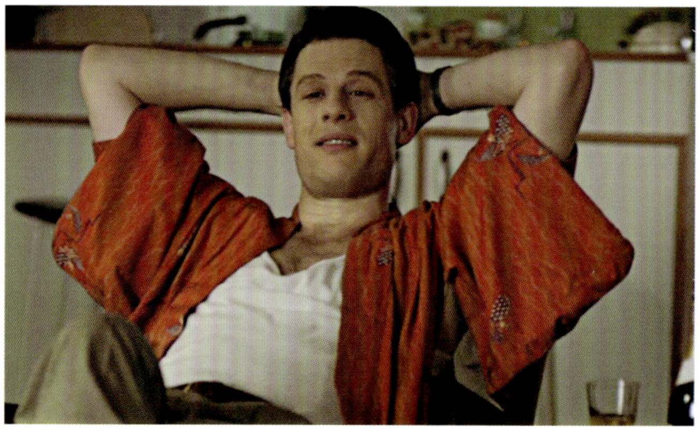

98. James Norton in *The Trial of Christine Keeler* (2019), dir. Andrea Harkin, Leanne Welham

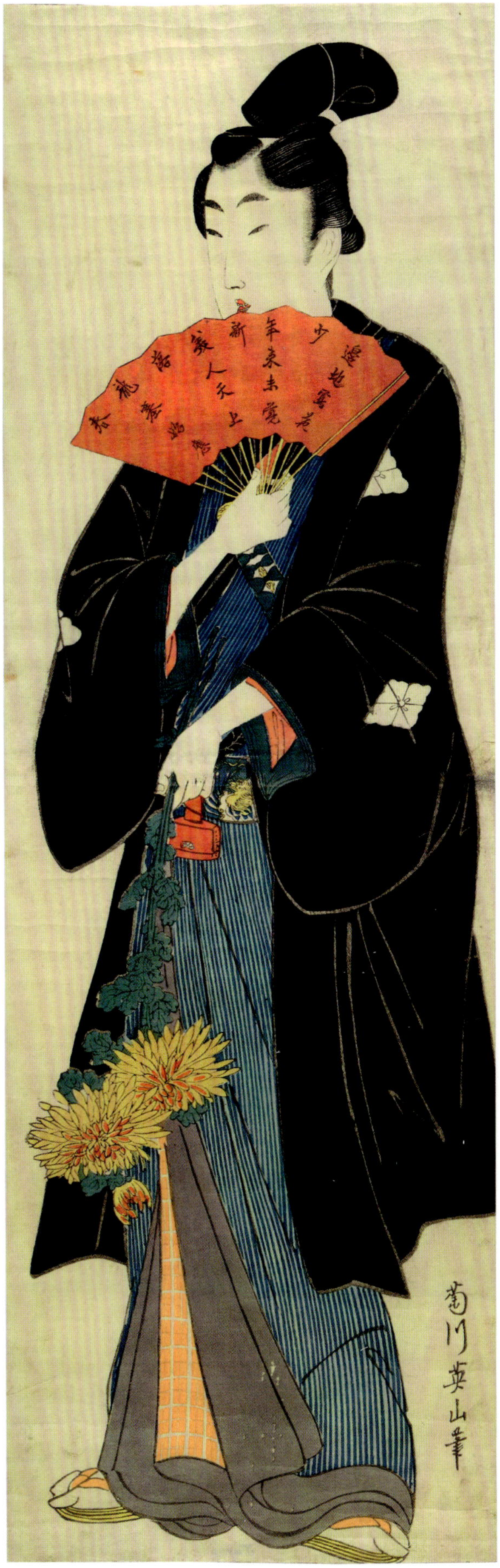

99. Kikukawa Eizen (1787–1867), *Fashionable Youth (wakashū)*.
Woodblock print, 72.2 × 23.6 cm. Edo (Tokyo), 1804–18. V&A: E.13312-1886

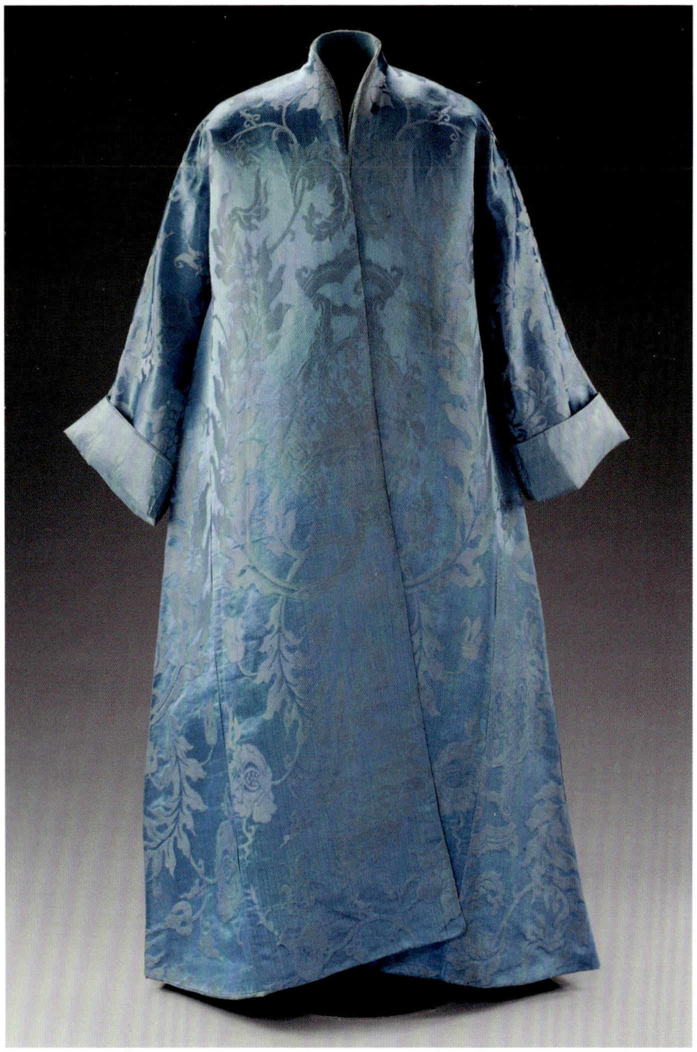

100. Night gown. Silk damask. Tailored in England or the Netherlands from imported Chinese fabric, 1690–1700. V&A: T.31-2012

CULTURAL EXCHANGE

For the Edo-period dandy wishing to absorb more exotic elements into his personal style, foreign fabrics brought to Japan by the Dutch East India Company were extremely popular. The checks and stripes that were such fashion favourites were derived from Indian fabrics, while brightly patterned cottons were especially prized. A number of men's under-kimono made from such fabric survive, but the cloth was expensive and was often cut up and used for accessories such as tobacco pouches and pipe cases. For most of the Edo period, Japan imposed a 'closed country' policy that severely restricted foreign relations. The Dutch were the only Europeans permitted to trade in the country, their headquarters being in Dejima, a tiny artificial island in Nagasaki Bay in the far south-west of the country where they were kept under close scrutiny.[8] Very few Japanese ever actually saw a Dutchman, but these 'red-haired people', or *kōmōjin*, aroused great curiosity and came to occupy a place within popular imagination as is seen in their depiction on men's fashion accessories such as *inrō* and *netsuke*.[9]

Textiles formed an important part of trade and diplomacy, and the Dutch were presented with kimono by the *shōgun* and regional lords (*daimyō*). Surviving Japanese records list kimono and kimono fabrics that formed part of the cargos loaded onto Dutch ships bound for Amsterdam, which included high-quality garments such as, in 1711: 'two Japanese figured satin silk [kimono with] gold hem embroidery' and 'three Japanese habutae [lightweight] silk kimono with foil patterns', the latter a reference to resist-dyed garments with impressed gold or silver foil.[10] The wearing of long, loose robes was not unknown in Europe, such garments being donned for informal gatherings or to provide additional warmth while sitting in a library or at a desk. The colourful, silk kimono caused an immediate stir, however, fetching high prices at East India Company auctions. Realizing the commercial opportunities for these 'Japonse Rock', as they were called in the Netherlands, the Dutch began to commission from Japan a particular style of kimono with modified sleeves and thick wadding. European robes had been lined with heavy fur, but Japanese wadding was of silk, which was wonderfully warm, soft and lightweight. It became a much sought-after commodity in its own right, as reflected in a poem of 1658 by Constantijn Huygens:[11]

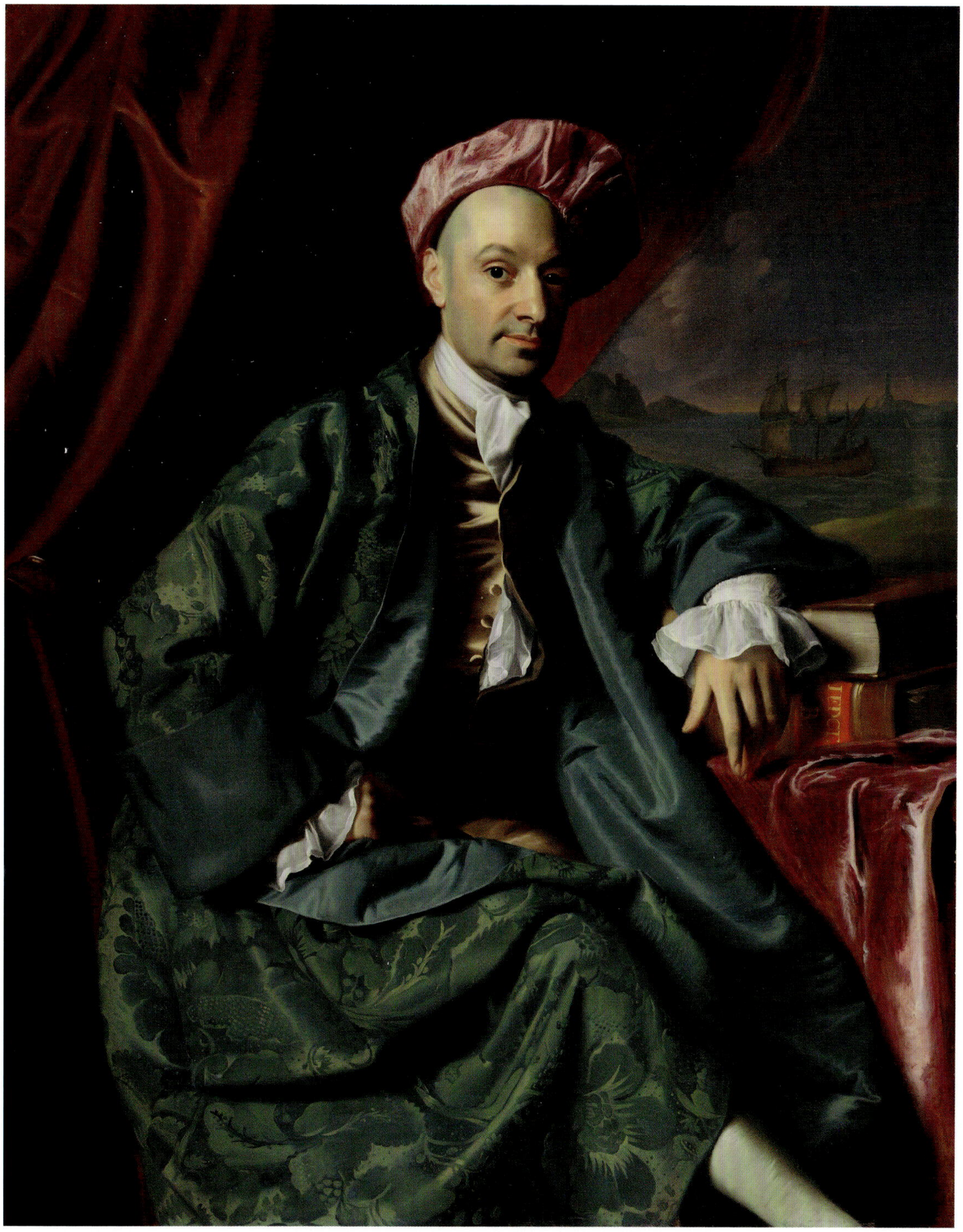

101. John Singleton Copley (1738–1815), *Nicholas Boylston*.
Oil on canvas, 127.3 cm × 101.1 cm. United States, 1767.
Harvard Art Museums, Harvard University Portrait Collection,
Bequest of Ward Nicholas Boylston to Harvard College, 1828 (H90)

I liken Kitty to Japanese wadding
Either in virtue or in weight
For both Kitty and wadding
Are very warm and very light

The Japanese could not keep pace with the demand for these garments, and the Dutch East India Company was soon commissioning robes from the Coromandel Coast of India. By 1663 specialist tailors in Amsterdam and Rotterdam were also making them from European and imported silk and the fashion for these robes soon spread throughout Europe and later America (100). Although sometimes worn by women, they were predominantly a male form of dress. Charles II seems to have started the craze in England, where the robes were called 'night gowns'. They were not for wearing in bed, but as informal garments around the home. It was certainly acceptable to wear a night gown to receive guests and to be depicted in one. Indeed, they marked one out as wealthy, stylish and cosmopolitan (101).[12]

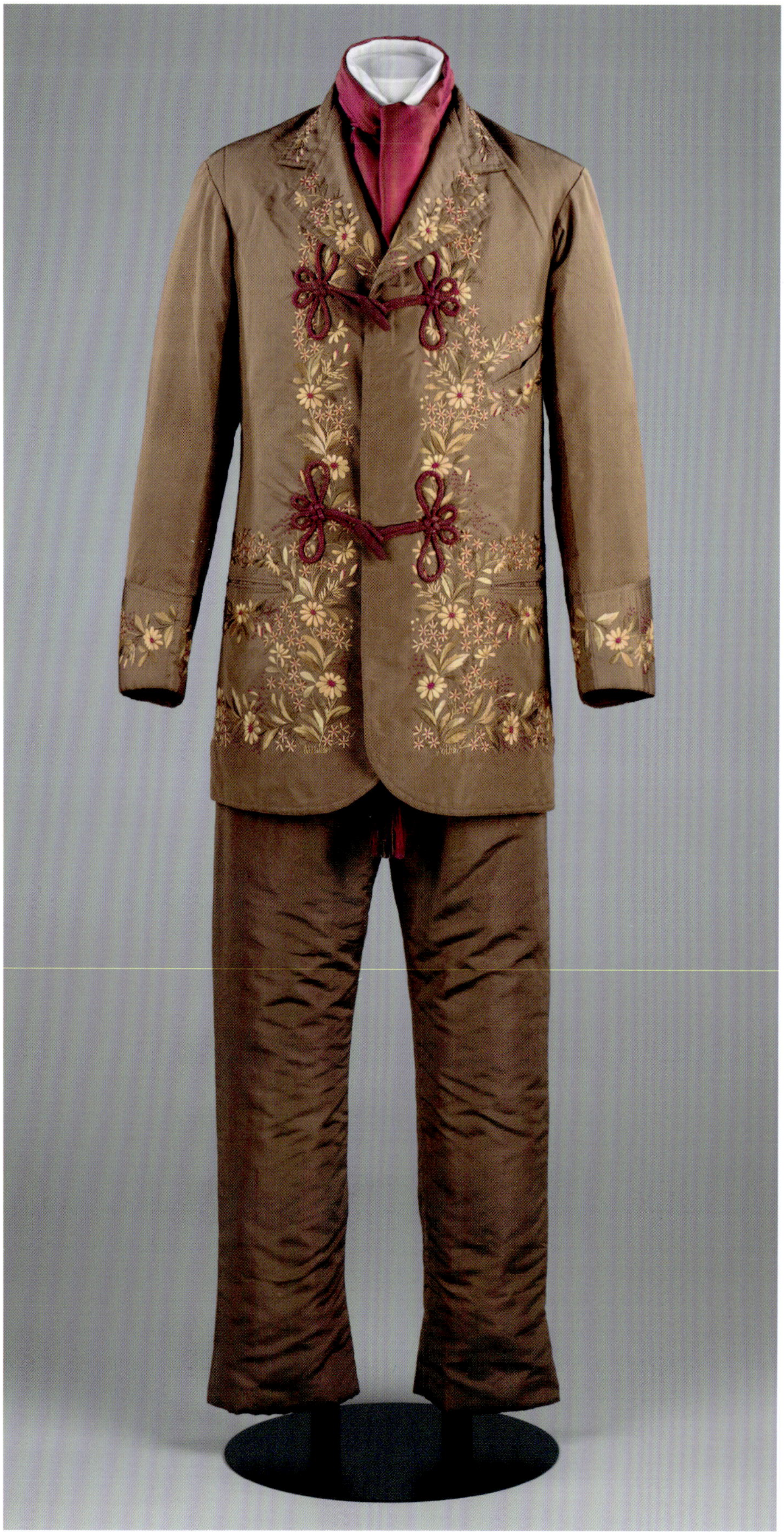

102. S. Shobey, Smoking suit. Plain weave silk, embroidery in silk threads and silk braid (kumihimo). Japan, probably Yokjohama, 1865–75.
V&A: FE.259:1,2-2020

AESTHETIC TASTES

Very few actual Japanese garments reached Europe in the seventeenth to mid-nineteenth centuries, but all this changed in the 1850s when Japan was forced to open its ports to foreign powers. This external pressure, coupled with internal unrest, led in 1868 to the overthrow of the *shōgun* and the restoration of the power of the emperor who moved his court from Kyoto to Edo, which was renamed Tokyo. Japanese silk merchants were quick to realize the potential of new markets, creating western-style garments initially for the increasing numbers of Europeans and Americans arriving in Japan, and then for direct export. Shiino Shōbei established what was arguably the world's first global fashion brand, S. Shobey, opening a shop in the treaty port of Yokohama in 1859.[13] This smoking jacket and trouser suit was probably created in his workshop (102). The shape is European, but the materials and techniques are distinctly Japanese. The layers of soft silk and fine wadding must have held the same tactile appeal as the robes that had arrived in Europe two centuries earlier, while the embroidery and braid (*kumihimo*) closures lent the jacket a similarly exotic appeal.[14] This style of male apparel indicated informality, but also suggested a loosening of the normal constraints of social behaviour and dress.

Garments from the S. Shobey Silk Store, as well as other Japanese manufacturers were sold in shops such as Liberty & Co. of London. This famous store was established by Arthur Lasenby Liberty in 1875 and catered for a growing craze for all things Japanese. Its wares attracted those eager to demonstrate a taste and lifestyle inspired by the 'art for art's sake' doctrine of the Aesthetic Movement. The culture of Japan, seemingly both traditional and avant-garde, offered artists and designers – as well as shoppers – an important alternative to established artistic canons.[15] Japanese woodblock prints, particularly erotic images (*shunga*), had a great impact on the subversive style of Aubrey Beardsley, with many of the garments worn by the figures he portrayed being reminiscent of the flowing forms of Japanese kimono. James Abbott McNeill Whistler's debt to Japan is well known, and he often depicted women wearing kimono. In the late nineteenth century it was women who generally adopted the garment, often as an indicator of an artistic, bohemian lifestyle. While it is tempting to think of Beardsley and Whistler as wearers of kimono, any evidence is yet to come to light.[16] Whistler's pupil Mortimer Menpes, however, was photographed wearing a kimono while painting in his home in Cadogan Square, designed in Japanese style by Arthur Heygate Mackmurdo in 1888, and incorporating elements the artist had brought back from

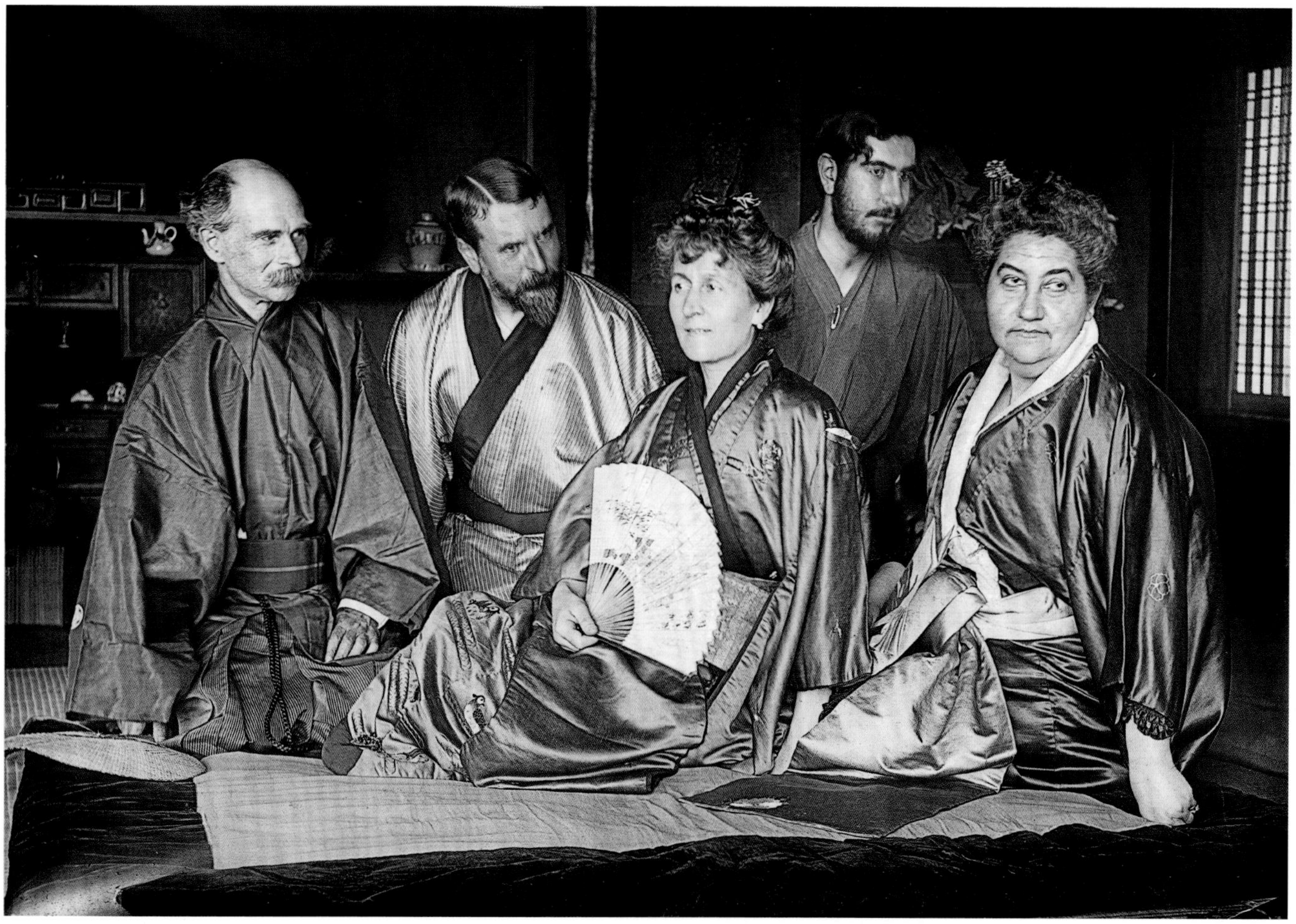

103. Hugues Krafft (1853–1935), Siegfried Bing, Louis Gonse, Mme Roujon, Emmanuel Gonse and Mme Gonse at Midori-no-sato. Photograph. France, 9 July 1899. Krafft Archives, Collection de la Société des Amis du Vieux Reims, Musée Le Vergeur, Reims

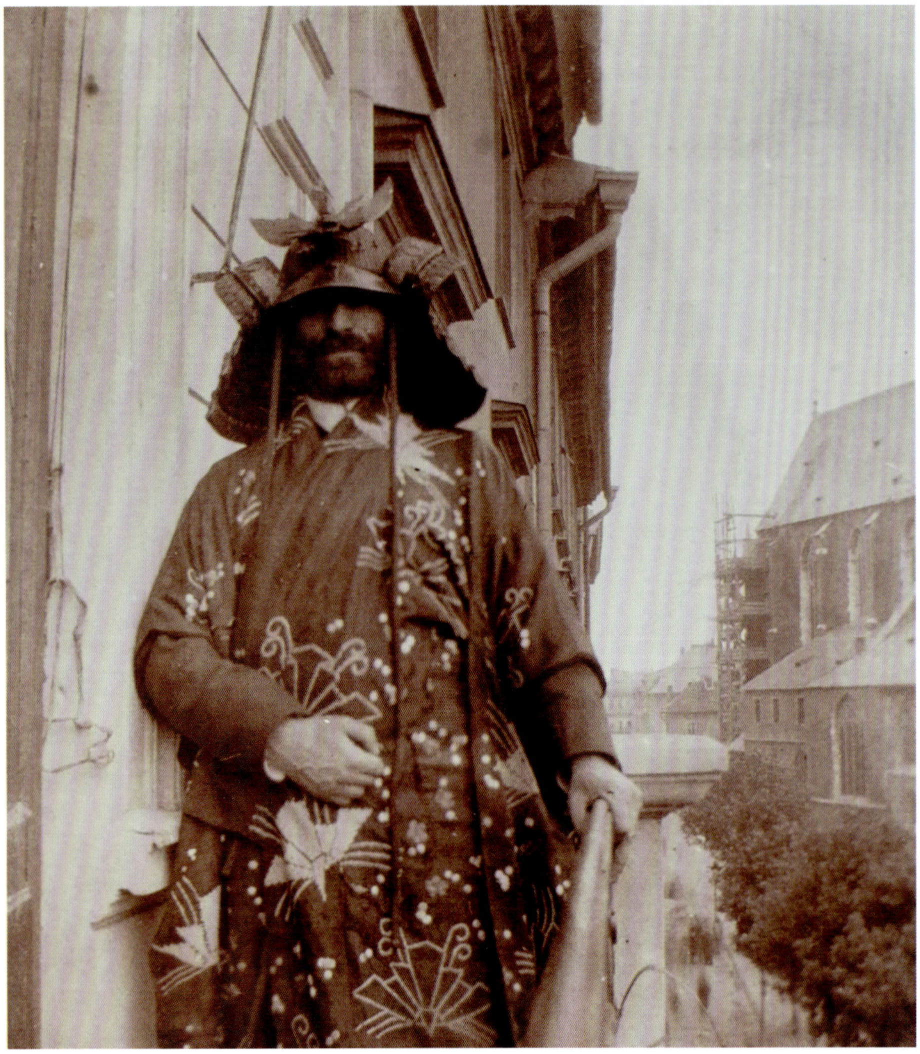

104. Feliks Jasieński on the balcony of his apartment in Krakow, 1903–4

Japan the previous year.[17] French photographer Hugues Krafft also visited Japan in the 1880s, returning with an entire house, which Japanese craftsmen installed for him in Reims. At Midori-no-sato, as it was called, Krafft lived – and dressed – in Japanese style. In 1899 noted dealer of Japanese art Siegfried Bing was photographed there with other Japanese enthusiasts including writer and collector Louis Gonse. All are wearing kimono (103). Bing's garment is fastened close to the neck perhaps with a safety pin, suggesting a seriousness of dedication to Japanese culture rather different from that of British aesthetes, for whom such a style denoted an artful decadence.[18] Feliks Jasieński was also a noted collector of Japanese art, and a leading figure of Krakow's bohemian milieu. His eccentric personality is captured in one photograph that shows him on the balcony of his apartment wearing pieces from his own collection: a samurai helmet and a woman's kimono, in red, from a wedding ensemble (104).[19] The kimono offered a way of dressing that allowed liberation from the restrictions of western clothing. For women, this meant potential freedom from corsets; for men, the enveloping garment with its flowing lines negated the tight, angularity of their customary style of dress.

STYLE AND CONFORMITY

A close friend and neighbour of Whistler, diplomat Algernon Mitford, had served in the British Legation in Japan in the 1860s. Back in London he helped create one of the most fanciful, and enduring, images of Japan, advising Sir William Schwenck Gilbert and Sir Arthur Seymour Sullivan on their 1885 production *The Mikado*. Recalling an event during a further visit to Japan in 1906 when he and British guests wore kimono, Mitford observed that 'a more comfortable dress it would be difficult to find, cool in summer and cosy in winter.' He goes on to ask: 'why did the Japanese abandon it for our clumsy costume?'[20] Dress was a very visible symbol of difference as the government of the new emperor sought to establish Japan as a modern nation equal to any of the West. In September 1871 the emperor proclaimed that:

> The national polity is firm, but manners and customs should be adaptable. We greatly regret that the uniform of our court has been established following the Chinese custom, and it has become exceedingly effeminate in style and character...

> The Emperor Jimmu, who founded Japan, and the Empress Jingu, who conquered Korea, were not attired in the present style. We should no longer appear before the people in these effeminate styles. We have therefore decided to reform dress regulations entirely.[21]

With this statement the emperor distanced his court from Japan's seriously weakened continental neighbour, implied that he was a firm and masculine ruler and established a connection between western dress and that worn by heroic figures from the country's mythical history. The suggestion that the imperial court's adoption of European clothing was somehow more 'Japanese' created continuity with the past and made the enormous transformations of the present a little less daunting. Courtiers thus abandoned the high lacquered caps and wide-sleeved robes they had worn for centuries in favour of formal western clothing. The Meiji emperor first appeared publicly in western dress in 1872 and was subsequently always depicted, in photographs and popular prints, in European-style uniform.

There was no sudden nor wholesale acceptance of western dress in Japan, but as the government sought to transform Japan, items of European apparel became useful symbols of allegiance to the state cause. Men started to wear leather shoes, bowler hats, capes and umbrellas with kimono, the adoption of foreign accessories being easier, and cheaper, than wearing an entire outfit. In 1860 the social reformer Fukuzawa Yukichi had accompanied Japan's first delegation abroad, travelling to Europe and the United States. Members of the delegation wore Japanese dress, which caused much curiosity and helped to brand them, Fukuzawa feared, as picturesque rather than as a nation to be taken seriously. Travelling again to Europe in 1862 and America in 1867, Fukuzawa became an expert on all matters western. His first book, *Conditions of the West (Seiyō jijō)*, was published in 1866 and *Western Clothing, Food and Homes (Seiyō ishokujū)* in 1867, on the eve of the Meiji restoration. The latter, which included illustrations and a phrasebook, advised readers on how to eat, dress and even urinate in western style (105).[22]

By the 1880s, full western garb had been adopted in the public arena by men of the new elite. Even in rural areas, where changes were less dramatic, farmers would have a western suit for smart occasions. This new form of dress was called a *sebiro* – a transliteration of 'Savile Row'. Most men however, would change into kimono when they were in the privacy of their own homes. Women, by contrast, who predominantly occupied the domestic sphere, continued to wear kimono and came to embody traditional

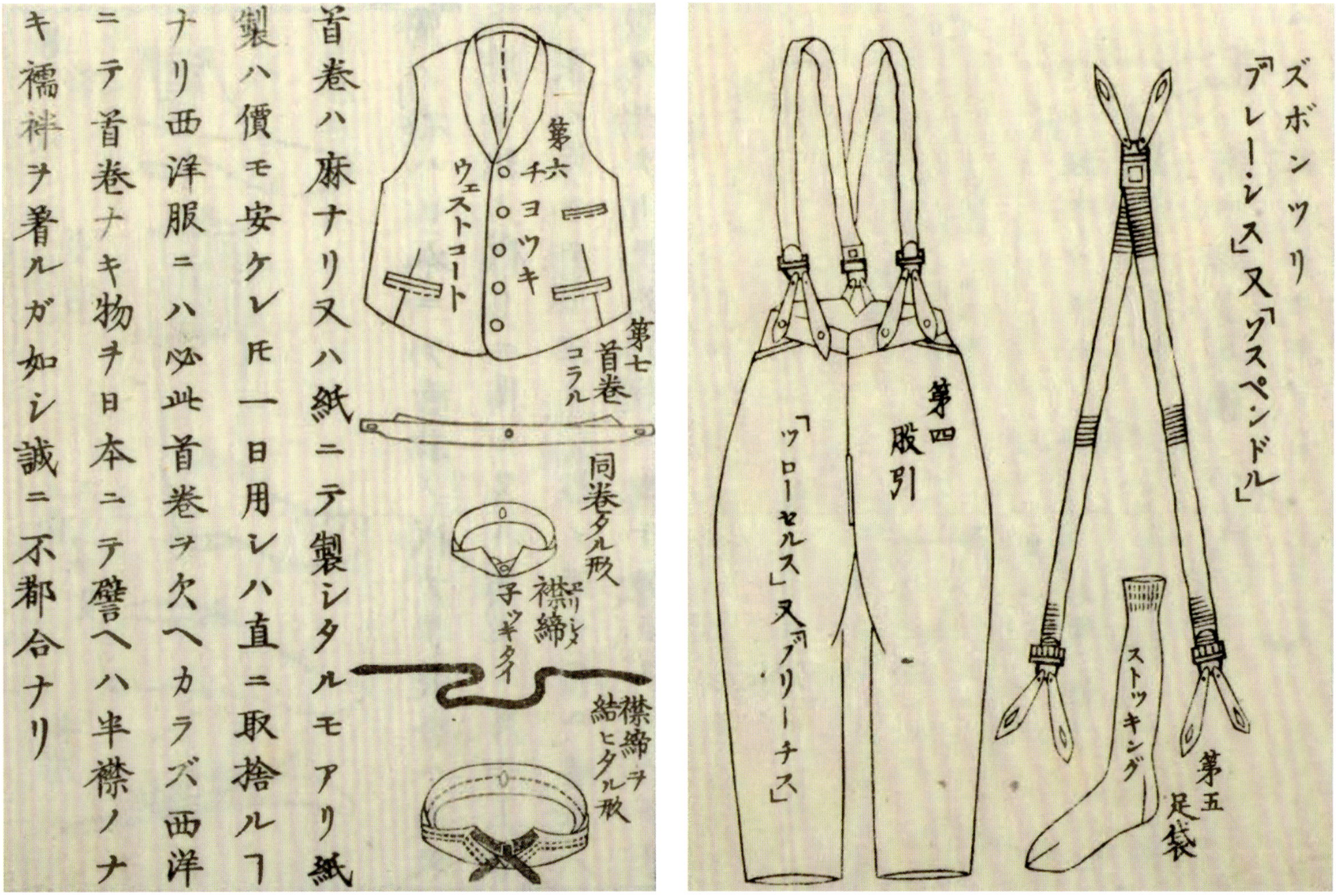

105. Fukuzawa Yukichi (1835–1901), *Western Clothing, Food and Homes* (Japan, 1867). Keiō University Library, Tokyo

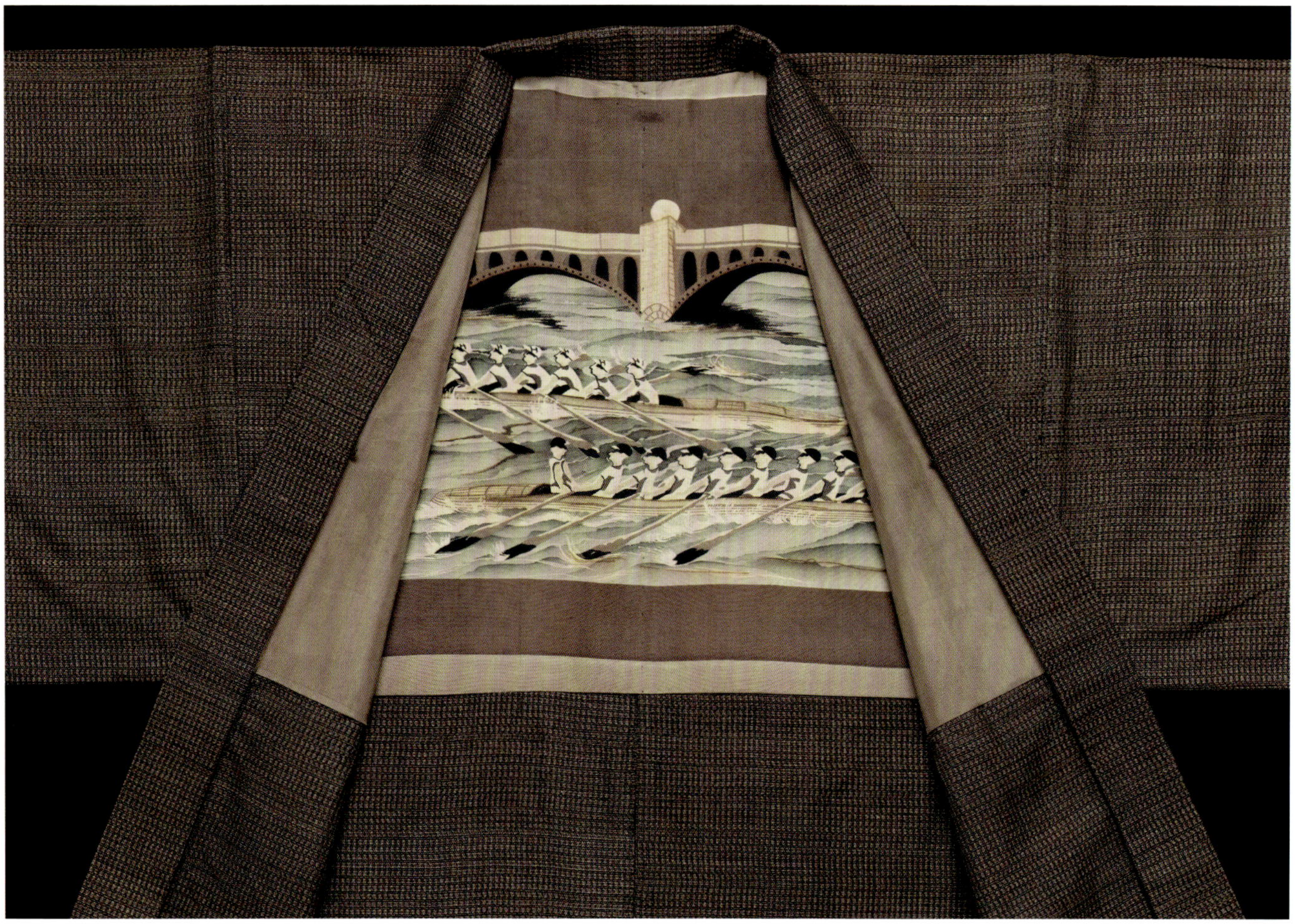

106. Haori (kimono jacket). Silk with selectively pre-dyed yarns (*kasuri*) with printed lining of plain weave silk. Japan, 1920–40. V&A: FE.27-2016

Japanese values. Even into the twentieth century, some men continued to wear Japanese clothing. Male dress was still characterized by sober colours and subtle patterning, yet a subdued exterior could hide a more exuberant interior. Thus the Edo-period fashion for using vibrant, but hidden, designs endured, with linings for men's kimono jackets (*haori*) and under-kimono (*juban*) often bearing images inspired by modern life. Such designs are known as *omoshirogara*, which roughly translates as 'novelty designs'. Motifs such as aeroplanes, skyscrapers, jazz bars and sporting activity, all symbols of Japan's progress and modernity, became increasingly popular. This *haori* lining features an image of a boat race between Keiō University and Waseda University on the Sumida River in Tokyo, an event modelled on the annual Oxford and Cambridge race on the River Thames in London (106).[23]

THE KIMONO RESURGENCE

Until recently, it seemed such garments might mark the last echo of Edo-period sensibilities in Japanese menswear. After the Second World War, the wearing of kimono declined dramatically. The garment ceased to be a form of everyday clothing and became instead a revered symbolic costume. The association of the garment with conservative femininity was reinforced and it became rare to see a man in a kimono. Although the indigenous fashion culture had lost its vitality in Japan, the kimono continued to have a wide-ranging influence internationally. Japan is often seen as a place where past and future happily coexist, giving its dress styles a timelessness and ambiguity that proved attractive for performers.[24] Like a modern-day *kabukimono*, flamboyant performer Freddie Mercury used kimono to challenge notions of gender and sexuality, while the kabuki theatre influenced David Bowie when crafting his futuristic alter ego Ziggy Stardust, created in collaboration with Japanese designer Kansai Yamamoto. Yamamoto has related his work to *basara*, a Japanese aesthetic concept of the Muromachi period (1336–1573), which connotes eccentricity and a lack of restraint. The designer's extravagant and colourful patterning is certainly in stark contrast to the work of his contemporaries Rei Kawakubo, Issey Miyake and Yohji Yamamoto, whose pioneering designs caused such a seismic shift in 1980s European fashion. Although each is unique in approach, these designers share a collective debt to historic Japanese dress, manifested through innovative forms that are not related or subordinate to the shape of the body. Yohji Yamamoto's fluid modernism is seen in his menswear collections, which feature unstructured suits, ambiguous silhouettes and layers of cloth that drape and sway, revealing Edo-style glimpses of unex-

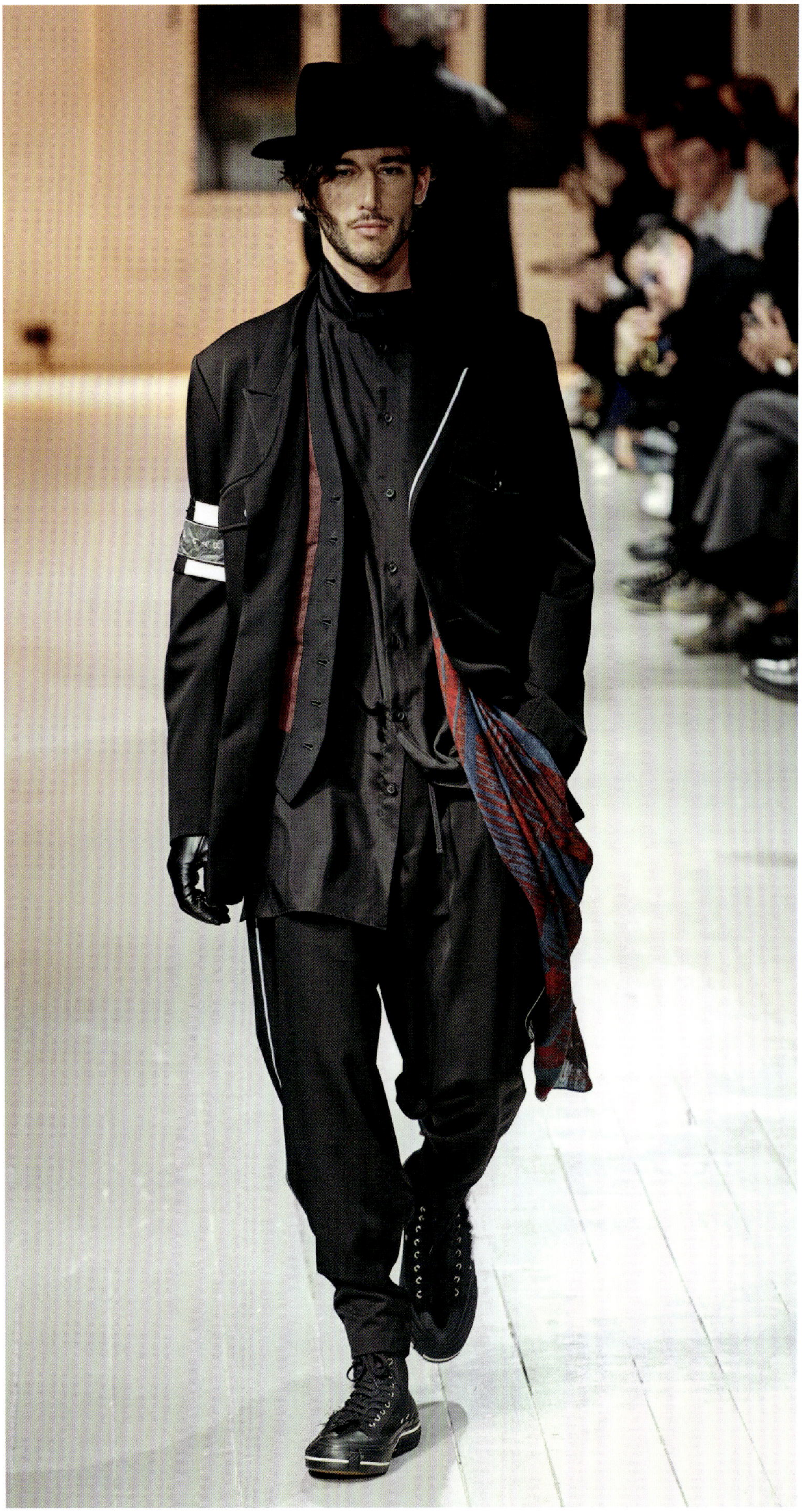

107. Yohji Yamamoto (1943–), Ensemble. Autumn/Winter 2020.
Model: Lou Gaillot

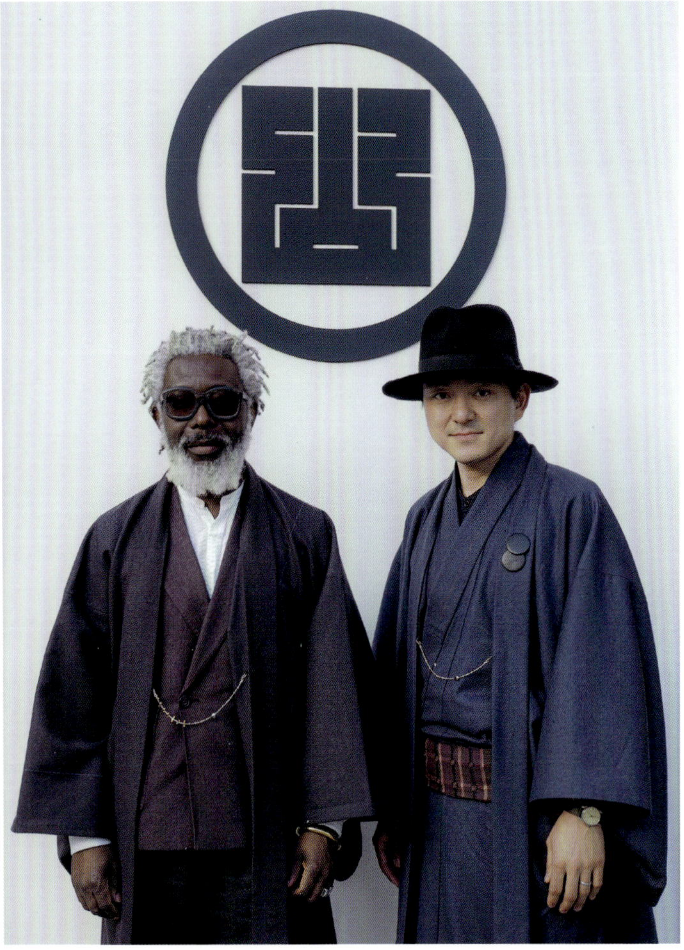

108. T-Michael and Takayuki Yajima, Director of Y & Sons, in T-Kimono ensemble, Tokyo, 2017. Courtesy of Y & Sons

pected colour (107). The designer has always sought to dissolve gender distinctions in fashion. This is also true of the kimono range he created in 2005 for Chiso, to mark this celebrated Kyoto textile firm's 450th anniversary.

Japan is currently witnessing a kimono revival as a younger generation adopts the garment as an item of fashionable dress once again. Photographer and stylist Akira Times is dedicated to breaking down the barriers of kimono conservatism, his self portraits recording his own inventive and often irreverent style (109). Akira mixes vintage and contemporary kimono, the latter from a new wave of designers who approach the creation of kimono in fresh and sometimes subversive ways. Some cater particularly for the growing men's market. Fujikiya Mikisuke tailors kimono of pinstripe fabric to be worn with a shirt and tie as business attire; Ueoka Tarō, founder of Robe Japonica, has brought colour back to men's kimono; and Hyōgō Sōyu, with his brand Wazigen Shizukuya, seeks to restore a sense of samurai swagger to Japanese male dress. The kimono has always transcended cultural and geographic borders, and this is seen in the T-Kimono range, a collaboration between Norwegian designer T-Michael and the Japanese company Y & Sons, a subsidiary of major kimono retailer Yamato. Echoing the understated elegance of Edo-period men's dress, the aim is to make kimono a staple in the modern man's wardrobe (108). The brand increasingly appeals to women as well as men, and indeed a number of kimono makers, from the catwalk designer Jōtarō Saitō to the independent studio Rumi Rock, are consciously making garments that are less binary.

The gender fluidity of the kimono is one reason for its growing influence on western fashion. Tom Stubbs, writing in the British men's magazine *GQ* in 2018, described the garments as 'simultaneously classic and modern, their draped style is at the intersection of where elegance and sophisticated fabric meet minimal restriction. Factor in they're gender-fluid and can command dressy evening clout without looking remotely stuffy and *kapow*!'[25]

The old stereotypes of Japanese men in kimono as old-fashioned and non-Japanese men in kimono as disreputable are now being broken. Hopefully the garment will continue to challenge the conventional constraints of masculine fashion, offering instead more fluid possibilities for creative individualism.

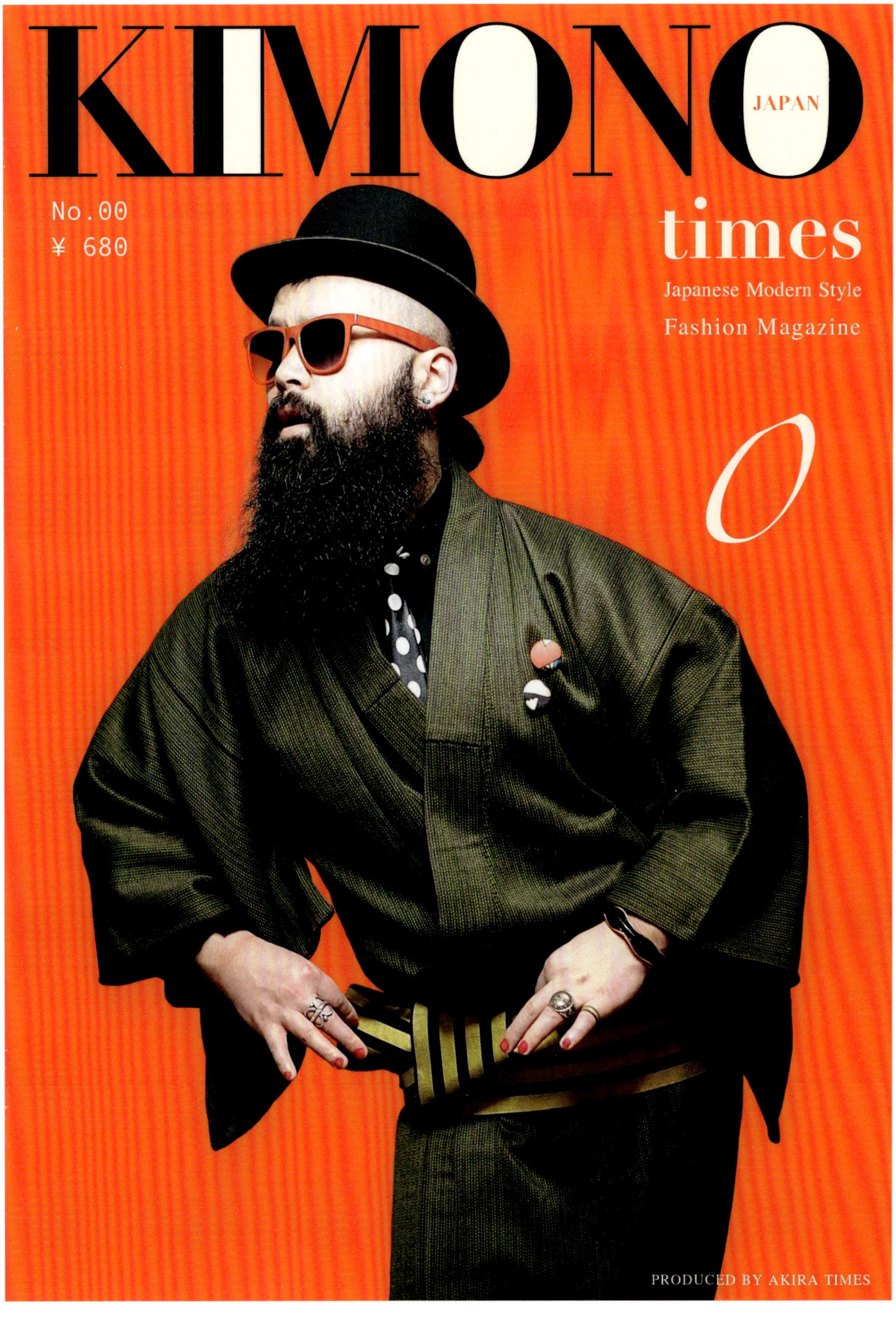

109. Akira Times (1980–), *Kimono Times – Japan* (February 2013)

ORLANDO AS A BOYETTE

ROSALIND McKEVER

> Vain trifles as they seem, clothes have, they say,
> more important offices than merely to keep us warm.
> [...] In every human being a vacillation from one sex
> to the other takes place, and often it is only the
> clothes that keep the male or female likeness,
> while underneath the sex is the very opposite of
> what it is above.[1]

In Virginia Woolf's 1928 novel, *Orlando: A Biography*, the eponymous s/hero travels through time, gender and a wardrobe tailored accordingly. At the start of the story, Orlando is a young man of fashion but, halfway through, he awakes to discover 'he was a woman'. Orlando's previously easy movement through life is impeded by social constraints that find form in 'coiling' skirts and 'dragging' crinolines. Flouting social convention and biblical proscription, Lady Orlando regularly dresses in her younger self's masculine apparel.[2]

Orlando is fiction styled as biography. It is also a love letter to, and portrait of, Vita Sackville-West. Woolf even illustrated the book with portraits of Sackville-West's aristocratic ancestors, irreverently captioned 'Orlando as a Boy' and 'Orlando as Ambassador', and photographs of Vita herself as Lady Orlando. Sackville-West regularly adopted masculine clothing, and sometimes with it the masculine identity 'Julian'. She had done so since April 1918 when she first donned the breeches worn by women in the Land Army and – experiencing 'unaccustomed freedom' – discovered the masculine as well as feminine elements of her gender, and her bisexuality.[3]

When Woolf was writing *Orlando* in 1927–8, the connection between women in masculine dress and sexuality was not yet fixed in public perception. This process had begun by the time it was published, due to the obscenity trial of another novel, *The Well of Loneliness* (1928). This brought into circulation photographs of its author Radclyffe Hall, with her short 'shingle' haircut and elegant tailored jacket in watered silk, and cigarette and monocle in hand (110).[4] Before it exemplified 1930s lesbian chic, Hall's aesthetic was high fashion. British magazines of the mid-1920s instructed their readers – many of whom had worn masculine attire for their wartime work – on how to dress as a 'boyette'.[5] In Paris the style was known as *la garçonne* – the title of Victor Margueritte's 1922 novel about a liberated young woman.[6] Gabrielle Chanel wore clothing borrowed from her male lovers and designed practical and elegant trousers and tailoring for women.[7]

Orlando articulates the layered motivations and connotations of real-life women adopting masculine dress in the late 1920s. The novel's chronological trajectory also intimates the subversive sartorial history of boyettes *avant la lettre* – from English Renaissance queens to Harlem Renaissance drag kings – who adopt masculine clothing for safety and adventure, expression and disguise, acquiescence to, and rebellion against, patriarchal and heteronormative conventions.

HE – FOR THERE COULD BE NO DOUBT OF HIS SEX, THOUGH THE FASHION OF THE TIME DID SOMETHING TO DISGUISE IT.

Woolf's novel begins in the mid- to late sixteenth century, and the name Orlando references two Renaissance texts in which transvestism destabilizes gender roles: Ludovico Ariosto's epic poem *Orlando Furioso* (1532) and William Shakespeare's play *As You Like It* (1599). In the latter, Orlando is a young man in love with the duchess Rosalind. Forced to flee into the forest of Arden, Rosalind dresses like a man for safety, and in her male guise of Ganymede teaches Orlando how to woo his beloved. In the theatre this genderplay and its homoerotic undercurrents were amplified as roles like Rosalind, and Jessica in *The Merchant of Venice* (1605) who adopts 'the lovely garnish of a boy', were played by men playing women playing men. In Jessica's sixteenth-century Venice, breeches were commonly worn by courtesans under their skirts, as seen in prints by Pietro Bertelli, with a flap for the viewer to lift (111).[8] This attire was somewhat pragmatic for a courtesan, and certainly arousing for a clientele for whom young men, as well as women, were objects of lust.

The sartorial gender ambiguity of the late 1500s is alluded to by the opening words of Woolf's novel; the tumescent codpieces of earlier in the century had receded and men's formerly short jackets and tight hose swelled in tandem with women's farthingale skirts. The fashion favoured by young men of the European courts like Orlando was captured in a portrait of Prince Alessandro Farnese at 15 by Sofonisba Anguissola, a painter particularly attuned to dress (112). Her skill in picking out the intricate embellishment of Farnese's cape equalled that of the men – and exceptional women like Francesca di Giesù – who wove such ornate textiles, and to whose work Anguissola's contemporaries compared her.[9] Women working in male-dominated professions often donned a mantle of masculinity. In her self portraits, Anguissola usually wears black, an expensive-to-produce colour worn chiefly by noblemen like her father, and advised for courtiers by Baldassare

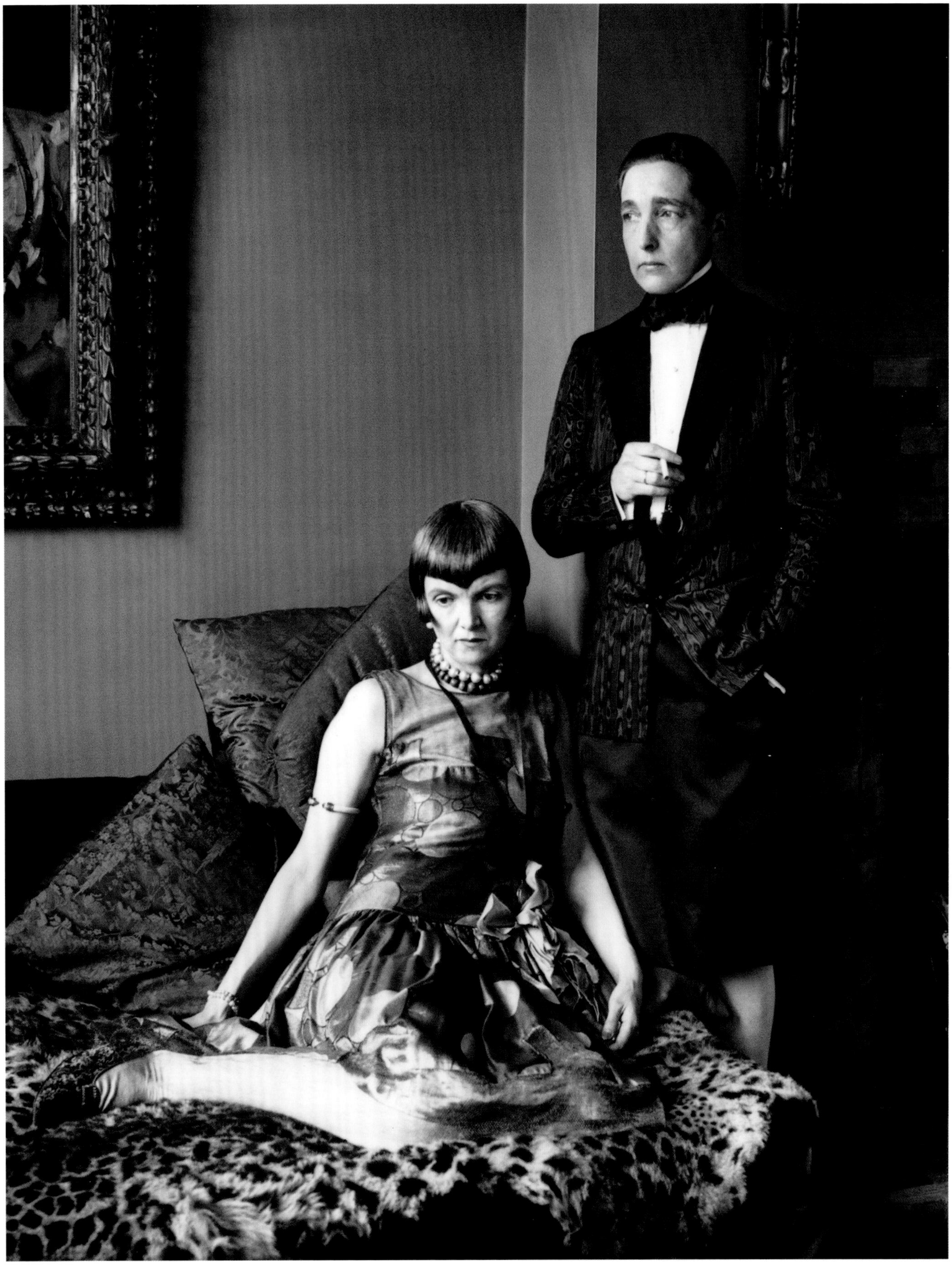

110. Radclyffe Hall (right) and Lady Una Troubridge, London, 1927

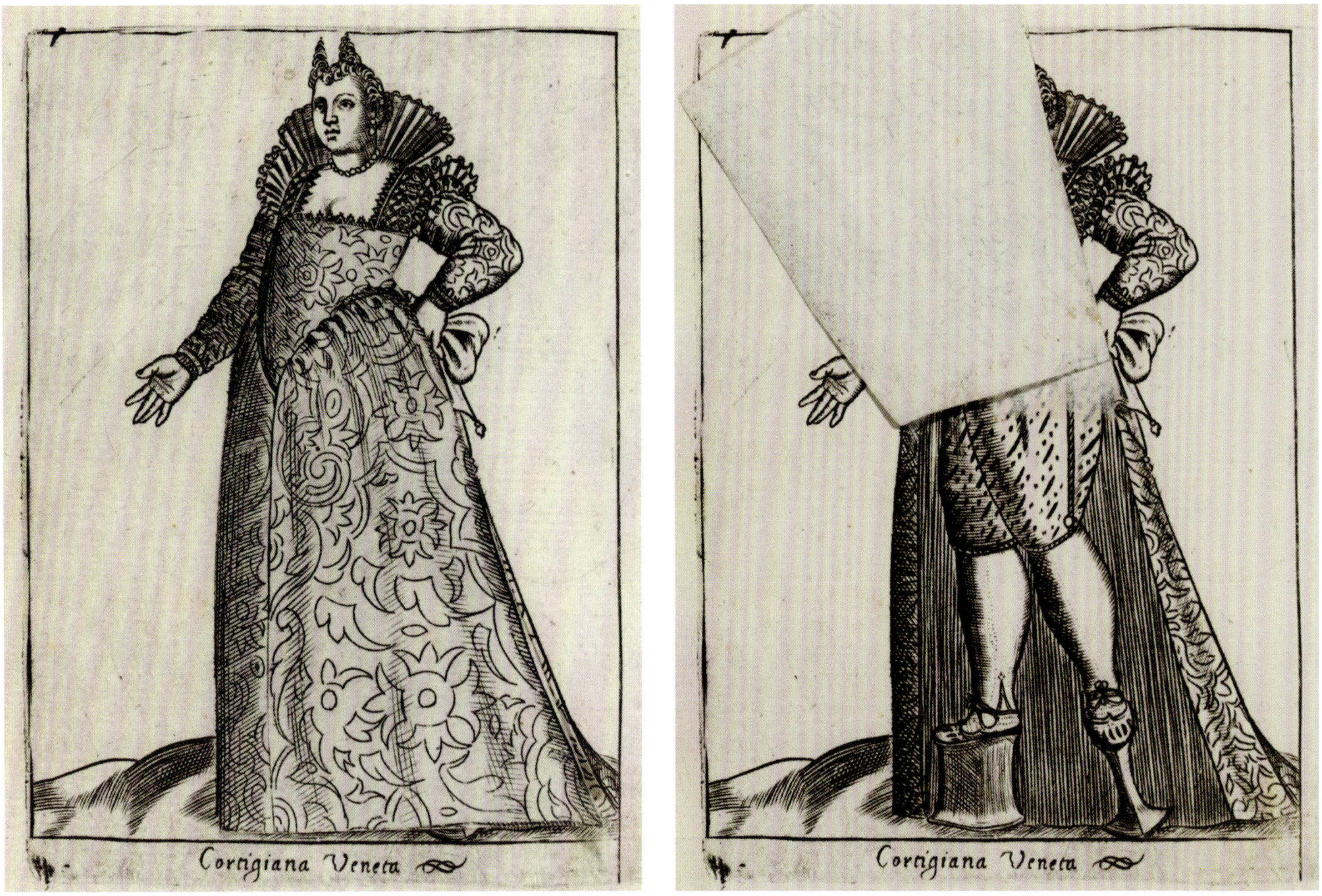

111. Pietro Bertelli (active 1571–1621), 'Cortigiana Veneta', *Diversarum nationum habitus* (Padua, 1589). V&A: National Art Library 87.D.21

Castiglione and for artists by Anguissola's contemporary Paolo Pino. By wearing black Anguissola, who worked at the Spanish court, demonstrated her social and professional status while making no attempt at disguise.[10]

In the same period, Queen Elizabeth I, who features in Woolf's novel, had to square her self-presentation as the Virgin Queen with the perceived masculinity of the monarchy. She purportedly dressed androgynously when making her famous speech at Tilbury in 1588 in which she declared: 'I know I have the body butt of a weake and feble woman, butt I have the harte and stomack of a king, and of a king of England too.'[11] For her subjects, Elizabeth prized the power of a dress code. She issued more edicts against 'excess of apparel', dictating who could wear what by class and gender boundaries, than any other British monarch.[12] The aim was to eradicate confusion about social status, but an unintended result was that ambiguity itself became fashionable. By the end of the century, many writers had documented the fashion for women wearing clothing previously considered the purview of men, and court cases record that women of all classes were involved.[13]

THERE IS MUCH TO SUPPORT THE VIEW THAT IT IS CLOTHES THAT WEAR US AND NOT WE THEM; WE MAY MAKE THEM TAKE THE MOULD OF ARM OR BREAST, BUT THEY MOULD OUR HEARTS, OUR BRAINS, OUR TONGUES TO THEIR LIKING.

When Orlando wakes up in the seventeenth century, his preoccupations are literary rather than sartorial. Writers in the 1610s sought new words like 'ganimeds' and 'girleboyes' for the spreading phenomenon of women opting for the new century's less restrictive menswear.[14] *Roaring Girl,* a play based on the true story of legendary highway woman Moll Cutpurse (real name Mary Frith), and *Hic Mulier* (Latin for 'masculine woman'), a satirical pamphlet, were both illustrated with prints showing their protagonists in masculine attire, linking their clothing choices to lascivious and violent behaviour. The perceived connection led to harsh punishments for many women who braved breeches in the seventeenth century, even death sentences.[15]

High-status women, however, had greater freedom in their attire, and none more so than Christina Vasa, the Swedish monarch who increasingly dressed in masculine clothing after abdicating in June 1654. Christina's biological sex, sexuality and gender presentation have been the sub-

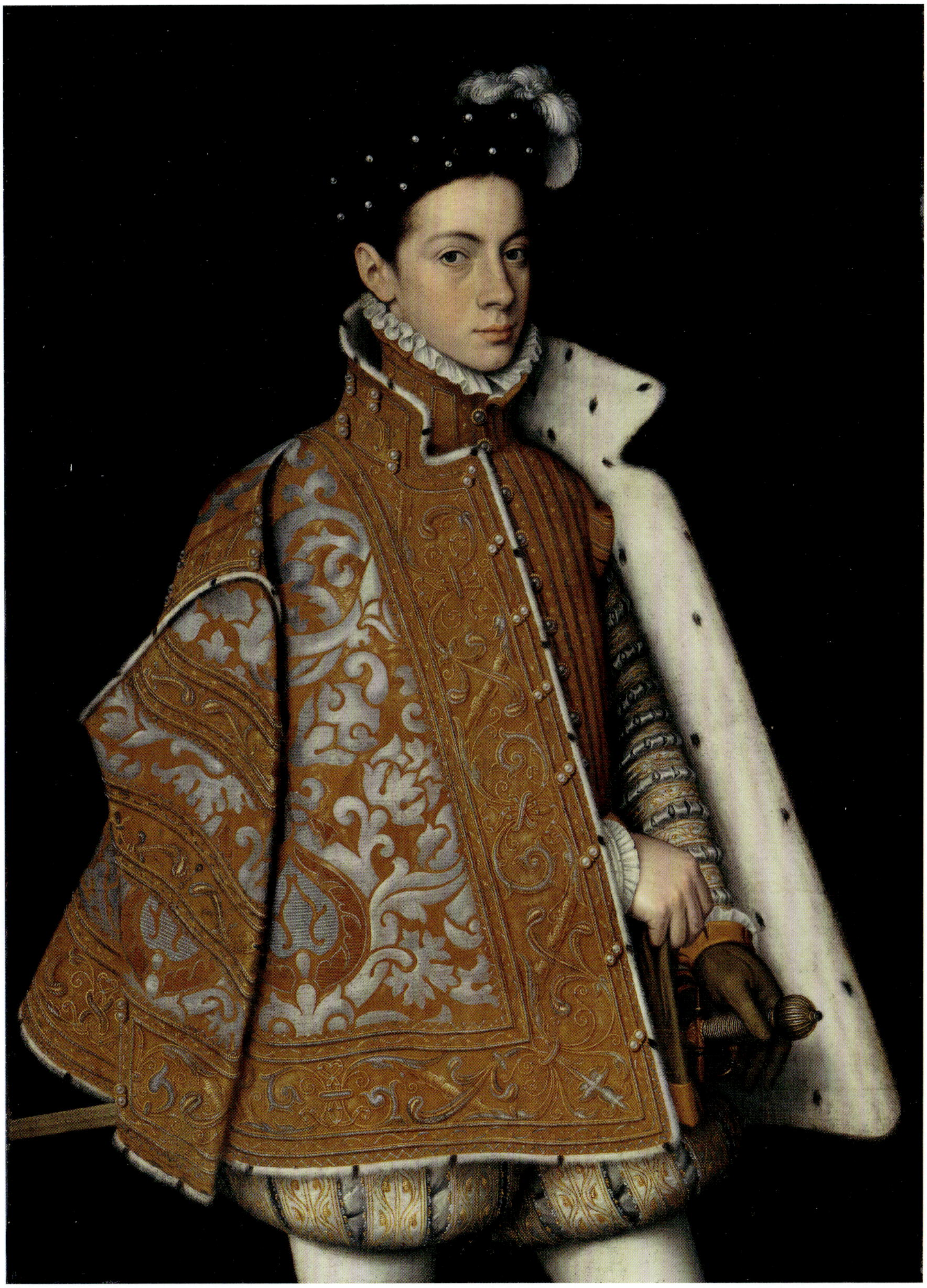

112. Sofonisba Anguissola (*c.*1532–1625), *Prince Alessandro Farnese*.
Oil on canvas, 107×79 cm. Spain, *c.*1560.
National Gallery of Ireland, Dublin: NGI.17

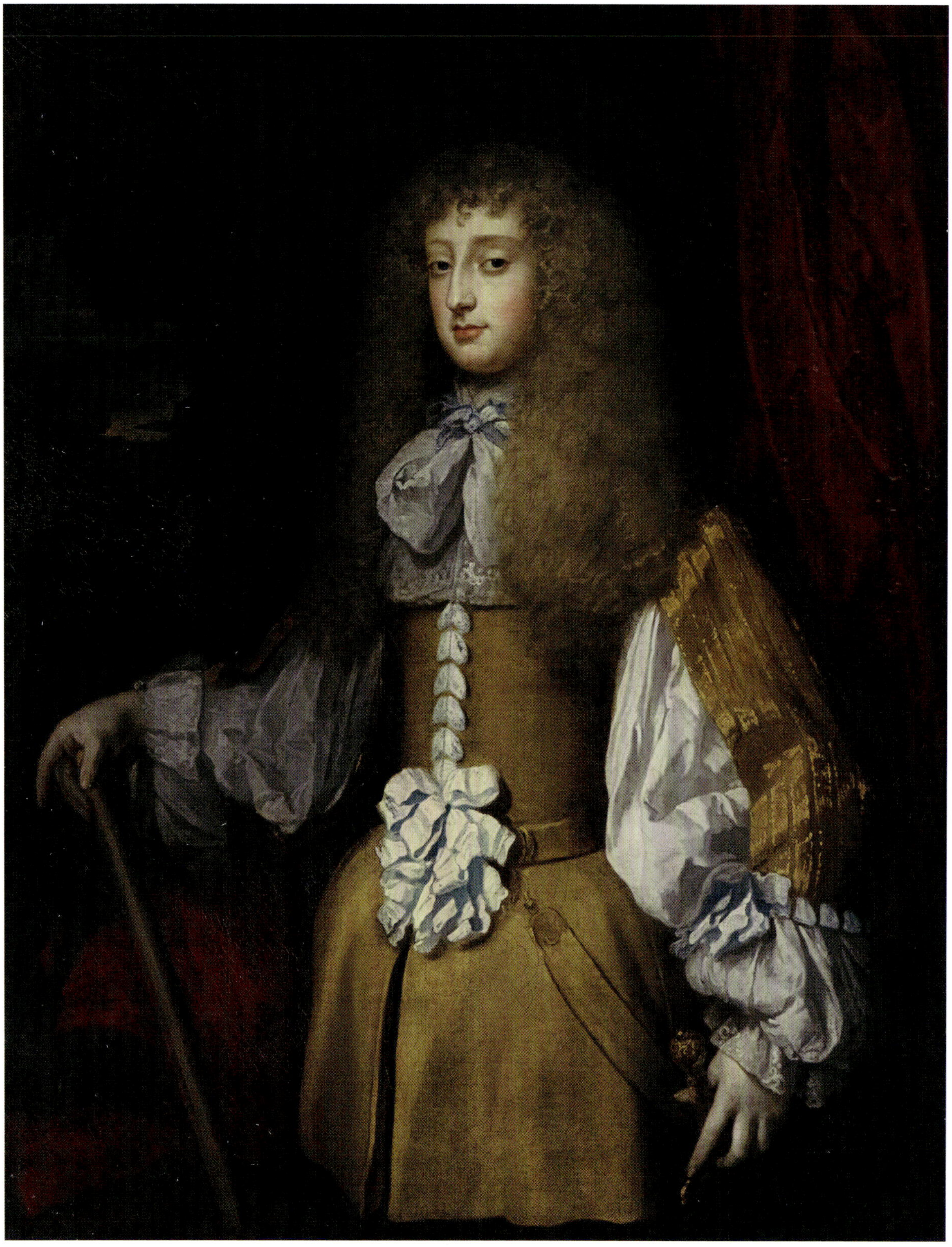

113. Jacob Huysmans (*c.*1633–1696), *Frances Stewart, later Duchess of Richmond*.
Oil on canvas, 127.7 × 104.4 cm. Great Britain, *c.*1664.
Royal Collection Trust: RCIN 405876

ject of much speculation. Her lifelong aversion to women's clothing was related also to her upbringing and lifestyle, and her need to establish her authority.[16] This convergence is evident in portraits of 1653 by court painter Sébastien Bourdon. In one she appears swathed in black (the dominant colour in her wardrobe) with a white blouse fastened at the collar with a black ribbon, a detail common to masculine dress at her court (120).[17] In another, an equestrian portrait commissioned by Philip IV of Spain, she wears riding attire that appears masculine from the waist up, but her side-saddle pose and full skirts signal her gender.[18] She continued to don riding clothing following her abdication, wearing it with men's shirts and shoes, and receiving special dispensation from the Pope to do so.[19]

The following decade, masculine riding clothes became fashionable for English women. In June 1666 diarist Samuel Pepys logged his disapproval:

> Walking here in the galleries I find the Ladies of Honour dressed in their riding garbs, with coats and doublets with deep skirts, just for all the world like mine, and buttoned their doublets up the breast, with perriwigs and with hats; so that, only for a long petticoat dragging under their men's coats, nobody could take them for women in any point whatever; which was an odde sight, and a sight did not please me.[20]

Pepys's discomfort at this encounter contradicts his earlier praise for Jacob Huysmans's portrait of Frances Stewart, a legendary court beauty with whom Charles II was infatuated, wearing a soldier's buff coat and with her left hand fondling the hilt of her sword (113).[21] The portrait tantalizingly stops at the bottom of the coat, denying a glimpse of whether the sitter – rendered androgynous by her garb and wig – is dressed in decorous skirts or seditious breeches. In 1667 one of the first female actors, Nell Gwyn, played her first 'breeches role', the cross-dressing Florimel in John Dryden's *Secret Love, or the Maiden Queen*, and received great praise from Pepys. In so doing Gwyn showed off her legs, subverted theatrical norms and reiterated the fashionability of masculine attire for women at the English court, where she would soon become mistress to Charles II.[22]

IT IS A STRANGE FACT BUT A TRUE ONE, THAT UP TO THIS MOMENT SHE HAD SCARCELY GIVEN HER SEX A THOUGHT. PERHAPS THE TURKISH TROUSERS WHICH SHE HAD HITHERTO WORN HAD DONE SOMETHING TO DISTRACT HER THOUGHTS.

As ambassador to Constantinople in the late seventeenth century, Orlando dresses in Turkish attire. This includes the amply cut trousers worn by men and women in parts of south-east Europe, the Middle East and South Asia, known in Turkey as *şalvar*. Awaking as a woman, Orlando's clothing, and identity, is unchanged. Locating these events in Turkey is indicative of Woolf's exoticized view of gender and gendered dress outside Europe as being more fluid. Her orientalism is a repetition, or more generously a parody, of that of the woman who first brought Turkish trousers to Britain: Lady Mary Wortley Montagu.[23]

In the late 1710s, mere decades after Orlando's fictional period as envoy, Montagu was in Turkey as wife of the ambassador to Constantinople. She wrote home about her experiences in letters that would be published posthumously.[24] In 1717 she told her sister, Lady Mar, about her clothing:

> I am now in my Turkish habit… The first piece of my dress is a pair of drawers, very full, that reach to my shoes and conceal the legs more modestly than your petticoats. They are of a thin rose-coloured damask brocaded with silver flowers, my shoes of white kid leather embroidered with gold. Over this hangs my smock of a fine white silk gauze edged with embroidery. This smock has wide sleeves hanging halfway down the arm and is closed at the neck with a diamond button, but the shape and colour of the bosom very well to be distinguished through it. The *antery* [*entari*] is a waistcoat made close to the shape, of white and gold damask, with very long sleeves falling back and fringed with deep gold fringe, and should have diamond or pearl buttons.[25]

Montagu's description translates her new wardrobe into the vocabulary of British menswear, suggesting that she felt herself to be in masculine attire, even if it was not perceived as such in the Turkish context.[26] Notable too, is that she related Turkish women's attire to the greater liberty she perceived them to have, the anonymity provided by their veils as much as the freedom of movement of their *şalvar* – fashionably voluminous at this date – in contrast to the restricting stays of her European dress.[27]

Returning to England, Lady Mary's dress and portraiture, like her letters, brought an orientalist *turquerie* which was absorbed into European fashion. The amply cut trousers, however, would return to fashion in different contexts in nineteenth-century America and early twentieth-century Paris.

COULD I, HOWEVER, LEAP OVERBOARD AND SWIM IN CLOTHES LIKE THESE? NO! THEREFORE, I SHOULD HAVE TO TRUST TO THE PROTECTION OF A BLUE-JACKET.

When Orlando changes out of her Turkish trousers and into eighteenth-century European women's dress, she is immediately conscious of how her skirts constrain her compared to the male crew of 'blue-jackets' aboard the *Enamoured Lady*.[28] In fact, the crew of an eighteenth-century ship was not so unlikely a place to find a woman in a uniform designed for men. The military – even piracy in the case of Mary Read and Anne Boney – offered activities and identities, as well as attire, not otherwise available to women.

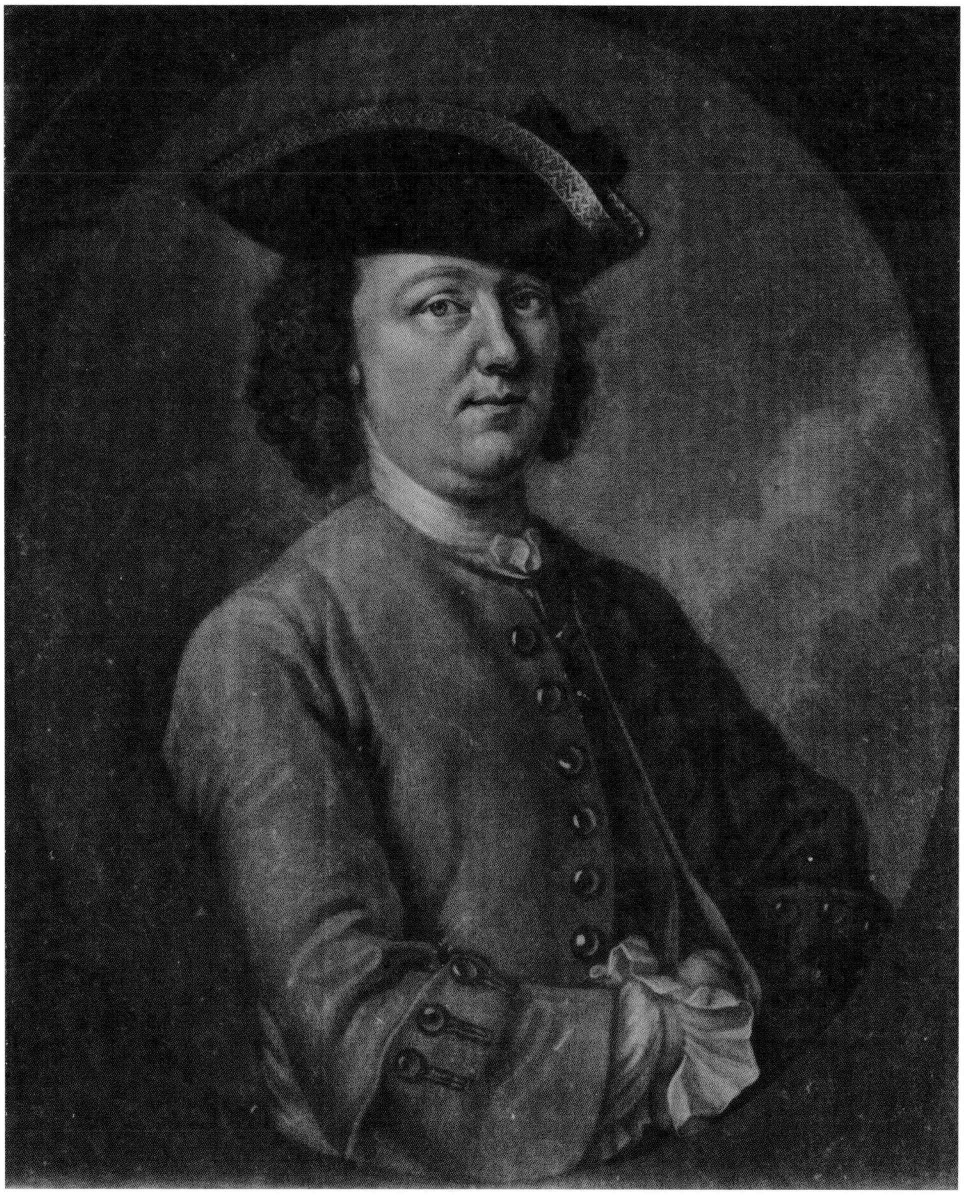

114. John Faber (*c.*1684–1756) and John Johnson, after James Wardell, *Hannah Snell*. Mezzotint 30 × 22.8 cm. Great Britain, 1771–6. The British Museum, London: 1851,0308.641

This was part of a longer tradition of female transvestism; women had donned uniforms to fight in the English Civil War well before Frances Stewart sat for her portrait in the guise of a soldier.[29] The greater opportunities available to men meant that women dressing in masculine clothing was more common than the reverse.[30] The exception that proves the rule is the Chevalier d'Éon, a French soldier, diplomat and spy living in London, who presented as a man and as a woman for periods of their life. There was much speculation over their sex (on the stock exchange as well as on the streets), and for the second half of their life following legal rulings on both sides of the Channel, the Chevalier was wrongly assumed to be biologically female; they may have been intersex.[31]

Unlike Stewart and d'Éon, most female soldiers who wore the uniform of their company were of humble origins, and their names, stories and images are lost to history. Those remembered in portraiture gained notoriety after the fact, through published autobiographies with images that focus on their masculine attire. Between Christian 'Kit' Cavanagh at the start of the century, and Mary Anne Talbot, known as John, at its end, the most famous and portrayed of these was Hannah Snell.

Snell, daughter of a hosier and dyer, first adopted masculine clothing when going in search of the husband who had abandoned her. According to her autobiography, *The Female Soldier* (1750), she first joined the army and then in 1747 the Royal Marines, all in the name James Gray – that of the man from whom she had borrowed a suit.[32] In the subsequent years she fought battles at Pondicherry and Devicotta in India. She only revealed her sex after returning to Britain in 1750, and gained celebrity status as 'a famous Woman in Men's Cloaths'.[33] Extraordinarily, one of the most circulated images of Snell (114) was adapted from a portrait of Clement Lemprière, a military draughtsman, which left the male sitter's clothing unchanged.[34]

SHE FOUND IT CONVENIENT AT THIS TIME TO CHANGE FREQUENTLY FROM ONE SET OF CLOTHES TO ANOTHER.

At the grey dawn of the nineteenth century, Orlando falls in love with Marmaduke Bonthrop Shelmerdine, Esquire, feels herself increasingly to be a woman, and finds it harder to switch between knee-breeches and skirts.[35] Her experience reflects tightening gender norms across Europe.

In 1800 a French prefectural decree outlawed women dressing as men, except for the period of Carnival.[36] Seven years previously, it had been declared that men dressing as women in France would face the guillotine. Women needing to don masculine attire for medical reasons, could request a *permission de travestissement*. This referred primarily to wearing trousers, as the redingote (a long coat, adapted from 'riding coat') had been tailored to a feminine silhouette, and the formerly exclusive colour black would become more accessible to all thanks to cheaper aniline dyes in the second half of the century.

The writer George Sand boldly adopted a masculine name and attire – without a permit – both with a view to practicality. With a man's name, she would get more work, and with his wardrobe, she could move through the streets of Paris with greater freedom, and dress herself at half the price. Sand was aided by the boxy shapes favoured by men's tailoring:

> At that period, the fashion was singularly helpful to the disguise ... So, I had a 'sentry box redingote' made for myself out of thick grey cloth, with matching trousers and vest. With a grey hat and a wide wool tie, I was the perfect little first year student.[37]

Sand wanted to blend in, but the portrait of her in male guise painted by Eugène Delacroix and commissioned by her editor shows that her clothing was attracting attention.[38] Delacroix's sepia-toned image of Sand, which anticipated its printed reproductions, resembles the portrait of Shelmerdine in Woolf's novel (115 and 116). Yet as seen in other portraits, photographic and painted, Sand – who took a great interest in her wardrobe – often wore dresses.

The painter Rosa Bonheur also adopted trousers for comfort and inconspicuousness in the all-male workplaces she painted, such as the horse fair that she depicted to great acclaim in the 1850s. While unlike Sand she did not change her name, Bonheur deviated from gender norms in other ways: she had short hair, smoked and had a female partner. And she did obtain the *permission de travestissement*.

Crucially, Bonheur did not wear trousers all the time, to the disappointment of visitors.[39] In portraits Bonheur is generally seen in a skirt, or an indistinct garment, yet a rare and unusual set of porcelain dolls of Bonheur issued in her lifetime show her in the masculine attire for which she became known. The dolls were a hit in 1860s America, where the wearing of 'pants' was connected to women's rights, and to Amelia Bloomer who gave her name to the version of *şalvar* she popularized in the United States.

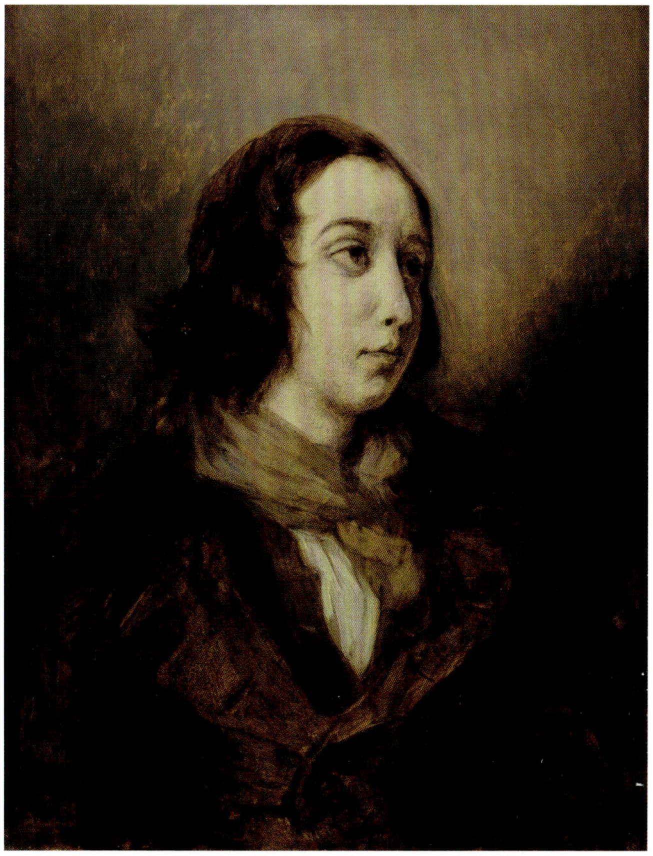

115. Eugène Delacroix (1798–1863), *George Sand Dressed as a Man.* Oil on panel, 26×21.5 cm. France, 1834. Musée national Eugène Delacroix, Paris: MD 2016-1

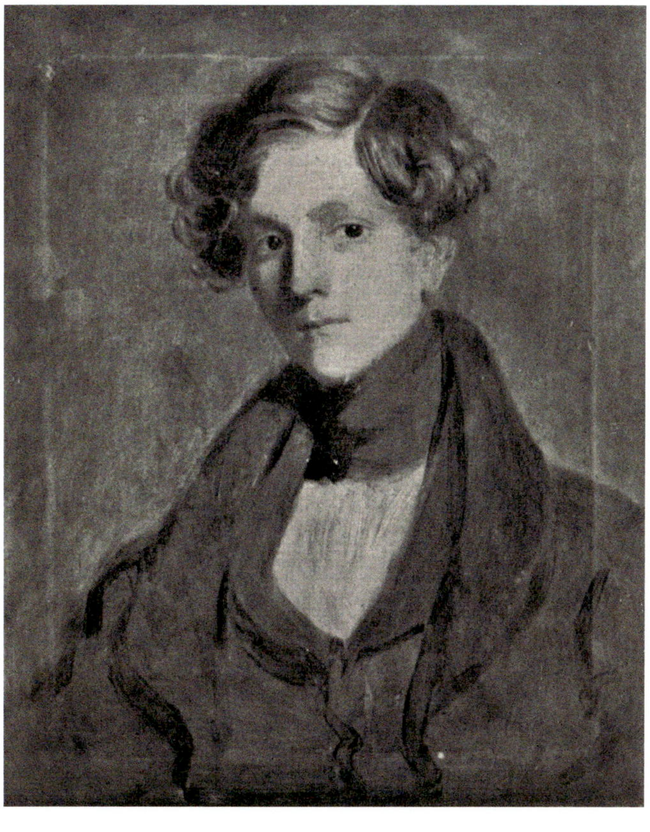

116. 'Marmaduke Bonthrop Shelmerdine, Esquire', *Orlando* (London, 1928)

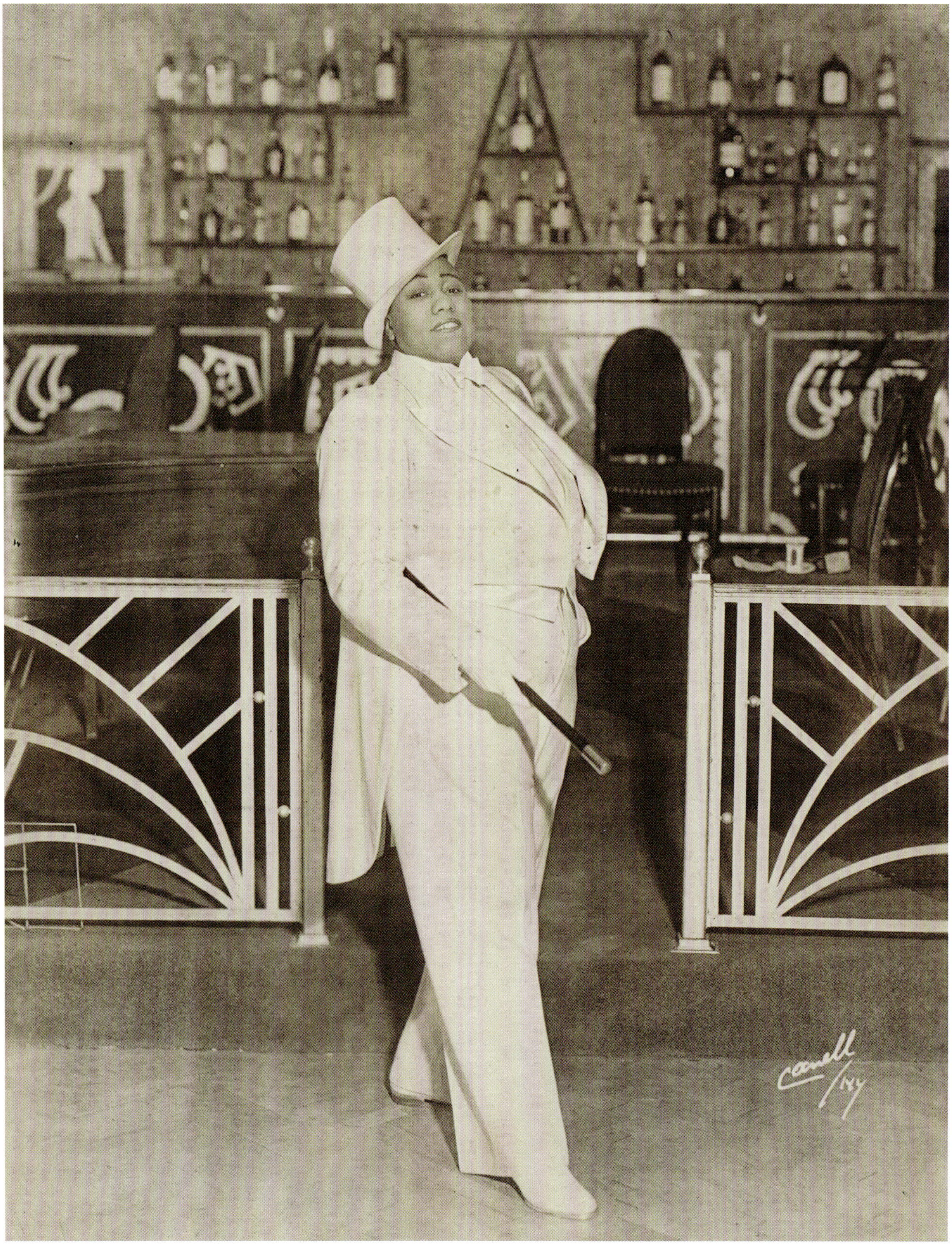

117. *Gladys Bentley*. Photograph, silver gelatin print, 23.7×18.6 cm. New York, *c.*1940. Collection of the Smithsonian National Museum of African American History and Culture: 2013.46.25.82

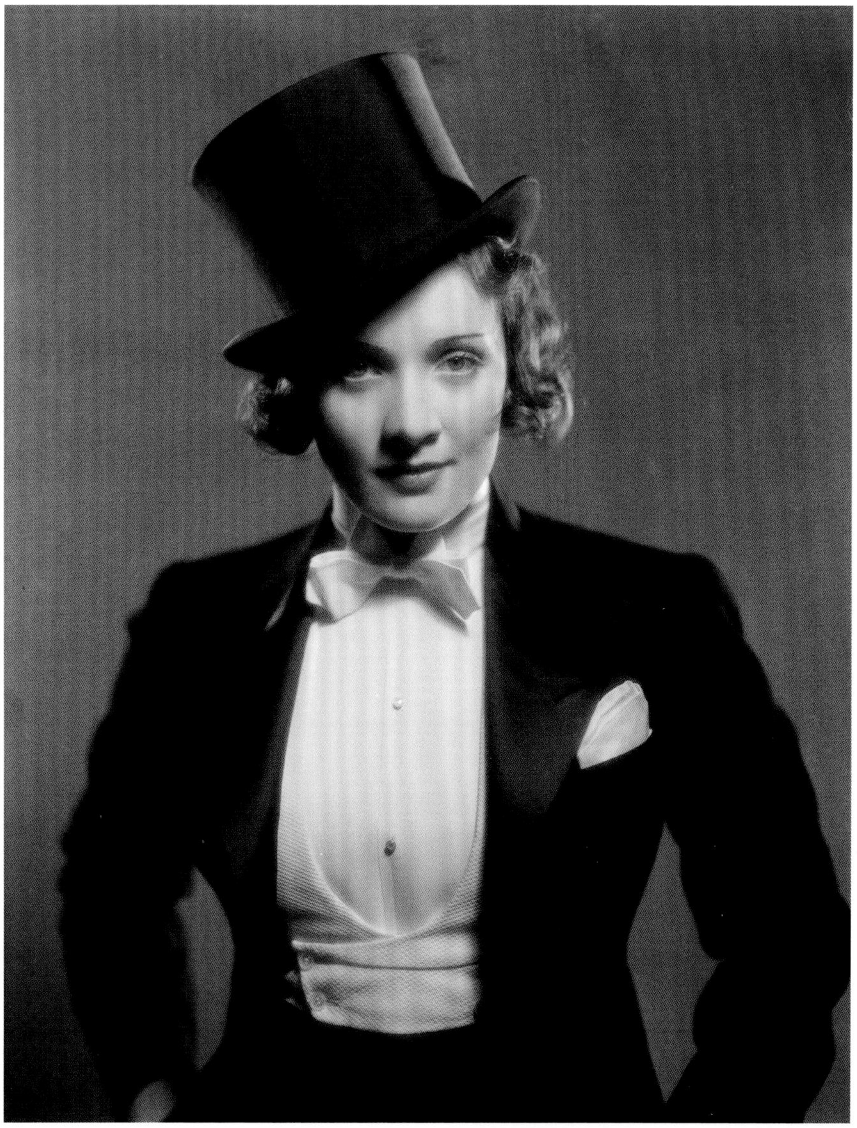

118. Eugene Robert Richee (1896–1972),
Marlene Dietrich in *Morocco* (1930),
dir. Josef von Sternberg

FOR THE PROBITY OF BREECHES SHE EXCHANGED THE SEDUCTIVENESS OF PETTICOATS AND ENJOYED THE LOVE OF BOTH SEXES EQUALLY.

Orlando's final chapter takes place at a time when the fashionability of the 'boyette' style and its new connotations of same-sex desire were perpetuated through photography and the cinema.[40] The aforementioned photograph of Radclyffe Hall (110) was far more widely reproduced than Romaine Brooks's painting of Hall's partner Una Troubridge (135)[41] in similar attire, made more subversive with the addition of pinstripe trousers (Hall wore a pencil skirt). Photographs of the lesbian nightclub Le Monocle taken by Brassaï show that the 'boyette' aesthetic had also become fashionable in Paris.

Queer nightclub performers, more so than their clientele, became the emblematic women in tuxedos between the world wars. Unlike their predecessors in turn-of-the century British music hall, such as Vesta Tilley who played a variety of male roles,[42] these performers adopted the tuxedo to express their own identities. The bisexual entertainer and activist Josephine Baker performed in a tuxedo at her Paris nightclub, and was repeatedly photographed in this outfit. Baker was subverting expectations in terms of class and race, as well as gender.

For Baker's fellow American, the blues singer Gladys Bentley, who sometimes performed under the name Bobbie Minton, a white tuxedo and top hat were their primary performance attire (117).[43] Bentley – described by poet Langston Hughes as a 'masculine lady, whose feet pounded the floor while her fingers pounded the keyboard'[44] – performed in the nightclubs of New York's Harlem, both at the gay speakeasy the Clam House, and the Cotton Club where Black entertainers performed for white audiences. There, her 'bulldagger' identity – a pejorative slang term for masculine, Black, queer women – which saw her marginalized in society, became her selling point on stage.

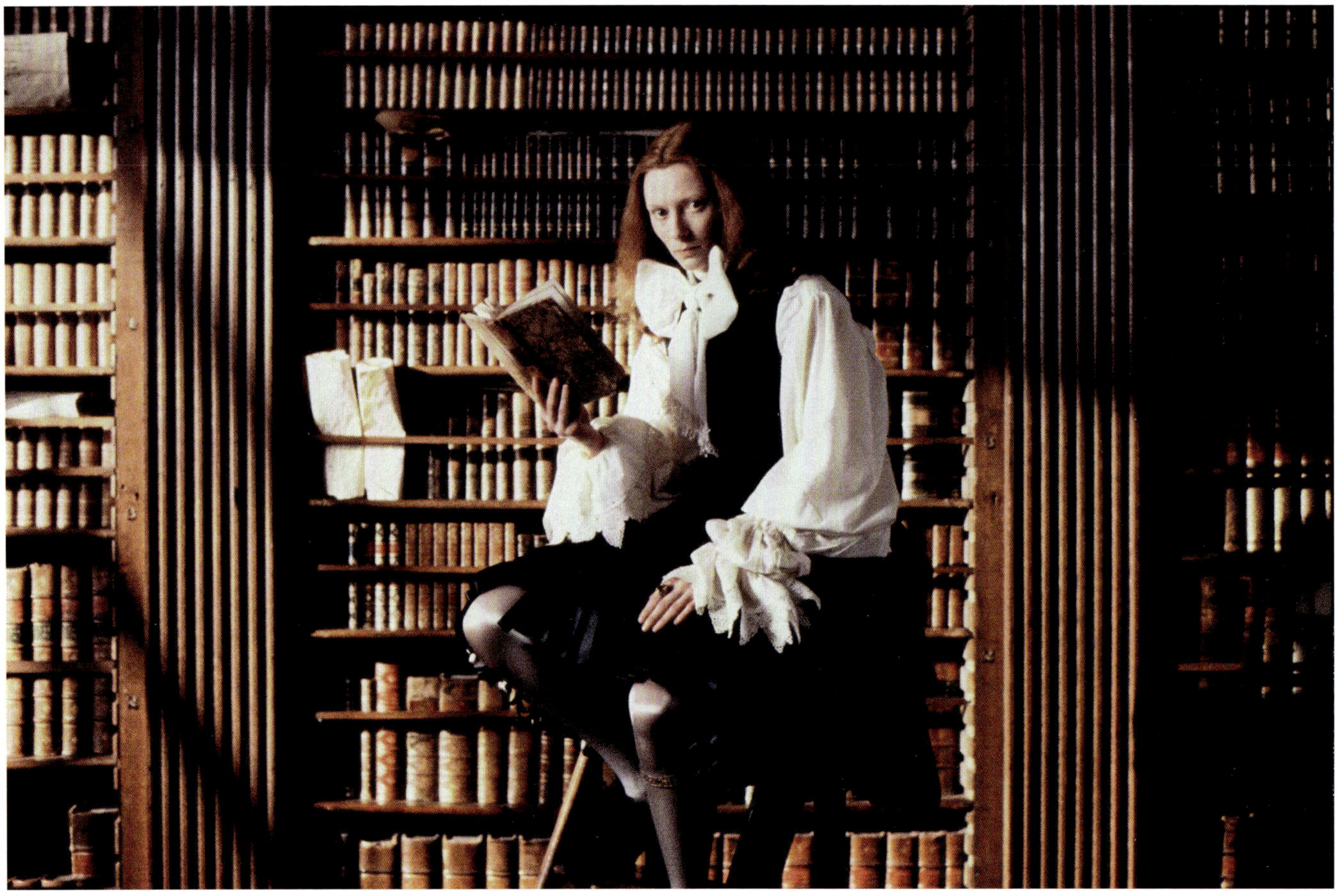

119. Tilda Swinton in *Orlando* (1992), dir. Sally Potter, costume design by Sandy Powell

120. Sébastien Bourdon (1616–1671), *Christina, Queen of Sweden*. Oil on canvas, 72×58 cm. Sweden, 1653. National Museum, Stockholm: NM 1072

Following Baker and Bentley, it was Marlene Dietrich's performance as nightclub singer Amy Jolly in *Morocco* (1930) (118) that cemented the queer connotations of a woman in a tuxedo. In the now iconic scene, a tuxedoed Jolly sings *Quand l'amour meurt* and kisses a woman in the audience. For the rest of the film, a story structured around her choice between two male lovers, Jolly wears dresses. Yet, Dietrich's personal commitment to masculine tailoring, which she pursued throughout her life, was arguably more central in the popularization of trousers for women in the United States than Chanel's designs.[45]

A century after Vita and Virginia first met, women wearing tailoring and trousers has been normalized (if in France only legalized in 2013), the (sartorial) gender binary is under pressure and *Orlando* has become a byword for androgyny. The film adaptation of the book, directed by Sally Potter and with Orlando played by Tilda Swinton, has heightened its androgynous vision, the costumes by Sandy Powell evoking many of the portraits described above (119).[46] In 2019 an operatic version was commissioned with costumes by fashion designer Rei Kawakubo.[47] For her Spring/Summer 2020 menswear presentation in Paris, Kawakubo also sought inspiration from Orlando's wardrobe of doublets and breeches, ruffles and frockcoats, bustles and petticoats and the 1920s *garçonne* silhouette (121). Kawakubo's company – which has always subverted gender norms – is aptly named Comme des Garçons.

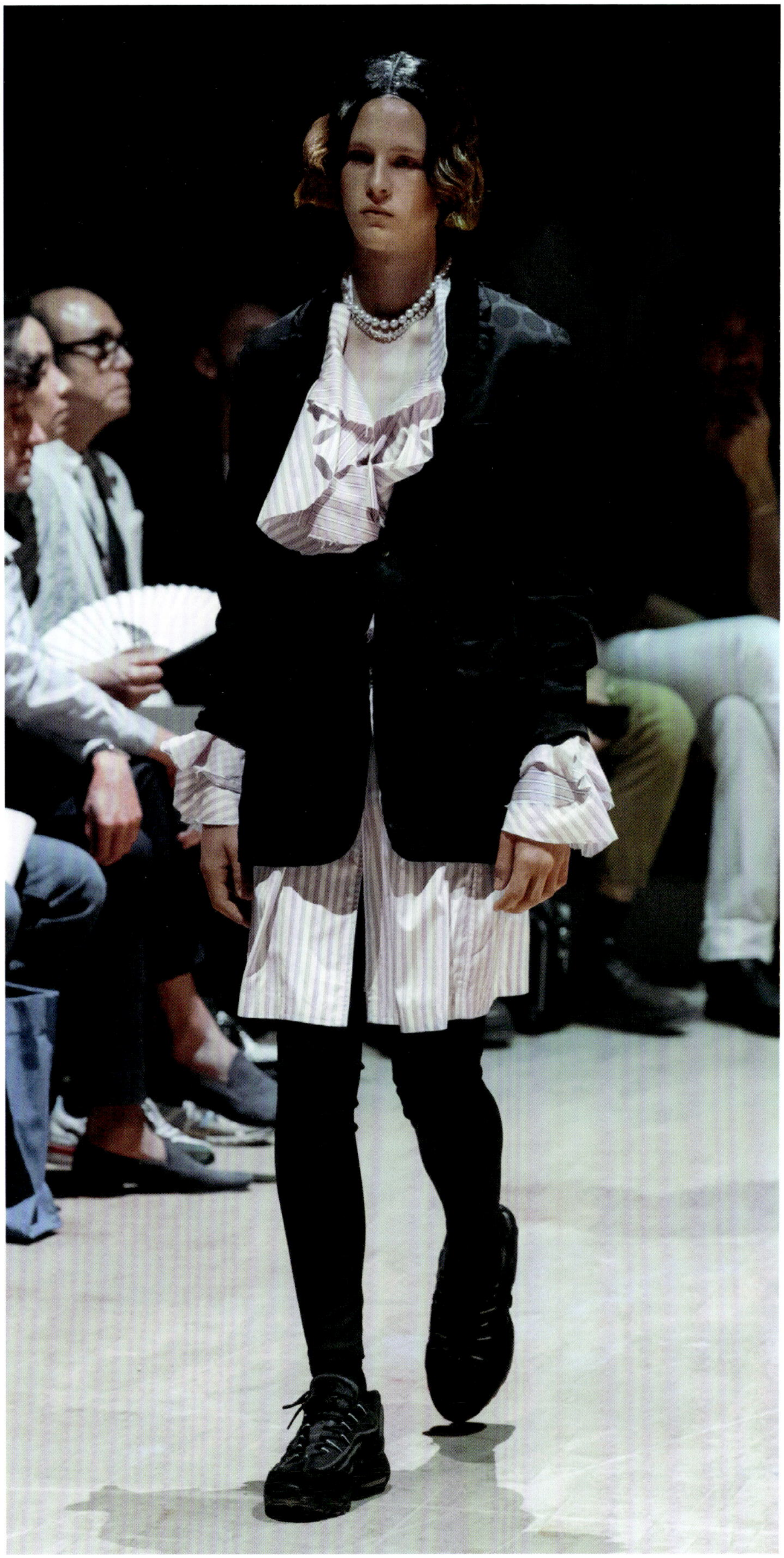

121. Rei Kawakubo (1941–) for Comme des Garçons Homme Plus.
Ensemble. Spring/Summer 2020. Model: Tibor Rozanc

A HIBISCUS PRINT

CHER POTTER

Lagosian fashion designer Adebayo Oke-Lawal, founder of Orange Culture, describes his label as a community rather than a brand. According to Oke-Lawal, the distinctive prints and hues of his softened menswear silhouettes promote a group awareness for men on the margins. 'Our clothes allow softer men to recognize each other as part of an empathetic community – the garments create a collective space where flower boys can blossom.'[1] He uses the terms 'softer men' and 'flower boys' to express a broader spectrum of male gender identities.

As both fashion label and social concept, Orange Culture endorses wardrobe androgyny and actively subverts established codes of masculine dress. The cultural theorist Grace Ebunlola Adamo, in her study of Nigerian dress as a symbolic language, explains that in contemporary Nigeria, masculine colours are brown, blue and grey, while feminine colours are pink, red and orange.[2] Much as in the UK, men who wear bright colours are seen as contravening the established societal code. Orange Culture is a defiant reclamation of so-called 'feminine' hues by a Nigerian menswear label. Oke-Lawal is adamant, 'In our studio, no colour or cut is gendered.'[3]

The flamboyant hibiscus-print trouser and blouse set held in the V&A collection is part of Orange Culture's Autumn/Winter 2020 'Flower Boy' range (122). The title alludes to remarks Oke-Lawal himself received as a young boy, now recast as a celebration of masculine sensitivity and emotionality. The Roselle hibiscus, native to West Africa and a common feature in Oke-Lawal's childhood settings, is magnified and digitally rendered in vivid oranges, reds and greens against a brilliant blue background. The intricate and entwined design produces a lace-like effect, while the two-dimensional graphic treatment evokes the wax-resist patterns of Yoruba *adire* prints.

The trousers and blouse are oversized, lightweight and simply cut with a politicized dedication to the comfort of the wearer. A delicately pleated collar borrows from womenswear and produces a petal-like effect, from which the head protrudes. When worn in sunlight, the fine-spun silk-cotton fabric is translucent and reveals the body's contours. All elements of the garments' construction are designed to communicate ideas of liberation, tenderness and ease.

Oke-Lawal describes such ensembles as a kind of uniform for flower boys. By uniform, he does not imply a uniformity of dress, but rather a certain conspicuousness, whereby the charismatic, polychrome garments produced by Orange Culture generate recognition and identification amongst their wearers. In this way, he deploys fashion and florals to both support and activate alternative masculine identities.

His strategy of expressing group identity through dress draws directly from the Yoruba dress culture in Nigeria known as *aṣọ ebì*. The term translates as 'family cloth' or 'solidarity uniform' and refers to the distinctive matching outfits worn by Yoruba families at social occasions. Unique custom-printed textiles or hand-woven *aṣọ ebì* fabrics for men (combined with imported lace and brocade for women) are used to create beautifully co-ordinated ensembles that allow for easy identification of kin and close friends during festivities.[4]

The origins of *aṣọ ebì* are debated among historians. Early Christian missionaries and colonial authorities in Yorubaland (which includes present-day Nigeria) are thought to have facilitated its intensification.[5] The dress code of Yoruba men was initially described by mid-nineteenth-century British and American missionaries as exceedingly stylish, colourful and able to rival that of any 'civilized' society.[6] However, following the British annexation of Lagos in 1861, the customary brightly coloured, loose-fitting trousers, shirts and gowns donned by Yoruba men came to be seen as an affront to Victorian notions of decency and 'appropriate' male moral codes. The British suit was heralded as a more appropriate choice.

In the final decades of the nineteenth century, as Victorian ideas of racial hierarchy became more rigid, an intellectual minority began to contest the enthusiasm for the British suit and advocate for a return to pre-colonial dress and values.[7] A dress reform initiative was established by the Lagosian intelligentsia and the so-called 'sartorial battle' of Lagos ensued.[8] The vibrant *agbada* (also known in Hausa as the *riga*), which had served as a masculine identity marker for hundreds of years prior to British imperial rule, was reintroduced as formal attire (123). The wide-sleeved robes, beautifully embroidered with abstracted flora, fauna and geometrics, became a powerful language of protest.

Clothing became a way for Yoruba men to signify their continued allegiance to pre-colonial social bonds. Yoruba family heads encouraged what became known as 'traditional clothing' at all social gatherings. Flamboyant and exclusive prints were created to identify family and friendship groups as part of a growing *aṣọ ebì* culture. The uniform practice expanded over the following decades to distinguish members of clubs and youth or political organizations.

With Nigeria's independence and an oil-related economic boom in the 1960s, widespread migration to Lagos radically altered the urban social structures within the city. The meanings of friendship, solidarity and camaraderie within the burgeoning hub became more complex, composite and cross-cultural. *Aṣọ ebì* spread well beyond the Yoruba families and clubs to demonstrate wider affiliations to businesses, co-operative groups and church associations.

Today, this dress culture has been adopted across geographies, by neighbouring countries and their diaspora.

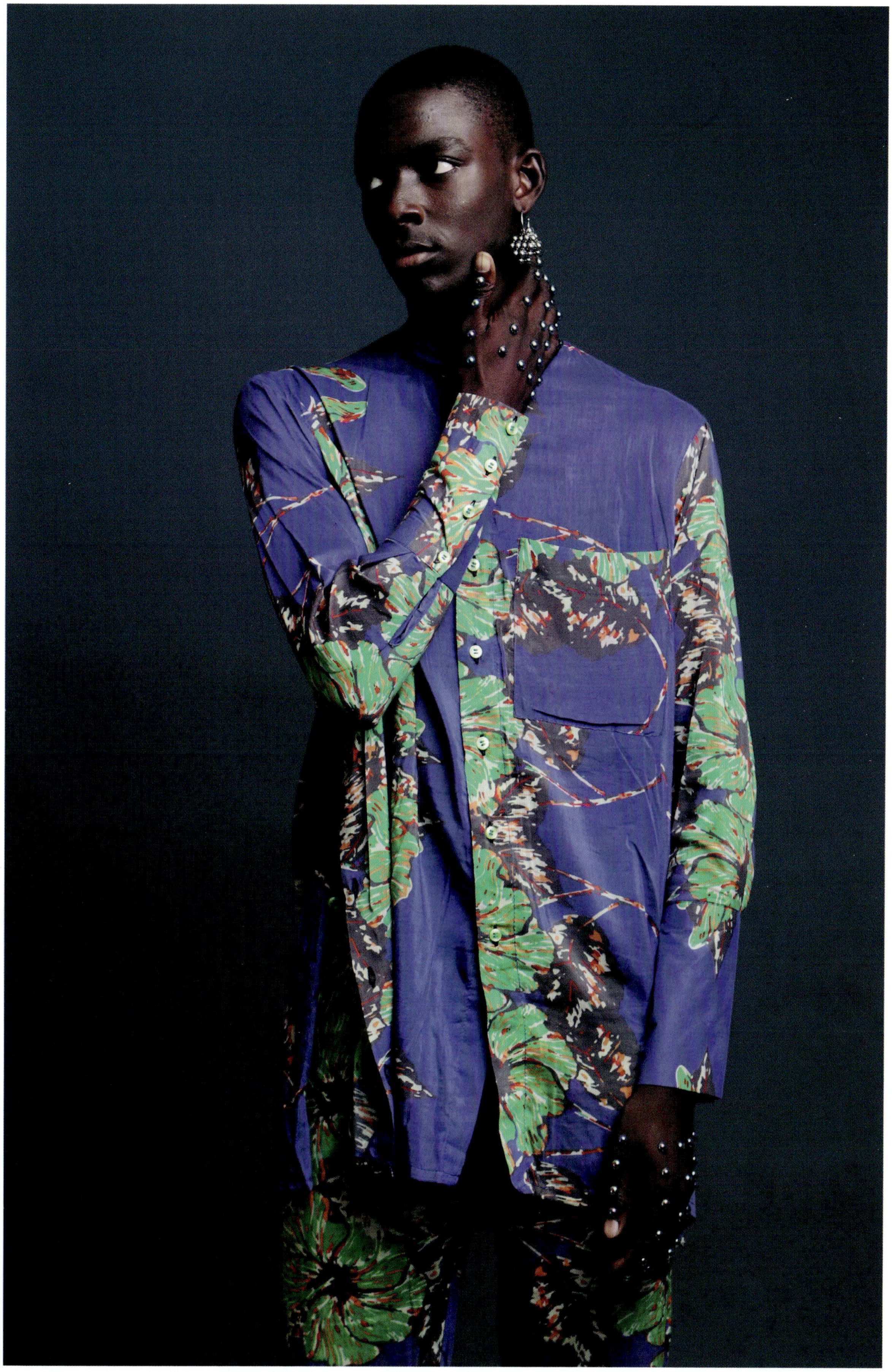

122. Adebayo Oke-Lawal (1990–) for Orange Culture, 'Flower Boy' blouse and trouser set. Autumn/Winter 2020. Model: Richy Blanson

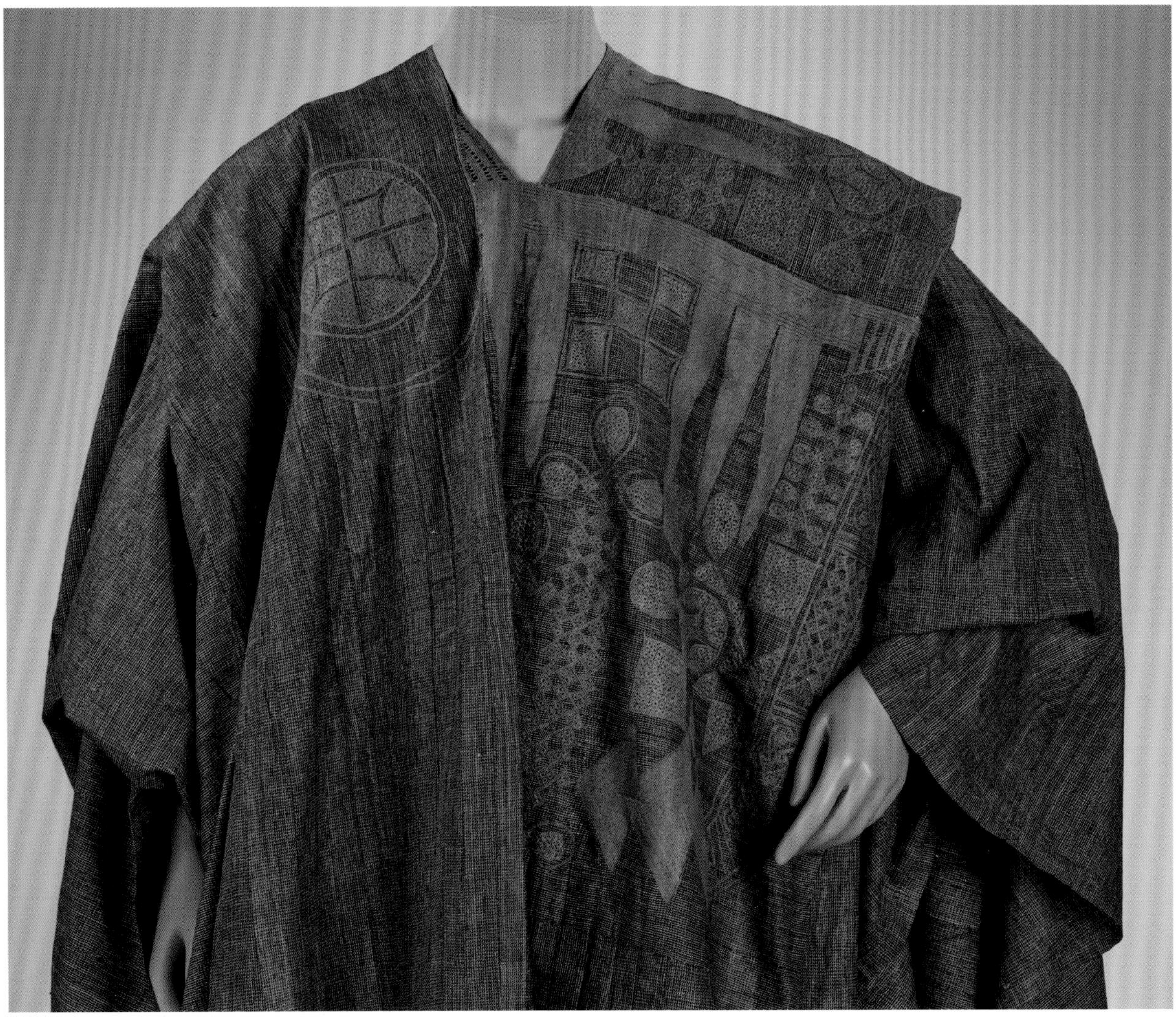

123. Robe. Cotton, embroidered with silk.
Nigeria, 1870–99. V&A: T.699-1994

Across the United Kingdom and United States of America, specialist services source and deliver *asọ ebì* nationwide for celebratory occasions. In Lagos itself, the sartorial practice is more powerful than ever for expressing visual identity and commonality.[9] Designers like Oke-Lawal are now expanding the practice of uniform dressing once more, to establish and announce a distinctive twenty-first-century collective identity for 'softer men'.

The launch of Lagos Fashion Week in 2011 and the growth of the Nigerian fashion scene have connected other aspects of *asọ ebì* to the globalized fashion system. Labels such as Orange Culture produce collections for international fashion retailers, alongside so-called 'traditional' silhouettes with custom-made matching print patterns for Lagos's uniformed attire. These interconnected practices result in a novel approach to fashion design that, according to Nigerian journalist Sean Williams, explores 'the space between traditional and modern tailoring... is often bright... and unmistakably Nigerian.'[10]

Designers such as Oke-Lawal and Kenneth Ize have over the last decade featured predominantly on Lagos, Paris and London menswear catwalks, as well as in the coveted Louis Vuitton and Moët Hennesey (LVMH) and Woolmark global fashion prizes. Like Oke-Lawal, Ize cites a desire to challenge the strict remit of masculinity in Nigeria through his eponymous label and to see 'more vulnerability in men, less power'.[11]

Ize's Spring/Summer 2019 collection pioneered international menswear styles that intercut the tailored suit jacket with the *agbada*, the *buba* (a loose-fitting blouse) and the *sokoto* (drawstring trousers) (124). Garments were produced in the finely striped *asọ oke* silks that are synonymous with men's attire in *asọ ebì* culture, but now with a sharp hibiscus pink injection. 'We're reviving, reinterpreting and giving new context to artisan techniques that have given meaning to West African identity,' Ize told the *New York Times*.[12]

Both Oke-Lawal and Ize work with artisans in Yoruba weave centres such as Ilorin and Iseyin, which date back as far as the fifteenth century. They modify and re-invent the colour codes and graphic applications of such historic textiles to challenge patterns of masculinity in Nigeria. On the international stage, they are refashioning masculinity by injecting bright colour, Yoruba draping and voluminous tailoring into a menswear canon long dominated by variations of the British suit.

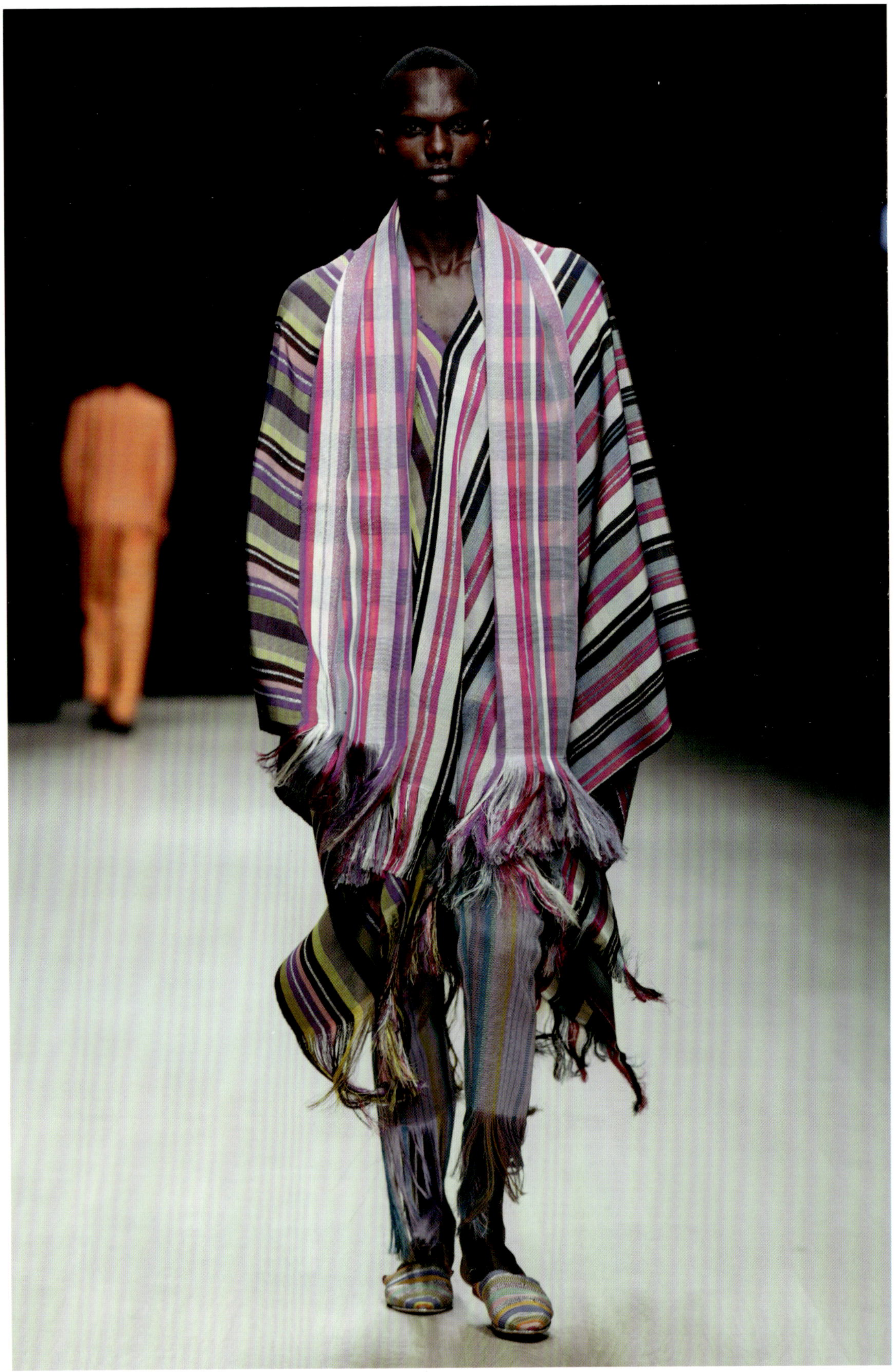

124. Kenneth Ize (1990–), Ensemble. Spring/Summer 2019.
Model: Nelson Oghenekevwe

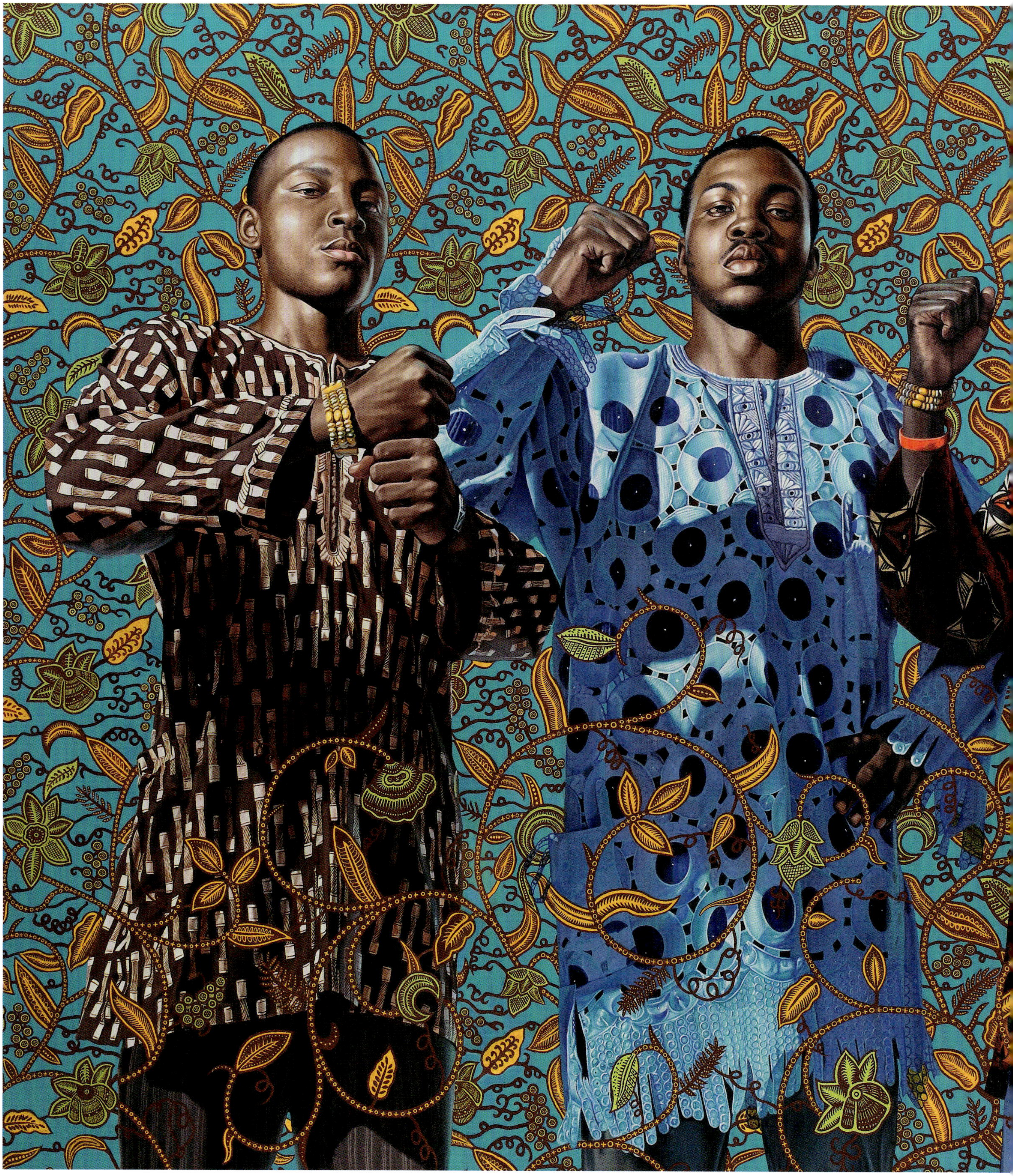

125. Kehinde Wiley (1977–), *Three Wise Men Greeting Entry into Lagos*. Oil on canvas, 182.8×241.9 cm. Nigeria, 2008. Pennsylvania Academy of the Fine Arts, Philadelphia: 2009.20

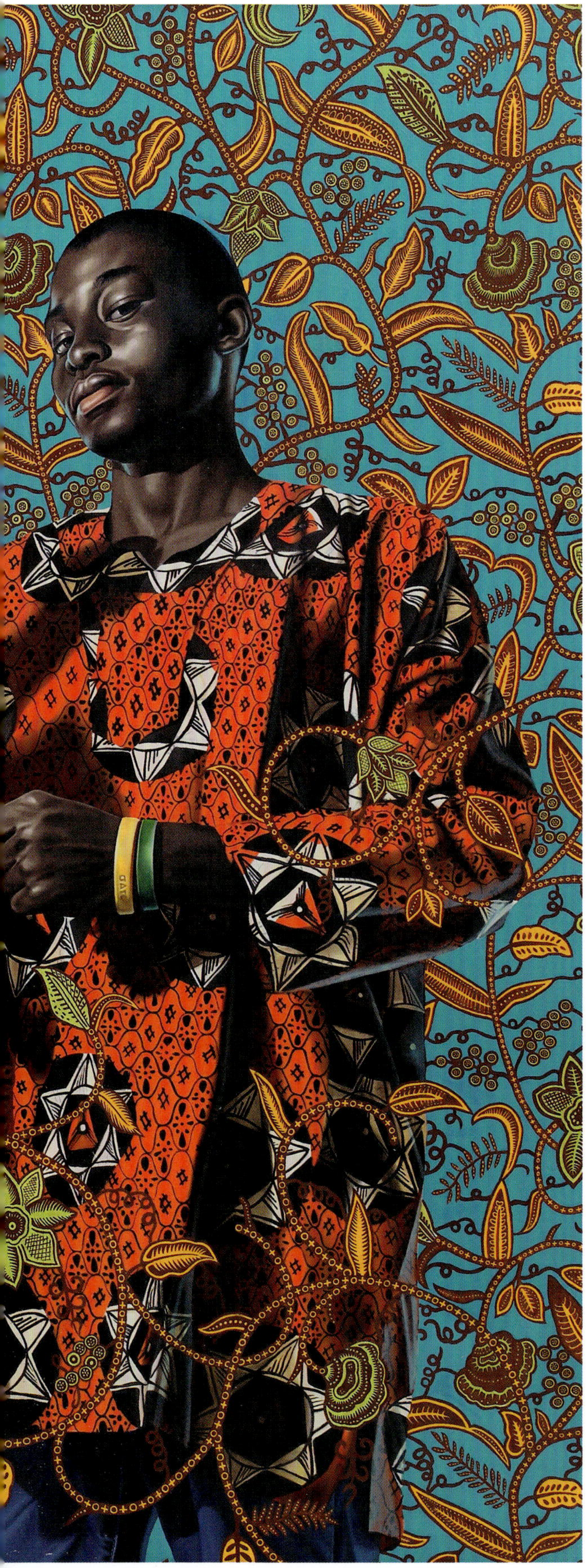

Oke-Lawal and Ize are part of a new era of Nigerian writers, designers and artists who defy dominant gender perceptions and test new forms of sensitivity in expression. This generation has been labelled 'Third Generation' within literary circles.[13] Associated with this group is Chimamanda Ngozi Adichie, author of acclaimed novels such as *Purple Hibiscus* (2003). Within her books, she too uses fashion and floral motifs as symbols of freedom and fragility in her efforts to 'remake masculinity from the narrow cage for men into a humane, expansive idea'.[14]

The use of fashion and florals was similarly explored by the American Nigerian portrait artist Kehinde Wiley in his interrogation of Black male masculinity in Nigeria. His 2008 series 'The World Stage: Africa' is based on time spent in Lagos. Within it, he examines his own patrilineal Yoruba heritage in relation to a Eurocentric art historical tradition defined by Titian, Sir Joshua Reynolds, Jean-Auguste-Dominique Ingres and John Singer Sargent. He incorporates the bold colours and designs of West African textiles to interrupt the Eurocentric genre of portraiture.

His painting *Three Wise Men Greeting Entry into Lagos* (2008) depicts a self-assured group of young Nigerian men, their poses mimicking Lagos's *Three Elders/Welcome to Lagos* (1991) statue by Bodun Shodeinde which celebrates independence from colonial rule (125). They wear contemporary *adire* print shirts and stand against a background of flat wax-resist floral patterns. The two-dimensional feminine florals envelop the three-dimensional masculine figures. Wiley has fused two- and three-dimensional artistic conventions, fashion and motifs to portray a generation of African youth that confronts both racial and gender stereotypes.

In the words of Oke-Lawal: 'It is important for people to think outside of a particular type of African man. We can be emotional, vulnerable and express ourselves however we want to, without being seen as anything less than African.'[15]

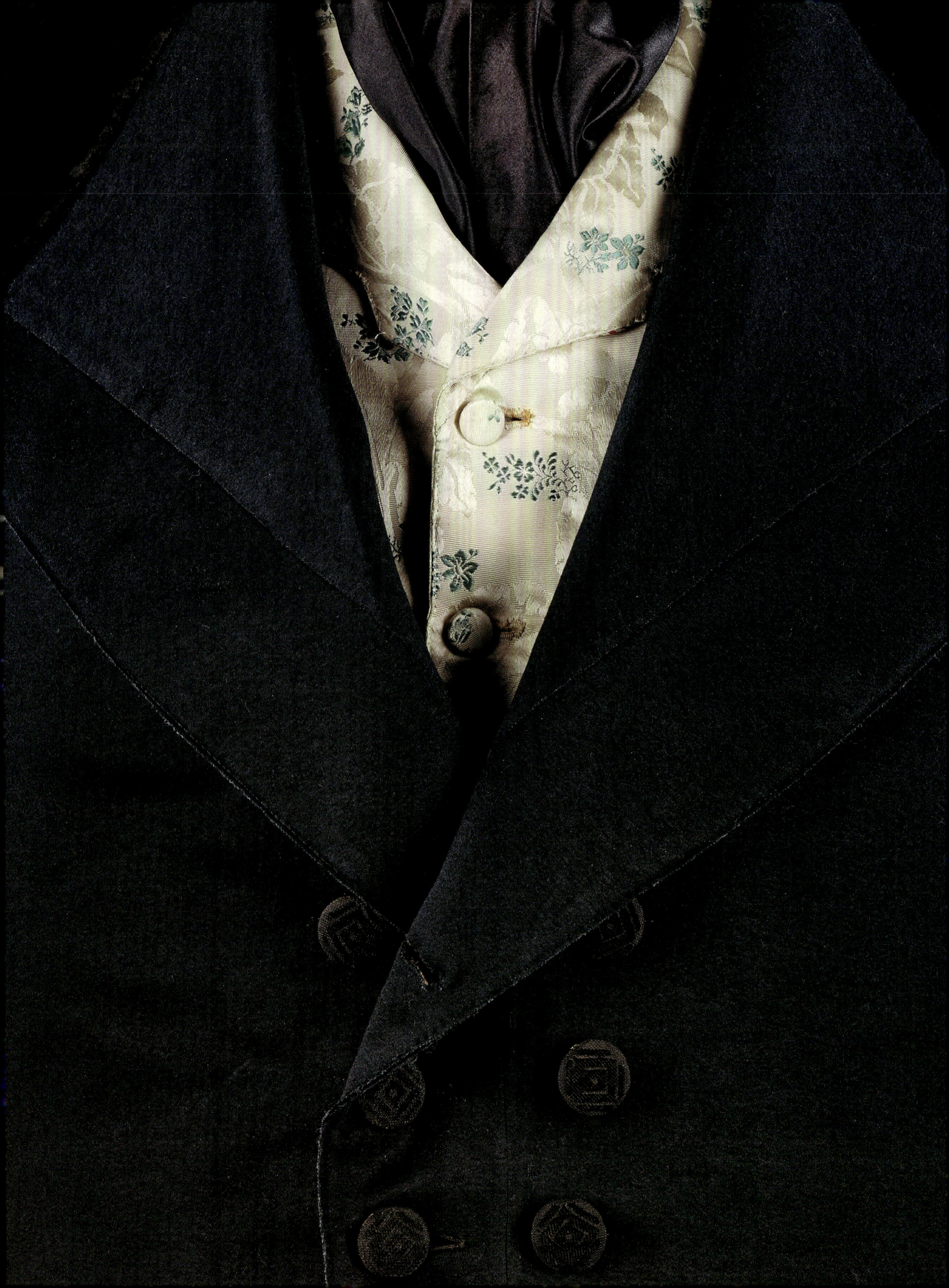

REDRESSED

I THINK THAT BLACK IS MORE PLEASING IN CLOTHING THAN ANY OTHER COLOUR

BALDASSARE CASTIGLIONE
1528

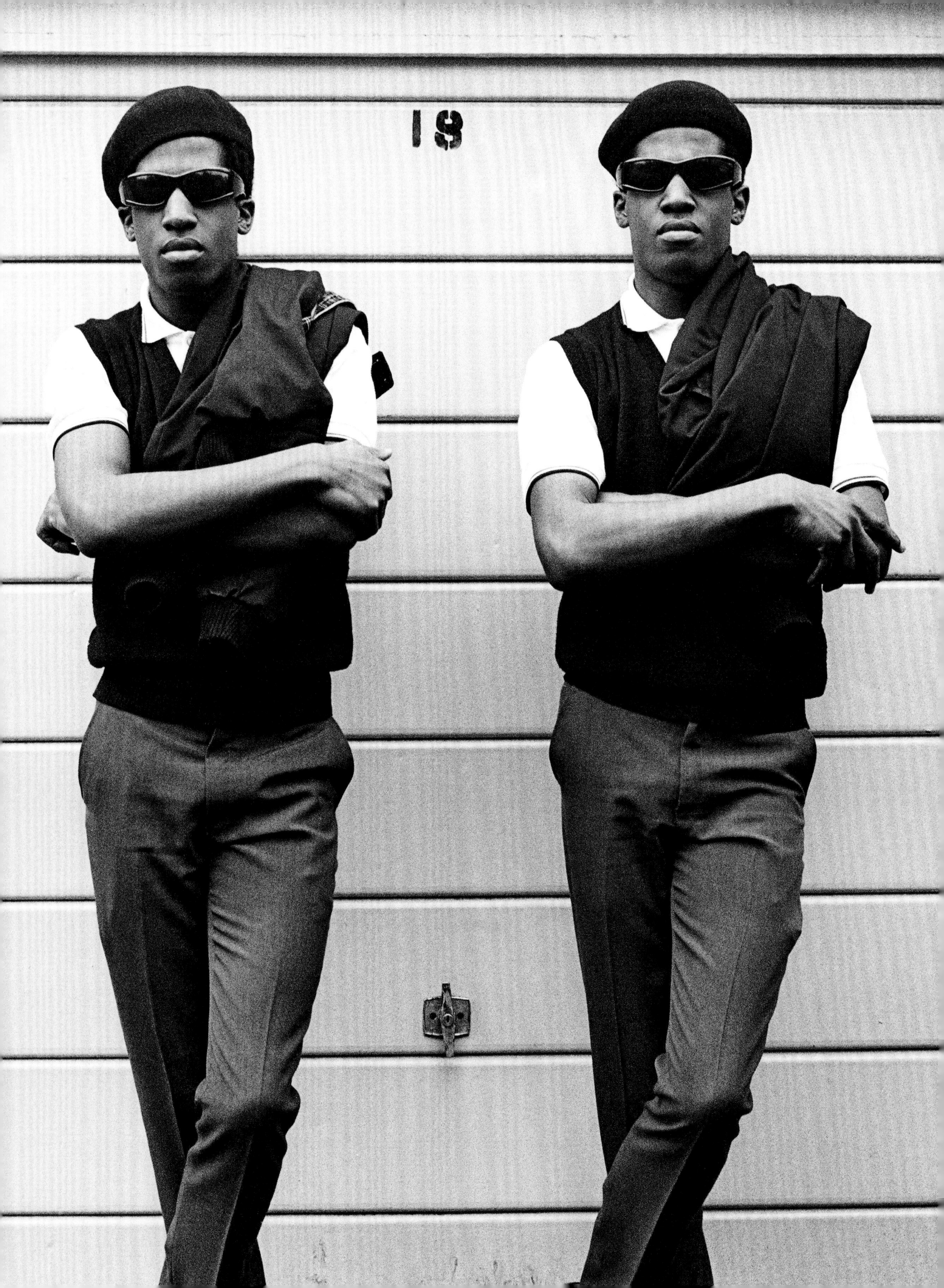
19

MONOCHROME MAN

CHRISTOPHER BREWARD

In darkness let me dwell, the ground shall sorrow be
The roof despair to bar all cheerful light from me
The walls of marble black that moistened still shall weep
My music hellish jarring sounds to banish friendly sleep
Thus wedded to my woes, and bedded to my tomb
O let me living die, til death do come.

John Dowland, *A Musical Banquet*, 1610

The publication of *The Psychology of Clothes* by psychologist and psychoanalyst John Carl Flügel in 1930 introduced perhaps the most influential theory ever proposed in the study of masculine dress. The act of vestimentary 'renunciation' has subsequently become the dominant discourse for understanding the preference for dark colour and simplified form that many writers and critics have ascribed to men's taste in clothing past and present. In his own words, Flügel adopts a mournful register to describe the process by which men, in his view, abandoned the pleasures of self-adornment:

> Men may be said to have suffered a great defeat in the sudden reduction of ... sartorial decorativeness which took place at the end of the eighteenth-century... Men gave up their right to all the brighter, gayer, more elaborate, and more varied forms of ornamentation, leaving these entirely to the use of women, and thereby making their own tailoring the most austere and ascetic of the arts... Man abandoned his claim to be considered beautiful. He henceforth aimed at being only useful.[1]

Flügel was a sophisticated and daring thinker and writer, one of a generation of public intellectuals committed to progressive social reform in a Britain rapidly modernizing its approach to education, housing, health and what we might now term as psychological well-being. Victorian constructions of class, gender and attitudes towards sexuality were increasingly seen by Flügel and his peers as a constraint on modernization, and in this context it is perhaps no surprise that questions of repression, prohibition, uniformity, shame and modesty should have preoccupied the author in his analysis of the development of male fashion. Beyond this Flügel was also arguing for a political aesthetic of men's clothing in the present that allowed for free expression, and an escape from the irrational and neurotic fear of the beauty of the human body that he believed had imprisoned the natural evolution of masculine style in the nineteenth century.[2]

In my own work as a fashion historian, Flügel's legacy has certainly cast a long shadow. My doctoral research on young men's engagement with fashion in late nineteenth-century London set Flügel and his theories of renunciation up as shibboleths to be tested and disproved.[3] Twenty years on, the arrogance of youth tempered a little, I have come to see how his thinking offers a valuable intellectual construct through which to explain the undeniable persistence of seemingly unchanging platonic clothing forms, including the suit in the male wardrobe.[4] In this essay, dedicated to Flügel's contribution to fashion scholarship and the meanings of masculine clothing, I want to reconsider those questions of suffering, self-restraint, sacrifice, abandonment, austerity and asceticism that float beneath the renunciatory turn. The dark, plain raiment of masculinity bespeaks a sense of loss and grieving, but also an engagement with power and indeed perverse desire that deserves a second look. There is perhaps a sweet pleasure to be had in the adoption and reading of the monochrome dress of men?

MONOCHROME MAGNIFICENCE: BLACK AND THE MAN OF STATUS

In one respect Flügel's simple before and after account of the rise of 'plain and uniform' costume, if read too literally, also does a disservice to the importance of dark and simplified garments in the choices available to fashionable men before 1800. It was not as if 'gorgeous and varied' clothing alone dominated the sartorial lexicon up to this point. Literary historian John Harvey, in his work on the symbolism of the colour black in cultural history and the history of men's fashion, offers a number of contexts in which dark attire played a major role in Renaissance and early modern court cultures. Darkness, as the words of John Dowland's lute song of 1610 suggest, was something of a social obsession for those living in court societies from Burgundy in the fourteenth century, to Spain and Holland in the seventeenth century. In Harvey's words, inky hues:

> ... weighed on aristocracies in a world prone to apocalyptic epidemics, where priests in black had power over the soul as physicians in black had power over death, while lawyers in black had power over goods, which one had bought from merchants in black with money one had borrowed from bankers in black who offered at interest the loans which caused [rich] families and royal families to be increasingly in debt.[5]

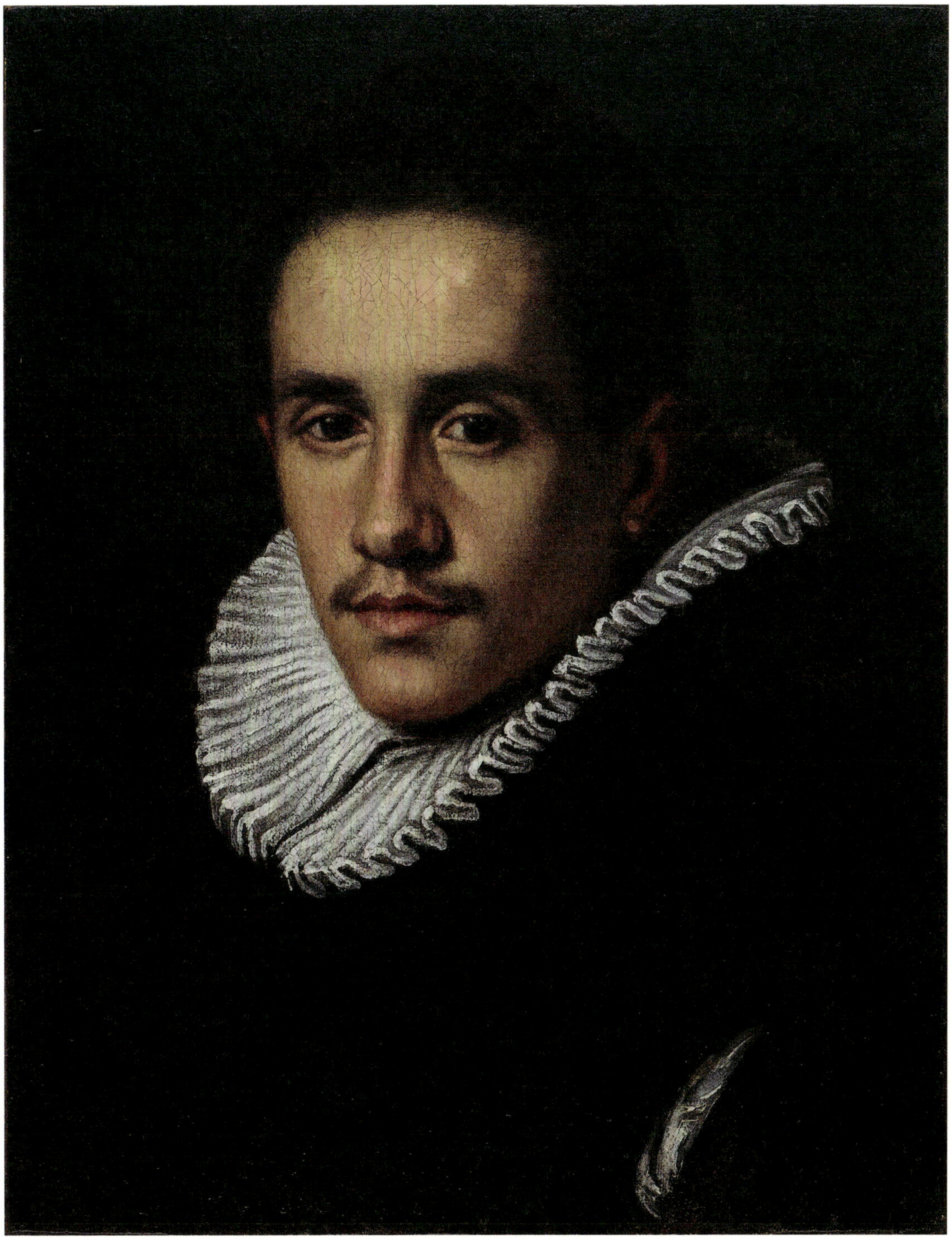

126. North Italian painter, *A Young Man in a White Ruff*.
Oil on canvas, 49.5 × 39.4 cm. Italy, *c*.1580–1600.
Bequeathed by Constantine Alexander Ionides. V&A: CAI.102

But the ubiquity of black clothing for men was tempered by the modulations of status and taste. As an expression of rank and style, quality black garments indicated wealth, authority and a restrained sensibility for fashion. In fundamental material terms, the production of a pure and long-lasting dark shade in silk, fine wool or leather was expensive and time-consuming. A deep and durable tone required several dips in the dyeing vat and fixing treatment with metal mordants if the resulting black cloth was not to fade in sunlight or take on the greenish bloom of cheaper goods.[6] And as contemporary portraits reveal, the dark foil of black fabric was an excellent companion for lace, embroidery, passementerie, pinking and slashing, metalwork and gemstones, either black on black or of a contrasting colour, particularly white (126).[7] Its subtle elegance drew out the noble qualities inherent in a princely demeanour, and justified the recommendations for dark clothing that pepper sixteenth-century guides to courtly conduct. Read, for example, Baldassare Castiglione's famous advice to ambitious young men in the Duchy of Urbino in *The Courtier* of 1528 (first published in English in 1561):

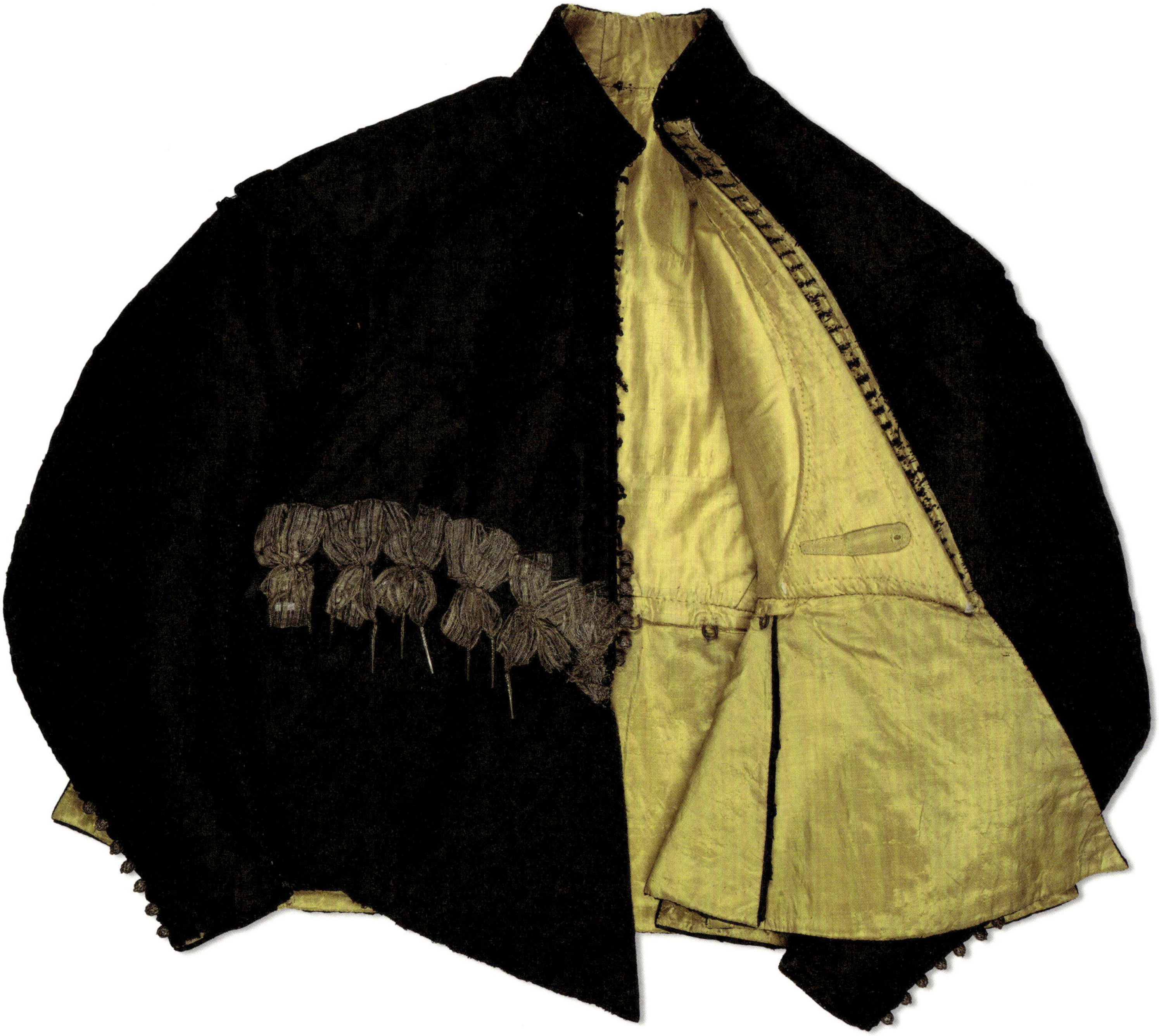

127. Doublet. Silk, linen, silver, bents.
Italy and England, 1630–5. V&A: 185-1900

> I think that black is more pleasing in clothing than any other colour; and if not black then at least some colour on the dark side. I mean this of ordinary attire, for there is no doubt that bright and gay colours are more becoming on armour, and it is also more appropriate for gala dress to be trimmed, showy and dashing... As for the rest, I would have our courtier's dress show that sobriety which the Spanish nations so much observe, since external things often bear witness to inner things.[8]

Monochrome dressing thus assumed both a moral and aesthetic dimension closely tied to concepts of an almost masochistic asceticism; *almost* ascetic in that the materials, workmanship and mastery of style involved in the production of such simple beauty came at no mean price; *almost* masochistic in that woeful black seemed to suppress desire for brighter tones with a drama and panache, suggesting that a control over pleasure was in itself pleasurable. Such properties are captured perfectly in an elegant black shot silk doublet with silver ribbon points around the waist, its darkness set off by the contrasting yellow lining (127). This is not dissimilar perhaps to a suit of doublet, breeches and cloak in grey wrought satin, edged with silver gilt and lace ordered by Charles I in 1633–4, costing £97 4s 6d (twice the price of the £40 paid for Sir Anthony van Dyck's portrait of Queen Henrietta Maria with Jeffrey Hudson and monkey of the same year).[9]

Similar costume was adopted by men of taste across Europe through the 1630s and 1640s. In Van Dyck's oeuvre alone, the monochrome man disports in the melancholy luxury of black silk and white linen many times. Charles's cousin James Stuart, Duke of Lennox, wore it with Order of the Garter insignia on the occasion of his investiture in 1633, its glossy sheen offset by the quivering muscle and tan coat of his adoring greyhound. Poet, playwright and courtier Thomas Killigrew chose it in a simpler, almost dishevelled form to commemorate his mourning for the death of his wife Cecilia Crofts in 1638. This was the same year in which Sir Thomas Hammer, page to the king and celebrated horticulturalist, accented his black doublet with bright ivory silk gloves (interestingly, Hammer had also sported a black and white ensemble when he sat for painter Cornelius Johnson as a younger man, with plaited lovelock, tied with a red bow, in 1631). Henry Peacham, poet of emblems and England's Castiglione (he wrote to guide the moral and aesthetic choices of fashionable young men), saw an obvious resemblance between that love for the contrast of black and white in modish self-presentation and the supposed fastidiousness of the ermine. What might have looked sharp, restrained and stylish on the surface, could not wholly disguise the shameful imperfection of the soul beneath. It was imperative that the man of fashion kept pride and shame in precarious balance:

> The Ermine here, whome eager houndes doe chase
> And hunters have, around environ'd in,
> (As some doe write) will not come neere the place,
> That may with dirt, defile his daintie skinne:
> But rather chooseth, than the same should soile,
> Be torn with dogges, or taken with the toile.
> Me thinks even now, I see a number blush,
> To heare a beaste, by nature should have care,
> To keepe his skinne, themselves not care a rush,
> With how much filth their mindes bespotted are;
> Great Lordes and Ladies turne your cost and art,
> From bodies pride, t'enrich your better part.[10]

MONOCHROME MODERNITY: BLACK AND THE MAN OF REVOLUTION

If black dress in the early modern world, in its denoting of social hierarchies and spiritual purity, signified an adherence to a sense of order and the common good, by the turn of the nineteenth century a new cult of romanticism and individualism set monochrome fashion at the centre of an entirely new and revolutionary set of moral and sartorial codes. The English novelist Edward Bulwer-Lytton captured the spirit in his novel *Pelham* of 1828, in which the eponymous hero sets down some instructions for modern self-presentation:

> Keep your mind free from all violent affections at the hour of the toilet. A philosophical severity is perfectly necessary for success...
>
> A man must be a profound calculator to be a consummate dresser... there is no diplomacy more subtle than dress...
>
> The most graceful principle of dress is neatness – the most vulgar is preciseness...
>
> Dress contains the two codes of morality – private and public. Attention is the duty we owe to others – cleanliness that which we owe to ourselves...
>
> Avoid many colours and seek by one prevalent and quiet tint to sober down the others. Apelles used only four colours, and always subdued those which were florid by a darkening varnish...
>
> Inventions in dressing should resemble Addison's definition of fine writing, and consist of 'refinements which are natural, without being obvious.[11]

Fictional characters like Pelham abound in the novels, satires and plays of the early 1800s. Elegant, elite and exclusive, and most often represented dressed in exquisite black and white, they intensified the magnificent dark exuberance of the Renaissance courtier, refashioning it for a more democratic age: more a refinement perhaps, than a renunciation? Loosely based on the habits of just a few metropolitan men, made famous through their collective tendency to promote their celebrity through the singularly severe arrangement of their costumes and manners, these cyphers of pared-back modernity, styled 'dandy' in contemporary terminology,

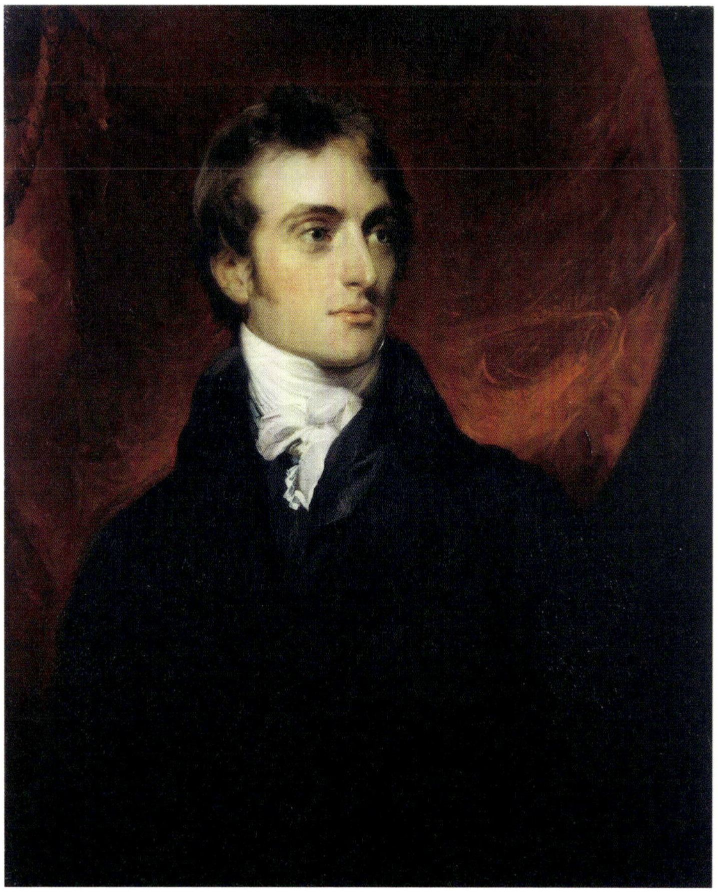

128. Thomas Lawrence PRA (1769–1830), *Sir Codrington Edmund Carrington*. Oil on canvas, 74.3 × 61.9 cm. London, *c*.1801. Bequeathed by Miss L.M. Carrington. V&A: 1359-1874

stood as a new, universal code of fashionable behaviour. The idea of dandyism, though perhaps trivial in itself, revealed in its broader cultural agency the ways in which urbanism, capitalism, industrialization, colonialism and enlightenment theories of truth were dissolving older sureties around commonweal and *droit de seigneur* in favour of the individualistic credo associated with the heroism of modern life.

The English socialite George Bryan 'Beau' Brummell stood out as a semi-fictional exemplar of the dandy attitude (semi-fictional because, although history records that he was born in London in 1778 and died in Caen, France, in 1840, the facts of his life survive as a palimpsest of myths and anecdotes retold in subsequent biographies).[12] The son of a minor equerry at court, through wit, sheer force of personality and the ability to make social connections, Brummell established himself as an expert in etiquette and a master of the art of dressing. His opinions influenced fashionable life from the top down. During the 1810s he cultivated a personal aesthetic that drew on aristocratic tailoring styles evolved to suit sporting pursuits, court ceremonial, club land business and the whirl of salons and balls that constituted the London season. Brummell's genius lay in reconfiguring these staples as a revolutionary costume for modern times, establishing a rule of taste based on subjective aesthetic criteria and the careful exercise of personal choice, rather than deference to status earned through family lineage or traditional forms of power exchange.

The most striking thing about the new wardrobe was its relative subtlety: spotless white linen, expertly tailored dark blue swallowtail coat, buff waistcoat and breeches and polished riding boots for the morning, and a more severe arrangement of black silk, fine wool and velvet for eveningwear. Fashion plates of the era, produced for the journals and shop displays of the burgeoning tailoring and menswear industries, record a fairly stable fashionable ensemble for men designed along these lines that remained dominant templates well into the nineteenth century. Similarly, portraits produced for Britain's landowners, politicians, colonial adventurers and industrial entrepreneurs by Sir Thomas Lawrence and other leading painters during the final years of the Hanoverian reign fall back on the same pattern. Lawrence's sumptuous painterly shorthand was particularly well suited to delineating the elongated black silhouettes of an elite generation of sitters, most often shown against a sweep of red velvet curtain (128). Some art critics praised a style of dressing and representation that was 'simple, natural and unostentatious ... an air of courteous suavity pervades the whole.' For others, the artist's talent was 'thrown around the representations of the most ordinary things, and in his hands, the unpicturesque costume of modern times – the coats and waistcoats of modern man – lose their common place appearance.'[13]

Critics of the 1820s were well ahead of their time in drawing attention to the quotidian, and intrinsically modern aspects of the monochrome suit. Four decades later, the Paris art world of the 1860s and 1870s was divided in its debates on the merits of contemporary dress as represented in the work of the Impressionists and their associates. Dress historian Aileen Ribeiro cites the writer Charles Blanc, whose reflections on modern fashion in *Art in Ornament and Dress* (1875) seem to find echoes in the work of painters including Gustave Caillebotte, James Tissot and Edouard Manet:

> [Blanc] claimed that both architecture and dress – particularly that of men ... were governed by similar rules, such as symmetry, repetition (variety had charm but 'repetition has more grandeur') and economy of decoration. These features of modern life, however, often created a sense of alienation and isolation. The predominant darkness of outdoor clothing was linked to the greyness of buildings and streets, and created a tendency for people to merge into their surroundings, lose their individuality, and retreat into their own private worlds.[14]

The great poet of Parisian modernity Charles Baudelaire had observed the attendant melancholy and ennui induced by such atmospherics in the revolutionary 1840s. His radical biographer Walter Benjamin notes:

> With the July Monarchy, blacks and greys began to predominate in men's clothes. Baudelaire concerned himself with this innovation in his 'Salon de 1845'. In the conclusion of his first work he wrote: 'More than anyone else ... the true painter, will be the man who extracts from present-day life its epic aspects and teaches us in lines and colours to understand how great and poetic we are in our patent-leather shoes and neckties...' One year later he wrote: 'Regarding the attire, the covering of the modern hero ... does it not have a beauty and charm of its own?... Is this not an attire that is needed by our epoch, suffering and dressed up to its thin black narrow shoulders in the symbol of constant mourning? The black suit and the frock coat not only have their political beauty as an expression of general equality, but also their poetic beauty as an expression of the public mentality... We all observe some sort of funeral. The unvarying livery of hopelessness is proof of the equality... And haven't the folds in the material, which make grimaces and drape themselves around mortified flesh like snakes, their secret charm?[15]

Certainly the dark wool frock and lounge coats and glossy beaver-skin top hats that have survived the pawnbrokers, thrift merchants and theatrical costumiers of the intervening years to enter museum collections bear witness to Baudelaire's lamentations (129 and 130). And yet, while their monochrome uniformity seems to speak to visions of mill chimneys, dehumanizing machinery, sooty pollution and graveyard protocol, there is also something in their sharp seriality that suggests the beauty of an affecting and artificial minimalist aesthetic (131). Contemporaries recognized the harmonious role that a controlled and subdued palette might have as part of the broader social milieu, particularly when it came to considering menswear as a foil for the more colourful excesses of women's dress. As one author of a guide for enjoying the nightlife of Paris noted in 1878:

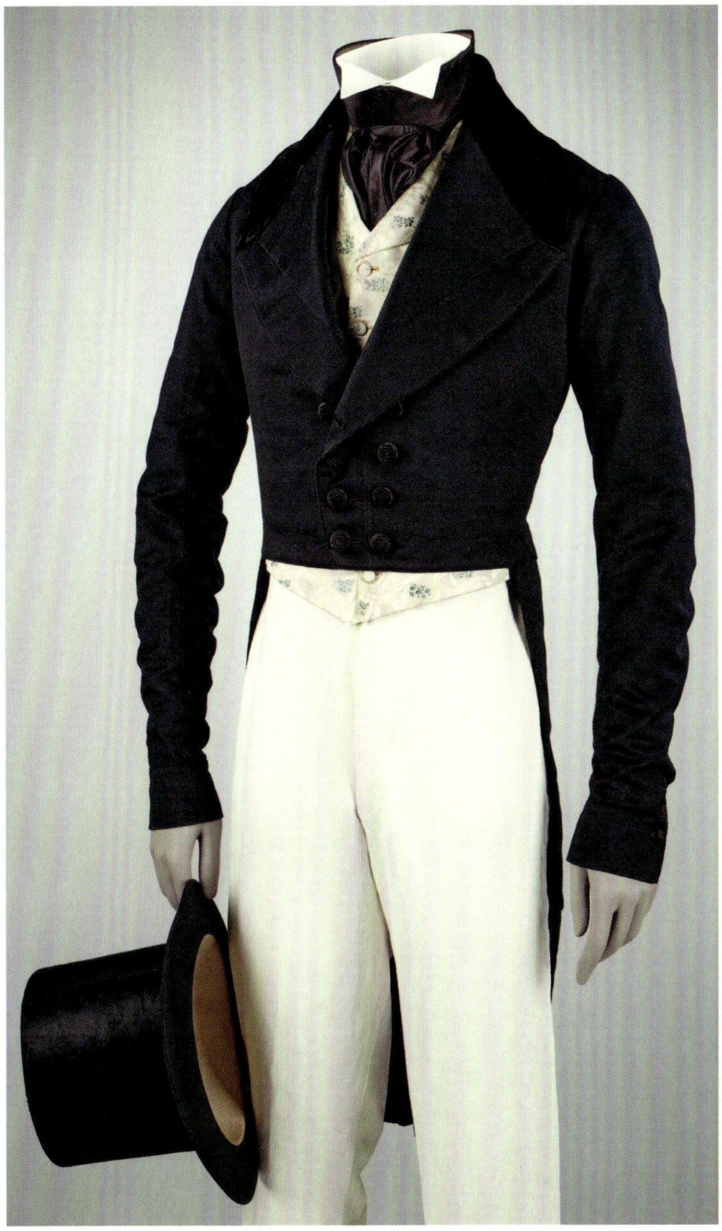

129. Coat. Wool and silk velvet. USA, 1845–53. V&A: T.176&A-1965. Waistcoat. Silk damask, cotton. England, 1850–3. Given by Miss C.M. Higgs. V&A: T.121-1949; Trousers. Linen. USA, 1845–53. Given by Captain Raymond Johnes. V&A: T.177-1965. Cravat. Satin. England, 1840–50. Given by Miss C. Wigginton. V&A: T.215-1966; Top Hat. Silk plush. England, *c.*1855. Given by Mr Hubert Arthur Druce. V&A: T.19-1918

> We are the lining of the jewelry box against which the eternal diamond stands out... Civilized man, from the point of view of his clothing, is nothing more than the accompanist of woman, he allows her to sing the symphony of white, pink and green as a solo.[16]

Following pages: 130. Coat, 1860–70, USA. Wool, lined with satin and cotton. V&A: T.4-1982; Lounge coat. Wool. Great Britain(?), 1870–5. Given by Mark Wallis. V&A: T.463-1997; Double-breasted frockcoat. Fine wool. Ireland, 1871. Given by Mr A.W. Furlong. V&A: T.47-1947; Frockcoat. Wool, lined with satin. Paris, 1885. Given by Mrs Frederick Ferraboschi. V&A: T.44A-1932

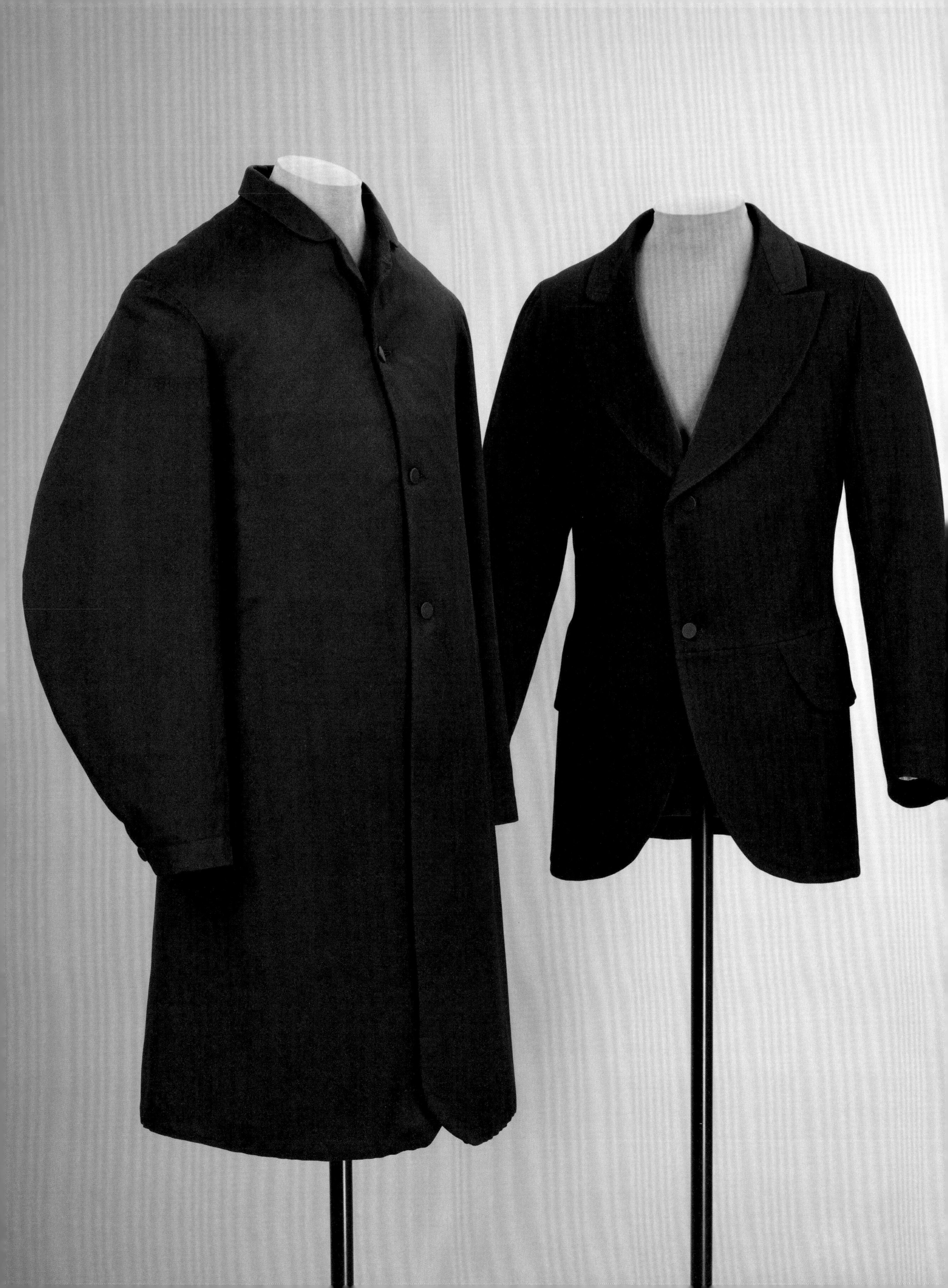

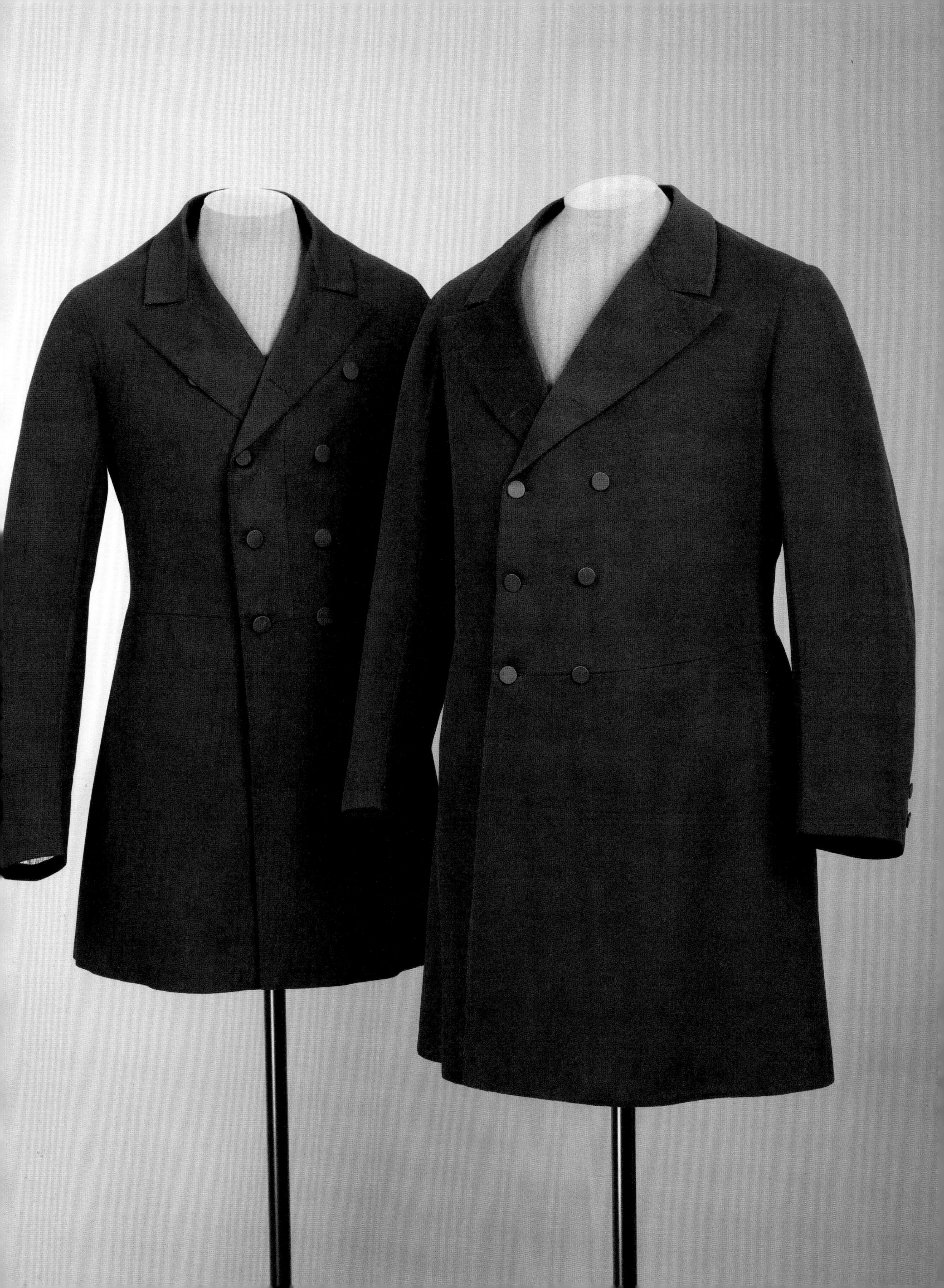

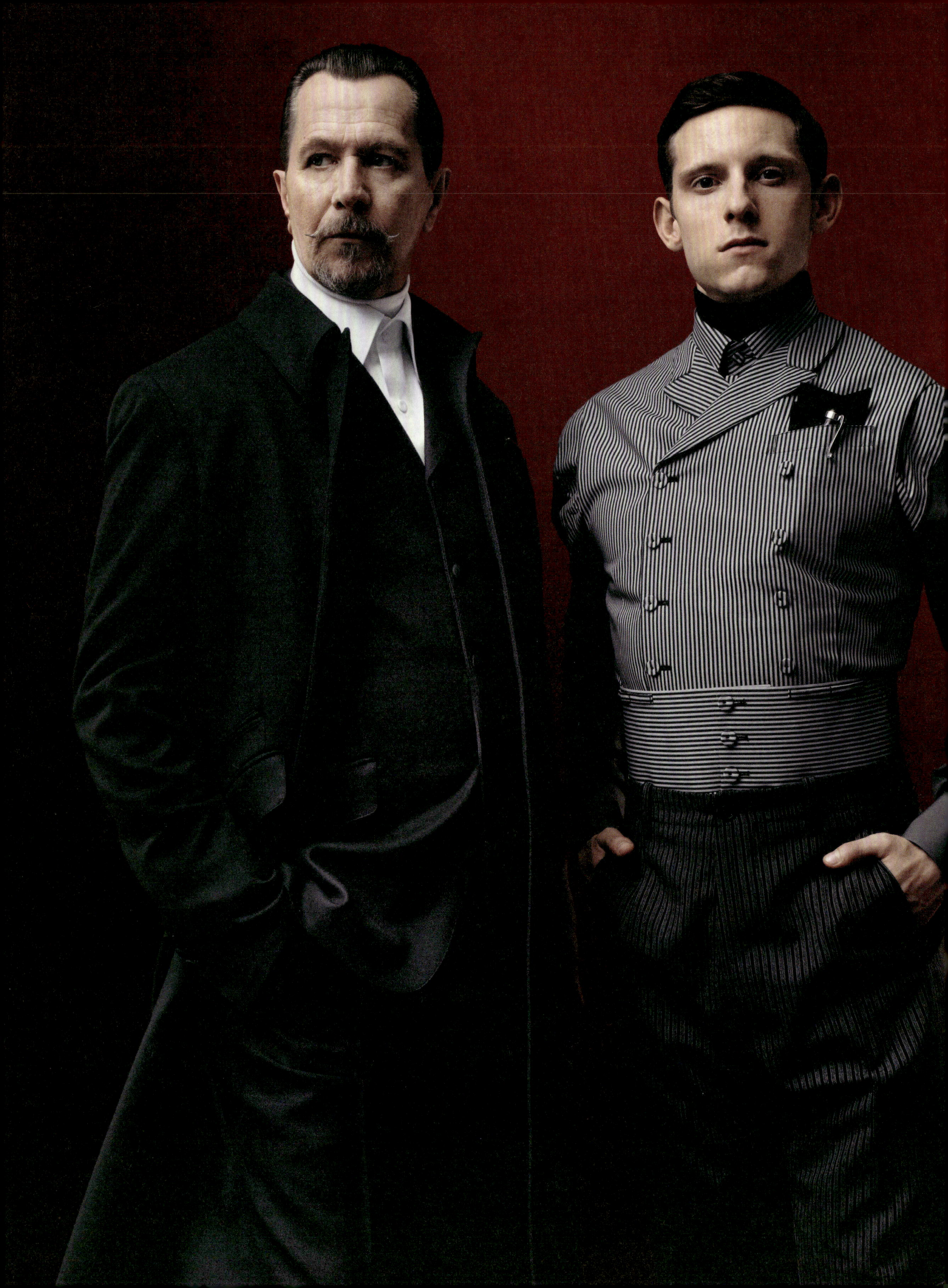

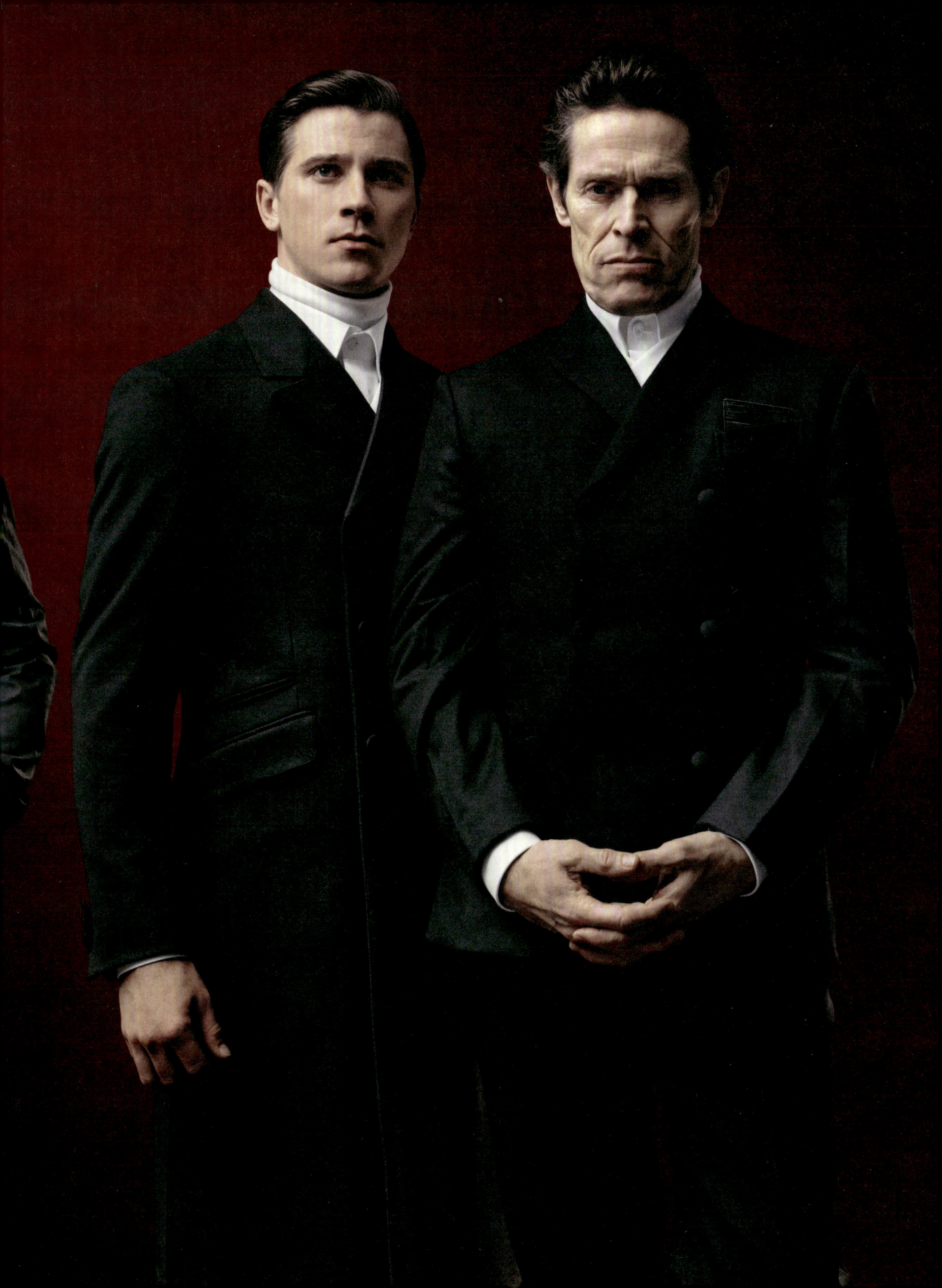

The inverse of such restraint was decadence. By the end of the century, the symbolism of black and white had taken on other, more sinister associations, as J.K. Huysmans's notorious dandy Jean des Esseintes set out to prove in the novel *À Rebours* (first published in 1884 and a key influence for Oscar Wilde's *The Picture of Dorian Gray* of 1890), blackness signalling an unsettling and shocking depravity:

> He won a considerable reputation as an eccentric – a reputation which he crowned by wearing suits of white velvet with gold-laced waistcoats, by sticking a bunch of Parma violets in his shirt front in lieu of a cravat, and by entertaining men of letters to dinners... One of these meals ... had been a funeral feast to mark the most ludicrous of personal misfortunes. The dining-room, draped in black, opened out onto a garden ... the paths being strewn with charcoal, the ornamental pond edged with black basalt and filled with ink... The dinner itself was served on a black cloth adorned with baskets of violets and scabious... Dining off black bordered plates, the company had enjoyed ... Russian rye bread, ripe olives from Turkey, caviar, mullet botargo, black puddings from Frankfurt, game served in sauces the colour of liquorice and boot-polish, truffle jellies, chocolate creams, plum puddings ... and black-heart cherries ... And after coffee and walnut cordial, they rounded off the evening with kvass, porter and stout.[17]

MONOCHROME METROPOLITANS: BLACK AND THE MAN OF STYLE

> You're the top!
> You're an Arrow collar.
> You're the top!
> You're a Coolidge dollar.
> You're the nimble tread of the feet of Fred Astaire,
> You're an O'Neill drama,
> You're Whistler's Mama,
> You're Camembert![18]

The witty lyrics written by Cole Porter for the Broadway musical *Anything Goes* in 1934 are a generation away from Huysmans's *fin-de-siècle* morbidity, but in their sophisticated referents (stylishly monochrome: from starched collars, to Astaire, to Whistler's famous painting of his mother) and the image they conjure up of fleet-footed dancers, celebrating on a cruise ship, the men in crisp swallow-tailed evening dress, they share the same cultural lineage. The renunciatory moment, having moved through courtly, Brummellian and decadent phases, found a new relevance in the context of the glamorous early twentieth century.

It was perhaps the well-tailored black suit that anchored it all. The V&A has several impeccable examples dating from the 1910s through to the 1930s, some of them, tailored for dinner or dancing, owned by the archetypal English dandy Max Beerbohm (132). Beerbohm's diminutive but

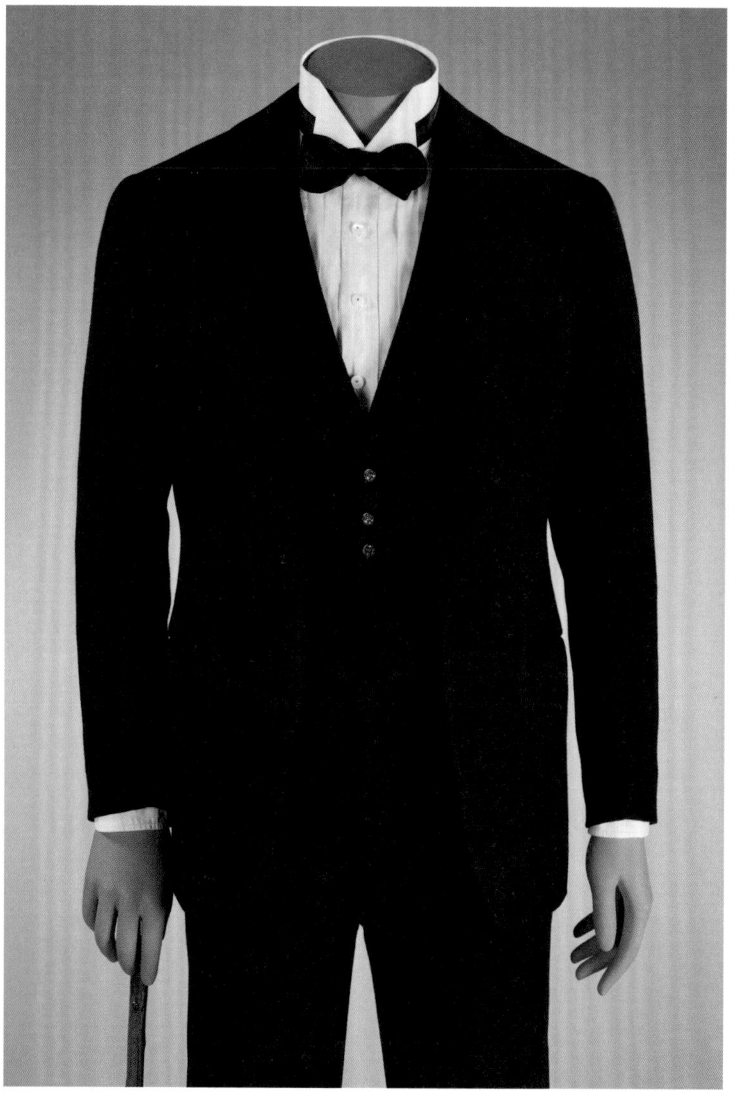

132. Dinner suit. Barathea, silk, steel, lined with satin and linen. Worn by Max Beerbohm. England, 1928. Bequeathed by Lady Beerbohm. V&A: T.212 to B-1960

dapper figure, together with his biting sense of humour, had marked him out, through his writings and caricatures, as a natural chronicler of the circle of Oscar Wilde and Aubrey Beardsley in the 1890s, during which decade he also authored the definitive essay on the nature and history of dandyism ('Dandies and Dandies'). From his self-exile to a villa in Rapallo in 1910 until his death in 1956, Beerbohm continued to make acerbic contributions to British cultural life in reviews and BBC broadcasts, ever immaculately dressed. Focusing in on the character of Beerbohm's art and self-presentation, literary theorist Robert Viscusi offers a useful interpretation of his style, entirely in keeping with renunciatory thinking, but posed for twentieth-century mass-consumption:

> Dandies make themselves. Whatever they may be by birth and nurture, dandies are born anew as dandies when they dress themselves according to the dandy code. The dandy self, naked and fresh, is a figure in black and white. Completely dressed, almost completely monochrome, he is, to put it simply, a written thing.[19]

Previous pages: 131. David Sims (1966–), Advertising campaign for Prada Autumn/Winter 2012. Models: Gary Oldman, Jamie Bell, Garrett Hedlund and Willem Dafoe

133. Max Beerbohm (1872–1956), *Caricature of Aubrey Beardsley*. Pen and ink, 31.9 × 25.8 cm. England, *c.*1894. Given by Mrs G.R. Halkett. V&A: E.1379-1931

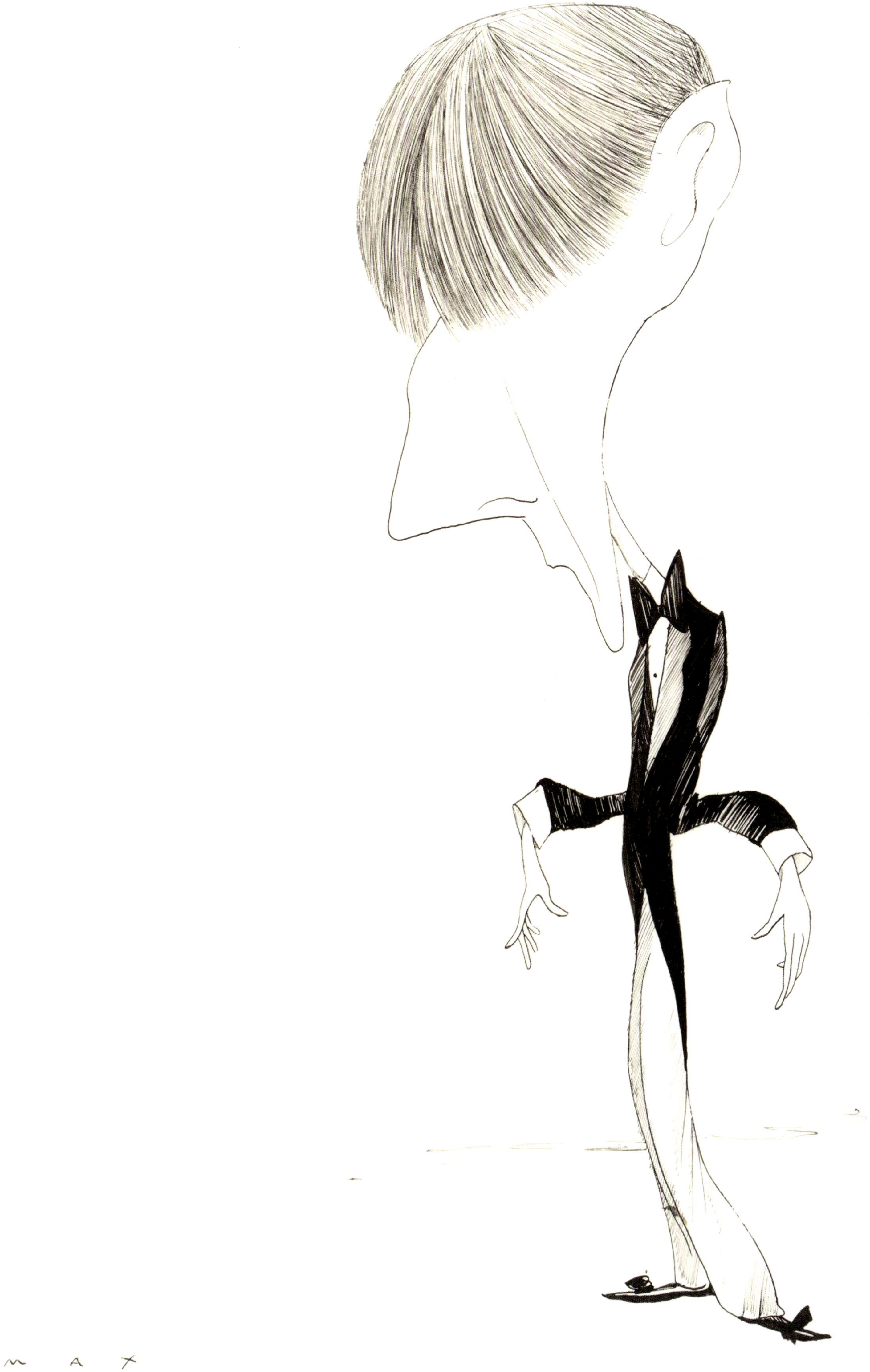
MAX

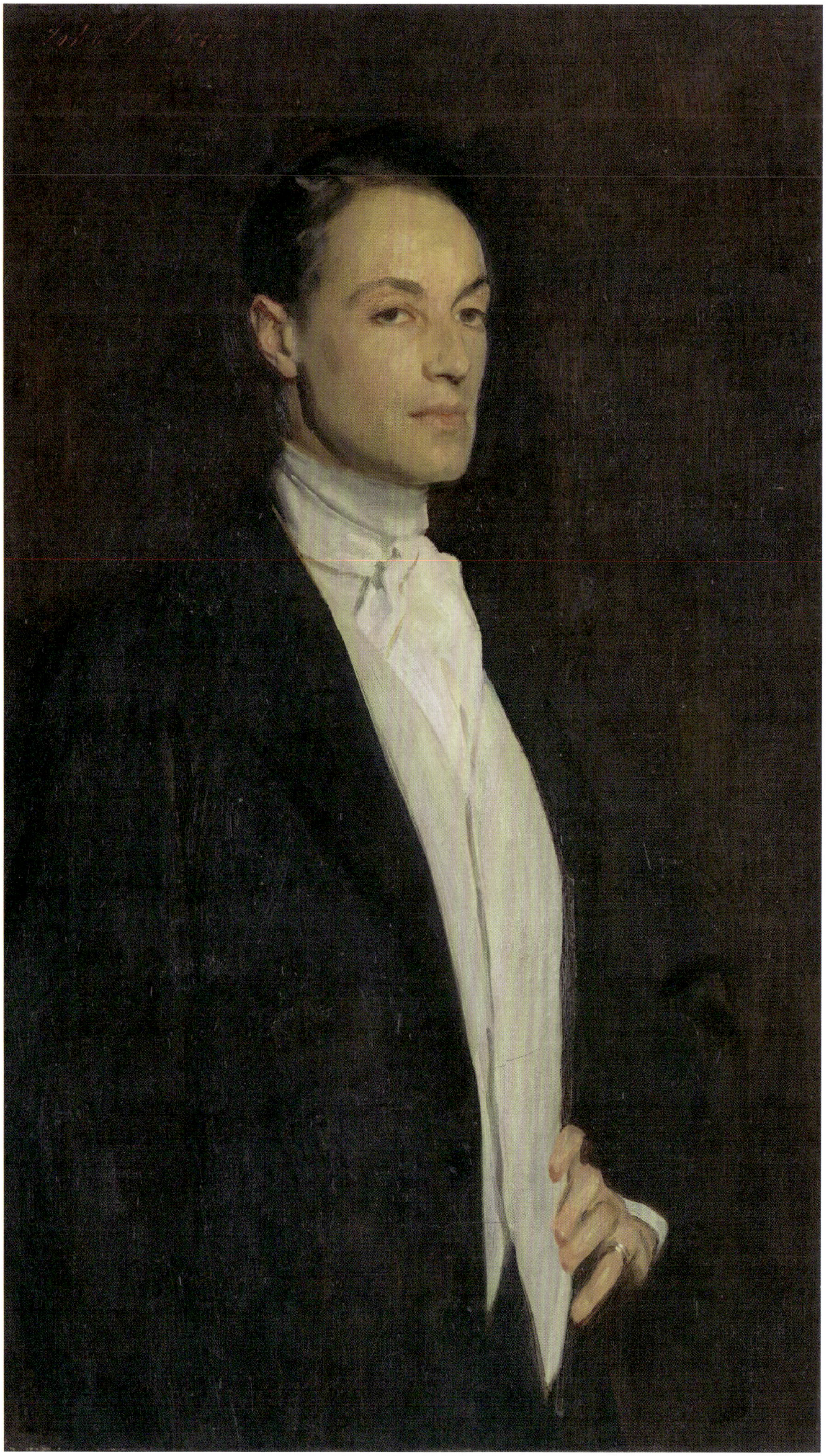

134. John Singer Sargent (1856–1925), *Sir Philip Sassoon*.
Oil on canvas, 95.2 × 57.8 cm. Great Britain, 1923. Tate, London: N05052

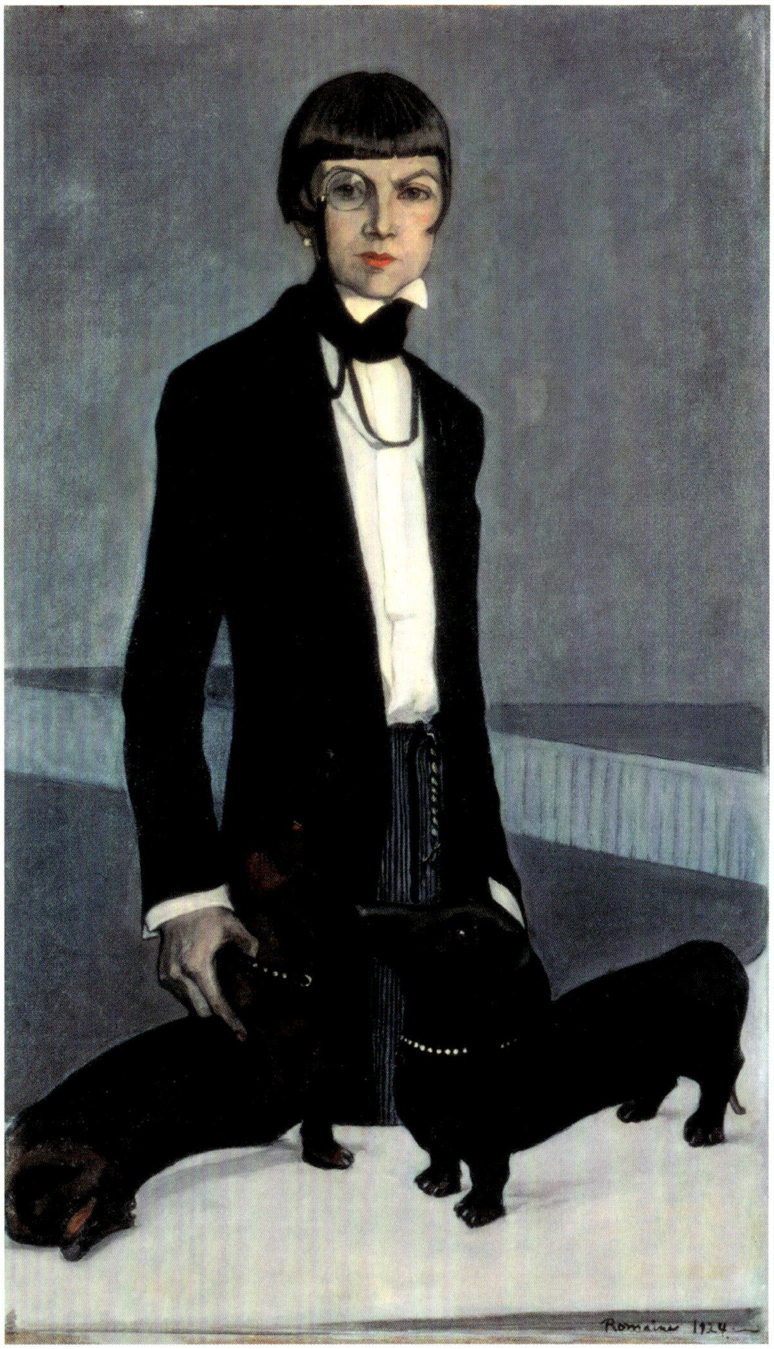

135. Romaine Brooks (1874–1970), *Una, Lady Troubridge*. Oil on canvas, 127.3 × 76.4 cm. Great Britain, 1924. Smithsonian American Art Museum, Washington DC: 1966.49.6

The 'pose' was replicated across all forms of visual and literary culture from the First World War through to the 1940s, often masking origins, tendencies or intentions otherwise unpalatable for populist modern moralities. It is there in countless Hollywood archetypes, from Fred Astaire to Marlene Dietrich. It is there in cartoons and fashion posters, by illustrators from H.M. Bateman to Tom Purvis. And it is there in the elegant portraits of socialite and politician Philip Sassoon painted by John Singer Sargent (134) and Glyn Philpot in 1913–14, the more scandalous likeness of Una Lady Troubridge in male evening attire and monocle, with dachshunds, by Romaine Brooks of 1924 (135), or the Maharaja of Indore captured in art deco splendour by painter and fashion illustrator Bernard Boutet de Monvel in 1929 (136). Jewish heritage, homosexuality or inherited power and wealth: all vulnerabilities were protected, momentarily, from vulgar attack by the armour of the dandy's monochrome wardrobe. As Harvey has observed: 'men have long been drawn or driven into uniforms – as soldiers or servants, as senators or executives – and the dinner jacket is perhaps the ultimate uniform, shorn of all duty but impersonal smartness.'[20]

This metropolitan style of renunciation, elite and elegant, found a final outing in Norman Parkinson's iconic photograph of 1950, part of a double-page spread in *Vogue* magazine in April of that year (137). Three archetypal English gentlemen stand on the pavement of Savile Row in the hazy spring sunshine. Two of them, Peter Coats and William

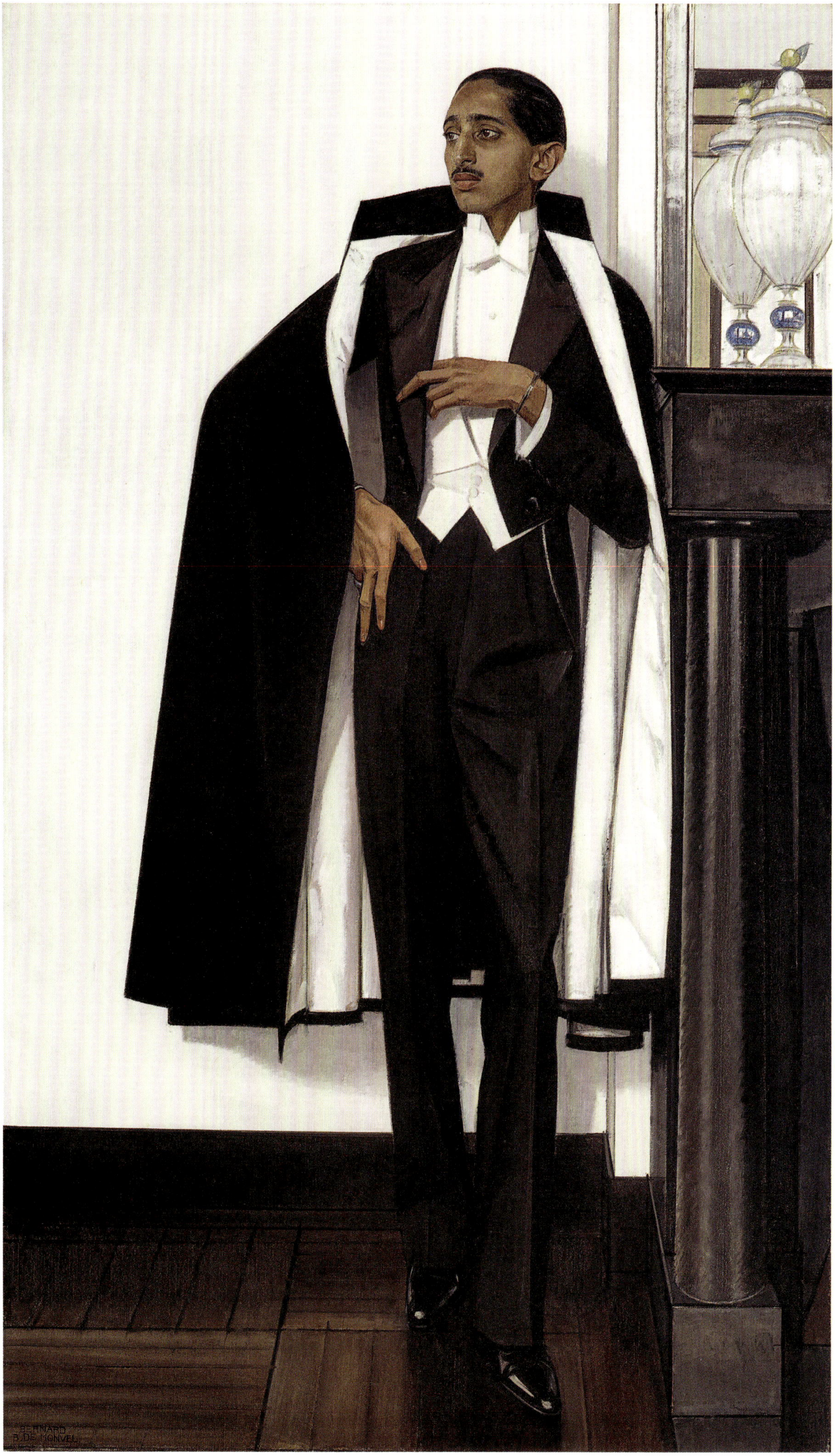

136. Bernard Boutet de Monvel (1881–1949), *Maharaja Yeshwant Rao Holkar II of Indore in Western Dress*. Oil on canvas, 194.5 × 116.5 cm. France, 1929. The Al Thani Collection

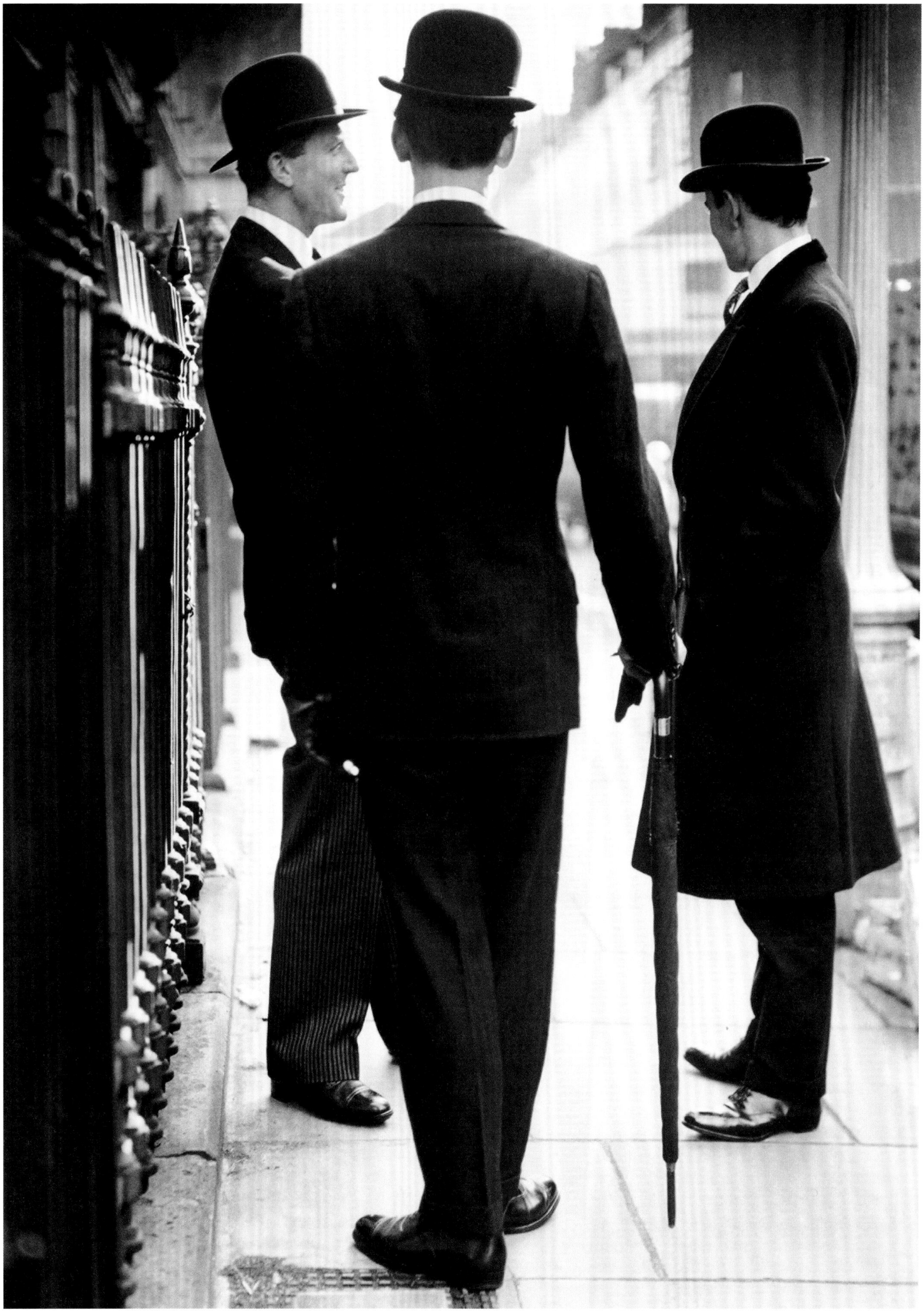

137. Norman Parkinson (1913–1990), *The New Mayfair Edwardians (Peter Daniel Coats; Sir William Miles Aykroyd, 3rd Bt; Mark Newman Gilbey)*.
Photograph, bromide print on card mount, 49.7 × 39 cm. London, 1950.
National Portrait Gallery, London. Given by Norman Parkinson,
1981: NPG X30089

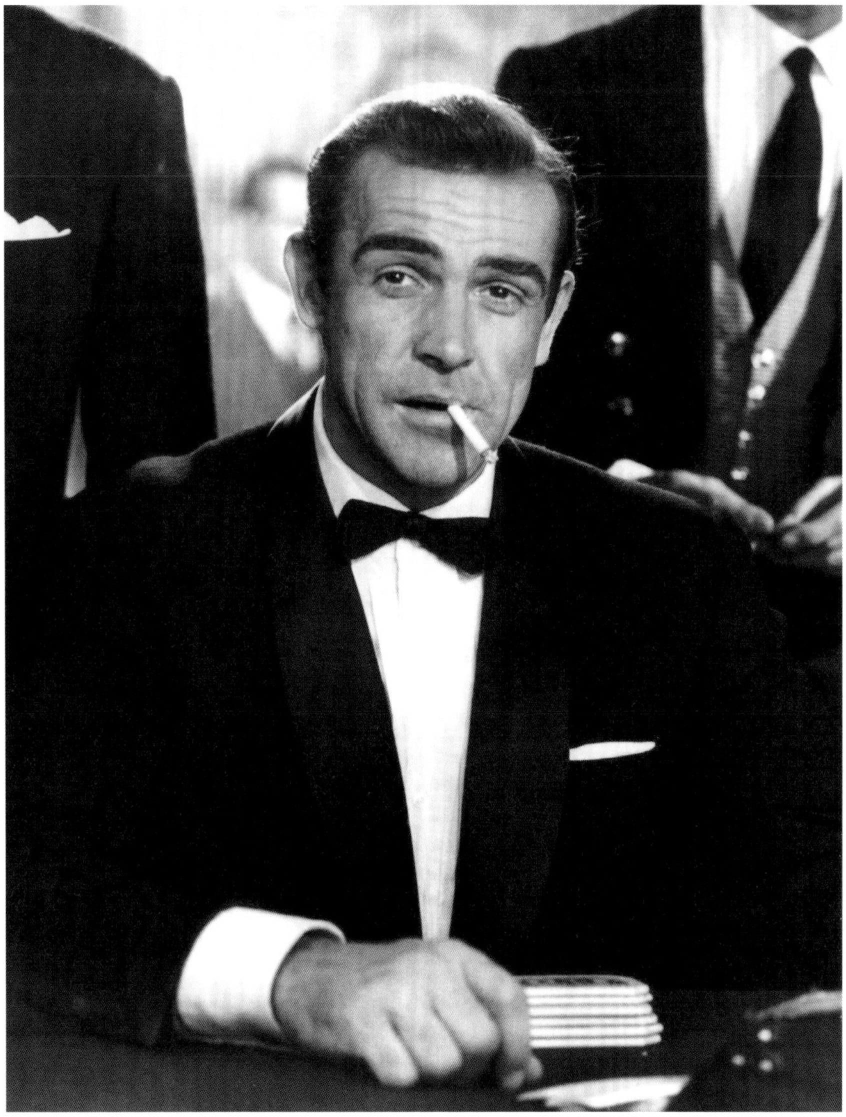

138. Sean Connery in *Dr No* (1962),
dir. Terence Young

Ackroyd, had enjoyed illustrious wartime military careers, and the sharp neatness of their black coats and suits, polished shoes, bowler hats and stiff white shirt collars bespeak the pin-sharp regulations of the parade ground.[21] 'Back To Formality' is the title of the feature, and there is something both elegiac and aloofly judgemental in their poised silhouettes, an implicit and reactionary rejection of the sloppy demob informality of contemporary youthful fashion styles that threatened to subsume post-war British culture with loud American pop and affordable Italian glamour.[22] In some ways the stark monochrome shot encapsulates what art historian Lynda Nead has described as a state of grey enervation in the attitudes of the British ruling class at the time:

> Loss of colour was a metaphor for all that was wrong with the post-war settlement: rather than celebrating the poetics of chiaroscuro and atmospheric contrast, grey became the symbol of stasis: of a ruined society, a government that was failing to modernize and a country that was bogged down in the past.[23]

The renunciatory moment in men's dress had come to its inevitable end as democracy in politics, society and fashion put an end to that masochistic, aristocratic prerogative to retreat into the luxury of black. From the 1960s onwards it survived only in the stylish anti-hero stereotypes of Joseph Losey's films (*Eva*, *The Servant* and *Darling*), or the more popular equivalent of Sean Connery's James Bond, fitted out in tailor Anthony Sinclair's dinner jackets and dress shirts for battle at the casino table (138) – to be replicated in a million suburban black-tie dinner dances and Rotary Club fundraisers across Europe and North America for the next 40 years.[24] As Harvey has it:

> By mid-century one could say – for the first time since the fourteenth century – that black had disappeared from the general daily dress of men. But not from their dress in the evening. When men's black began its territorial expansion, at the start of the nineteenth century, it arrived first in evening wear. And it is in evening wear, still, that black has been the last to leave.[25]

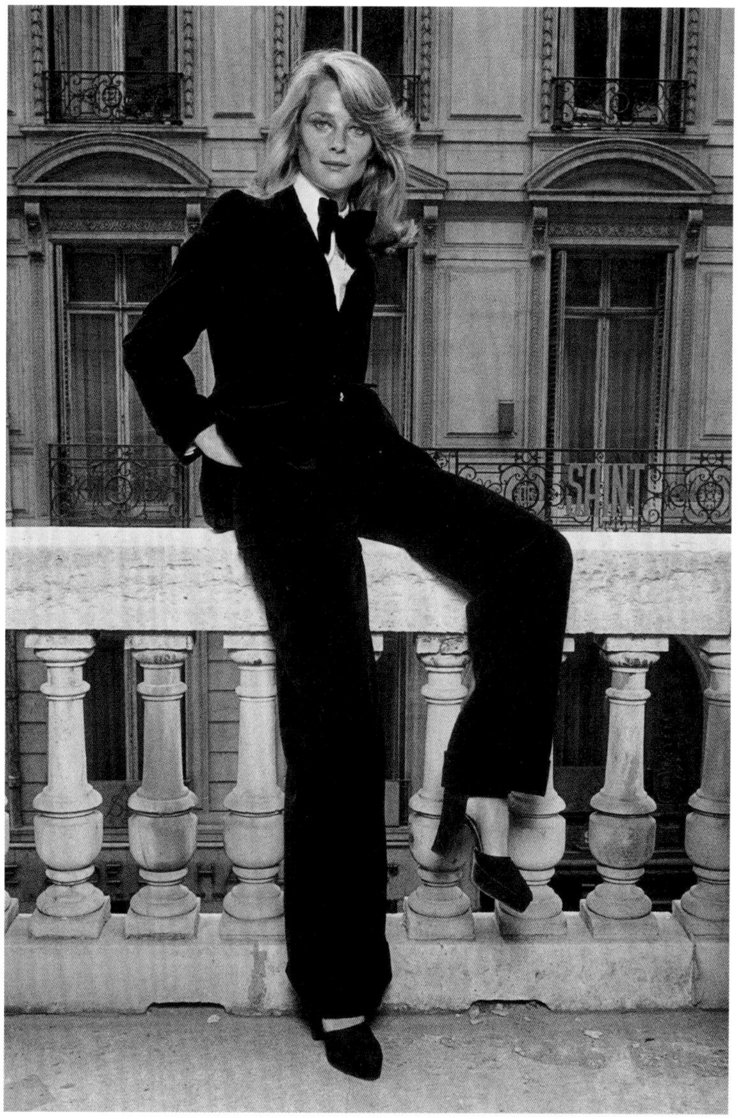

139. Alain Dejean, Charlotte Rampling in Yves Saint Laurent 'Le Smoking' trouser suit, 1972

POSTSCRIPT: MONOCHROME MODE

The bathetic fall to the netherworld of hire and fancy dress has not quite put paid to black's place in the progressive lexicon of masculine dress, however. In the domain of high fashion and street expression, the soigné sophistication of monochrome dressing and its association with subversive or counter-cultural practices have meant that the dark, renunciatory palette has found its niche and a perennial slot in the work of late twentieth-century and post-millennial fashion auteurs, who will often conjure up black ghosts from the past. A generation of Paris-based Japanese designers from Yohji Yamamoto to Rei Kawakubo, and their counterparts in Antwerp, has fallen back on the mournful repertoire of inky, priest-like hues and textures, well suited to creative clients set to minister the last rites in the fields of film, architecture and advertising. Gothic introversion has become the favoured style of a new court society located in the gentrified districts of New York, Paris, London and Berlin.

But beyond this uniform, Flügel's refugees also retain the power to provoke. None more so than Yves Saint Laurent, whose appropriation of masculine evening dress for women in the 1970s went to the root of that pleasurable, kinky masochism in monochrome dressing with which this chapter commenced. In 1966, building on the precedent set by women in the 1920s and '30s, he experimented for the first time with the formal dinner suit, elongating its line to drape around the curves of the female body, finding in the tension and confusion between genders a new freedom (139). 'Le Smoking' became a staple in Saint Laurent's repertoire, captured most famously in Helmut Newton's brooding photographs for *Vogue* in 1975 and 1979. As cultural theorist Stephen Gundle has noted, the two men – Saint Laurent a gay man born in French colonial North Africa and Newton a refugee from Nazism – were well versed in the fact that 'corruption, authoritarianism and sexual perversion were never far from the centre of the bourgeois subconscious... The cultural climate of the seventies allowed them to bring their convictions about the bourgeoisie into the commercial and artistic mainstream.'[26] Sharp tailoring, black and white photography and a fetishistic spin on old-style Flügellian dandyism provided them with the tools.

They were not the only mid-twentieth-century stylists for whom a monochrome palette offered a point of resistance and hope. Writing at the tail end of 2020, a year in which pandemic and political turmoil across the world ripped fashionable obsessions apart and recast mourning as a dominant cultural trope, it seems especially appropriate to conclude with the wardrobe of the Black Panthers (140). The power salute of these civil rights campaigners of late 1960s and early 1970s America endures as a universal symbol of the Black Lives Matter movement 50 years later, following the murder of George Floyd by Minneapolis police in May 2020. The Black Panther Party itself, formed in 1966 by Bobby Seale and Huey P. Newton as a more radical manifestation of the impetus for change initiated by Malcolm X's Nation of Islam, drew its sartorial power from the same jazz-inflected version of monochrome Black 'cool'.[27] But where Malcolm X had favoured the slim graphic black suit and tie of modern jazz, itself a repudiation of Zoot Suit excess, the Panthers looked to a more emphatic statement of revolutionary intent. The black felt beret and roll-neck sweater of the inter-war artistic avant-garde joined military blue shirts and black leather coats as an expression of struggle.

As a visible renunciation of racism and proud signifier of Black identity, the Panther look is as enduring, at least in a symbolic sense, as its Flügellian counterpart, and remains a powerful reminder of the sense of loss that black in men's fashion has always carried with it, and which this essay attempts to read. For British and American style magazines, its simple elegance has formed a useful shorthand for the particular rigour of Black dandyism, described so elegantly by Monica L. Miller.[28] In 1980 for example,

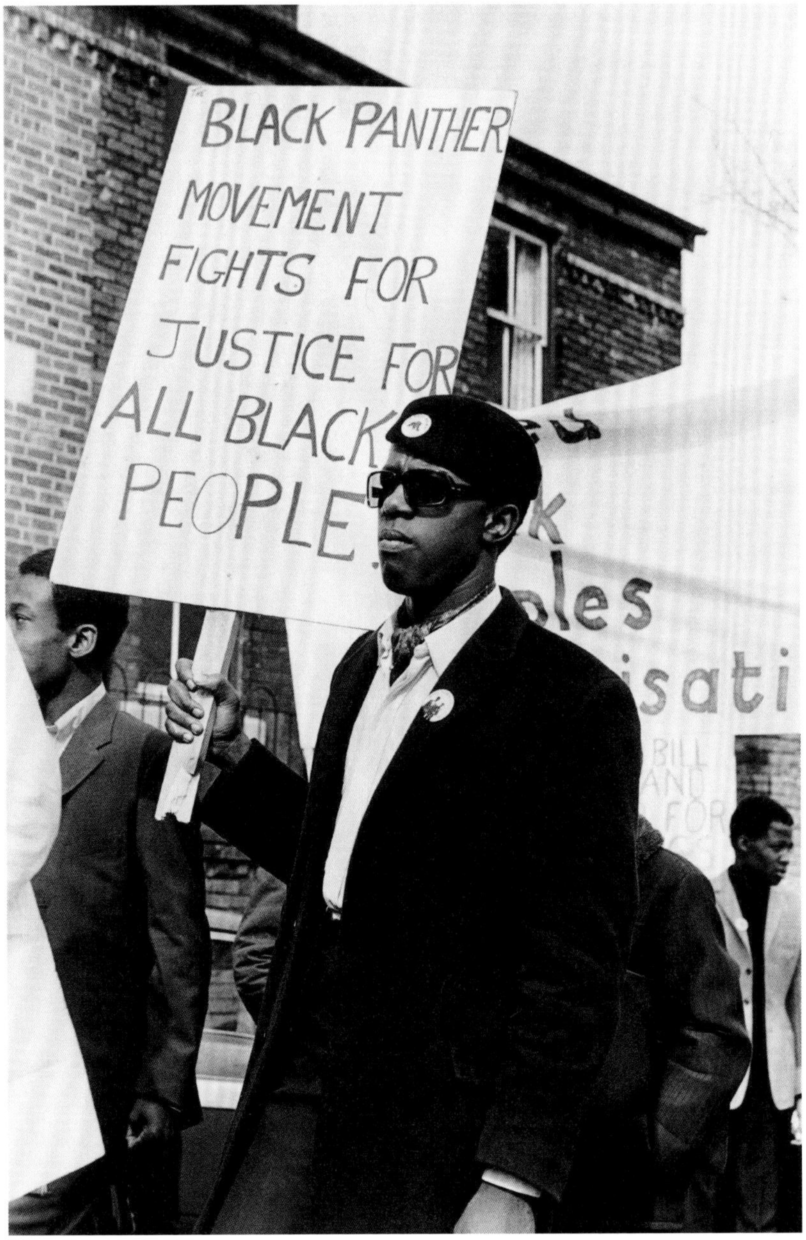

140. Neil Kenlock (1950–), *Untitled*.
Photograph, gelatin silver print, 45.6 × 30.8 cm. London, 1971.
Supported by the National Lottery Heritage Fund. V&A: E.218-2012

141. Janette Beckman (1959–), London Rude Boy twins Chuka and Dubem Okonkwo, published in *The Face* (London, May 1980)

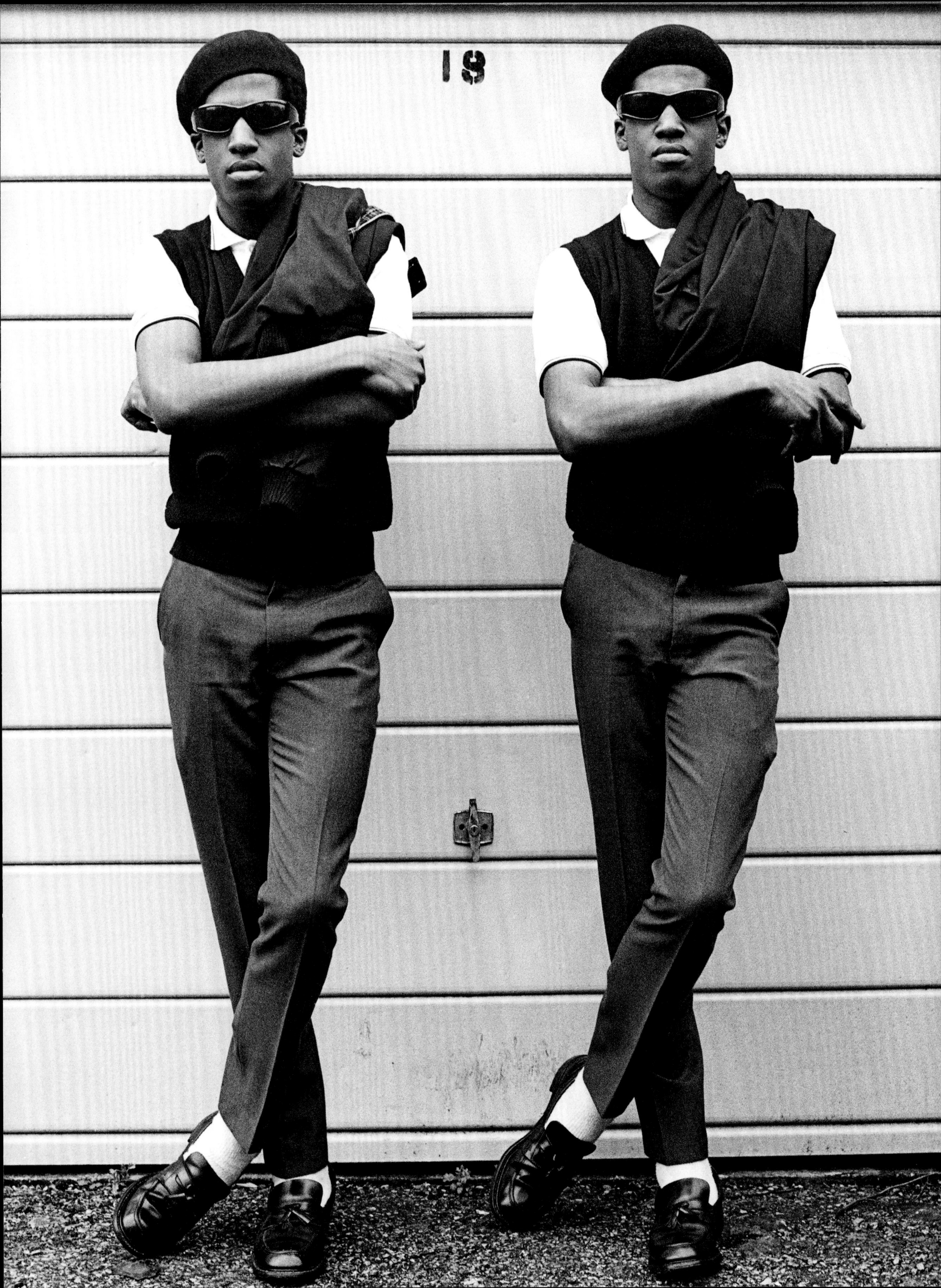
19

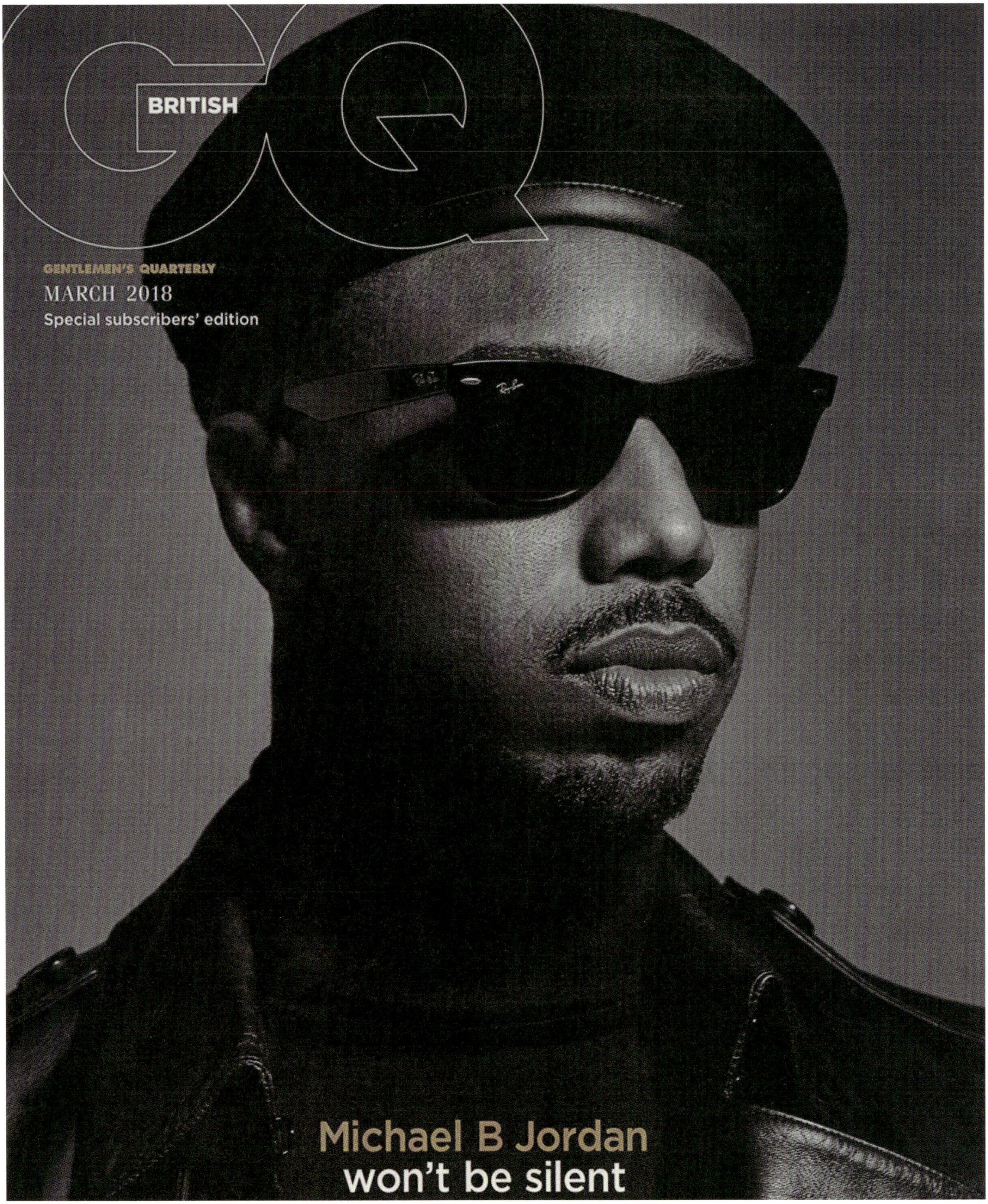

142. Gavin Bond (1970–), Michael B. Jordan,
published on the cover of *GQ* (March 2018)

Janette Beckman photographed twins Chuka and Dubem Okonkwo for *The Face*: London 'rude boys' bricolaging the Fred Perry sports shirts, Sta-Prest trousers, Harrington jackets and tasselled loafers of British Jamaican ska music, with the berets and sunglasses of Black Panther protest (141). Nearly 20 years later, in 2018, American actor and director Michael Bakari Jordan adopted a black beret, roll neck, leather coat and Ray-Ban sunglasses in Gavin Bond's cover shot for British *GQ* (142).

Not all was lost to chic Hollywood reappropriation in this slick piece of sartorial PR. There is authentic soul here. Bobby Seale has recorded that the fundamentals of the Panther style were borrowed from the words of a Broadway jazz standard *(What did I do to be so) Black and Blue*, adapted from a blues lament of violent discrimination from the pre-war segregationist South. Written by Harry Brooks, Andy Razaf and Fats Waller for the musical *Hot Chocolates* of 1929, and reprised by Louis Armstrong and other Black stars for decades after, the song was a showstopper. Seale understood that 'the American community is all beat up, black and blue from over 200 years of racist discrimination' and demanded 'let's make this the uniform.'[29] There is something of John Dowland's dark lament in the song's entreaty. Monochrome man is not dead yet:

Cold empty bed, springs hard as lead
Feel like old Ned, wished I was dead
What did I do to be so black and blue?
Even the mouse ran from my house
They laugh at you and scorn you too
What did I do to be so black and blue?
I'm white inside, but that don't help my case
'Cause I can't hide, what is in my face
How would it end? Ain't got a friend
My only sin is my skin
What did I do to be so black and blue?

A FULL MONTY

MIRIAM PHELAN

'The need for clothes confidence overcomes economic hesitations', was the conclusion of a Mass Observation survey in 1939, and that it was thanks to 'the miracle wrought by Montagu[e] Burton' which enabled every man, of any class, to 'enjoy the satisfaction of being well-dressed'.[1] Montague Burton was a Jewish immigrant whose contribution to men's fashion in Britain earned him the title of 'The Tailor of Taste'.[2] Burton was born Meshe David Osinsky, and he immigrated to Britain in 1900 to escape the harsh persecution of Jews in Russia. Many Jewish immigrants to Britain started in the rag trade selling old clothes in markets and on street corners. Osinsky quickly established himself in the clothing trade, renting premises in Chesterfield in 1904 and began selling ready-to-wear suits under the anglicized name Montague Burton (146).[3] From these humble beginnings, Burton became a household name, dominating the wholesale bespoke and made-to-measure industry into the 1960s. War changed many aspects of life in Britain from 1914 and beyond 1945, and tailoring was no exception. Burton, knighted in 1939 for his contribution to the war effort, seized the opportunity presented by periods of uncertainty to further the availability of made-to-measure and challenge the exclusivity of bespoke tailoring.[4]

From the end of the nineteenth century, firms like Hepworth's were already providing wholesale bespoke suits at an affordable price. Wholesale bespoke was an efficient factory system whereby the customer would select each of the different elements of his suit, from fabric and buttons to linings and pockets. Once the customer's measurements were taken, all this information was sent to the factory for the suit to be made through a standardized manufacturing process.[5] This service provided men with an alternative to the vastly more expensive bespoke suit, and it was not long before Burton offered wholesale bespoke alongside his ready-to-wear stock. From 1909 to 1914, Burton experienced a surge in demand, with 14 shops open before the outbreak of the First World War.[6] At this time, bespoke tailoring and wholesale bespoke were divided along class lines. The working classes were catered for by companies like Burton, mainly based in northern counties, thus having little to no impact on the elite clientele who frequented tailors like Henry Poole or Gieves Ltd on Savile Row in London.[7] The First World War, however, challenged this sartorial divide and set in motion the democratization of the tailored suit.

At the outbreak of war in 1914, bespoke tailors were still providing a made-to-measure service for both civilian dress and military uniform. Distinctions of class and rank were maintained for those who could afford to have their uniforms tailored in line with British army regulations. As Siegfried Sassoon noted: 'Ordering my uniform from Craven & Sons was quite enjoyable – almost like getting hunting clothes.'[8] The majority of recruits from the lower and work-

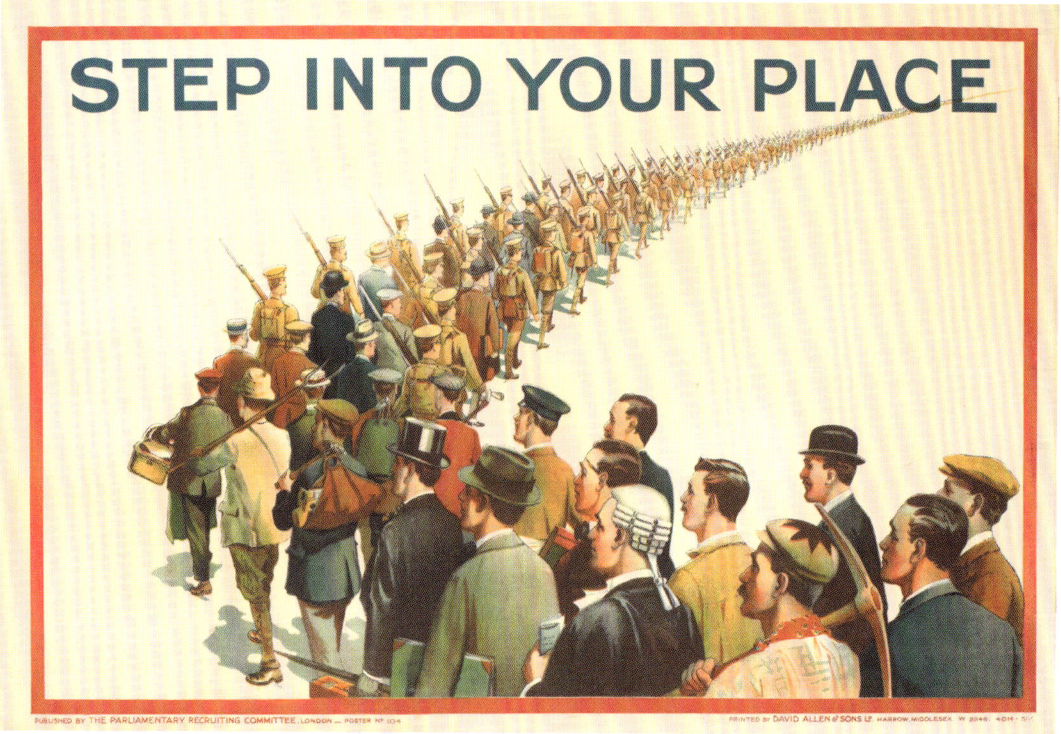

143. Recruitment poster. Lithograph, 50.6 × 75.8 cm. Great Britain, 1915. Imperial War Museum, London: Art.IWM PST 11855

144. Montague Burton (1885–1952), Suit. Tweed. England, 1935. Worn with single-breasted knitted woollen waistcoat by Arthur Shepherd, 1940–50. Given by Mr Raymond Burton CBE. V&A: T.13:1 to 4-2006

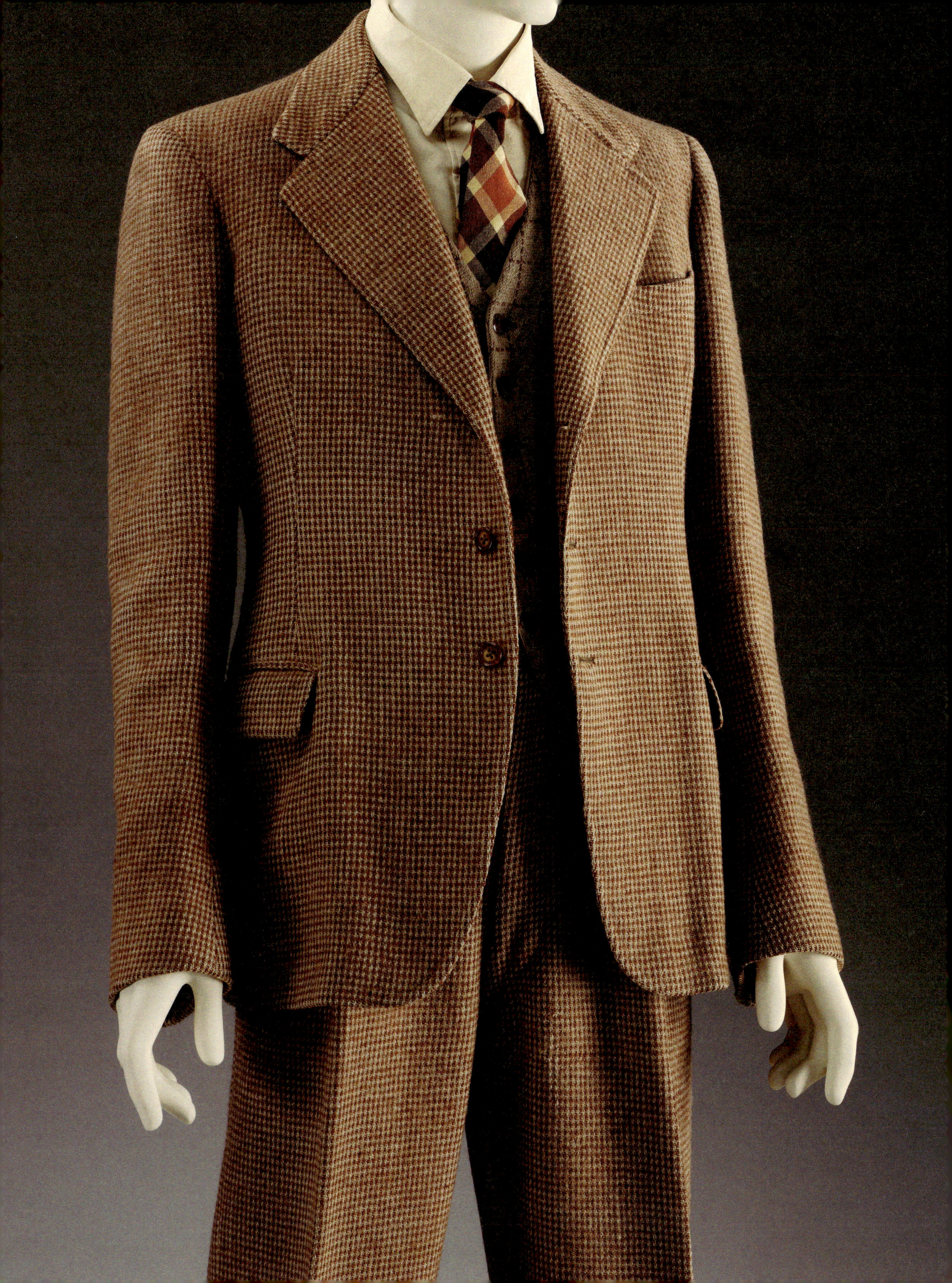

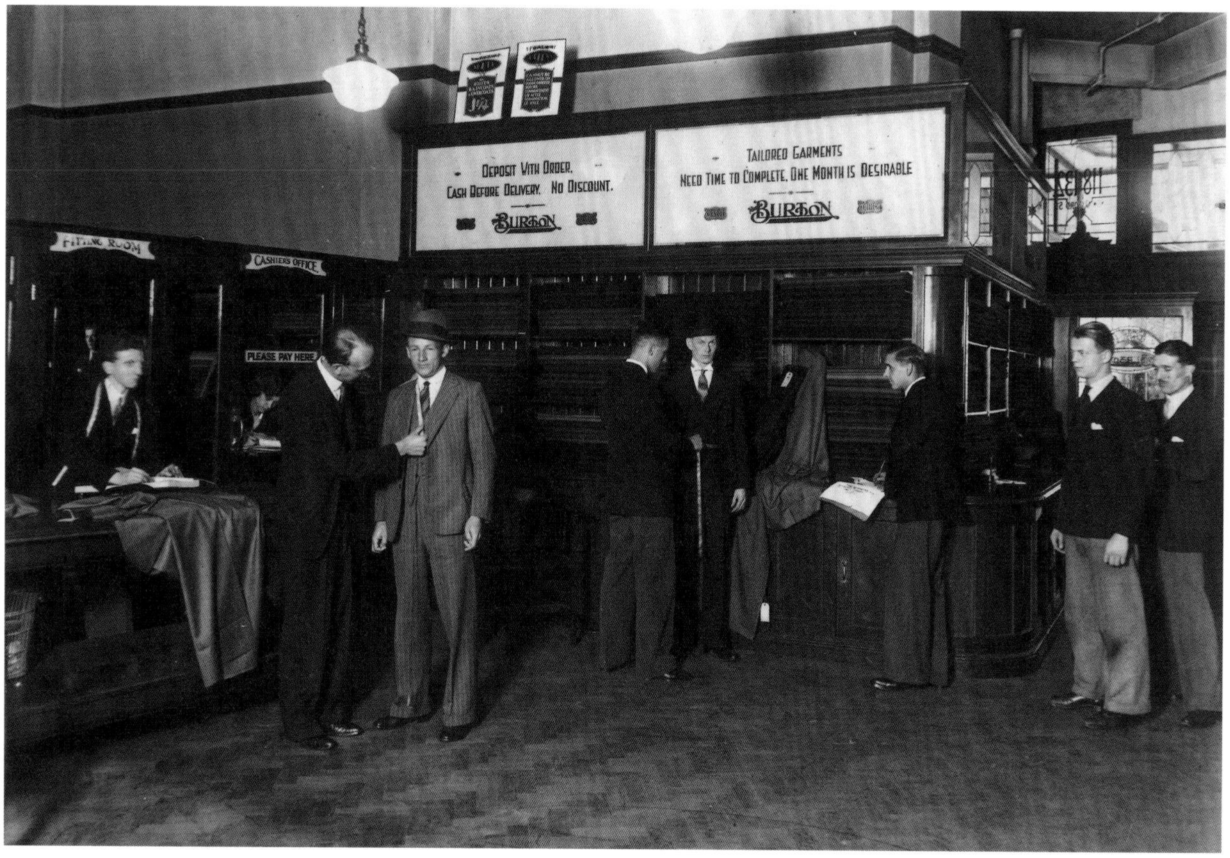

145. Australian cricketer Don Bradman and others being measured for a Burton suit, 1938. West Yorkshire Archive Service: WYL1951

ing classes had to make do with mass-produced, ill-fitting uniforms. These divisions in class among British army recruits quickly became blurred as the devastating impact of the war became apparent.[9] Mounting casualties and the vast numbers of recruits required to maintain the front line meant that uniform production needed to be upscaled to meet demand.

As the war dragged on, men were united across class boundaries in their experience of war, and recruitment drew on this idea of a singular military masculinity, as shown in the poster *Step Into Your Place* (143). This poster shows men from all social strata changing from their flat caps and shirts and top hats and tails into the khaki uniform. Although bespoke tailored uniforms were still available, the expansion of firms like Burton through the manufacture of uniforms democratized the industry in civilian life through affordable tailoring. Montague Burton himself was exempt from war service on the grounds of poor health, but from the early days of the war, the company expanded production to supply uniforms. These uniform contracts triggered rapid growth in the company's production capacity, and Burton opened a further 26 shops throughout the war period, including eight in Ireland.[10] This expansion enabled Burton to explore the potential of affordable wholesale bespoke suits in a post-war economy.[11]

After the end of the war in 1918, demobilized men were presented with a ready-made suit or a voucher to purchase their own suit for their reintroduction into civilian life.[12] This was not a comfortable transition for many because, following a war that focused public attention on men's clothing through recruitment and demobilization, men of all classes were self-conscious about their position in society out of uniform.[13] Following his success throughout the war period, Burton was ideally placed to provide men with an affordable tailored suit to ease this transition. A shrewd businessman, Burton understood from his retail experience that men wanted to be made to feel important and retain a sense of individuality. Burton shop interiors began to mimic those of the Savile Row tailors, with little to no stock on the shop floor, and instead reams of fabrics and drawers of buttons: this was the tailor-made experience for the man with a modest budget. This promotional photograph of a Burton shop interior captures Australian cricketer Don Bradman being measured for a suit in 1938, during his tour of England (145). Associating Burton's wholesale bespoke service with sports stars like Bradman highlighted Burton's informal tailoring, which drew on popular ideals of sports and leisure. Made in 1935, a Montague Burton suit in the V&A collection encapsulates these ideals, which became so popular in the inter-war period. Worn by Burton's son Raymond Burton, the suit is made of Harris tweed, a popular fabric for hunting clothes, while the single-breasted jacket with two buttons is typical of the informal lounge suit style (144). By the time the suit was made, Burton was dominating the wholesale bespoke market, and when the Second World War broke out in 1939, Burton was, once again, best placed to provide the British army with well-made, mass-produced uniforms.[14]

146. Maurice, later Montague, Burton outside his first shop in Holywell Street, Chesterfield, *c.*1904. West Yorkshire Archive Service: WYL1951/280/18

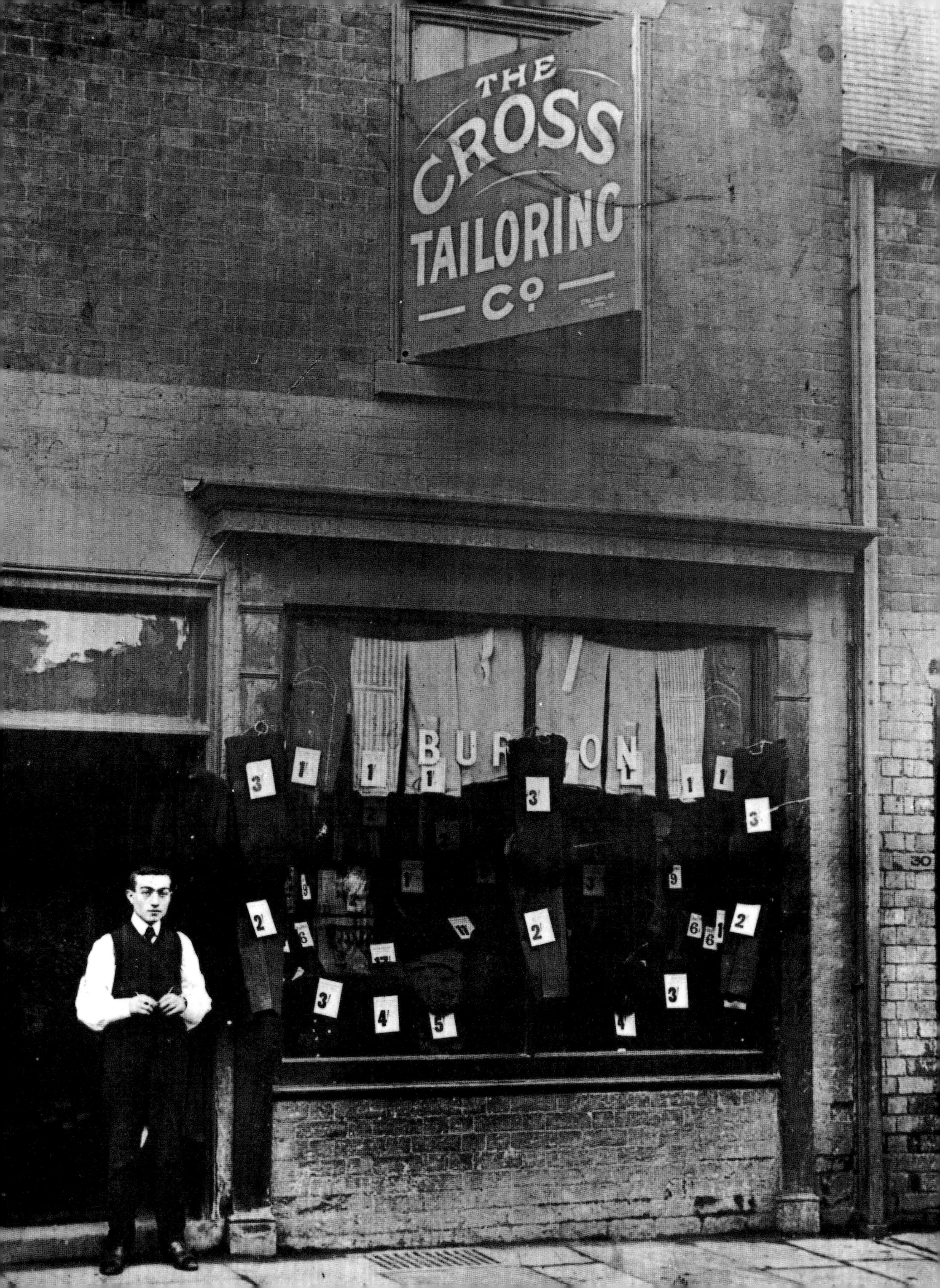
THE CROSS TAILORING Co
BURTON
30

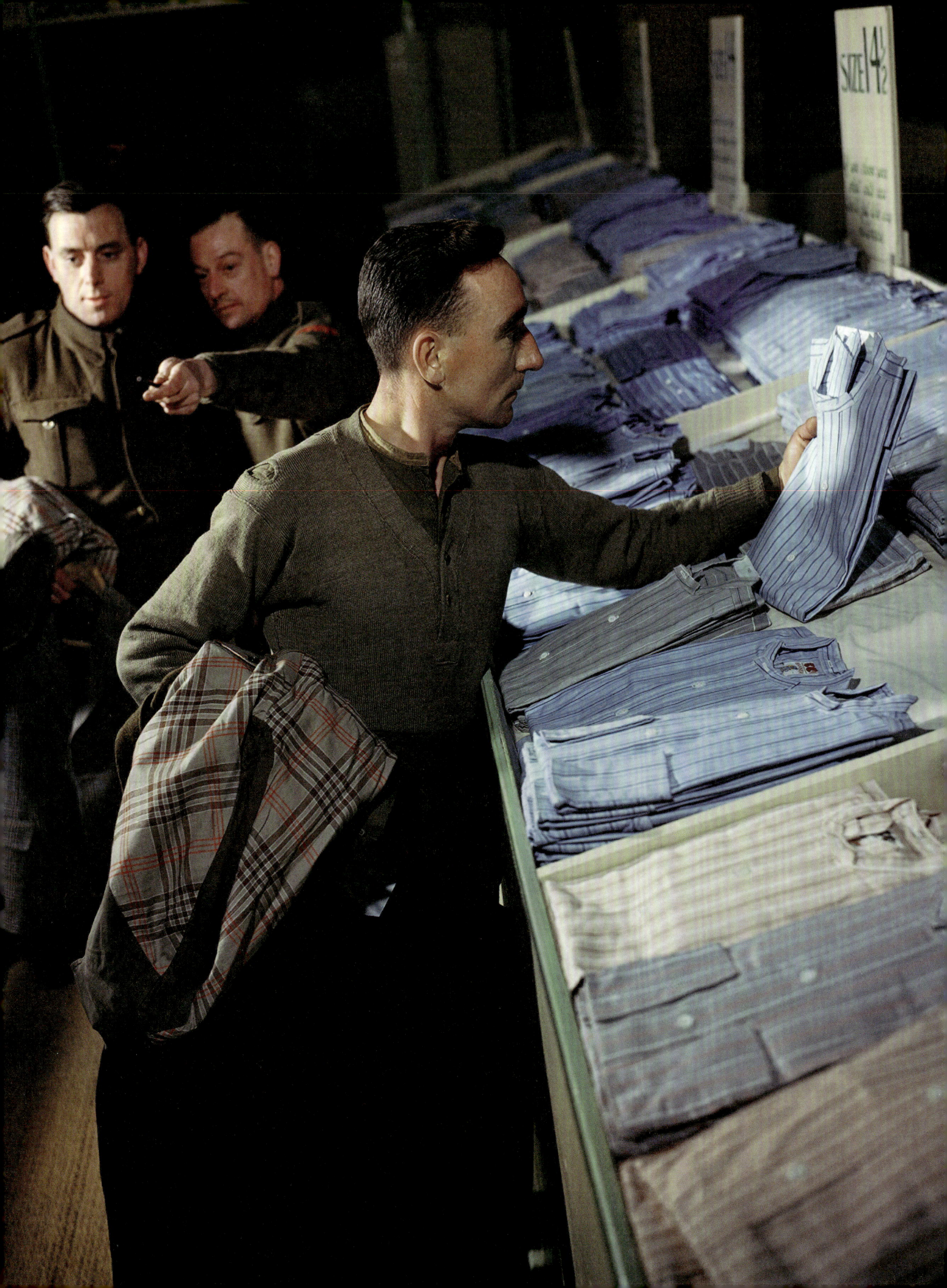
SIZE 14½

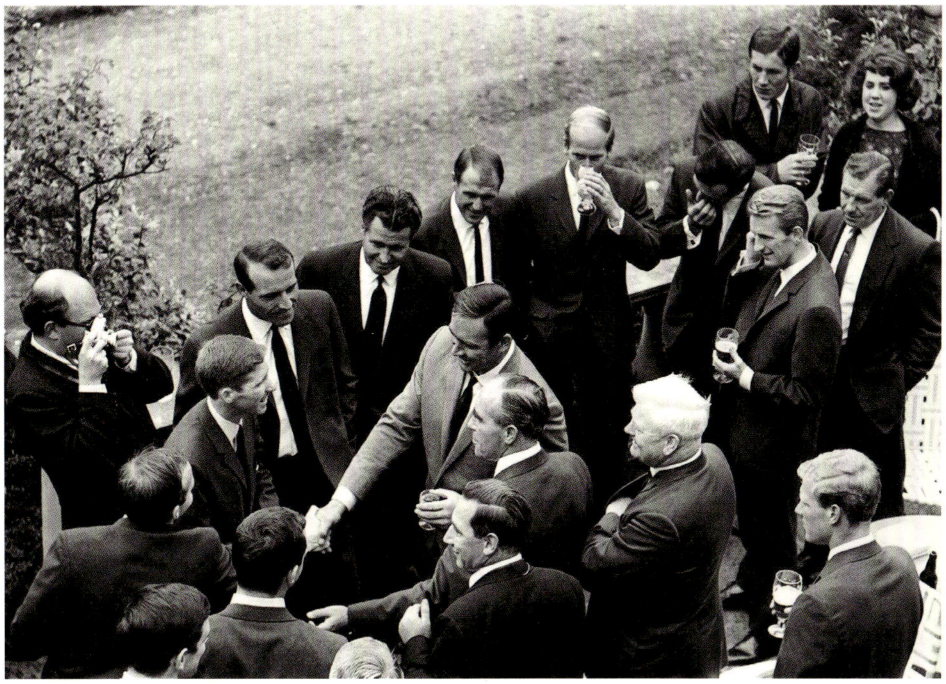

148. Members of the England World Cup football team meet Sean Connery during a visit to Pinewood Studios. 12 July 1966

Rationing during the war had a significant impact on all aspects of the clothing industry in Britain; however, the sheer scale of production of uniforms kept the Burton company afloat.[15] The bespoke tailors of Savile Row suffered throughout the Second World War, with the Blitz destroying 14 of Gieves's shops, as well as Meyer & Mortimer, J. Dege & Sons and many others.[16] However, the greatest threat to the bespoke tailoring trade was affordable clothing, continued rationing and the Civilian Clothing Order of 1942, which set out to regulate the manufacture and distribution of clothing in wartime. The Second World War saw men's fashions move away from the traditions of formal dressing as affordability became an increasingly important factor for customers of all classes.

The end of the war in 1945 brought a new opportunity for Burton in the form of the 'demob' suit. Upon leaving the armed forces, men would make their way through a demobilization centre, pick their outfit from the available selection, and begin the transition from soldier to civilian. The Montague Burton demob suit, which became known as 'The Full Monty', was an entire wardrobe that provided men with underwear, shoes, a hat, a coat and a three-piece suit.[17] Burton made over a third of all demob suits issued between 1944 and the early 1950s.[18] Once again, men's dress was the focus of public attention as men, no longer wearing the uniform that defined their position in society, came back to civilian life after six years of war. The utopian vision of the demobilization scheme was that all ranks and classes were offered the same suit in a bid towards a more democratic post-war society (147). This official colour photograph from the Ministry of Information of a demobilization centre in 1944 captures the process as a seamless transition. In reality, however, ill-fitting suits with limited styles and colours available left some critics feeling they were simply swapping one uniform for another. Others were impressed with the quality of the demob suits and continued to wear them long after rationing ended.[19]

The First and Second World Wars had a lasting impact on the clothing industry, and for Burton, this meant the successful expansion of wholesale bespoke manufacturing. In 1942 around 75 per cent of all Burton suits sold were made-to-measure.[20] When the war ended in 1945, the marketing of Burton suits continued to focus less on an aspirational gentleman and more on the 'everyman' who needed a good-quality, stylish suit at an affordable price. Maintaining the post-war notion of a uniform masculinity, the demob suit encapsulated Burton's 'affirmation of a collective male culture' and cemented the company as a leader in the democratization of men's fashion.[21]

Following Montague Burton's death in 1952, the brand experienced a period of change under new management. Burton's responded to a shift in consumer culture towards a more casual silhouette and a desire for fashionable clothing among younger men by moving away from wholesale bespoke manufacture and towards retail.[22] Marketing again played an essential role in Burton's rebranding, and in 1966, the company made suits for the English football team during their winning World Cup tour, were photographed in their suits alongside movie stars such as Sean Connery and Yul Brynner (148).[23] Retail became a new space of sartorial democracy and post-war Britain set the stage for Burton's to become a giant of the high street aimed at a new younger consumer for whom the experience of war, uniform and the demob suit belonged to an older generation. A new generation of young men wanted to access fashionable clothing not just as a means of social mobility but of creative self-expression.

147. A demobbed soldier selecting a shirt at a demobilization centre, 1944. Ministry of Information Second World War Colour Transparency Collection, Imperial War Museum, London: TR 1581

A SUITABLE HAT

ORIOLE CULLEN

At the beginning of the nineteenth century, the top hat reigned supreme within the upper levels of the rigid British social order. Initially developed in England as a tall riding hat with a drawstring around the rim to keep it in place, it was transformed in Paris in the late eighteenth century into a fashionable city hat. Replacing the bicorn and tricorn as the headwear for the stylish male, by the 1820s it had become the only hat for a gentleman to be seen in. Its tall foreboding silhouette morphed in height and proportion, casting its hegemonic shadow throughout the rest of the century (149).

As Britain's empire expanded, its hat trade grew. The fur felt trade was centred in the north-west of England, in towns such as Denton, Stockport, Hyde, Manchester and Bury, while the straw hat industry was based in the south-east at Luton. Hundreds of thousands of hats were produced each year for both the home and export market. By the turn of the twentieth century, 10,000 men, women and children were employed in the hatting industry in Stockport alone.[1]

In the House of Commons, the seat of power and privilege, strict rules surrounded the wearing of hats, with the top or tall hat coming to be, in the nineteenth century, the accepted form of dress.[2] In 1892 Britain's first socialist MP Keir Hardie caused a sensation when he entered the House wearing a tweed wool cap in place of a top hat (150). Hardie believed that he should dress like those he represented, thus visibly manifesting a strata of society not usually seen in this rarefied environment. His fellow politicians and the press poured scorn upon his choice of hat, suggesting that he had been mistaken for a workman and that 'Perhaps after a few days experience, Mr Keir Hardie will come to the conclusion that there is nothing to be gained by the display, and will accept the more conventional costume.'[3] He didn't.

The top hat's associations with power and gentility inevitably attracted those who aspired to social mobility such as the Swells, nineteenth-century working-class young men often mocked for their flamboyant style. The 'topper' would see out its last days of popularity as a uniform choice for certain sections of the working class. In 1913 the *Liverpool Echo* mourned the top hat's decline, noting that 'Apart from its ordinary ceremonial use the most frequent appearance of the tall hat used to be on the head of the ... good old cabby ... the bus-driver, and the private coachman...' who had now all become 'flat-capped chaffeurs'.[4] Considering the impracticality of the tall, cumbersome top hat, its reign was surprisingly long, but the arrival of the motor car, with its small enclosed space, signalled its end as an everyday hat. Its lingering presence is preserved through ceremonial events, racing and weddings.

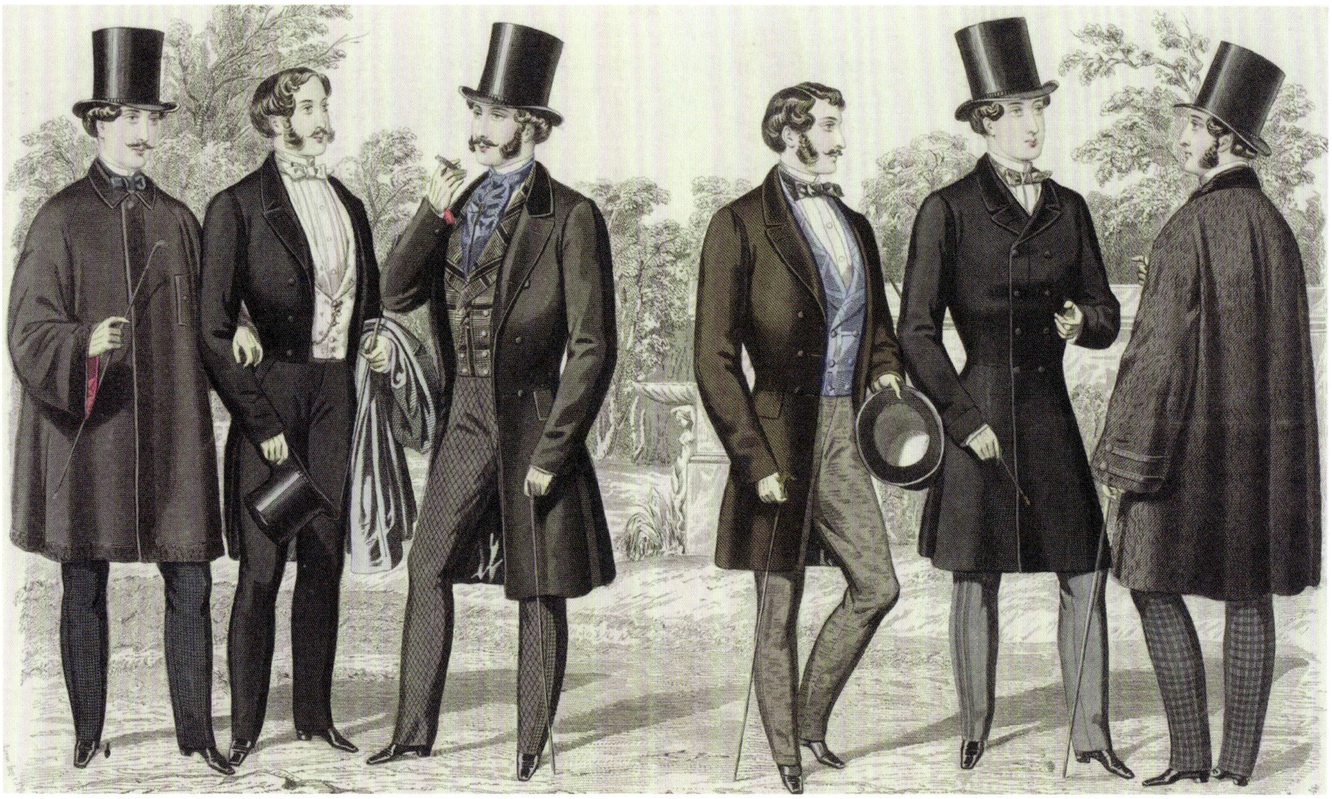

149. Edward Minister & Son, Gazette of Fashion. Lithograph, 25.5 cm × 33 cm. London, 1856. Given by Mrs E. M. Bridgland. V&A: E.585-1946

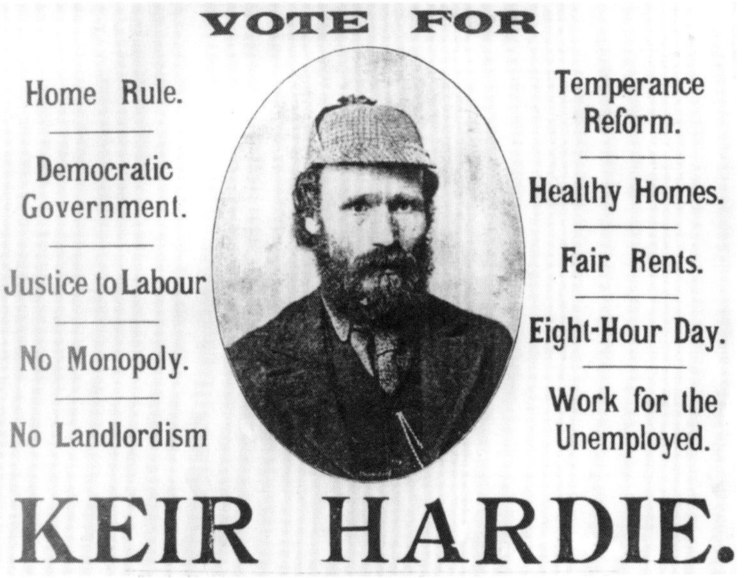

150. Election campaign poster for Scottish socialist and Labour leader James Keir Hardie, *c.*1895

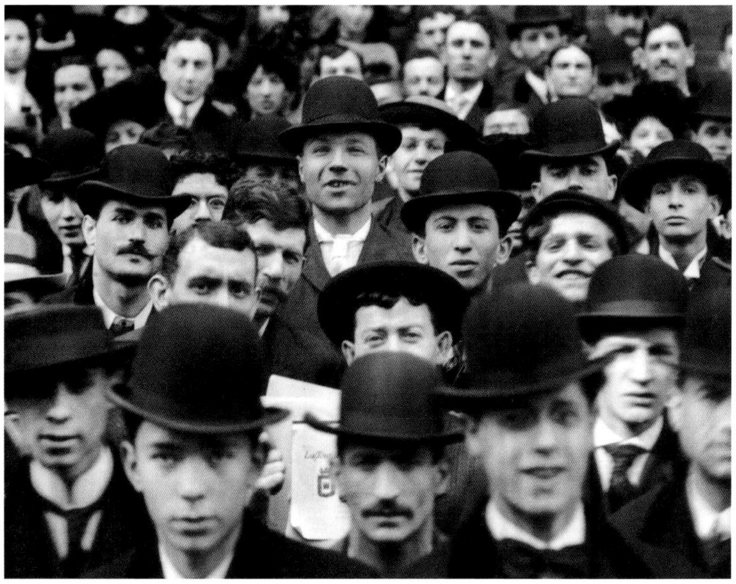

151. A crowd, mostly men wearing bowler hats, gathers for a picture, 1903

With the top hat's demise, the bowler hat emerged. Originally developed in the mid-nineteenth century as a protective rigid felt sporting hat with a solid curved crown and flat brim,[5] by the 1870s the bowler, with its brim now curling up, had become the hat of choice to wear around town (151). In America it was worn by race goers, earning itself the name of the 'derby' hat. It vied with the homburg, a stiff felt hat with a crease in the crown, popularized by King Edward VII who brought the style back from a spa trip to Bad Homburg, Germany, in 1882, and that later reached notoriety on the heads of British politicians Sir Winston Churchill and Sir Anthony Eden. But the bowler won out. Following the First World War it came to replace the top hat as the formal choice for politicians and city gentlemen. Concurrently, an informal short-brimmed felt hat with a soft dented crown, the trilby, emerged. It was named after the eponymous female character in the 1895 bestselling novel *Trilby* by George du Maurier and popularized when worn as part of Trilby's own costume in an onstage adaptation.

While Keir Hardie did not wear an actual flat cap into Parliament – rather, a tweed deerstalker style of cap with ear flaps tied up on the crown – the cloth or flat cap is very much tied to the image of the working man. Cheap, practical and portable, the cap was described in 1928 as 'the most proletarian of headwear',[6] and yet, like the top hat worn by cabbies, it also crossed the social divide. In the later nineteenth century, it was adopted by those wealthy enough to pursue sporting activities. Marketed as the 'golf cap', it was touted as the perfect hat for cycling, golfing and sailing among other sports, and also recommended for travelling. In 1896 hat retailers Reed & Sons promoted their 'golf caps' as 'Just the kind of cap to have with you on your holiday... A close fitting golf cap which hugs the head and defies the wind is indisposable.'[7] The Prince of Wales, an important arbiter of style, was a fan of the flat cap, often made in his signature Prince of Wales checked fabric. A 1925 portrait by John Saint Helier Lander depicts the prince in a knitted Fair Isle sweater and flat cap, holding his beloved terrier (152). Widely disseminated on the cover of the Christmas edition of the popular *Illustrated London News*, the image was strikingly informal, the prince glancing shyly from under his wide cap: a complete rejection of the strict sartorial protocol observed by his father Edward VII in his characteristic homburg.

In 1911 there were 12,494 people employed in the British felt hat-making industry. By 1922 this had fallen by a third, yet it was still producing over 9 million hats per year.[8] However, despite these numbers, there could be no disguising the fact that the ubiquity of the hat was in decline. In the post-war period, the younger generation no longer viewed the hat as essential. Nevertheless, some hats retained their popularity throughout the 1950s, especially the trilby and the round-crowned, narrow-brimmed porkpie hat,[9] sported by jazz and blues musicians and later popularized by the Rude Boy subculture of the Jamaican diaspora. But these styles alone could not keep the industry afloat. The young and handsome presidential candidate John F. Kennedy was well aware of the power of his image and media visibility. His thick thatch of hair assured no self-conscious concerns over receding lines or balding patches that might be caught by the ever-present cameras. In 1961, just eight years after his predecessor Dwight D. Eisenhower had caused outcry for choosing to wear a homburg instead of a top hat to his inauguration, Kennedy chose to become the first president to go hatless, for evermore accused of putting the final nail in the coffin of the American men's hat industry.

In July 1968, under the title of the 'The Big Male Robbery', the British papers reported from the New York millinery shows 'What used to be "his" is now "hers"' stating: 'The designers of hats for women have taken from the men such items as the classic tailored Fedora...; the visored newsboy cap...; the head-hugging leather-gear of the motorcycle set... Women are in the man-tailored era ... why not the hats too?'[10] Like the trilby, the fedora started life as a woman's

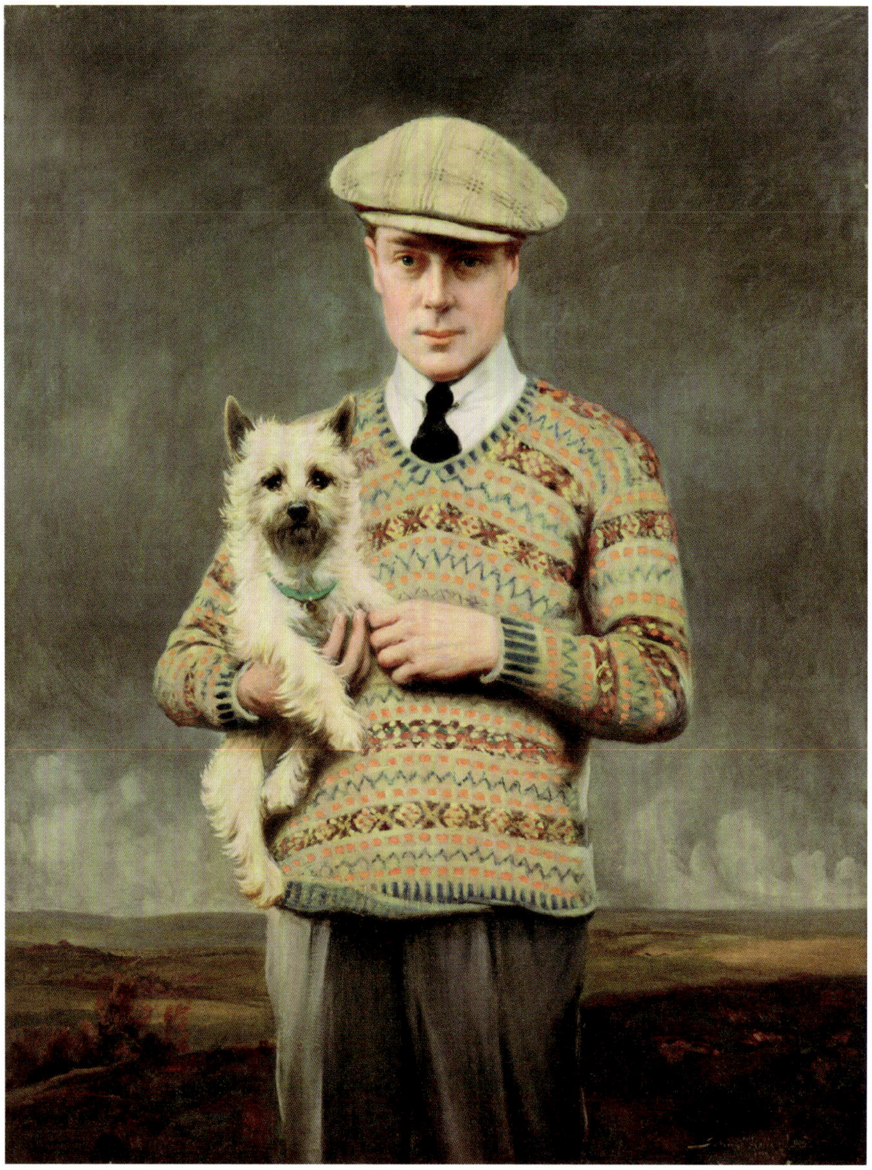

152. John Saint Helier Lander (1869–1944), *HRH The Prince of Wales*. Oil on canvas, 112 × 86.3 cm. Great Britain, 1925. Lotherton Hall, Leeds Museums and Galleries, LEEAG.PA.1926.0687, gift from the *Illustrated London News*

hat, popularized by the actor Sarah Bernhardt as she toured America in 1889 in the role of Princess Fedora Romanov in Victorien Sardou's play of the same name. Revived for men in the 1920s by the Prince of Wales, the malleable wide-brimmed fedora lends the wearer an alluring, somewhat feminine appeal. From Quentin Crisp, to David Bowie and Boy George, it has been the hat of choice for those who played with the narrow boundaries of traditional gender roles.

Within the V&A's collection, this gendered millinery transgression is evident in an impressive olive-green fedora of long-haired melusine felt, with a soft crown and floppy brim, and a thick petersham ribbon band.[11] Made by London hatters Herbert Johnson, the unisex fedora was one of its top sellers in the late 1960s, worn by rock stars and celebrities. This particular fedora belonged to the young museum director Sir Roy Strong, who experienced an epiphany in 1967 when *Vogue* magazine commissioned photographer Sir Cecil Beaton to take his portrait.[12] Following its publication, Strong was catapulted into the stratosphere of a glamorous and stylish social set and recalled this time as an 'emancipating period', when he would 'wear a Regency frockcoat' if he fancied.[13] He subsequently became known for his flamboyant dress sense, including his wide-brimmed hats (153). While hats certainly continued to be worn throughout the twentieth century, they were no longer an expected or necessary marker of correct dress. The hat now became the choice of the performer and the rebel, someone who wanted to stand out rather than blend in. In the north-west of England, the hatting industry declined, with just one traditional firm, Christys', still in existence in the 2020s. Yet milliners and hat-makers from the world of fashion had much success with men's hats alongside their womenswear creations. Stephen Jones sprang to prominence designing imaginative statement hats for the New Romantics of the early 1980s, and Philip Treacy's coloured trilbys became a feature of high-fashion menswear in the 1990s. These two decades also saw the rise of the baseball cap, out of the sportsworld and into the realms of music and fashion, championed by the hip-hop community and still going strong today.

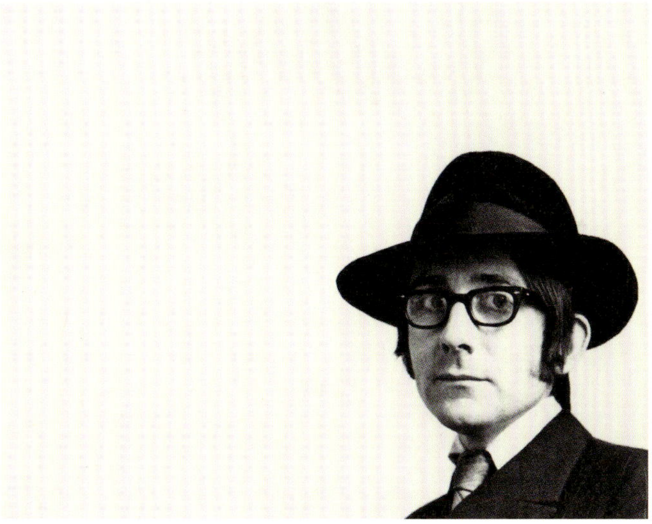

153. Godfrey Argent (1937–2006), *Sir Roy Strong*.
Photograph, bromide print, 28.5 × 37.7 cm. Great Britain, 21 March 1969.
National Portrait Gallery, Photographs Collection, NPG X28791

The early twenty-first century saw the return to popularity of the flat cap. As with its earlier incarnation there was a dichotomy representing two sides of the British class system, yet this time around it was soaked in nostalgia for a fantasy past. The cap was worn by celebrities such as singer Madonna and her then husband film director Guy Ritchie, who reimagined the upper-class country lifestyle at their manor house, Ashcombe, the former home of Sir Cecil Beaton. Ritchie, director of gangster movies such as *Lock, Stock and Two Smoking Barrels* (1998), also referenced the proletarian angle. Footballer and style icon David Beckham, a working-class boy made millionaire, frequently championed the flat cap, sporting it in advertisements for heritage brands such as Barbour and Kent & Curwen, a company in which he invested personally.

Towards the end of the second decade of the twenty-first century, a rise in nationalistic feelings and notions of a bygone Britain were fuelled by popular television shows such as *Downton Abbey* and *The Crown* in which the flat cap was sported by young aristocrats and salt-of-the-earth farmers and servants alike. For those who preferred their nostalgia tinged with a harder edge, in 2013 the release of television series *Peaky Blinders* furthered the demand for 'news boy' or 'baker boy' caps with a looser crown made from eight sections with a covered button in the centre (154). Based around a series of stylishly suited and booted gangsters at the turn of the twentieth century, the title of the show came from the slum-dwelling gangs of the New Inkleys area of Birmingham.[14] A contemporary report refers to the name 'peaky blinder' as '... acquired by reason of their peculiar headdress. They were violent characters and pulled over one eye they wore a peaked cap. The peak often contained a sharp piece of steel or metal which could be made a very formidable weapon.'[15]

A sure marker of the flat cap's universal appeal was its addition to the 2019 British Consumer Price Index, as an item of apparel most likely to be found in the average shopping basket. Milliner Noel Stewart, who became Creative Director of Christys' hats in 2013, attests to the popularity of the flat cap as a bestseller for the company. He noted that, unlike the aesthetic, playful displays of women's millinery, Christys' merchandise its men's hats in the traditional way, stacked up by size, so that men can go directly to their section and feel instantly reassured.[16] In the twenty-first century, despite lack of social expectations, and regardless of which social aspect they may choose to channel, the purchase of a suitable hat remains a serious business.

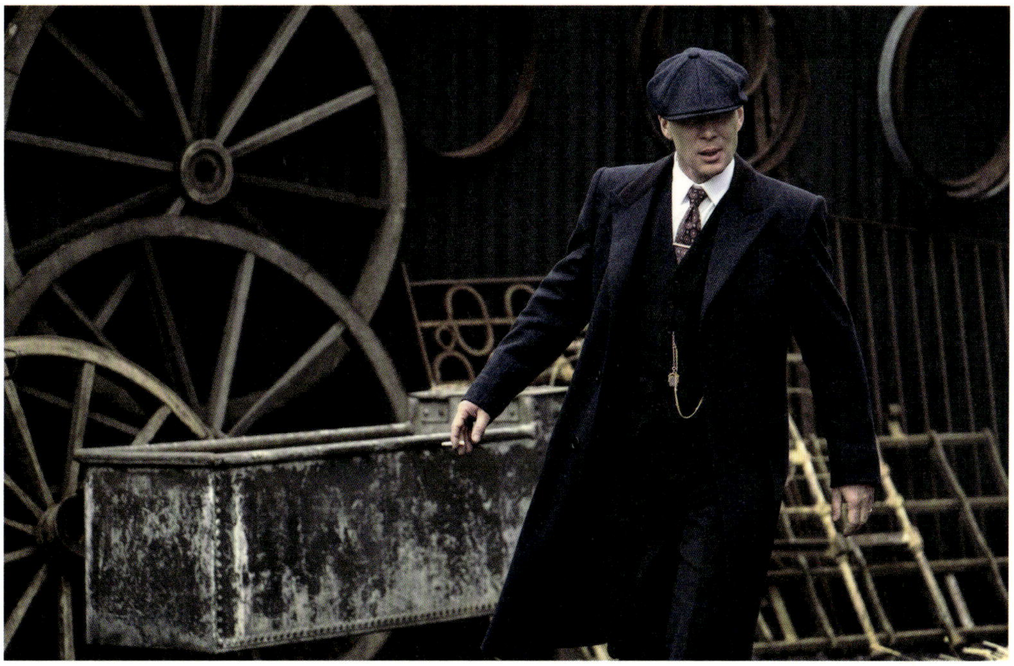

154. Cillian Murphy in *Peaky Blinders* (2015),
dir. Anthony Byrne, costume design by Alison McCosh

THE HYBRID OF IT ALL: THE MAKING OF BLACK BRITISH STYLE

EKOW ESHUN

ASSIMILATION OR ALIENATION

From the beginnings of mass Commonwealth immigration to Britain, Black men were judged on their appearance. They arrive in a war-scarred nation where an 'atmosphere of stale weariness' prevails.[1] Fog and dust chokes the streets. The modish colours of the season are 'donkey brown' and 'greige'.[2] What then to make of the immigrants in their vivid fashions, their rakishly tilted hats, their outsized zoot suits?

Just three months after the *Empire Windrush* docks at Tilbury, on 22 June 1948, the trade journal *Tailor and Cutter* runs a story about the fashions of its Black, mostly male, passengers. Headlined 'The Psychology of the Zoot Suit', the article ties dress sense indivisibly to racial identity (156). The 'sartorial exaggerations' of the zoot suit are 'a reflection of the Negro's connections with the tropics – where his instincts were attuned to extremes of growth and colour and heat and excitement.'[3]

Could the coloured man shed his vulgar clothes and learn to fit in with the customs and culture of his new country? Could he be socialized into Britishness? Or did being Black leave him subject to brutish impulses and miscreant behaviour, a stranger always to the British way of life? Assimilation or alienation? What path would the immigrant population follow? This was the question that vexed the country in the aftermath of the *Windrush*'s arrival. It was, of course, a false dichotomy. Not all Caribbeans were flashily dressed. They were not, by nature, irredeemably savage. But the 'colour problem' continued to reverberate across society.[4] As historian Kathleen Paul has described the problem as viewed in 1948, 'The British People were not "coloured" and conversely "coloured" people were not ... and never could be, "British".'[5]

Black men, the targets of discrimination at school, work and in the justice system, continued to be judged by their appearance over the decades. This essay examines how the young Black men that came to adulthood in the 1970s and 1980s responded to persistent discrimination by using style as a way to assert selfhood; and how, in doing so, they evolved a distinctive Black British cultural identity, characterized by an exhilarating fusion of fashion, art, music and politics.

THE PRACTICE OF REFUSAL

On a Friday evening in 1977 the photographer John Goto set up a makeshift studio at the back of Lewisham Youth Centre and began to take pictures. Out front, the Black teenagers who attended the centre were transforming the site into a dance hall. A huge sound system was brought in. Vibrations from the bass bins shook the floor. Against a plain, slightly crumpled backdrop, Goto captured the young people getting ready for the night.

In *Lovers' Rock*, the series of portraits he produced from that evening, most of his subjects are modestly dressed. Girls wear pleated skirts. Hair is straightened and flicked, or curled into a 1940s-style chignon. Boys are in smart, wide-lapelled jackets (155). One wears a sheepskin. Another a trench coat. Afros are neatly tended. There are porkpie hats and flat caps. An abundance of polo necks and cardigans. Their clothes are similar to those their parents might wear and perhaps this should not be surprising. The post-war immigrants were Christian, God-fearing, culturally conservative, and they raised their children to follow the same values. The pious headwraps and below-the-knee skirts of the girls and the smart coats and hats of the boys give at least the appearance of fidelity to those principles. But there are also signs of dissent. One youth sports an army surplus look, with khaki trousers and a military jacket decorated with the flag of Ghana. Like a few other boys, he wears a crochet-knit tam, beneath which short dreadlocks are visible, peeking out from the rim. With its references to Rastafarianism and pan-African liberation, his style signals some of the wider political and cultural fault lines of the period. It also illustrates how the fashion choices of young Black men like him functioned as a form of opposition to the challenges of the 1970s, a decade in which rising unemployment, police harassment and the anti-immigration rhetoric of politicians made conditions 'miserable in too many ways to count' for Black people.[6]

This is the period when a moral panic about mugging has seized the country and when the perpetrator is invariably cast as young, male and Black, such crimes becoming 'identified not merely as those which blacks are most likely to commit, but as crimes which are somehow expressive of the ethnicity of those who carry them out.'[7] A period when Sir Kenneth Newman, Commissioner of the Metropolitan Police, can typify Blacks as inveterate trouble-makers: 'In the Jamaicans you have a people that are constitutionally disorderly... It's simply in their make-up, they're constitutionally disposed to be anti-authority.'[8]

This despite the fact that Black people are more often the victims of crime than its culprits, as the journal *Race & Class* reports:

> Black places of worship, black shops, black centres are targets for brutal attack, vandalism and fascist daubings. Nor is there safety inside the house – bricks may be thrown through windows and burning petrol-soaked rags pushed through letter-boxes. Day in, day out black people, young and old, men and women, are subjected to abuse and assault.[9]

155. John Goto (1949–), *Lovers' Rock*. London, 1977

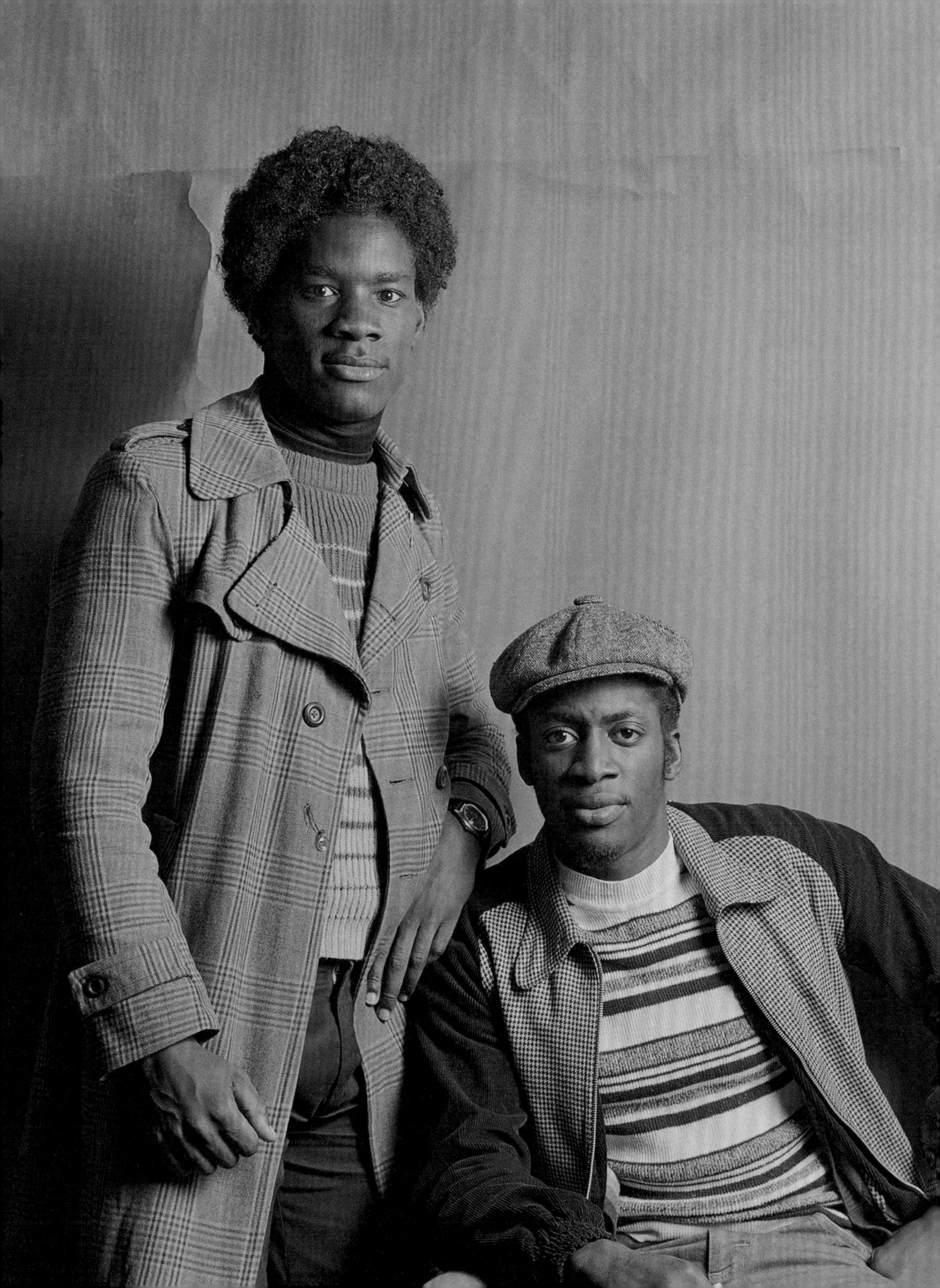

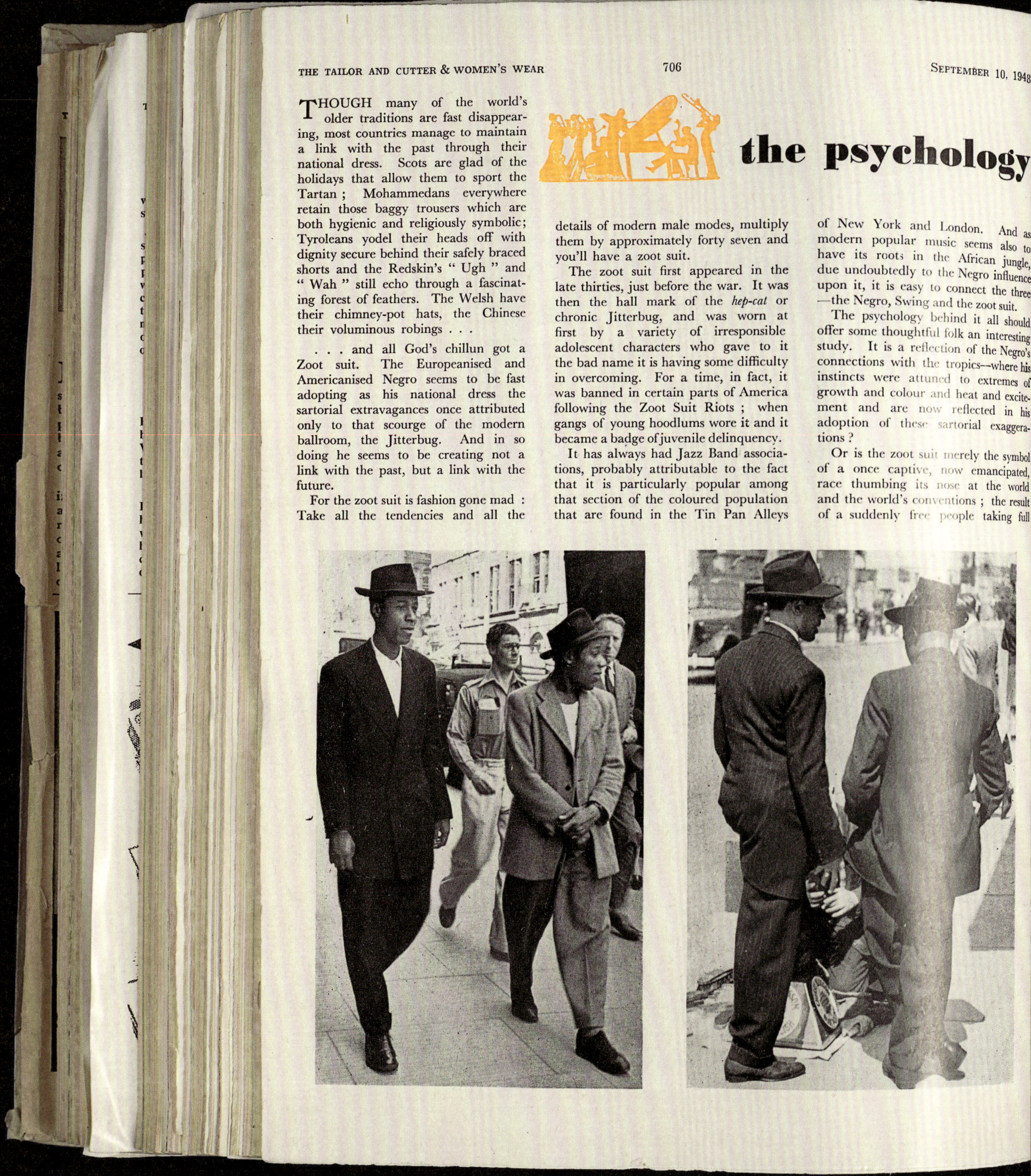

the psychology

THOUGH many of the world's older traditions are fast disappearing, most countries manage to maintain a link with the past through their national dress. Scots are glad of the holidays that allow them to sport the Tartan ; Mohammedans everywhere retain those baggy trousers which are both hygienic and religiously symbolic; Tyroleans yodel their heads off with dignity secure behind their safely braced shorts and the Redskin's " Ugh " and " Wah " still echo through a fascinating forest of feathers. The Welsh have their chimney-pot hats, the Chinese their voluminous robings . . .

. . . and all God's chillun got a Zoot suit. The Europeanised and Americanised Negro seems to be fast adopting as his national dress the sartorial extravagances once attributed only to that scourge of the modern ballroom, the Jitterbug. And in so doing he seems to be creating not a link with the past, but a link with the future.

For the zoot suit is fashion gone mad : Take all the tendencies and all the details of modern male modes, multiply them by approximately forty seven and you'll have a zoot suit.

The zoot suit first appeared in the late thirties, just before the war. It was then the hall mark of the *hep-cat* or chronic Jitterbug, and was worn at first by a variety of irresponsible adolescent characters who gave to it the bad name it is having some difficulty in overcoming. For a time, in fact, it was banned in certain parts of America following the Zoot Suit Riots ; when gangs of young hoodlums wore it and it became a badge of juvenile delinquency.

It has always had Jazz Band associations, probably attributable to the fact that it is particularly popular among that section of the coloured population that are found in the Tin Pan Alleys of New York and London. And as modern popular music seems also to have its roots in the African jungle, due undoubtedly to the Negro influence upon it, it is easy to connect the three —the Negro, Swing and the zoot suit.

The psychology behind it all should offer some thoughtful folk an interesting study. It is a reflection of the Negro's connections with the tropics—where his instincts were attuned to extremes of growth and colour and heat and excitement and are now reflected in his adoption of these sartorial exaggerations ?

Or is the zoot suit merely the symbol of a once captive, now emancipated, race thumbing its nose at the world and the world's conventions ; the result of a suddenly free people taking full

156. 'The Psychology of the Zoot Suit', *Tailor and Cutter & Women's Wear* (10 September 1948)

of the zoot suit

advantage of the chance to wear and do exactly what they please ; an instinctive reaction embodied in a pathetic attempt to outwhiteman the white man ?

Whatever the psychologist's decide, they must accept the fact that the zoot suit is rather more than a kind of sartorial sickness. It is too exaggerated to be mere exaggeration and too popular among its wearers to be dismissed merely as " bad taste."

We don't consider an Evzone as wanting in taste because he wears odd clothes—nor do we curl our lip at the Esquimaux because their sartorial habits fail to conform with our own.

So it is with the gentleman who wears the zoot suit. He may feel that it's ugly—but at least he knows it's all his own.

On the extreme left on the facing page are two pretty conservative zoot suiters we photographed in London recently. These are definitely zoot suits—but only just. Often with the zoot suit either the tie is abandoned or a crew neck shirt is worn. Ties, if adopted, are usually pretty noisy. Most zoot suits are seen in London in the Charing Cross Road.

The two gentlemen enjoying a shoe shine demonstrate the overall length of the zoot jack-et. Notice that the jacket on he left almost reaches the ack of the knee. The photo-raph on the right shows gentleman with an in-ividual flair even among ot suiters. Three button stening, square fronts d vertical pockets are usual touches.

Notice, too, the mbrero type hat th wide band and im to match.

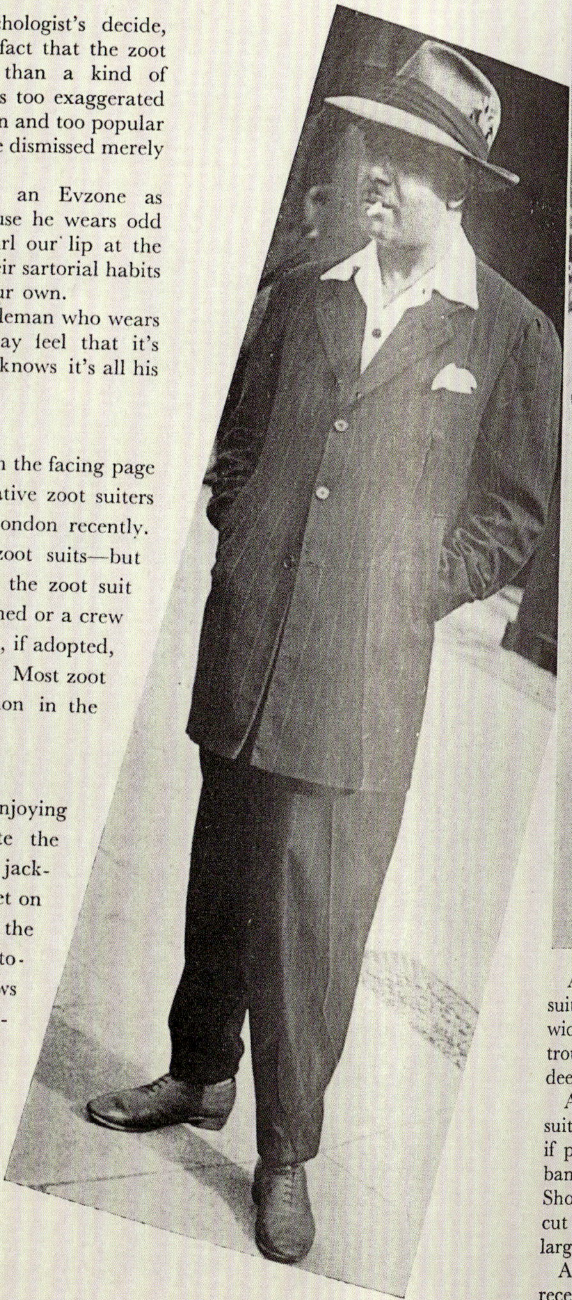

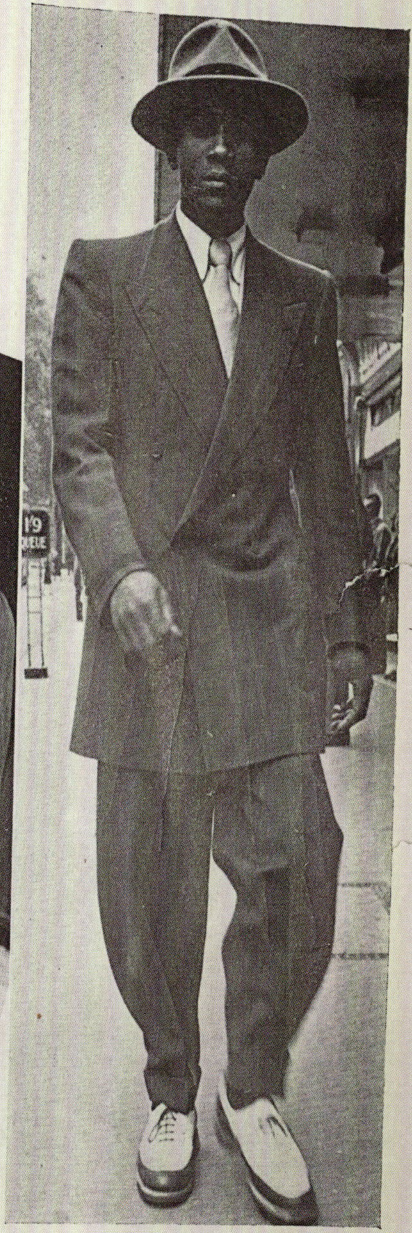

Above is an example of the classic zoot suit : Extra long jacket, extra long lapels, wide shoulders, nipped in waist, peg-topped trousers with extra narrow bottoms, extra deep turn ups.

Accessories are important with the zoot suit. Hat must have very wide brim with, if possible, a coloured band and feathers in band. Ties are bright and generously tied. Shoes are usually two-toned. Trousers are cut high under the arm pits and usually a large metal watch chain is sported.

All these photographs were taken in London recently by *The Tailor and Cutter* cameraman.

E

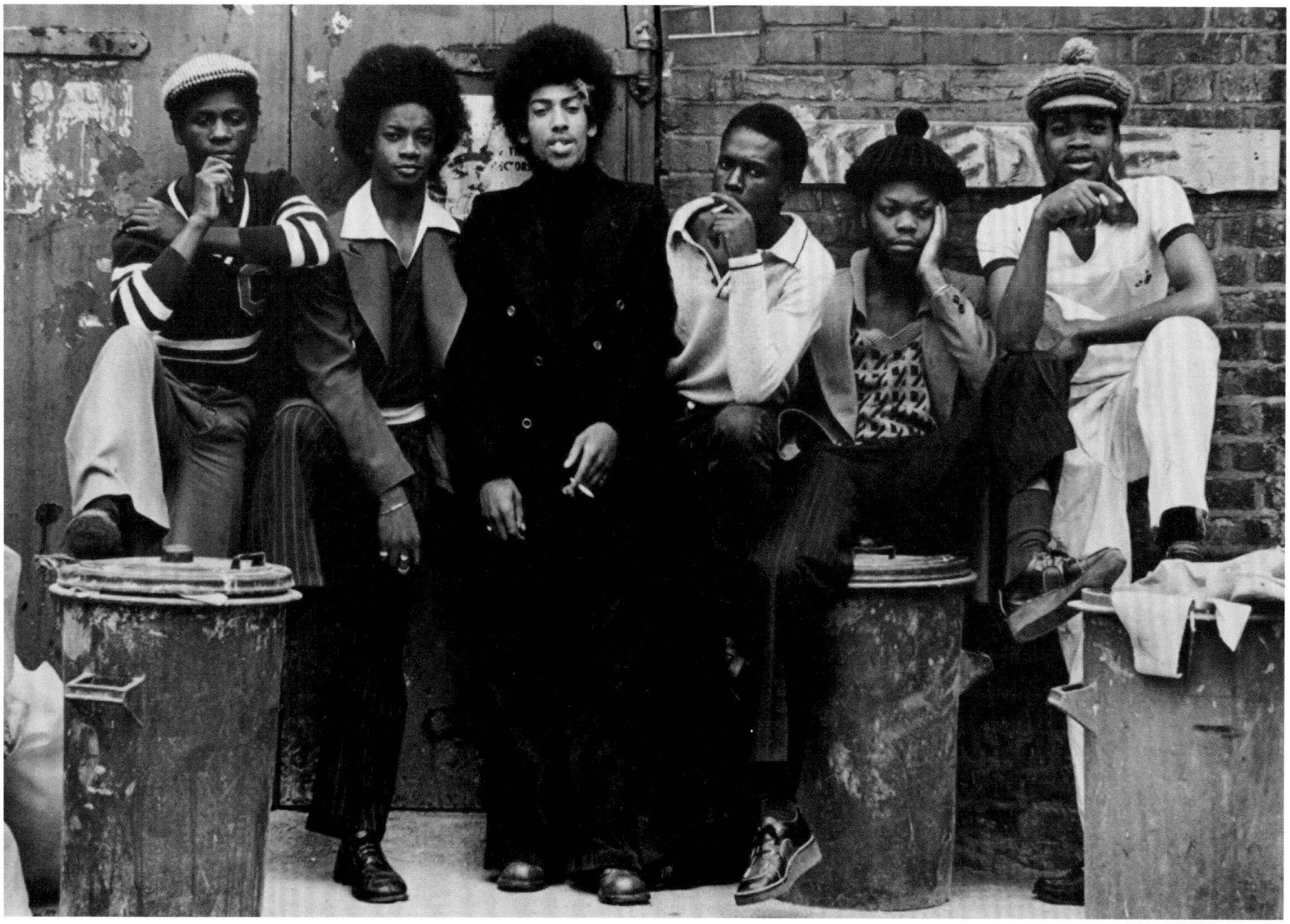

157. Colin Jones (1936–2021), 'The Black House', *c.*1973

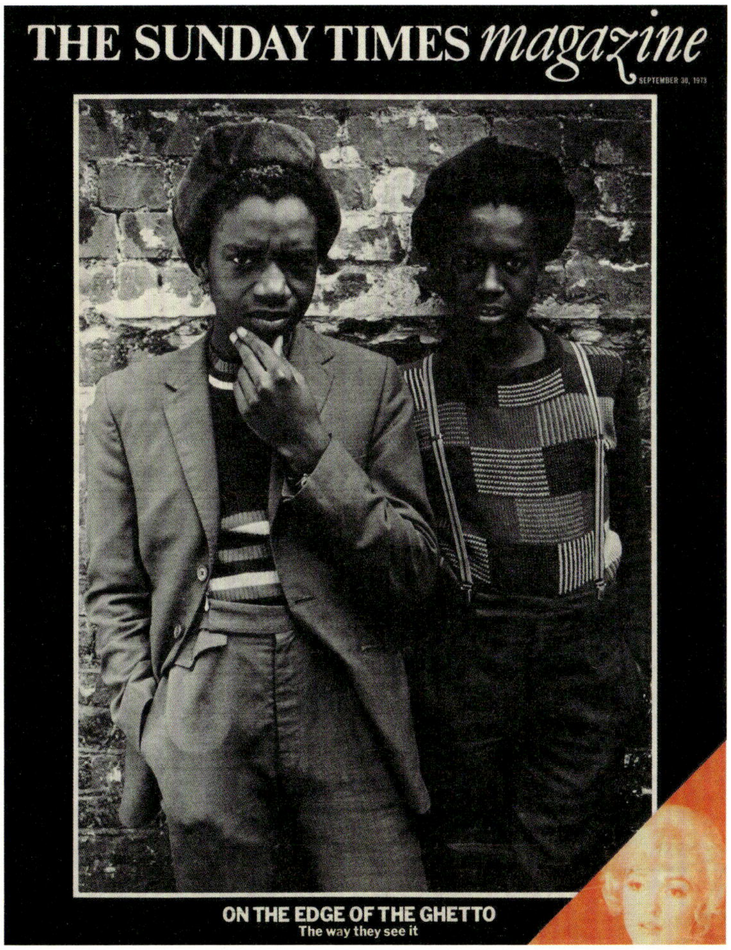

158. Colin Jones (1936–2021), 'On the Edge of the Ghetto', published on the cover of *Sunday Times Magazine* (30 September 1973)

In response to an environment of such concerted antipathy, young African Caribbeans gather together at house parties and dance halls and places like Lewisham Youth Centre, seeking to create spaces of sanctuary and solidarity. In 1973 the *Sunday Times Magazine* ran a story on one such site, a hostel on the Holloway Road, north London, colloquially known as the Black House (158). Its habitués were troubled young Blacks struggling to find their footing in life. Some had been thrown out by their families or been in and out of Borstal or prison. The Black House was a place for them to take shelter, study for qualifications, or just smoke weed and play cards. Under the heading, 'On the Edge of the Ghetto', the article emphasized the bleak conditions of the hostel. Black and white photographs by Colin Jones showed bare rooms with broken furniture and boarded-up windows where boys slept three to a bed.

But after publication, Jones continued to visit the Black House and his subsequent images tell a more nuanced story. The hostel youths wear clothes that are sometimes shabby and stained, even as they carry themselves with a defiant self-regard. Their relationship to clothes stands in contrast to that of the post-war immigrants. For the earlier generation dressing in smart Sunday-best clothes represented a route to upward mobility. It signalled a desire 'to be someone, to be proud and good-looking; respectable and upstanding; an aspiration to betterment and middle-class prosperity.'[10]

We should be wary here of setting up the responses of the second generation against the first. As art historian Eddie Chambers has noted, from sport to culture and cuisine the response of the original Caribbean immigrants to the widespread prejudice they encountered was more resourceful and complex than can be accommodated in the binary opposition of assimilation versus alienation.[11]

Nevertheless, at least when it comes to the sartorial choices of the generations, we might talk about a divide between strategies of convention and non-conformity. And we can say that, for their offspring, style was not a path to success. It was a form of resistance.

In one of Jones's Black House images, six young men stand together against a brick wall (157). The figure at the centre of the group wears a dark double-breasted blazer over a polo neck. A puff of smoke escapes from his mouth. Next to him, another young man wears a jacket with the white collars of a shirt spread wide across the lapels. There is a slim bracelet around his wrist and rings on a couple of his fingers. Both youths have large, carefully tended Afros. The others are more casually attired, in polo shirts and jumpers, flat caps and tams. They are conscious of being looked at, perhaps all too much so in the era of Sus (suspected person) laws. Yet each of them regards the camera with dandyish poise. They exude a knowing pride as if demanding to be seen on their own terms, for once.

The assurance of their gaze brings to mind feminist theorist Tina Campt's notion of the practice of refusal: 'a refusal to recognize a system that renders you fundamentally illegible and unintelligible; the decision to reject the terms of diminished subjecthood with which one is presented. Using negation as a generative and creative source of disorderly power to embrace the possibility of living otherwise.'[12]

The most potent form of refusal you could practise in the 1970s as a young Black man was to grow dreadlocks in line with the tenets of Rastafari. 'You were creating problems for yourself in relation to work, to the police and to the general attitudes which associated locks with uncleanliness. You were accepting a kind of pariah status',[13] reflects Paul Gilroy, who began to grow his hair as a student in 1977.

Rastafari gained popularity in Britain through the righteous, socially conscious roots of Bob Marley, Burning Spear and other reggae artists. But the credo that developed in the UK was less an overarching belief system than an 'aesthetic' that was 'inflected to suit the needs of second-generation immigrants ... stripped of nearly all its original religious meanings: a distillation, a highly selective appropriation of all those elements within Rastafarianism which stressed the importance of resistance and black identity.'[14] Its signature elements included a red, gold and green tam, khaki fatigues culled from local army surplus stores, Clarks desert boots or Wallabees, and suede-trimmed Gabicci cardigans.

We can glimpse the popularity of the look in a photograph by Vanley Burke taken at a public rally in Handsworth, Birmingham to mark African Liberation Day in 1977 (159). Burke's picture shows a multitude of Black faces. Hats and hairstyles catch the eye. Amid the Afros, watch caps, baker

Following pages: 159. Vanley Burke (1951–), African Liberation Day in Handsworth Park, 1977

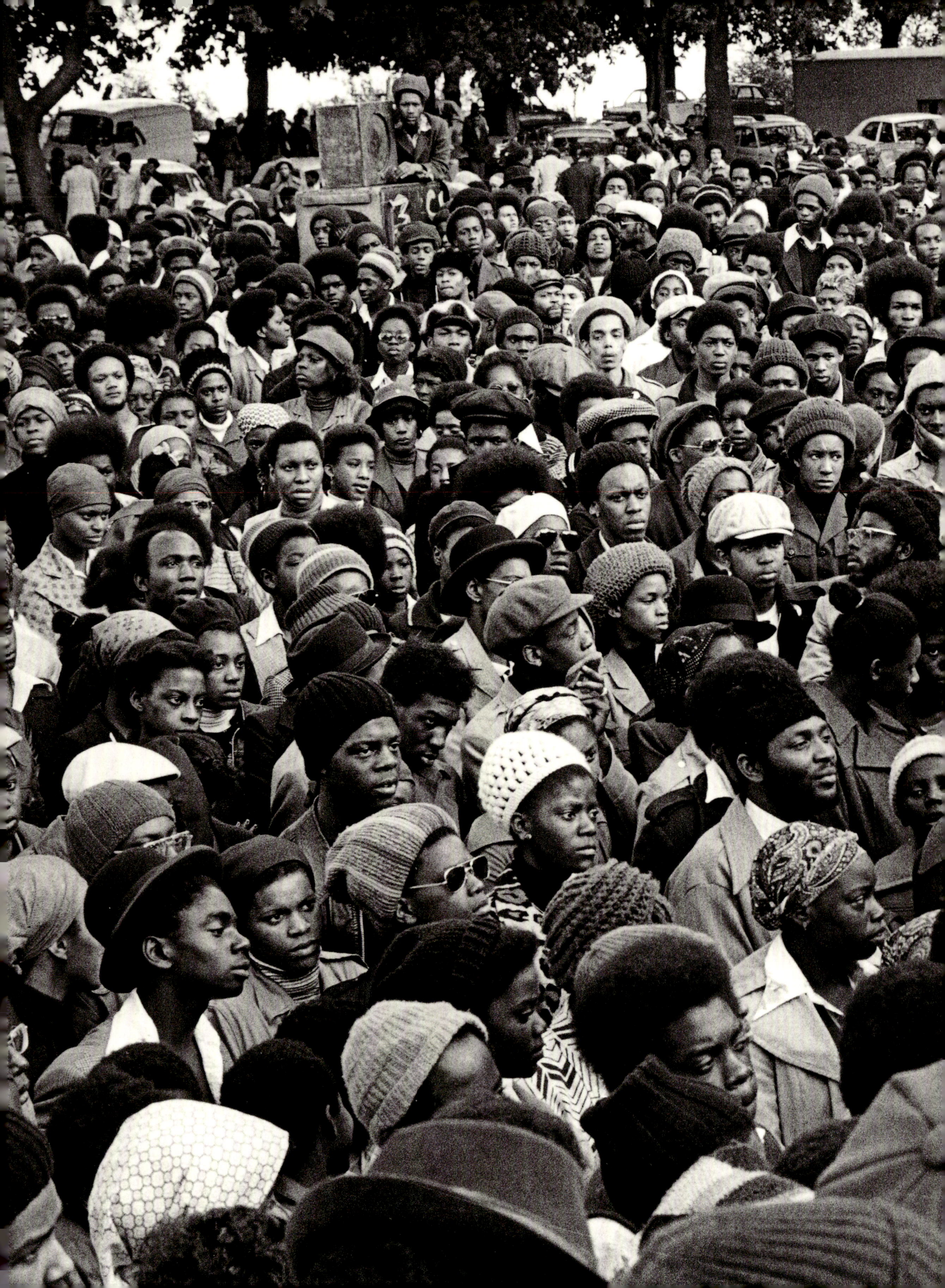

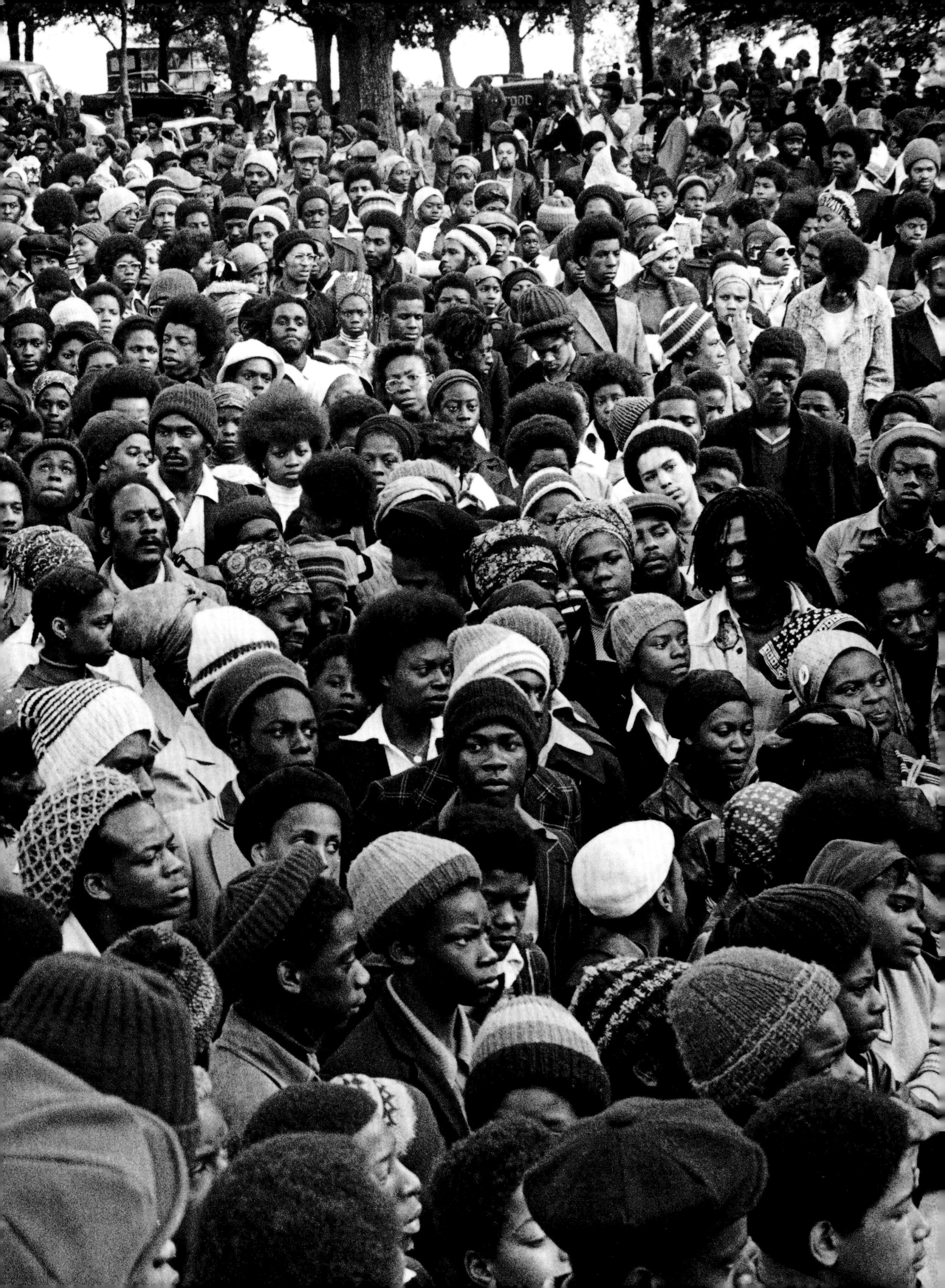

boy hats and headwraps, the tam is a recurring feature, worn by men and women scattered throughout the crowd, some with dreadlocks, others not, its presence offering an illustration of how Rastafari acted as a powerful 'means of fashioning an identity' for Black youth across the country.[15]

BLACK *AND* BRITISH

But the presence of Rastafari could also be oppressive. Its influence contributed to the perpetuation in Britain of patriarchal gender norms carried over from the Caribbean. As Jamaican author Carolyn Cooper has noted, some Rastafari values were 'an extreme manifestation of the duplicitous gender ideology that pervades Jamaican society [which] is ultimately derived, via Victorian England, from Judeo-Christian theology.'[16] In Britain, that meant women were 'accorded a subordinate status' in the family or in communal spaces such as the reggae dance hall.[17] But it also meant that men, too, could be trapped within restrictive roles, caught in a performance of overt toughness that affirmed their maleness even as it left little room for them to express their feelings or vulnerabilities. In this 'masculinised and patriarchal terrain',[18] style was a loaded indicator of racial and gender identity. Records like Bob Marley's 'Crazy Baldhead' made derisive mention of baldheads: men without dreadlocks who identified with the values of the bourgeois white mainstream and were therefore not real men at all (Marley proposed to chase them out of town on the record). There was particular scorn for men whose dress sense placed them outside the narrow parameters of authentic Black masculinity.

As a teenager in 1970s Acton, the DJ Norman Jay defined himself as a soul boy, a subculture with its own style codes: 'You'd wear a Ben Sherman shirt; a tank top from Shepherds Bush Market, always woollen never nylon; high-waisted bags, tailored not off the peg; and crepe-soled shoes from Sacha on Kensington High Street, or Ivy Brogues.'[19]

Jay's choice of clothes brought him into regular conflict with the censorious attitude of the local Black community:

> Enough times in the Seventies, I'd be getting chased down the street and called a black queer 'cos of wearing certain styles of clothes. So, when I'd been out, on the way back home, I'd have to get changed and put my clothes in a duffel bag. When everyone around you was in dungarees and dreadlocks and listening to dub reggae, and you bowl down the street in bright yellow or orange jeans, then you're asking for trouble.[20]

After the death of Marley in 1981, reggae's influence waned in the UK, and Black youth began to look beyond Jamaica and Rastafari for their style cues.

African Caribbeans had long been barred from centrally located nightclubs and bars by racist door policies. They had been forced to stage their own blues parties and dance hall nights in school halls and private houses on the urban fringes instead. But in the early 1980s it became impossible to ignore the new sounds and styles developing in metropolitan centres across the country: Birmingham's Two-Tone movement, Soho's flamboyant New Romantics; the Sheffield synthpop of ABC, Heaven 17 and the Human League; and from abroad, New York's raw, dynamic hip-hop scene.

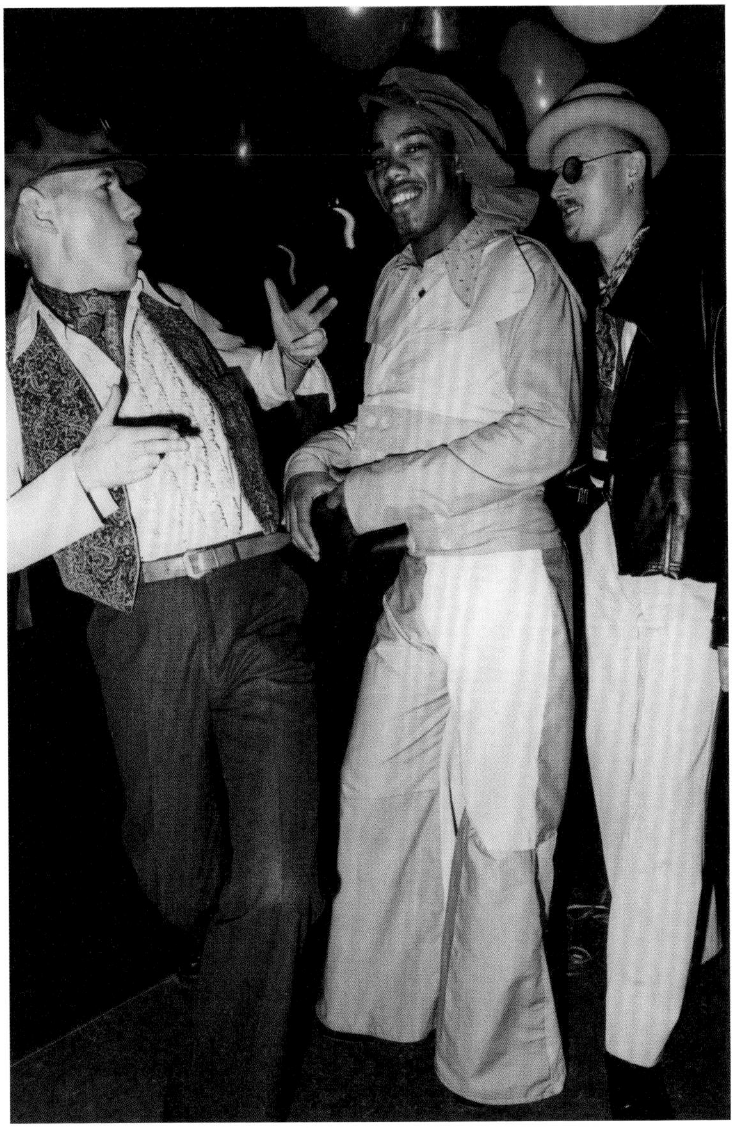

160. Dave Swindells (1961–), Shak Shak at Spats: Gary Haisman, Constantine Weir and Johny Rocca, November 1987, published in *The Face* (London, September 1988)

Young African Caribbeans aspired to be in the heart of the city rather than confined to the peripheries. As an 18-year-old growing up in Hackney, the DJ Trevor Nelson found the neighbourhood increasingly parochial. 'Hackney was so closeted, so limited in its attitude... You would see the same people everywhere and every party was a reggae party.'[21] Instead, Nelson began to frequent the Electric Ballroom in Camden, dressing for the occasion with extravagant individuality:

> For going out I had all kinds of shoes I bought in Carnaby Street; blue patent pony skin and brown patent. In 1982 you could go to the King's Road and buy some outlandish leopard-skin top with chains and Wild Youth written on it. You could go to Laurence Corner and get your second-hand army

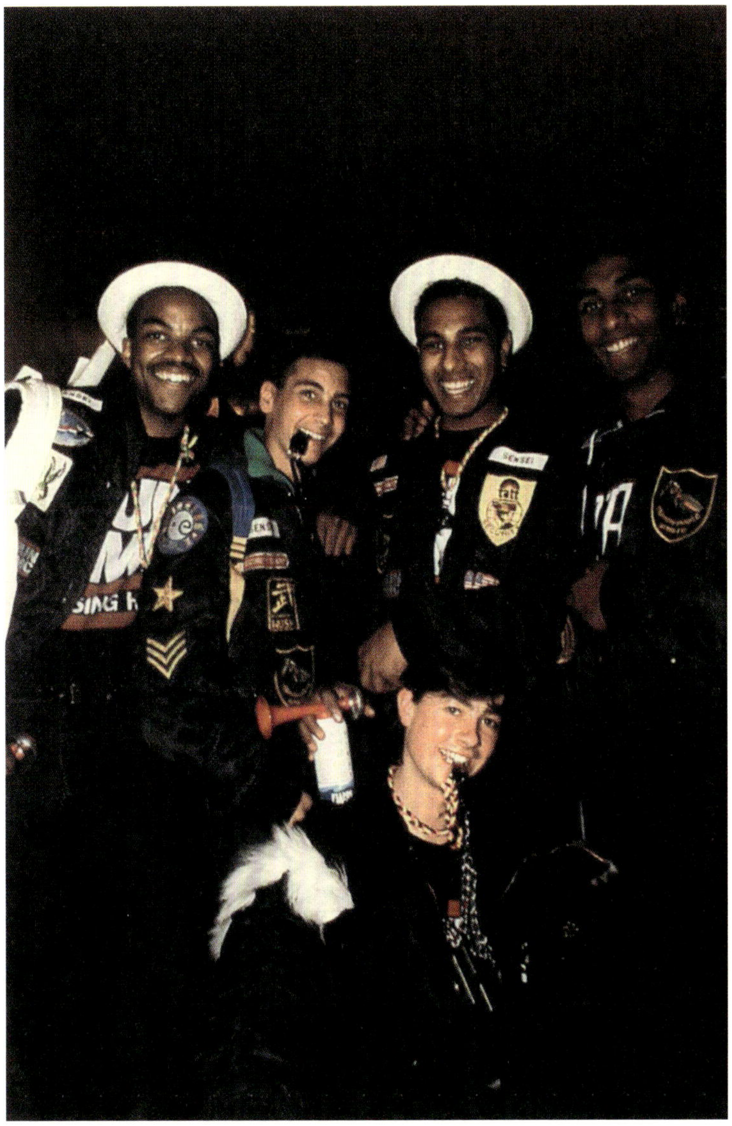

161. Derek Ridgers (1950–), Run-DMC/Beastie Boys concert, Brixton Academy, London, 23 May 1987, published in *The Face* (London, July 1987)

> gear or a band-leader jacket...I had the Raiders of the Lost Ark kinda look, which was sick. I would wear, literally, a Harrison Ford hat with a brown, distressed leather flight jacket, ankle boots and trousers tucked into them. At some point you even had the leg warmer action going over the very tight jeans.[22]

The increasing desire by Black youth to participate more fully in city centre nightlife helped fuel the development of London's warehouse scene. A wave of illicit parties between 1982 and 1987, the scene drew thousands of clubbers to atmospheric abandoned industrial sites across the capital where they danced to hip-hop and gritty 1970s funk (160).

Warehouse parties represented a geographical and racial realignment of the city's dance underground. They brought DJs like Jay, a pivotal figure on the scene, to the fore and, via the championing of pirate radio and style magazines like *The Face* and *i-D*, led to the development of a fashion-conscious, multicultural audience. As Jay said of his own Shake 'n' Fingerpop parties: 'The revellers would come from every social circle: mad punks, Sloanes, lazy college liggers and clued-up yardies could all be found raving together in some run-down, empty factory or warehouse in areas such as King's Cross, Docklands, Southwark.'[23] In contrast to the culturally conservative environment of the dance hall, here was an exhilarating new space for Black youth that 'opened up new, albeit fragile and temporary, aesthetic and social possibilities where the "old boundaries" of race, gender and class might be challenged.'[24]

The impact on Black style was startling. A photo story from *The Face*, July 1987, shows second-generation Black teenagers, captured at night, in heavily accessorized black MA-1 flight jackets (161). Their dress sense owes a clear debt to the influential aesthetic of *The Face*, but it is also clear from the accompanying text that the teens are forging an exuberant identity of their own: 'The look is pure London – a mutant blend of *The Face* stylist Ray Petri's Buffalo look, retro rockabilly, Soho fashion casualty and US B-Boy: dungarees, black Levi's, flight jackets, baseball caps, straw hats, safety pins, badges, cartoon characters, chains, car emblems and slogans that change week to week.'[25]

At the same time as African Caribbean youth were making themselves more visible at night, pioneering figures in the arts, politics and the academy were also bringing heightened prominence to the Black presence across society more broadly. Significant names here include talented visual artists Lubaina Himid, Sonia Boyce, Keith Piper and Donald Rodney; the film-making groups Sankofa, Ceddo and Black Audio Film Collective; photographers Rotimi Fani-Kayode (46) and Ingrid Pollard; pop stars Sade, Loose Ends and Neneh Cherry; and writers Ben Okri and Caryl Phillips. In addition, there was the quartet of MPs (Diane Abbott, Paul Boateng, Bernie Grant and Keith Vaz) who, in 1987, became the first Black politicians elected to the Houses of Parliament; and the influential theorists of Birmingham University's Centre for Contemporary Cultural Studies, Stuart Hall, Paul Gilroy and Hazel Carby.

In the rising profile of such figures there is evidence of a generation coming of age, a generation whose cosmopolitan outlook signals what Hall describes as 'the end of the essential black subject.'[26] The end, that is, of the idea that being Black meant having a single, unchanging identity – mugger, Rasta, baldhead – and instead, the notion that Blackness is a mutable proposition, a hybrid state of being shaped and reshaped by culture, politics and history. Instinctively, this generation, observed Hall, works:

> ... across cultural boundaries and vocabularies. They work with and on 'difference'. But they do not have a binary, either/or, conception of it... They know that everyone comes from somewhere, speaks from some place, is multiply positioned. But they don't see cultures as autonomous, self-sufficient entities that bind people forever into common scripts or seal them off from a wider dialogic conversation.[27]

The example of high-profile cultural practitioners in music and fashion in the late 1980s offers an illustration of how the second generation was actively reimagining questions of race, place and belonging through style.

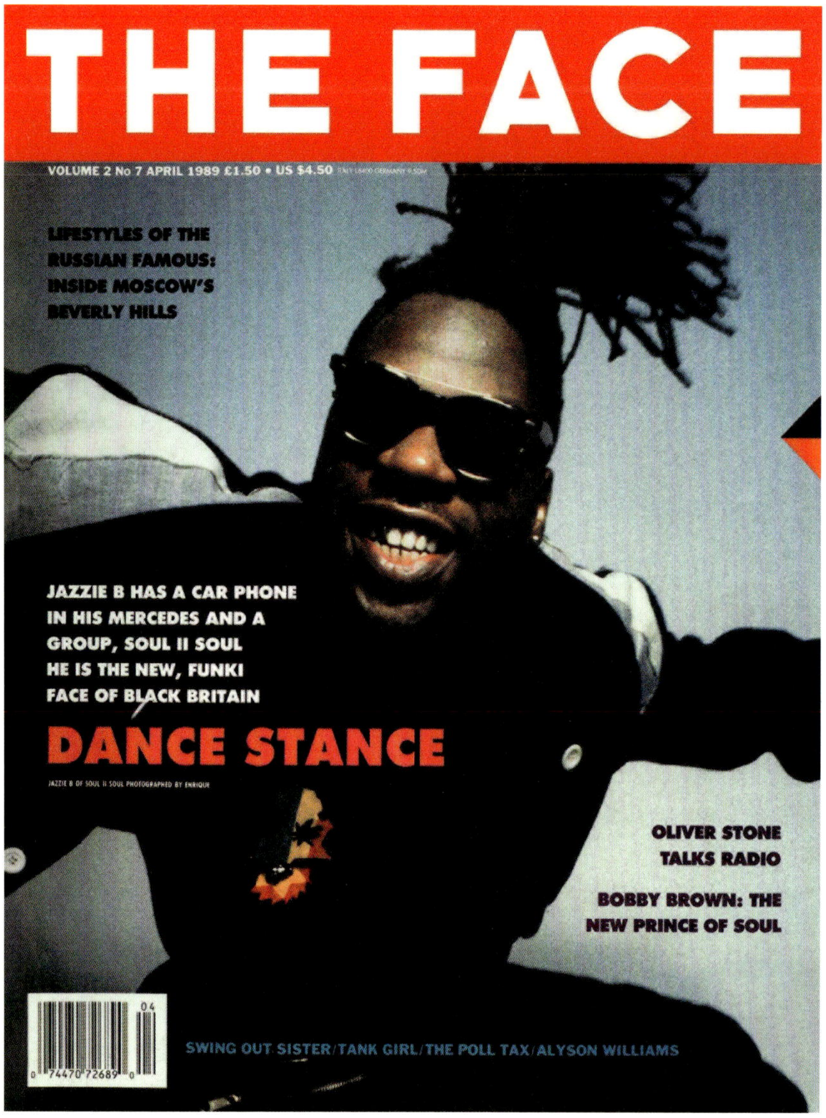

162. Soul II Soul as 'Funki Dreds' on the cover of *The Face* (London, April 1989)

In 1989 the music collective Soul II Soul scored an international hit record with 'Keep on Movin'. The group had begun life as a north London-based reggae sound system called Jah Rico. 'In those days, we were West Indian kids growing up in a country where we didn't fit in. We were born in the UK but nothing in the culture related to us',[28] reflected their leader, Jazzie B. After changing their name, and broadening their approach to include soul, funk and hip-hop, they played a significant role as DJs on the warehouse party scene. But the collective was also influential as style leaders. Pioneering an eclectic style that married their own Soul II Soul branded streetwear, sold in their Camden record store, with avant-garde designs by labels such as Comme des Garçons, Vivienne Westwood, Christopher Nemeth and John Moore, they refashioned themselves as the 'Funki Dreds' (162).[29] The nickname was a reference to their distinctive hairstyles – short on the sides, dreadlocks on top – a look intended to represent their second-generation Caribbean British identity and 'the multiculturalism of London at that time ... where we were much more about the hybrid of it all'.[30]

Soul II Soul's success marked the fusion of 'music and fashion and attitude' that defined the identity of a newly self-assured and creative young Black Britain. 'Soul II Soul created the first definably black British look ever', argues Jay. 'It broke the black stereotype. "Blacks are just muggers. We've just got locks. We just smoke dope all day." No, well, actually, we don't. We're sculptors, we're artists, we're fashion designers. We're music makers. We're cultural icons. We're all of these things and Soul II Soul embodied that for us.'[31]

The idea of a self-fashioned formulation of Blackness and Britishness also helped shape the work of menswear designer Joe Casely-Hayford, who similarly came to prominence in the 1980s. Casely-Hayford was born in Britain to a storied Ghanaian family and saw fashion as a way to both articulate and complicate questions of origin and belonging. He liked to cite the influence of his grandfather, J.E. Casely-Hayford, the author of *Ethiopia Unbound* (1911), one of the first novels to be published in English by an African writer. For Casely-Hayford, the book provided an illuminating exploration of W.E.B. Du Bois's notion of double consciousness: 'the idea that when you're black you're never just one identity; you're aware of both yourself and how you're viewed by the majority at all times.'[32]

A formally trained tailor, he described his designs as a mix of classical elegance and punk spirit. 'English sartorialism and British anarchy' went the slogan. In laying simultaneous claim to Ghanaian and British cultural influences, Casely-Hayford sought to deliberately confound expectations about what it meant to be a Black creative practitioner:

> I was always classified as a 'black designer', so I had to struggle to work against that. I was into punk. I made clothes for The Clash. There weren't African elements in my clothes until later in my career, even though people always expected them. I wanted to be seen as 'the designer'. I just felt the idea of hip-hop culture being the focal point of black identity was something quite narrow, and that there should be other diverse elements. As a young kid I liked rock and heavy metal.[33]

In the breadth of outlook of figures like Casely-Hayford and Jazzie B we see a decisive refutation of the canard that the Black presence in Britain came down to a choice between assimilation or alienation. Casely-Hayford's elegant designs and cosmopolitan sensibility suggest that in the matter of taste versus race you could have both at once. As Hall put it, 'Blacks in the British diaspora must ... refuse the binary black or British. The aim of the struggle must be, instead, to replace the "or" with the potentiality or the possibility of an "and". You can be black *and* British.'[34]

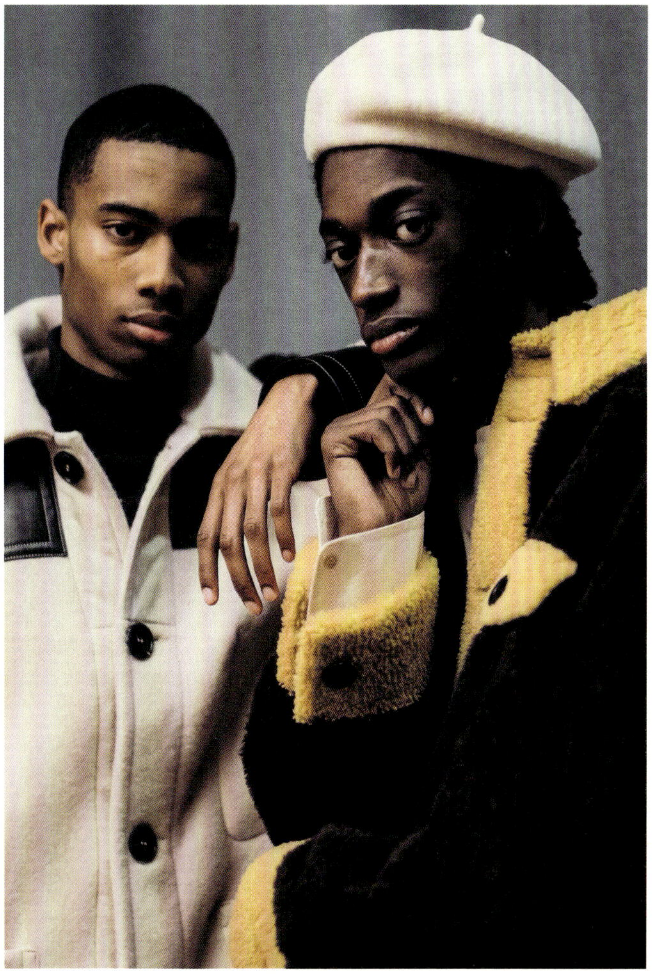

163. Inès Manai (1994–), Wales Bonner, Autumn/Winter 2020

LOVERS' ROCK

The Autumn/Winter 2020 men's fashion show by Grace Wales Bonner, the British designer, took place at the Royal Horticultural Halls in Westminster. The collection drew inspiration from the music and style culture of second-generation African Caribbean youth. An enormous speaker stack playing a commissioned soundtrack of reggae and dubstep dominated one end of the room. Jamaican patties and fruit punch were served. Guests watched models process by in tailoring and sportswear threaded through with West Indian influences: a navy twill pea coat fastened with Jamaican gold brass buttons; knitted beanies in red, gold and green (163). The show was called 'Lovers' Rock' after John Goto's 1977 photo series, a key reference for the collection.

Goto, in turn, took his title from the music genre of the same name, a style of reggae noted for its romantic sound and content. Because the majority of its performers were women, and its songs centred on affairs of the heart, lovers' rock was often seen as soft, feminine and less consequential than the portent-filled masculinity of roots reggae.

Such a characterization was misleading. When it was played at clubs and dance halls, the mellifluousness of lovers' rock created a shared space of intimacy that was likely to be treasured by men as much as women. As sociologist Lisa Amanda Palmer has observed, the music offered a route for men to 'move beyond notions of patriarchal domination' towards more 'redemptive liberatory models for social change'.[35]

This idea of lovers' rock as a crucible for emotional connection is mirrored in Goto's images, where teenage boys and girls are often pictured in couples, laughing, flirting, heads so close that two Afros merge into one. It is also apparent in Wales Bonner's show where female models presented the collection alongside men, the presence of both sexes suffusing the show with a mood of intimacy and desire.

In both works there is a looking beyond fixed ideas of Black maleness and an evocation instead of masculinity as provisional and fluid. And perhaps this tendency was always present. Perhaps, with hindsight, we can locate the first stirrings of a hybrid Black British style in the 1970s, not the 1980s.

In the 1970s style could be a carapace. A practice of refusal. A means of resistance to the hostile mainstream. But it might also act as a shared language by which young Black men could signal a more complex range of emotions than mere strength or hardness.

In the ease and intimacy of Goto's portraits, we see youths who have not surrendered to dichotomy: boys who are not quite men, caught between youth and adulthood, vulnerability and toughness, maleness and femaleness. The sum of the whole greater than the parts.

A TAILORED SARI

AVALON FOTHERINGHAM

Over his 50-year career, designer Jean-Paul Gaultier earned a reputation as a fearless boundary-crosser. Gaultier's work blended streetwear with haute couture, blurred categories of gender and sexuality, played with religious symbolism and iconography, and indiscriminately appropriated from global cultures of dress. Dubbed *'l'enfant terrible de la mode'*, his creations provoked, titillated and amused, while pushing the limits of fashion and its meanings in the modern world.

Gaultier's Sari Suit – dating to the same year as his debut haute couture collection – perfectly encapsulates the designer's 'nothing sacred' approach (164). The ensemble combines a European tailored suit with an Indian-inspired 'sari', mashing together an ancient and iconic garment of Indian womanhood with western fashion's most emblematic uniform of twentieth-century masculinity.

Indian dress holds a special fascination for Gaultier, who first visited the country in the 1970s. He repeatedly returned to Indian source material over the course of his career, once claiming 'In every collection I have done, there is always an Indian inspiration.'[1] Of his sari-inspired Autumn/Winter 2017 collection, the designer explained: 'Embracing tradition makes us stronger. I have taken the cherished garment and created something new ... something that offers a new expression, while respecting its original form.'[2]

Perhaps it is no surprise Gaultier would claim inspiration from India, as experimentation and hybridity are core to the history of Indian dress. The incredible diversity of India's clothing cultures is the result of millennia of assimilations and adaptations. In addition to indigenous tailored and wrapped garments (consisting of purpose-woven lengths of cloth draped around the body), styles of clothing from as far as the Mediterranean and North Africa, the Middle East, and Central, East and Southeast Asia were introduced through commerce, immigration and martial invasions.[3]

Over centuries these foreign clothes were modified to suit local Indian climates and tastes. It has been suggested that the Indian *jama,* for example, may have roots in the warm and heavy robes of ancient Central Asia.[4] Yet by the time it had been adopted as the male uniform of the Mughal court, the *jama* had developed into a uniquely Indian garment of lightweight cotton with flowing skirts and fastenings on either the right or left side of the body, distinguishing the wearer as Muslim or Hindu.

Seen in the context of Gaultier's overall body of work, the Sari Suit can be interpreted as an experimental transgression of boundaries of both gender and geography, which in some ways relates to India's own history of sartorial experimentation. However, Gaultier's specific pairing of a European man's tailored suit with an Indian woman's sari taps into a particularly dark chapter in Indian dress history: that of Indian dress under British colonialism.

During this period, racist strictures of what constituted 'civilized' and 'masculine' dress versus 'uncivilized' and 'feminine' dress were used to control, disenfranchise and oppress Indians living under British colonial rule. Over the nineteenth and early twentieth centuries, the European-style tailored suit became the symbolic dress of the powerful, while Indian dress – especially wrapped dress – was denigrated as the clothing of the powerless.

Unlike previous instances, in which India had borrowed from the fashions of other cultures and regions, the restrictive tailoring, dark, heavy fabrics and comparatively high expense of nineteenth-century European clothing made it neither comfortable nor attractive. Lacking any inherently desirable qualities, its adoption was instead a result of the expansion of British control in India.

The first formal experiments in Indian adoption of European clothes might be traced to the uniforms of eighteenth-century British East India Company Indian soldiers, or sepoys (165). The earliest sepoy uniforms combined British-style military jackets with Indian *cholnas* (shorts) and turbans. This uniform evolved over time and as different regiments customized their looks: incorporating more-or-less Indian dress; fusing Indian fabrics with British cuts, frogging, buttons and trim; negotiating styles of footwear; and adjusting turban styles and clothing materials in line with various Indian caste distinctions and religious beliefs. The success of these stylistic experiments depended on compromise; instances in which British commanders refused to adjust uniforms in accordance with sepoy demands resulted in protest and sometimes mutiny.[5]

But as British martial power increased, so too did the influence of British fashion. European dress began to be perceived as a symbol of status, while Indian dress began to be judged as – at worst – indecent and uncivilized and – at best – effeminate and therefore symbolic of weakness. Whereas in previous decades many Europeans in India had adopted aspects of Indian life and culture including Indian dress, such experimentation was increasingly discouraged. In 1830 the East India Company went so far as to issue an edict banning European men in their employ from wearing Indian dress in public. Those who continued to wear it in private were disparaged as lowering their status by 'going native'.[6]

At the same time, the British began to discourage Indians from adopting European dress, even instituting dress codes for Indians attending official functions to ensure they were clothed in an appropriately 'oriental manner'.[7] Colonial control of male dress in particular became part of 'a more general process by which the politically dominant group tried to define the Indian male as powerless and subordinate in his own country'.[8] Clothing became a means by which to distinguish, segregate and exclude Indians from positions of authority; a way to maintain a divide between the British

164. Jean-Paul Gaultier (1952–), Sari Suit. Rayon. Designed in France, tailored in Italy, 1997. Given by Mark Reed. V&A: T.51-2011

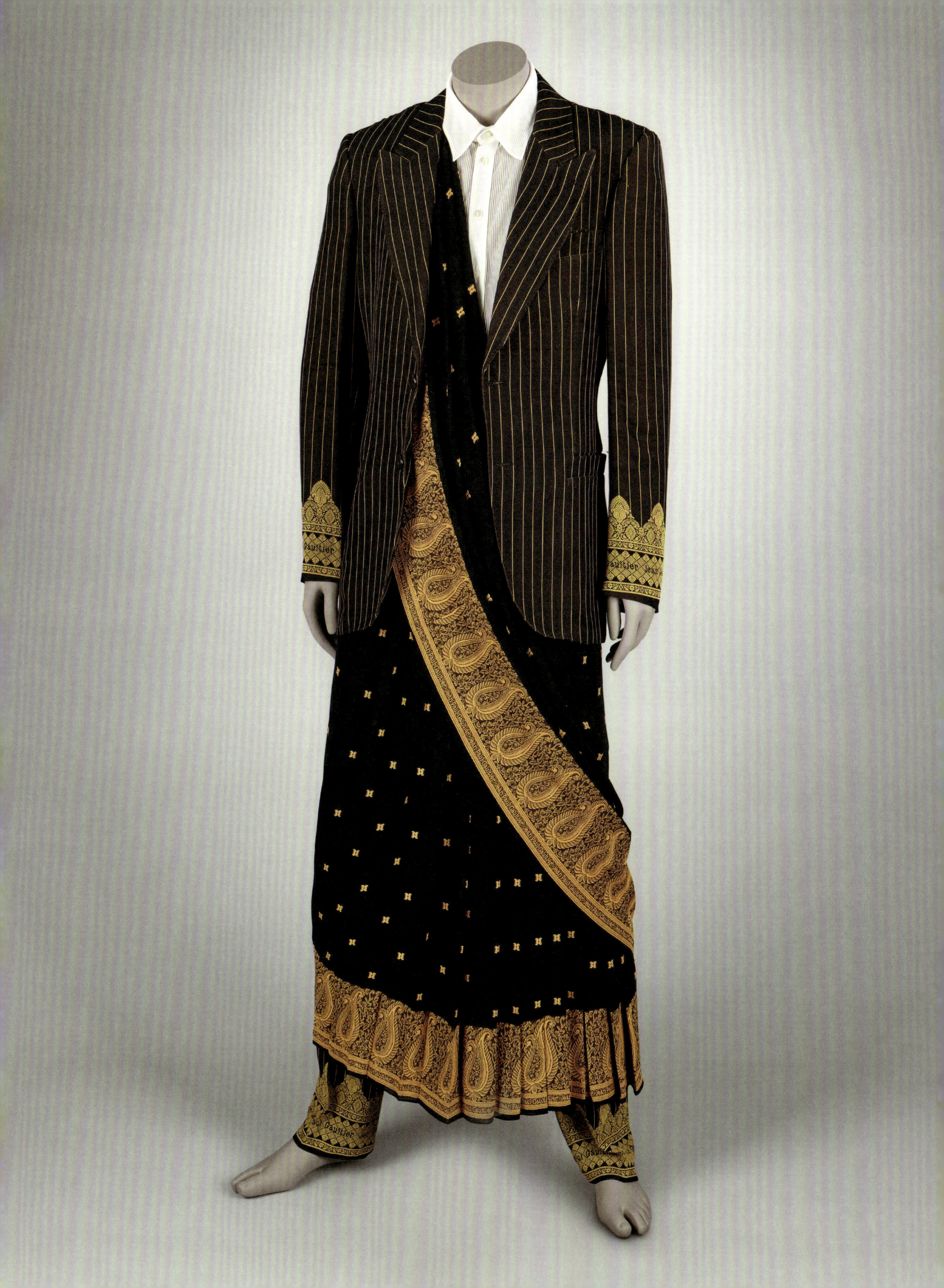
Gaultier

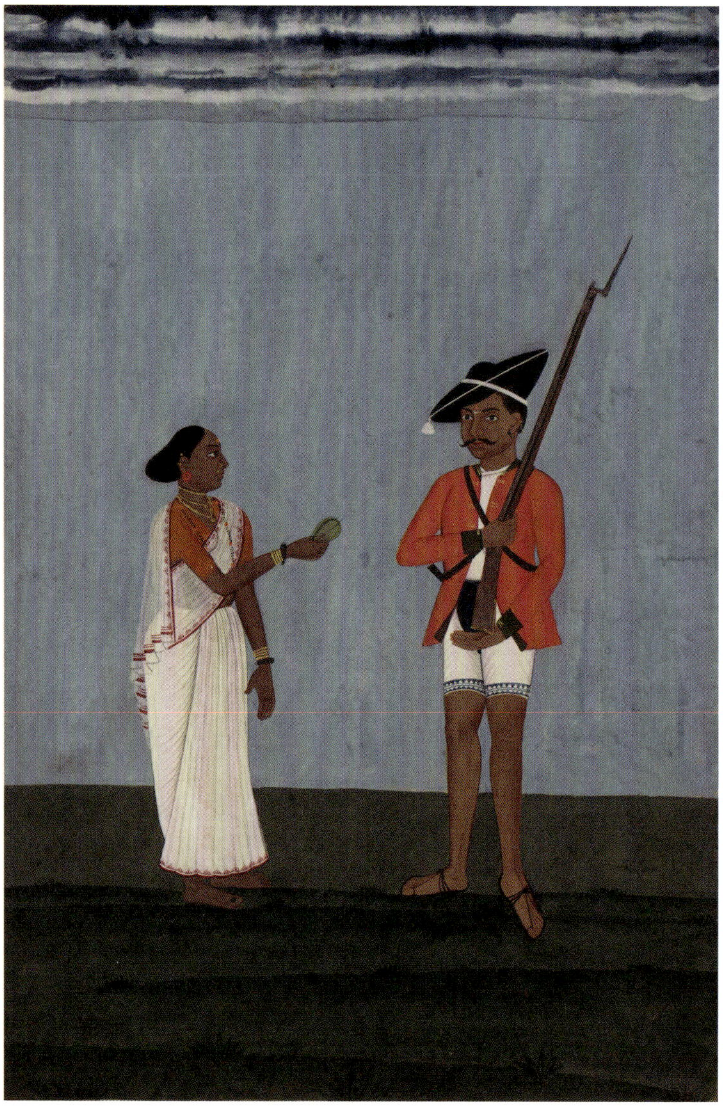

165. 'A South Indian Sepoy and his Wife', from an album of 36 paintings of castes and occupations of South India. Gouache, 34 × 25 cm. Thanjavur, Tamil Nadu, *c.*1770. V&A: AL.9128:10

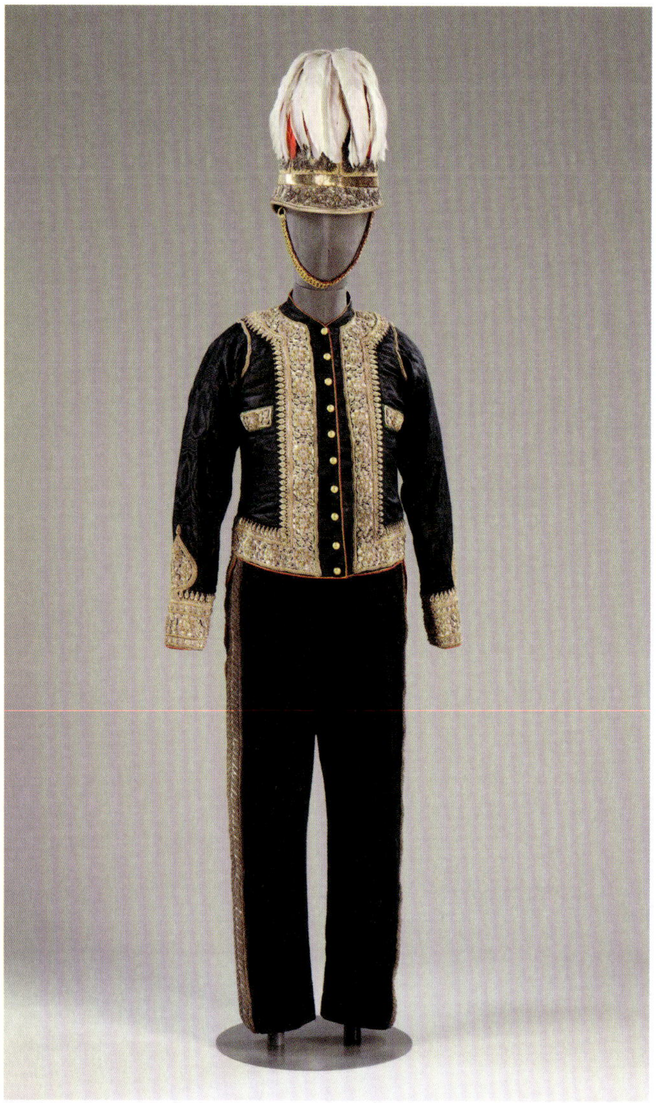

166. Ceremonial uniform of the Gaekwad of Baroda. Silk with silver-gilt embellishments. Vadodara, Gujarat, *c.*1873. V&A: 0716(IS), 0717(IS)

as the 'masculine' and 'civilized' ruling power and the 'feminine' and 'uncivilized' Indians they ruled.

In order to operate within the structural racism of this system, Indian men faced difficult choices with respect to dress. For men of India's elite and emerging urban middle classes, adopting European-style clothing promised an elevation in status and increased respect. As Bengali poet Michael Madhusudan Dutta explained when asked why he had attended a party in full European dress: 'If I came wearing [a *dhoti* and *chadar*] I'd have to help carry pitchers and napkins; but these are the clothes of the Ruling Race; so there's no fear of that.'[9]

Of course, the adoption of European-style clothing was not without tension. Conflict between professional ambition versus 'values and tastes [as well as] notions of loyalty to family, self, caste, religion and race' made the wearing of European dress difficult to navigate.[10] Over the nineteenth century, urban middle- and upper-class Indian men devised numerous strategies for fusing European and Indian clothing in ways that both reflected their cultural identities and enabled their professional aspirations.

Initial methods included tailoring and embellishing European-style clothes using Indian materials, as seen in the *zardozi*-embellished silk European-cut military uniform of the Gaekwad of Baroda (166). New styles of garment were also developed, which combined aspects of pre-colonial Indian menswear fashions with European uniform and suit tailoring techniques. Indian drawstring *paijama* were tailored to mimic European trouser cuts, while Kashmiri pashmina, Varanasi brocades and Lucknowi jamdani were made into close-fitting *sherwani* jackets with rounded armholes, standing collars, pockets and button fasteners (167).

By the turn of the century, new ensembles that instead combined elements of both European and Indian dress became fashionable in select urban centres. Full European suits were worn with turbans and embroidered Indian shawls, while stiff European jackets, shirts and ties were paired with *angarkha*, *paijama* and fine *dhotis*.[11] But even in fully British dress, Indian men could not escape the inherent racism of the colonial period. The artist Gaganendranath Tagore aptly illustrated the futility of attempting to circumvent structural prejudice with cloth-

167. Sherwani. Jamdani muslin. Lucknow, Uttar Pradesh, *c.*1912. Given by Mr Muhammed Zaheer. V&A: IS.8-1971. Dhoti. Muslin. Purchased in Mumbai, Maharashtra, 2014. Private collection

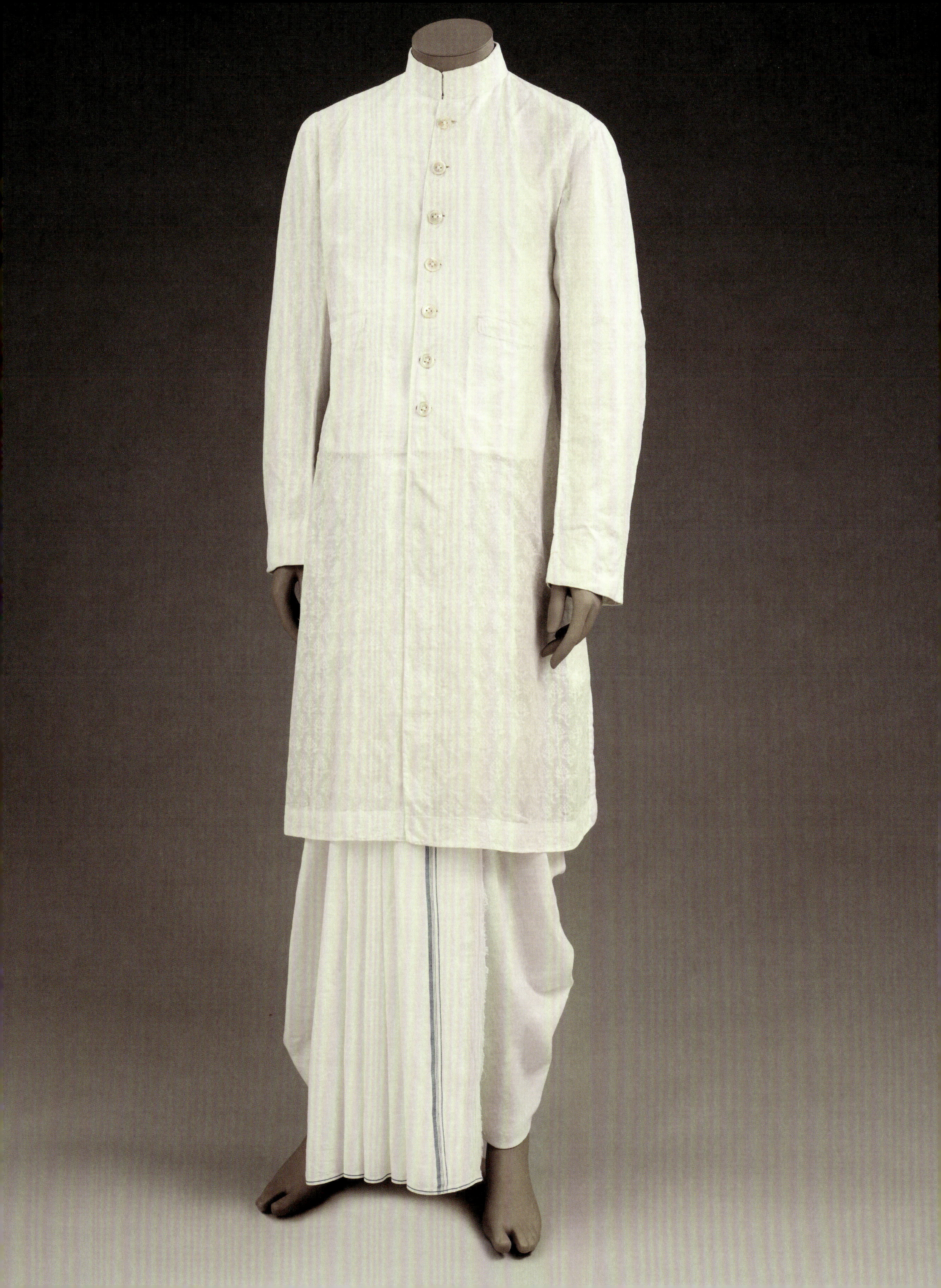

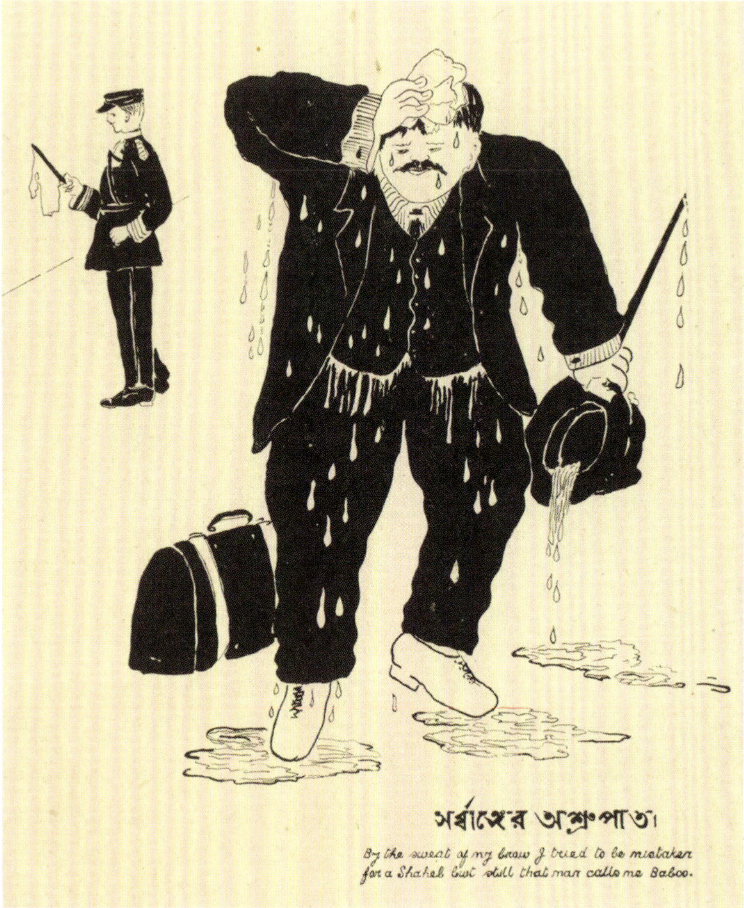

168. Gaganendranath Tagore (1867–1938), *By the Sweat of My Brow*. Lithograph, 44.5 × 30.7 cm. Kolkata, 1917. V&A: IS.5:7-1987

ing in his satirical cartoon *By the Sweat of My Brow* (168). An Indian man is depicted sweating in a three-piece European suit – complete with derby hat, walking stick and travelling case – as he walks away from a white train guard. The caption reads 'By the sweat of my brow I tried to be mistaken for a Shaheb [European] but still that man called me Baboo' – a term then used to disdainfully describe Indian men perceived to be 'aspiring' to the status of Europeans.

It is therefore unsurprising that dress would become so central to the Indian independence movement. Upending British judgements of Indian dress as uncivilized and effeminate, Indian men used their clothing as a powerful form of protest. *Dhoti*, *kurta*, *paijama* and *sherwani* took on new importance as the clothing of India's male political freedom fighters, who encouraged all Indians to reject European cloth and clothing as forms of economic, social and cultural oppression. These ensembles remain popular, even as globally homogenous styles from international fast-fashion brands have entered the Indian market.

Ironically, despite British colonial perceptions of European dress as superiorly civilized, India was able to adopt and adapt European methods of dress but Europe has yet to master Indian methods. While many European designers have been inspired by Indian wrapped garments, the pleats and folds of their constructions are always tailored illusions, sewn, hooked, or buttoned into place to compensate for the skills required to properly drape wrapped clothing.[12] Gaultier's Sari Suit is no different: the 'sari' itself is assembled from several panels of custom Gaultier-branded silk, the pleats of which are stitched into place and fastened around the waist with buttons.

Gaultier's pairing of an Indian sari with a European suit is therefore much more than a playful blurring of gender and geography. It is also a reflection of the tense history of fashion's relationship with colonialism: how Indian clothing – especially male clothing – was imbued with imbalanced value, used to other, control and segregate, and then reappropriated as a tool in the fight for Indian independence. Imbued with all this history, the fusion of Indian wrapped and European tailored dress is a powerful combination for any designer, and one Gaultier only borrowed. Pioneered in India generations ago, the many permutations and meanings of 'Indo-western style', as it is known today, are still being explored by leading Indian designers including Tarun Tahiliani, Anju Modi (169) and Rajesh Pratap Singh, among many others. Doubtless European dress will constitute only one more sartorial assimilation in India's long and rich fashion history.

169. Anju Modi, Ensemble. Lakme Fashion Week Winter Festival, 2014

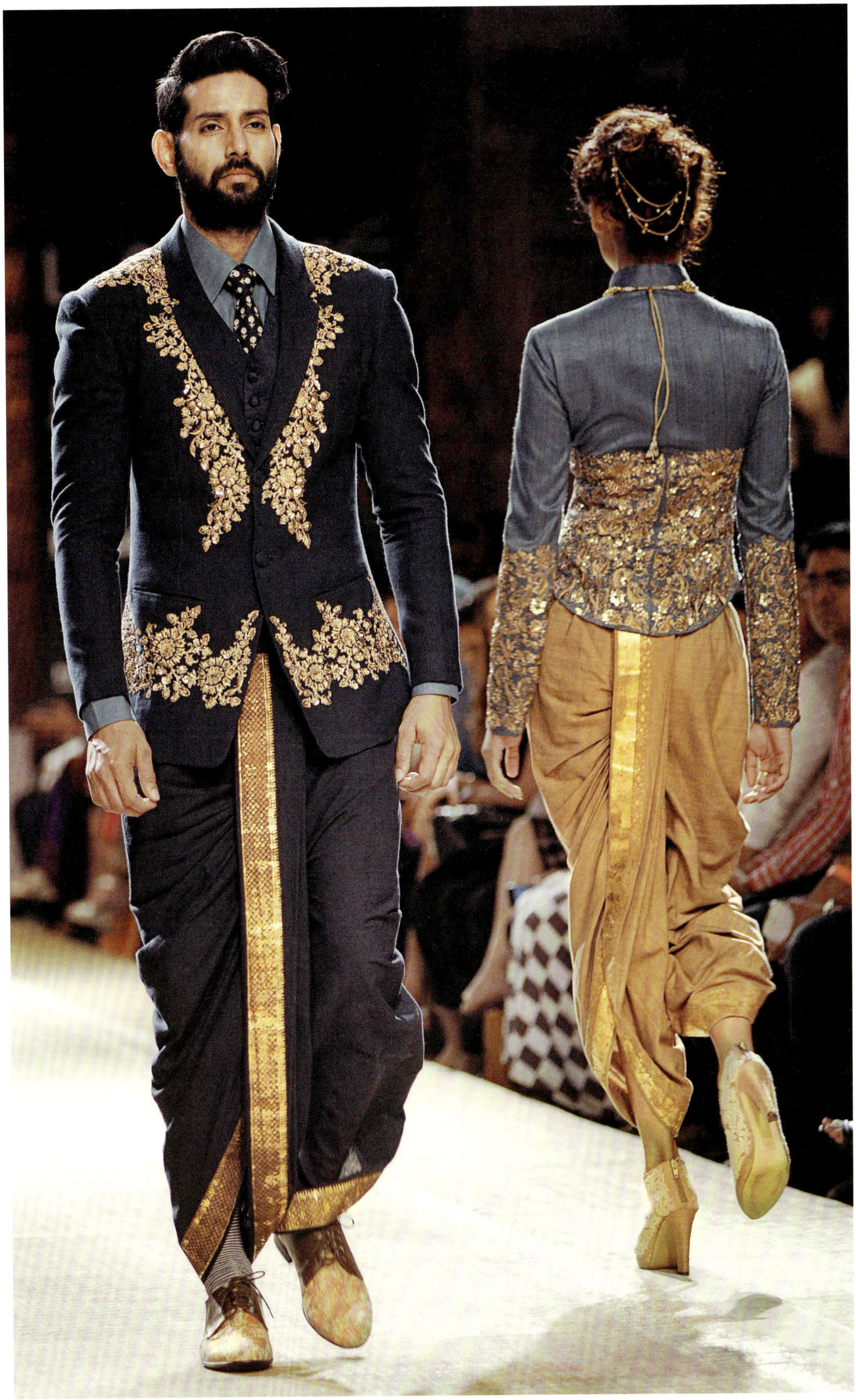

A BROKEN SUIT

MARTA FRANCESCHINI

Italian designer Romeo Gigli made clothes for men and women that were *sensual*. They seemed to come directly from the senses, and they spoke to the senses, revealing how fashion is not a just a system of communication with the outside world, but also a physical practice, experienced through sight and touch. Architect and critic Enrico Morteo defined Gigli's approach to fashion design as a 'quest for a discipline of emotions'.[1] Gigli's womenswear was praised by the international press for its 'cocoons', tracing silhouettes that protected the intimacy of ethereal and bashful femininities. Close observation of Gigli's menswear reveals a more nuanced interpretation of his own aesthetic, and a consideration of how the Italian fashion system has dealt with masculinities.

A velvet and wool suit held in the V&A collection stands as the material result of the intricate itinerary of a sartorial network, whose systemization started in the early twentieth century (170). It is a *spezzato* – literally meaning 'broken' – a word traditionally used to indicate a suit in which the fabric of the trousers and jacket do not match, a popular style in Italian menswear since at least the 1950s.

The fiery red velvet is soft but structured enough to sustain the relaxed cut of the jacket and fitted waistcoat; the wool trousers are straight, almost slouchy at the top, due to the central pleats, and narrower towards the hemline. Both fabrics accommodate the body without constraint, serving as a threshold to the outer world; or, as the philosopher Jacques Derrida put it, embodying 'betweenness', the state of transition between the experience of exteriority and interiority, both tangible and conceptual.[2]

In the late 1990s, Gigli's menswear was produced by Ermenegildo Zegna S.p.A in a Swiss factory in Lugano, just across the Italian border, that specialized in men's clothing. Zegna is central to the history of the Italian menswear system. First established in the province of Biella in 1910, one of many wool mills in this north-eastern region of Italy, Zegna produced fine cloth for Italian tailors. The company also fostered the publication of fashion magazines for men, such as *Arbiter* and *Petronio*, and supported the establishment of the Festival della Moda Maschile di Sanremo, launched in 1952, an event that showed the work of tailoring schools, and later, ready-made clothing firms too, from all over Italy and Europe. The festival was talked about in the national press mostly for the presence of male models, who walked the runways in casinos and classy hotels and also paraded on the streets of the city, turning it into a stage for male performance, which was unprecedented and unexpected for the rather conservative Italian society (171). A similar kind of peacockery would later become associated with Pitti Uomo, an event attracting men's fashion enthusiasts to Florence since 1972.

Italian textile manufacturers started venturing into ready-made clothing in the 1950s. In 1957 Nino Cerruti, of the Lanificio Cerruti, founded Hitman, the first luxury ready-to-wear line of men's clothing, and others soon followed. The preferred strategy for launching these new lines was to collaborate with established tailors to create mass-produced suits that balanced customer taste with the creation of a distinctive Italian style. Cerruti appointed tailor Osvaldo Testa, with whom he developed the 'Flying Cross' line in 1962; Lebole, a mass-manufacturer from Ancona, hired Angelo Litrico (known for being Nikita Khrushchev's tailor) to design his lines at the beginning of the 1960s; finally, Zegna established the ready-to-wear line 'Emilio Pucci per Ermenegildo Zegna' in 1967, before founding its own brand In.Co Gritti in 1968.

The gradual shift from traditional tailoring to high-quality ready-to-wear led to the development of a specifically Italian style of men's fashion, first in design and standardized production, and then in consumption. According to historian Mario Lupano, what defined this style, a mix of tailoring traditions and industrial values, was its commitment to attitude and individual taste.[3] Outside Italy, and especially among Britain's working-class subcultures, 'Italian Style' came to signify an attitude of 'experiencing' clothes. From the late 1950s, it was associated with the mods. Riffing on the teddy boys' ironic take on rigid Edwardian tailoring and proletarian attitude and poses, the mods exploited the 'Italianicity' of their clothes, related primarily to the emergence of the body underneath them: 'with its lightweight materials, brighter colours and slimline jackets and trousers, Italian style emphasized the contours of men's bodies, especially their legs and thighs, rather than camouflaging them under the weight of heavy fabrics'.[4] It is no surprise then, that the short and tight mohair jacket designed by Nazareno Fonticoli of Brioni, a tailoring company founded in 1945, epitomizing the fashionable 'Roman Style', was taken up by designer and retailer Cecil Gee and turned into the even-shorter, even-tighter 'bumfreezer'.[5]

The carefree attitude and elegantly subversive flair of Brioni's designs attracted British youth, but also captivated the attention of American men. The success of Italian fashion, in its 'national' connotations, relates specifically to post-Second World War geopolitics. From 1948 the Marshall Plan not only provided the money needed to kick-start Italy's post-war recovery, but also crafted an exquisitely exportable image of the country, its products and its people.[6] While helping to rebuild the country devastated by war, America opened its doors to Italian products and their carefree elegance often referred to as *sprezzatura*. Men's fashion was one of many areas that exploited the value of Italian taste, stripping a nation of their 'sacks' and providing clothes that promised refinement.[7] Actors such as Clark Gable and Sidney Poitier contributed to the popularity of the *bella figura*, preferring Italian labels – both clothing and acces-

170. Romeo Gigli (1957–), *Spezzato* suit. Velvet, wool and cotton. Designed in Italy, made in Switzerland, 1997. Given by Mark Reed. V&A: T.30:1 to 4-2011

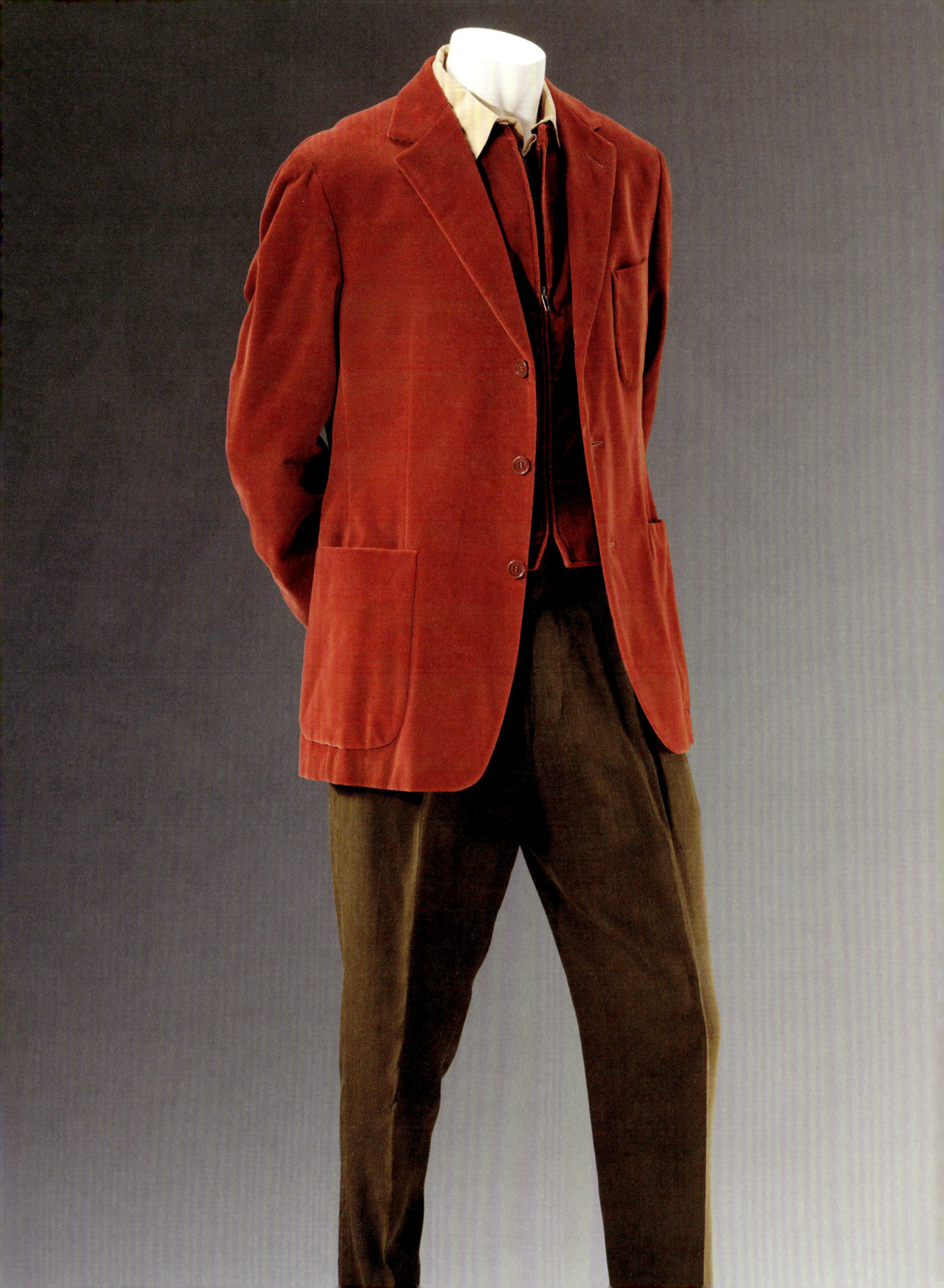

da Sanremo

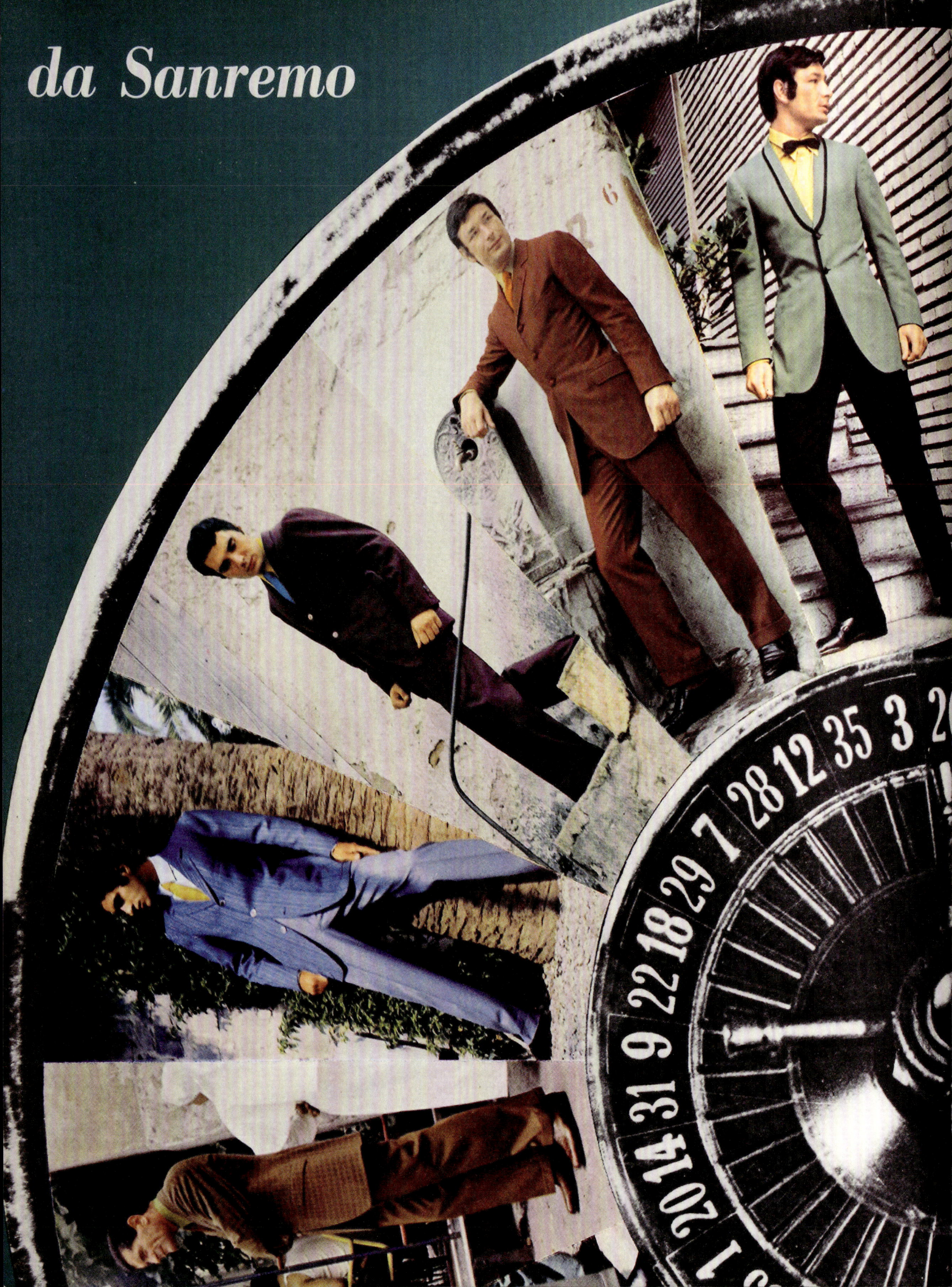

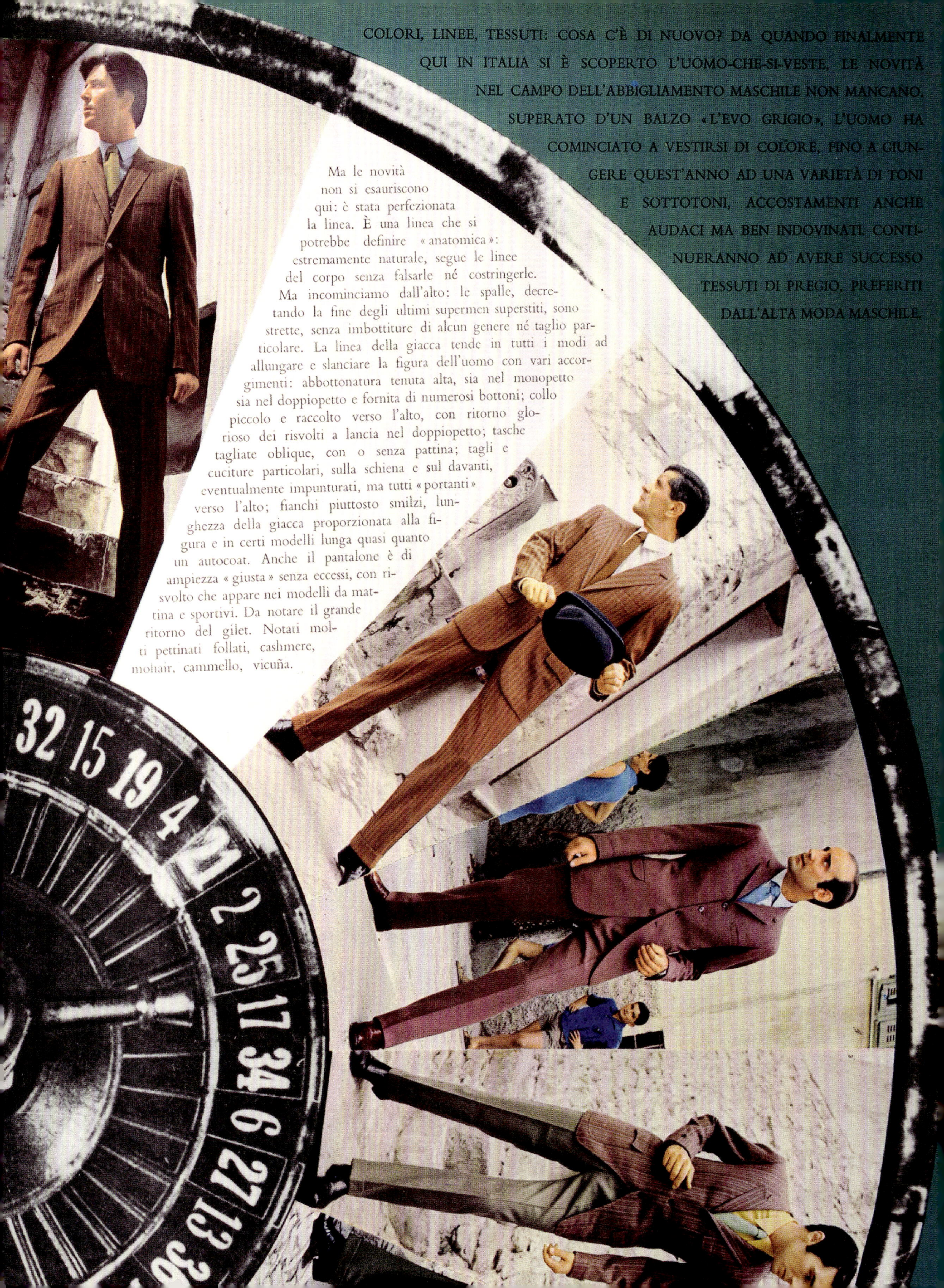

COLORI, LINEE, TESSUTI: COSA C'È DI NUOVO? DA QUANDO FINALMENTE QUI IN ITALIA SI È SCOPERTO L'UOMO-CHE-SI-VESTE, LE NOVITÀ NEL CAMPO DELL'ABBIGLIAMENTO MASCHILE NON MANCANO. SUPERATO D'UN BALZO «L'EVO GRIGIO», L'UOMO HA COMINCIATO A VESTIRSI DI COLORE, FINO A GIUNGERE QUEST'ANNO AD UNA VARIETÀ DI TONI E SOTTOTONI, ACCOSTAMENTI ANCHE AUDACI MA BEN INDOVINATI. CONTINUERANNO AD AVERE SUCCESSO TESSUTI DI PREGIO, PREFERITI DALL'ALTA MODA MASCHILE.

Ma le novità non si esauriscono qui: è stata perfezionata la linea. È una linea che si potrebbe definire «anatomica»: estremamente naturale, segue le linee del corpo senza falsarle né costringerle. Ma incominciamo dall'alto: le spalle, decretando la fine degli ultimi supermen superstiti, sono strette, senza imbottiture di alcun genere né taglio particolare. La linea della giacca tende in tutti i modi ad allungare e slanciare la figura dell'uomo con vari accorgimenti: abbottonatura tenuta alta, sia nel monopetto sia nel doppiopetto e fornita di numerosi bottoni; collo piccolo e raccolto verso l'alto, con ritorno glorioso dei risvolti a lancia nel doppiopetto; tasche tagliate oblique, con o senza pattina; tagli e cuciture particolari, sulla schiena e sul davanti, eventualmente impunturati, ma tutti «portanti» verso l'alto; fianchi piuttosto smilzi, lunghezza della giacca proporzionata alla figura e in certi modelli lunga quasi quanto un autocoat. Anche il pantalone è di ampiezza «giusta» senza eccessi, con risvolto che appare nei modelli da mattina e sportivi. Da notare il grande ritorno del gilet. Notati molti pettinati follati, cashmere, mohair, cammello, vicuña.

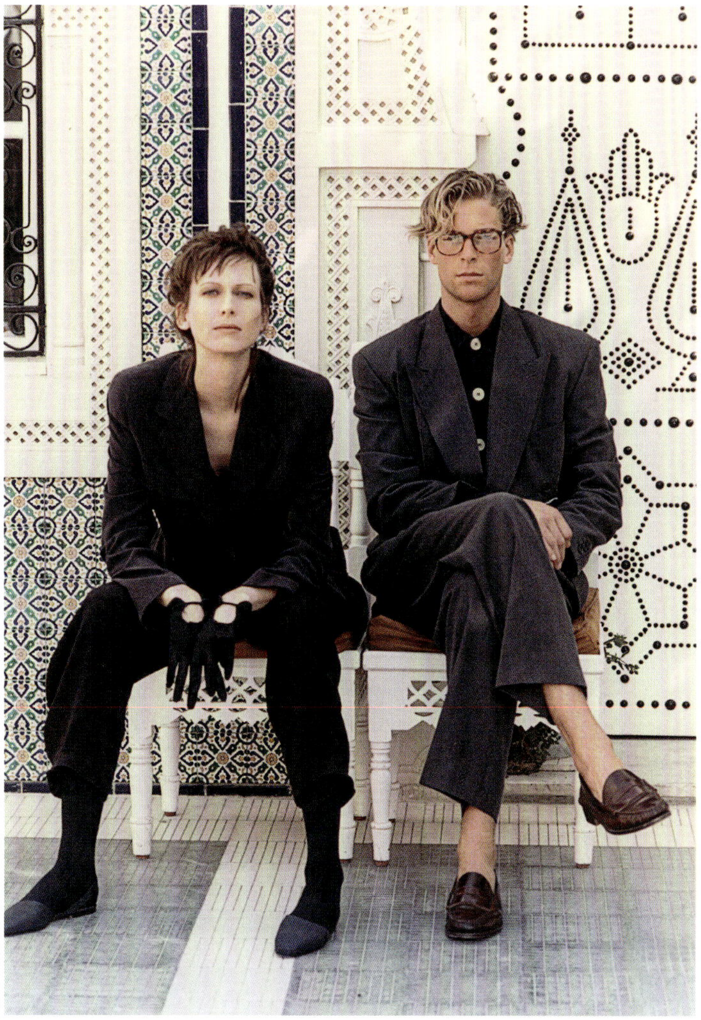

172. Aldo Fallai (1943–), Advertising campaign for Giorgio Armani, Spring/Summer 1989. Models: Gina di Bernardo and Sam Alderson

sories – for their appearances on and off duty, enriching Italian menswear with Hollywood glamour.

Celebrity culture gave Italian menswear a stage on which to perform the peculiarities of its style. And it was not only actors championing these dapper, sensual clothes; the tailors themselves acted as models, taking part in events and featuring in glossy magazines. In England John Stephen and Tommy Nutter were the first to model their flared-legged trousers and wide-lapelled jackets, and in Italy Bruno Piattelli and Carlo Palazzi paraded in the streets wearing suits with daring prints or *spezzati*, sleek and fitted to slender and unashamedly garish silhouettes. The ensembles worn – and advertised – by these star-tailors mixed together influences from the sartorial traditionalism preferred by the bourgeoisie and the 'factious elegance' of what Pier Paolo Pasolini called 'popular dandyism'.[8]

The masculine qualities exuding from this ambivalent 'stylistic verve' were a novelty in the 1950s.[9] Their popularity then exploded in the 1960s, boosted by a brazen use of nudity, as seen on catwalks and at events such as MareModa Capri, a fashion festival held on the glamorous island near Naples. This provocative setting further enhanced the well-established international appeal of designs by Walter Albini and Nino Cerruti.[10]

In an interview with the magazine *Artribune*, Flavio Lucchini retraced the motivations that led him to found the magazine *L'Uomo Vogue* in September 1967: 'For guys, traditional dress was violated in every way, even with different coloured sleeves or with inserts of various fabrics… This was the moment and the climate that favoured and allowed the birth and success of this magazine… In Italy *L'Uomo Vogue* was the banner of change.' [11]

The magazine became the house organ of the menswear system. Designers used it to present and promote their products, and to articulate their views on the relationship between dress and different masculine attitudes, fuelled by the air of revolt and renovation that pervaded Milan throughout the 1970s and 1980s. The designer immersed in this vibrant Milanese atmosphere, who led the way in deconstructing tailoring, was Giorgio Armani.

During his time as *stilista* at Hitman,[12] Armani learned about the rules of cut and construction, only to challenge them with his own label from 1974, updating tailoring with a more relaxed, almost classical, approach to draping cloth over the body. As British fashion designer Hardy Amies put it, Armani fulfilled his 'plan to impose softness where there was once rigidity, to insist on reduction of weight, to reject linings – allowing the body to feel the wool.'[13] Stripping the

Previous pages: 171. 'da Sanremo', *TOP Magazine* (III, 1968). Fondazione Zegna Collection jacket of its mid-layers and internal structures, and preferring nude, earthy shades and flowing fabrics, he gave material form to the desire for a more intimate experience of men's sensibility through clothing (172). Armani's methodology appeared as a rational way to bring together the mechanical act of making clothes with a response to the needs of an ever-more diversified, fragmented, postmodern society: 'My fashion is not unisex; it demands softness for men and strength for women'.[14]

While Armani offered men formal attire that would not hide their new-found grace, other types of masculinity demanded to be dressed. Designs by Mauro Calugi and Danilo Giannelli, Domenico Dolce and Stefano Gabbana and, most notably, Gianni Versace (173), clad the male body in leather and studs, pumped its volume with knitted armour enmeshed with metal threads, and replied to the quest for overtly (homo)erotic and hyper-masculine 'men without ties'.[15]

The tension between traditional making and vitalistic eroticism in Italian menswear was resolved in the mid-1990s, when American designer Tom Ford became Creative Director of Gucci.[16] Founded in 1921, Gucci focused on high-luxury leather goods, expertly made by artisans from Florence and the surrounding area. Its products attracted women and men alike, as proved by photographs of actor Peter Sellers, writer Samuel Beckett and former first lady Jackie Kennedy Onassis casually wearing their Hobo Bags. From his appointment in 1994, Ford's interpretation of masculinity pervaded the heritage of the brand with the designer's very personal reminiscences of New York club

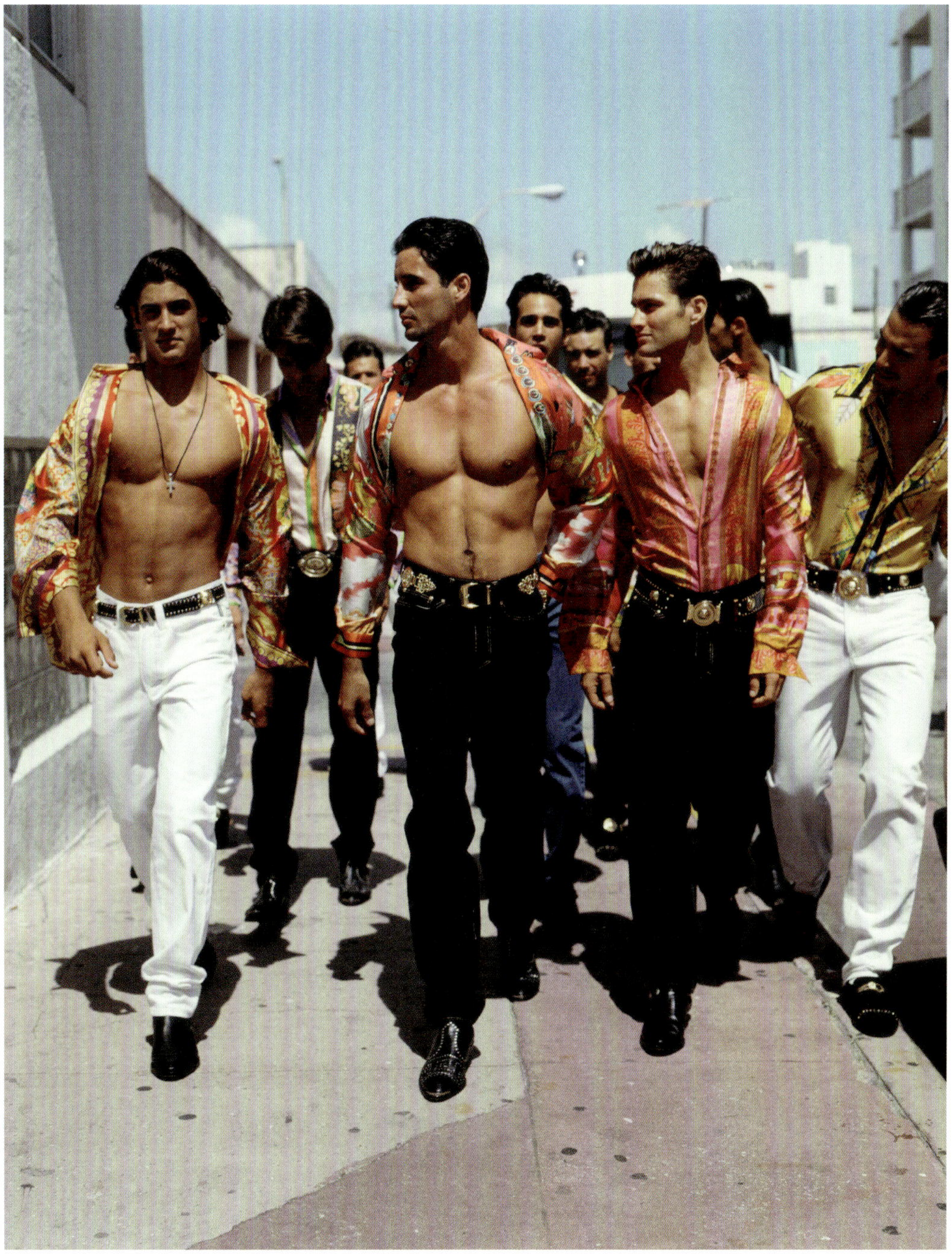

173. Doug Ordway (1962–), advertising campaign for Versace Jeans Couture, Spring/Summer 1994. Models: Hansel Rodriguez, Horacio Le Don, Joel Guzman (et al.)

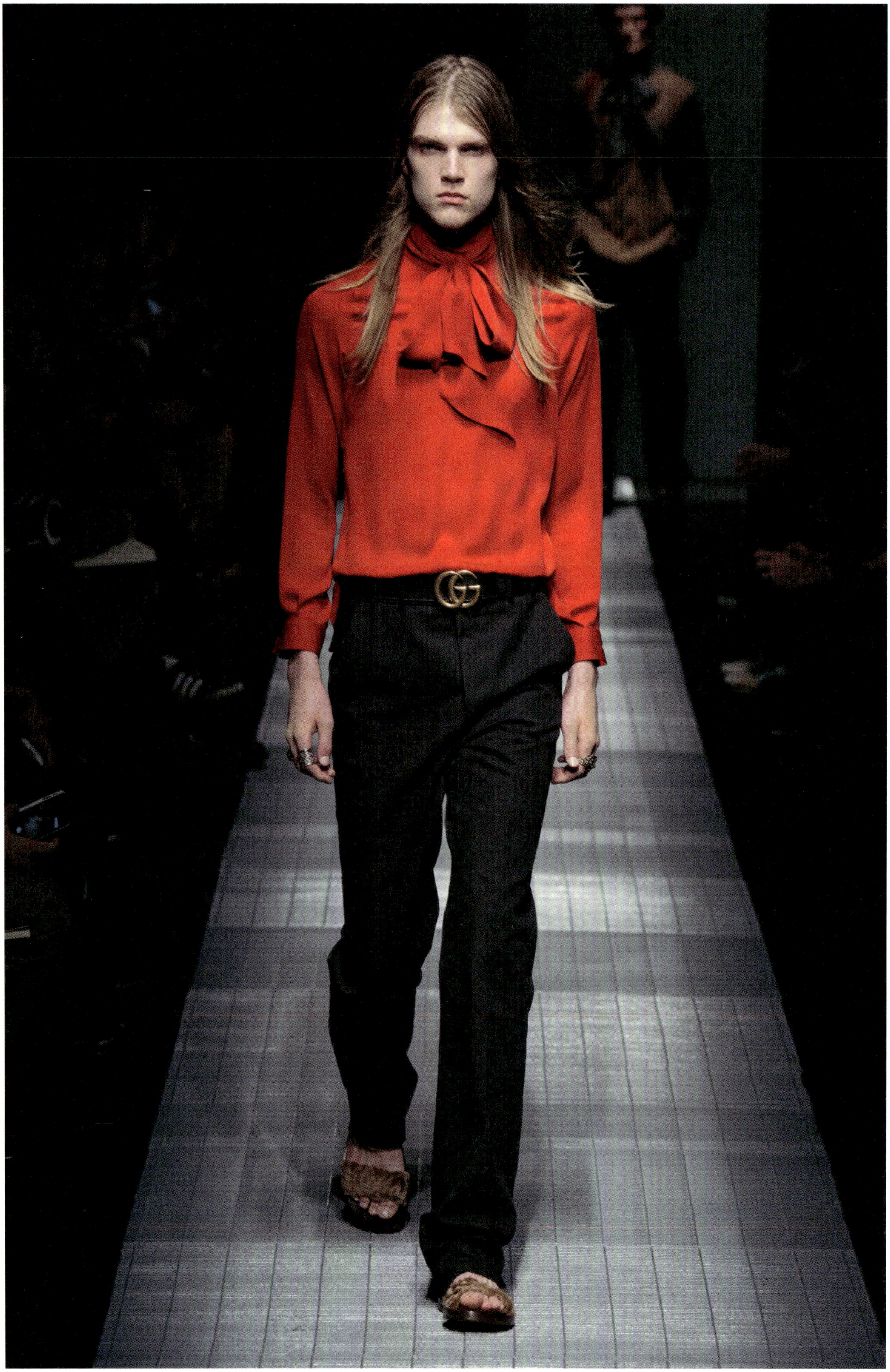

174. Alessandro Michele (1972–) for Gucci. Ensemble.
Autumn/Winter 2015 Menswear. Model: Hugo Goldhoorn

Studio 54.[17] Virility and langour were translated into boxy proportions balanced by deep necklines and a preference for flashy, haptic materials such as lace, leather, silks and velvets, selected from the refined creations of Italian manufacturers.

Ford's work had a direct impact on his contemporaries, and his aesthetic was recently revisited by Alessandro Michele, who became Gucci's Artistic Director in 2015 (174). Since presenting a slouchy pussy-bow shirt paired with tailored trousers in his first runway show, Michele's collections have been identified as manifestos of queerness, challenging traditional gender performance and identity: '...it seems necessary to suggest a desertion, away from patriarchal plans and uniforms. Deconstructing the idea of masculinity as it has been historically established... It's not about suggesting a new normative model, rather to release what was constrained.'[18]

The Gucci Autumn/Winter 2020 menswear collection was titled 'Masculine, plural'. It acknowledged Michele's intention to 'release the constraint' of a norm, paying respect to Ford's legacy, recapturing the vibe of the 1970s Italian fashion scene and realigning it to the demands of today's social awareness.

As Romeo Gigli did with his take on the *spezzato*, Michele distorts the same recognizable codes to form his own design lexicon; he imagines 'certainly uncertain' men, dressed in muslin and lurex, soft in gait and not worried about defining their sexuality according to traditional canons. Designing uniforms for desertion, Michele today channels the sensuous needs of the male body, updating the sophisticated reflection on masculinity that, in Italy, has been historically – and powerfully – expressed through fashion.

THE JACKET
ERODED, BORROWED, EVOLVED

ALISTAIR O'NEILL

In the twenty-first century, the wearing away of the formal codes that uphold men's dress is ascribed to the influence of casual and sporting dress on the male wardrobe. In the case of the suit, there is a focus around the loss of the tie as means of fastening the shirt collar tight to the neck, covering the shirt's placket and buttons, and finishing the outfit. This opening up at the neck exposes an underlying assumption that it marks the decline of the suit as a symbol of male armour, appropriateness and acumen.

This essay argues that the erosion of the suit is also informed by alternative jacket styles that had an impact on western men's dress in the post-war period, undermining the authority of the formal business suit: the Bleu de Travail, the Mao, the Nehru, the Safari. All offer a different kind of formality, either by covering the tie at the neck, or by dispensing with it entirely. It is a practically minded but curious range, drawn from military and occupational dress, and from the Global South, purportedly worn by every man, but championed by men who live and work beyond the realm of the ordinary, in the unlikely pairing of artists and politicians. Such clothes have allowed men to articulate how a uniform can be worn as a marker of individuality, expressing artistic, cultural and political affiliations. These are jackets that enact a sartorial position of difference and potential, worn to dream the world awake.

ARTISTS' WORKWEAR

The formulation of the modern artist in Paris in the mid-nineteenth century, evolved two stylized modes of dressing to mark the white, male construct as opposed to bourgeois masculinity. Art historian Amelia Jones describes them as either:

> ... align[ing] themselves with the working class, taking on the sartorial signifiers of the peasant or the labourer (used jackets, rumpled fabrics, messy hair, or, in the case of Vincent van Gogh and Paul Cézanne, actual peasants' clothing) or to construct themselves through the aristocratic codes of the dandy or his peripatetic colleague, the *flâneur*.[1]

By the turn of the twentieth century, artists working in Paris turned to the working clothes of tradesmen to express their investment in everyday life as a commitment to modernity (175). At the Rotonde, a café frequented by artists in Montparnasse, British artist Nina Hamnett arrived in 1914 wearing her brightly coloured Omega Workshop clothes and patterned stockings. Her biographer, Denise Hooker, writes that she is noticed not only for her gender, but also because she stands out from the male artists dressed like

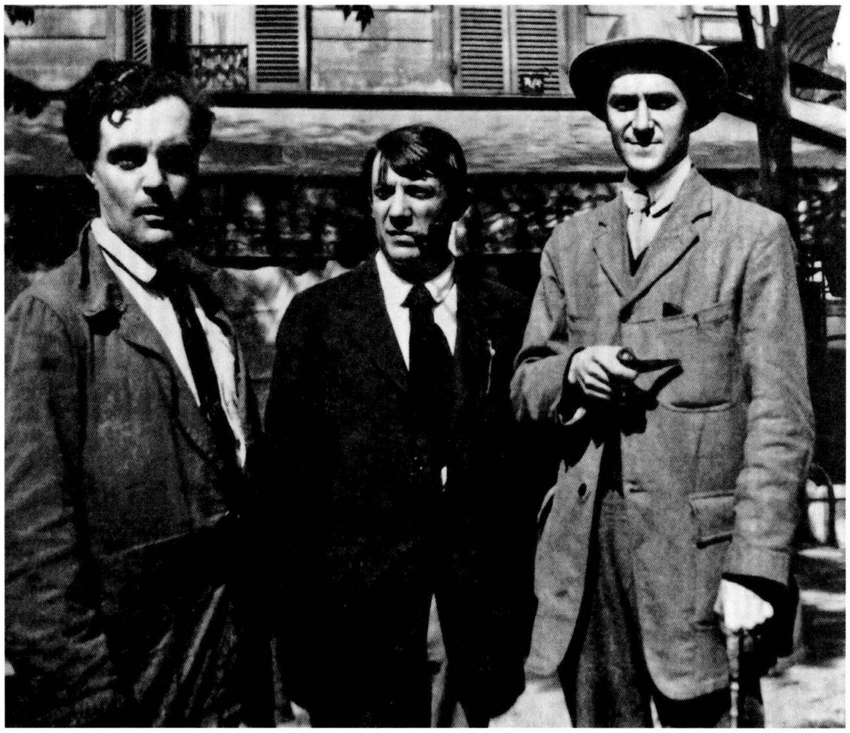

175. Jean Cocteau (1889–1963), Amedeo Modigliani, Pablo Picasso and André Salmon in front of Café de la Rotonde, Paris, *c.*1915

the workpeople of the quarter: 'Derain, Vlaminck, Matisse and Van Dongen would appear wearing bowler hats, while Kisling always dressed in a blue boiler suit and was described by André Salmon as looking like an Eskimo plumber. Picasso sported both a workman's cap and a gold watch chain.'[2]

The male artists adopted workers' clothes dyed indigo, hydrone blue (a cheaper, vat dye alternative) and black in robust fabrics such as cotton drill, denim, moleskin and corduroy known as *bleu de travail* (work blues). Tradesmen such as carpenters, craftsmen, mechanics and railway and sanitation workers were recognized by these factory-made clothes; the oldest surviving company is Lafont (1844), later followed by Le Mont Saint Michel (1913), Vetra (1927) and Le Laboureur (1956). The artists who now wore them did so not just for practical but also for political reasons: to claim their distinction from white-collar workers (office-based) who were petit bourgeois; and to show their solidarity with the working class, identified as blue-collar (defining those engaged in physical rather than mental work).

Artists in the Soviet Union and Eastern Europe subsequently made their own interpretations of workers' clothing to represent the ideals of a new utopia. Russian Aleksandr Rodchenko and Hungarian Lázló Moholy-Nagy invested in the ideal of the 'artist-constructor' as an artist committed to working with industry to make useful products rather than pure art. They were intended as machines for living, as well as for teaching art in. Moholy-Nagy wore his overalls as Bauhaus Master in Dessau from 1925, as head of metalwork and leading the preliminary foundation course.

Galina Chichagova, a young art student, recounted seeing Rodchenko as her teacher for the first time:

> A man walked into the studio, from his appearance he looked like a combination of pilot and motorist. He was wearing a beige jacket of military cut, Gallifet-breeches of a grey-green color, on his feet were black boots with grey leggings. On his head was a black cap with a huge shiny, leather peak... I immediately saw that this was a new type of man, a special one.[3]

In 1922 Rodchenko designed his own worksuit, comprising matching shirt and trousers in plain grey wool fabric, with a black leather trim at the collar, cuffs, pockets and waistband. In the photograph of him wearing it, standing amongst a set of wooden geometric shapes – shaved head, pipe to mouth, hand on hip – he appears primed to design a radical future (176).

In Italy, the Futurist artists Ernesto Michahelles (aka the fashion illustrator Thayaht) and his brother Ruggero Michahelles created the TuTa in 1919 as 'a one piece, straight line garment' (177). The all-in-one was made from a length of cotton, cut into a T-shape, to which a collar, patch pockets, gussets, buttons and a belt were added. The intention of the TuTa was to 'initiate a transformation similar to an "industrial revolution"' of fashion'. While the manifesto blessed the 'ECONOMY OF FABRIC CONSUMPTION, ECONOMY OF EFFORT, ECONOMY OF TIME and ECONOMY OF ENERGY', Thayaht preferred a TuTa made from hemp worn with a Robespierre-collared white shirt and 'Forte dei Marmi' leather sandals, an outfit that resists, even in descriptive terms, the political notion of economy supposedly rationalized in the design of the garment.

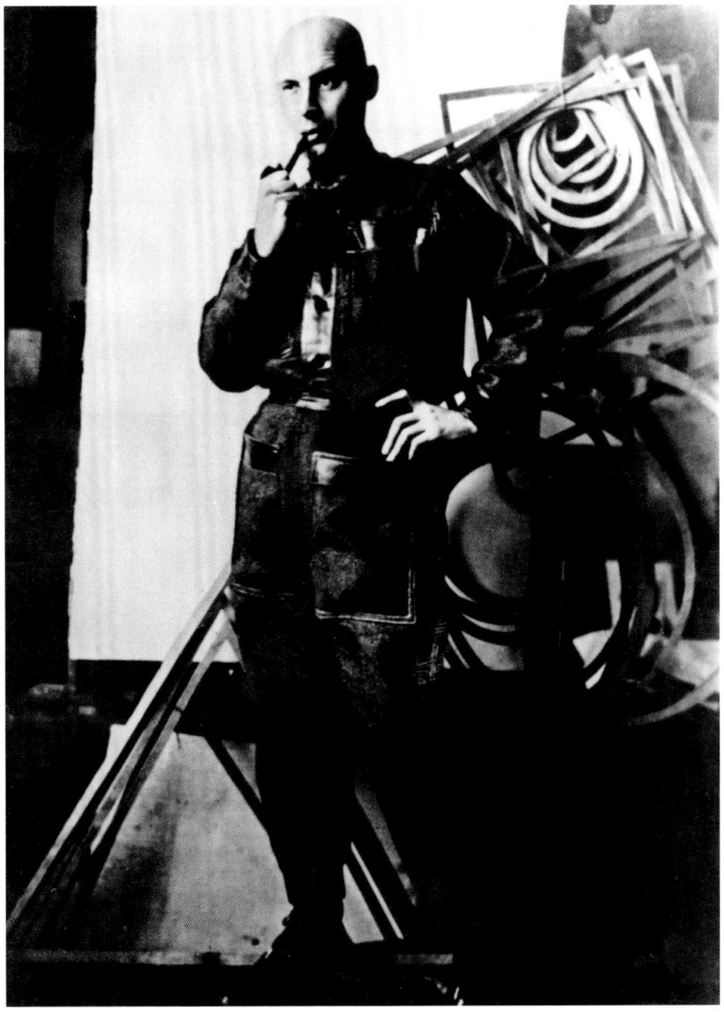

176. Mikhail Kaufman (1897–1980), Aleksandr Rodchenko, 1922

Bleu de travail (French blue workwear) is now enshrined in male artist's dress, as 'the worker artist has become the mainstay of traditional narratives of modern art history',[4] exemplified by Jackson Pollock dressed in overalls, dripping paint. However, it can also be a disguise. The anti-modernist painter, Balthus, wore a navy workwear smock to signal the artist. He once told Alberto Giacometti that he 'needed a château more than a workman needed a loaf of bread',[5] but he continued to wear the same smock for over 60 years. Artist Katerina Jebb has made life-size representations of the smock using a high-resolution scanner (178), which were exhibited at Dover Street Market New York to coincide with a Balthus exhibition at the Metropolitan Museum of Art in 2014, which drew criticism for a lack of critical engagement around the many portraits of young girls Balthus painted in his studio (including the daughters of his servants). The forensic detail of Jebb's images gives the smock a chilling quality, more reminiscent of an item in a crime scene photograph than a portrait of the artist.

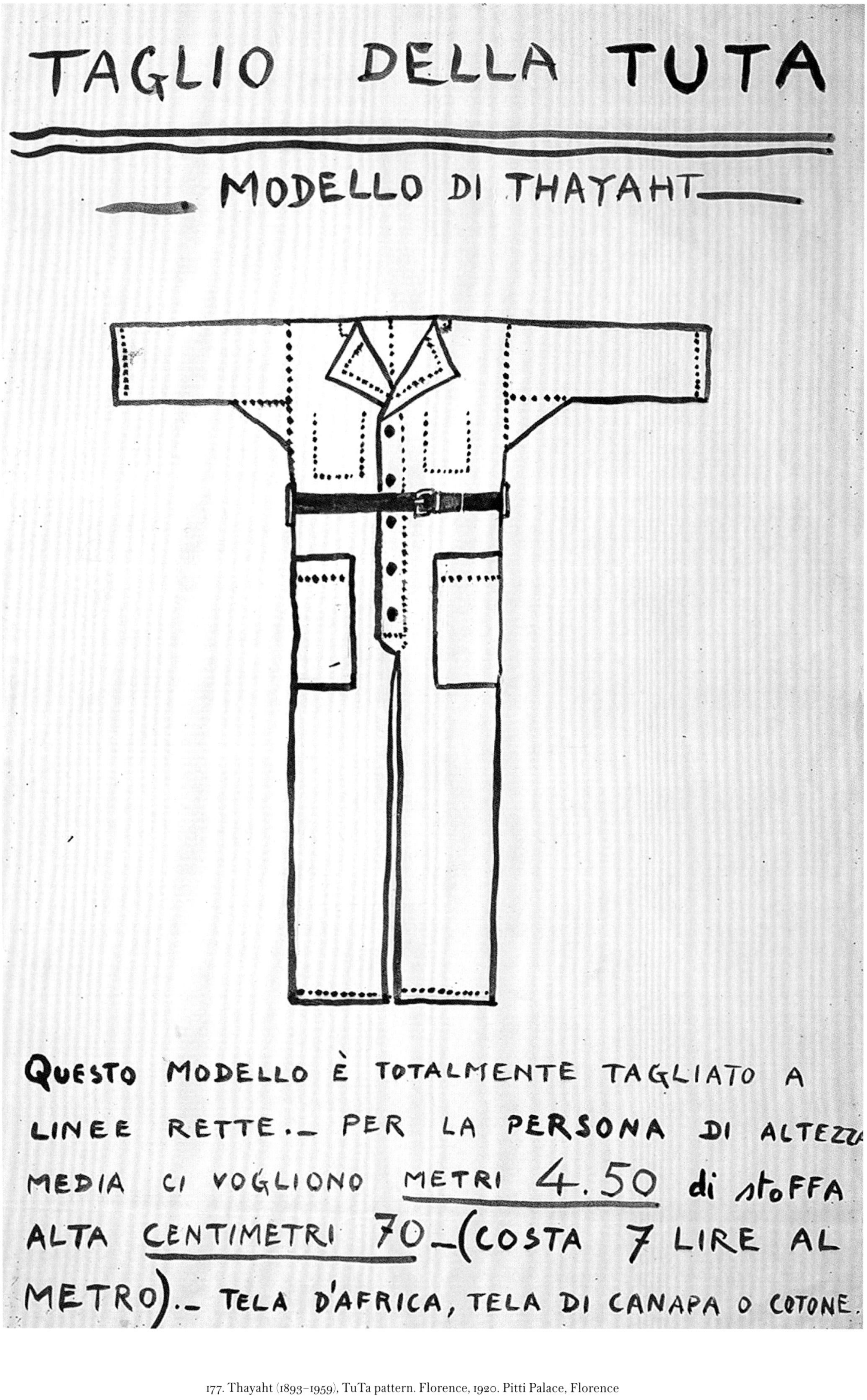

177. Thayaht (1893–1959), TuTa pattern. Florence, 1920. Pitti Palace, Florence

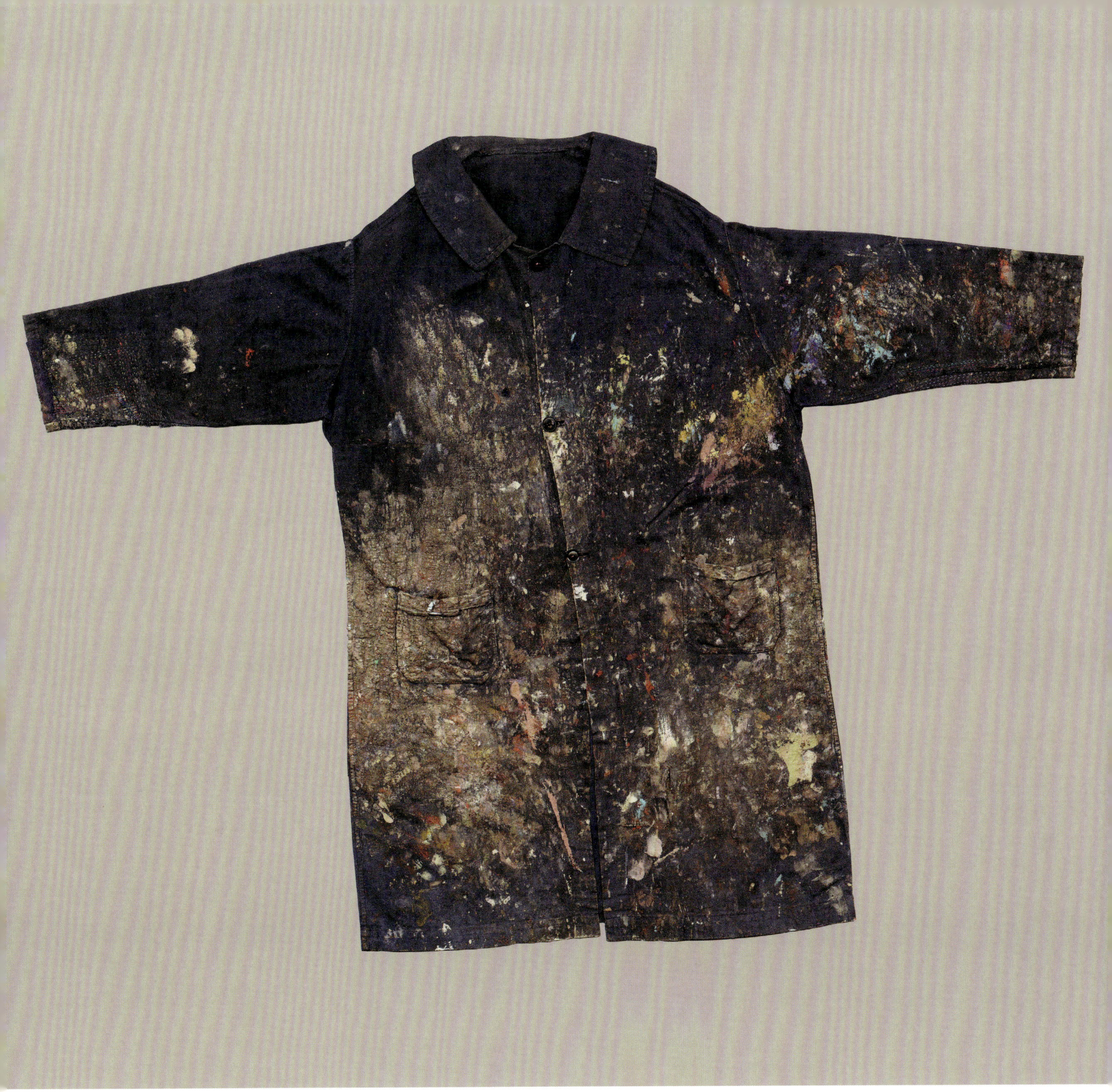

178. Katerina Jebb (1962–), *Tablier de Balthus, The Balthus Inventory*.
Digital scan on paper, 150 × 150 cm. Switzerland, 2011

THE MAO SUIT

In the 1960s, *bleu de travail* was appropriated once again, this time by students and anti-establishment radicals in Paris, who wanted to reject consumerism and invest in unregulated forms of clothing, free from fashion. It is here that it comes into contact with another type of blue workwear, hailing from China. The Mao suit originates in the Zhongsam suit, developed by the founding father of the Republic of China, Sun Yatsen Zhongsam, and named to commemorate his death in 1925. The jacket style is based on western and Japanese military uniform, featuring a turn-down collar and flapped patch pockets. The formation of the People's Republic of China in 1949, led by Mao Zedong, took the suit and inlaid its design features with the symbolism of its political doctrine. The four pockets would now embody the four cardinal principles of propriety, honesty, justice and shame, while the five-button front closure would exemplify the five branches of the Communist government.[6] The revised design was made by tailor Tian Atong, and referenced Chinese peasant tunics to valorize the humble sartorial traditions of the proletariat. In turn, the suit came to symbolize the figurehead of Chairman Mao and the militarization of the Chinese people, as an army dressed in the very same outfit as their leader.

The suit's appearance in Paris in the 1960s was due to pro-Chinese attitudes held by western European intellectuals and socialists, motivated by a zealous anti-colonial agenda. But it was a film-maker rather than a political leader or fashion designer who made young men want to wear the Mao suit.

La Chinoise, directed by Jean-Luc Godard and released in 1967, is a film that deals with a group of students in thrall to Maoism (the ideology developed by the Chinese Communist Party), and the spirit of revolutionary politics. The film anticipates the May 1968 student uprising in Paris, and the workwear and casual separates the young people wear – in a palette of blue, red, yellow and black – are a salient feature of the film's reductive use of political colours in its pop art-infused production design. While not technically a Mao jacket, the pale blue workwear jacket worn by the lead protagonist (played by Jean-Pierre Léaud), is given explicit reference points in a key scene from the film, where he speaks directly to camera standing between a newspaper article showing Mao Zedong wearing his Mao suit in Yan'an, the birthplace of the Chinese Revolution, with the headline, 'Go Among the Masses and Investigate Reality', and a graphic illustration of a traditional Chinese dragon head (179). The idea of film as a political art was a central aim for Godard at this point, and the collaging of such imagery was intended to prompt a visualization of China as a mode of thought over a western imaginary. But what is so interesting about the way the scene is visually structured, is how it posits that a third meaning could arise out of what the young man in the middle might choose to wear to express direct action.

In another scene from the film *La Chinoise*, a student (played by Anne Wiazemsky) relays her experiences of studying at Nanterre University, the origins of the student uprising, how she learnt about Marxism by speaking to the workers still completing the construction of the buildings the students were expected to study in, and the immigrants who lived in the Paris suburb. In one of the only scenes of the film shot outside, it shows labourers in their blue workwear gathering at the train station that connected the university site to Paris, prosaically called *La Folie* (*The Folly*) (180). The film therefore draws a link between proletariat clothing and class struggle, turning *bleu de travail* into *lán máo tàozhuāng* (Chinese blue Mao suit). This aspect of the film did not escape *Cahiers du cinéma* film critic Iannis Katsahnias, who noted in a later Godard retrospective season: 'Perhaps *La Chinoise* is not a political pamphlet, but a comedy about the relationship between fashion and ideology.'[7]

In line with the film's release, Parisian boutiques such as Gilbert Féruch prêt-à-porter, and Charles Glenn's Mayfair offered upmarket versions of the Mao suit, while chain stores such as Prisunic and Monoprix offered imported Chinese workers' uniforms, and department stores such as La Samaritaine offered similar styles in their work clothes department. All catered to young men who were students or working in creative professions, eager to

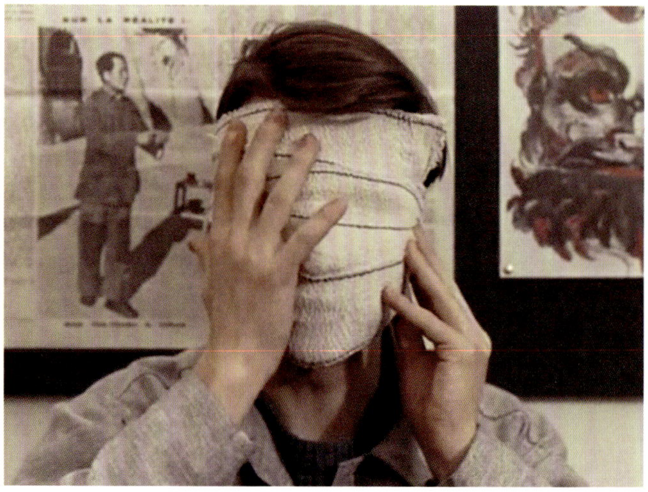

179. Jean-Pierre Léaud in *La Chinoise* (1967) dir. Jean-Luc Godard

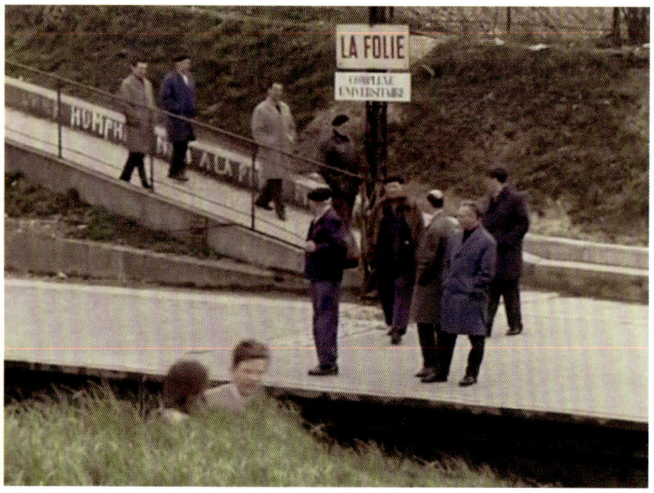

180. Still from *La Chinoise* (1967) dir. Jean-Luc Godard

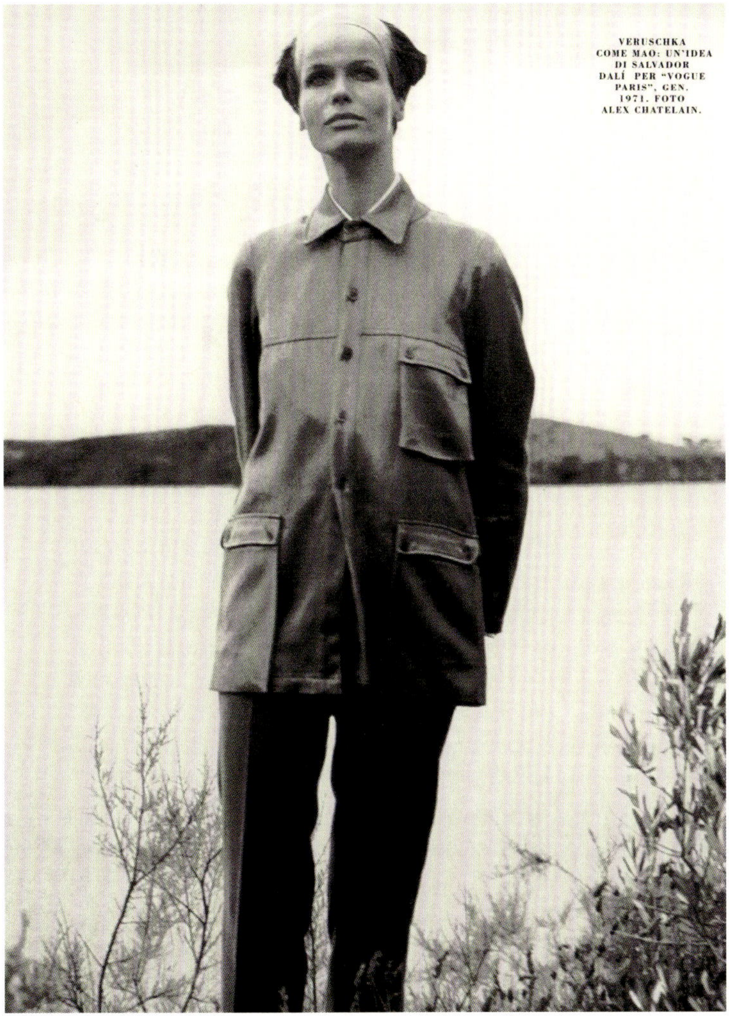

181. Alex Châtelain (1941–), 'Veruschka as Mao Zedong', first published in *Vogue Paris* (December 1971), reprinted in *Vogue Italia* (March 1997)

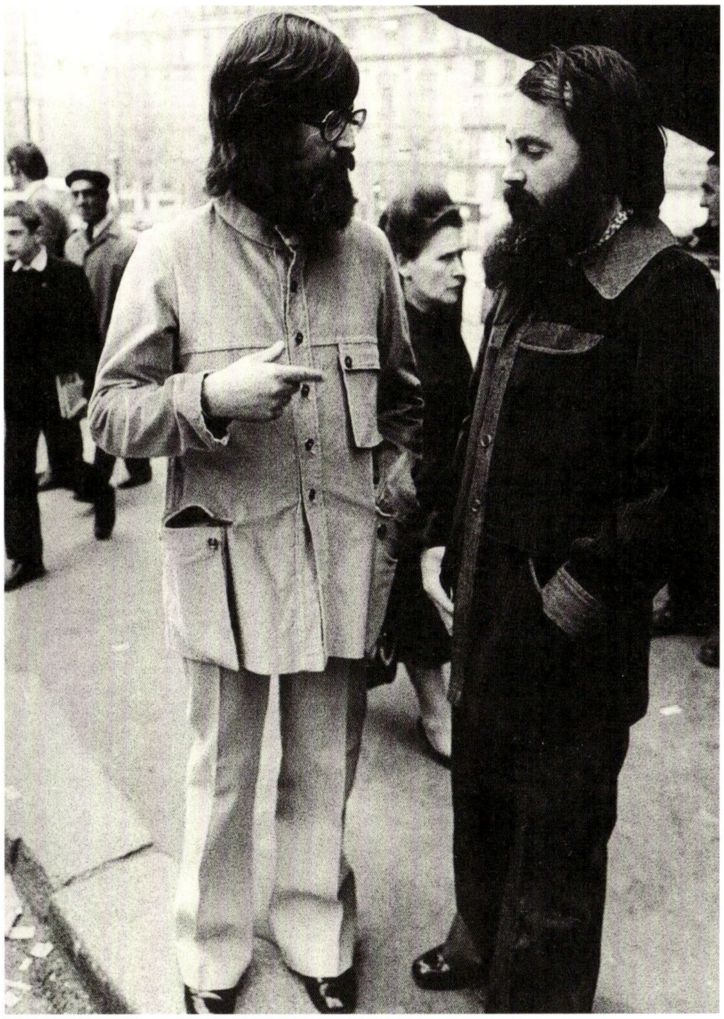

182. Michel Schreiber (right) and Patrick Hollington, Paris, *c.*1972

express their nonconformist credentials. But the attack on the formality of the business suit as a symbol of western capitalism's pecuniary values, also existed at the upper end of the market.

For the December 1971 issue of *Vogue Paris*, guest editor Salvador Dalí presented a disquieting fashion plate of the model Veruschka, standing by the Yangtze river in China posing as Mao Zedong (181). She wears a theatrical wig by Bertrand, which gives her the Chairman's receding hairline and curtained mop, and a blue two-piece that could pass as a Mao suit: except it is not a masquerade costume (the masthead describes the transformation as *Moa-ifie*), but an ensemble by progressive Paris menswear designers Michel Schreiber and Patrick Hollington (182).

The editorial may seem a dream image in the Surrealist idiom, but it is more exact to claim it as an imaginary of the possibilities of menswear in the post-war era, an impossible conversation – lost in translation – between an artist and a political leader. Dalí may well have been in thrall to the idea of using China's modern image as antithetical to the kind of chinoiserie fashion is known for playing with, but returning the suit to its supposed origins reveals how it differs from the Mao in lacking one patch pocket, surely pointing to its dishonesty in interpreting the garment's ideological design concept.

A suit by Schreiber and Hollington was certainly not a casual exercise in cultural appropriation or the reverse engineering of workwear; it was more a treatise on how men could dress reductively. A jacket design was an exercise in elimination: interfacing, linings, shoulder pads, darts, vents and waist emphasis were all removed. It might look like workwear in its simplistic form, but the cloth was of the highest quality, with attention paid to how it draped on the body. Schreiber apprenticed at Paul Portes, a tailor known for producing the finest men's suiting for film costumes; Hollington worked first as a journalist, then in a textile purchase office servicing the Paris fashion houses, and also at Cacharel.

They addressed a generation of educated men who were familiar with workwear, 'who had already adopted a uniform consisting of a prisoner's heavy twill and the moleskin fabric of coal men.'[8] They espoused a philosophy that was concerned with 'how to dress the man better',[9] and the haute workwear they offered was in itself an early kind of designer clothing for men. It was worn by the cream of Parisian intelligentsia, including philosopher Michel Foucault, psychoanalyst Jacques Lacan, sculptor César, film director Peter Brook, fashion designer Paco Rabanne, graphic designer Peter Knapp and product designer Roger Tallon.

THE NEHRU JACKET

Fashion historian Simona Segre Reinach has identified the Mao and Nehru jacket styles as existing within a culture of exoticism in fashion in the late 1960s, which projected the East 'as a place immune from a consumer society under attack'. She argues such associated indigenous forms of dress were 'informal and soft', compared to an earlier era of orientalism in the 1910s, when oriental expressions in dress were, 'complicated, rich, [and] luxurious',[10] typified by the influence of the Ballets Russes on early twentieth-century fashion. It is therefore fascinating that the artist Nicholas Roerich, Diaghilev's set and costume designer, who did so much to establish the colours, shapes and forms of western oriental style in the 1910s, would play his part in the adoption of the Nehru-collared jacket by men's fashion in the 1960s.

Roerich travelled extensively throughout his career, eventually settling in the Himalayas, where he studied Indian and eastern philosophies and art. His interest in the preservation of cultural artefacts, borne out of the destruction he witnessed in the First World War and the Russian Revolution, was formalized as the Roerich Pact, an international treaty for the protection of all sites of cultural heritage. It brought him into contact with political leaders, including the leader of the India independence movement, Jawaharlal Nehru, after whom the jacket collar style is named.

The Roerichs hosted Nehru and his daughter, Indira Gandhi, in 1942 at their ashram over a fortnight, and a surviving photograph of the group shows Nehru wearing a *sherwani* jacket, traditionally worn by Hindu nobles in the Indian royal courts (183). The *sherwani* jacket has a closed stand collar, undefined waist, and is knee length and usually unlined. Roerich, by contrast, sports an outfit of his own devising: a Chinese skullcap, and a pale silk suit of baggy plus-fours and a jacket with two patch pockets and a stand collar (although this is hard to ascertain due to the imposing volume and length of his white beard). The other name for a stand collar is a mandarin, named after the Chinese mandarins of imperial China, although this style of collar was higher and included a hook fastener. After India gained independence from Britain in 1947, Nehru wore the *sherwani* as India's first prime minister at home and on diplomatic trips abroad.

Pierre Cardin was the first European menswear designer to make use of the Nehru jacket style in his ready-to-wear collection for men in 1960, titled the *Cylindre* (Cylinder), although in his interpretation there was no stand collar (184). Reviewing the collection, the *New York Times* took pains to draw a parallel between the young male models and the young men in the unfolding Algerian War of Independence (1954–62):

> A bearded young French man, who has chosen law as his career, sparked a revolution this week. The place, however, was not Algiers but Paris' Crillon Hotel, and the young man was not Pierre Lagaillarde but one of a handful of students whom Pierre Cardin, the widely known designer of women's fashions, had chosen to model his new collection of ready-to-wear clothes for men.[11]

Lagaillarde was the lawyer turned politician at the heart of the uprising against French colonial rule, and the article suggested that students and their choice of clothes were all the power needed for change. As with Schrieber and Hollington, it was an earlier reductive experiment, of single-breasted jackets with a single vent and buttonless sleeves, complemented by cuffless stovepipe trousers. A press release promoted the suits as raising 'male necklines by eliminating lapels', which 'button all the way to the neck' finishing in an 'officer collar'.[12] But the fabrics – corduroy for winter, striped cotton for summer – are drawn from workwear fabric stock, giving the collection a modernity that tailoring innovation alone could not provide.

Cardin's true revolution lay in offering prêt-à-porter fashion for men before it was developed as an industrial system for womenswear in the mid-1960s. The legacy of the Cylinder collection is how London tailor Dougie Millings, who specialized in dressing music performers, gave the high-buttoned, collarless style to the Beatles to complement their mop top haircuts, thus turning them into a pop phenomenon. But in the hands of tailors such as Gilbert Féruch in Paris and Oleg Cassini in New York, the Nehru collar evolved into a rather refined countercultural statement for men, dutifully referencing its noble origins, but offsetting it by how it was accessorized, often with a roll-neck underneath (the traditional shirt to accompany a Nehru is collarless) and a medallion worn over the top.

The Nehru continues as a perennial jacket style offered by Comme des Garçons, the clothing brand led by Rei Kawakubo, who has associated it with the figure of the artist. Between 1986 and 1989 the catalogue for the Homme menswear line was photographed by Timothy Greenfield-Sanders and modelled by New York artists and critics, including Francesco Clemente, Julian Schnabel, Brice Marden, Hilton Kramer and Calvin Tomkins. Peter Halley, the neo-conceptualist artist and co-founder of *Index* magazine, modelled a Nehru jacket in a collection that amplified the jacket proportions with wide shoulders, deep armholes and enlarged buttons (185). Other styles produced a similar collar style by pulling the lapels up and fastening with a concealed button; another assimilated the line of a kimono collar.

Although Halley had worn Comme des Garçons since its Soho shop opened in 1983 (at the time, an abandoned district of artists' studios), he only met the designer at a party at Greenfield-Sanders's Lower East Side home, given in honour of Kawakubo in 1992, where he 'asked for her forgiveness for the Brooks Brothers shirt he was wearing with her suit'.[13] The theme of artists modifying dress to their own concerns was reprised by Comme des Garçons in 2007 in a show that featured a group of British artists and men invested in personal style. Michael Costiff, who ran the shop World in 1980s London, selling clothing and accessories bought during his global travels, started the show. He was followed by artist Duggie Fields, who spearheaded the 1950s style revival in the early 1970s, then Andrew Logan, host of

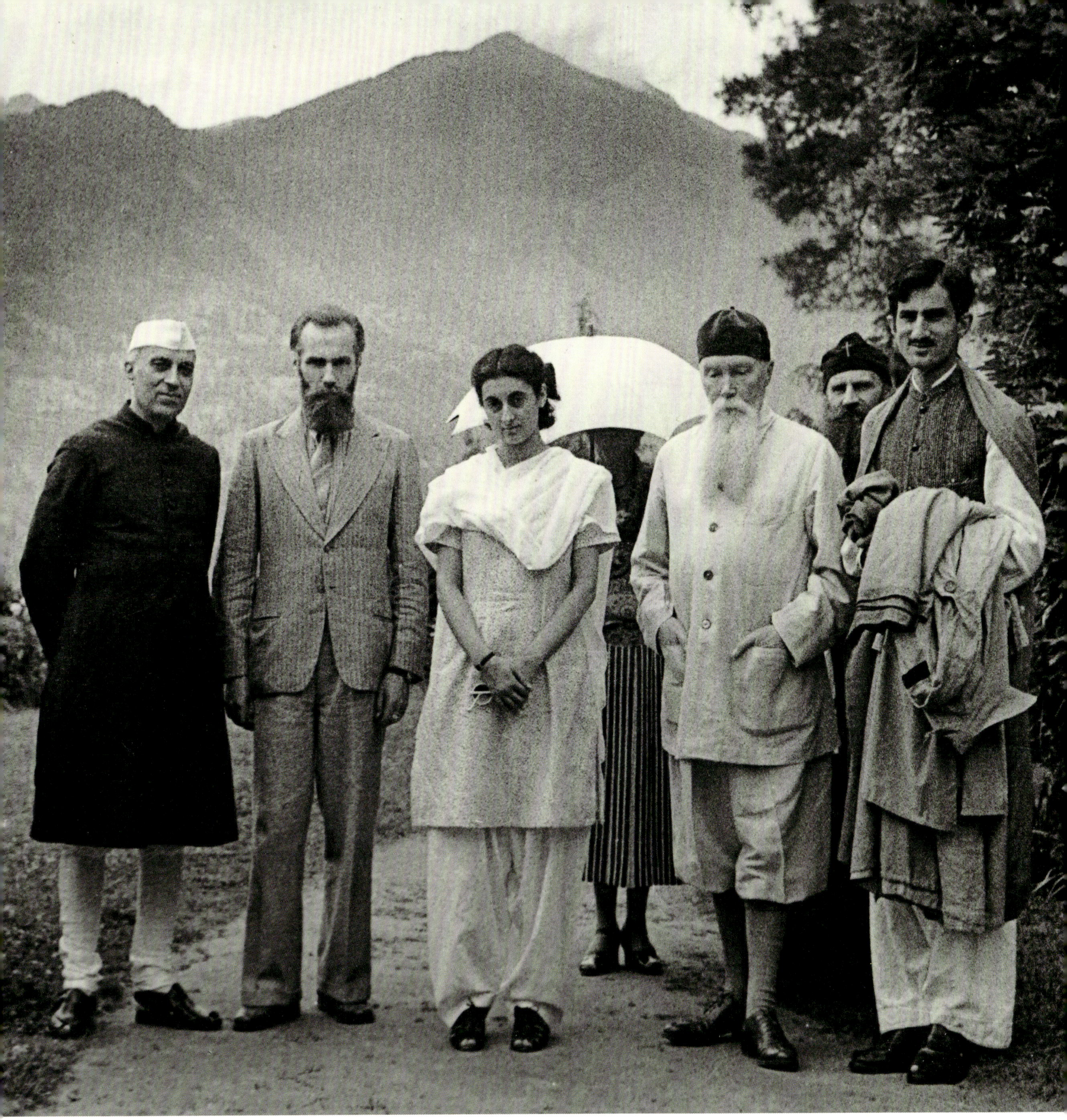

183. Jawaharlal Nehru, Swetoslav Roerich, Indira Gandhi, Nicholas Roerich and Helena Roerich, Naggar, India, 1942. NRM archive: 401802

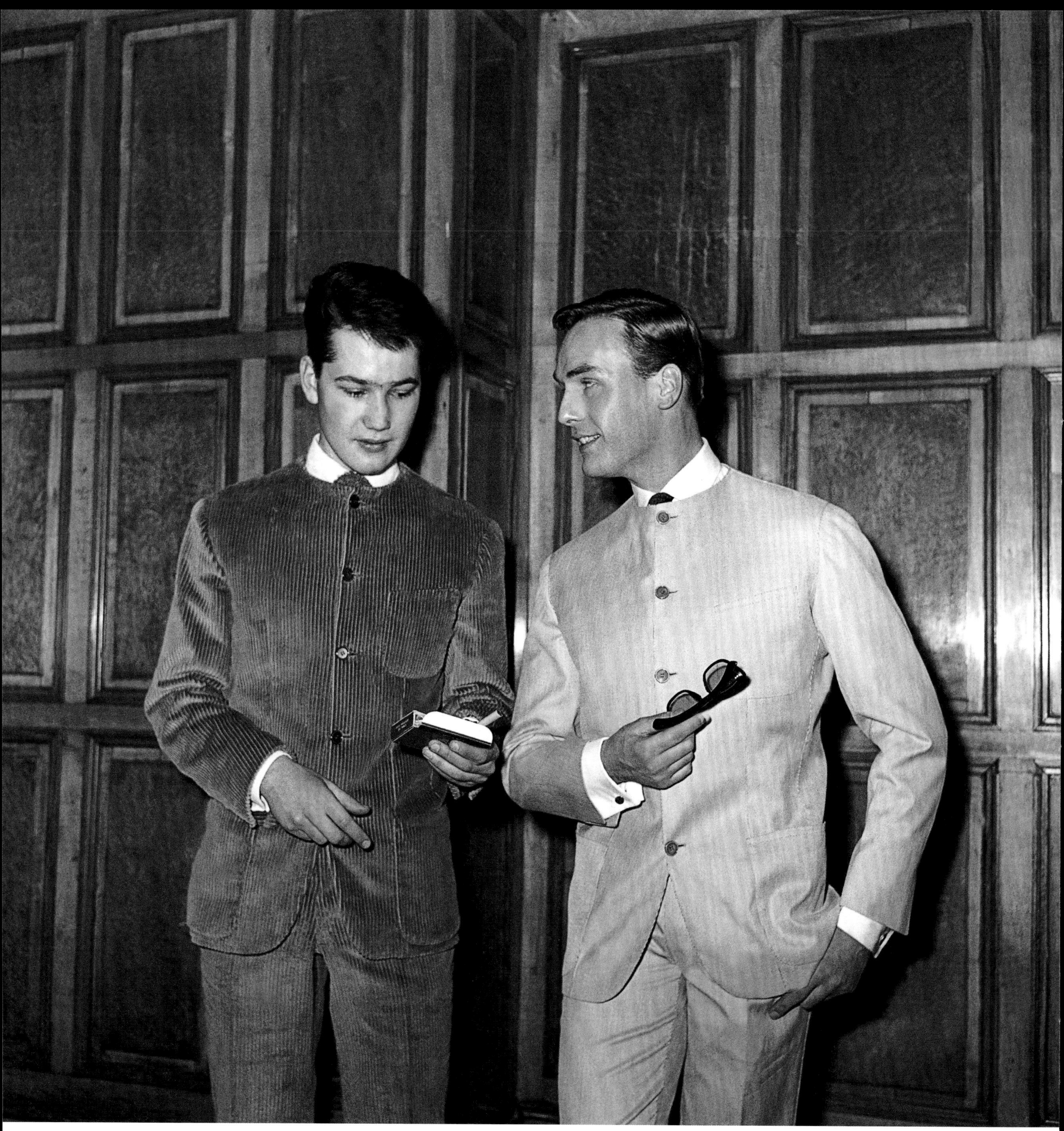

184. Pierre Cardin (1922–2020), First menswear collection, 26 February 1960

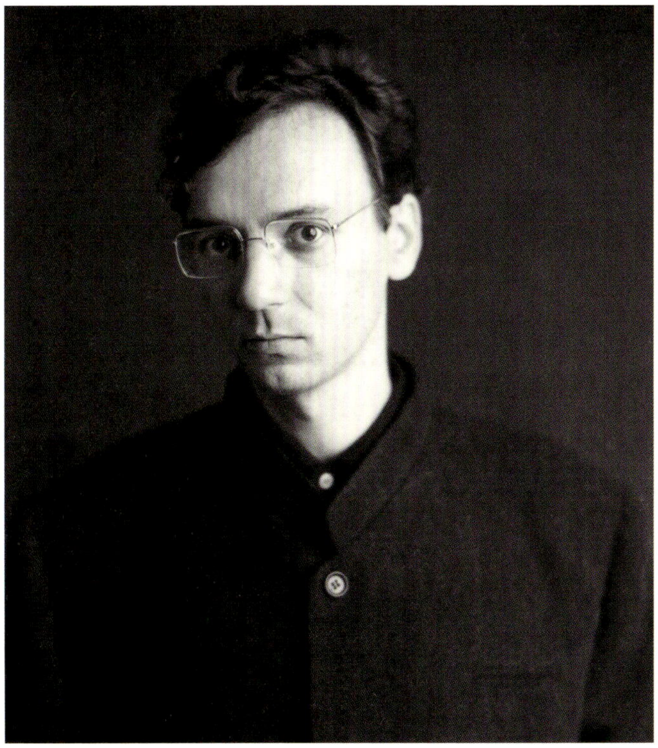

185. Timothy Greenfield-Sanders (1952–), Comme des Garçons Homme catalogue, Autumn/Winter 1986. Model: Peter Hally

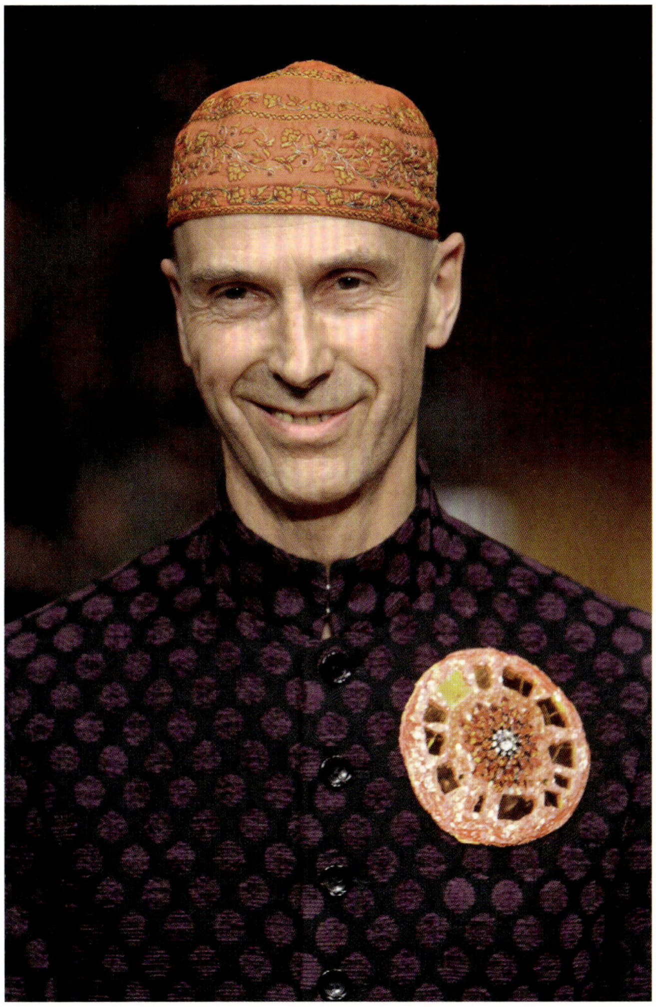

186. Rei Kawakubo (1941–) for Comme des Garçons. Ensemble. Autumn/Winter 2007. Model: Andrew Logan

the Alternative Miss World competition, sculptor and jewellery designer and finally, Soho dandy Sebastian Horsley. Logan wore a Nehru-collared brocade suit with an embroidered skullcap and a mirrored mosaic brooch of his own making, a reflection of his long-standing interest in Indian culture (186). The male models that followed him wore similar styles, one bearing an embroidered garter running across the chest with a mirror mosaic garter star brooch: a curious amalgam of colonial ceremonial regalia and post-independence hippy jewellery, demonstrating a cultural and historical awareness of the jacket style's rich legacy.

THE SAFARI JACKET

The Safari jacket is perhaps the most contentious of jacket styles. Its origins lie in the tropical uniforms developed for officers serving in the British colonies in Africa and India in the late nineteenth century; the original white poplin fabric was found to quickly stain the colour of the ochre dust, so they were dyed a similar colour, called regulation khaki. The jacket style has a number of features, partly drawn from its military lineage, and also by being adopted by tailors specializing in expedition clothing for jungle hunting and desert treks, such as Norton & Sons on Savile Row. The principal features are four large bellow patch pockets and shoulder epaulet straps; it usually has an inverted centre pleat in the yoke, a single vent, and is either belted or waisted. Additional features are a quilted recoil pad, to protect the shoulder from gun use and gun cartridge loops and a spectacle pocket set on one arm.

It duly became essential kit for actors in adventure and action films in 1930s Hollywood, and American outfitter Willis & Geiger, who was known for aviation and explorer clothing, developed a bush jacket in poplin in 1932. It is an extremely functional piece of workwear, developed to address a specific terrain. This has meant that the Safari's adoption as a metropolitan jacket style has not gone unnoticed, even though the original meaning of the word 'safari' in Swahili is 'to sojourn'. In a *New Yorker* magazine profile on Ernest Hemingway's visit to New York in 1950, it portrays the American author buying a bush jacket at Abercrombie & Fitch on Fifth Avenue. When trying the jacket on, Hemingway raises his arm as if aiming a rifle to test if there is enough allowance in the jacket, to which the clerk incredulously asks: 'You going to use it for *shooting*, sir?'[14]

The first European fashion designer to propose the style to men was Yves Saint Laurent (187), offering it in cotton gabardine in 1969, although it was offered to women two years earlier as another borrowing from the male wardrobe in line with 'Le Smoking' (see pp. 181–2). Cardin offered a jacket named the Cabot, after *King Kong* (1933) actor Bruce Cabot; many other menswear designers followed, deeming it a classic, if somewhat misplaced, jacket style. In 1974 the *New York Times* reported on the saturation of the style in the marketplace, and a number of pending court cases due to Abercrombie & Fitch registering the name in relation to the design for the American market. It also described how the jacket style could be found on the streets of the city:

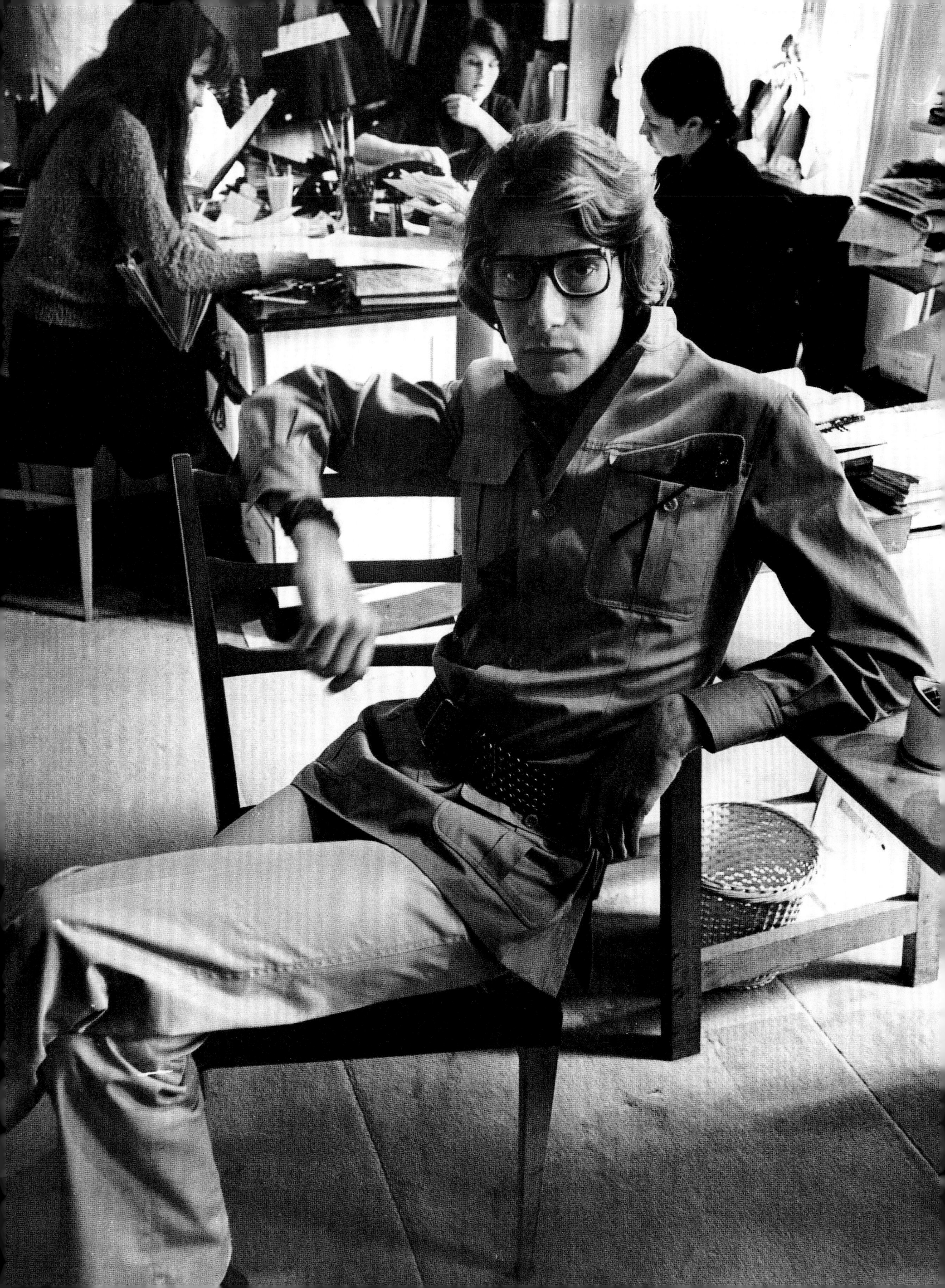

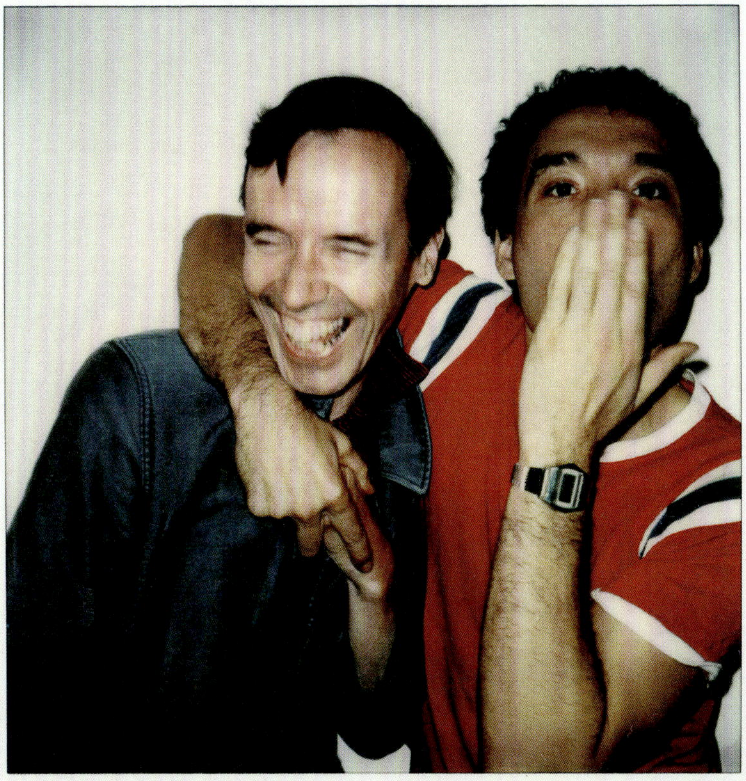

188. Bill Cunningham and Antonio Lopez, polaroid by Juan Ramos, 1978

> Meanwhile back in the Manhattan jungle, one spots enough safari suits to costume twelve chapters of a Tarzan serial. Under the sheltering palms of the Plaza's Palm Court, a male in a blue denim safari suit, polka-dotted bow tie and Gucci loafers sips tea. A movie buff at a Third Avenue cinema wears a khaki bush jacket, hounds tooth-checked slacks and platform shoes. At Mangnaro's food emporium on Ninth Avenue, a shopper orders a pound of prosciutto wearing a short-sleeved bush jacket with epaulettes, matching shorts, knee-length white socks, white shoes and a pith helmet.[15]

It is a testament to the way that the Safari, the Nehru, the Mao and *bleu de travail* were worn in the western fashion capitals of the 1970s as a casual alternative to the standard suit, but with the capacity to make a style statement in how it was worn as part of an outfit.

The law of this sartorial jungle has resonated ever since, and its great chronicler, Bill Cunningham, never wavered from wearing his regulation blue workwear jacket as the poster boy for this quiet revolution (188). He reportedly bought it from a Paris flea market as he was looking for something practical; but, of course, it is never that straightforward. Barneys window dresser Simon Doonan described him as 'an enigma wrapped in a bright blue French sanitation worker's jacket'.[16] The jacket, his Nikon camera and Biria bicycle are now part of the permanent collection of the New York Historical Society, and while they do speak of New York and of Cunningham's long-standing career as a street fashion photographer – the junction of Fifth Avenue and 57th Street is now known as Bill Cunningham Corner – his jacket refers elsewhere.

It returns him to Paris in the 1970s with his friends the illustrator Antonio Lopez and art director Juan Ramos; to a more carefree time, when designer fashion was still very much in its infancy. As Cunningham recalled, 'Everyone was free as a bird. The kids talk about being liberated today, we never used the word but by god, Antonio and Juan were the most liberated.'[17] To wear such a jacket was a badge of allegiance for a generation that was discovering dead stock workwear and decommissioned military clothing from the flea markets and second-hand dealers. Kenzō Takada, whose first boutique in Paris was called Jungle Jap, patchworked

187. Yves Saint Laurent (1936–2008) wearing a Safari Suit from his collection, 9 May 1969

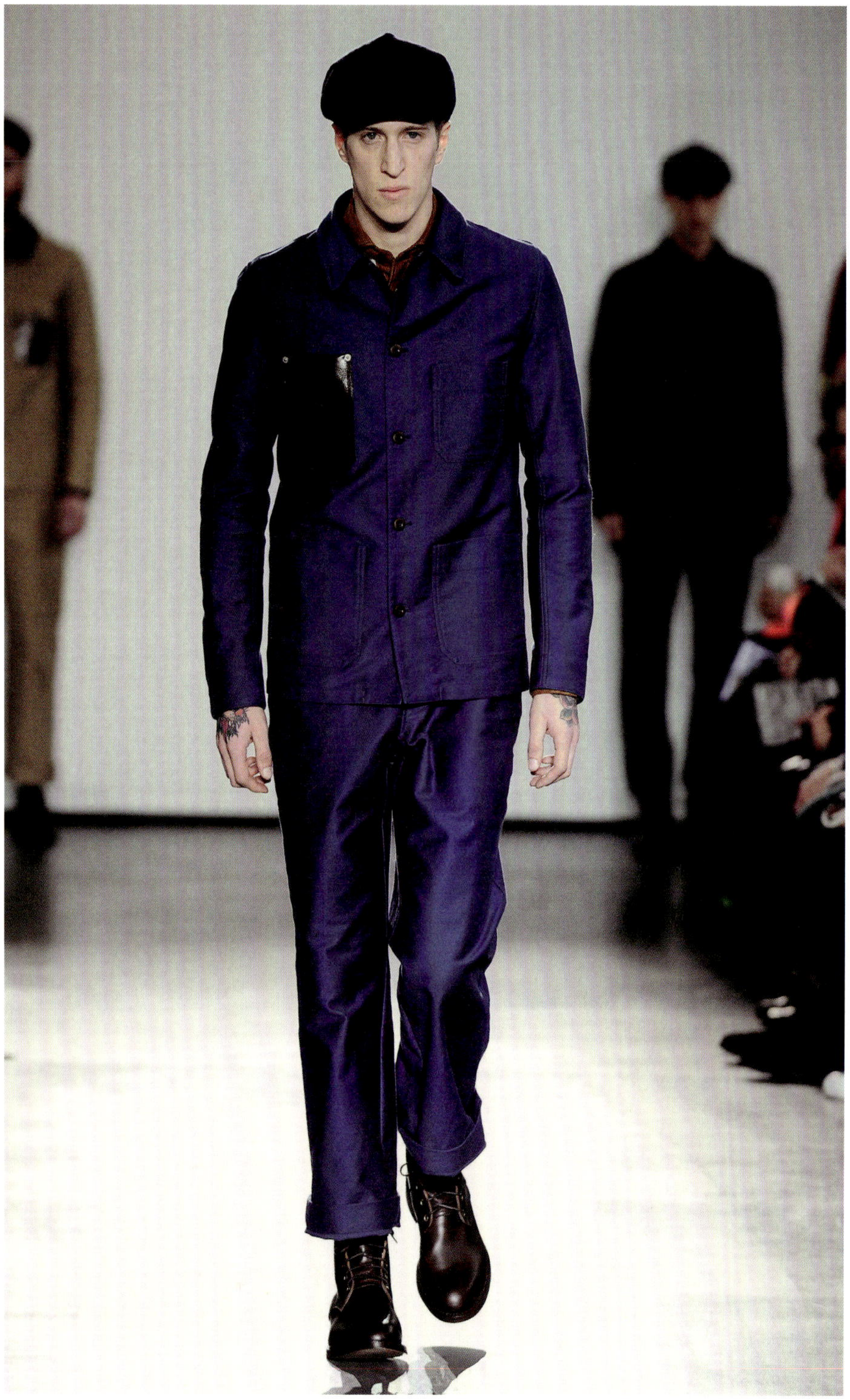

189. Junya Watanabe (1961–). Ensemble. Autumn/Winter 2012

workwear and kimono into new womenswear designs. These jackets were worn to late breakfasts and make-up sessions at Café de Flore, and to dinner and dancing at Le Sept.

Cunningham was fond of saying that 'Money's the cheapest thing. Liberty and freedom is the most expensive',[18] and many thought this lay behind how he negotiated control of his work: not getting paid for the photos he took for *Details* magazine in the 1980s meant he got to art direct the pages in which his work appeared; at all the society parties he photographed, he always refused the glass of water the host or party organizer offered. But freedom for Cunningham also referred to the era of gay liberation, to a moment when workwear stood for playing up to roles, an ironic uniform that stood for the fun that fashion bestowed in that rare moment. He spent the rest of his career looking for it through his lens, forever dressed in his *bleu de travail*.

More recently, workwear has become a focal point for a number of menswear designers, notably Junya Watanabe (189), Nigel Cabourn and Craig Green. In the hands of women designers, workwear is employed to broker dialogue across gender, as in Margaret Howell's MHL range for men

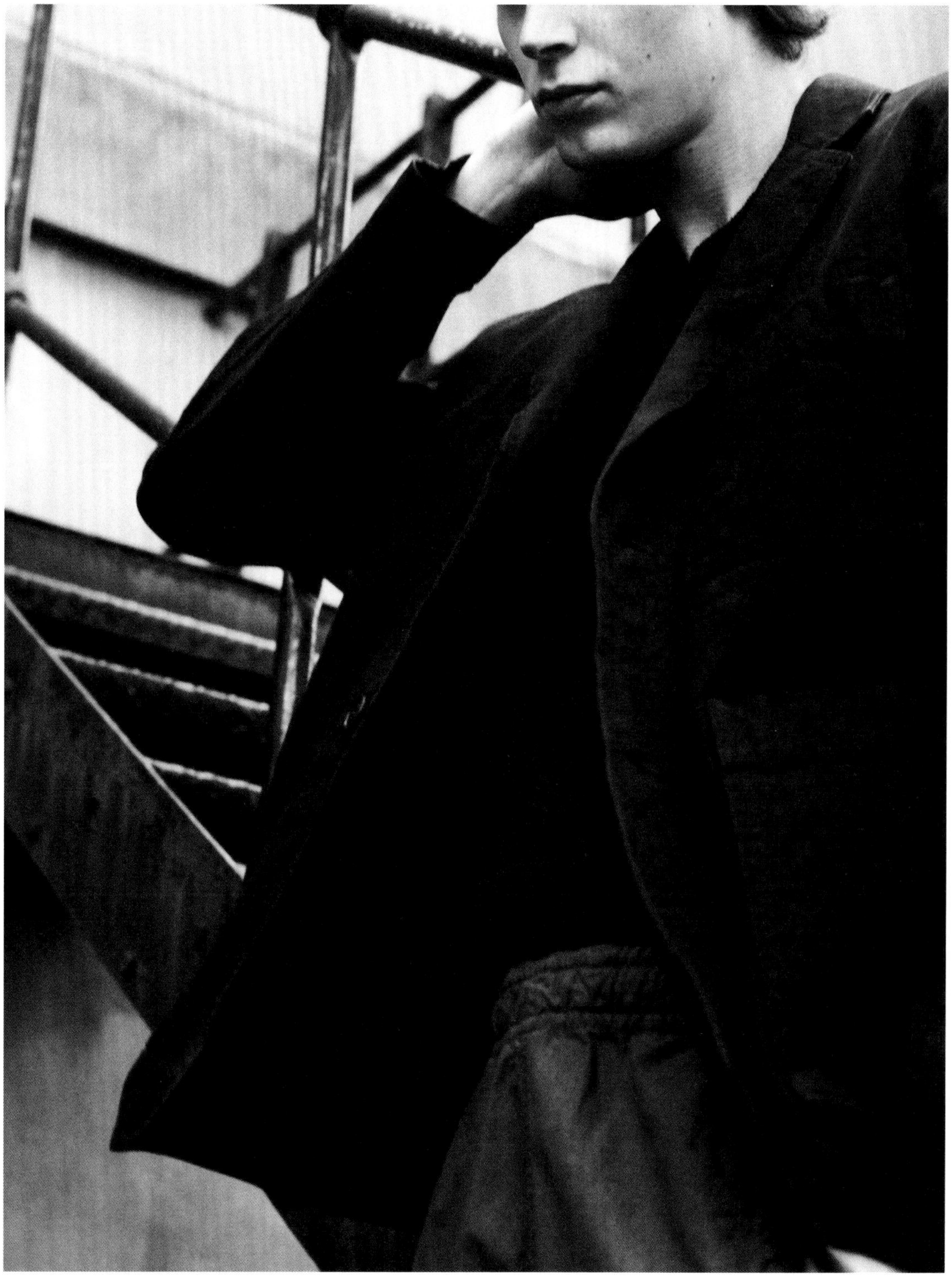

190. Margaret Howell (1946–), MHL. Spring/Summer 2020

and women (190), and in the gender-neutral clothing by Toogood, designed by sisters Faye and Erica Toogood.

Workwear is now accepted as a staple of men's fashion, even recognized in the sphere of business wear. Robert Armstrong, US Financial Editor for the *Financial Times*, now writes for the weekend edition on matters of men's style. Although his column photo shows him in jacket and tie, he recently revealed he owns a Carhartt jacket and Red Wing boots even though his work, 'pushing keyboard buttons', means he has 'no need to own anything with a pocket to hold a tool'. And yet, Armstrong acknowledges the hazards involved in wearing such things on the job. He may not wear them into the office, but he has been seen online; divulging that there are 'risks involved in what my editor calls the "I just whittled a chair in my lunch hour" look.'[19]

It is a good example in underlining that workwear continues to refer to non-white-collar work, and that the work it does refer to is no longer trade based or occupation specific. Instead, it refers to a creative and craft-based approach, that honours the legacy of artist's dress, and the desire to dress differently.[20]

WHAT EVER HAPPENED TO CONTEMPORARY MENSWEAR?

CHARLIE PORTER

In 1983 my parents took me to the V&A. We lived a hundred miles from London, but visited regularly. At the time, the V&A was home to an independent exhibition space called the Boilerhouse Project, which eventually evolved into the Design Museum. On this trip, it was showing *Better Living*, an exhibition by Pippa Garner, who was then known by her pre-transition name. I was 10.

It was the beginning point of my alertness to menswear. Garner's work played with the consumerist idealism of post-war America, creating fantastical products that never existed. Rollerskate stilettos! A two-person hat! There, in the middle of the exhibition, was a black and white photograph of Garner wearing the HALF-SUIT (191). It was regular tailoring – Garner walking out of an office building carrying the *New York Times* – except the suit, shirt and tie had been slashed horizontally, halfway down the body, entirely exposing the midriff.

Another option was the OFF-SHOULDER SHIRT: a regular shirt and tie, complete with tie pin, only the right side of the collar went under the right armpit, leaving the whole shoulder and arm exposed. It was so subversive, so powerfully counter to the usual images of masculinity. By exposing vulnerable flesh, Garner had cut through the alleged armour of what men wore.

I was captivated and bought the poster. The images were on my bedroom wall my whole adolescence. I was already awakened to those using clothes to question gender: Boy George, Kenny Everett's character Cupid Stunt. Garner herself transitioned in the 1980s. Her work showed it was also possible to use menswear itself to puncture masculinity.

I educated myself. My first copy of *The Face* was April 1986. I was 12. It featured a fashion shoot by the Buffalo collective: styling by Ray Petri, photographs by Jamie Morgan. On the first spread, the model – handsome, muscled – wore, on his top half, a pin-striped, strong-shouldered blazer over a tank top, or a Jean-Paul Gaultier white crew-neck jumper. On his bottom half: a pair of black briefs that look from the front like a jockstrap. In the main image, the model wore a white belt, customized with gold metal hardware: buttons, a knuckle-duster. It was by Judy Blame (192).

Here it was again: ostensibly masculine garments subverted, toughened up and queered. I still have the issue now. Its cover star is Nick Kamen. A coverline reads 'FASHION SPECIAL EXTRA!' Nowhere does it say 'menswear'. It features clothes by BodyMap and John Crancher, news about Christopher Nemeth. Then, it seems, menswear was considered an equal part of fashion.

1980s BRITAIN: WHERE WERE THE MENSWEAR DESIGNERS?

Inside that issue of *The Face*, a news feature on the new Comme des Garçons men's store states that, according to its founder and designer Rei Kawakubo, 'menswear is in a much more interesting phase than women's clothing. It's also growing much faster as a business.'[1]

A few pages before is an interview with Jean-Paul Gaultier. He talks of his love of London fashion. But, the writer notes: 'He believes that the British government does not give enough support to British designers; unlike the situation in France where designers are financially assisted and encouraged.'[2]

In 1987 a leaflet was delivered to every home in the UK. I remember it coming through our door. AIDS: DON'T DIE OF IGNORANCE. I was 13. It was the same year that Ray Petri, the Buffalo stylist, discovered he was HIV-positive. The stock market crashed on 19 October 1987. Two years later, Petri was dead, a victim of the AIDS crisis.

When I moved to London in 1992, it not only felt like any optimism about menswear in London had vanished: it was like it had never existed. I was a broke student, already well adept at scouring the bargain bins in Kensington Market stalls like Sign of the Times. There were rave T-shirts, one-off bits made for clubs, vintage. I loved it. But where were the designers? Where were the names?

At the time, I did not dwell. I had grown up in a culture obsessed with cyclical change: hippie replaced by glam rock, replaced by disco, replaced by punk, replaced by New Romantic… It was easy to think: London menswear was over.

A NEW MILLENNIUM

In 2003 a young designer called Kim Jones wanted to show his menswear at London Fashion Week. Jones was friends with Alexander McQueen, who had scattered some menswear looks in his early London shows: transparent shirt and trousers in *The Hunger*, Spring/Summer 1996; denim bumsters in *Dante*, Autumn/Winter 1996 (193). In 2001 Jones had graduated from the MA course at Central Saint Martins. He was a favourite of its course leader, Professor Louise Wilson. John Galliano had bought half his graduate collection.[3] His name was feted.

The British Fashion Council told Jones the only way he could get a slot on-schedule was to show womenswear.[4] Menswear was not allowed at London Fashion Week. Let us take a minute with the implication of those words. In the early years of the twenty-first century, the British Fashion Council did not consider men's clothing worthy of London

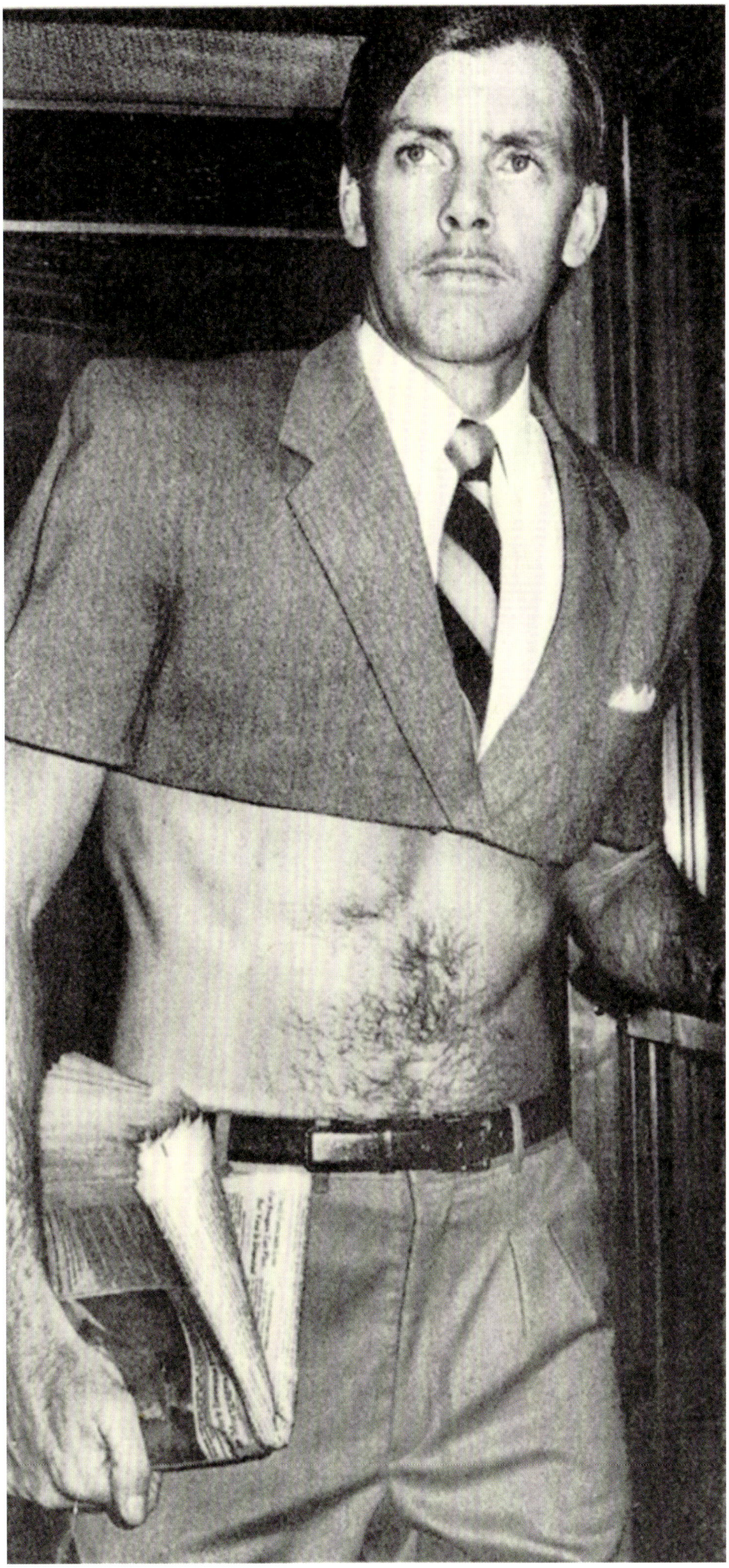

191. Pippa Garner (1942–), 'HALF-SUIT', *Better Living*
(London, The Boilerhouse Project, V&A, 1983)

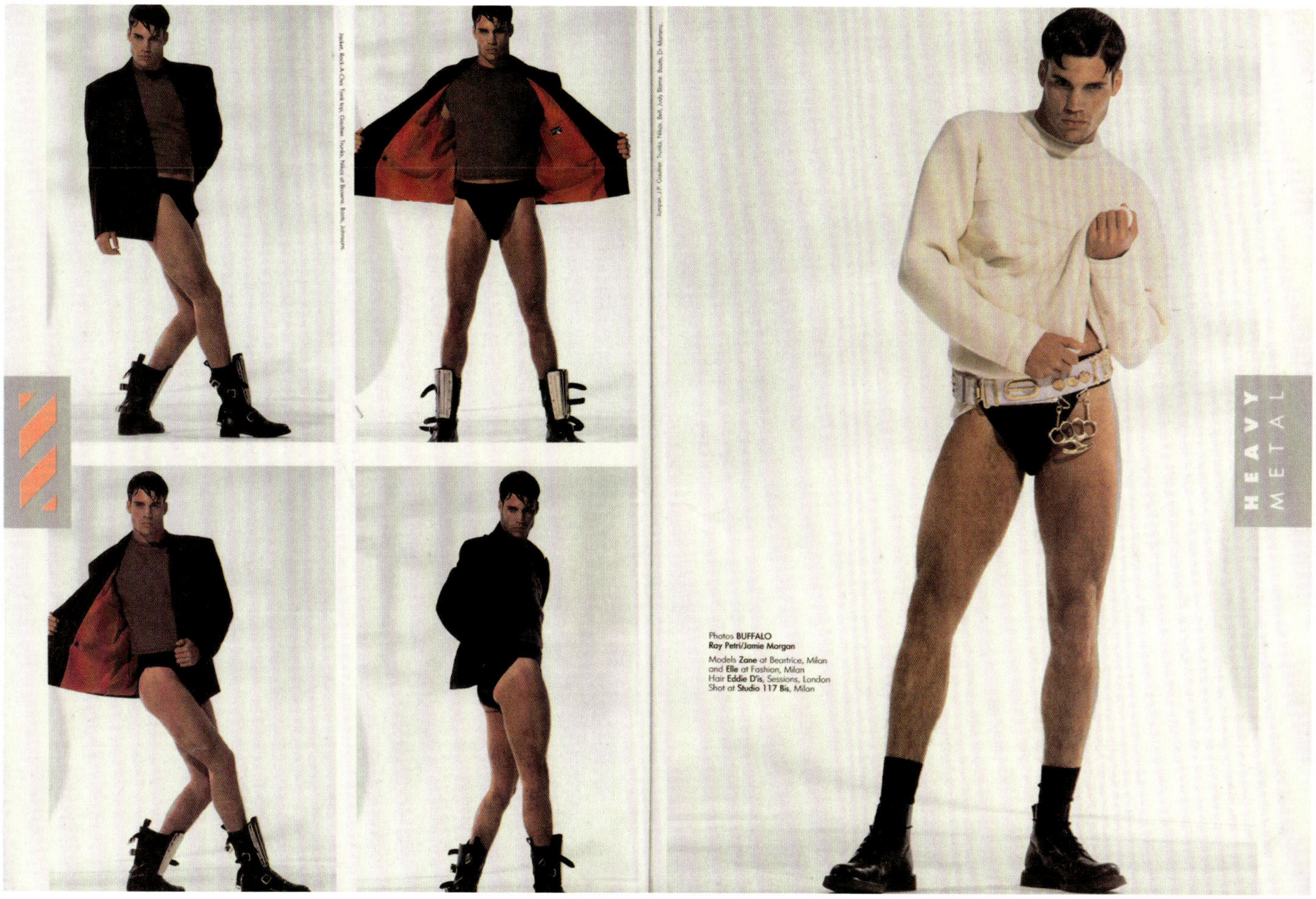

192. Jamie Morgan, *The Face EXTRA* (London, April 1986)

Fashion Week. A designer had to show women's clothing. The implication: fashion = womenswear. It shocks me now as much as it did then.

Jones called on his friend Marios Schwab, another recent Central Saint Martins graduate, to design some women's pieces to show alongside his men's. On 23 September 2003 Jones debuted his menswear for the first time (194), but if you look at the runway coverage on *Vogue*'s website, the lead image is women's.[5]

I was there. I remember the show vividly. It was in an old church off the Hackney Road, which was home to the wild Sunday night party Radio Egypt. Jones's menswear was sensational: sexy, optimistic, approachable. It was a fresh language of sports casual that was so prescient of what was to follow. The clothes, and the way the models wore them, had a new take on that idealism, that confidence of menswear from before.

The menswear had so much energy. At the end, Jones did not come out to take a bow. The audience clapped, then eventually went silent. No one moved. We sat there forever. What did we do now?

Jones had no patience for it. The following season, he showed in Paris, where menswear was accepted on its own terms. He is now Artistic Director of menswear at Dior and Artistic Director of women's at Fendi, a global award-winning designer.[6] London had no place for him. How did this happen? Why was this allowed to be?

THE EFFECTS OF THE AIDS CRISIS ON BRITISH MENSWEAR

It is only in the past few years that I have begun to see that there could be a correlation with the AIDS crisis, with the vacuum left by those who died. I am 48. Friends around my age often talk about being on the edge of a cliff: the generation before me died, or had to live with grief.

The counterculture figure Scarlett Cannon talked to me about it once. Cannon did the door at the Cha Cha Club, was a coverstar of *i-D*, modelled for Thierry Mugler, was friends with Judy Blame, Leigh Bowery. 'There were about four years where every couple of months you'd go to a funeral', she said. 'And I do remember getting to a point and thinking, I actually don't think I can go to another funeral. Because I was just devastated the whole time.'[7]

I have no facts to present here, because we are talking about the stolen lives of those unseen. This is parallel to the important work by Sarah Schulman in her book *Gentrification of the Mind* – a memoir of how the AIDS crisis wiped out the radicalism of New York's downtown arts scene. 'None of this can be proven', she says in her introduction.[8] This is a history that needs to be explored in other ways.

As Cannon said, 'so many creative lives gone, so many people, the unsung heroes gone, before they had a chance to have their time to come around.'

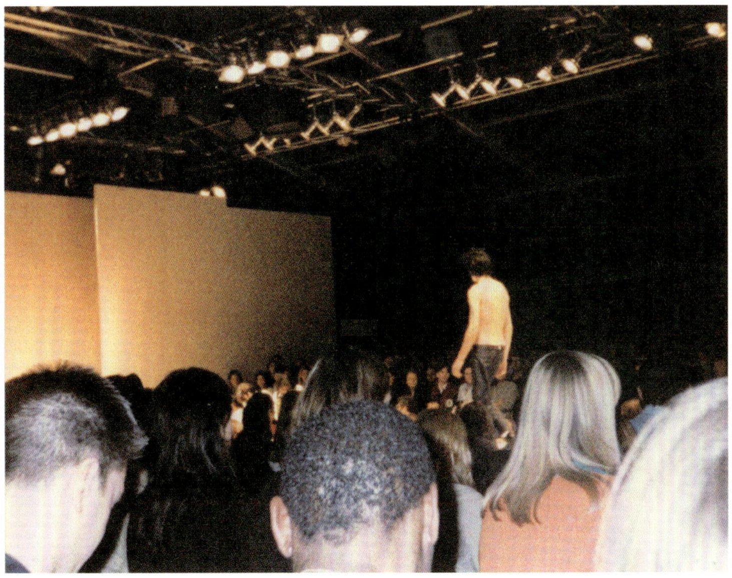

193. Alexander McQueen (1969–2010), 'The Hunger' ensemble. Spring/Summer 1996. Photo by Charlie Porter

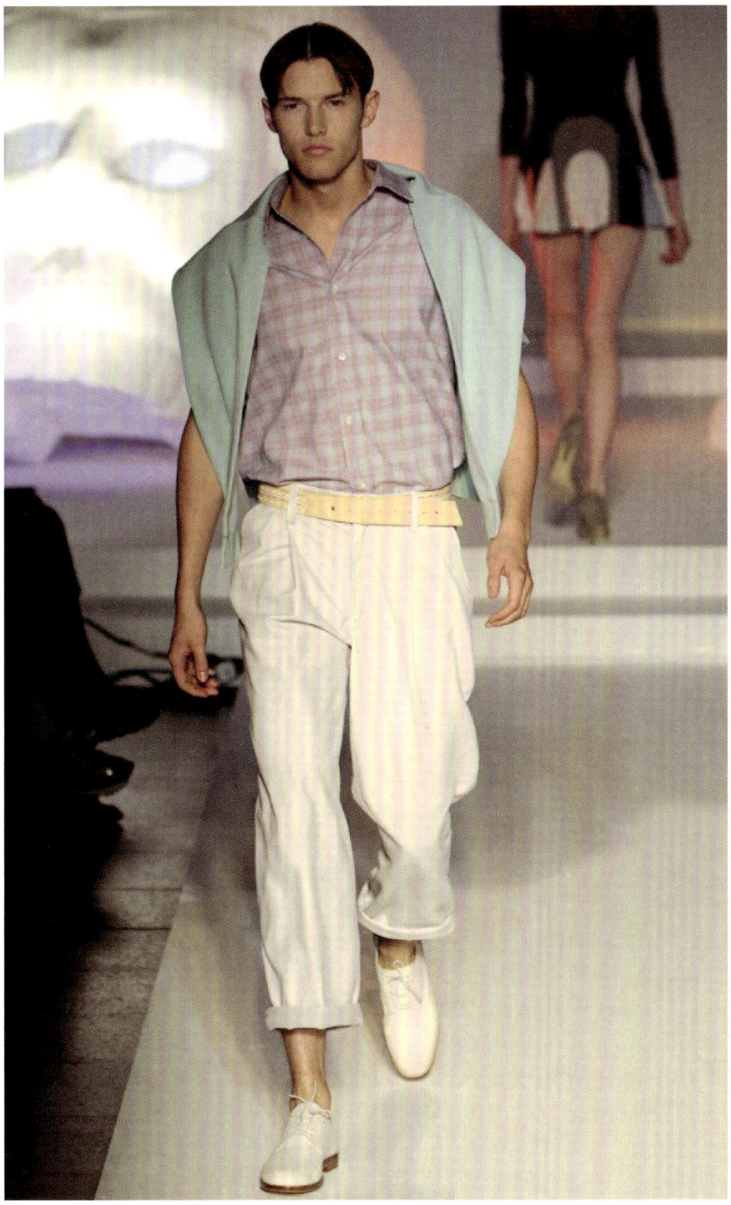

194. Kim Jones (1973–). Ensemble. Spring/Summer 2004

Think about those young men and women who would have studied fashion, would have been designers. Think about the stylists, such as Ray Petri, and those who would have become stylists. Same for hairdressers, make-up artists, photographers. Then think about those who worked in shops. Think about the customers, or those who would have become customers, if they had lived, if they had not died in a pandemic.

It was a whole ecosystem, decimated. It was only 40 years after the end of the Second World War. That ecosystem was still evolving, still establishing its roots. Radical, pioneering British menswear did not survive. And, because the general mood then was to look away from the AIDS crisis, to pretend everything was OK, no one took action to support, nurture and encourage what creativity was left.[9]

How come radical menswear at the time still existed in Paris, Tokyo, Antwerp, Milan? Look back at what Gaultier said about French government support. Further evidence comes in the December 1983 issue of *The Face*, which reported on the first London Fashion Week. Both men's and women's designers and brands showed. Much of the article is about designer's debt: Katharine Hamnett raising a £200,000 loan from a French bank to secure an extra £500,000 of income; BodyMap needing to see half of orders worth £100,000 'before a penny is earned'.[10]

Many designers are quoted. 'I went to Japan because I was ripped off here and left with huge debts', said Stephen Linard. Boy George had modelled for him while studying at Central Saint Martins. 'It's the business people who think small and don't understand fashion who are giving Britain a bad name.'[11]

The feature ends with a plea. 'What is urgently needed for a clothing industry with sales potential in the same league as motor cars is a trouble-shooting minister to see that a few 24-year-old managing directors get appointed, as they do in Japan, and to go bang a drum for our cottage industrialists.'

At the time, the Secretary of State for Trade and Industry was Norman Tebbit, who, even in 2017, said, 'it is perfectly sensible to argue that a homosexual act is a sin.'[12]

Radical young menswear designers, many of them queer, who pushed for an alternative to the patriarchal power messaging of the suit, never stood a chance.

RADICAL NEW MENSWEAR

In February 2005 a designer called Christoffer Lundman graduated from the Menswear MA of Central Saint Martins. I thought his collection of menswear was exceptional. Little sweaters and tailored jackets; high-waisted pale denim jeans with a roll at the ankle; lace-up shoes with stacked cork soles. I remember afterwards Lulu Kennedy of Fashion East saying, why was there no place for this in London Fashion Week?

Kennedy took matters into her own hands. Seven months later, Fashion East staged its first MAN show. It was the same set-up as its women's shows, which the not-for-profit had been running for five years. Three designers were given

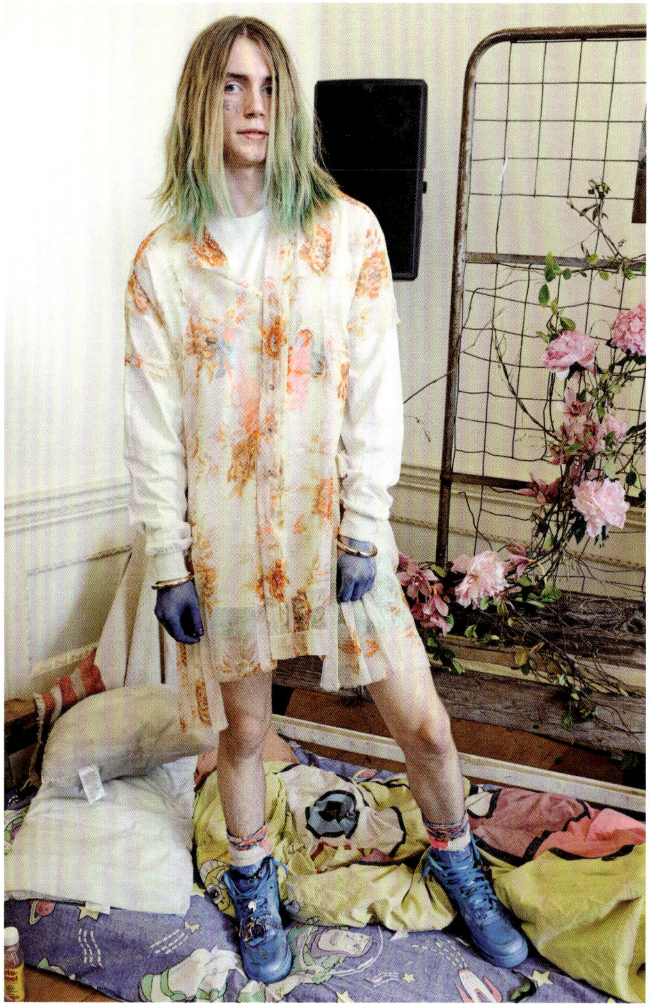

195. Meadham Kirchhoff. Ensemble. Spring/Summer 2013

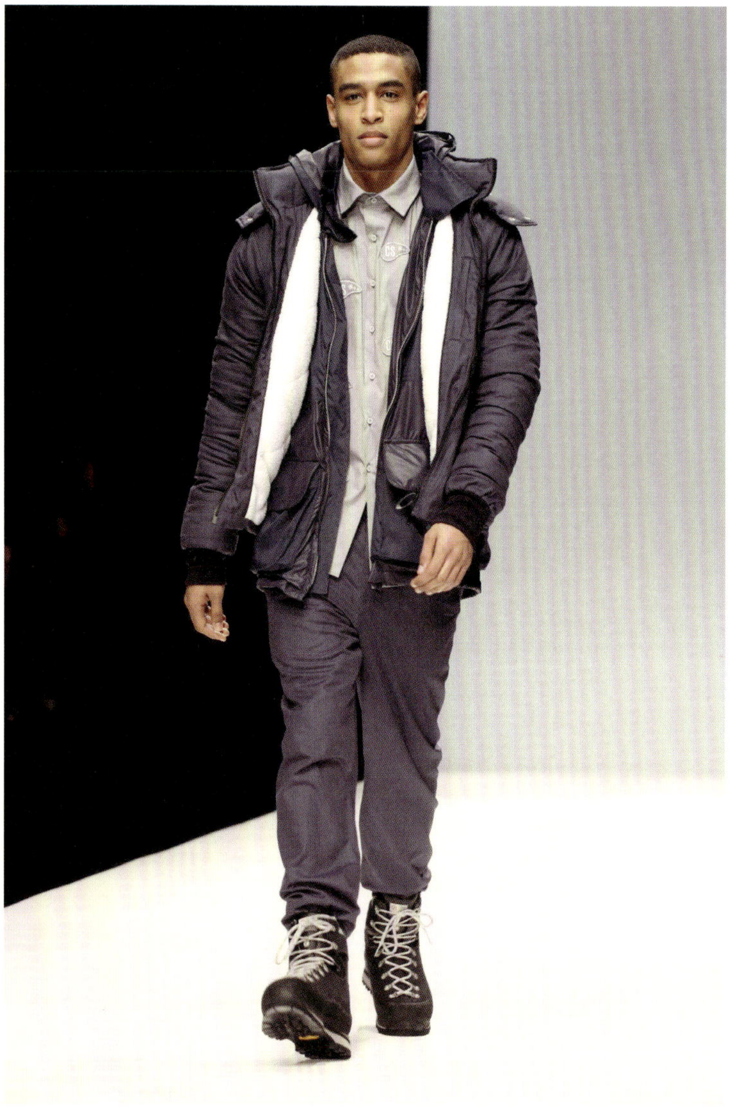

196. Christopher Shannon (1978–). Ensemble. Autumn/Winter 2010

financial support and the chance to show together. Each designer could show for a maximum of three seasons, meaning there was always an influx of new. Crucially, Kennedy believed in resetting to zero: if a designer gained success while part of Fashion East, whoever took their slot was not expected to follow in their footsteps. Everyone was allowed to work on their own terms.

Kennedy persuaded the British Fashion Council to give them a slot on the London Fashion Week schedule, helped by the fact that her sponsor and collaborator was Topman. It was the last show on the last day, a time that no-one else wanted. The show was a riot. Kim Jones presented a video. Benjamin Kirchhoff, later half of Meadham Kirchhoff, showed cropped sweaters, bleached jeans, wrestler singlets, all worn with jelly sandals. I would love to show you a photo of one such look, but we can find no high-resolution images from the show. There is so much from this crucial period, pre-smartphones, that is in danger of being forgotten because imagery is not easily accessible. This image is from a later show by Meadham Kirchhoff, presented in collaboration with Fashion East (195).

It was the beginning of a resurgence. It was righting a wrong: there should always have been a platform for radical menswear in London. Finally, someone was allowing it to happen. Somebody was encouraging true self-expression and unshackled creativity in menswear.

Fashion East kept staging its MAN shows, giving space for fresh menswear designers: Christopher Shannon, James Long, Martine Rose (97), Sibling, Astrid Andersen, J.W. Anderson, Nasir Mazhar. Eventually, others started to stage shows before or after. It grew into an afternoon of menswear, then a whole day at the end of London Fashion Week. These were vital, giddy times. Difference in thinking was given a platform.

It happened as society was pivoting. The internet, broadband strength and public Wi-Fi changed work habits. Apple's iPhone was introduced in 2007. For many men, work could now take place on the move, on their laptop, away from an office. Meanwhile, new tech industries, from app development to digital marketing, encouraged a creative atmosphere in their workplaces. That meant more freedom in dressing. For them, the tailored suit became obsolete.

London's young designers were suggesting fresh ways of dressing. Christopher Shannon grew up in Liverpool and made fashion from what was familiar to him: tracksuits, zip-up windcheaters, polo necks, T-shirts (196). He cut them, spliced them, played with them, subverted them. His point: fashion is false if it is all luxurious and untouchable. Fashion is what we see, in front of us, if we are willing to look.

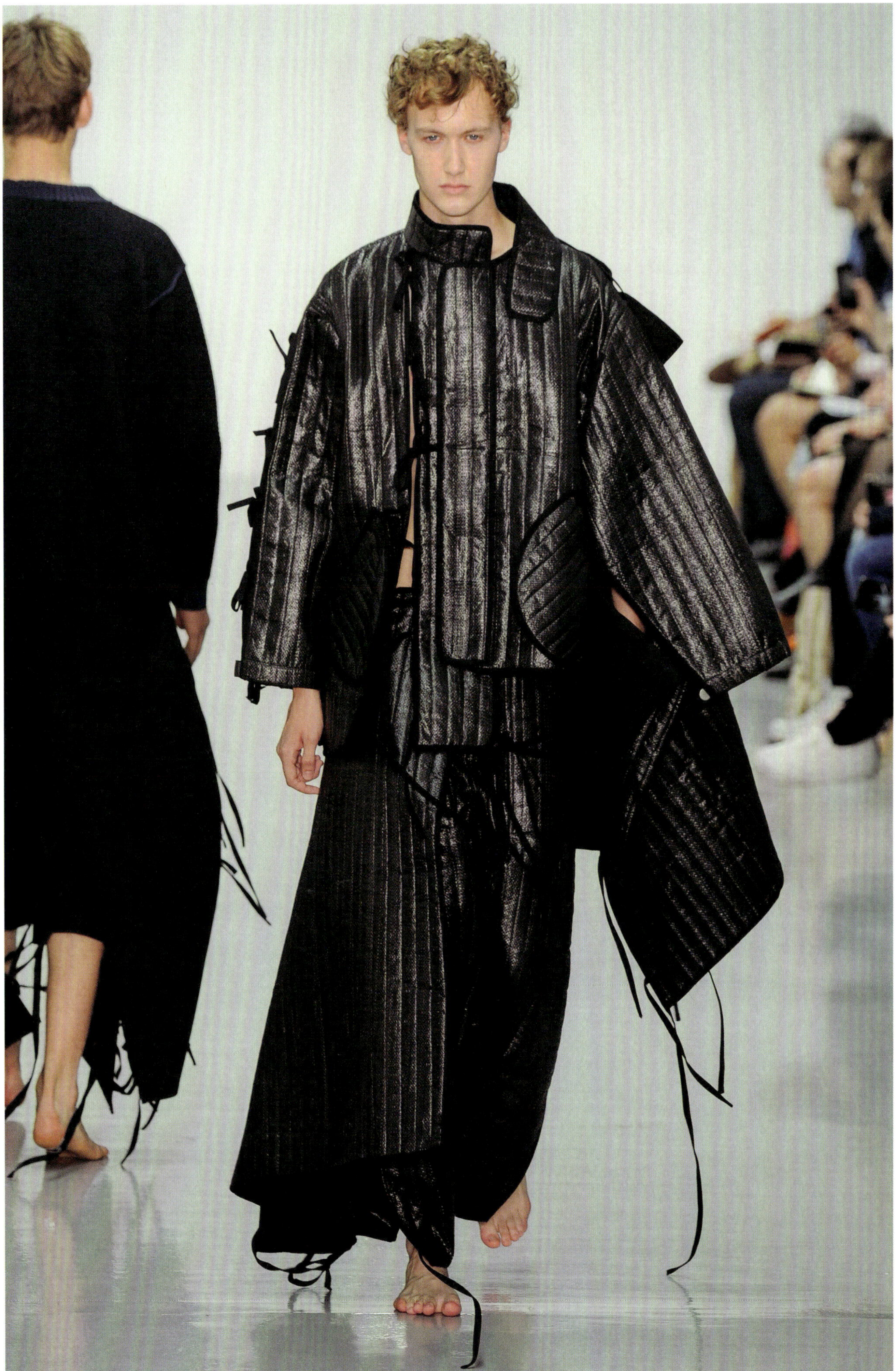

197. Craig Green (1986–). Ensemble.
Spring/Summer 2015. Model: Stefan Cooke

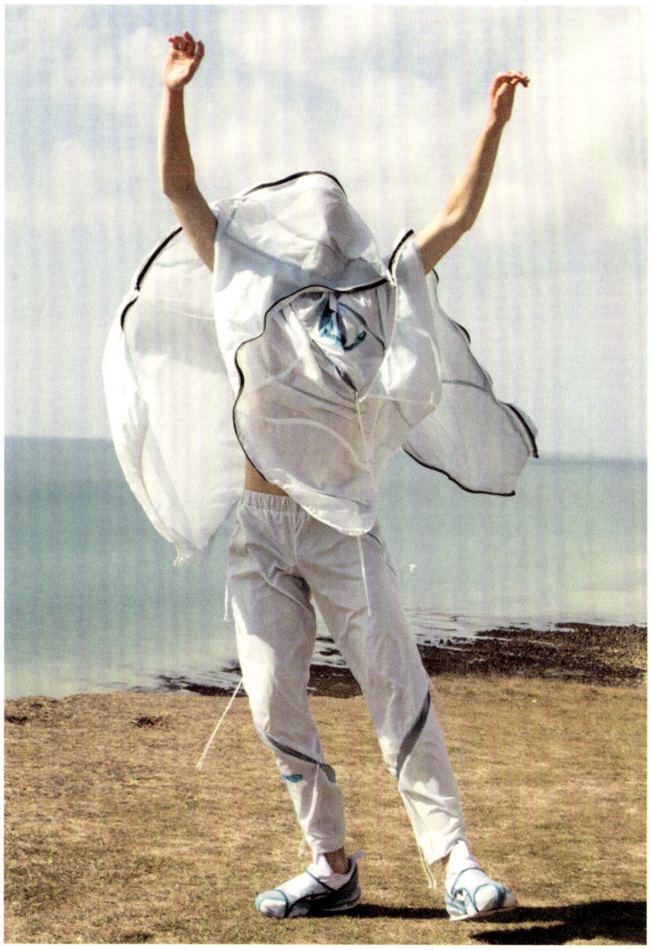

198. Saul Nash (1992–). Ensemble. Spring/Summer 2021.
Model: Sam Josiah Dilkes

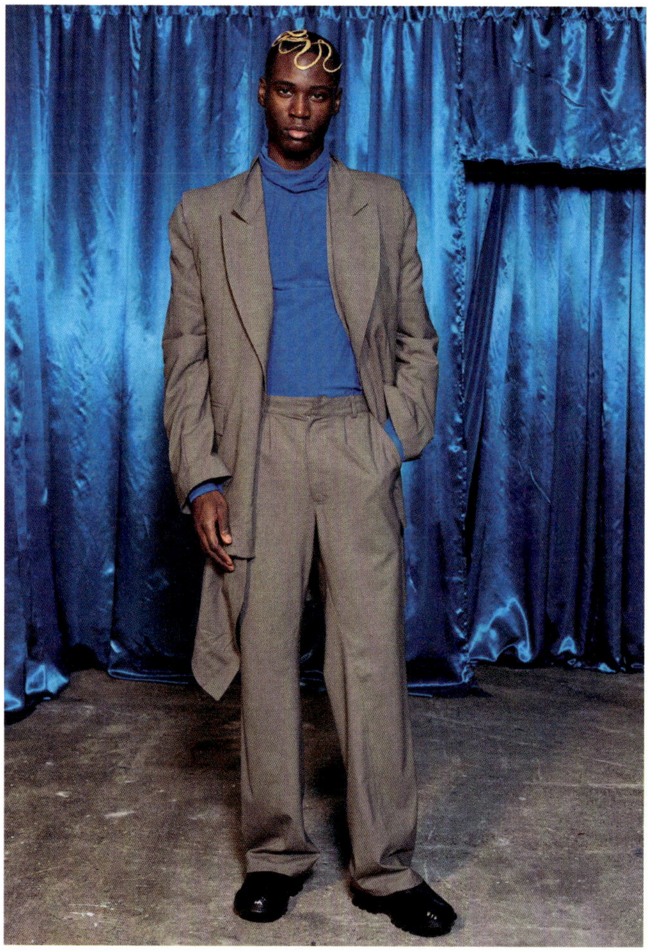

199. Bianca Saunders (1993–). Ensemble. Autumn/Winter 2020.
Model: Edge Lheureux

At the time, his work was not particularly understood. Nor was that of Astrid Andersen, who showed lace baseball shirts and logo hoodies, or Nasir Mazhar, whose streamline, ergonomic millinery had more to do with illegal raves than Ascot.

This was clothing that reflected working-class culture, as well as disenfranchised communities. Critically, these young designers were using fashion to reflect society in a way that was uncomfortable for many. It was particularly uncomfortable for those who believed that menswear should focus on suit/shirt/tie, with all of the power structures of wealth and privilege that such tailoring denotes.

As the London Olympics of 2012 approached, the city was awash with sponsorship money. The British Fashion Council finally took the plunge and announced the launch of London Collections Men, a stand-alone menswear schedule in line with the men's shows in Milan and Paris. Making his debut that June was Craig Green, a graduate from the Central Saint Martins MA. He showed a few pieces made from raw-cut cheesecloth and calico on static models at the Fashion East Installations. The work was gripping: a mix of open-eyed innocence and the ancient knowledge of paganism.

The next season, Green made his catwalk debut as part of Fashion East's MAN show. I thought it was an extraordinary collection, complete in its own internal logic. The opening look featured a worker's jacket, which has gone on to become his signature piece. The cut of everything was roomy, wearable, desirable. Looks were shadows of each other, with many of the models wearing structures of wooden planks that completely covered their faces. It was like watching hidden emotion suddenly exposed.

He continued to strike chords. He staged his first stand-alone show in June 2014. The show was based around a succession of outfits, many of them repeating, rendered in block colours: white, black, navy, sky blue (197). The opening look was like a straitjacket unravelled and sliced. Jackets were attached by strings tied together. One model walked in the simplest of sweaters, worn with trousers wide and gathered. Some models walked with banners of simple cloth attached to frames behind them.

The work was plaintive, stirring. It was the first show by Green since his tutor and friend Professor Louise Wilson lost her life to cancer, aged 52. I remember when the last model walked past thinking, I am going to cry. I looked up and across the catwalk from me. Others had the same look on their face. It was overwhelming, what his work had done to us. We wept. Backstage, Green was weeping. It brings tears to my eyes writing these words now.

This emotional connection with Green's work is important, beyond the pull that it gives to his clothing. Many men have trouble expressing how they feel. Society has only recently started to talk about male mental health. Clothing plays a part in it: the expression 'buttoned-up' says everything. Green is making a vital cultural contribution by using fashion to express what cannot be said.

Many others have made similar cultural contributions. Grace Wales Bonner has brought to attention stories from the African diaspora, at a time when designers of colour are still a minority (201). The duo Rottingdean Bazaar have questioned the nature of fashion consumption itself, even showing an entire collection of hired novelty costumes. Meanwhile, Priya Ahluwalia draws attention to the appalling waste of fast fashion, an industry that dumps its unwanted excesses in countries such as Nigeria and India, presuming it will remain out of sight.

We are now in a place where menswear can go beyond what is shown on the catwalk. I am very much taken by the work of John Alexander Skelton, a deeply political designer whose belief in sustainability runs through his entire practice. Skelton sources as many materials as possible within the UK, employing historical methods for work that is very much by the hand. He presents his collections once a year, always on Twelfth Night. One presentation saw his brother, Ryan Skelton, recite from memory *Under Milk Wood* (1954) by Dylan Thomas, while revealing mannequins dressed in the collection that were hidden under sheets.

The designer Saul Nash is also a choreographer, his understanding of movement informing the cut of his tracksuits, coats and shorts. This movement is a signature of his shows, whether on the catwalk or on film, like his extraordinary footage of his Spring/Summer 2021 collection shot high on the Seven Sisters cliffs on the coast of East Sussex (198). Nash also collaborates on movement with his friend Bianca Saunders, whose work is a constantly evolving exploration of cut, line and silhouette. For her breakthrough collection in January 2020, Saunders staged a presentation with models dancing (199), 'like they would normally do in a club, in the dark, when no one's watching.' In the summer of 2021, Saunders won the prestigious ANDAM Award, previous winners of which include Martin Margiela, Anthony Vaccarello and Marine Serre.[13]

THE FUTURE OF MENSWEAR IN LONDON

I have recently been doing some teaching on the BA Fashion Design course at the University of Westminster. The final year classes have been full of brilliant individuals, whose eyes are wide open to the reality of climate crisis and the limitations of the traditional fashion system. When, in the summer of 2020, fashion graduates faced grim job prospects, it was a thrill to watch some of the young talents take matters into their own hands. Steven Stokey-Daley had made his graduate collection using deadstock material donated by Alexander McQueen, using this luxury cloth to create pieces that looked at the public-school homo-socialism of the British ruling classes (201). He is from Liverpool. Since graduating, he had moved back to the city, set up his own website, and is now selling his wide cut shirts and ultra-pleated pants directly to customers. Within a year, the wider fashion world has taken notice: Harry Styles wore his pieces in the video for 'Golden', while Josh O'Connor was dressed in an S.S. Daley bespoke suit for the 2021 BAFTAs. His debut catwalk show, for Spring/Summer 2022, featuring members of the National Youth Theatre, was seen by many as the high point of that season's London Fashion Week.

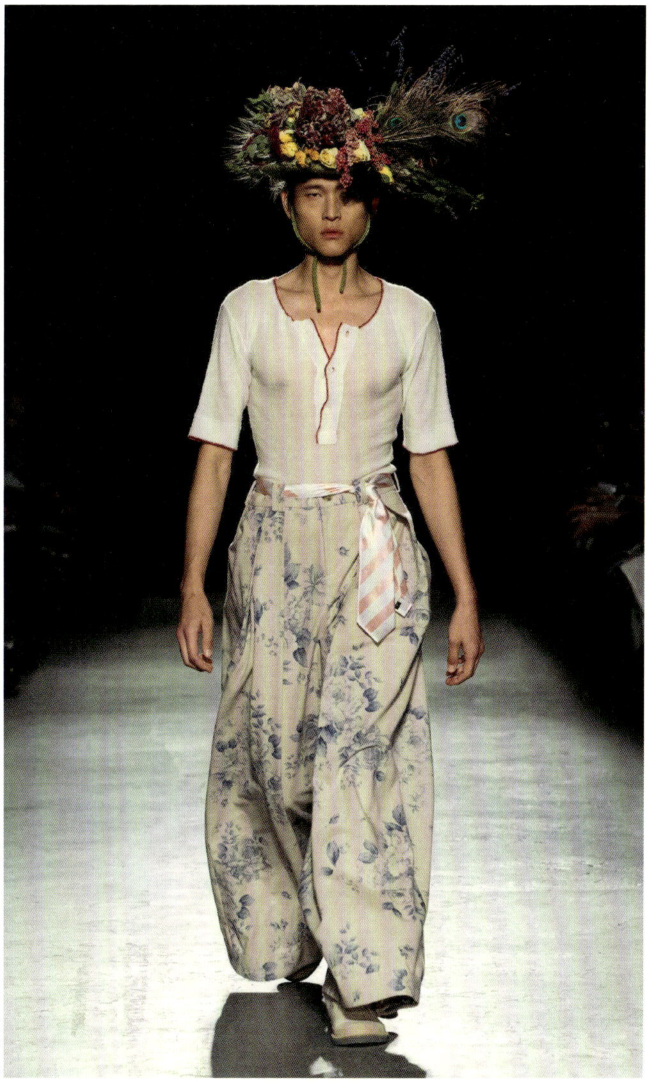

200. Steven Stokey-Daley (1996–). Ensemble. Autumn/Winter 2021. Model: Sheldon Chang

One of Steven's classmates was Jonty K. Mellmann, whose graduate collection was about his beloved hardcore rave scene. Hardcore raves do not follow fashion seasons, why should Jonty's clothes? Since graduating, he has started selling pieces as he makes them, often at the store Fantastic Toiles in Forest Gate, set up by designer Nasir Mazhar to champion one-off pieces by young, independent and radical designers.

This is the lifeblood that needs to be nurtured and protected. London is stereotyped as a city of wild creativity. I see otherwise. It is a place that can allow raw and true emotional connection. That is what made the work of Malcolm McLaren and Vivienne Westwood so visceral. That is what fuelled Alexander McQueen. Fashion is usually written about in terms of commercial success, about who got which job where. That is not the real story. What matters are individuals, their ability to express themselves, and their effect on others.

Following pages: 201. Grace Wales Bonner (1992–), Fashion in Motion at the V&A, 2015

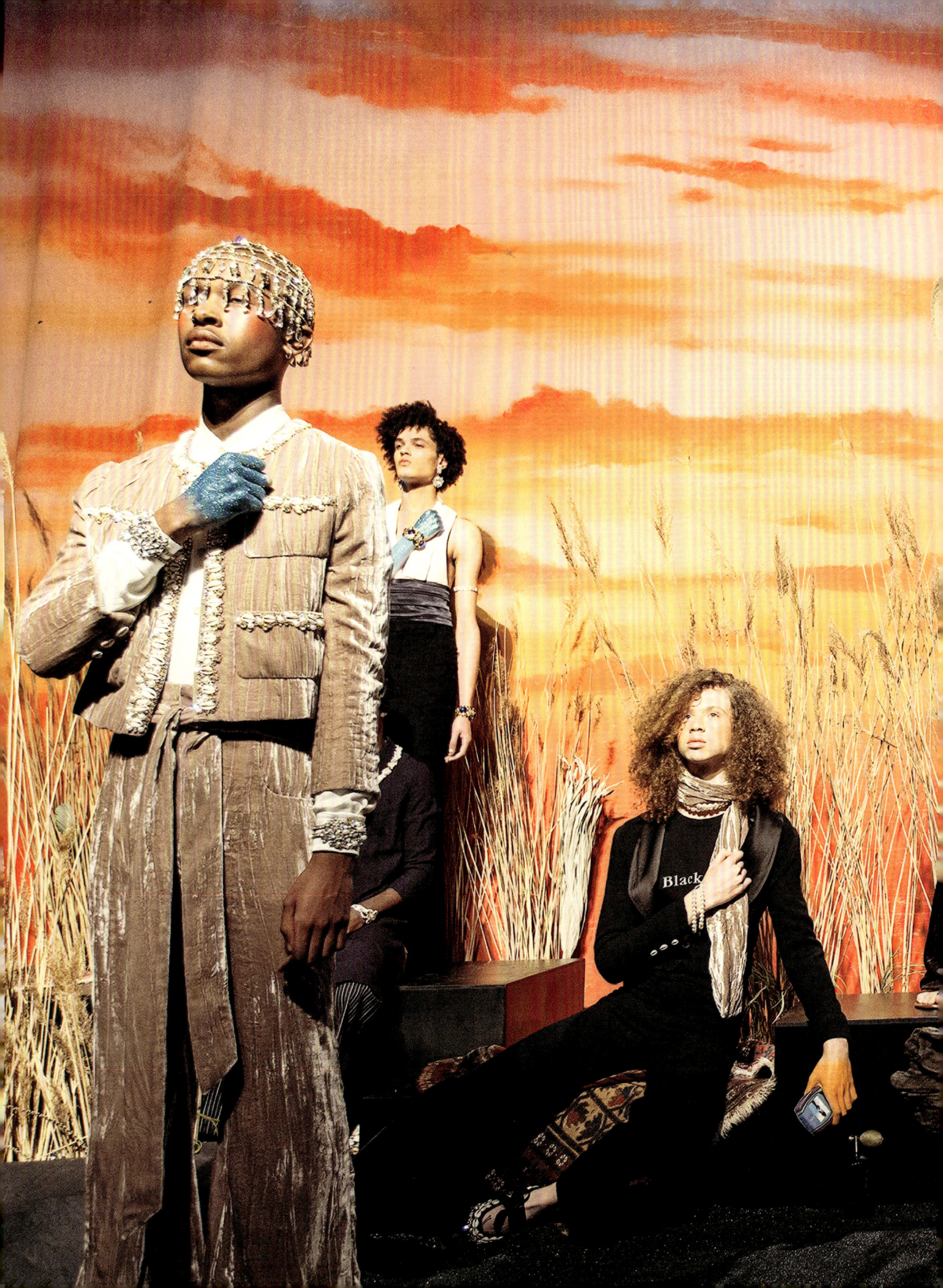
Black

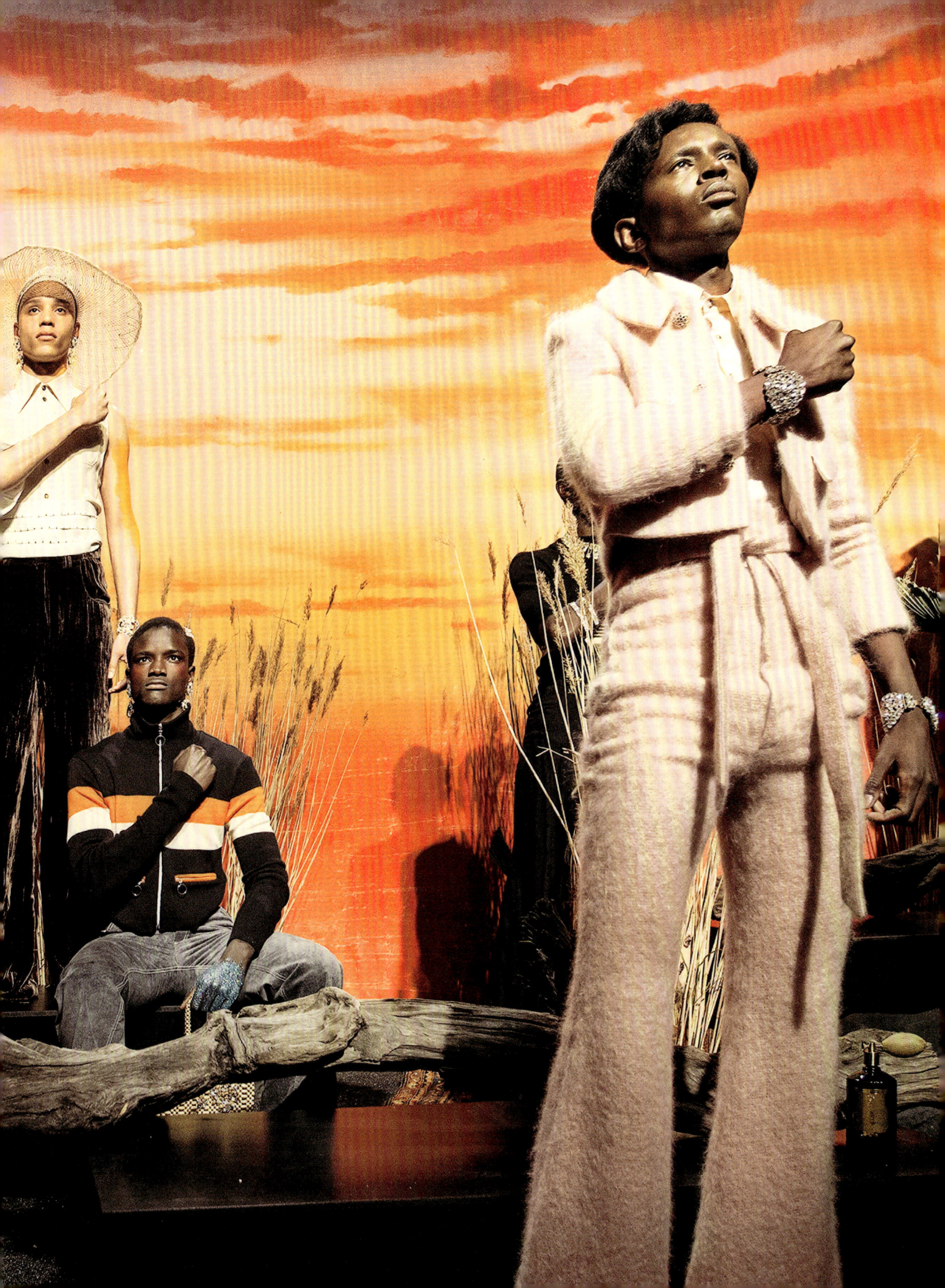

EPILOGUE

GUS CASELY-HAYFORD

In early 1996, just after Alexander McQueen took the helm at Givenchy, I asked Karl Lagerfeld at the rival atelier Chanel what he thought of this luminous young talent. After affectionately welcoming McQueen to Paris, praising his astounding gifts, Lagerfeld delivered a coda: he told me that he saw great design as having particular potential to map both past and future, to act simultaneously, as he put it, as 'archaeology and oracle', to operate as a temporal lens with the power to locate and connect us. As Lagerfeld spoke, I was reminded of that exquisite passage, drawn from Jacques Lacan's 1964 seminar lectures, in which he argued that art at its very best can have a prophetic quality, that it can be mined to give up glimpses of our collective motivations, it can be read to offer access to an otherwise hidden set of cultural mechanics that might open portals to possible futures.[1]

These are compelling visions of culture as a window through which we might further our understanding of ourselves, our heritage, our futures – they also capture the most beguiling overall conclusion of this enquiry into *fashioning masculinities*: that beyond the extrinsic benefits of men's fashion, there lies a rich hinterland of revelatory value in the sartorial choices that define masculinity. Great menswear has been the therapeutic couch upon which a gender has reclined. Rarely serving as an effective carapace, men's fashion is a burnished lens through which we have been able to steal views across our psyches, open up vistas across time and geography, to gain perspective upon the shifting plates of power and gender. And it is a two-way lens, both with the capacity to reveal something of our personal disposition, but also with the power to cast light upon incipient attitudes and ambient aspirations. Fred Hoffman in his interviews with Jean-Michel Basquiat reflected that the artist showed an 'innate capacity to function as something like an oracle distilling his perceptions of the outside world down to their essence and, in turn, projecting them outward through his creative acts' (202).[2] And the most compelling vision of men's fashion is perhaps as a similar kind of multi-dimensional lens, a glass through which we might gaze backward and forward – but also critically, laterally and inwardly, coaxing us to acknowledge and accommodate the peripheral, suppressed and alternate voices.

My earliest menswear encounters were gathered in the mid-1980s among that gilded generation of designers who graduated from Central Saint Martins alongside my eldest brother, Joe Casely-Hayford. John Galliano, Andrea Sargeant, Ninivah Khomo, Alistair Blair, John Flett, Nick Coleman, Rifat Ozbek – they were part of a dazzling moment in menswear history, a generation who seemed driven by that same compelling pursuit of those 'other' voices (203). I was still a child when I first saw their work, but there was something about their talent that simply translated.

In an era of Margaret Thatcher, power-dressing and the Filofax, I particularly remember the young Galliano's audacious weaponization of menswear, turning the suit into a canvas for deconstructing the ambient politics and culture. It was a zeitgeist-shifting series of collections that evoked revolution: both a 'villagers with pitch-forks' Hegelian uprising and, somewhat presciently, a kind of Fukuyama-esque foretelling of the end to historical discourse. They asked difficult questions of my ideas of menswear, not by wanting to raze clothing tradition, but through a careful investment in unpicking the conventional history of men's fashion, deliberately mining its archaeology, and fastidiously deconstructing my suburban views. What especially fascinated me was that they did not just reference history or choose to deconstruct Enlightenment notions of progress; they solicited us to concertedly consider the sources of inspiration for men's fashion narratives, forcing their work into a richer global context. I learned later that Galliano's own fashion awakening had taken place in the bazaars and souks of Morocco on childhood trips with his mother. And beyond being spellbound by the intoxicating visual wealth of what he encountered, he had learned what it was like to stand on a shore and to gaze at the West from afar, what it was like to feel alien, what it was like to feel excluded. Perhaps understandably, like so many of his generation, he would use that appetite and that alienation to corral and disrupt fashion and its conventions into telling his own stories. Once you stand on that shoreline it is hard to forget the view, it is difficult to not want to nurture, seek out and invest in those other perspectives wherever you might find them. I think that is what I identified with most in reading the rich and evocative texts in this book; it is what they coax from beneath the façade of received fashion history, a rich archaeology of other stories. Not romantic fashion fairy-tales, but a corroborable set of rich and involving alternative narrative routes across our fashion history.

In July 1324 a long camel train, laden with gold, drifted off the Sahel into Cairo. Even for a cosmopolitan desert port fuelled by camel caravans, this was unlike anything the city had seen before. This camel train was led by a young man riding an Arabian stallion: the Malian emperor, Mansa Musa, the richest man who ever lived, and the mastermind of one of the most celebrated pilgrimages to Mecca of all time. Musa and his retinue had walked and ridden every tough mile from Niani in West Africa but had done so in a style that was a sight to behold. It was said that each night when they made camp, they assembled a city in the desert, building irrigation systems, even constructing a portable mosque. The journey had been long in the planning. By the time that Musa's thousands of followers descended upon Cairo, the city already anticipated his arrival. Scholars travelled from the newly established university in Salamanca,

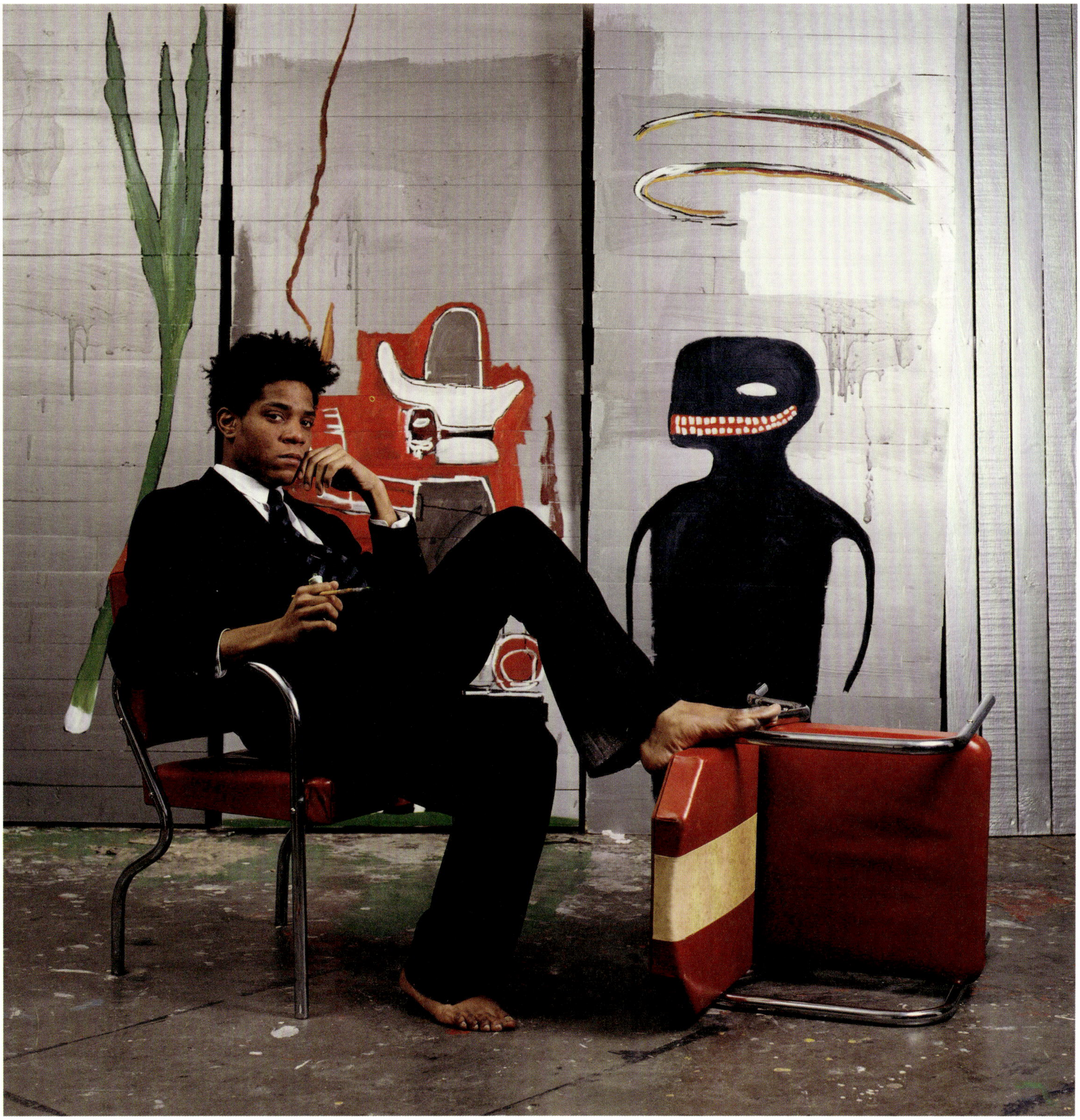

202. Lizzie Himmel (1953–), Jean-Michel Basquiat wearing Giorgio Armani, published on the cover of the *New York Times Magazine* (February 1985)

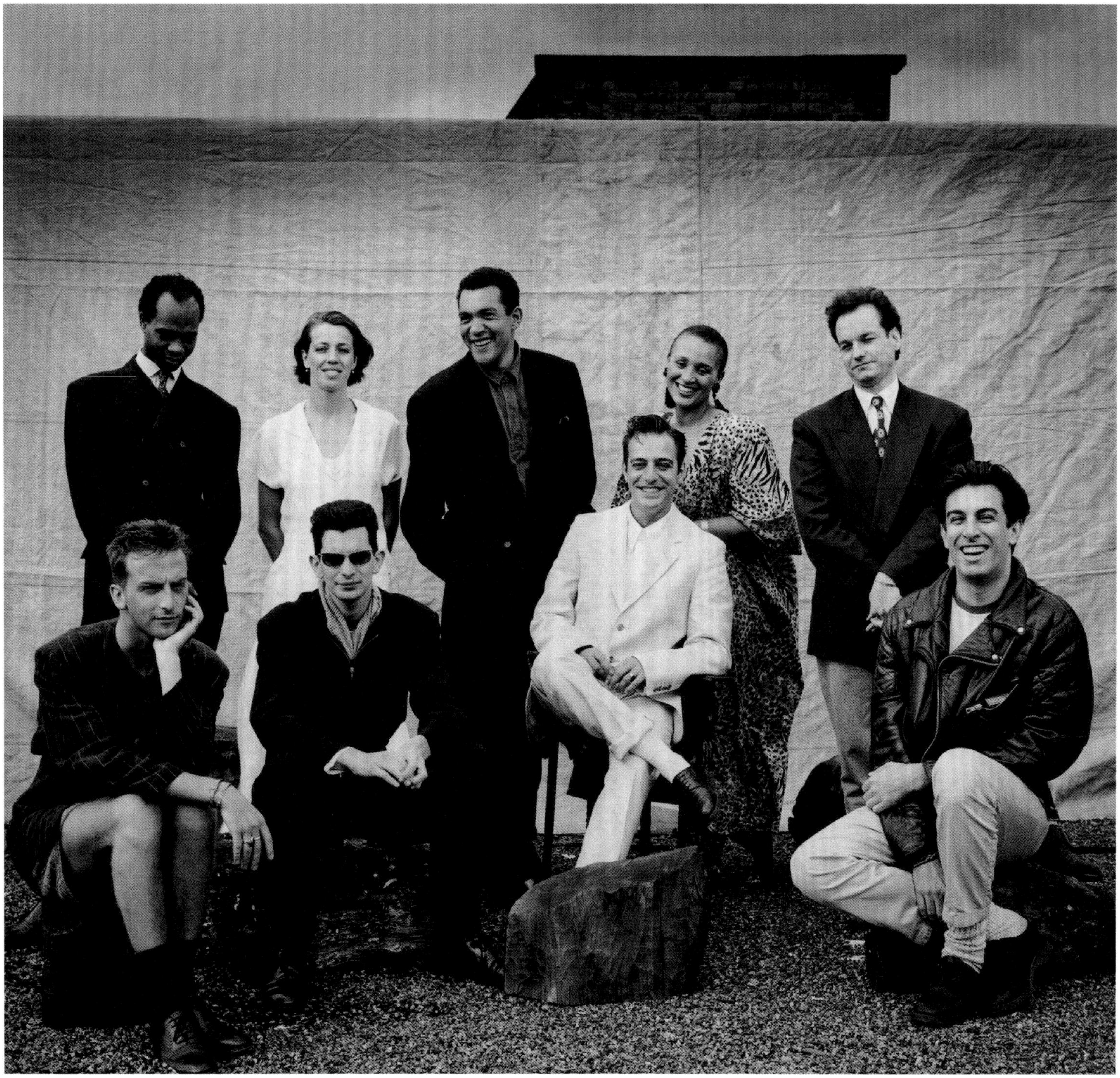

203. Eamonn J. McCabe (1959–), St Martin's School of Art Alumni,
L–R (back row) Joe Casely-Hayford, Andrea Sargeant, Bruce Oldfield, Ninivah Khomo, Alistair Blair
(front row) John Flett, Nick Coleman, John Galliano and Rifat Ozbek, 1985

from the ancient Berber centres of academic excellence in North Africa and southern Spain, from the courts of Venice and the Madrassas of the burgeoning Ottoman empire to intercept the caravan, to witness the arrival of one of the great personalities of the medieval world, and to join him on his final leg of this spectacular hajj. In part they were attracted by Musa's unfathomable wealth, but also by this man's famed sophistication, charisma and style.

Cairo fell under the young emperor's spell. Al-Makrizi, the Egyptian historian wrote, 'he appeared amidst his companions magnificently dressed and mounted and surrounded by more than ten thousand subjects. He brought gifts and presents that amazed the eye with their beauty and splendor'. He would famously give away so much of his fortune, spoiling his hosts and followers, that there would be an impact on the price of gold for years to come.

Musa's spectacular hajj was not just a statement about a powerful man's religious commitment, or a sign of an African empire's economic ambition, but a conscious exhibition of how a new kind of diplomacy might operate in a burgeoning transnational cultural arena. As once disparate cultures sought increasingly substantive international engagement, a new kind of cultural power was being brokered in the uncharted space. From Bruges to Cairo, from Venice to Constantinople, the great centres of exchange saw profound cultural shifts as they adapted to become better conduits of the latest thinking. This gave rise to a rash of new universities, madrasas and libraries, new centres of intellectual innovation being constituted in the heart of the great trading cities. When late-medieval artists sought to reimagine the story of the Three Wise Men for their time, it was in part from this phenomenon that they drew their inspiration, seeing the Magi as worldly symbols of wisdom, wealth and the very future itself. They knew that the most thrilling kinds of innovation were being forged at the point of convergence of some of the great international cultural narratives. Perhaps the most accessible and compelling instantiation of that phenomenon would be the sartorial statements that men began to make, the conscious borrowing of textile and line, of style and form, of adornment and refinement that spoke to that nascent cosmopolitanism.

It would be within this spirit of cultural borrowing that the tenets of recognizable international men's wardrobe would emerge. Its constituent parts would be bought and bartered in marketplaces across vast expanses of geography, pulled into an endlessly interconnected, ever-evolving arena of dynamic discourse and development. During the course of the Renaissance, wardrobes would become the most potent symbols of that quickening change, maps of time and culture that could be worn on your back, an exoskeleton that could both protect and promote, and yet, for those with the interpretative tools to decode it, an open book. While this process of fashioning a gender became increasingly tightly controlled by smaller numbers of people, its industrial engine and influence became increasingly global and expansive. The burgeoning of European imperial ambition, the colonialism and industrialized enslavement that would follow, would only serve to exacerbate the consolidation of these globalized hierarchies, to enrich western fashion and expand its reach, while diminishing the interconnected cultures and peoples that serviced and so often inspired it. I have always imagined that it was the ghosts of these narratives that thrilled young Galliano in the markets of Marrakesh, and it would be to the same shoreline that many of us would return to for inspiration again and again.

By the time that Mansa Musa returned from the hajj, seemingly with the world in his pocket, I think he had quietly come to understand that however powerful he was perceived to be, he was vulnerable to marginalization, and likely to be written out of the future he hoped to shape. Understandably, he sought to carve himself indelibly into history, by building his own libraries, his own university, his own legacy, leaving his lasting material mark upon culture. How can we argue with those instincts? Globalized culture – global fashion – has indeed exploited the cultures of the geographic periphery and then excluded many of those peoples from narratives within which they played a significant part. And as anyone who has shared that shoreline will remind us, the story of *fashioning masculinities*, like so much else, is not the exclusive preserve of any region, or people – it belongs to us all.

The story of menswear is, in its history, economics, its inspiration, a global one, and that remains so well evidenced in the sartorial archaeology of the contemporary wardrobe. The shirt, in great part being drawn from a long tradition of light linen garments worn in Egypt and North Africa for more than a thousand years, was fashioned from materials that were being traded in the foothills of the Caucasus mountains 30,000 years earlier. The shirt would find aspects of its jacket in the eastern European *zupan*, which was probably in turn inspired by *achkans* and *sherwanis* made in India, themselves no doubt borrowed from the Central Asian *chapan*, or kaftan. You sense that heritage of practicality and style in the *justacorps* frockcoats that would be worn by seventeenth-century European aristocrats, garments that in form and materials flaunt those beautifully complex origins. It has been said that the word cravat is a corruption of the word 'Croat', but the neckerchief might again have had more complex and heterogenous set of histories. It was across these vast geographies that the inspiration for the modern suit would be negotiated, crafted, catalysed into being, iterated through trade, wars, migration, imperialism. Its waistcoat said to have been introduced by the court of Charles II, became a canvas upon which the most exotic and expensive Asian silks could be shown off – a projection of our imperial ambition rendered in fabric. Every detail of the suit, from cuff, to buckle to button of is part of a sartorial geography across which one could also map power, control and ambition.

Men's fashion has offered a window onto our dreams and fantasies, it has been deployed to offer us cover and camouflage, and has been a powerful mechanism for encouraging conformity or expressing our individuality. It has also obscured the archaeology of the fashion industry's wider story, of its part in the creation and maintenance of many of the powerful inequalities evidenced in class, race, gender and geography. Perhaps its greatest instantiation, the suit, was never just a garment, but a suit of armour, a weapon of sexual politics, a map, a clock, a piece of political geography, through which we might understand something of the nature of the rich, complex, contested story of us – both the good and the bad. Its most conspicuous constituent parts were not crafted or curated by any atelier, but rather evolved as a cultural reflection of irresistible wider global forces, its form and function worn and eroded under the inexorable weight of huge socio political plates. And perhaps that rich dark archaeology remains men's fashion's most poignant beauty: that wonder, iniquity and sadness are woven through our fashion story, warp and weft, its inescapable undergirding.

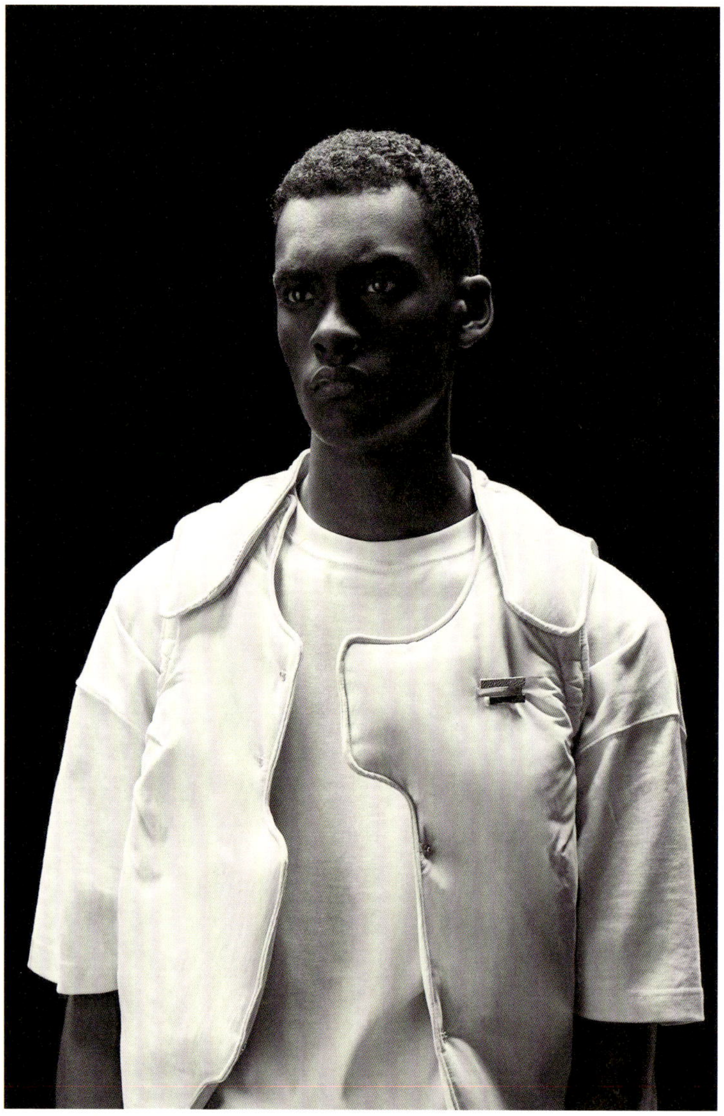

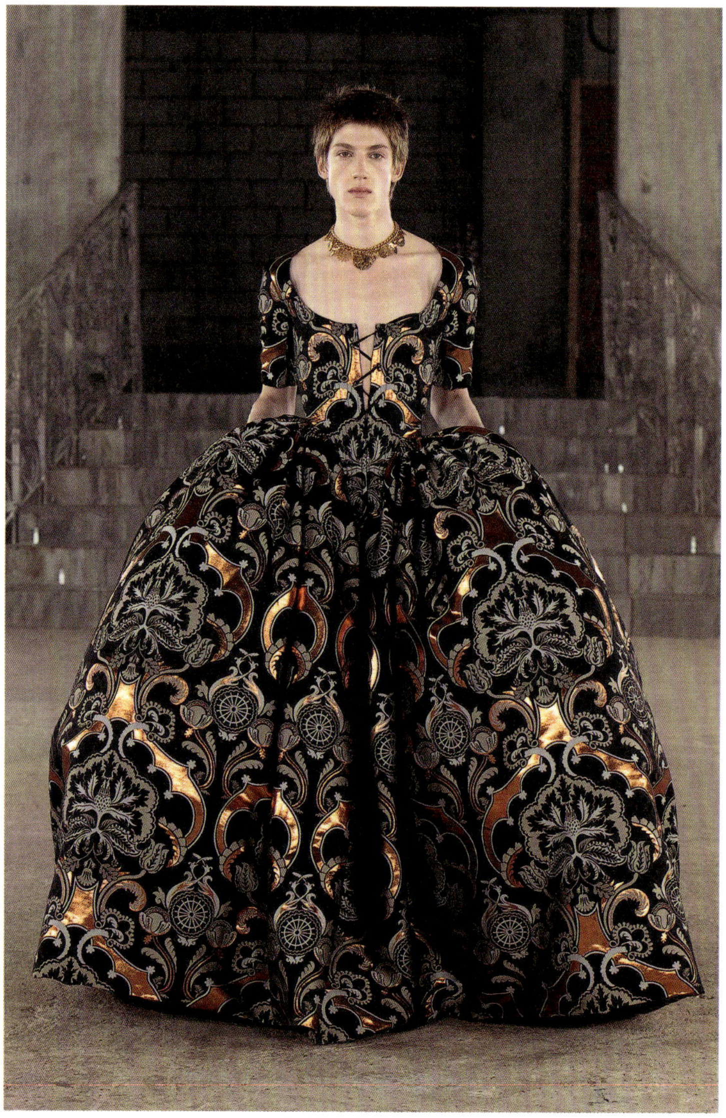

204. Samuel Ross (1991–) for A-Cold-Wall*. Ensemble. Spring/Summer 2021.
Model: Samer Rahma

Blending sportswear with sharp tailoring, and focusing on technical materials, ergonomic efficiency and innovative silhouettes, Samuel Ross's A-Cold-Wall* is revolutionizing streetwear. Trained in graphics and product design, Ross worked with Virgil Abloh before starting A-Cold-Wall* as an art project. With references ranging from architecture to class systems to the combat styles of this ensemble, his designs remain intrinsically political.

205. Edward Crutchley (1980–). Ensemble. Spring/Summer 2022.
Photo: Chris Yates. Model: Siddharta Van Der Sluis

Edward Crutchley's encyclopaedic knowledge of textiles and their histories permeates his collections. Crutchley, who is also Director of Fabric for Dior Homme, was inspired by eighteenth-century botanical silk designer Anna Maria Garthwaite for this floral print. It enhances the silhouette of the tight corset, modelled to fit a male torso, and imbues the full-length skirt with drama, queering the 'robe à l'Anglaise'.

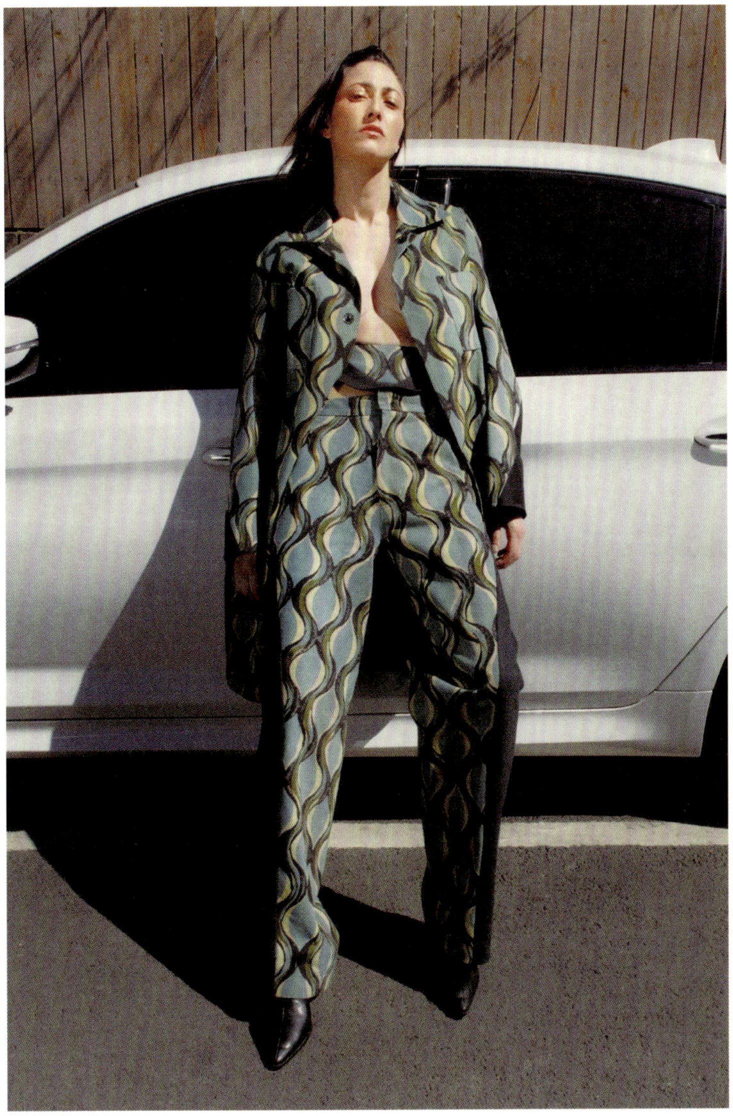

206. Rahemur Rahman (1992–). Ensemble. Collection 3 – Children of the Rag Trade. Photo: Daniele Fummo. Model: Jessica Tesoniero

Rahemur Rahman retells stories of South Asian identity through his designs. His fabrics are wood-block-printed by artisans in Bangladesh, re-activating a traditional technique. Assembling the garments in London, Rahman mixes tailoring and draping techniques to shape a gender-neutral silhouette. The uniqueness of the handmade fabric connects wearers and makers across different geographies, updating the values associated with the label 'Made in Bangladesh.'

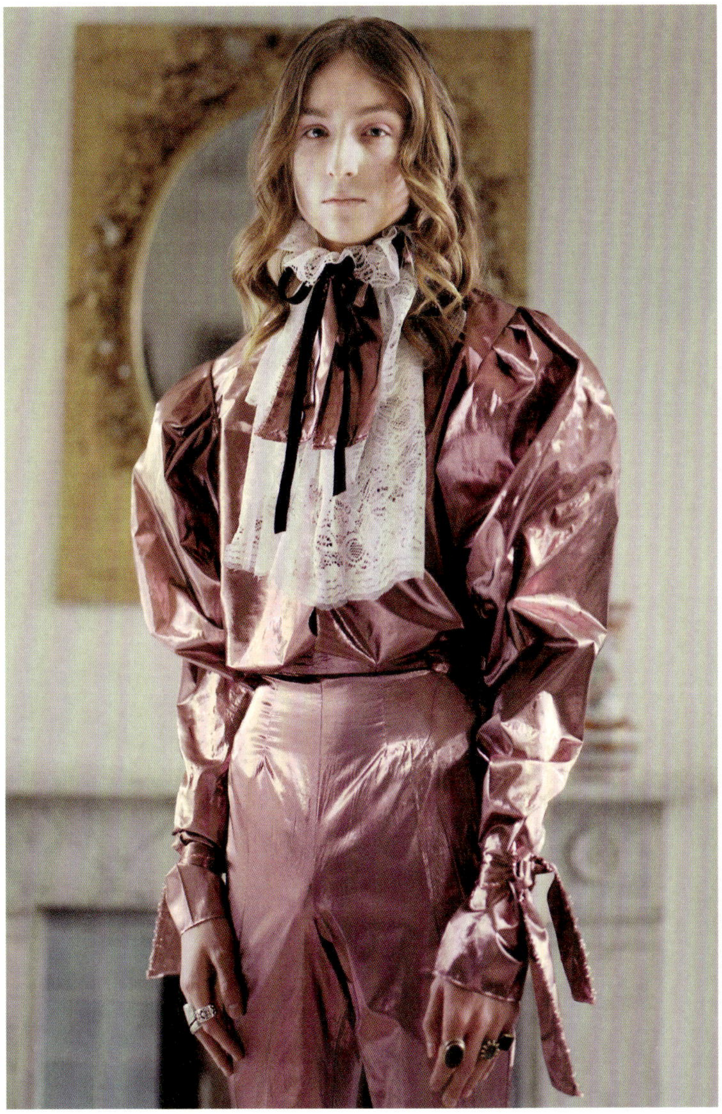

207. Harris Reed (1996–). Ensemble. Fluid Romanticism 001, 2017. Photo: Giovanni Corabi. Model: Harris Reed

As a student at Central Saint Martins, Harris Reed's imaginative and tolerant vision was informed by looking to the past. This ensemble from his first collection pays homage to 1970s glam rock, while puffed sleeves and a lace jabot evoke historical portraiture. The designer, who often models his own creations, describes his work as fighting for 'the beauty of fluidity'.

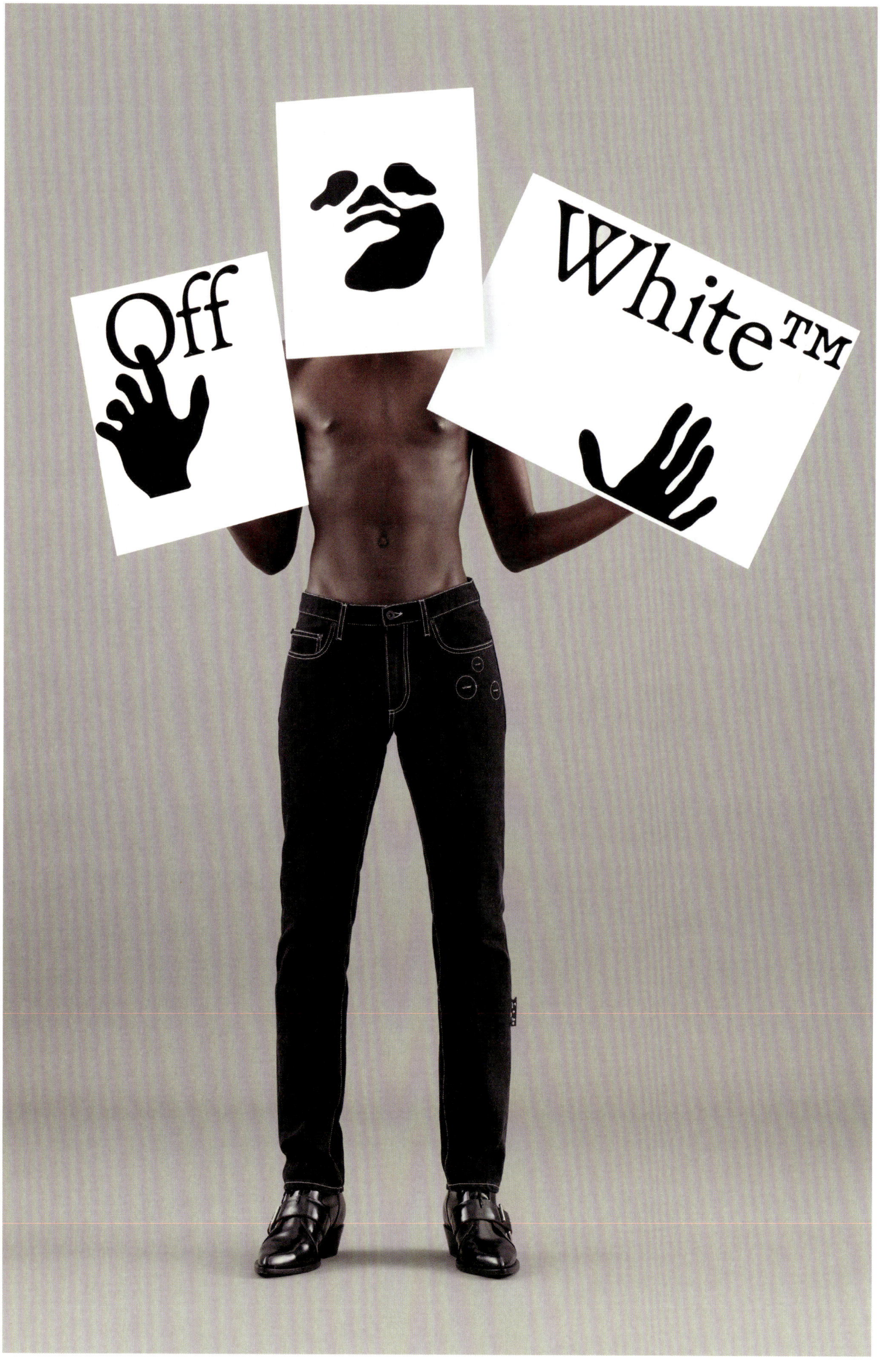

208. Virgil Abloh (1980–2021) for Off-White, Resort 2021

It has always been a belief of mine that clothing has the opportunity to place all beings on an even playing field. It allows us to blur long held, and often outdated, social norms. We can challenge and break down societal barriers such as the lines between classes, differences in race, opposing belief systems, and superfluous gender norms. It has long been part of my ethos to question the notion of what has traditionally been viewed as 'masculine' versus 'feminine' within my work. My ideology is to create for all people, of all ages, and from all backgrounds to offer a singular language that we can collectively understand and communicate through.

VIRGIL ABLOH

NOTES

DO CLOTHES MAKE THE MAN?
Rosalind McKever

1. Mark Twain is sometimes cited as the originator of the phrase, with the additional line 'Naked people have little or no influence on society.' 'Clothes make the man', John Simpson and Jennifer Speake (eds), *The Oxford Dictionary of Proverbs* (Oxford 2009). https://www.oxfordreference.com (accessed 9 Feb 2021).
2. Philip Dormer Stanhope, *The Works of Lord Chesterfield including His Letters to His Son, &c.* (New York 1860) p. 135
3. Harold Koda and Richard Martin's 1989 exhibition *Jocks and Nerds: Men's Style in the Twentieth Century* at the Fashion Institute of Technology, New York and Anne Hollander's *Sex and Suits* (New York, 1994) anticipated a deluge of scholarship in the mid-2010s, including the exhibition *Reigning Men: Fashion in Menswear 1715–2015* at Los Angeles County Museum of Art in 2016, and the books Christopher Breward, *The Suit: Form, Function and Style* (London 2016); Elizabeth Currie, *Fashion and Masculinity in Renaissance Florence* (London 2016); Peter McNeil, *Pretty Gentlemen: Macaroni Men and the Eighteenth Century* (New Haven and London 2018) and Jay McCauley Bowstead, *Menswear Revolution: The Transformation of Contemporary Men's Fashion* (London 2018). For perceptive analysis and statistical data on the place of menswear in fashion exhibitions over the past 45 years, see the scholarship of Jeffrey Horsley, especially 'The Absent Shadow: Reflections on the Incidence of Menswear in Recent Fashion Exhibitions', *Critical Studies in Men's Fashion*, Vol. 4, No. 1 (2017), pp. 11–29: https://ualresearchonline.arts.ac.uk/id/eprint/12317/1/CSMF_Horsley-2.pdf.

MARBLE MARVELS AND CLASSICAL IDEALS
Sarah Goldsmith

1. Addison 1705, p. 341
2. These sculptures are now at the Vatican Museums (Rome), the Musée du Louvre (Paris) and the Museo Archeologico Nazionale (Naples) respectively.
3. Redford 1996, pp. 7–9, 14–15; Cohen 1996, pp. 54–63; Goldsmith 2020, Introduction
4. Sweet 2012, especially chapter 3 for an excellent account of how tourists engaged with antiquity.
5. Haskell and Penny 1981, p. 221; Scott 2004, p. 57
6. Ansell 2018, pp. 1446–77; Misson 1714, pp. 10; 69
7. For an accessible introduction to this topic and key scholars, see https://www.newyorker.com/magazine/2018/10/29/the-myth-of-whiteness-in-classical-sculpture (accessed 18 Apr 2021).
8. Raguenet 1723, p. 176
9. Richardson 1754, p. 126; Winckelmann 1764, quoted in Potts 1994, p. 84
10. Raguenet 1723, pp. 177–8
11. Ibid; Richardson 1754, p. 276
12. Winckelmann 1764, quoted in Potts 1994, p. 118; Spence 1755, p. 84
13. Quoted in Potts 1994, pp. 126–7
14. Spence 1755, p. 114
15. Raguenet 1723, p. 60
16. Winckelmann 1764, quoted in Potts 1994, pp. 63, 179–80
17. Misson 1714, Vol. 3, p. 69
18. Raguenet 1723, p. 19
19. Ibid., pp. 19, 21
20. Postle 1997, p. 80
21. Wilton-Ely 2004, p. 152; Redford 1996, pp. 8–9. See also the work of John Locke and Anthony Ashley Cooper, 3rd Earl of Shaftesbury.
22. Turnbull 1740, pp. 8, 84, 129, quoted in Barrell 1989, p. 103. See Myrone 2005, pp. 58–67 and see Goldsmith 2021 for a wider commentary on this.
23. Coltman 2009, p. 171; Adams 2009, p. 82; Barrell 1989, pp. 101–31
24. Raguenet 1723, pp. 178–9
25. Winckelmann 1754, quoted in Potts 1994, p. 172
26. Quoted in Chard 1999, p. 224
27. Hogarth, Paulson (ed.) 1997, p. 4
28. See, for example, Sir Wyndham Knatchbull-Wyndham (1758–9) and Sir Gregory Page-Turner (1768–9). Bowron and Kerber 2008, pp. 55–7, 62, 69
29. Harvey 2015, p. 798
30. Ibid., p. 802
31. Hollander 1994, p. 67
32. Breward 2016, p. 24
33. Walpole, Lewis (ed.) 1961 p. 294
34. Quoted in Radford 2012, pp. 172–3
35. Postle 1997, pp. 84–5
36. Vertue 1938, pp. 21–2
37. See Pointon 1978, pp. 131–3; Callen 2018, pp. 80–8
38. Leoussi 2016, p. 51
39. Farington, Cave (ed.) 1982, p. 3301
40. Quoted in Honour 2019, pp. 8–12
41. Ibid., p. 7
42. Salzmann 1800, pp. 24–6, 196
43. Grimes 2013, p. 273
44. See Mangan 1981
45. Quoted in Park 2005, p. 372
46. Zweiniger-Bargielowska 2006, pp. 598–9
47. See Budd 1997; Dutton 1995, p. 21
48. Dutton 1995, pp. 121–8. See also Chapman 1994
49. Quoted in Park 2005, p. 383
50. Begiato 2016, pp. 11; 121; Kestner 1995, p. 53
51. Quoted in Budd 1997, p. 68
52. Dutton 1995, p. 131. For further information on the men and women who purchased such photography for aspirational, aesthetic and erotic purposes, see Mitchell Snow 2019, pp. 135–55.
53. See Hau 2003; Mangan 2013; Carden-Coyne 2009
54. For insight on the scholarship surrounding this topic, see Mackenzie 2003, pp. 302–36
55. See Turner and Withey 2014, pp. 775–9
56. My sincere thanks to Susan North for bringing this artefact to my attention.
57. See, for example, National IPED Info Survey reports (2013–16): https://www.ipedinfo.co.uk (accessed 31 Mar 2020); Sirin Kale, '"Get shredded in six weeks!" The problem with extreme male body transformations', *The Guardian* (27 Jun 2018): https://www.theguardian.com/lifeandstyle/2018/jun/27/get-shredded-in-six-weeks-the-problem-with-extreme-male-body-transformations (accessed 31 Mar 2020).
58. Brown 2010, p. 45
59. Ibid., pp. 43, 45
60. Ibid., pp. 42–3
61. Jack Poolet, '10 Actors Who Got SERIOUSLY Ripped To Play Superheroes,' *WhatCulture* (8 Jun 2018): https://whatculture.com/film/10-actors-who-got-seriously-ripped-to-play-superheroes?page=6 (accessed 31 Mar 2020); Comments Section, 'A Scientifically Proven Way To Build The Perfect Male Body', fitmole (16 Aug 2014): https://www.fitmole.org/perfect-male-body/comment-page-1/ (accessed 31 Mar 2020)
62. Holly Pyne, 'Anthony Mackie talks Captain America 2', *ShortList* (25 Mar 2014): https://www.shortlist.com/news/anthony-mackie-talks-captain-america-2 (accessed 31 Mar 2020)
63. Edith Zimmerman, 'Chris Evans: American Marvel', *GQ* (14 Jun 2011): https://www.gq.com/story/chris-evans-gq-july-2011-cover-story (accessed 31 Mar 2020)

A POLISHED IMPRESSION
Alun Withey

1. 'An Essay on the Nature, Marks and Principles of Politeness', *The Universal Magazine* (Dec 1775), p. 308
2. Withey 2016, p. 66
3. Withey 2021, pp. 232–4
4. Andry 1743, p. 59. See also Withey 2016, pp. 77–8
5. Withey 2016, pp. 81–2
6. Advertisement, 'Cast Steel Razors by R. Sangwine', *St James Chronicle or the British Evening Post* (7–10 Feb 1778)

BEHIND CLOTHES: FASHIONING MEN AT THE MUSEUM
Satish Padiyar

1. Acknowledgement: I warmly thank Susan Siegfried for crucial bibliographic advice on this essay, and Rosalind McKever and Claire Wilcox for many helpful discussions in the course of writing it. Morley 1852, pp. 265–70
2. See Burton 1999, pp. 32–3
3. On a vogue, commencing in the 1840s, for bizarre patterns on men's trousers, including horizontal stripes, see Chenoune 1993, p. 70.
4. Burton 1999, p. 30
5. On 'unmentionables', see Chenoune 1993, p. 24.
6. I thank Ella Ravilious for bringing this photograph to my attention.
7. On opposition to the more elitist Royal Academy's perceived neglect of a broadly applicable training in British design, which drove the inception of the V&A, see Bryant 2019, p. 18; and Burton 1999, pp. 15–18.
8. Burton 1999, p. 28

9. Although the V&A's continuing teaching of the skill of drawing also came under attack in the second half of the nineteenth century by critics such as John Ruskin and Edward Poynter for narrowing students' vision. See Burton 1999, p. 127.
10. Alberti 1956, p. 73
11. By contrast, the medium of sculpture technically incorporated cloth. Renaissance sculptors dressed clay models and life-size mannequins with cloth or wettened paper to ascertain the behaviour of folds. On this, see Hills 2018, pp. 104–5.
12. Alberti 1956, p. 73
13. The acquisition of plaster casts of male nude sculptures – as well as of architectural ornament and models – was fundamental to the accruing collections of the Victoria and Albert Museum, culminating in the opening of the museum's Cast Courts in 1873. The most prominent cast of a heroic male nude (still a highlight of the collection today) was Michelangelo's *David*, gifted to the Museum by Queen Victoria in 1857.
14. Audran 1683.
15. On the history of the reception of these statues, see Haskell and Penny 1981.
16. See Matthews David 2007, pp. 142–64; and Hobson 2004, pp. 33–49
17. Audran 1683, 'la correction du Dessin', Preface, unpaginated
18. Reynolds 1988, p. 62
19. Ibid., p. 187. On the gendering of colour and line (or drawing), as, respectively, feminine and masculine, see Lichtenstein 1993.
20. Brown 1989
21. Hills 2018, pp. 127–47
22. As cited in Squire 1970, p. 8
23. These neoclassical conceptions of drapery are summarized, for example, by Aubin-Louis Millin, in his article 'Draperie', in *Dictionnaire des Beaux-Arts* (Paris 1818), pp. 467–9
24. Georg Wilhelm Friedrich Hegel, *Lectures on Fine Arts*, Part 3, Section II, Sculpture, 'Draping (or Clothing)'. The lectures were delivered in Berlin and Heidelberg between 1818 and 1829.
25. See Celant and Ippolitov 2004

A DEVELOPED PHYSIQUE
Zorian Clayton

1. See https://iucat.iu.edu/kinsey/13540183
2. Campbell *c.*1937
3. William Hamo Thornycroft, lecture to the sculpture students of the Royal Academy, 1885.
4. Meeker 2006
5. Mizer 1954
6. Aldrich 1993, p. 32.
7. Keiley 1899, p. 125. A review of a publication entitled *The Photogram* in the *Leeds Mercury* (10 Dec 1903) states that Gloeden's frontispiece with a study of an Italian boy 'possessed a remarkable, almost hypnotic fascination'. He was also widely praised for exhibiting at the 38th annual Royal Photographic Society show in London in 1893, with 21 figure study photographs.
8. George Platt Lynes, Orpheus and Eros, a poem of 1936
9. Mercer 1991, p. 192
10. Bourland 2019, p. 88
11. Ibid., p. 89
12. Fani-Kayode 1988
13. See visualaids.org/artists for the largest online database of works by artists with HIV/AIDS.
14. Morrisroe 2016, p. 87
15. Ibid.
16. Bourland 2019, p. 186
17. In place from May 1988 to June 2000, Section 28 of the Local Government Act 1988 stated that a local authority 'shall not intentionally promote homosexuality or publish material with the intention of promoting homosexuality' or 'promote the teaching in any maintained school of the acceptability of homosexuality as a pretended family relationship'.
18. Benyon 2002, pp. 98–102

UNDERPINNINGS: THE NEXT BEST THING TO NAKED
Shaun Cole

Title and subheading quotations taken from:
'Next best thing to Naked', Jockey men's underwear advertisement, 1940s
'Keep Your Shirt On!', Munsingwear advertisement, 1940
'So comfortable, so smooth to the skin', Courtaulds Ltd advertisement, 1930
'Design is one thing, fit is the other ... In situations like this you should be able to rely on your underwear', Wolgang Jessner, quoted in Cole 2010, p. 131
'It's an erogenous zone that we can brand literally', quoted in Dan Shaw, 'Unmentionable: not when they have designer labels', *New York Times* (14 Aug 1994), p. 52
'An overt bulge', quoted in Bennett-England 1967, pp. 40–1

1. Steele 1989, p. 56
2. Vigarello 1988, p. 62
3. *The Workwoman's Guide* (London 1840), p. 59
4. Steele 1989, p. 59
5. Laver 1968, p. 21
6. William Jesse, *Life of Brummell* (1844), quoted in Laver 1968, p. 70
7. Arnold Bennett, *Riceyman Steps* (London 1923)
8. Newton 1974
9. Harris 1931, p. 114
10. Shove 2003, p. 124
11. By altering the needle selection on circular knitting machines, the density of knit could be changed to create ribbed outlines around the crotch pouch area and a pre-formed pouch, allowing for a better fit on the wearer for greater comfort.
12. Quoted in Petersen 2008
13. Bennett-England 1967, pp. 41, 45
14. Martin and Koda 1992, p. 26
15. Gaines and Churcher 1994, p. 294
16. Bordo 1999, p. 190
17. Quoted in Steele 1996, p. 129
18. Davis 1991, pp. 5, 17

YOUNG ENGLISHMEN BEHAVING BADLY (AND DRESSING OUTRAGEOUSLY)
Susan North

1. Fielding 1763, p. 42
2. According to the OED, the word 'masculinity' appeared in English in 1748: 'Besides the Prerogative of his Sex, or Masculinity (as the French call it)'.
3. Bailey and Hentschell 2010; Harvey 2005; Shepard 2005; Breitenberg 1996; Griffiths 1996; Ben-Amos 1994
4. A proclamation vvith certayne clauses of diuers statutes, 1579 and A proclamation for the observation of certein statutes, 1562.
5. London Metropolitan Archives, Journal, Proceedings of the Common Council, CL/CC/01/02/001, Vols 18, 20, 21
6. LMA, CL/CC/01/02/001 v21, fol. 161–2
7. LMA, CL/CC/01/02/001 v28, 161–2
8. Dendy 1895, p. 20
9. Ibid., p. 21
10. Ibid., p. 23
11. Stubbes 1583, Dvii verso
12. Ibid., Dviii recto
13. Ibid., E6 recto, E3 recto
14. Ibid., Dvi recto, verso, Dvii recto, verso, E4 recto
15. Ibid., q7 recto-verso
16. Ibid., Cii verso
17. Allestree 1682, p. 128
18. Cleland (1612) 1948, pp. 215–16
19. Anon., *The Institucion of a gentleman* (London 1555), Bvi verso–Ciii verso
20. Mandeville 1715, p. 103
21. Wildeblood and Brinson 1965, p. 181
22. Dendy 1895, p. 21
23. Patterson 2009, pp. 58, 63, 69–70
24. Dendy 1895, p. 21
25. Churchyard 1593, p. 60
26. Banks 2010, pp. 2, 52–3
27. Bailey 2007, pp. 4, 19, 24, 93
28. Earle 1628, D9 verso–D11 recto
29. Brooke 1681, p. 123
30. Carter 2001, pp. 21, 68, 73, 131
31. Constable 1738, p. 24
32. Anon. 1699, p. 30
33. Williams 1995 pp. 46–7
34. Anon. 1706, p. 23
35. Anon. 1699, p. 47
36. Mancinus 1570, p.E6 verso; 'The English Courtier 1586' in Hazlitt 1868, p. 69
37. Anon. 1699, p. 50
38. Mackie 2009, pp. 35–44; Statt 1995, pp. 179–99
39. Anon. 1763, p. 24
40. Defoe 1742, p. 106
41. Elyot (1531) 1970, p.C1 recto
42. Whitchurch 1772, pp. 68–9
43. Ibid., p. 73.
44. Casa 1576, pp. 18–19
45. de Courtin 1671, pp. 83–4
46. Dare 1673, pp. 14–15
47. Jones 1735, p. 11
48. Anon. 1747; Campbell 1747; Collyer 1761
49. Campbell 1747, p. 197
50. Anon. 1555, p.J7 verso–J8recto
51. Etherege 1676, pp. 42–3
52. Cohen 1996, pp. 54–63
53. Hurd 1764, p. 68
54. Yarwood 1970, p. 53
55. Evelyn 1661, pp. 11–12
56. Anon. 1675a, pp. 3–4
57. Anon., 1675b, pp. 5–6
58. Staves 1982, p. 416

A WELL-TURNED LEG
Elisabeth Gernerd

1. Farrell 1992, pp. 9–10
2. See Pointon 2013; Gernerd 2015
3. A pair of stockings, which have been padded

with unspun wool, 1770–1800, Acc. No. 50.104.5 A & B, survive in the National Museums Liverpool, Walker Art Gallery. See Cunnington and Cunnington 1992, pp. 80–1.
4. McNeil 2000
5. See McNeil 2018
6. *Town and Country Magazine or Universal Repository of Knowledge, Instruction and Entertainment*, Vol. IV (May 1772), p. 243
7. *Walker's Hibernian Magazine: or Compendium of Entertaining Knowledge* (Aug 1786), p. 408
8. McNeil 2000, p. 404
9. Admiral Nelson's striped stockings that he wore at Tenerife *c.*1797 survive in the National Maritime Museum, Acc. No. TXT0381-2; for example, see *Virginia Gazette and Daily Advertiser*, 27 Jul 1791.
10. Gernerd 2015, p. 20
11. White silk was the most expensive and hardest to keep clean.
12. Walpole 1985, p. 151
13. John Mountstuart was born in 1744, married first in 1766 to Charlotte, daughter of the 2nd Viscount Windsor; secondly in 1800 to Frances, daughter of Thomas Coutts, Esq. He was created Marquesss of Bute in 1796 and died in 1814; Lady Sarah Bunbury to Lady Susan O'Brien, 9 Jan 1776; Napier 1902, p. 180
14. Coltman 2019, p. 26
15. Ibid., p. 27
16. Letter CCLVIII, 10 Jun 1751. Stanhope 1860, p. 415
17. See Whitenier (Jr) 2016
18. Friedman 2016
19. Riello 2006, p. 62
20. Mansel 2005, p. 15
21. The court and the gentry continued to wear a 'high' heel into the 1740s.
22. Joseph Addison, *The Tatler*, No. 294 (22–7 Feb 1711); Semmelhack 2017, p. 170
23. For example, *The Seventh Earl of Northampton*, *c.*1758, oil on canvas, 237.7 × 149.2 cm, The Fitzwilliam Museum (accession No. PD.4-1950) and *Sir Sampson Gideon and an unidentified companion*, 1767, oil on canvas, 275.6 × 189 cm, National Gallery of Victoria (Acc. No. 1325-5).
24. *Middlesex Journal* (5 Jun 1771)
25. A visual example of a macaroni in red heels is *A Decoy for the Old as well as for the Young*, *c.*1773, printed for Carrington Bowles, mezzotint, 35.2 × 25 cm, Lewis Walpole Library, Farmington
26. McNeil 2018, p. 19
27. *Public Advertiser* (7 Jun 1779)
28. McNeil and Riello 2005, p. 184
29. Letter CLXIX, 14 Nov 1749; Stanhope 1860, p. 292

BRAGGADOCIO: A BRIEF HISTORY OF SWAGGER
Elizabeth Currie

1. Written by Caleb Speir, Keith Ernesto Harris, William Adams, Kanye Omari West, John Roger Stephens, Estelle Swaray, Joshua Lopez, Kweli Ebon Washington.
2. Oware 2018, p. 48
3. Metal jewellery worn over one or more teeth and sometimes inlaid with gemstones. Nowadays, teeth grills are usually detachable and custom-made from a dental mould.
4. Falls 2014, pp. 133–4
5. hooks 2004, pp. 15–32
6. Zadie Smith, Jay Z interview, *T Magazine*, 9 Sep 2012, p. 109: https://www.nytimes.com/2012/09/09/t-magazine/the-house-that-hova-built.html (accessed 22 Mar 2020)
7. See Williams 2013
8. https://www.rocawear.com/about/ (accessed 22 Mar 2020)
9. Kaiser, Rabine, Hall and Ketchum 2004, pp. 62–5
10. Chandler and Chandler Smith 2005, pp. 229–54
11. Lewis 2010, p. 415
12. Suterwalla 2013, pp. 229–32. I am grateful to the author for sharing her expertise with me.
13. Cover design by Hales Curtis: https://www.designweek.co.uk/issues/25-november-1-december-2019/stormzy-second-album-cover/ (accessed 22 Mar 2020)
14. Edmund Spenser, *The Faerie Queene* (London 1596), Book III, p. 515
15. Ibid., Book I, pp. 22, 47, 97
16. John Florio, *Queen Anna's New World of Words* (London 1611), p. 67
17. Eliav-Feldon 2009, pp. 276–91. One example of this link is discussed in Moffitt 2004, p. 48.
18. Langdon 1998, p. 91
19. For a pattern, detailed photography and X-ray images of this doublet, see Braun, Costigliolo, North, Thornton and Tiramani 2016, pp. 88–102.
20. Currie 2019, p. 122
21. There is a burgeoning literature on the codpiece see, for example, Bruna 2015 and Glover 2019.
22. Long after the introduction of standardized uniforms in the mid-seventeenth century, military finery retained its colourful and elaborate nature, as evidenced by the desirability of regimental uniforms in the writings of Jane Austen. See Davidson 2019 and Muir 2019.
23. Tlusty 2011, p. 19
24. Leather coat, Swedish, *c.*1630, Livrustkammaren, 31123 (20:26)
25. Strype 1824, p. 296
26. Calvi 2002, p. 491

FINE AND DANDY
Claire Wilcox

1. Pepys (6 Apr 1661): https://www.pepysdiary.com/diary/1661/04/06/ (accessed 16 Oct 2021)
2. Evelyn 1661, p. 12
3. Pepys (7 Aug 1663): https://www.pepysdiary.com/diary/1665/10/28/ (accessed 16 Oct 2021)
4. Pepys (28 Oct 1665): https://www.pepysdiary.com/diary/1666/10/17/ (accessed 17 Oct 2021)
5. Chapter 5, *Intricacy*: https://arthistoryproject.com/artists/william-hogarth/the-analysis-of-beauty/chapter-5-intricacy/ (accessed 21 Oct 2021)
6. See, for example, James Thomson's *The Seasons* (1735)
7. Quoted in Razzall 2006
8. The average price of a horse in 1790, according to the National Archives: https://www.nationalarchives.gov.uk/currency-converter/#currency-result (accessed 20 Oct 2021)
9. *Old Bailey Proceedings Online* (Sep 1790): www.oldbaileyonline.org (17900915) (accessed 3 Jan 2021)
10. V&A: 1414–1869
11. Alexander Pope, *The Rape of the Lock* (London 1712), canto 4, line 132
12. Ibid., canto 5, line 84
13. Ashton 1890, chapter 14: https://www.gutenberg.org/files/48780/48780-h/48780-h.htm (accessed 20 Oct 2021). Petersham always wore brown, favoured Cossack trousers instead of breeches and boots, and gave his name to the Petersham coat.
14. Anon. 1818
15. Virginia Woolf, *The Common Reader Vol. II 1932* (London 2003), p. 150
16. Jesse 1844, p. 48
17. Kelly 2005, p. 1
18. Honoré de Balzac, *Treatise on Elegant Life* (1830), Jules Barbey d'Aurevilly, *On Dandyism and George Brummell* (1845) and Charles Baudelaire, *The Painter of Modern Life* (1863).
19. Windsor 1960, p. 30
20. Ibid., pp. 13–14
21. Quoted in Kuhn 2006, p. 169.
22. The St Louis *People's Organ* (12 Apr 1842). See Collins 1981, p. 54
23. V&A: 3504–1953 and 3503–1953. The photographer was John J.E. Mayall.
24. Strong 2020
25. Quoted in Nick Piercey, 'A Brief History of Public Parks before 1870': https://www.playingpasts.co.uk/articles/the-great-out-doors/a-brief-history-of-british-public-parks-before-1870/ (accessed 21 Oct 2021).
26. Quoted in Hart 1998, p. 68.
27. Lucy Kumara Moore, 'An Interview with Designer Martine Rose About "Sexness"', anothermag.com: https://www.anothermag.com/fashion-beauty/11447/lucy-kumara-moore-an-interview-with-designer-martine-rose-about-sexness (accessed 22 Mar 2021)
28. Sarah Mower, 'Martine Rose Spring 2020 Menswear', *Vogue:* https://www.vogue.com/fashion-shows/spring-2020-menswear/martine-rose (accessed 23 Mar 2021)

SARTORIAL ENCOUNTERS: THE KIMONO AND MASCULINE STYLE
Anna Jackson

1. The history of the kimono dates back a thousand years, but it was from the early sixteenth century that it became the garment as we think of it today and was worn by all. The term 'kimono' literally means 'the thing to wear', although this came to be widely used only in the late nineteenth century. It was previously known as a 'kosode', meaning 'small sleeves', a reference to the sleeve opening that is just wide enough for the hand and arm to pass through. For more information on both men's and women's dress and the sumptuary laws issued to curb conspicuous consumption, see Jackson 2020, pp. 37–78.
2. The warrior, or samurai, class had controlled Japan from the twelfth century, the emperor being a mere figurehead. The supreme military ruler was called the *shōgun*. In the early seventeenth century Japan was unified by the general Tokugawa Ieyasu who took the title *shōgun* in 1602 and fought his last, and decisive, battle in 1615. He established his capital in Edo (modern-day Tokyo), which gives the period its name, and his descendants ruled Japan until 1868.
3. See Mostow, Ikeda and Matsuba 2016
4. The latter would have taken place at the age of 11 or 12, with the long forelocks usually being shaved off at the end of the teenage years.

5. The poem is *Watching Princess Yongle Journey to the Frontier* by Sun Ti (696–761):
Orioles and blooms are few on the frontier;
Nothing is newly felt year by year.
Not until the fair lady descends from the sky;
Does spring arrive at the dragon fortress far and nigh.
6. The word for the drama form, however, came to be rewritten with different characters meaning, literally, 'song', 'dance' and 'technique'. Commoners were the primary audience for kabuki, the samurai supposedly – but not always in reality – shunning it in favour of classical Nō theatre.
7. *Onnagata* actors wore their hair in women's styles, but still had the shaved crown of men. Kabuki continues to be highly popular in Japan, all parts still performed by men.
8. The Portuguese had been the first Europeans to reach Japan in 1543, followed by the Spanish, Dutch and English. Japan's rulers sensed that the religion that the Portuguese and Spanish brought with them was a threat to their authority and expelled them. The English venture had proved a failure, leaving only the Protestant Dutch to trade in Japan. As well as being part of popular culture, the Dutch were the subject of scholarly enquiry known as *Rangaku* (from *Oranda*, the Japanese for 'Holland' and *gaku* meaning academic disciple), which represented an important alternative to dominant intellectual practices derived from China.
9. *Netsuke* are the toggles that act as a counterbalance to the *inrō* when they are hung from the sash.
10. The registers of the *Tōban Kamotsuchō [the Cargo List of Chinese and European Ships]* record the products imported and exported by Chinese and Dutch ships entering and leaving Nagasaki between 1709 and 1713. See Oyama 2020.
11. Quoted in Breukink-Peeze 1989, p. 56
12. See North 2020
13. Names in this chapter are expressed in Japanese order, with family name followed by given name. The exceptions are modern and contemporary designers who have an international profile and/or brand name that is written in western order. Shiino Shōbei adapted his name, operating under S. Shobey, feeling it was easier for foreigners to pronounce his given name, especially with a y instead of an i.
14. The jacket is of soft habutae silk, the lining being quilted with fine silk wadding between the two layers. The trousers are of the same two fabrics but without the quilting or wadding.
15. See Jackson 2000, pp. 100–13
16. Painter E.A. Walton, one of the Glasgow Boys and a great admirer and later friend of Whistler, dressed himself as the Japanese artist Hokusai for a fancy-dress ball organized by the Glasgow Arts Club in 1889, while his fiancée came as Whistler's butterfly.
17. *Mr Mortimer Menpes* published in Marion Hepworth Dixon, 'The Art of Mortimer Menpes', *The Lady's Realm*, Vol. 9 (Nov 1900 – Apr 1901) p. 214
18. The women in the image wear their kimono incorrectly wrapped, right over left.
19. The kimono that Jasieński is wearing, which survives, would have been one of probably three garments – in matching design but different colours – worn by the bride during the wedding banquet.
20. Cortazzi 2001, p. 231
21. Quoted in Dalby 1993, pp. 66–7
22. See Meech-Pekarik 1986, pp. 64–72
23. Keio University, Japan's oldest higher education establishment, was founded in 1858 by Fukuzawa Yukichi, while Waseda was founded in 1882 by Meiji-period politician and former Prime Minister Ōkuma Shigenobu (1838–1922).
24. For more on kimono in film and music performance see Rout 2020.
25. Tom Stubbs, 'Going Kimono Should Be Your Next Fashion Step', *GQ* (9 Jun 2018): https://www.gq-magazine.co.uk/article/mens-kimono-trend (accessed 1 Apr 2020).

ORLANDO AS A BOYETTE
Rosalind McKever

Subheading quotations taken from Woolf 1993, pp. 11, 132, 108, 109, 153.

1. Woolf 1993, pp. 131–3
2. 'A woman must not wear men's clothing, nor a man wear women's clothing', Deuteronomy 22:5.
3. Nicholson 1973; reprint 1990, p. 99. Laura Doan chronicles this moment in her discussion of the impact of women adopting uniform in the First World War in chapter 3 of her *Fashioning Sapphism*. See Doan 2001, pp. 64–94. My thanks to Francesco Ventrella for highlighting the importance of Doan's book at an early stage of our exhibition research.
4. Doan 2001, pp. 95–125
5. As articulated in Doan 2001, p. 105, this short-lived neologism ensured this style did not carry connotations of masculine power by referring to boy, rather than man, and adding the diminutive '-ette'.
6. Victor Magueritte, *La garçonne* (Paris 1922)
7. Evans 2020
8. I thank Kit Heyam for bringing this print to my attention, and for his wider insights as part of the Arts and Humanities Research Council funded project Gendered Interpretations of the V&A and Vasa Museums.
9. Cole 2020, p. 76
10. Garrard 1994 p. 586. See also Pino, Pardo (ed.) 1984 and Castiglione, Singleton (trans.) 1959
11. British Library Harley MS 6798; see also Montrose 1983
12. Garber 1992, p. 26
13. Clark 1985, p. 160. See also Bullough and Bullough 1993, p. 75
14. Clark 1985, p. 167, Saccardi 2018
15. Jonsson 2018, p. 44
16. 'As a young girl I had an overwhelming aversion to everything that women do and say. I couldn't bear their tight-fitting, fussy clothes. [...] I couldn't stand long dresses and I only wanted to wear short skirts.' quoted in Buckley 2008, p. 91.
17. Holm 2019, p. 189; Ångström Grandien 2018, p. 6
18. This portrait is in the collection of the Museo del Prado, Madrid, inv. No. P001503.
19. Bolich 2007, p. 155. For accounts of Christina's male attire, see Ångström Grandien 2018, p. 12; Willborg Jonsson 2018, p. 44.
20. Samuel Pepys (12 Jun 1666) https://www.pepysdiary.com/diary/1666/06/ (accessed 1 Oct 2020)
21. 'Mayds of Honour (particularly Mrs Steward in a buff doublet like a solder) as good pictures, I think, as ever I saw'. Samuel Pepys (26 Aug 1664) https://www.pepysdiary.com/diary/1664/08/ (accessed 1 Oct 2020)
22. 'But so great performance of a comical part was never, I believe, in the world before as Nell do this, both as a mad girle, then most and best of all when she comes in like a young gallant; and hath the notions and carriage of a spark the most that ever I saw any man have.' Samuel Pepys, 2 Mar 1667: https://www.pepysdiary.com/diary/1667/03/02/ (accessed 1 Oct 2020). See chapter 4 of Bax 1932, pp. 87–96; p. 89.
23. Seshagiri 2010, especially chapter 3, pp. 140–91. The satire perspective is presented by Beeber 2015, pp. 104–9
24. A robe supposedly worn by Lady Mary Wortley Montagu is found in the V&A collection, T.225–1958.
25. Montagu, Heffernan and O'Quinn (eds) 2012, p. 113
26. Garber 1992, p. 312
27. Pointon 1993, especially chapter 3, pp. 141–57. Scarce 1987, especially chapter 4, pp. 38–89
28. Ibid., p. 108
29. Dekke and van de Pol 1989, Stoyle 2018
30. Bullough and Bullough 1993, p. 134
31. Kates 2001, pp. 184, 249
32. Snell 1750
33. See entry for 21 May 1778 in Woodforde 2011, p. 100. See also Bullough and Bullough 1993, p. 134.
34. This is noted in the object file for the V&A's own print of Lemprière (E.18–1965). I thank Zorian Clayton for bringing this to my attention and for his comments on this essay.
35. Ibid., p. 159
36. Van Slyke 1998
37. Sand, Jurgrau (trans.) 1991, p. 893
38. Siegfried and Finkelberg 2020, p. 8. I thank Satish Padiyar for bringing this essay to my attention.
39. Van Slyke 1998, pp. 321–35
40. For example, the highly fictionalized depiction of Queen Christina in the 1933 film starring Greta Garbo amplifies both her wearing of masculine attire and her relationship with Ebba Sparre.
41. Troubridge was cropped out of the photograph of Hall used in relation to the trial.
42. Aston 1988
43. Garber 1998
44. Hughes 1940, p. 226
45. Steele 2017, pp. 214–27
46. Swinton in turn inspired an androgynous runway in the form of Viktor and Rolf's Autumn/Winter 2003 collection, in which an army of models styled as Swinton, copper-haired and pale-faced, marched down the catwalk in a menswear-inspired collection.
47. This was commissioned by Vienna State Opera, composed by Olga Neuwirth, with a libretto by Neuwirth and Catherine Filloux, and directed by Polly Graham.

A HIBISCUS PRINT
Cher Potter

1. Adebayo Oke-Lawal, interview with the author, 9 Oct 2020, Lagos
2. Adamo 2011, p. 6
3. Adebayo Oke-Lawal, interview with the author, 9 Oct 2020, Lagos
4. *Aṣọ oke* is the name given to cloth woven

for a variety of special ceremonies of Yoruba-speaking people in south-western Nigeria. The cloth is decorated with elaborate patterns made from dyed strands of fabric that are woven into strips. These strips are sewn together to form larger pieces.
5. This is argued by the art historian Okechukwu Nwafor in his definitive thesis on *aṣọ ebì*, 'Photography and the Spectacle of *Aṣọ Ebì* in Lagos, 1960–2010' (unpublished PhD thesis, University of the Western Cape, 2011). However, dress historian Tunde M. Akinwumi believes that *aṣọ ebì* has much older origins. He suggests that *aṣọ ebì* is a contraction of *aṣọ ti ebì da jo*, which were special cloths brought by Yoruba families to funerals to wrap their deceased, dating back many centuries. See Akinwumi 1990, p. 171
6. As described by the American nineteenth-century missionary William H. Clarke his journal *Travels and Discoveries in Yorubaland 1854–1858*. Edited and published by Joseph Adebowale Atanda, Clarke 1972, p. 237
7. Yoruba textiles scholar Duncan Clarke, personal communication, 29 Jun 2021, London
8. This expression was published in the title of an editorial in *Lagos Record* (6 Aug 1887), p. 6.
9. Nwafor 2012, p. 493
10. Williams 2018
11. Kenneth Ize quoted in Seward 2020
12. Coop 2019
13. Chigozie Obioma, 'Boys Must Cry: Masculinity in Nigerian Fiction', *The Guardian* (24 Nov 2016)
14. Chimamanda Ngozi Adichie, 'We Should All Be Feminists', TEDx Euston (1 Dec 2012)
15. Adebayo Oke-Lawal, interview with the author, 9 Oct 2020, Lagos

MONOCHROME MAN
Christopher Breward

1. Flügel 1966, pp. 110–11
2. Carter 2003, pp. 97–119
3. Breward 1999, pp. 24–5
4. Breward 2016, pp. 15–20
5. Harvey 2013, p. 99
6. Reynolds 2013, p. 161
7. Hayward 2020, pp. 34–5. Recent conservation of this portrait revealed his apparel was possibly once red. We thank Carolina Jiménez Gray for bringing this to our attention.
8. Currie 2016, p. 28
9. North 2009, p. 126
10. Henry Peacham, *Minerva Britannia, or a Garden of Heroical Devices* (London 1612), cited in Breward 1995, p. 66
11. Bulwer-Lytton 1842, pp. 180–2
12. Cole 1978; Walden 2002; Kelly 2005
13. Funnell 2011, p. 23
14. Ribeiro 2012, p. 186
15. Benjamin 1989, pp. 76–7
16. Thiebaut 2012, p. 136
17. Huysmans 1959, p. 27
18. Eisen and McHugh 2019, pp. 97–9
19. Viscusi 1986, p. 28
20. Harvey 2013, p. 262
21. Mort 2010, p. 80
22. Breward 2004, p. 126
23. Nead 2017, p. 129
24. Breward 2004, p. 197
25. Harvey 2013, p. 260
26. Gundle 2008, p. 325
27. Tulloch 2016, pp. 127–50
28. Miller 2009
29. Shola von Reynolds, 'Retracing the Creative Legacy of the Black Panthers', *AnOther Magazine*, (19 Oct 2016)

A FULL MONTY
Miriam Phelan

1. Mass-Observation, Personal Appearance and Clothing 1938–54, 18/1/C: Bolton clothes 1939, p. 4
2. Mort and Thompson 1994, p. 106
3. Sigsworth 1990
4. Mort and Thompson 1994, p. 110
5. Honeyman 2000, pp. 53–5
6. Sigsworth 1990, p. 24
7. Breward 1999, p. 28
8. Quoted in Tynan 2011, p. 141
9. Tynan 2013, p. 60
10. Sigsworth 1990, p. 27
11. Honeyman 2000, p. 55
12. Tynan 2013, p. 163
13. Biddle-Perry 2017, pp. 43–5
14. Ugolini 2007, p. 175
15. Sprecher 2020, p. 115
16. Sherwood 2010, p. 114
17. Sprecher 2020, p. 108. See also Summers 2015, pp. 171–2
18. Mort 1996, p. 135
19. Sprecher 2020, pp. 119–22
20. Ibid., p. 125
21. Ibid., p. 138
22. Honeyman 1993, pp. 186–217
23. Bailey 2012, pp. 180–96

A SUITABLE HAT
Oriole Cullen

1. McKnight 2000, chapter 4
2. They were to be worn in the Chamber but removed when addressing the Chamber. To raise a point of division a Member was required to be seated and wearing his hat. This arcane ruling remained in place until 1998, requiring the presence of two collapsible top hats in the Chamber that would be passed to the Member who wished to make their point. Interestingly, women MPs were exempt from this.
3. *Pall Mall Gazette* (6 Aug 1892)
4. *Liverpool Echo* (11 Mar 1913)
5. The bowler hat was created in 1849 by hat-maker Thomas Bowler for Locks of London. Locks had been charged with supplying a protective hat for the gamekeepers of Edward Coke, younger brother of the Earl of Leicester. The bowler hat was created with fur felt and shellac to build up a rigid waterproof crown.
6. *Sheffield Daily Telegraph* (13 Apr 1928)
7. *Reading Observer* (22 Aug 1896)
8. Michael Nevell et al., 'Denton and the Archaeology of the Felt Hatting Industry', *Archaeology of Tameside*, Vol. 7 (2007), p. 18
9. So-called as it resembled the shape of a porkpie, this style of hat was originally popular for women in the 1860s.
10. *Coventry Evening Telegraph* (12 Jul 1968)
11. Given by Sir Roy Strong: V&A: T.195–1979
12. Cecil Beaton also owned a fedora from Herbert Johnson, which is now in the V&A collection: T.160–1980.
13. BBC4 television, 'When Lucy Met Roy: Sir Roy Strong at 80' (24 Mar 2015): https://www.bbc.co.uk/programmes/b067fm60 (accessed 1 Jul 2020)
14. In 1901 a newspaper report noted that 9000 people were housed in just 1200 dwellings in this area of Birmingham. *Bolton Evening News – Bolton, Lancashire, England* (14 Dec 1901)
15. *Warwick and Warwickshire Advertiser* (2 Nov 1929)
16. Ibid.

THE HYBRID OF IT ALL: THE MAKING OF BLACK BRITISH STYLE
Ekow Eshun

1. Nead 2017, p. 5
2. Ibid.
3. Ibid.
4. David Olusoga, 'Windrush: Archived Documents Show the Long Betrayal', *The Guardian* (16 Jun 2019)
5. Quoted in Nead 2017, p. 153
6. Young 2013, p. 13
7. Gilroy 1987, p. 117
8. Gilroy 2002, p. 72
9. Fryer 2010, p. 396
10. Quoted in Nead 2017, p. 196
11. Chambers 2016
12. Tina Campt, 'Refusal', *Black Visual History: A Glossary* (24 Jul 2018) https://www.fotomuseum.ch/de/2018/07/24/refusal/ (accessed 5 Jul 2021)
13. Quoted in Caspar Melville, 'Roots', *New Humanist* (7 Jul 2008): https://newhumanist.org.uk/articles/1819/roots (accessed 1 May 2020)
14. Hebdige 1979, p. 43
15. Chambers 2016, p. 86
16. Quoted in Palmer 2017, p. 127
17. Melville 2019, p. 91
18. Palmer 2017, p. 17
19. Cunningham, Eshun and Lazarides (eds) 2001, p. 68
20. Ibid.
21. Ibid.
22. Ibid.
23. Quoted in Kureshi and Savage (eds) 1995
24. Melville 2019, p. 91
25. R. Derrick, K. Flett and J. Strongman, 'Chillin' (not Illin')' *The Face* (Jul 1987)
26. Hall 2006, p. 444
27. Hall 2011, p. 35
28. Quoted in *The Guardian* (11 Apr 2013): https://www.theguardian.com/fashion/fashion-blog/2013/apr/11/jazzie-b-fashion-soul-ii-soul (accessed 1 May 2020)
29. A Soul II Soul T-shirt is held in the V&A collection: T.93-2016.
30. Quoted in *Interview* (21 Jan 2017): https://www.interviewmagazine.com/music/jazzie-b (accessed 1 May 2020)
31. BBC, 'Jazzie B's 1980s': https://www.bbc.co.uk/programmes/b084flz4 (accessed 20 Apr 2020)
32. Quoted in Alex Frank, 'Casely-Hayford's Inherited Resistance', *The Fader* (11 Mar 2011) https://www.thefader.com/2011/03/11/feature-casely-hayfords-inherited-resistance (accessed 13 Apr 2020)
33. Ibid.
34. Hall 1987, p. 111
35. Palmer 2017, p. 128